ANOTHER BLOCK-BUSTER YEAR AT GUINNESS!

THE 1989 *GUINNESS BOOK OF WORLD RECORDS*
THE LARGEST EVER,
CHOCK-FULL OF BIZARRE, BREATHTAKING, BRAND-NEW
RECORDS SUCH AS . . .

- **DAREDEVILS!** . . . Mathias Rust, the young West German who landed in Kremlin Square after a 540-mile flight through Soviet-defended zones
- **SPEED QUEENS!** . . . American speed skater Bonnie Blair, the fastest woman on skates
- **BREADWINNERS!** . . . Bill Cosby, the highest-paid man on TV
- **LEAPFROGGERS!** . . . the record-smashing long-jumping Madagascar frog
- **CUP SWEEPERS!** . . . Pirmin Zurbriggen of Switzerland, the skier who won 4 World Cup events

---

PLUS!!!

- THE 38-INCH FINGERNAILS!
- THE MOTHER OF 69 CHILDREN!
- THE ARTIST WHO CAN PRODUCE A CREDITABLE PAINTING IN 30 SECONDS!
- THE 100-FOOT DRESS!
- THE 100-FOOT, 6-INCH PIZZA!

AND

- THE MAN WHO ATE A BICYCLE!

All this and much more . . . the best and the worst, the most beautiful and the most grotesque, the wackiest and the most memorable, all captured in one super-spectacular book.

GUINNESS BOOK OF WORLD RECORDS

Bantam Books in the Guinness Series

GUINNESS BOOK OF OLYMPIC RECORDS, 1988
GUINNESS BOOK OF WORLD RECORDS, 1989

1989 GUINNESS® BOOK OF WORLD RECORDS

EDITORS
Donald McFarlan
Norris D. McWhirter, *Editorial Advisor*

David A. Boehm, *American Editor-in-Chief*
Cyd Smith, *Assistant Editor*
Jim Benagh, *Sports Editor*
Gene Jones, *Associate Editor*
Robert Obojski, *Contributing Editor*

BANTAM BOOKS
NEW YORK • TORONTO • LONDON • SYDNEY • AUCKLAND

This edition contains the complete text of the original hardcover edition.
NOT ONE WORD HAS BEEN OMITTED.

GUINNESS BOOK OF WORLD RECORDS 1989

A Bantam Book / Published by arrangement with
Sterling Publishing Co., Inc.

PRINTING HISTORY
American Guinness edition published October 1956
Bantam edition / October 1963
Revised Bantam edition April 1964
Revised and enlarged Bantam Special edition / June 1966
Revised and enlarged new Bantam edition / March 1968
Revised and enlarged new Bantam edition / May 1970
Revised and enlarged new Bantam edition / April 1971
Revised and enlarged new Bantam edition / March 1973
Revised and enlarged new Bantam edition / February 1974
Revised and enlarged new Bantam edition / February 1975
Revised and enlarged new Bantam edition / March 1976
Revised and enlarged new Bantam edition / January 1977
Revised and enlarged new Bantam edition / March 1978
Revised and enlarged new Bantam edition / March 1979
7 printings through October 1979
Revised and enlarged new Bantam edition / March 1980
9 printings through October 1980
Revised and enlarged new Bantam edition / March 1981
4 printings through October 1981
Revised and enlarged new Bantam edition / March 1982
5 printings through August 1982
Revised and enlarged new Bantam edition / April 1983
4 printings through October 1983
Revised and enlarged new Bantam edition / April 1984
3 printings through July 1984
Revised and enlarged new Bantam edition / April 1985
3 printings through August 1985
Revised and enlarged new Bantam edition / April 1986
4 printings through October 1986
Revised and enlarged new Bantam edition / April 1987
Revised and enlarged new Bantam edition / April 1988
Revised and enlarged new Bantam edition / April 1989

For information address: Sterling Publishing Co., Inc., 2 Park Avenue, New York, NY 10016.

For information address: Sterling Publishing Co., Inc., 2 Park Avenue, New York, NY 10016

ISBN 0-553-27926-2

Published simultaneously in the United States and Canada

Bantam Books are published by Bantam Books, a division of Bantam Doubleday Dell Publishing Group, Inc. Its trademark, consisting of the words "Bantam Books" and the portrayal of a rooster, is Registered in U.S. Patent and Trademark Office and in other countries. Marca Registrada: Bantam Books, 666 Fifth Avenue, New York, New York 10103.

PRINTED IN THE UNITED STATES OF AMERICA

O 0 9 8 7 6

CONTENTS

The Story Behind the Guinness Book / Preface vii

Is It a Record? viii

1. The Human Being 1
Dimensions . . . Origins of Man . . . Longevity . . . Reproductivity . . . Physiology and Anatomy

2. The Living World 44
Animal Kingdom . . . Mammals . . . Domesticated Animals . . . Birds . . . Reptiles . . . Amphibians . . . Fishes . . . Starfishes . . . Arachnids . . . Crustaceans . . . Insects . . . Centipedes . . . Millipedes . . . Segmented Worms . . . Mollusks . . . Ribbon Worms . . . Jellyfishes and Corals . . . Sponges . . . Extinct Animals . . . Plant Kingdom . . . Fruits and Vegetables . . . Garden Flowers and Plants . . . Trees . . . Kingdom Protista . . . Kingdom Fungi . . . Kingdom Procaryota . . . Parks, Zoos, Aquaria and Oceanaria

3. The Natural World 126
Structure and Dimensions . . . Oceans . . . Land . . . Weather . . . Earthquakes . . . Volcanoes . . . Geysers

4. The Universe & Space 150
The Moon . . . The Sun . . . Planets . . . Stars . . . The Universe . . . Rocketry and Missiles

5. The Scientific World 166
Elements . . . Drink . . . Photography . . . Telescopes . . . Gems . . . Numerals . . . Physical Extremes (Terrestrial)

6. The Arts & Entertainment 190
Painting . . . Sculptures . . . Language and Literature . . . Music . . . Theatre . . . Radio Broadcasting . . . Television . . . Motion Pictures . . . Recorded Sound

7. The World's Structures 244
Earliest Structures . . . Buildings for Working . . . Buildings for Living

. . . Structures for Entertainment . . . Towers and Masts . . . Bridges . . . Canals . . . Dams . . . Tunnels . . . Specialized Structures . . . Borings and Mines

8. The Mechanical World 277
Ships . . . Road Vehicles . . . Railroads . . . Aircraft . . . Power Producers . . . Engineering

9. The Business World 341
Commerce . . . Finance . . . Land . . . Manufactured Articles . . . Collections . . . Antique Sales at Auction . . . Agriculture . . . Livestock Sales Records

10. The Human World 378
Political and Social . . . Countries . . . Cities . . . Standards of Living . . . Government . . . Military and Defense . . . Judicial . . . Crime and Punishment . . . Economic . . . Labor . . . Food and Drink . . . Transportation and Mass Communications . . . Education . . . Religions . . . Accidents and Disasters

11. Human Achievements 431
Endurance and Endeavor . . . Marriage and Divorce . . . Marine Records . . . Stunts and Miscellaneous Endeavors . . . Eating . . . Wealth and Poverty . . . Honors, Decorations and Awards

12. Sports, Games & Pastimes 507
Auto Racing . . . Baseball . . . Basketball . . . Bowling . . . Boxing . . . Cycling . . . Fishing . . . Football . . . Games . . . Golf . . . Gymnastics . . . Harness Racing . . . Hockey . . . Horse Racing . . . Ice Skating . . . Marathons (Running) . . . Motorcycling . . . Skiing . . . Soccer . . . Softball . . . Swimming . . . Tennis . . . Track and Field . . . Endurance Marathons

Newly Verified Records 675

Index 678

THE STORY BEHIND THE GUINNESS BOOK

On 12 September 1954, Sir Hugh Beaver invited Norris and Ross McWhirter to see if their fact and figure agency in London could help settle arguments about records. An office was set up at 107 Fleet Street, London, and work began on the first 198-page book. The printers bound the first copy on 27 August 1955. Before Christmas the *Guinness Book* was No. 1 on the best-sellers list. It has occupied this position every year since except 1957 and 1959 when it was not republished.

The first US edition appeared in New York in 1956 followed by editions in French (1962) and German (1963). In 1967 there were first editions in Japanese, Spanish, Danish and Norwegian, while the following year editions were published in Swedish, Finnish and Italian. In the seventies there followed Dutch (1971); Portuguese (1974); Czechoslovak (1976); Hebrew, Serbo-Croat and Icelandic (all in 1977) and Slovenian (1978). In the 1980's translations into Greek, Indonesian, Chinese, Turkish, Hindi, Malay, Arabic, Thai, Tamil, Telugu, Malayalam, Kannada and Hungarian brought the total to 262 editions in 35 languages.

By 1974 the *Guinness Book* earned its own place in the *Guinness Book*. It had become the top-selling copyright book in publishing history. By October 1988 the global sales had risen to more than 60 million, which is equivalent to 168 stacks, each as high as Mount Everest.

October 1988

Iveagh
[BENJAMIN GUINNESS]
EARL OF IVEAGH, President
Arthur Guinness & Sons, PLC

PREFACE

Many events and feats reported to us do surpass all other known claims yet are not included in each new edition of the book. The *Guinness Book of World Records* is not a compendium of every record ever set, but a rather subjective selection of those that the editors *in their sole discretion* find to be the most significant and/or interesting. Moreover, in order to give succeeding editions of the book variety, some records and photos, and even some whole categories of records, are dropped from time to time even when they have not been exceeded.

This 27th US edition has been brought up to date by the editors and provided with many new photos.

We wish to thank correspondents from the many countries of the world for raising and settling various editorial points. Strenuous efforts have been made to improve the value of the material presented and this policy will be continued in future editions.

Sterling Publishing Co, Inc
Two Park Ave, New York, NY 10016

IS IT A RECORD?

Categories

We are *likely* to publish only those records which improve upon previously published records or which are newly significant in having become the subject of widespread and, preferably, worldwide competition. Records in our sense essentially have to be both measureable and comparable to other performances in the same category.

It should be stressed that unique occurrences, interesting peculiarities and the collecting of everyday objects, are not themselves necessarily records. Records which are *qualified* or limited in some way—for example, by age, handicap, day of the week, etc.—cannot be accommodated in a reference work so general as the *Guinness Book of World Records*.

We do not publish records in gratuitously hazardous categories, such as the lowest starting height for a handcuffed, free-fall parachute jump, or the thinnest burning rope suspending a man in a straitjacket from a helicopter. World records claimed on TV specials are not always set according to Guinness rules. Certain innately dangerous but historically significant activities, such as tightrope walking, are included but are best left to professionals. Other categories which have reached the limits of safety, such as sword swallowing and Volkswagen stuffing, have been retired and either are so marked or have been deleted. No further claims will be considered for publication.

We reserve the right to determine in our sole discretion the record to be published and/or deleted and the use of the name of the record holder for purposes of inclusion in the book.

Rules and Procedures

A record attempt should compete *exactly* with the record in the book and the conditions under which it was set. Where there is doubt about the rules, it is recommended that the strictest interpretation be adopted. Contact with the Guinness editorial offices at 33 London Road, Enfield, Middlesex, England or the American editors (212-532-7160) for clarification should be made well in advance of a planned attempt.

If there is a recognized world or national governing body for an activity, that body should be consulted for rules and one of its representatives, whenever possible, should be involved in officiating. For any attempt, expert officiating by impartial witnesses is desirable.

In marathon or endurance events, five-minute rest intervals are permitted, but only AFTER each *completed* hour, except for a few "non-stop" categories in which minimal intervals may be taken only for purposes other than for resting. These rest breaks are optional and may be accumulated (for example, 3 hours of activity earns 15 minutes of rest time, etc.). Violation of the rest-interval rules will disqualify an attempt. The accepted record will be the gross time (that is, the total elapsed time, including rest intervals, from start to finish). However, unused accumulated rest break time cannot be added to the final figure.

In recent years there has been a marked increase in efforts to establish records for sheer endurance in many activities. In the very nature of record-breaking, the duration of such "marathons" will tend to be pushed to greater and greater extremes, and it should be stressed that marathon attempts are not without possible dangers. Those responsible for marathon events would be well counseled to seek medical advice before, and surveillance during, marathons which involve extended periods with little or no sleep.

Documentation and Verification

• We do *not* normally supply personnel to monitor, invigilate or observe record attempts, but reserve the right to do so. In any case, the burden of proof rests with the claimant. No particular form is required, and no entry fee is payable. Guidelines for documentation are provided below. We cannot accept as accurate any claim that is insufficiently documented.

• Claimants should obtain independent corroboration in the form of local or national newspaper, radio or TV coverage. Newspaper clippings must be annotated with the name of the newspaper, its place of publication and the date of the issue in which the article appeared. When possible, the name of the reporter and black-and-white and/or color action photographs should also be supplied. Videotapes and audio cassettes should not be sent, but held in reserve in the event further documentation is requested.

• Claimants should send signed authentication by independent, impartial adult witnesses or representatives of organizations of standing in their community. Where applicable, a signed document showing ratification by a governing body should be supplied (see above). A claim is naturally enhanced by a witness with a high degree of expertise in the area of endeavor.

• Signed log books should show there has been unremitting surveillance in the case of endurance events. These log books must include, in chronological order, the times of activity and the times and durations of all rest breaks taken. The log books must be legible and readily decipherable. They must include signatures of witnesses with times of entering and leaving (at least two *independent* witnesses must be on hand at all times). Where applicable, scoresheets must be kept to demonstrate a satisfactory rate of play.

All submissions become the property of the publishers. The publishers will consider, but not guarantee, the return of material, only if a self-addressed stamped envelope or wrapper is supplied *with sufficient postage*.

Revisions

Notwithstanding the best efforts of the editors, errors in the book, while rare, may occur. In the event of such errors, the sole responsibility of the publishers will be to correct such errors in subsequent editions of the book.

If there are discrepancies between entries in one edition and another, it may be generally assumed that the *later* entry is the product of up-to-date research.

Editorial Offices

Please consult the latest edition of the book before phoning or writing the editorial offices, which are primarily concerned with maintaining and improving the quality of each succeeding edition. **We do not offer advice on choosing a record for anyone to attempt breaking.** Also, we are unable to perform the function of a free general information bureau for quiz competitions and the like. However, we are always happy to hear about new record attempts.

From the American Editors of *Guinness*

Chapter 1

The Human Being

1. DIMENSIONS

Tallest Men

The true height of human giants is frequently obscured by exaggeration and commercial dishonesty. The only admissible evidence on the actual height of giants is that collected in this century under impartial medical supervision. Unfortunately, medical papers themselves are not blameless in including fanciful, as opposed to measured, heights.

The assertion that Goliath of Gath (*c.* 1060 BC) stood 6 cubits and a span (9 ft 6½ in) suggests a confusion of units or some over-enthusiastic exaggeration by the Hebrew chroniclers. The Hebrew historian Flavius Josephus (b 37 or 38 AD, d *c.* 100 AD) and some of the manuscripts of the Septuagint (the earliest Greek translation of the Old Testament) attribute to Goliath the wholly credible height of 4 Greek cubits and a span (6 ft 10 in).

Modern opinion is that the tallest recorded man of whom there is irrefutable evidence was the pre-acromegalic giant Robert Pershing Wadlow, born at 6:30 a.m. in Alton, Ill, on Feb 22, 1918. Weighing 8½ lb at birth, his abnormal growth started at the age of 2, following a double hernia operation.

At the age of 9 he was able to carry his father, Harold, later mayor of Alton, who stood 5 ft 11 in tall and weighed 170 lb, up the stairs of the family home. On his 13th birthday, he stood 7 ft 1¾ in tall, and at the age of 17 had reached 8 ft 0½ in and measured again at 8 ft 11.1 in, on June 27, 1940. He died 18 days later, at 1:30 a.m. on July 15, 1940, in Manistee, Mich. He was buried in Oakwood Cemetery, Alton, Ill, in a coffin measuring 10 ft 9 in long, 32 in wide, and 30 in deep.

His greatest recorded weight was 491 lb on his 21st birthday. He weighed 439 lb at the time of death. His shoes were size 37AA (18½ in long) and his hands measured 12¾ in from the wrist to the top of the middle finger. His arm span was 9 ft 5¾ in and he consumed 8,000 calories daily. He wore a size 25 ring.

The only other men for whom heights of 8 ft or more have been reliably reported are listed on page 8. In seven cases gigantism was followed by acromegaly, a disorder which causes an enlargement of the nose, lips, tongue, lower jaw, hands and feet, due to renewed activity by an already swollen pituitary gland, which is located at the base of the brain.

Giants exhibited in circuses and exhibitions are routinely under contract not to be measured and are, almost traditionally, billed by their promoters at heights up to 18 in in excess of their true heights. Notable examples of such exaggeration were listed in the 1982 *Guinness Book of World Records*.

HEIGHT MADE WADLOW A CELEBRITY: When he visited St Louis in 1939, the crowds found his height of almost 9 feet hard to believe. ▲

◄ TALLEST LIVING MAN: The 418-lb Mozambique circus giant Monjane is not Wadlow's height, but at 8 ft 0¾ in, he is the tallest person living.

Tallest Living Man

Gabriel Estavao Monjane (b 1944) in Mozambique measured 7 ft 5 in at the age of 16 and 7 ft 10 in when he was 21. He has not been anthropometrically assessed since joining a Portuguese circus in May 1967 when he was billed as 8 ft 8.3 in. This exaggerated height compares with an estimated actual height of 8 ft 0¾ in.

Tallest Twins

The tallest (identical) twins ever recorded are Michael and James Lanier (b Nov 27, 1969) of Troy, Mich, who both measure 7 ft 4 in.

Tallest Living Woman

The tallest living woman is Sandy Allen (b June 18, 1955, in Chicago), who now lives in Shelbyville, Ind. On July 14, 1977, she measured 7 ft 7¼ in at age 22, when she underwent a pituitary gland operation to inhibit further growth. A 6½-lb baby, her acromegalic growth began soon after birth. Her greatest weight has been about 462 lb. She takes a size 16EEE shoe.

Tallest Giantess

Giantesses are rarer than giants but their heights are still spectacular. The tallest woman in history was the acromegalic giantess Zeng Jinlian (pronounced San Chung Lin) (b June 26, 1964) of Yujiang village in the Bright Moon Commune, Hunan Province, central China.

TALLEST LIVING WOMAN: Sandy Allen, 7 ft 7¼ in tall, on her 26th birthday, was given a party by her friends in Niagara Falls, Ont, Canada. (*Gordon Counsell*)

TALLEST PEOPLE
(apart from Robert Wadlow)

		ft	in
John F. Carroll (1932–69) of Buffalo, NY	(a)	8	7¾
John William Rogan (1871–1905) of Gallatin, Tenn	(b)	8	6
Văinö Myllyrinne (1909–63) of Helsinki, Finland	(f)	8	3
Don Koehler (1925–81) of Denton, Mont, later Chicago	(d)	8	2
Bernard Coyne (1897–1921) of Anthon, Iowa	(e)	8	2
Patrick Cotter O'Brien (1760–1806) of Kinsale, County Cork, Ireland	(g)	8	1
"Constantine" (1872–1902) of Reutlingen, W. Germany	(h)	8	0.8
Gabriel Estavao Monjane (b 1944–*fl.* 1987) of Monjacaze, Mozambique	(j)	8	0.75
Sulaiman 'Ali Nashnush (b 1943–*fl.* 1986) of Tripoli, Libya	(i)	8	0.4

(a) Carroll was a victim of severe kypho-scoliosis (two-dimensional spinal curvature). The figure represents his height with assumed normal spinal curvature, calculated from a standing height of 8 ft 0 in, measured Oct 14, 1959. His standing height was 7 ft 8¼ in shortly before his death.
(b) Measured in a sitting position. Unable to stand owing to ankylosis (stiffening of the joints through the formation of adhesions) of the knees and hips. Weighed only 175 lb. Still growing at time of death.
(d) Abnormal growth started at age 10. He had a twin sister who is 5 ft 9 in tall. His father was 6 ft 2 in tall, his mother 5 ft 10 in.
(e) Eunuchoidal giant ("daddy-longlegs" syndrome). He was rejected by the US Army in 1918 when he stood 7 ft 9 in.
(f) Stood 7 ft 3½ in at the age of 21. Experienced a second phase of growth in his late thirties and measured 8 ft 1.2 in at the time of his death.
(g) Revised height based on skeletal remeasurement after bones exhumed Dec 19, 1972.
(h) Height estimated, as both legs were amputated after they turned gangrenous. He claimed a height of 8 ft 6 in. Eunuchoidal.
(i) Glandular injections in Rome in 1960 to check abnormal growth.
(j) Eunuchoidal. Now walks with aid of a stick after breaking his hip in a fall.

She could not stand erect, due to scoliosis, but was 8 ft 1¾ in long when she died on Feb 13, 1982. She began to grow abnormally from the age of 4 months and stood 5 ft 1½ in before her 4th birthday and 7 ft 1½ in when she was 13. Her hands measured 10 in and her feet 14 in in length. Her parents are 5 ft 4 in and 5 ft 1½ in while her brother was 5 ft 2 in tall at age 18.

Tallest Couple

Anna Hanen Swan (1846–88) of Nova Scotia, Canada, was billed at 8 ft 1 in but actually measured 7 ft 5½ in. In London, June 17, 1871, she married Martin van Buren Bates (1845–1919), of Whitesburg, Letcher County, Ky, who stood 7 ft 2½ in, making them the tallest married couple on record.

Shortest Little People

The strictures which apply to giants apply equally to dwarfs, except that exaggeration gives way to understatement. In the same way 9 ft may be regarded as the limit toward which the tallest giants tend, so 23 in must be regarded as the limit toward which the shortest mature dwarfs tend (*cf.* the average length of new-born babies is 18 to 20 in). In the case of child dwarfs their *ages* are often enhanced by their agents or managers.

TALLEST MARRIED COUPLE: The Canadian giantess Anna Hanen Swan, 7 ft 5½ in tall, married Martin van Buren Bates (not shown here) in London in 1871. Bates was only 3 in shorter than his wife. (*Gary Doidge*)

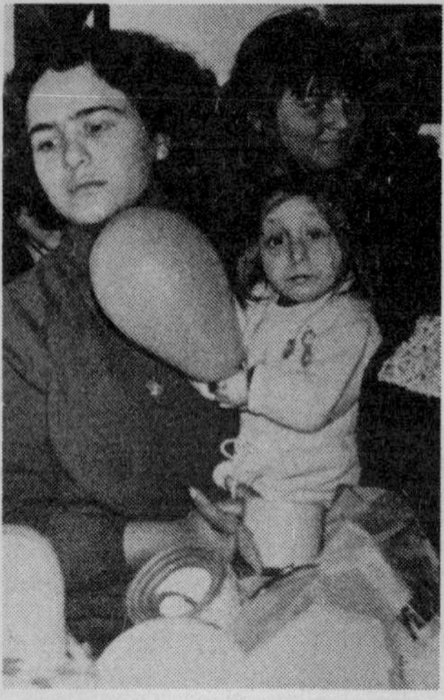

SHORTEST AND LIGHTEST GIRLS: (Above left) The little Greek girl, Stamatoula, photographed at age 9. In this picture, she weighed 4 lb 4 oz. (Left) Lucia Zarate of Mexico weighed 4.7 lb at age 17, after weighing 2½ lb at birth in 1863. (Above right) "Princess Pauline" Musters, a Dutch midget, weighed 9 lb at her heaviest and reached 23.2 in at age 19.

There are many forms of human dwarfism, but those suffering from ateliosis (midgets) are generally the shortest. They have essentially normal proportions but suffer from growth hormone deficiency. Such dwarfs tended to be more diminutive in the past due to lower nutritional standards.

The shortest mature human of whom there is independent evidence was Pauline Musters ("Princess Pauline"), a Dutch midget. She was born at Ossendrecht Feb 26, 1876, and measured 11.8 in at birth. At the age of 9 she was 21.65 in tall and weighed only 3 lb 5 oz. She died, at the age of 19, of pneumonia, with meningitis, in New York City on Mar 1, 1895. Although she was billed at 19 in, she had earlier been medically measured and found to be 23.2 in tall. A *post mortem* examination showed her to be exactly 24 in (there was some elongation after death). Her mature weight varied from 7½ lb to 9 lb and her "vital statistics" were 18½–19–17, which suggests she was overweight.

In 1979 a height of 19.68 in and a weight of 4 lb 6 oz were reported for a 9-year-old Greek girl named Stamatoula (b Sept 1969). She measured 5.9 in at birth. When she died on Aug 22, 1985, at the Lyrion Convent, Athens, she measured 26.4 in and weighed 11 lb. The child, believed to be the survivor of twins, suffered from Seckel's "bird-head" syndrome; victims have prominent eyes and noses. In Mar 1988 an unconfirmed height of 25.5 in was reported for a woman named Mary Bester (b 1965) living in S Africa.

Shortest Males

In 1938 a height of 19 in was attributed to Paul Del Rio (b Madrid, Spain, 1920) by *Life Magazine* when he visited Hollywood, but the fact that he created no "fuss" in the film capital and weighed as much as 12 lb suggests he was closer to 26 in tall.

The shortest recorded adult male dwarf was Calvin Phillips, born in Bridgewater, Mass, Jan 14, 1791. He weighed 2 lb at birth and stopped growing at the age of 5. When he was 19 he measured 26½ in tall and weighed 12 lb with his clothes on. He died two years later, in Apr 1812, from progeria, a rare disorder characterized by dwarfism and premature senility.

The shortest known mobile living adult human is Nelson de la Rosa (b June 1968), an ateliotic dwarf of Santo Domingo, Dominican Republic. On Apr 2, 1987, he was examined by the head of the nation's medical association who revealed this tiny man measured 28.3 in in height, weighed only 15 lb, had a 17½ in chest and 16 in waist. The doctor also reported Nelson had stopped growing. The rest of his family is normal-sized.

William E. Jackson, *alias* "Major Mite" (b Oct 2, 1864, Dunedin, New Zealand), measured 9 in long and weighed 12 oz at birth. In Nov 1880, he stood 21 in and weighed 9 lb. He died in NYC, on Dec 9, 1900, when he measured 27 in.

The most famous midget in history was Charles Sherwood Stratton, *alias* "General Tom Thumb," born Jan 4, 1838. When he came into the clutches of the circus proprietor P. T. Barnum, his birth date was changed to Jan 4, 1832, so that when he was billed as standing 30½ in at the age of 18 he was in fact only 12 years old.

At the age of 25, he married Lavinia Warren (2 ft 8 in) on Feb 10, 1863 while she was also in P. T. Barnum's Circus. Two thousand people attended the wedding at NYC's Grace Episcopal Church. At the hotel reception that followed, the bridal couple stood on top of a piano to greet the guests, then cut into a wedding cake that weighed more than they did together. Later, President Lincoln gave a reception for them at the White House, and they went on to 29 years of married life.

He died of apoplexy on July 15, 1883 in his birthplace of Bridgeport, Conn, aged 45 (not 51), and was then 3 ft 4 in tall.

Shortest Twins

The shortest twins ever recorded were the primordial dwarfs Matjus and Bela Matina (b 1903–*fl.* 1935) of Budapest, Hungary, who later became naturalized Americans. They both measured 30 in. The world's shortest living twins are John and Greg Rice (b Dec 1951) of West Palm Beach, Fla, who both measure 34 in.

Oldest Little People

There were only two centenarian dwarfs on record. The first was Miss Anne Clowes of Matlock, Derbyshire, England, who died Aug 5, 1784, at the age of 103. She was 3 ft 9 in tall and weighed 48 lb.

TALL TRIBESMAN: This member of the Tutsi of Central Africa, one of the tallest tribes, is seen here in a traditional native dance. (*Hutchinson Library*)

Hungarian-born Susanna Bokoyni ("Princess Susanna") of Newton, NJ, died, aged 105 years, on Aug 24, 1984. She was 3 ft 4 in tall and weighed 37 lb.

Tallest Tribes

The tallest major tribes are the slender Tutsi (also known as the Watutsi), herdsmen of Rwanda and Burundi, Central Africa, and the Dinka of the Sudan where the average adult height of the males is more than 6 ft. The S American Tehuelches of Patagonia, long regarded as of gigantic stature (7–8 ft average) have in fact an average adult male height of 5 ft 10 in. The same height is reported for the Montenegrins of Yugoslavia.

SHORTEST LIVING TWINS: The Rice brothers, John and Greg, of West Palm Beach, Fla, 34 in tall, love their special-size motorcycles.

SHORTEST LIVING MAN: Nelson de la Rosa poses in the indoor market place in his home town, Santo Domingo, Dominican Republic, with American "amigo," Richard L. Finkler. He is 19 years old, measures 28.3 in tall and weighs 15 lb.

Shortest Tribes

The smallest pygmies are the Mbuti, with an average height of 4 ft 6 in for men and 4 ft 5 in for women, with some groups averaging only 4 ft 4 in for men and 4 ft 1 in for women. They live in Zaïre, Africa.

Most Variable Stature

Adam Rainer, born in 1899 in Graz, Austria, measured 3 ft 10.45 in at the age of 21. But then he suddenly started growing at a rapid rate, and by 1931 he had reached 7 ft 1¾ in. He became so weak as a result that he was bedridden for the rest of his life. He measured 7 ft 8 in when he died on March 4, 1950, aged 51, and was the only person in medical history to have been both a dwarf and a giant.

Most Disparate Couple

Nigel Wilks (6 ft 7 in) of Kingston-upon-Hull, Eng, married Beverly Russell (3 ft 11 in), both aged 21, on June 30, 1984. Their son, Daniel, was 9 lb 5 oz, when born on Mar 22, 1986.

WEIGHT

Heaviest Men

The heaviest human in medical history was Jon Brower Minnoch (1941–83) of Bainbridge Island, Wash, who was carried on planking by a rescue team of 12 firefighters to a ferryboat to University Hospital, Seattle, in March 1978. Dr Robert Schwartz, the endocrinological consultant, estimated that he was "probably more" than 1,400 lb, a great deal of which was water accumulation due to his congestive heart problem. His highest actually recorded body weight was 975 lb in Sept 1976. It took 13 attendants to roll him over in his hospital bed. After nearly 2 years on a 1200-calorie-per-day diet he was discharged at 476 lb. He had to be readmitted in Oct 1981 having reportedly gained 200 lb in 7 days. This former taxicab driver stood 6 ft 1 in tall. He was 400 lb in 1963; 700 lb in 1966; and about 975 lb in late 1976. When Minnoch died in Sept 1983, he weighed more than 800 lbs and had to be rolled in his hospital bed to the funeral home and buried in a double-size wooden casket that took up two cemetery plots.

Fattest Living Man

On Sept 14, 1987 Walter Hudson (b Nov 1954) of NYC, made the headlines when he became wedged in his bedroom doorway and had to be rescued by firemen. It took 9 men to carry him back to the reinforced bed in which he had been virtually a prisoner for 27 years. Later, when an attempt was made to weigh him on an industrial scale which registered up to 1,000 lb, the machine broke down, but the 6-ft heavyweight was estimated to weigh somewhere between 1,050 and 1,200 lb. He measures 106 in around the chest and now 110 in around the waist. Hudson went on a special weight-loss program and by Mar 1988 had lost about 280 lb.

Heaviest Twins

The heaviest were the performers Billy Leon and Benny Loyd McCrary, *alias* Billy and Benny McGuire (b Dec 7, 1946) of

Hendersonville, NC, who were normal in size until the age of 6, when they contracted German measles. In Nov 1978, they were weighed at 743 lb (Billy) and 723 lb (Benny) and had 84-in waists. As professional tag wrestling performers, they were *billed* at weights up to 770 lb. Billy died of heart failure on July 13, 1979, in Niagara Falls, Canada, after falling from his mini-bike. He was buried in a cubic coffin with a total weight of over 1000 lb in Hendersonville. A hydraulic lift was needed to lower the coffin to its final resting place. After one 6-week slimming course in a hospital, they emerged weighing 5 lb more each.

HEAVIEST TWINS: ▲ Benny and the late Billy McCrary (McGuire) weighed almost 1,500 lb together. They were normal at birth.

HEAVYWEIGHT: ► Mrs Flora Mae Jackson, 5 ft 9 in, known in show business as "Baby Flo" (b 1930 Shuqualak, Miss) weighed an authenticated 841 lb on Dec 9, 1965, just before she died.

HEAVIEST MEN

	lb
Jon Brower Minnoch (1941–83) US 6 ft 1 in	1,400
Walter Hudson (b Nov 1954) US 6 ft	1,200
Michael Walker (*née* Francis Lang) (b 1934) US 6 ft 2 in	1,187 (1)
Robert Earl Hughes (1926–58) US 6 ft ½ in	1,069
Mohamed Naaman (b 1946) Kenya 6 ft	1,050
Mills Darden (1798–1857) US 7 ft 6 in	1,020
"Big Tex" (1902 —*fl* 1956) US 6 ft 1 in	924
John Hanson Craig (1856–94) US 6 ft 5 in	907 (3)
Arthur Knorr (1914–60) US 6 ft 1 in	900 (4)
T. J. Albert Jackson (b 1941) Canton, Miss 6 ft 4 in	898 (5)
Albert Pernitsch (b 1956) Grafkorn, Austria 5 ft 9 in	880 (6)
Toubi (b 1946) Cameroon	857½
Ron High (b 1953) Chicago	853 (7)
T. A. Valenzuela (1895–1937) Mexico 5 ft 11 in	850
Chief Wise Owl (b 1939) US 5 ft 4 in	850 (2)
Joseph Schorr (1934–80) US 6 ft 4 in	846

1. Peak weight 1971. Reduced to 369 lb by Feb 1980.
2. Weight not independently corroborated. Winner of National Enquirer "Biggest Belly" contest announced Sept 9, 1986. Waist reputedly 111 in.
3. Won $1,000 in "Bonny Baby" contest in NYC in 1858.
4. Gained 300 lb in last 6 months of his life.
5. Born Kent Nicholson, 22 lb.
6. His left arm is tattooed "Nobody is perfect." Girth 78¾ in in July 1984.
7. Reduced by dieting to 340 lb in 16 months by Jan 6, 1987.

Heaviest Women

The heaviest woman ever was the late Mrs Percy Pearl Washington (b Louisiana, 1926) who died in a hospital in Milwaukee, Wis, Oct 9, 1972. The hospital scales registered only up to 800 lb, but she was believed to weigh about 880 lb. She was 6 ft tall and wore a size 62 dress. The previous weight record for a woman was set 84 years earlier at 850 lb although a wholly unsubstantiated report exists of a woman, Mrs Ida Maitland (1898–1932) of Springfield, Miss, who reputedly weighed 911 lb.

Lightest Humans

The lightest adult human on record was Lucia Zarate (b San Carlos, Mexico, Jan 2, 1863, d Oct 1889), an emaciated ateliotic dwarf of

26½ in who weighed 4.7 lb at the age of 17. She "fattened up" to 13 lb by her 20th birthday. At birth she had weighed 2½ lb.

The thinnest recorded adults of normal height are those suffering from Simmonds' disease (hypophyseal cachexia). Losses up to 65% of the original body weight have been recorded in females, with a "low" of 45 lb in the case of Emma Shaller (b St Louis, Mo, July 8, 1868, d Oct 4, 1890) who stood 5 ft 2 in tall.

Edward C. Hagner USA (1892–1962), *alias* Eddie Masher, is alleged to have weighed only 48 lb at a height of 5 ft 7 in. He was also known as "the Skeleton Dude." In Aug 1825 the biceps measurement of Claude-Ambroise Seurat (b Apr 1, 1797, d Apr 6, 1826), of Troyes, France, was 4 in and the distance between his back and his chest was less than 3 in. According to one report, he stood 5 ft 7½ in and weighed 78 lb, but in another account was described as 5 ft 4 in and only 36 lb.

It was recorded that the American performer Rosa Lee Plemons (b 1873) weighed 27 lb at the age of 18.

Greatest Weight Differential

The greatest recorded for a married couple is *c.* 1,300 lb in the case of Jon Brower Minnoch (see page 10) and his 110-lb wife Jeannette in Mar 1978. She bore him two sons.

Slimming

The greatest recorded slimming feat was that of William J. Cobb (b 1926), *alias* "Happy Humphrey," a professional wrestler of Augusta, Ga. It was reported in July 1965 that he had reduced from 802 lb to 232 lb, a loss of 570 lb, in 2½ years. His waist measurement declined from 101 to 44 in. In Oct 1985, "Happy" reported he was back to a normal 432 lb.

The US circus fat lady Mrs Celesta Geyer (b 1901), *alias* Dolly Dimples, reduced from 553 lb to 152 lb 1950–51, a loss of 401 lb in 14 months. Her vital statistics diminished *pari passu* from 79–84–84 to a svelte 34–28–36. Her book "How I Lost 400 lb" was not a best seller. In Dec 1967, she was reportedly down to 110 lb.

By July 1979, Jon Brower Minnoch (see page 10) had reduced to 476 lb; if the peak weight quoted for him was authentic, this indicates a weight loss of 924 lb in 16 months, a speed record of 14.4 lb per week.

Richard Stephens of Birmingham, Ala, slimmed from 467 lb to 305¾ lb in 157 days from Apr 12 to Sept 1985.

Roly McIntyre (b 1952, N Ireland) reduced from 592 lb to 187 lb between Apr 1983 and Feb 1985, a loss of 405 lb in 22 months, or 18.4 lb per month.

Ron Allen (b 1947) sweated off 21½ lb of his 250- lb frame in Nashville, Tenn in 24 hours in Aug 1984.

The speed record for slimming was established by Paul M. Kimelman, 21, of Pittsburgh, Pa, who from Jan 1, 1967 to Aug 3, 1967, went on a crash diet of 300 to 600 calories per day to reduce from 487 lb to 130 lb, a total loss of 357 lb. He later stabilized at 175 lb.

Weight Gaining

The reported record for gaining weight was set by Jon Minnoch (see page 10) when in Oct 1981 he was readmitted to University Hospital, Seattle, Wash, having re-gained 200 lb in 7 days.

Arthur Knorr (see page 12) gained 300 lb in the last 6 months of his life.

Miss Doris James of San Francisco is alleged to have gained 325 lb in the 12 months before her death in Aug 1965, aged 38, at a weight of 675 lb. She was only 5 ft 2 in tall.

2. ORIGINS OF MAN

The earliest known primates appeared in the Paleocene period about 69 million years ago. The earliest members of the sub-order Anthropoidea are known from both Africa and South America in the early Oligocene period, 34–30 million years ago.

Earliest Man

Characteristics typical of the Hominidae, such as the large brain and bipedal locomotion do not appear until much later. The earliest undoubted hominid relic found is an Australopithecine jawbone with two molars 2 in in length found near Lake Baringo, Kenya, in Feb 1984 and dated at 4 million years by associated fossils, and to 5.6–5.4 million years through rock correlation by potassium-argon dating.

The most complete of the earliest skeletons of *Homo* is that of "Lucy" (40% complete) found by Dr Donald C. Johanson and T. Gray at Locality 162 by the Awash river, Hadar, in the Afr region of Ethiopia on Nov 30, 1974. She was estimated to be about 40 years old when she died about 3 million years ago, and she was 3½ ft tall.

Parallel tracks of hominid footprints extending over 80 ft were discovered at Laetoli, Tanzania, in 1978, in volcanic ash dating to 3.5 million years ago. The height of the smallest of the seemingly three beings was estimated to be 3 ft 11 in.

OLDEST MAN WHO EVER LIVED: At a verified 120 years 237 days before he died in Feb 1986, Shigechiyo Izumi of Japan is the undisputed record holder.

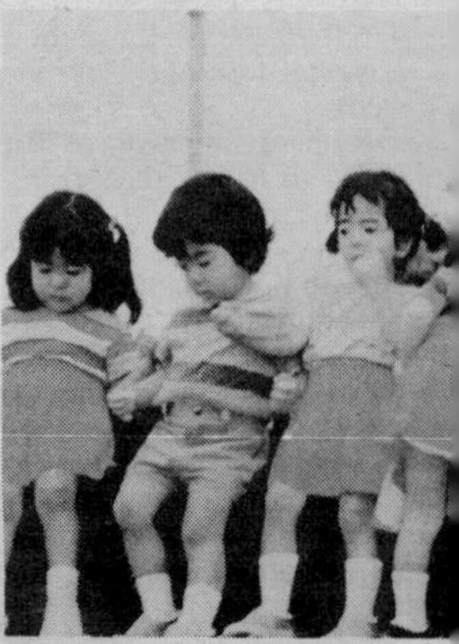

The earliest species of the genus *Homo* is *Homo habilis* or "Handy Man" named by Prof. Raymond A. Dart (b 1893, Australia) in 1964. The greatest age attributed to fossils is for the skull "1470" discovered by Bernard Ngeneo at Koobi Fora, North Kenya. It is dated to 1.9 million years old and was reconstructed by Dr Meave Leakey (*née* Epps).

The earliest stone tools are abraded core choppers dating from *c.* 2.5 million years. They were found at Hadar, Ethiopia in 1976 by Helene Roche (France). Finger- (as opposed to fist-) held quartz dicers found by Roche close to the Hadar site by the Gona River are also dated to *c.* 2.5 million years.

What is believed to be the earliest *Homo erectus* (upright man), the species directly ancestral to *Homo sapiens,* was discovered by Kamoya Kimen on the surface at the site of Nariokotome III to the west of Lake Turkana, Kenya, in 1984. The skeleton of a 12-year-old boy is the most complete of this species ever found, only a few small pieces being missing.

The earliest evidence for the presence of man in the Americas could date from at least 50,000 BC or "more probably 100,000 BC" according to the late Dr Louis Leakey after the examination of some hearth stones found in the Mojave Desert, Calif, and announced in Oct 1970. The earliest human relic is a skull found in the area of Los Angeles, dated in Dec 1970 to be from 22,000 BC.

3. LONGEVITY

Centenarians

No single subject is more obscured by vanity, deceit, falsehood and deliberate fraud than the extremes of human longevity. Extreme claims are generally made on behalf of the very aged rather than *by* them.

Many hundreds of claims throughout history have been made for persons living well into their second century and some, insulting to the intelligence, for people living even into their third. The facts are that centenarians surviving beyond their 113th year are of the extremest rarity and the present absolute limit of proven human longevity does not admit of anyone living to celebrate any birthday after their 120th.

It was announced in Feb 1984 that the 1982 census in China revealed only 2,450 centenarians of whom two thirds were women, from a population of more than 1 billion. In the US the mid-1983 figure was 32,000. Birth and death registration, however, became complete only in 1933 and was only 30.9% complete by 1915.

Oldest Authentic Centenarians

The greatest *authenticated* age to which any human has ever lived is a unique 120 years 237 days in the case of Shigechiyo Izumi of Asan, Tokunoshima Island, Japan. He was born on the island on June 29, 1865, and recorded as a 6-year-old in Japan's first census of 1871. He died at his home, a double-glazed bungalow, at 12:15 GMT on Feb 21, 1986 after developing pneumonia.

Oldest Living Person

At age 112 on Aug 3, 1988, Mrs Birdie May Vogt (née Musser) (b Akron, O) is the oldest living person for whom there is adequate authentication. She was married on Nov 10, 1929 and now resides in a retirement village in Miami, Fla.

(A table of oldest persons in each country appears in all the annual "Guinness" editions prior to this one.)

4. REPRODUCTIVITY

Most Children

The greatest officially recorded number of children produced by a mother is 69 by the first of the 2 wives of Feodor Vassilyev (b 1707–*fl.* 1782), a peasant from Shuya, 150 miles east of Moscow. In 27 confinements she gave birth to 16 pairs of twins, 7 sets of triplets and 4 sets of quadruplets. The children, of whom almost all survived to their majority, were born in the period *c.* 1725–1765. At least 67 survived infancy. The case was reported to Moscow by the Monastery of Nikolskiy Feb 27, 1782. Empress Ekaterina II (The Great) (1762–96) was reputed to have evinced wonderment.

Currently the world's most prolific mother is reported to be Leontina Albina (*née* Espinosa) (b 1925?)—she claims to be 3 years younger—of San Antonio, Chile, who prior to May 1988 produced 59 children. Her husband Gerardo Secundo Albina (b 1921?)—he admits to 73, she says "he's really pushing 80"—states that they were married in Argentina in 1943 and they had 5 sets of triplets (all boys) before coming to Chile.

Septuplets

The only birth of 7 at a time in the US occurred on May 21, 1985, when septuplets were born to Patti Jorgenson (Mrs) Frustaci of Orange, Calif, a 30- year-old English teacher who had been taking a fertility drug. One baby was stillborn. The infants who lived ranged in weight from 1 lb upwards. In the weeks that followed, 3 more babies died, leaving 3 that survived.

Oldest Mother

Medical literature contains extreme but unauthenticated cases of septuagenarian mothers such as Mrs Ellen Ellis, aged 72, of Four Crosses, Clwyd, Wales, who allegedly produced a stillborn 13th child May 15, 1776, in her 46th year of marriage. Many very late maternities are cover-ups for illegitimate grandchildren. The oldest recorded mother of whom there is satisfactory verification (provided by the doctor who attended her) was Mrs Ruth Alice Kistler (*née* Taylor), formerly Mrs Shepard (1899–1982), of Portland, Ore. She was born in Wakefield, Mass, June 11, 1899, and gave birth to a daughter, Suzan, in Glendale, Calif, Oct 18, 1956, when her age was 57 years 129 days.

OLDEST MOTHER: When she was more than 57 years old, Mrs Ruth Kistler bore daughter Suzan. (*"Family Doctor" magazine* (*IPC*))

Quindecaplets

It was announced by Dr Gennaro Montanino of Rome that he had removed the fetuses of 10 girls and 5 boys from the womb of a 35-year-old housewife July 22, 1971. A fertility drug was responsible for this unique and unsurpassed instance of quindecaplets.

"Siamese" Twins

Conjoined twins derived the name ''Siamese'' from the celebrated Chang and Eng Bunker (known in Thailand as Chan and In) born at Meklong, on May 11, 1811 of Chinese parents. They were joined by a cartilaginous band at the chest and married in Apr 1843 the Misses Sarah and Adelaide Yates of Wilkes County, NC, and fathered 10 and

MULTIPLE BIRTHS

Highest number reported at single birth (Decaplets): 10 (2 male, 8 female), Bacacay, Brazil, Apr 22, 1946 (also report from Spain, 1924, and China, May 12, 1936).

Highest number medically recorded (Nonuplets): 9 (5 male, 4 female), to Mrs Geraldine Brodrick at Royal Hospital, Sydney, Australia, June 13, 1971. 2 males were stillborn. Richard (12 oz) survived 6 days. 9 (all died), to patient at University of Penn, Philadelphia, May 29, 1972. 9 (all died), reported from Bagerhat, Bangladesh, *c.* May 11, 1977, to 30-year-old mother.

Highest number and percent surviving: 6 out of 6 sextuplets (3 males, 3 females), to Mrs Susan Jane Rosenkowitz (*née* Scoones) (b Colombo, Sri Lanka, Oct 28, 1947) at Mowbray, Cape Town, South Africa, Jan 11, 1974. In order of birth they were: David, Nicolette, Jason, Emma, Grant and Elizabeth; 24 lb 1 oz. was their total weight. 6 out of 6 (4 males, 2 females) to Mrs Rosanna Giannini (b 1952) at Careggi Hospital, Florence, Italy, on Jan 11, 1980. They are Francesco, Fabrizio, Giorgio, Roberto, Letizia and Linda. 6 out of 6 (all female) to Mrs Janet Walton (b 1952) at Liverpool Maternity Hospital, England, Nov 18, 1983.

Quintuplets (Heaviest): 25 lb to Mrs Lui Saulien, Chekiang, China, June 7, 1953. 25 lb to Mrs Kamalammal, Pondicherry, India, Dec 30, 1956. (Most sets): No recorded case of more than a single set.

Quadruplets (Heaviest): 22 lb 13 oz to Mrs Ayako Takeda, Tsuchihashi Maternity Hospital, Kagoshima, Japan, Oct 4, 1978 (4 girls). (Most sets): 4, to Mme Feodor Vassilyev (d *ante* 1770), of Shuya, Russia.

Triplets (Heaviest): 26 lb 6 oz (unconfirmed), Iranian case (2 male, 1 female), March 18, 1968. (Most sets): 15, to Maddalena Granata (1839–*fl.* 1886), Nocera Superiore, Italy. Mrs Anna Steynvaait of Johannesburg, South Africa, produced 2 sets within 10 months in 1960.

Twins (Heaviest): 27 lb 12 oz (surviving), 14 lb and 13 lb 12 oz, to Mrs J. P. Haskin, Fort Smith, Ark, Feb 20, 1924. (Most sets): 16, to Mme Vassilyev (*see p 16*). 15, to Mrs Mary Jonas (d Dec 4, 1899), of Chester, England, all sets were boy and girl. Mrs Barbara Zulu of Barbeton, South Africa, bore 3 sets of girls and 3 mixed sets in 7 years (1967–73).

12 children, respectively. They died within three hours of each other on Jan 17, 1874, aged 62.

Longest Interval Between Twins

Mrs. Danny Berg (b 1953) of Rome, Italy, who had been on hormone treatment after suffering two miscarriages, gave birth normally to a baby girl, Diana, on Dec 23, 1987, but the other twin, Monica, was not delivered until Jan 30, 1988 and then by Caesarean section.

Multiple Great-Grandparents

The report in 1983 that Jane Kau Pung (1877–1982) had left 4 great-great-great-great-grand- children has proved to be incorrect. She in fact proved to be one of many cases of great-great-great- grandparents. Of these cases the youngest person to learn that their great-granddaughter had become a grandmother was Mrs Ann V. Weirick (1888–1978) of Paxtonville, Pa, who received news of her great-great-great-grandson Matthew Stork (b. Sept 9, 1976) when aged only 88. She died on Jan 6, 1978.

SEXTUPLETS: The Walton girls, just prior to their third birthday, face the camera. Left to right: Hannah, Sarah, Kate, Lucy, Ruth and Jenny. Mother, Janet Walton of Liverpool, Eng, not shown. *(Camera Press)*

Lightest Twins

The lightest recorded birth weight for surviving twins is 2 lb 3 oz in the case of Mary (16 oz) and Margaret (19 oz) born to Mrs Florence Stimson of Peterborough, England, delivered by Dr Macaulay, Aug 16, 1931.

Oldest Twins

The chances of identical twins both reaching 100 are said to be one in 50 million. The oldest recorded twins were Eli and John Phipps, born Feb 14, 1803, in Affinghton, Virginia. Eli died at the age of 108 years 9 days Feb 23, 1911, in Hennessey, Okla, at which time John was still living, in Shenandoah, Iowa. Identical twins Mildred Widman Philippi and Mary Widman Franzini, born in St Louis, Mo, missed reaching their 105th birthday together, by 44 days, when Mildred died on May 4, 1985.

The oldest living twins are Allie Hill and Maggie Lambeth (*née* Grubb), who reside in Mountain Vista Health Park, Denton, NC, born on Jan 13, 1884, and who celebrated their 104th birthday in 1988.

Longest-Separated Twins

Twins Lloyd Ecre and Floyd Ellswerk Clark were born on Feb 15, 1917 in Nebraska. They were separated when only 4 months old and lived under their adopted names Dewayne William Gramly (Lloyd) and Paul Edward Forbes (Floyd). Both men knew that they had been born twins, but it wasn't until June 16, 1986 that they were reunited, having been separated for over 69 years.

Most Twins, Geographically

In Chungchon, South Korea, it was reported in Sept 1981 that there were unaccountably 38 pairs in only 275 families—the highest ratio ever recorded.

Descendants

In polygamous countries, the number of a person's descendants soon becomes incalculable. The last Sharifian Emperor of Morocco, Moulay Ismail (1672–1727), known as "The Bloodthirsty," was reputed to have fathered a total of 525 sons and 342 daughters by 1703, and a 700th son in 1721.

In April 1984 the death was reported of Adam Borntrager, aged 96, of Medford, Wis, who had had 707 direct descendants of whom all but 32 were living. The total comprised 11 children, 115 grand, 529 great-grand and 20 great-great grandchildren. The family is Amish-Mennonite, eschews cars, telephones, electric light, and higher education.

Most Living Ascendants

Megan Sue Austin (b May 16, 1982) of Bar Harbor, Maine, had a full set of grandparents and great-grandparents and five great-great-grandparents making 19 direct ascendants.

Oldest Quadruplets

The world's oldest quads are the Ottman quads of Munich, W Germany—Adolf, Anne-Marie, Emma and Elisabeth. They celebrated their 76th birthday on May 5, 1988.

Oldest Triplets

The longest-lived triplets on record were Faith, Hope, and Charity Caughlin, born Mar 27, 1868, in Marlboro, Mass. Mrs (Ellen) Hope Daniels was the first to die, Mar 2, 1962, when 93.

Fastest Triplet Birth

The fastest recorded natural birth of triplets has been 2 minutes in the case of Mrs James E. Duck of Memphis, Tenn (Bradley, Christopher and Carmon) March 21, 1977.

Longest Pregnancy

Claims up to 413 days have been widely reported, but accurate data are bedevilled by the increasing use of oral contraceptive pills, which can be a cause of amenorrhea. Some women on becoming pregnant erroneously add some preceding periodless months to their pregnancy. In the pre-pill era, English law had accepted pregnancies with extremes of 174 days (1939), and 349 days (1949).

In May 1961 a Burmese woman in Rangoon aged 54 gave birth to a 3-lb calcified baby after 25 years gestation.

Most Premature Birth

Ernestine Hudgins was born (weighing 17 oz) about 18 weeks premature in San Diego, Calif, on Feb 8, 1983. This has been equaled by Alexander McGlade, born in Middlesbrough, Cleveland, Eng on May 20, 1986 at the same weight. Exactly a year later, a 22-oz baby was born 18 weeks (126 days) premature, to Brenda and James Gill of Ottawa, Ont, Canada.

Birth After Death

A woman who had been kept alive by breathing mechanically gave birth to a 3-lb 11-oz baby girl 84 days after she had had a seizure, the longest time a fetus has been carried in a clinically-dead mother and survived. The event occurred in Roanoke (Va) Memorial Hospital July 5, 1983.

BABIES

Heaviest Babies

The heaviest viable baby on record of normal parentage was a boy of 22 lb 8 oz born to Signora Carmelina Fedele of Aversa, Italy, in Sept 1955. Tying the record at 22 lb 8 oz, a boy named Sithandive was delivered by Caesarean section to Mrs Christina Samane on May 24, 1982, at Sipetu Hospital, Transkei, S Africa. He weighed 77 lb at 16 months, and 112 lb at age 5.

Mrs Anna Bates, *née* Swan, the 7-ft-5½-in Canadian giantess (see Tallest Couple), gave birth to a boy weighing 23 lb 12 oz (length 30 in) at her home in Seville, Ohio, on Jan 19, 1879, but the baby died less than 24 hours later. Her first child, an 18-lb girl (length 24 in), was stillborn when she was delivered in 1872.

On Jan 9, 1891, Mrs Florentin Ortega of Buenos Aires, Argentina, produced a stillborn boy weighing 25 lb.

In May 1939 a deformed baby weighing 29 lb 4 oz was born in a hospital at Effingham, Ill, but died two hours later from respiratory problems.

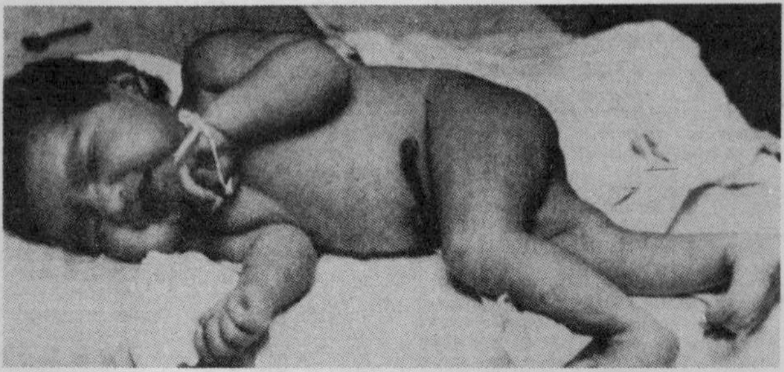

FIRST TEST TUBE BABY: Louise Brown weighed 5 lb 12 oz at birth. She was conceived externally in England in 1977.

LEAP-YEAR BABIES: The 3 children of the Henriksen family of Andenes, Norway—Heidi (b 1960); Olav (b 1964) and Lief-Martin (b 1968)—all celebrate their birthday infrequently because these all fall on Leap Year Day—Feb 29.

MOST PREMATURE BABY: James Elgin Gill, 22 oz at birth May 20, 1987, was 128 days premature, one of 3 similar cases.

Most Bouncing Baby

The most bouncing baby on record was probably James Weir (1819–21) whose headstone in the Old Parish Cemetery, Wishaw, Strathclyde, Scotland, lists him at 112 lb, 3 ft 4 in in height, and 39 in around the waist at the age of 13 months.

T.J. Albert Jackson (see Heaviest Living Man) claimed that he weighed 105 lb and stood 4 ft 1 in tall at the age of 12 months.

Brazil's "super-baby" Veridiano dos Santos (b 1978) weighed 143 lb aged 5, and 187 lb aged 7, with a 43-in waist.

Theresebabies Parentean, who died in Rouyn, Quebec, Canada, aged 9, May 11, 1936, weighed 340 lb (*cf.* 378 lb for Robert Earl Hughes at 10 years of age).

Lightest

The lowest birth weight recorded for a surviving infant, of which there is definite evidence, is 10 oz in the case of Mrs Marion Taggart *née* Chapman, born 6 weeks prematurely on June 5, 1938, in South Shields, northwest England. She was born unattended (length 12¼ in) and was nursed by Dr D. A. Shearer, who fed her hourly for the first 30 hours with brandy, glucose and water through a fountain-pen filler. At three weeks she weighed 1 lb 13 oz and by her first birthday her weight had increased to 13 lb 14 oz. Her weight on her 21st birthday was 106 lb. She died May 31, 1983.

A weight of 8 oz was reported on March 20, 1938, for a baby born prematurely to Mrs John Womack, after she had been knocked down by a truck in East St Louis, Ill. The baby was taken alive to St Mary's Hospital, died a few hours later. On Feb 23, 1952, it was reported that a 6 oz baby only 6½ in in length lived for 12 hours in a hospital in Indianapolis. A twin was stillborn.

Earliest Test Tube Baby

Louise Brown (5 lb 12 oz) was delivered by Caesarean section from Lesley Brown, 31, in Oldham General Hospital, Lancashire, England, at 11:47 p.m. July 25, 1978. She was externally conceived on Nov 10, 1977.

Earliest Frozen Embryo Birth

A 5½-lb infant girl named Zoe was reported by the Associated Press on Apr 10, 1984 as having been born in Melbourne, Australia from an embryo that had been frozen. An ovum from the mother had been fertilized in a laboratory with her husband's sperm and then frozen for 2 months, before being implanted in the mother's uterus where it developed normally until delivery by Caesarean section.

Coincidental Birth Dates

While July 4 is celebrated by 225 million Americans, it has special significance for the Williams family of Wilmington, NC. Ralph Bertram Williams IV was born on July 4, 1982, his father (same name, but III) was born on July 4, his grandfather (same name, but Jr) was born on July 4, and his great-grandfather (Sr) was born on July 4, 1876, exactly 100 years after the Declaration of Independence.

The only verified example of a family producing five single children with coincidental birthdays is that of Catherine (1952), Carol (1953), Charles (1956), Claudia (1961) and Cecilia (1966), born to Ralph and Carolyn Cummins of Clintwood, Va, all on Feb 20th. The random odds against five such births occurring singly on the same date would be 1 to 17,797,577,730—more than 3½ times the world's population.

Catherine and Les Rittenhouse of Alliance, Alberta, Canada became grandparents of 3 girls within 3 hours from 12:17 to 3:28 PM on Feb 28, 1988. The 3 babies were born to 2 daughters and one son of the Rittenhouses. The mothers did not know that their sisters and sister-in-law were in the hospital having babies at the same time.

---

5. PHYSIOLOGY AND ANATOMY

Longest Bones

The longest recorded bone was the *femur* of the 8-ft German giant Constantine, who died in Mons, Belgium, March 30, 1902, aged 30. It measured 29.9 in. The *femur* of Robert Wadlow, the tallest man ever recorded, measured an estimated 29½ in.

Smallest Brain

The lightest "normal" or non-atrophied brain on record weighed 2 lb 6.7 oz, belonging to a 31-year- old woman. It was reported by Dr P. Davis and Prof E. Wright of King's College Hospital, London, in 1977.

Largest Brains

The brain of an average adult male (*i.e.*, 20–55 years) weighs 3 lb 2.2 oz, falling to 3 lb 1.1 oz. The heaviest brain ever recorded was that of a 50-year-old male which weighed 4 lb 8.29 oz, reported by Dr Thomas F. Hegert, chief medical examiner for District 9, Fla, on Oct 23, 1975.

Prof Marian Diamond of the Univ of Calif, at Berkeley, announced on Feb 13, 1985 that the neuron-to-glial-cell ratio in Section 39 of the brain of Albert Einstein (1879–1955) was 1.12 as opposed to the standard 1.936.

Human Memory

Bhandanta Vicitsara recited 16,000 pages of Buddhist canonical texts in Rangoon, Burma, in May 1974. Gou Yan-ling, 26, has memorized more than 15,000 telephone numbers in Harbin, China, according to the Xinhua News Agency. Rare instances of eidetic memory, the ability to reproject and thus "visually" recall material, are known to science.

Creighton Carvello memorized a random sequence of 6 separate packs of cards (312) on a single sighting with only 4 errors including an all correct straight run of 139 cards at the New Marske Institute Club, Cleveland, Eng on Mar 21, 1985. Jonathan Hancock (b Feb 12, 1972) of Middlesbrough, Cleveland, achieved a rarer accomplishment by memorizing a random sequence of 6 packs shuffled all together on Apr 30, 1988 with only 6 errors at the Dolphin Leisure Centre, Darlington, Durham, Eng.

Most Expensive Skull

The Swedish Academy of Sciences paid $9,900 on Mar 6, 1977 for the skull of Emanuel Swedenborg (1688–1772), a famous Swedish philosopher and theologian.

Human Computer

The fastest extraction of a 13th root from a 100-digit number is in 1 min 28.8 sec by Willem Klein (The Netherlands, 1914–86), on Apr 7, 1981 at the National Laboratory for High Energy Physics (KEK), Tsukuba, Japan.

Mrs Shakuntala Devi of India demonstrated the multiplication of two 13-digit numbers 7,686,369,774,870 × 2,465,099,745,779 picked at random by the Computer Department of Imperial College, London on June 18, 1980, in 28 sec. Her correct answer was 18,947,668,177,995,426,462,773,730. Some eminent mathematical writers have questioned the conditions under which this was apparently achieved and predict that it would be impossible for her to replicate such a feat under highly rigorous surveillance. However, during 1987, she convinced experts in the US of her skill, and in addition performed other feats to prove her ability to calculate.

Highest IQ

Intelligence quotients or IQ's comprise the subject's mental age divided by his chronological or actual age multiplied by 100, so that an 8-year-old more gifted than an average 16-year-old would have an IQ of $\frac{16}{8} \times 100 = 200$. The highest childhood score has been achieved by Marilyn (née vos Savant) Jarvik of St. Louis, Mo, who as a 10-year-old achieved a ceiling score for 23-year-olds, thus giving her an IQ of 228.

In adult High IQ clubs, admission requirements are not on IQ points but are gauged in percentiles. An IQ exhibited by 1 person in 10,000 for instance coincides with 158 on the Stanford-Binet scale but 187 on the Cattell scale. The most elite ultra-high IQ society is the Mega Society with 26 members with percentiles of 99.9999, or 1 in a million. The topmost scorer in the Mega admission test, devised by its founder Ronald K. Hoeflin, has been 46 out of 48 by Marilyn Jarvik (see above).

The highest IQ published for a national population is 115 for the Japanese born in 1960–61. At least 10 percent of their whole population has an IQ over 130.

Memorizing Pi

Hideaki Tomoyori (b Sept 30, 1932), of Yokohama, Japan, recited pi from memory to 40,000 places in 17 hours 21 min including 4 hours 15 min breaks Mar 9–10, 1987 at the Tsukuba University Club House. On a Japanese TV program, Mr Tomoyori also demonstrated his ability to recite correctly the 20 consecutive digits following a randomly selected series of numbers.

(Note: It is only the *approximation* of π at 22/7 which recurs after its sixth decimal place and can, of course, be recited *ad nauseam*. The true value is a string of random numbers fiendishly difficult to memorize. The average ability for memorizing random numbers is barely more than 8, as proved by the common inability to memorize 9 or 10 digit telephone numbers.)

Smallest Waists

Queen Catherine de Medici (1519–89) decreed a standard waist measurement of 13 in for ladies of the French court. This was at a time when females were more diminutive. The smallest recorded waist among women of normal stature in the 20th century is a reputed 13 in in the cases of the French actress Mlle Polaire (1881–1939) and Mrs Ethel Granger (1905–82) of Peterborough, England, who reduced from a natural 22 in over the period 1929–39.

Largest Chest Measurements

The largest chest measurements are among endomorphs (those with a tendency toward globularity). In the extreme case of Robert Earl Hughes of Monticello, Mo (one of the heaviest recorded humans), this was 124 in. The next largest measurement was 96 in attributed to William Campbell (GB), Britain's second heaviest man who weighed 750 lb.

Among muscular subjects (mesomorphs) of normal height *expanded* chest measurements above 56 in are extremely rare. Gentleman Dan

WAIST: ▲
13
in:
Ethel
Granger
(Eng).

LARGEST MUSCULAR CHEST: ▲
"Gentleman" Dan Bernhardt of Salt Lake City, U, shows his 70-in expanded chest.

◄

LONGEST NECKS: The Padaung women of Burma are much admired for the length of their necks. The copper coils, however, make neck turning difficult and the muscles tend to atrophy. *(Planet News)*

Bernhardt of Salt Lake City, Utah had a 70-in expanded chest in 1977. Vasili Alexeyev (b 1942), the 6-ft-1¼-in Russian super-heavyweight weight-lifting champion, had a 60½-in chest at his top weight of 350 lb.

Arnold Schwarzenegger (b 1948, Graz, Austria), the 6-ft-1-in former Mr Universe and "the most perfectly developed man in the history of the world," had a chest measurement of 57 in at his best body weight of 235 lb.

Largest Biceps

Isaac (Dr Size) Nesser (b Apr 21 1962) has biceps of over 26⅛ in cold (not pumped). He has a chest measurement of 68¹⁄₁₆ in, a waist of 43¹⁄₁₆ in, and weighs 362 lb.

Longest Necks

The maximum measured extension of the neck by the successive fitting of copper coils, as practiced by the Padaung or Kareni people of Burma, is 15¾ in. The neck muscles become so atrophied that the removal of the rings produces asphyxiation in some cases. In others, the muscles shrink back to their normal size.

Most Fingers and Toes

At an inquest held on a baby at Shoreditch, East London, England, on Sept 16, 1921, it was reported that the boy had 14 fingers and 15 toes.

Fewest Toes

The two-toed syndrome exhibited by some members of the Wadomo tribe of the Zambezi Valley, Zimbabwe, and the Kalanga tribe of the eastern Kalahari Desert, Botswana, is hereditary via a single mutated gene. These "ostrich people," as they are known, can walk great distances without discomfort.

Touch Sensitivity

The extreme sensitivity of the fingers is such that a vibration with a movement of 0.02 of a micron can be detected.

Strongest Hair

In a test on BBC-TV *Record Breakers* on Sept 9, 1984 a hair from the head of Miss Pham Thy Lan broke at a strain of 6¼ oz.

Longest Hair

Swami Pandarasannadhi, the head of the Tirudaduturai monastery, Tanjore district, Madras, India, was reported in 1949 to have hair 26 ft in length. In 1780 a head of hair measuring 12 ft in length and dressed in a style known as the Plica Polonica (hair closely matted together) was sent to Dresden, Germany, after adorning the head of a Polish peasant woman for 52 years. The head of hair was a foot in circumference.

The length of the hair of Miss Skuldfrid Sjorgren (b Stockholm) was reported from Toronto, Canada, in 1927 to have attained twice her height at 10 ft 6 in.

LONGEST FINGERNAILS: Shridhar Chillal of India is proud of his left hand with its nails that total 163 in in length. However, it's a handicap in his job as a photographer, and as for typing, that's impossible. He keeps them covered when he sleeps, too.

LONGEST HAIR CONTENDER: Diane Witt, Worcester, Mass, last cut her hair in 1981. On May 24, 1988 it was measured at a length of 10 ft 3 in. It is growing at a rate of ½ in per month, and by 1989 is expected to tie the 10½ ft record. She takes 4 hours for a shampoo.

Longest Beard

The longest beard preserved was that of Hans N. Langseth (1846–1927) of Norway, which measured 17½ ft at the time of his burial in Kensett, Iowa, in 1927 after 15 years residence in the US. The beard was presented to the Smithsonian Institution, Washington, DC in 1967.

The beard of the bearded lady Janice Deveree (b Bracken County, Ky, 1842) was measured at 14 in in 1884. The beard of Mlle Helene

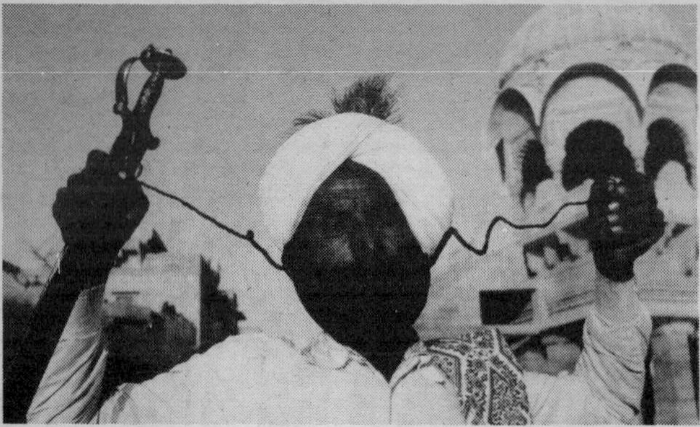

NEXT TO LONGEST MOUSTACHE: Prisoner in New Delhi, India, Karna Ram Bheel (1928-81) had a 7-ft-10-in moustache. Longest (over 8 ft) belongs to a Swede. *(Gamma)*

Antonia of Liège, Belgium, a 17th century exhibitionist, was said to have reached her hips.

Longest Moustache

The longest moustache until now was that of Masuriya Din (b 1908), a Brahmin of the Partabgarh district in Uttar Pradesh, India. It grew to an extended span of 102 in between 1949 and 1962. However, from 1973 to Jan 25, 1988 the moustache of Birger Pellas (b Sept 21, 1934) of Malmö, Sweden, has grown to a record length of 110½ in.

Longest Fingernails

The longest known set of nails now belongs to the left hand of Shridhar Chillal (b 1937), of Poona, India. The five nails on his left hand, by Mar 25, 1988, had achieved a measured aggregate length of 163 in (thumb 38 in) uncut since 1952. Human nails normally grow from cuticle to cutting length in from 117 to 138 days, 4 times faster than toenails.

Most Teeth

Cases of the growth in late life of a third set of teeth have been recorded several times. A reference to an extreme case in France of a fourth dentition known as Lison's case was published in 1896. A triple row of teeth was noted in 1680 by Albertus Hellwigius.

Earliest Dentition

The first deciduous or milk teeth normally appear in infants at 5 to 8 months, these being the mandibular and maxillary first incisors. There are many records of children born with teeth, the most distinguished example being Prince Louis Dieudonné, later Louis XIV of France, who was born with two teeth on Sept 5, 1638. Molars usually appear at 24 months, but in Pindborg's case published in

Denmark in 1970, a 6-week premature baby was documented with 8 natal teeth of which 4 were in the molar region.

Most Dedicated Dentist

Brother Giovanni Battista Orsenigo of the Ospedale Fatebenefratelli, Rome, Italy, a dentist, conserved all the teeth he extracted as a dentist in three enormous boxes during the time he exercised his profession from 1868 to 1904. In 1903, the number was counted and found to be 2,000,744 teeth, indicating an average of 185 a day.

Strongest Bite

In August 1986, Richard Hofmann (b 1949) of Lake City, Fla, achieved a bite strength of 975 lb for approx 2 sec in a research test using a gnathodynometer at the College of Dentistry, Univ of Fla. This figure is over 6 times normal biting strength.

Most Valuable Tooth

In 1816 a tooth belonging to Sir Isaac Newton (1643–1727) was sold in London for £730 (now $1,100). It was purchased by a nobleman who had it set in a ring which he wore constantly.

Earliest False Teeth

From discoveries made in Etruscan tombs, partial dentures of bridge-work type were being worn in what is now Tuscany, Italy, as early as 700 BC. Some were permanently attached to existing teeth and others were removable.

Leading Cause of Death

The leading cause of death in industrialized countries is arteriosclerosis (thickening of the arterial wall), which underlies much coronary and cerebrovascular disease.

Longest Coma

The longest recorded coma was that of Elaine Esposito (b Dec 3, 1934) of Tarpon Springs, Fla. She never stirred after an appendectomy on Aug 6, 1941, when she was six, in Chicago. She died on Nov 25, 1978, aged 43 years 357 days, having been in a coma for 37 years 111 days.

Heart Stoppage

The longest recorded heart stoppage is 4 hours in the case of a Norwegian fisherman, Jan Egil Refsdahl (b 1936), who fell overboard in the icy waters off Bergen on Dec 7, 1987. He was rushed to nearby Haukeland Hospital after his body temperature fell to 77 degrees and his heart stopped beating, but he made a full recovery after he was connected to a heart-lung machine normally used for heart surgery.

"Mammalian diving effect" can be triggered in humans falling into water cooler than 70° F.

Allen Smith, aged 2, on Oct 9, 1986 fell into the swollen waters of the Stanislaus River at Oakdale, Calif. He was spotted 90 min later and rushed to Modesto Memorial Hospital, and it was another 2 hours before his heart began beating again spontaneously.

Heart Transplants

The first human heart transplant operation was performed on Louis Washkansky, aged 55, at the Groote Schuur Hospital, Cape Town, South Africa, between 1:00 and 6:00 a.m. Dec 3, 1967, by a team of 30 headed by Prof Christiaan N. Barnard (b 1922). The donor was Miss Denise Ann Darvall, aged 25. Washkansky died Dec 21, 1967, after living for 18 days.

The first transplantee to give birth was Betsy Sneith, 23, with a baby girl Sierra (7 lb 10 oz) at Stanford University, Calif on Sept 17, 1984. She had received a donor heart in Feb 1980.

The longest surviving heart transplantee was Emmanuel Vitria of Marseilles, France (b Jan 24, 1920), who received a heart transplant from Pierre Ponson, 20, on Nov 27, 1968, and lived until May 9, 1987.

The youngest heart transplantee was Paul Holt of Vancouver, BC, Canada who underwent a heart transplant at Loma Linda Hospital, Calif, on Oct 16, 1987 aged 2 hours 31 min. He was born 6 weeks premature at 6 lb 6 oz.

Artificial Heart

On Dec 1–2, 1982 at the Utah Medical Center, Salt Lake City, Dr Barney B. Clark, 61, of Des Moines, Iowa, received an artificial heart. The surgeon was Dr William C. De Vries. The heart was a Jarvik Mark 7 designed by Dr Robert Jarvik. Dr Clark died on Mar 23, 1983, 112 days later.

William J. Schroeder survived 620 days in Louisville, Ky from Nov 25, 1984 to Aug 7, 1986.

Multiple Transplants

The first triple transplant (heart-lung-liver) took place on Dec 17, 1986 at Papworth Hospital, Cambridge, Eng, when Mrs. Davina Thompson (b Feb 28, 1951) underwent surgery for 7 hours by a team of 15, headed by chest surgeon Mr John Wallwork and Prof Sir Roy Calne.

Tabatha Foster (b June 10, 1984) of Madisonville, Ky, when aged 3 years 143 days, received 5 transplants: liver, pancreas, small intestine and portions of stomach and large intestine, in a 15-hour operation at Children's Hospital, Pittsburgh, on Oct 31, 1987. She had never eaten solid food before the operation.

Highest Body Temperature

Sustained body temperatures of much over 109° F are normally incompatible with life, although recoveries after readings of 111° F have been noted. Marathon runners in hot weather attain 105.8° F.

Willie Jones, a 52-year-old black, was admitted to Grady Memorial Hospital, Atlanta, Ga, on July 10, 1980 with heat stroke on a day when the temperature reached 90° F with 44% humidity. His temperature was found to be 115.7° F. After 24 days he was discharged "at prior baseline status."

Lowest Body Temperature

There are three recorded cases of patients surviving body temperatures as low as 60.8° F. Dorothy Mae Stevens (1929–74) was found in an alley in Chicago Feb 1, 1951. Vickie Mary Davis of Milwaukee, Wis, at age 2 years 1 month was admitted to the Evangelical Hospital, Marshalltown, Iowa, Jan 21, 1956 after having been found unconscious on the floor of an unheated house. Michael Trode, aged 2, was found in the snow near his home in Milwaukee, Wis, on Jan 19, 1985. All three had a temperature of 60.8° F, when found. People may die of hypothermia with body temperatures of 95° F.

Pulse Rates

A normal adult pulse rate is 70–72 beats per min at rest for males and 78–82 for females. Rates increase to 200 or more during violent exercise or drop to 12 in extreme cold weather, low-body-temperature situations like Dorothy Mae Stevens (see above) and Jean Hilliard (b 1962) of Fosston, Minn on Dec 20, 1980. When Charles Thompson of Cwmbran, Gwent, Wales was admitted to a hospital for hip-joint replacement surgery on Aug 16, 1987, he was found to have a record resting pulse of 28.

Most Acute Vision

Dentist Veronica Seider of Stuttgart, W Germany (b 1951) possesses a visual acuity 20 times better than average. She can identify people at a distance of more than a mile, and specialises in microwriting without

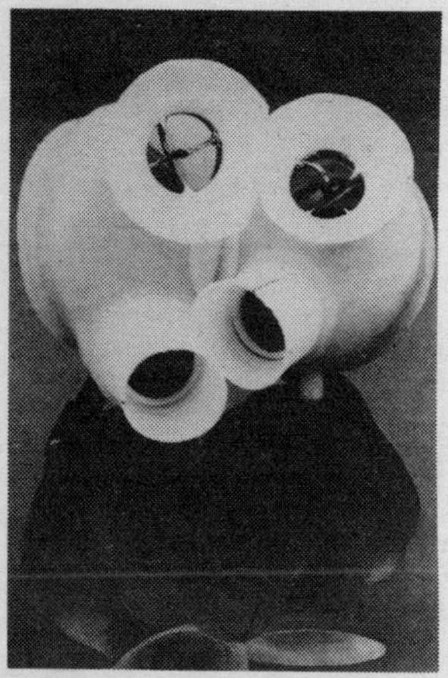

ARTIFICIAL HEART: The Mark 7 heart designed by Dr Robert K. Jarvik (US). The first artificial heart recipient was Dr Barney B. Clark, 61, who survived for 112 days, Dec 1, 1982–Mar 23, 1983. Later, with Mark 7, William J. Schroeder survived for 620 days Nov 25, 1984–Aug 7, 1986. ◄

HEART TRANSPLANT ► PIONEER: Dr Christiaan Barnard in 1967 in Cape Town, South Africa, completed the first of his spectacular operations successfully.

the use of artificial aids. In one test she examined what seemed to be a thread of cotton and then announced that it was actually four threads twisted tightly together. Magnification proved her right.

Color Sensitivity

The unaided human eye, under the best possible viewing conditions, comparing large areas of color, in good illumination, using both eyes, can distinguish 10,000,000 different color surfaces.

About 7.5 percent of men and 0.1 percent of women are color blind. The most extreme form of color blindness, monochromatic vision, is very rare. The highest rate of red-green color blindness exists in Czechoslovakia and the lowest rate among Fijians and Brazilian Indians.

Commonest Diseases

The commonest non-contagious disease is periodontal disease, such as gingivitis, which afflicts some 80% of the US population. In Great Britain 13% of the people have lost all their teeth before reaching 21. During their lifetime few completely escape its effects.

Infestation with pinworm (*Enterobius vermicularis*) approaches 100% in some areas of the world.

The commonest contagious illness in the world is coryza (acute nasopharyngitis) or the common cold.

Highest Mortality

Rabies in humans has been regarded as uniformly fatal when associated with the hydrophobia symptom. A 25-year-old woman, Candida de Sousa Barbosa of Rio de Janeiro, Brazil, after surgery by Dr Max Karpin, was believed to be the first to survive the disease in Nov 1968, though some sources give priority to Matthew Winkler, 6, who, on Oct 10, 1970, survived a bite by a rabid bat.

Most Infectious Disease

The most infectious of all diseases is the pneumonic form of plague, as evidenced by the Black Death of 1347–51. It has a mortality rate of 99.99%.

AIDS (Acquired Immune Deficiency Syndrome), was first recognized in 1978, and was first identified in Jan 1983 at the Pasteur Institute, Paris by Luc Montagnier, Francoise Barre-Sinoussi and Jean-Claude Chermann as a human T-lymphotrophic virus Type III (HTLV III).

The US death toll from AIDS has been predicted to reach 179,000 by 1991, with care costs possibly reaching $16 billion. Uncertainty on the percentage of sero-positive HIV carriers and the duration of incubation only make it possible to say the toll will be of the order of 100,000 to 300,000 by 1991.

Blood Groups

The preponderance of one blood group varies greatly from one locality to another. On a world basis Group O is the most common (46%), but in some areas, for example Norway, Group A predominates.

The rarest blood group on the ABO system, one of 14 systems, is AB. The rarest blood is a type of Bombay blood (sub-type h-h) found so far only in a Czechoslovak nurse in 1961 and in a brother (Rh positive) and sister (Rh negative) named Jalbert in Mass, reported in Feb 1968. The brother has started a blood bank for himself.

Champion Blood Donor and Recipient

Since 1966 Allen Doster, a self-employed beautician, has (to Mar 1988) donated a total of 984 platelets by both manual and machine plasmapheresis at Roswell Park Memorial Institute, NY. The current limit in the US on machine platelet pheresis donations is 24 per year.

Warren C. Jyrich, a 50-year-old hemophiliac, required 2,400 donor units (2,283 pints) of blood when undergoing open heart surgery at the Michael Reese Hospital, in Chicago, in Dec 1970.

Swallowing

The worst reported case of compulsive swallowing was an insane woman, Mrs H., aged 42, who complained of a "slight abdominal pain." She was found to have 2,533 objects in her stomach, including 947 bent pins. They were removed by Drs Chalk and Foucar in June 1927 at the Ontario Hospital, Canada.

The heaviest object ever extracted from a human stomach was a 5-lb 3-oz ball of hair, from a 20-year- old woman at the South Devon and East Cornwall Hospital, England, March 30, 1895.

Sword "Swallowing"

Edward Benjamin, known as Count Desmond (b July 30, 1941, Binghamton, NY), swallowed thirteen 23-in-long blades to below his xiphisternum and injured himself in the process. *This category has now been retired and no further claims will be entertained.*

Largest Tumor

The largest tumor ever recorded was Spohn's case of an ovarian cyst weighing 328 lb from a woman in Tex in 1905. She recovered fully.

Largest Stone

The largest stone or vesical calculus reported in medical literature was one of 13 lb 14 oz removed from an 80-year-old woman by Dr Humphrey Arthure at Charing Cross Hospital, London, on Dec 29, 1952.

Pill Taking

The highest recorded total of pills swallowed by a patient is 555,439 from June 9, 1967 to Jan 31, 1988, by C. H. A. Kilner (b 1926) of Bindura, Zimbabwe, following a successful operation to remove a cancerous pancreas on May 26, 1966.

Longest Operation

The most protracted reported operation for surgical as opposed to medical control purposes was one of 96 hours performed on Mrs Gertrude Levandowski (b 1893) of Burnips, Mich, for removal of a cyst which reduced her weight by 308 lb, Feb 4–8, 1951. The patient suffered from a weak heart and the surgeons had to exercise the utmost caution during the operation.

Most Operations by a Doctor

Dr Denton A. Cooley of Houston, Tex, has performed more than 75,000 open heart operations with his group, 1956–88, with two-thirds performed by him personally. In addition, under his direction at the Texas Heart Institute, an equal number of vascular surgeries were performed.

Dr. M.C. Modi, a pioneer of mass eye surgery in India since 1943, with his staff, has performed as many as 833 cataract operations in one day, and a total of 564,834 to Jan 1987.

Most Major Operations on a Patient

Joseph Ascough (b 1935) of Nottingham, England, underwent his 337th operation (for the removal of papillomas from his windpipe) on Dec 9, 1986. These wart-like growths which impede breathing first formed when he was 18 months old.

Oldest Subject Operated On

The greatest recorded age at which a person has been subjected to an operation is 111 years 105 days in the case of James Henry Brett, Jr. (b July 25, 1849, d Feb 10, 1961) of Houston, Tex. He underwent a hip operation Nov 7, 1960.

Longest Survival in Iron Lung

The longest recorded survival by an iron lung patient is 37 years 58 days by Mrs Laurel Nisbet (b Nov 17, 1912) of La Crescenta, Calif, who was in an iron lung continuously from June 25, 1948, to her death on Aug 22, 1985.

Earliest Anesthesia

The earliest recorded operation under general anesthesia was for the removal of a cyst from the neck of James Venable by Dr Crawford Williamson Long (1815–78), using diethyl ether $(C_2H_5)_2O$, in Jefferson, Ga, on Mar 30, 1842.

Fastest Amputation

The shortest time recorded for the amputation of a leg in the pre-anesthetic era was 13 to 15 sec by Napoleon's chief surgeon, Dominique Larrey. There could have been no ligation.

Earliest Appendectomy

The earliest recorded successful appendix operation was performed in 1736 by Claudius Amyand (1680–1740). He was Serjeant Surgeon to King George II (reigned 1727–60) of Great Britain.

Laryngectomy

On July 24, 1924, John I. Poole of Plymouth, England, then aged 33, after diagnosis of carcinoma, underwent total laryngectomy in

Edinburgh, Scotland. He died on June 19, 1979, after surviving 55 years as a "neck-breather." Mr F. B. Harvey of Plymouth, England, has been a neck-breather since 1929.

Most "Ills"

The most extreme recorded case of the rare and incurable condition known as "Munchausen's syndrome" (a continual desire to have medical treatment) was William McIlroy (b 1906), who cost the British National Health Service an estimated £1 million during his 30-year career as a hospital patient. During that time he had 23 major operations, and stayed at 68 different hospitals using 22 aliases. The longest period he was ever out of a hospital was for 6 months. In 1979 the Irishman hung up his bedpan for the last time, saying he was sick of hospitals, and retired to an old people's home in Birmingham.

Earliest Kidney Transplant

R. H. Lawler (b 1895, US) performed the first transplantation of a human kidney in 1950. The longest survival, as between identical twins, has been 20 years.

Hiccoughing

The longest recorded attack of hiccoughs is that which afflicted Charles Osborne (b Dec 18, 1894) of Anthon, Iowa, from 1922 for 66 years. He contracted it when slaughtering a hog and hiccoughed about 430 million times in the interim period. He was unable to find a cure, but led a reasonably normal life in which he had two wives and fathered eight children. He did admit, however, that he could not keep in his false teeth. In July 1986, his rate went up to 20–25 times from 10 hics per min in 1985, and an earlier high of 40.

Sneezing

The most chronic sneezing fit ever recorded is that of Donna Griffiths (b 1969) of Pershore, England. She started sneezing on Jan 13, 1981, and surpassed the previous duration record of 194 days on July 27, 1981. She sneezed an estimated million times in the first 365 days. She achieved her first sneeze-free day on Sept 16, 1983—the 978th day.

The highest speed at which expelled particles have been measured to travel is 103.6 mph.

Yawning

In Lee's case, reported in 1888, a 15-year-old female patient yawned continuously for a period of five weeks.

Loudest Snore

The highest measured sound level recorded by any chronic snorer was a peak of 87.5 decibels on June 28, 1984 at a distance of 1 meter from the recorder, in the case of Melvyn Switzer of Totton, Hants, Eng, whose wife Julie is deaf in one ear.

Research has shown that differences in lung capacity and pharynx shape account for snoring. In general the pharynx was smaller in snorers.

Voice

The highest and lowest recorded notes attained by the human voice before this century were a staccato E in *alt-altissimo* (*e'' ''*) by Ellen Beach Yaw (US, 1869–1947) in Carnegie Hall, New York City, Jan 19, 1896, and an A1 (55 Hz cycles per sec) by Kaspar Foster (1617–73).

Madeleine Marie Robin (1918–60), the French operatic coloratura, could produce and sustain the B flat above high C in the Mad Scene in *Lucia di Lammermoor*.

Since 1950 singers have achieved high and low notes far beyond the hitherto accepted extremes. Notes, however, at the bass and treble extremities of the register tend to lack harmonics and are of little musical value.

Fräulein Marita Günther, trained by Alfred Wolfsohn, has covered the range of the piano from the lowest note A,, to c^{v}. Of this range of 7¼ octaves, 6 octaves are considered to be of musical value.

Roy Hart, also trained by Wolfsohn, has reached notes below the range of the piano. Barry Girard of Canton, Ohio, in May 1975 reached the e (4,340 Hz) above the piano's top note.

The highest note put into song is G^{v} first occurring in *Popoli di Tessaglia* by Mozart.

The lowest vocal note in the classical repertoire is in Mozart's *Il Seraglio* by Osmin who descends to low D (73.4 Hz). Dan Britton reached the 4th E below middle C at 20.6 Hz at Anoka County Fair, Minn, on July 31, 1984. Stefan Zucker sang A in *alt-altissimo* for 3.8 sec in the tenor role of Salvini in the world premiere of Bellini's *Adelson e Salvini* in Carnegie Hall, New York City, Sept 12, 1972.

Greatest Range

The normal intelligible outdoor range of the male human voice in still air is 200 yards. The *silbo*, the whistled language of the Spanish-speaking Canary Island of La Gomera, is intelligible across the valleys, under ideal conditions, at 5 miles. There is a recorded case, under freak acoustic conditions, of the human voice being detectable at a distance of 10½ miles across still water at night. It was said that Mills Darden (see *Heaviest Men*) could be heard 6 miles away when he bellowed at the top of his voice.

Shouting

Because of their more optimal frequency, female screams generally register higher readings on decibel meters than male bellows, but the International Town Criers' championship at 113 dBA was won by a man, Donald H. (Bod) Burns of St. George's, Bermuda, on Sept 15, 1984.

The highest scientifically measured emission has been one of 123.2 dBA by the screaming of Neil Stephenson of Newcastle-upon-Tyne, Eng on May 18, 1985.

Lowest Detectable Sound

The intensity of noise or sound is measured in terms of pressure. The pressure of the quietest sound that can be detected by a person of normal hearing at the most sensitive frequency of *c.* 2,750 Hz (cycles per sec) is 2×10^{-5} pascal. One tenth of the logarithm to this standard provides a unit termed a decibel (dBA). A noise of 30 decibels is negligible.

Highest Noise Levels

Prolonged noise above 150 decibels will cause immediate permanent deafness while above 192 dBA a lethal over-pressure shock wave can be formed. Equivalent continuous sound levels (LEQ) above 90 dBA are impermissible in factories, but this compares with 125 emitted by racing cars, 130 (amplified music) and 170 (some toy guns).

Highest Detectable Pitch

The upper limit of hearing by the human ear has been regarded as 20,000 Hz (cycles per sec). Experiments in the USSR have conclusively proved that oscillations as high as 200,000 Hz can be heard if the oscillator is pressed against the skull.

Fastest Talker

Extremely few people are able to speak *articulately* at a sustained speed above 300 words per min. The fastest broadcaster has usually been regarded to be Gerry Wilmot (b Oct 6, 1914, Victoria, BC, Canada), the ice hockey commentator in the post-World War II period. Raymond Glendenning (1907–74), the BBC horse-racing commentator, once spoke 176 words in 30 seconds while reporting a greyhound race. In public life the highest speed recorded is a 327-words-per-min burst in a speech made in Dec 1961, by John Fitzgerald Kennedy (1917–63), then President.

Fasting

Most humans experience considerable discomfort after an abstinence from food for even 12 hours, but this often passes off after 24–48 hours. Records claimed without unremitting medical surveillance are inadmissible.

The longest period for which anyone has gone without solid food is 382 days by Angus Barbieri (b 1940) of Tayport, Fife, Scotland, who lived on tea, coffee, water, soda water and vitamins from June 1965 to July 1966 in Maryfield Hospital, Dundee, Angus, Scotland. His weight declined from 472 lb to 178 lb.

The longest recorded case of survival without food *and* water is 18 days by Andreas Mihavecz, 18, of Bregenz, Austria, who was put in a holding cell April 1, 1979, in a local government building in Höchst, Austria, but was totally forgotten by the police. On April 18, 1979, he was discovered close to death, having had neither food nor water. He had been a passenger in a car crash.

Hunger Strike

The longest recorded hunger strike was 385 days from June 28, 1972 to July 18, 1973 by Denis Galer Goodwin in Wakefield Prison, W Yorkshire, Eng, protesting his innocence of a rape charge. He was force fed by tube orally.

The longest recorded hunger strike without force feeding was one of 94 days by 9 men in Cork Prison, Ireland, from Aug 11 to Nov 12,

1920. These 9 survivors owed their lives to expert medical attention and an appeal by the nationalist leader, Arthur Griffith.

Most Tattoos

The seeming ultimate in being tattooed is represented by Wilfred Hardy of Huthwaite, Nottinghamshire, England. Not content with a perilous approach to within 4% of totality of his outer skin, he has been tattooed on the inside of his cheek, his tongue, gums and eyebrows.

Walter Stiglitz of N Plainfield, NJ, in Mar 1988 claimed 5,473 separate tattoos by 6 artists.

The most decorated woman is strip artist Krystyne Kolorful of Seattle, Wash, whose 95% body suit took 10 years to complete and cost $15,000.

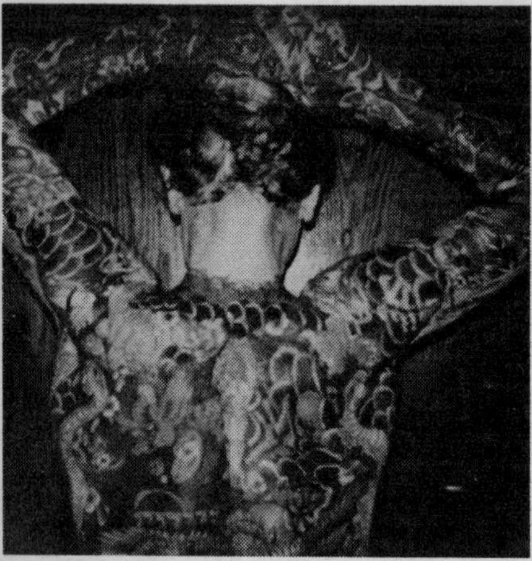

MOST TATTOOED MAN: Wilfred Hardy (Eng) left very little of his body without artistic embellishment. He even has tattoos on his tongue, gums and inner cheeks.

Longest Dream

Dreaming sleep is characterized by rapid eye movements (known as REM), discovered in 1953 by William Dement of the University of Chicago. The longest recorded period of REM is 2 hours 23 min, set by Bill Carskadon on Feb 15, 1967, at the Department of Psychology, University of Illinois, Chicago. His previous sleep had been interrupted.

In July 1984 The Sleep Research Centre, Haifa, Israel, recorded nil REM in a 33-year-old male who had a shrapnel brain injury.

Extrasensory Perception

The two most extreme published examples of ESP in scientific literature have been those of the Reiss case of a 26-year-old female at Hunter College, NY, in 1936 and of Pavel Stepének (Czechoslovakia) in 1967–68. The importance which had been attached to their cases was diminished by subsequent developments. The Reiss subject refused to undergo any further tests under stricter conditions. When Stepének was retested at Edinburgh University with plastic cards he "failed to display any clairvoyant ability." Much smaller departures from the laws of probability have, however, been displayed in less extreme cases carried out under strict conditions.

g Forces

The acceleration due to gravity (g) is 32 ft 1.05 in per sec per sec at sea level at the Equator. A *sustained* force of 25 g was withstood in a dry capsule during astronautic research by Dr Carter Collins of Calif.

The highest g value endured was 82.6 g for 0.04 sec on a water-braked rocket sled by Eli L. Beeding, Jr., at Holloman Air Force Base, NM, May 16, 1958. He was put in the hospital for three days.

A man who fell off a 185-ft cliff survived a *momentary* g force of 209 in decelerating from 68 mph to stationary in 0.015 sec.

In a crash, race car driver David Purley survived a deceleration from 108 mph to zero in 26 in at the Silverstone circuit, Northamptonshire, England, July 13, 1977, which involved a force of 179.8 g. He suffered 29 fractures, 3 dislocations and 6 heart stoppages.

A land diver of Pentecost Island, New Hebrides, dove from a platform 81 ft 3 in high on May 15, 1982 for a TV show. He had liana vines attached to his ankles, his body speed was 50 ft/sec (34 mph) and the force of the jerk transmitted a momentary g force in excess of 110.

Sleeplessness

The longest recorded period for which a person has voluntarily gone without sleep is 453 hr 40 min by Robert McDonald of California in a rocking chair on Mar 14–Apr 2, 1986. Victims of the very rare condition chronic colestites (total insomnia) have been known to go without definable sleep for many years. Jesus de Frutos (b 1925) of Segovia, Spain asserts that he has only dozed since 1954.

Motionlessness

The longest recorded time that anyone was involuntarily made to stand at attention was 132 consecutive hours without food or water while a prisoner of the Japanese in Osaka from 8 a.m. Aug 15 until 8 p.m. Aug 20, 1944, by Everett D. Reamer (b 1923) of Havasu City, Ariz. Whenever he slumped, he was beaten; finally he dropped to the ground.

The longest that anyone has continuously remained motionless is 24 hours by William Fuqua at Glendale, Calif, on May 17–18, 1985 while sitting on a motorcycle.

An Indonesian teacher named Sunardi (b 1960) continuously *stood* motionless for 15 hours 25 sec on July 21, 1986 at a Motionlessness Festival in Semarang, Indonesia.

Isolation

The longest period for which any volunteer has been able to withstand total deprivation of all sensory stimulation (sight, hearing

MOTIONLESSNESS: Voluntary and involuntary: Sunardi (left) (b 1960), an Indonesian teacher, continuously stood motionless for 15 hours 25 sec on July 21, 1986 to set a record at the Motionlessness Festival in Semarang, Indonesia. As a prisoner in Osaka, Japan, Corp Everett D. Reamer (US Army) (right) was made to stand motionless for 132 consecutive hours, Aug 15–20, 1944.

and touch) is 92 hours, recorded in 1962 at Lancaster Moor Hospital, Eng.

Electric Shock

People in aircraft in thunder clouds may be at 30 million volts relative to the earth without harm. In some "bare hand" laboratory work in France experimenters in insulated cabins have experienced 5 million volts.

People walking on nylon carpets on dry days may go up to 10,000 volts relative to earth and yet experience only mild shocks. Contacts with exposed high tension power lines with system voltages of 765,000 have occurred in the US. A person in contact with earth via ladders, dinghy masts, crane jibs, etc, normally suffers instant death due to a heavy current arc or flashover flowing through the body. That shocks received from high tension cables by Brian Latasa (230,000 volts in Griffith Park, Los Angeles on Nov 9, 1967) and Harry F. McGrew (340,000 volts in Huntington Canyon, Utah, on Oct 7, 1977) were non-lethal underlines their idiosyncratic nature when compared with the mere 2,500 volts used since 1890 in judicial electrocution.

Underwater Duration

The record for voluntarily staying underwater is 13 min 42.5 sec by Robert Foster, aged 32, an electronics technician of Richmond, Calif, who stayed under 10 ft of water in the swimming pool of the Bermuda Palms at San Rafael, Calif, on March 15, 1959. He hyperventilated with oxygen for 30 min before his descent. *It must be stressed that record-breaking of this kind is extremely dangerous.*

Highest Temperature Endured

The highest dry-air temperature endured by naked men in US Air Force experiments in 1960 was 400° F and for heavily clothed men 500° F. (*Steaks require only 325° F.*) Temperatures of 284° F have been found quite bearable in sauna baths.

Fire-Walking

A group of 11 people led by Steven Neil Bisyak of Redmond, Wash, participated in a fire-walk with an average temperature of 1,546°F on Dec 19, 1987 at Redmond.

Fire-Eating

Reg Morris blew a flame from his mouth to a distance of 31 ft at the Miner's Restaurant, Chasetown, Eng on Oct 29, 1986.

On Mar 17, 1987 Morris also extinguished 20,035 torches of flame in his mouth in 1 hour 48 min 14 sec at Cinders Night Club, Willenhall, Eng.

Sipra Ellen Lloyd set a female record of 8,357 at Port Lonsdale, Vic, Australia on July 26, 1986. *Fire-eating is potentially a highly dangerous activity.*

Chapter 2

The Living World

ANIMAL KINGDOM (*ANIMALIA*)

Largest and Heaviest Animal

The longest and heaviest mammal, and the largest animal ever recorded is the blue or sulphur-bottom whale (*Balaenoptera musculus*), also called Sibbald's rorqual. The longest specimen ever recorded was a female landed at the Compania Argentina de Pesca, Grytviken, South Georgia, Falkland Islands, in 1909 which measured 110 ft 2½ in in length. During summer months an average-sized specimen consumes up to 3 million calories per day.

The tongue and heart of the 209-ton female taken by the *Slava* whaling fleet in the South Atlantic Ocean on Mar 20, 1947 weighed 4.72 tons and 1,540 lb, respectively.

Loudest Sound

The low frequency pulses (whistles) made by blue whales when communicating with each other have been measured up to 188 dB, making them the loudest sounds emitted by any living source. They are detectable 530 miles away.

Fastest Burrower

The champion burrower is the Eurasian blind mole-rat *Spalax microphthalmus*. One burrow found in the southern USSR measured 1191 ft in length, but this was dwarfed by another example which had a total of 114 mounds, the last two being 554 ft apart.

Smelliest Animal

The smelliest animal is the skunklike zorilla (*Ictonyx striatus*) of Africa. It can discharge a nauseous fluid from its anal glands which can be smelled over a radius of half-a-mile, and there is one record of a zorilla taking possession of a zebra carcass and keeping fully grown lions at bay for several hours.

Slowest Walker

A crab of the species *Neptunus pelagines* tagged in the Red Sea took 29 years to travel the 101.5 miles to the Mediterranean via the Suez Canal at an average speed of 3.5 miles a year.

MOST VALUABLE: ▲ Killer whales like "Orky" of Sea World, San Diego, Calif, are valued at about $2 million per pair.

TALLEST ANIMAL: ► George, the tallest giraffe in captivity, along with his friends, licked the telephone wires that ran past his pen, disrupting the system.

GIANT PANDA, the most costly zoo animal. One cub in the Madrid (Spain) Zoo is valued at $1.4 million. The one pictured here is in the San Diego (Calif) Zoo.

Longest Animal

The longest animal ever recorded is the ribbon worm *Lineus longissimus*, also known as the "boot-lace worm," which is found in the shallow coastal waters of the North Sea. In 1864 a specimen measuring more than 180 ft was washed ashore at St. Andrews, Fifeshire, Scotland, after a storm.

Tallest Animal

The tallest living animal is the giraffe (*Giraffa camelopardalis*), which is now found only in the dry savannah and semi-desert areas of Africa south of the Sahara. The tallest ever recorded was a Masai bull (*G. camelopardalis tippelskirchi*) named "George," received at Chester Zoo, England, Jan 8, 1959 from Kenya. His "horns" *almost* touched the roof of the 20-ft-high Giraffe House when he was 9 years old. George died July 22, 1969. Less credible heights of up to 23 ft between taxidermist's pegs have been claimed for bulls shot in the field.

Strongest Animal

The strongest animals in the world in proportion to their size are the larger beetles of the Scarabaeidae, which are found mainly in the tropics. In tests carried out on one unnamed species it was found that it could support 850 times its own weight on its back.

Toughest Animal

According to experiments carried out by Prof H. E. Hinton at Bristol University in England, the larva of the Chironomid fly (*Polypedilum vanderplanki*) can tolerate temperatures ranging from −454°F to −215.6°F, and is the most advanced organism so far known that can be totally dehydrated.

Most Valuable Animals

The most valuable animals in cash terms are race horses. *Shareef Dancer* was syndicated for $40 million in Aug 1983 by his owner Sheikh Mohammed al Maktoum when 40 shares were issued at $1 million each. (See *Horse Racing*.) The most valuable zoo exhibit is the giant panda (*Ailuropoda melanoleuca*). "Chi-Lin," (b Sept 1982) of the Madrid Zoo, Spain, the only panda cub in Europe, which has been valued at about $1.4 million. A 6th cub, born to "Mei mei" on Sept 20, 1987 at Chengdu Zoo, Sichuan province, China, is believed to be the most valuable mammal alive. There are only 14 giant pandas living in captivity outside China, and the wild population may now be as low as 600–700 despite full protection.

The most valuable marine exhibit is a pair of killer whales (*Orcinus orca*) named "Orky" and "Corky" at Sea World, San Diego, Calif. They are the world's only captive breeding pair of killer whales. Their value in 1985 was $2 million.

Longest-Lived Animal

Few non-bacterial creatures live longer than humans.

In 1982, a specimen of an ocean quahog (*Arctica islandica*), a thick-shelled clam, was found in the mid-Atlantic with 220 annual growth rings, indicating an age of 220 years.

Up until 1982 tortoises were regarded as the longest-lived such animals. The greatest authentic age recorded for a tortoise is 152-plus years.

Fastest Flying Animal

The fastest-moving animal is the peregrine falcon (*Falco peregrinus*), which has been timed electronically at 217 mph in Germany while making a stoop at a 45-degree angle of descent and 168 mph diving a 30-degree descent. The fastest bird in level flight is the red-breasted merganser (*Mergus serrator*) (US) which attained an air speed of 80 mph in 1960.

Commonest Animal

It is estimated that man shares the earth with 3×10^{33} (3 followed by 33 zeros) other living things. The number of nematode sea-worms has been estimated at 4×10^{25}. The house mouse (*Mus musculus*) is found on all continents.

Largest Concentration of Animal Life

The largest single concentration of animals ever recorded was an enormous swarm of krill (*Euphausia superba*) estimated to weigh 10 million tons tracked by American scientists off Antarctica in Mar 1981. The swarm was so dense it equaled about one-seventh of the world's yearly catch of fish and shellfish.

Most Prodigious Eater

The most phenomenal eating machine in nature is the larva of the Polyphemus moth (*Antheraea polyphemus*) of North America which, in the first 48 hours of its life, consumes an amount equal to 86,000 times its own birth weight. In human terms, this would be equivalent to a 7-lb baby taking in 301 tons of nourishment.

Rarest Animal

A number of mammals are known only from a single (holotype) specimen. An example is Garrido's hutia (*Capromys garridoi*), a rodent, known only from a single specimen collected on the islet of Cayo Maja off southern Cuba in Apr 1967.

The Thylacine or Tasmanian tiger (*Thylacinus cynocephalus*), feared extinct since the last captive specimen died in Beaumaris Zoo, Hobart, on Sept 7, 1936, was rediscovered in July 1982 when a wildlife ranger saw one of these predatory marsupials in the spotlight of his parked car. Since then, however, there have been no more positive sightings.

The rarest marine mammal is Longman's beaked whale (*Indopacetus pacificus*), which is known only from two skulls. The type specimen was discovered on a beach near MacKay, Queensland,

Australia, in 1922, and the second near Mogadiscio, Somalia, E. Africa, in 1955.

Largest Animal Town

The black-tailed prairie dog (*Cynomys ludovicianus*) of the western US and northern Mexico builds the largest colonies of any known animal. One single town discovered in 1901 was estimated to cover an area measuring 240 by 100 mi. It contained about 400 million individuals.

Longest Gestation

The viviparous amphibian Alpine black salamander (*Salamandra atra*) can have a gestation period of up to 38 months at altitudes above 4,600 ft in the Swiss Alps, but this drops to 24–26 months at lower altitudes.

Fastest and Slowest Growth

The fastest growth in the animal kingdom is that of the blue whale calf. A barely visible ovum weighing a fraction of a milligram (0.000035 of an ounce) grows to a weight of *c.* 29 tons in 22¾ months, made up of 10¾ months gestation and the first 12 months of life. This is equivalent to an increase of 30,000 millionfold.

The slowest growth in the animal kingdom is that of the deep-sea clam (*Tindaria callistiformis*) of the North Atlantic, which takes an estimated 100 years to reach a length of 0.31 in (8 mm).

Lowest Blood Temperature

The lowest mammalian blood temperature is that of the spiny anteater (echidna), (*Tachyglossus aculeatus*), a monotreme found in Australia and New Guinea, with a normal range of 22.2° to 24.4° C. The ice worm of Alaska has an internal temperature of 14° F.

Lowest Metabolism

The metabolism of the lizard-like tuatara (*Sphenodon punctatus*) of New Zealand is so reduced that it can go as long as 60 min without taking a breath.

Heaviest Brain

The sperm whale (*Physeter macrocephalus*) has the heaviest brain of any living animal. The brain of a 49-ft-long bull processed aboard the Japanese factory ship *Nissin Maru No. 1* in the Antarctic Dec 11, 1949 weighed 9.2 kg (20.24 lb), compared to 6.9 kg (15.38 lb) for a 90-ft blue whale. The heaviest brain recorded for an elephant was an exceptional 16.5 lb in the case of a 2.17-ton Asiatic cow. The normal brain weight for an adult African bull is 9¼–12 lb.

Thickest Nerve Fibers

Fast-swimming squids (*Cephalopoda*) have the thickest nerve fibers of any living animal. In the case of the Humboldt squid (*Ommastrephes gigas*) they have been measured up to 0.7 in in diameter, about 100 times thicker than human nerves.

Largest Eye

The giant squid *Architeuthis sp*. has the largest eye of any living animal. The ocular diameter may exceed 15 in, compared to less than 12 in for a 33⅓-rpm long-playing record and 4.72 in for a large blue whale.

Most Acute Sense of Smell

The most acute sense of smell exhibited in nature is that of the male emperor moth (*Eudia pavonia*), which, according to German experiments in 1961, can detect the sex attractant of the virgin female at the almost unbelievable range of 6.8 miles upwind. This scent has been identified as one of the higher alcohols ($C_{16}H_{29}OH$) of which the female carries less than 0.0001 mg.

Largest Egg

The largest egg laid by any known animal was that of the elephant bird (*Aepyornis maximus*) which lived in southern Madagascar until *c*. 900 AD. One huge example collected in 1841 and now in the Académie des Sciences, Paris, France measures 12.8 × 15.4 in and probably weighed about 27 lb with its contents.

The largest egg of any living animal is that of the whale shark (*Rhineodon typus*). One egg case measuring 12 in × 5.5 in × 3.5 in

"COOLEST" MAMMAL: The ▲ spiny anteater, from Australia and New Guinea, has the lowest blood temperature of any mammal. This one is a baby.

◄ SLOWEST MAMMAL: The ai or 3-toed sloth moves on the ground at 6–8 ft per min (or 4 mi per day).

was picked up June 29, 1953 at a depth of 186 ft in the Gulf of Mexico, 130 miles south of Port Isabel, Tex. The egg contained a perfect embryo of a whale shark 13.78 in long.

Highest g Force

The highest force encountered in nature is the 400 g *averaged* by the Click beetle *Athous haemorrhoidalis* (a common British species) when "jackknifing" into the air to escape predators. One example measuring *0.47 in* in length and weighing *0.00014 oz* which jumped to a height of *11¾ in* was calculated to have "endured" a peak brain deceleration of 2300 g at the end of the movement..

---

1. MAMMALS (*MAMMALIA*)

Largest and Heaviest Mammals

The blue whale (see details on page 44) holds the record.

Blue whales inhabit the colder seas and migrate to warmer waters in winter for breeding. Observations made in the Antarctic in 1947–8 showed that a blue whale can maintain speeds of 20 knots (23 mph) for 10 minutes when frightened. This means a 90-ft blue whale traveling at 20 knots would develop 520 hp. Newborn calves measure 21–28.5 ft long and weigh up to 3.3 tons.

It has been estimated that there were about 12,000 blue whales living throughout the oceans in 1986 as a result of overfishing—compared to a peak estimate of about 220,000 at the start of the 20th century.

The species has been protected *de jure* since 1967 although non-member countries of the International Whaling Commission (*e.g.* Panama and Taiwan) are not bound by this agreement. A worldwide ban on commercial whaling came into effect in 1986, but Iceland, S Korea, Norway and the Philippines are still killing whales.

Fastest Marine Animal

The fastest is the killer whale (*Orcinus orca*). On Oct 12, 1958, a bull measuring 20–25 ft in length was timed at 30 knots (34.5 mph) in the eastern Pacific.

Speeds of up to 30 knots also have been reported for short bursts by Dall's porpoise (*Phocoenoides dalli*).

Deepest Dive

The greatest *recorded* depth to which a whale has dived is 620 fathoms (3,720 ft) by a 47-ft bull sperm whale (*Physeter macrocephalus*) found with his jaw entangled with a submarine cable running between Santa Elena, Ecuador, and Chorillos, Peru, Oct 14, 1955. At this depth he withstood a pressure of 1,680 lb per sq in of body surface.

On Aug 25, 1969, another bull sperm whale was killed 100 miles south of Durban, South Africa, after it had surfaced from a dive lasting 1 hour 52 min, and inside its stomach were found two small sharks which had been swallowed about an hour earlier. These were later identified as *Scymnodon sp.*, a species found only on the sea floor. At this point from land the depth of water is in excess of 1,646 fathoms (10,476 ft) for a radius of 30–40 miles, which now suggests that the sperm whale sometimes may descend to a depth of over 10,000 ft when seeking food, and is limited by pressure of time rather than by pressure of pressure.

Ambergris

The heaviest piece of ambergris (a fatty deposit in the intestine of the sperm whale) on record weighed 1,003 lb and was recovered from a sperm whale (*Physeter macrocephalus*) Dec 24, 1912 by a Norwegian whaling company off Tasmania in Australian waters. The lump was sold in London for £23,000 (then $111,780).

Largest Animal on Land

The largest living land animal is the African bush elephant (*Loxodonta africana*). The average adult bull stands 10 ft 6 in at the shoulder and weighs 6½ tons. The largest specimen ever recorded, and the largest land animal of modern times, was a bull shot 25 miles north-northeast of Mucusso, southern Angola, Nov 7, 1974. Lying on its side this elephant measured 13 ft 8 in in a projected line from the highest point of the shoulder to the base of the forefoot, indicating that its standing height must have been about 13 ft. Other measurements included an overall length of 35 ft (tip of extended trunk to tip of extended tail) and a forefoot circumference of 5 ft 11 in. The weight was computed to be 26,998 lb.

Fastest Land Animal

The fastest of all land animals over a short distance (*i.e.* up to 600 yd) is the cheetah or hunting leopard (*Acinonyx jubatus*) of the open plains of East Africa, Iran, Turkmenia and Afghanistan, with a probable maximum speed of 60–63 mph over suitably level ground. Speeds of 71, 84 and even 90 mph have been claimed for this animal, but these figures must be considered exaggerated. Tests in London in 1937 showed that on an oval greyhound track over 345 yd a female cheetah's average speed over three runs was 43.4 mph (compared with 43.26 mph for the fastest race horse), but this specimen was not running at its best and had great difficulty negotiating curves.

The fastest land animal over a sustained distance (*i.e.* 1,000 yd or more) is the pronghorn antelope (*Antilocapra americana*) of the western US. Specimens have been observed to travel at 35 mph for 4 miles, at 42 mph for 1 mile and 55 mph for half a mile.

Smallest Mammals

The smallest recorded mammal is the endangered Kitti's hog-nosed bat (*Craseonycteris thonglongyai*), also called the bumblebee bat which is confined to about 20 limestone caves on the Kwae Noi River, Thailand. Mature specimens of both sexes have a wing span of about 6.29 in and weigh between 0.062 and 0.071 oz.

The smallest totally marine mammal in terms of weight is probably Commerson's dolphin (*Cephalorhynchus commersoni*) also known as

LARGEST CARNIVORE: The Kodiak bear from Alaska on average weighs 1,050 lb or more, but this 360-lb specimen was induced to perform in Minn for a beer commercial. *(Hamm's Beer)*

Le Jacobite, which is found in the waters off the southern tip of South America. In one series of six adult specimens the weights ranged from 50.7 lb to 77.1 lb. The sea otter (*Enhydra lutris*) of the north Pacific is of comparable size, weighing from 55 to 81.4 lb, but this species sometimes comes ashore during storms.

Slowest and Sleepiest Mammal

The slowest-moving land mammal is the ai or three-toed sloth (*Bradypus tridactylus*) of tropical America. The average ground speed is 6–8 ft per min (0.068 to 0.098 mph), but in the trees it can "accelerate" to 15 ft per min (0.170 mph). (Compare these figures with the 0.03 mph of the common garden snail and the 0.17 mph of the giant tortoise.)

The slowest swimming marine mammal is the sea otter (*Enhydra lutris*) which has a top speed of *c.* 6 mph. Some armadillos (*Dasypodidae*), opossums (*Didelphidae*) and sloths (*Bradypodidae*) spend up to 80 percent of their lives sleeping or dozing.

Largest Carnivore

The largest living terrestrial carnivore is the Kodiak bear (*Ursus arctos middendorffi*), found on Kodiak Island and the adjacent Afognak and Shuyak islands in the Gulf of Alaska. The average adult male has a nose-to-tail length of 8 ft (tail about 4 in), and weighs between 1,050 lb–1,175 lb. In 1894 a weight of 1,656 lb was recorded for a male shot at English Bay, Kodiak Island, whose *stretched* skin measured 13 ft 6 in from the nose to the tail. This weight was exceeded by a "cage-fat male" in the Cheyenne Mountain Zoological Park, Colorado Springs, Colo, which scaled 1,670 lb at the time of its death

Sept 1955. In 1981 an unconfirmed weight of over 2,000 lb was reported for a Peninsula giant bear (*Ursus a. gyas*) from Alaska on exhibition at the Space Farms Zoological Park at Beemerville, NJ.

Weights in excess of 2,000 lb have been reported for the Polar bear (*Ursus maritimus*), but the average adult male weighs 850–900 lb and measures 7¾ ft nose-to-tail. In 1960 a Polar bear allegedly weighing 2,210 lb before skinning was shot at Kotzebue Sound, Alaska, by Arthur Dubs of Medford, Ore. In April 1962 the 11 ft 1¼ in tall mounted specimen was put on display at the Seattle World Fair, but further details are lacking.

Smallest Carnivore

The smallest living carnivore is the least weasel (*Mustela rixosa*), also called the dwarf weasel, which is circumpolar in distribution. Four races are recognized, the smallest of which is the *M. r. pygmaea* of Siberia. Mature specimens have an overall length (including tail) of 6.96–8.14 in and weigh between 1¼ and 2½ oz.

Largest Marine Carnivore

The largest toothed mammal ever recorded is the sperm whale (*Physeter macrocephalus*), also called the cachalot. The largest specimen ever to be measured accurately was a bull 67 ft 11 in long captured off the Kurile Islands, in the northwest Pacific, by a USSR whaling fleet in the summer of 1950.

Longest-Lived Mammal

No other mammal can match the proven age of 120 years attained by man (*Homo sapiens*). It is probable that the closest approach is made by the Asiatic elephant (*Elephas maximus*).

The greatest age that has been verified with absolute certainty is 78 years in the case of a cow named "Modoc," who died at Santa Clara, Calif., on July 17, 1975. She was imported into the US from Germany in 1898 at the age of 2 years. Nepal's royal elephant "Prem Prased" was reportedly 81 years when he died at Kasra, Chitwan, on Feb 27, 1985, but his actual age was believed to have been 65–70 years.

The longest-lived marine mammal is Baird's beaked whale (*Berardius bairdii*) which has a maximum life span of *c.* 70 years.

Highest-Living Mammal

The highest-living wild mammal in the world is probably the yak (*Bos grunniens*), of Tibet and the Szechwanese Alps, China, which occasionally climbs to an altitude of 20,000 ft when foraging.

Largest Litter

The greatest recorded number of young born to a *wild* mammal at a single birth is 31 (of which 30 survived), in the case of the tail-less tenrec (*Tenrec ecaudatus*), found in Madagascar and the Comoro Islands. The normal litter is 12 to 15, although females can suckle up to 24.

Longest and Shortest Gestation Periods

The longest of all mammalian gestation periods is that of the Asiatic elephant (*Elephas maximus*), with an average of 609 days (or just over 20 months) and a maximum of 760 days, more than 2½ times that of a human. By 1981, only about 35,000 survived.

The gestation periods of the rare water opossum or yapok (*Chironectes minimus*) and the American opossum (*Didelphis marsupialis*) also called the Virginian opossum, both of central and northern South America and the eastern native cat (*Dasyurus viverrinus*) of Australia are all normally 12–13 days, but may also be on occasion as short as 8 days.

Youngest Breeder

The streaked tenrec (*Hemicentetes semispinosus*) of Madagascar is weaned after only 5 days, and females are capable of breeding 3–4 weeks after birth.

Longest Hibernation

The barrow ground squirrel (*Spermophilus parryi barrowensis*) of Point Barrow, Alaska, hibernates for 9 months of the year. During the remaining 3 months it feeds, breeds and collects food for storage in its burrow.

Largest Herds

The largest herds on record were those of the South African springbok (*Antidorcas marsupialis*) during migration across the plains of the western parts of southern Africa in the 19th century. In 1849, Sir John Fraser of Bloemfontein observed a herd that took three days to pass through the settlement of Beaufort West, Cape Province. Another herd seen in the same province in 1888 was estimated to contain 100 million head, although 10 million is probably a more realistic figure. A herd estimated to be 15 miles wide and more than 100 miles long was reported from Karree Kloof, Orange River, South Africa, in July 1896.

The largest concentration of wild mammals found living anywhere in the world today is that of the Mexican free-tailed bat (*Tadarida brasiliensis*) in Bracken Cave, San Antonio, Tex, where up to 20 million animals assemble after migration.

Largest Feline

The largest member of the cat family (Felidae) is the protected long-furred Siberian tiger (*Panthera tigris altaica*), also known as the Amur or Manchurian tiger. Adult males average 10 ft 4 in in length (nose to tip of extended tail), stand 39–42 in at the shoulder, and weigh about 585 lb. A male weighing 846.5 lb was shot in the Sikhote Alin Mountains, Maritime Territory, USSR in 1950.

The largest living feline is a 7½ year-old male Siberian tiger named "Jaipur" who weighs 932 lb and is 10 ft 11 in long. He is owned by animal trainer Joan Byron-Marasek of Clarksburg, N.J.

Smallest Feline

The smallest member of the cat family is the rusty-spotted cat (*Felis rubiginosa*) of southern India and Sri Lanka. The average adult male has an overall length of 25–28 in (tail 9–10 in) and weighs 3 lb.

Largest Pinniped (Seal, Sea Lion, Walrus)

The largest of the 34 known species of pinnipeds is the southern elephant seal (*Mirounga leonina*) which inhabits the sub-Antarctic islands. Adult bulls average 16½ ft in length (tip of inflated snout to the extremities of the outstretched tail flippers), 12 ft in maximum body girth and weigh 5,000 lb. The largest accurately measured specimen on record was a bull killed in Possession Bay, South Georgia, Falkland Islands, South Atlantic, Feb 28, 1913, which measured *c.* 22½ ft in length or 21 ft 4 in after flensing and probably weighed 9,000 lb. There are old records of bulls measuring 25, 30 and even 35 ft, but these figures must be considered exaggerated.

Smallest Pinniped

The smallest pinnipeds are the ringed seal (*Phoca hispida*) of the Arctic and the closely related Baikal seal (*P. sibirica*) of Lake Baikal and the Caspian seal (*P. caspica*) of the Caspian Sea, USSR. Adult specimens (males) measure up to 5 ft 6 in in length and reach a maximum weight of 280 lb. Females are about two-thirds this size.

Fastest and Deepest Pinnipeds

The highest speed measured for a pinniped is a 25-mph spurt for a California sea lion (*Zalophus californianus*). The deepest dive recorded for a pinniped is 2,067 ft by a female northern elephant seal (*Mirounga anguistirostris*) off Ano Nuevo Point, Calif, on Mar 1,

LARGEST LIVING FELINE: This Siberian tiger, "Jaipur," who weighs 932 lb and is almost 11 ft long, lives on a preserve with his lady owner-trainer in NJ. (*Marasek*)

1983. At this depth, the seal withstood a pressure of 919 lb per sq in of body area.

Most Abundant Pinniped

The most abundant species of pinniped is the crabeater seal (*Lobodon carcinophagus*) of Antarctica. In 1978 the total population was believed to be nearly 15 million.

Rarest Pinniped

The last reliable sighting of the Caribbean or West Indian monk seal (*Monachus tropicalis*) was on Serranilla Bank off the coast of Mexico's Yucatan peninsula in 1952. In 1974 two seals were sighted near the southeast Bahamas, but a search in 1979 found nothing. It has been suggested that they may have been California sea lions which had escaped from captivity and have been recorded in the Gulf of Mexico on several occasions.

Longest-Lived Pinniped

A female gray seal (*Halichoerus grypus*) shot at Shunni Wick in the Shetland Islands, Scotland, Apr 23, 1969 was believed to be at least 46 years old, based on a count of dentine rings. The captive record is an estimated 43 years for a bull gray seal "Jacob" held in Skansen (Stockholm Zoo) (1901–42).

Largest and Smallest Bat

The only flying mammals are bats (order Chiroptera), of which there are about 950 living species. The bat with the greatest wing span is the Bismarck flying fox (*Pteropus neohibernicus*) of the Bismarck Archipelago and New Guinea. One specimen preserved in the American Museum of Natural History has a wingspread of 5 ft 5 in, but some unmeasured bats probably reach 6 ft.

The smallest species of bat is the rare Kitti's hog-nosed or bumblebee bat.

Highest Detectable Pitch

Because of their ultrasonic echolocation, bats have the most acute hearing of any land animal. Vampire bats (*Desmodontidae*) and fruit bats (*Pteropodidae*) can hear frequencies as high as 120–210 kHz. (Compare with 20 kHz for the adult human limit, but 280 kHz for the common dolphin (*Delphinus delphis*).

Longest-Lived Bat

The greatest age reliably reported for a bat is 31 years 5 months for an Indian flying fox (*Pteropus giganteus*) which died at London Zoo on Jan 11, 1979.

Longest-Lived Primate

The greatest irrefutable age reported for a primate (excluding humans) is *c.* 59 years in the case of a male orangutan (*Pongo pygmaeus*) named "Guas," who was received by the Philadelphia Zoo May 1, 1931, when he was at least 13 years old, and died Feb 9, 1977.

SMALLEST PRIMATE: Related to the pen-tailed shrew is this Etruscan shrew.

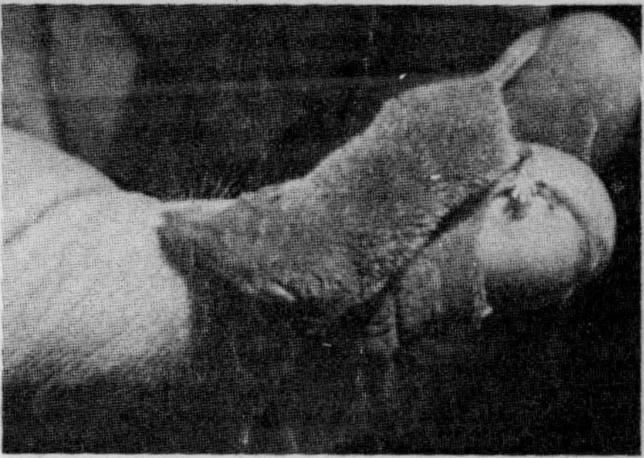

SMALLEST BAT: The rare bumblebee bat, discovered in Thailand by Kitti Thonglongya in Oct 1973.

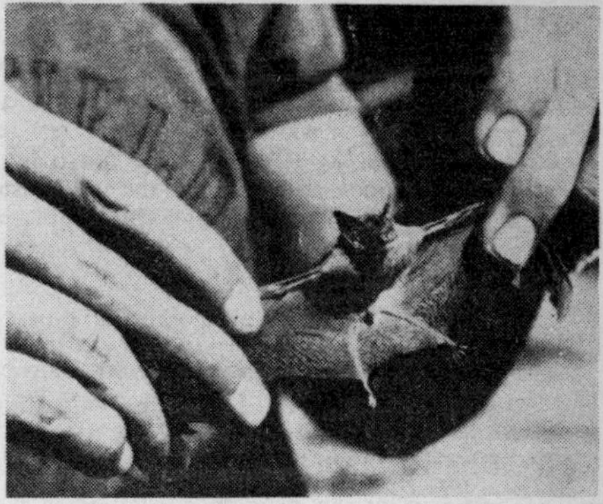

Smallest Living Primate

The smallest known primate is the rare pen-tailed shrew (*Ptilocercus lowii*) of Malaysia, Sumatra and Borneo. Adult specimens have a total body length of 9–13 in, a head and body length of 3.9–5.5 in, a tail of 5.1–7.5 in and weigh 1.23–1.76 oz. The pygmy marmoset (*Cebuella pygmaea*) of the Upper Amazon Basin and the lesser mouse lemur (*Microcebus murinus*) of Madagascar are also of comparable length but heavier, adults weighing 1.76–2.64 oz and 1.58–2.82 oz respectively.

Largest Living Primates

The largest living primate is the eastern lowland gorilla (*Gorilla g. graueri*) of the lowland forests of Zaire and Uganda. The average adult male stands 5 ft 9 in tall and weighs 360 lb. The mountain gorilla (*Gorilla g. berengei*) of the volcanic mountain ranges of Rwanda, Uganda and Zaire is also of comparable size, i.e. 5 ft 8 in and 343 lb, and most of the exceptionally large gorillas taken in the field have been of this race. The greatest height (top of crest to heel) recorded for a gorilla is 6 ft 4¾ in for a male collected by a German expedition at Alimbongo, N Kivu, Zaire on May 16, 1938.

The heaviest gorilla ever kept in captivity was a male of the mountain race named "N'gagi," who died in the San Diego Zoo, Calif, on Jan 12, 1944, aged 18 years. He scaled 683 lb at his heaviest in 1943, and weighed 636 lb at the time of his death. He was 5 ft 7¾ in tall and boasted a record chest measurement of 78 in.

Primate Strength

"Boma," a 165-lb male chimpanzee at the Bronx Zoo, NYC, in 1924 recorded a right-handed pull (feet braced) of 847 lb on a dynamometer (compare with 210 lb for a man of the same weight). On another occasion an adult female chimpanzee named "Suzette" (estimated weight 135 lb) at the same zoo registered a right-handed pull of 1,260 lb while in a rage. A record of a 100-lb chimpanzee achieving a two-handed dead lift of 600 lb with ease suggests that a male gorilla could, with training, raise 2,000 lb!

Rarest Primate

The rarest living primate is the broad-nosed gentle lemur (*Hapalemur simus*) of Madagascar, which reportedly became extinct in the early 1970s. In 1986 a group consisting of 35 animals was discovered in a remote rain forest in the southeastern part of the island by an expedition from Duke University, Durham, NC.

Albino Gorilla

The world's first recorded albino gorilla, blue-eyed "Snowflake" (b 1964), was captured in Equatorial Guinea in 1966, and later transferred to Barcelona, Spain. The gorilla shares his enclosure with 3 females and has fathered a number of offspring with similar coloring.

Test-Tube Primate

The first non-human primate conceived in a laboratory dish is a female black baboon, born on July 25, 1983, just 6 months after fertilization at the Southwest Foundation for Research and Education in San Antonio, Tex. The date was coincidentally exactly 5 years after the birth of Louise Brown, first human test-tube baby. The baby baboon was named E.T. (for embryo transfer).

Largest and Smallest Monkeys

The only species of monkey reliably credited with weights of more than 100 lb is the mandrill (*Mandrillus sphinx*) of equatorial West Africa. The greatest reliable weight recorded is 119 lb for a male, but an unconfirmed weight of 130 lb has been reported. Adult females are about half the size of males.

The smallest monkey is the pygmy marmoset (*Cebuella pygmaea*) of the Upper Amazon Basin.

Oldest and Rarest Monkeys

The oldest monkey was a male white-throated capuchin (*Cebus capucinus*) called "Bobo" owned by the American Cyanamid Company of Pearl River, NY, who celebrated his 53rd birthday in Oct 1987 and passed away on July 10, 1988.

The rarest monkey is the golden-rumped tamarin of southeastern

OLDEST MONKEY: "Bobo," a capuchin, celebrated his 53rd birthday on Oct 30, 1987, and died on July 10, 1988. ►

ALBINO GORILLA: The first of his coloring to be captured in the wild of equatorial Africa, "Snowflake" has fathered offspring in his Barcelona enclosure. ◄

LARGEST RODENT: The capybara doesn't look like a mouse, is aquatic and has webbed feet, but it is still in the rodent family. Venezuelans call it a fish. ▼

Brazil. In 1986 there were only 75–100 left, all of them in the state of Sao Paulo, and the species is now on the verge of extinction.

Largest Rodent

The largest rodent is the capybara (*Hydrochoerus hydrochaeris*), an aquatic animal with webbed feet, found in tropical South America. Mature specimens have a head and body length of 3¼–4½ ft and weigh up to 250 lb (cage-fat specimen). It is wrongfully classified as a fish by Catholics in Venezuela so it can be eaten during Lent.

Smallest Rodent

The smallest known rodent is the northern pygmy mouse (*Baiomys taglore*) of central Mexico, southern Ariz and Tex, which measures up to 5.3 in in total length and weighs 0.24–0.35 oz.

Longest-Lived Rodent

The greatest reliable age reported for a rodent is 27 years 3 months for a Sumatran crested porcupine (*Hystrix brachyura*) which died in the National Zoological Park, Washington, DC, on Jan 12, 1965.

Rarest Antelope

The rarest antelope is the Arabian oryx (*Oryx leucoryx*) which has not been reported in the wild since 1972 when 3 were killed and 4 others captured on the Jiddat-al Harasis plateau, South Oman, Arabian peninsula. Between Mar 1980 and Aug 1983, a total of 17 specimens, most of them born and bred at San Diego Zoo, were released into the open desert in South Oman under the protection of a nomadic tribe. Since then there have been at least 15 live births, and two antelopes born in Oman have bred. Another release has also been carried out in Jordan.

Largest Antelope

The largest of all antelopes is the rare giant eland (*Tragelaphus derbianus*) of West and Central Africa, which may surpass 2,000 lb. The common eland (*T. oryx*) of East and South Africa has the same shoulder height of up to 5 ft 10 in, but is not quite so massive, although there is one record of a 5 ft 5 in bull shot in Nyasaland (now Malawi) in *c.* 1937 which weighed 2,078 lb.

Smallest Antelope

The smallest known antelope is the royal antelope (*Neotragus pygmaeus*) of West Africa. Mature specimens measure only 10–12 in at the shoulder, and weigh only 7–8 lb, which is the size of a large brown hare (*Lepus europaeus*). Salt's dik-dik (*Madoqua saltina*) of northeast Ethiopia and Somalia weighs only 5–6 lb when adult, but this species stands about 14 in at the withers.

Largest Deer and Antler Span

The largest deer is the Alaskan moose (*Alces alces gigas*). Adult bulls average 6 ft at the shoulder and weigh about 1,100 lb. A bull standing 7 ft 8 in at the withers and weighing 1,800 lb was shot in Sept

Most Valuable Furs

The highest-priced animal pelts are those of the sea otter (*Enhydra lutris*), also known as the Kamchatka beaver, which fetched up to $2,700 each before their 55-year-long protection started in 1912. The protection ended in 1967, and at the first legal auction of sea otter pelts in Seattle, Wash, Jan 31, 1968, Neiman-Marcus, the famous Dallas department store, paid $9,200 each for four pelts from Alaska. (The sea otter is the slowest swimming marine mammal.)

In May 1970 a Kojah (mink-sable cross) coat costing $125,000 was sold by Neiman-Marcus to Welsh actor Richard Burton for his then wife, Elizabeth Taylor. In 1983 the most expensive full fur coat in NYC was $100,000 for a Russian lynx on sale at Ben Kahn and Maximilian.

1897 in the Yukon Territory, Canada. Unconfirmed measurements of up to 8½ ft at the withers and 2,600 lb have been claimed.

The record antler span or "rack" is 78½ in. They were taken from a moose killed near the headwaters of the Stewart River in the Yukon in Oct 1897 and are now on display in the Field Museum, Chicago.

Oldest Antelope

The greatest reliable age recorded for an antelope is 25 years 4 months for an addax (*Addax nasomaculatus*) which died in the Brookfield Zoo, Chicago, on Oct 15, 1960.

Oldest Deer

The greatest reliable age recorded for a deer is 26 years 8 months for a red deer (*Cervus elaphus scoticus*), which died in the Milwaukee Zoo, Wis, on June 28, 1954.

Smallest Deer

The smallest true deer (family Cervidae) is the northern pudu (*Pudu mephistopheles*) of Ecuador and Colombia. Mature specimens measure 13–14 in at the shoulder and weigh 16–18 lb. The smallest ruminant is the lesser Malay chevrotain (*Tragulus javanicus*) of SE Asia, Sumatra and Borneo. Adult specimens measure 8–10 in at the shoulder and weigh 6–7 lb.

Rarest Deer

The rarest deer is Fea's muntjac (*Muntiacus feae*), which until recently was known only from two specimens collected on the borders of Burma and Thailand. In Dec 1977 a female was received at the Dusit Zoo, Bangkok, followed by 2 females in 1981, and 3 males and 3 females from Xizang, Tibet, southwest China, Feb 1982–Apr 1983.

Largest Goat

"Shad," a 352-lb wether male (b May 1978) standing 41 in high at the shoulder, owned by Bill and Mickey Vestle of Modesto, Calif, is said to be the heaviest and largest goat.

Largest Insectivore (Insect-Eating Mammal)

The largest insectivore is the moon rat (*Echinosorex gymnurus*), also known as Raffles' gymnure, found in Burma, Thailand, Malaysia, Sumatra and Borneo. Mature specimens have a head and body length of 10.43–17.52 in, a tail measuring 7.87–8.26 in, and weight up to 3.08 lb. Although the much larger anteaters (family Tachyglossidae and Myrmecophagidae) feed on termites and other soft-bodied insects, they are not insectivores, but belong to the orders Monotremata and Edentata ("without teeth").

Smallest Insectivore

The smallest insectivore is Savi's white-toothed pygmy shrew (*Suncus etruscus*), also called the Etruscan shrew, which is found along the coast of the northern Mediterranean and southwards to Cape Province, South Africa. Mature specimens have a head and body length of 1.32–2.04 in, a tail length of 0.94–1.14 in, and weight of between 0.052 and 0.09 oz.

Longest-Lived Insectivore

The greatest reliable age recorded for an insectivore is 16+ years for a lesser hedgehog-tenrec (*Echinops telefairi*), which was born in the Amsterdam Zoo, Netherlands, in 1966 and was later sent to Jersey Zoo. It died on Nov 27, 1982.

Heaviest Tusks

The heaviest recorded tusks are a pair in the British Museum (Natural History), London, which were collected from an aged bull shot by an Arab with a muzzle-loading gun at the foot of Mt Kilimanjaro, Tanzania, in 1897. They originally weighed 240 lb (length 10 ft 2½ in) and 225 lb (length 10 ft 5½ in) respectively, giving a combined weight of 465 lb, but their combined weight today is 440½ lb.

The greatest weight ever recorded for one elephant tusk is 258 lb for a specimen collected in Benin (formerly Dahomey), West Africa, and exhibited at the Paris Exposition in 1900.

Longest Tusks

The longest recorded elephant tusks (excluding prehistoric examples) are a pair from Zaïre preserved in the National Collection of Heads and Horns, kept by the New York Zoological Society, Bronx Park. The right tusk measures 11 ft 5½ in along the outside curve and the left measures 11 ft. Their combined weight is 293 lb. A single tusk of 11 ft 6 in has been reported, but details are lacking. Ivory rose in market price from $2.30 to $34 per lb, 1970–80.

Longest Horns

The longest horns grown by any living animal are those of the water buffalo (*Bubalus arnee = B. bubalis*) of India. One huge bull shot in 1955 had horns measuring 13 ft 11 in from tip to tip along the outside

LONGEST TEXAS ▲ LONGHORN: This 10½-ft-long spread of a steer, the largest ever recorded, is on exhibit in the Heritage Museum, Big Spring, Tex.

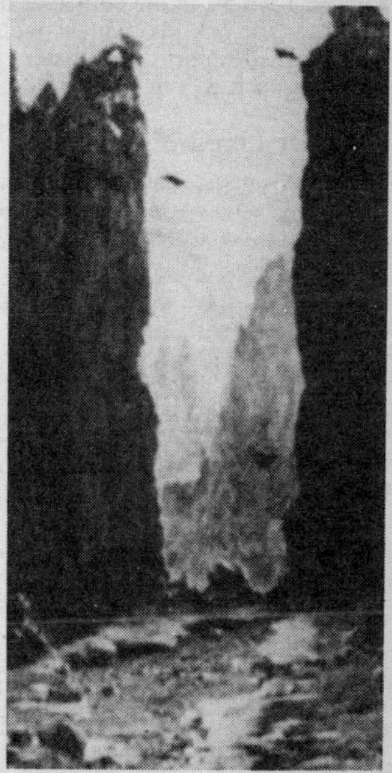

► JUMPERS: These ibex are crossing the canyon in escape from hunters by leaping back and forth.

curve across the forehead. The longest single horn on record was one measuring 81¼ in on the outside curve found on a specimen of domestic Ankole cattle (*Bos taurus*) near Lake Ngami, Botswana, Africa.

Largest Marsupial

The largest of all marsupials is the red kangaroo (*Macropus rufus*) of southern and eastern Australia. Adult males or "boomers" stand up to 7 ft tall, weigh up to 175 lb and measure up to 8 ft 1½ in along the curves of the body.

Smallest Marsupial

The smallest known marsupial is the very rare long-tailed planigale (*Planigale ingrami*), a flat-skulled mouse found only in northern Australia. Adult males have a head and body length of 2.16–2.48 in, a tail length of 2.24–2.36 in and weight of about 0.14 oz.

Fastest, Highest, Longest Marsupial Jump

The highest speed recorded for a marsupial is 40 mph for a young female eastern gray kangaroo (*Macropus giganteus*).

The greatest measured height cleared by a hunted kangaroo is 10 ft 6 in over a pile of timber. The longest recorded leap was reported in Jan 1951 when, in the course of a chase, a female red kangaroo made a series of bounds which included one of 42 ft. There is an unconfirmed report of an eastern gray kangaroo (*Macropus canguru*) jumping 44 ft 8½ in on the flat.

Longest-Lived Marsupial

The greatest reliable age recorded for a marsupial is 26 years 0 months 22 days for a common wombat (*Vombatus ursinus*) which died in London Zoo Apr 20, 1906.

DOMESTICATED ANIMALS

Horse Population

The world's horse population is estimated to be 75 million.

Oldest Horse and Pony

The greatest reliable age recorded for a horse is 62 years in the case of "Old Billy" (foaled 1760), believed to be a cross between a Cleveland and an Eastern blood. He was retired to a farm, where he died Nov 27, 1822. The skull of this horse is preserved in the Manchester Museum, and his stuffed head (fitted with false teeth) is now on display in the Bedford Museum.

The greatest reliable age recorded for a pony is 54 years for a stallion owned by a farmer in central France which was still alive in 1919.

The greatest age recorded for a thoroughbred racehorse is 42 years in the case of the bay gelding "Tango Duke" (foaled 1935), owned by Mrs Carmen J. Koper of Barongarook, Victoria, Australia. The horse died Jan 25, 1978.

Largest Horse

The largest and heaviest horse ever recorded was "Brooklyn Supreme," a purebred Belgian (Brabant) stallion (foaled Apr 12, 1928) owned by C. G. Good of Ogden, Iowa, which weighed 3,200 lb shortly before his death Sept 6, 1948, aged 20. He stood 19.2 hands (6 ft 6 in) and had a chest girth of 102 in.

In Apr 1973 the Belgian (Brabant) mare "Wilma du Bos" (foaled July 15, 1966), owned by Mrs Virgie Arden of Reno, Nev was reported to weigh 3,218 lb when in foal and being shipped from Antwerp. The mare stood 18.2 hands (6 ft 2 in) and normally weighed about 2,400 lb.

Tallest Horse

The tallest documented horse on record was the shire gelding named "Sampson" (later renamed "Mammoth") bred by Thomas Cleaver of Toddington Mills, Bedfordshire, Eng. This horse (foaled in 1846) measured 21.25 hands (7 ft 2½ in) in 1850 and was later said to have been 3,360 lb.

Smallest Horse

The smallest breed of horse is the Falabella of Argentina which was developed over a period of 70 years by inbreeding and crossing a small group of undersized horses originally discovered in the southern part of Argentina. Most adult specimens stand less than 30 in and average 80–100 lb. The smallest mature horse bred by Julio Falabella of Recco de Roca before he died in 1981 was a mare which stood 15 in and weighed 26¼ lb.

SMALLEST HORSE: The Falabella, an Argentine breed named for its developer, is hardly any bigger than a cockerel rooster and weighs 40–80 lb.

HEAVIEST DOG: Although St Bernards generally weigh more than any other breed, this Old English mastiff named "Alcama Zorba of La-Susa," set a record at 314½ lb in Sept 1987. *(Gerald L. Wood)*

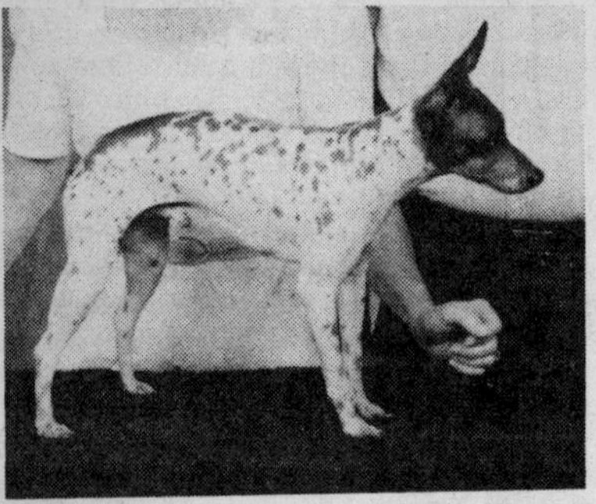

RAREST DOG: Replacing the Chinook as the rarest, this American Hairless Terrier was developed since 1972, with only 70 living examples, most of them in Trout, La.

Dr T. H. Hamison of the Circle Veterinary Center, Spartanburg, SC on Nov 30, 1975 certified that the stallion "Little Pumpkin" (foaled Apr 15, 1973) owned by J. C. Williams Jr. of Della Terra Mini Horse Farm, Inman, SC stood 14 in and weighed 20 lb.

Dog Population

In 1988 there were an estimated 49.4 million dogs in 37.2% of the households in the US.

In the city of Peking, China, all dogs even Pekingese are now banned because "pet-keeping has an adverse effect on social order and harms environmental sanitation." All pets had to be destroyed by Nov 1, 1983. A century before, Pekingese dogs were encouraged to sit on an emperor's lap and theft of a Pekingese was a crime punishable by death.

Oldest Dogs

Most dogs live between 8 and 15 years and authentic records of dogs living over 20 years are rare. The greatest reliable age recorded for a dog is 29 years 5 months for an Australian cattle dog named "Bluey," owned by Les Hall of Rochester, Vic, Australia. The dog was obtained as a puppy in 1910 and worked among cattle and sheep for nearly 20 years. He was put to sleep Nov 14, 1939.

Most Popular Dog Breeds

Cocker spaniels continued in 1987 to lead in new registrations (105,236) with the American Kennel Club. Poodles again were second (85,400). Labrador retrievers came in third (81,987) far ahead of golden retrievers (60,936), German shepherds (57,612), and chow chows (49,096).

Dog Strength and Endurance

The greatest load shifted by a dog was 6,400½ lb of railroad steel pulled by a 176-lb St Bernard named "Ryettes Brandy Bear," at Bothell, Wash, July 21, 1978. The 4-year-old dog, owned by Douglas Alexander of Monroe, Wash, pulled the weight on a four-wheeled carrier across a cement surface for a distance of 15 ft in less than 90 sec. Ten days earlier the same dog had moved 6,600 lb, but was 5 in short of the 15 ft minimum distance when the 90 seconds were up.

The strongest dog in the world in terms of most proportionate weight hauled is "Barbara-Allen's Dark Hans," a 97-lb Newfoundland, who pulled 5,045½ lb (= 52 lb per lb bodyweight) across a cement surface at Bothell, Wash, July 20, 1979. The dog, owned by Miss Terri Dickinson of Kenmore, Wash, was only 12 months old when he made the attempt.

In the annual 1,049 (not 1,135) mile dog sled race from Anchorage to Nome, Alaska, the record time is 11 days 2 hours 5 min by Susan Butcher's team of dogs in the 1987 race. It was her second consecutive win. The dogs wear booties to protect their paws from ice.

Heaviest Dog

The heaviest breed of domestic dog (*Canis familiaris*) is the St Bernard. The heaviest recorded example is "Benedictine Jr Schwarzwald Hof," owned by Thomas and Anne Irwin of Grand Rapids, Mich. He was whelped in 1982 and weighed 310 lb on Dec 3, 1984 (height at shoulder 39 in).

However, the heaviest individual dog ever recorded is "Alcama Zorba of La-Susa" (whelped Sept 26, 1981), an Old English mastiff owned by Chris Eraclides of London. In Sept 1987 this canine super-heavyweight tipped the scales at 314½ lb (shoulder height 35 in). If his diet was not strictly controlled his owner believes he would reach 336 lb without any trouble. Other statistics include a chest girth of 52 in, a 36½ in neck, and a nose-to-tail length of 8 ft 3 in.

Rarest Dog

The rarest breed of dog currently is the American hairless terrier, which at last count numbered only 70 living examples, 68 of them owned by Willie and Edwin Scott of Trout Creek Kennels, Trout, La. It is described as first appearing as a breed on Aug 2, 1972. (See photo.)

Tallest Dogs

The tallest breeds of dog are the Great Dane and the Irish

wolfhound, both of which can exceed 39 in at the shoulder. The extreme recorded example is the Great Dane "Shamgret Danzas" (whelped in 1975), owned by Mr and Mrs Peter Comley of Milton Keynes, Buckinghamshire, England. He stood 41½ in, or 42 in when his hackles went up, and weighed 238 lb. He died on Oct 16, 1984.

Smallest Dogs

The smallest breeds of dog are the Yorkshire terrier, the Chihuahua and the toy poodle, *miniature* versions of which have been known to weigh less than 16 oz when adult.

The smallest mature dog on record was a matchbox-sized Yorkshire terrier owned by Arthur F. Marples of Blackburn, Eng. This tiny atom, which died in 1945, aged nearly 2 years, stood 2½ in at the shoulder and measured 3¾ in from the tip of its nose to the root of its tail. Its weight was an incredible 4 oz.

Largest Litter

The largest recorded litter of puppies is one of 23 thrown on June 9, 1944, by "Lena," a foxhound bitch owned by Commander W. N. Ely of Ambler, Pa. All survived. On Feb 6–7, 1975, "Careless Ann," a St Bernard bitch owned by Robert and Alice Rodden of Lebanon, Mo, produced a litter of 23, but only 14 survived.

Most Prolific Dog

The dog who has sired the greatest recorded number of puppies was the greyhound "Low Pressure" nicknamed "Timmy," whelped in Sept 1957 and owned by Mrs Bruna Amhurst of Regent's Park, London. From Dec 1961 until he died in Nov 1969, he had fathered 2,414 registered puppies, with at least 600 others unregistered.

Most Valuable Dogs

Greyhound racing dogs are more highly valued than family dogs. The most highly valued is "Marathon Hound," worth $250,000 based on a sale of a half-interest for $125,000. The hound has won $225,000 in 4 years, and is now retired to stud at $750 per session.

In 1907 Mrs Clarice Ashton Cross of Ascot, Eng turned down an offer of £32,000 (equivalent to $1,380,000 in 1985!) from the American financier J. Pierpont Morgan for her famous Pekingese "Ch. Ch'erh of Alderbourne" (1904-*fl.*1914). Mr Morgan then came back with an "open" cheque, but again she turned him down.

The largest legacy to a dog was by Miss Ella Wendel of NYC who reputedly "left" her standard poodle "Toby" $75 million in 1931. Some say the amount was $4 million to the ASPCA.

Guide Dog

The longest period of active service is 14 years 8 months by Cindy-Cleo, a spayed female Labrador retriever, who died Apr 10, 1987, after serving Dr Aaron Barr of Tel Aviv, Israel, since Aug 1972.

Highest and Longest Dog Jumps

The canine "high jump" record for a leap and a scramble over a smooth wooden wall (without any ribs or other aids) is held by a

MOST VALUABLE DOG: ▲ A half-interest in "Marathon Hound" was sold for $125,000 in Aug 1984. In his career, this greyhound set a world record in winnings of $225,000. *(American Greyhound Track Operators)*

► TOP GERMAN SHEPHERD BITCH: "Ch Clayfield's Mon Ami" of W Des Moines, Iowa, owned by the Lea family won 10 dog shows on 4 continents.

◄ FASTEST DOG BREED: The Saluki is used in Arabia to hunt gazelles and has recorded a speed of 43 mph. *(Syndication International)*

German shepherd called "Max of Pangoula." He scaled an 11-ft-5⅛-in wall at Chikurubi prison's dog training school near Salisbury, Zimbabwe on Mar 18, 1980. His trainer was Chief Prison Officer Alec Mann.

"Duke," a 3-year-old German shepherd dog, handled by Corp. Graham Urry of RAF Newton, Nottinghamshire, scaled a ribbed wall with regulation shallow slats to a height of 11 ft 9 in on the BBC *Record Breakers* TV program on Nov 11, 1986.

The longest recorded canine long jump was one of 30 ft by a greyhound named "Bang," made in jumping a gate in coursing a hare at Brecon Lodge, Gloucestershire, England, in 1849.

Top Dog Trainer

The most successful dog trainer was Mrs Barbara Woodhouse of Rickmansworth, Hertfordshire, England, who trained 19,000 dogs to obey the basic commands during the period from 1951 to her retirement in 1985. She died July 10, 1988.

The fastest dog trainer is Armand Rabuttinio of Aston, Pa. His highest total for a single day (9 am–6 pm) is 132 dogs at a training marathon held at Upland, Pa, on June 12, 1982.

Top Show Dog

The greatest number of "Best-in-Show" awards won by any dog in all-breed shows is the 203 compiled by the Scottish terrier bitch "Ch. Braeburn's Close Encounter" (whelped Oct 22, 1978) up to Mar 10, 1985. She is owned by Sonnie Novick of Plantation Acres, Fla.

"Ch Clayfield's Mon Ami," owned by the Lea family of W Des Moines, Iowa, is a German shepherd bitch who has won 10 Dog Show Championships on 4 continents, 1975–84.

Cat Population

The estimated cat population in 1988 in the US of 57.8 million is the largest in the world, up from 23 million in 1981. Cats are kept in 30% of all households in the US, according to the Pet Food Institute in Wash, DC.

Oldest Cats

Cats are generally longer-lived animals than dogs. Information on this subject is often obscured by two or more cats bearing the same nickname in succession. The oldest cat ever recorded was probably the tabby "Puss," owned by Mrs T. Holway of Clayhidon, Devon, England, who celebrated his 36th birthday on Nov 28, 1939 and died the next day.

A more recent and better-documented case was that of the female tabby "Ma," owned by Mrs Alice St George Moore of Drewsteignton, Devon, Eng. This cat was put to sleep on Nov 5, 1957, aged 34.

Heaviest and Longest Cats

The largest of 330 cat breeds is the ragdoll, with males weighing 15–20 lb.

In the majority of domestic cats (*Felis catus*), the average weight of males (toms) at maturity is 6.2 lb compared to females (queens) averaging 5.4 lb. Neuters and spays average out somewhat heavier.

The heaviest weight for a domestic cat was recorded as 46 lb 15¼ oz at the time of his death, Mar 12, 1986, for a 10-year-old neutered male tabby named "Himmy," owned by Thomas Vyse of Cairns, Australia. His measurements were neck 15 in, waist 33 in, length 38 in.

Smallest Cats

The smallest breed of domestic cat is the Singapura or "Drain Cat" of Singapore. Adult males average 6 lb in weight and adult females 4 lb. In extreme cases of feline dwarfism weights of under 3 lb have been reliably reported. A male Siamese cross named "Ebony-Eb-Honey Cat," owned by Angelina Johnston of Boise, Idaho, tipped the scales at only 1 lb 12 oz in Feb 1984, when aged 23 months.

Most Prolific Cat

A cat named "Dusty," aged 17, living in Bonham, Tex, gave birth to her 420th kitten June 12, 1952.

Largest Cat Litter

The largest litter ever recorded was one of 19 kittens (4 stillborn) delivered by Caesarean section to "Tarawood Antigone," a 4-year-old brown Burmese, on Aug 7, 1970. Her owner, Mrs Valerie Gane of Kingham, Oxfordshire, England, reported that the litter was

HEAVIEST CAT: "Himmy" (on the ground), a 10-year-old tabby, weighed 46 lb 15¼ oz at the time of his death in Mar 1986.

LARGEST PET LITTERS

Animal	Number	Breed	Owner
Cat (1970)	15†	Burmese Siamese	Mrs Valerie Gane, Kingham, Oxfordshire, Eng
Dog (1944)	23	Foxhound	Cdr W. N. Ely, Ambler, Pa
(1975)	23	St Bernard	R. and A. Rodden, Lebanon, Mo
Rabbit (1978)	24	New Zealand White	Joseph Filek, Sydney, Cape Breton, Nova Scotia, Canada
Guinea Pig (1972)	12		Laboratory Specimen
Hamster (1974)	26*	Golden Hamster	L. and S. Miller, Baton Rouge, La
Mouse (1982)	34‡	House Mouse	Marion Ogilvie, Blackpool, England
Gerbil (1983)	14		Sharon Kirkman, Bulwell, Nottingham, England
(1960's)	15**		George Meares, geneticist-owner, gerbil breeding farm, St Petersburg, Fla.

† 4 stillborn
* 18 killed by mother
‡ 33 survived
** Uses special food formula

CAGED PET LONGEVITY TABLE

The greatest recorded ages for commonly kept pets are as follows:

	Years	Months	
Hamster, Golden	19		Reported, Cambridge, Eng 1984
Rabbit	18	10¾	"Flopsy" (owner Mrs L. B. Walker, Longford, Tasmania), caught Aug 6, 1964, d. June 29, 1983
Guinea Pig (*Cavia porcellus*)	14	10½	"Snowball," Nottinghamshire, Eng. Died 1979
Gerbil, Mongolian	8	4½	"Sahara," May 21, 1973–Oct 4, 1981 (owner Aaron Milstone) Lathrup Village, Mich
House Mouse (*Mus musculus*)	7	7	"Fritzy" (owner Mrs Bridget Beard. West House School, Birmingham, Eng) Sept 11, 1977–Apr 24, 1985
Rat (*Rattus sp.*)	5	8	Philadelphia. Died 1924

the result of mismating with a half-Siamese. Of the 15 survivors, 14 were male.

The largest live litter of which all survived was one of 14 kittens born in Dec 1974 to the Persian cat "Bluebell," owned by Mrs Elenore Dawson of Wellington, Cape Province, South Africa.

Richest Cat

When Mrs Grace Alma Patterson of Joplin, Mo died in Jan 1978, she left her entire estate worth $250,000 to her 18-lb white alley cat "Charlie Chan." When the cat dies, the estate, which includes a three-bedroom house, a 7-acre pet cemetery and a collection of valuable antiques, will be auctioned off and the proceeds donated to humane societies.

Most Valuable Cat

In 1967 Miss Elspeth Sellar of Grafham, England, turned down an offer of 2,000 guineas (then $5,880) from an American breeder for her 2-year-old international champion copper-eyed white Persian tom, "Coylum Marcus" (b Mar 28, 1965, d Apr 14, 1978).

Mousing Champion

The greatest mouser on record is "Towser," (b Apr 21, 1963), a female tortoiseshell cat owned by Glenturret Distillery Ltd, Scotland, who notched up an estimated score of 28,899 kills. She averaged three mice per day until her death on Mar 20, 1987.

Best Climbing Cat

On Sept 6, 1950 a 4-month-old kitten belonging to Josephine Aufdenblatten of Geneva, Switzerland, followed a group of climbers up to the top of the 14,691-ft Matterhorn in the Alps.

Rabbits

The largest breed of domestic rabbit (*Oryctolagus cuniculus*) is the Flemish giant. Adult specimens average 15.4–18.7 lb but weights up to 25 lb have been reliably reported. In Apr 1980 a 5-month-old female French lop weighing 26.45 lb was exhibited at the Reus Fair in northeastern Spain.

The heaviest recorded wild rabbit (average weight 3½ lb) was one of 8 lb 4 oz, killed by Norman Wilkie of Fife, Scotland while ferreting on Nov 20, 1982.

The smallest breeds of domestic rabbit are the Netherlands dwarf and the Polish, both of which reach a maximum of 2–2½ lb at maturity. In 1975, Jacques Bouloc of Coulommiers, France, announced a new cross of the above breeds which weighed 14 oz.

The most prolific domestic breeds are the New Zealand white and the Californian. Does produce 5–6 litters a year during their breeding life, each containing 8–12 young (compare with 5 litters and 3–7 young for the wild rabbit).

Longest Ears

In the lop family (French) ears exceeding 30 in have been measured.

Hares

In Nov 1956 a brown hare (*Lepus europaeus*), weighing a record 15 lb 1 oz, was shot near Welford, Northamptonshire, England. The average adult weight is 8 lb.

---

2. BIRDS (*AVES*)

Largest Bird

The largest living bird is the North African ostrich (*Struthio camelus camelus*) which is found in reduced numbers south of the Atlas Mountains from Upper Senegal and Niger across to the Sudan and central Ethiopia. Male examples of this flightless or ratite subspecies have been recorded up to 9 ft in height and 345 lb in weight.

The heaviest flying bird, or carinate, is the Kori bustard or paauw (*Otis kori*) of East and South Africa. Weights up to 40 lb have been reliably reported for cock birds shot in South Africa. The mute swan (*Cygnus olor*) resident in Britain can also reach 40 lb on occasion, and there is a record from Poland of a cob weighing 49.5 lb which could not fly.

The heaviest bird of prey is the Andean condor (*Vultur gryphus*), which averages 20–25 lb as an adult. A weight of 31 lb has been claimed for an outsize male California condor (*Gymnogyps californianus*) now preserved in the California Academy of Sciences, Los Angeles. This species is appreciably smaller than the Andean condor and rarely exceeds 23 lb.

Longest Bird Flights

The greatest distance covered by a ringed bird during migration is 14,000 miles by an Arctic tern (*Sterna paradisaea*), which was banded as a nestling July 5, 1955 in the Kandalaksha Sanctuary on the White Sea coast of the USSR, north of Archangel, and was captured alive by a fisherman 8 miles south of Fremantle, W Australia, May 16, 1956. The bird had flown south via the Atlantic Ocean and then circled Africa before crossing the Indian Ocean. It did not survive to make the return journey.

Fastest- and Slowest-Flying Birds

The fastest fliers are found among the ducks and geese (*Anatidae*), and some powerful species like the red-breasted merganser (*Mergus serrator*), the eider (*Somateria mollissima*), the canvasback (*Aythya valisineria*) and the spur-winged goose (*Plectropterus gambiensis*) can probably reach 65 mph in level flight and 80 mph in an escape-dive. The white-throated spinetail swift (*Hirundapus caudacutus*) of Asia and the alpine swift (*Apus melba*) are also extremely fast during courtship display flights, and the former has been timed at speeds up to *105.6 mph* in tests carried out in the USSR. Probably at least 50 percent of the world's flying birds cannot exceed an air speed of 40 mph in level flight.

A record for sustained speed was set by a semi-palmated sandpiper

(*Calidris pusilla*) tagged in Massachusetts in Aug 1985 and shot by a hunter in Guyana 2,750 miles away within 4 days, thus averaging some 30 mph above 5,000 ft.

The slowest-flying bird is the American woodcock (*Scolopax minor*), which has been timed at 5 mph without sinking.

LARGEST WING SPAN: This wandering albatross, a very old male caught in the Tasman Sea by members of the Antarctic research ship USNS *Eltanin* on Sept 18, 1965, had an 11-ft-11-in wing span. *(Robert Burton/Bruce Coleman)*

LARGEST BIRD: The ostrich shows how elastic are his jaws and throat and how tame he is.

HUMMINGBIRDS: Known for their speedy wing beat, these are identified by their thorntails. *(Arden London Ltd).* ◄

LONGEST IN AIR: ▼ The sooty tern remains aloft for 3–4 years.

◄
OLDEST BIRD: "George," a domestic gander, lived for 49 years 8 months, though the average longevity for a goose is 25 years.

Fastest and Slowest Wing Beat

The fastest recorded wing beat of any bird is that of the horned sungem (*Heliactin cornuta*) of tropical South America with a rate of 90 beats per sec.

Large vultures (family Vulturidae) sometimes exhibit a flapping rate as low as one beat per sec. Condors can cruise on air currents for 60 miles without beating their wings.

Highest-Flying

The highest acceptable altitude recorded for a bird is just over 27,000 ft for 30 whooper swans (*Cygnus cygnus*) flying from Iceland to winter at N Ireland. They were spotted by an airline pilot over the Outer Hebrides on Dec 9, 1967, and the height was also confirmed by air traffic control in N Ireland after the swans had been picked up on radar.

Rarest Bird

Because of the practical difficulties involved in assessing bird populations in the wild, it is virtually impossible to establish the identity of the rarest living bird. The strongest contender, however, was the dusky seaside sparrow (*Ammospiza nigrescens*), formerly of Titusville Marshes, Fla, with only a solitary captive male remaining at Discovery Island, Disney World, Orlando until its death June 16, 1987. (The last female was sighted in 1975.) In Mar 1987 one of the last two Californian condors (*Gymnogyps californianus*) still living in the wild was captured in an effort to save the species (total population 27) from extinction by breeding them in captivity.

Smallest Bird

The smallest bird is the bee hummingbird (*Mellisuga helenae*) found in Cuba and the Isle of Pines. Adult males (females are slightly larger) measure 2.24 in in total length, half of which is taken up by the bill and tail. It weighs 0.056 oz, which means it is lighter than a privet-hawk moth (0.084 oz).

The smallest bird of prey is the 1.23-oz white fronted falconet of northwestern Borneo (*Microhierax latifrons*), which is about the size of a sparrow.

The smallest sea bird is the least storm petrel (*Halocyptena microsoma*), which breeds on many of the small islands in the Gulf of Calif, Mexico. Adult specimens average 5½ in in total length and weigh about 1 oz.

Highest g Force in Bird World

Recent American scientific experiments have revealed that the beak of the red-headed woodpecker (*Melanerpes erythrocephalus*) hits the bark of a tree with an impact velocity of 13 mph. This means that when the head snaps back the brain is subject to a deceleration of about 10 g.

Most Airborne Birds

The most airborne of land birds is the common swift (*Apus apus*) which remains aloft for 2–3 years, until it is mature enough to breed.

But the sooty tern (*Sterna fuscata*) is the most aerial of all birds. It remains continuously aloft for 3 or 4 years after leaving the nesting grounds in a permanent state of insomnia before it returns to the breeding grounds.

Longest-Lived Bird

The greatest irrefutable age reported for any bird is 80+ years in the case of a male greater sulphur-crested cockatoo (*Cacatua galerita*) in the London Zoo 1925–82, which was fully mature when acquired.

In 1987 an unconfirmed age of *c.* 82 years was reported for a male Siberian white crane (*Grus leucogeranus*) named "Wolfe" at the International Crane Foundation, Baraboo, Wis. The bird was said to have hatched out in a zoo in Switzerland in *c.* 1905.

The oldest ringed bird on record is "Blue White," a 58-year-old female royal albatross (*Diomedea epomophora*), which nests annually at Taiaroa Head, Otago, New Zealand. Her mate "Green White Green" is 45.

Largest Nest

The largest bird's nest on record is one 9½ ft wide and 20 ft deep built by a pair of bald eagles (*Haliaeetus leucocephalus*) and possibly their successors near St Petersburg, Fla, reported in 1963. It weighed more than 6,700 lb.

Fastest Swimming and Deepest Diving Birds

The fastest swimmer is the gentoo penguin (*Pygoscelis papua*), which has a maximum burst speed of *c.* 17 mph. This is a respectable flying speed for some birds.

The deepest diver is the emperor penguin (*Aptenodytes forsteri*) of the Antarctic which can reach a depth of 870 ft and remain submerged for as long as 18 min.

Most Abundant Birds

The most abundant species of wild bird is the red-billed quelea (*Quelea quelea*) of the drier parts of Africa south of the Sahara with a population estimated at 10 billion of which a tenth are destroyed each year by pest control units.

The most abundant domesticated bird is the chicken, the domesticated form of the wild red jungle fowl (*Gallus gallus*) of Southeast Asia. In 1982 there were believed to be about 6½ billion in the world, or about 1.4 chickens for every member of the human race.

The most abundant sea bird is probably Wilson's storm petrel (*Oceanites oceanicus*) of the Antarctic. No population estimates have been published, but the number must run into hundreds of millions.

Incubation

The longest incubation period is that of the wandering albatross (*Diomedea exulans*), with a normal range of 75–82 days. There is an isolated case of an egg of the mallee fowl (*Leipoa ocellata*) of Australia taking 90 days to hatch. Its normal incubation period is 62 days. The shortest incubation period is the 10 days of the great spotted woodpecker (*Dendrocopus major*) and the black-billed cuckoo (*Coccyzus erythropthalmus*).

The idlest of cock birds include hummingbirds (family Trochilidae), eider duck (*Somateria mollis sima*) and golden pheasant (*Chrysolophus pictus*), among whom the hen bird does 100% of the incubation, whereas the female common kiwi (*Apteryx australis*) leaves this to the male for 75–80 days.

Largest Bird Eggs

Of living birds, the one producing the largest egg is the ostrich (*Struthio camelus*). The average egg weighs 3.63–3.88 lb, measures 6–8 in in length, 4–6 in in diameter and requires about 40 min for boiling. The shell, though 1/16th in thick, can support the weight of a 280-lb man.

Smallest Bird Eggs

The smallest egg laid by any bird is that of the Vervain hummingbird (*Mellisuga minima*) of Jamaica. Two specimens measuring less than 0.39 in in length weighed 0.0128 oz and 0.0132 oz respectively. The egg of the smallest bird, the bee hummingbird, weighs 0.0176 oz. Eggs emitted from the oviduct before maturity, known as "sports," are not reckoned to be of significance in discussion of relative sizes.

Longest and Most Feathers

The longest feathers grown by any bird are those of the cock Phoenix fowls, or onagadori (a strain of the red jungle fowl *Gallus gallus*), which has been bred in southwestern Japan since the mid-17th century. In 1972 a tail covert measuring 34 ft 9½ in was reported by Masasha Kubota of Kochi, Shikoku. Among flying birds the two central pairs of tail feathers of Reeve's pheasant (*Syrmaticus reevesi*) of central and northern China can exceed 8 ft. They serve as an escape brake.

In a series of "feather counts" on various species of birds, a whistling swan (*Cygnus columbianus*) was found to have 25,216 feathers, 20,177 of which were on the head and neck. The ruby-throated hummingbird (*Archilochus colubris*) has only 940, although hummingbirds have more feathers per area of body surface than any other living bird.

Birds with Most Acute Vision

Birds of prey (Falconiformes) have the keenest eyesight in the avian world. Their visual acuity is at least 8–10 times stronger than that of human vision. The golden eagle (*Aquila chrysaetos*) can detect an 18-in-long hare at a range of 2 mi, in good light and against a contrasting background, and a peregrine falcon (*Falco peregrinus*) can detect a pigeon at a range of over 5 mi.

Longest Bill

The longest bill grown by any bird in proportion to its body size is that of the male Toco toucan (*Ramphastos tocs*) of eastern S America, whose bill of 7.87 in compares with its 25.98-in total body length. The swordbill hummingbird (*Ensifera ensifera*) of the Andes is 4 in long, excluding tail, and its beak is longer.

Champion Bird-Spotters

The world's leading bird-spotter or "twitcher" is Norman Chesterfield (b Mar 8, 1913) of Wheatley, Ont, Canada. By Mar 1988 he had logged 6,260 of the 9,016 known species.

Peter G. Kaestner of Washington, DC, Dr Ira Joel Abramson of Miami, Fla, and Dr Martin H. Edwards of Kingston, Ont, Canada have all three seen at least one species of each of the world's 159 bird families.

Heaviest Chicken

The heaviest breed of chicken is the white sully developed by Grant Sullens of West Point, Calif, over a period of 7 years by crossing and recrossing large Rhode Island reds. One monstrous rooster named "Weirdo" reportedly weighed 22 lb in Jan 1973, and was so ferocious that he crippled a dog which came too close and killed two cats.

Chicken Flying

The record distance flown by a chicken is 630 ft, 2 in by "Sheena," a barnyard bantam owned by Bill and Bob Knox of Parkesburg, Pa which was videotaped flying the distance on May 31, 1985.

Heaviest Turkey

The greatest dressed weight recorded for a turkey (*Meleagris gallopavo*) is 81 lb 0¼ oz for a stag reared by British United Turkeys of Cheshire, Eng. It won the annual heaviest turkey competition held in London, Dec 9, 1986.

Longest-Lived Domestic Birds

The longest-lived domesticated bird (excluding the ostrich) is the domestic goose which normally lives about 25 years. A gander named "George," owned by Mrs Florence Hull of Lancashire, England, died on Dec 16, 1976, aged 49 years 8 months. He was hatched in Apr 1927. The longest-lived small cage bird is the canary (*Serinus canaria*). The oldest example on record was a 34-year-old cock bird named "Joey," owned by Mrs K. Ross of Hull, England. The bird was purchased in Calabar, Nigeria, in 1941, and died Apr 8, 1975.

Most Talkative Bird

The world's most talkative bird is a male African gray parrot (*Psittacus erythacus*) named "Prudle," owned by Mrs Lyn Logue of Golders Green, London, England, which won the "best talking parrot-like bird" title at the National Cage and Aviary Bird Show in London for 12 consecutive years (1965–76) before retiring undefeated. Prudle, who has a vocabulary of nearly 1,000 words, was taken from a nest in a tree about to be felled at Jinja, Uganda, in 1958.

3. REPTILES (*REPTILIA*)

(Crocodiles, snakes, turtles, tortoises and lizards)

Largest and Heaviest Reptiles

The largest reptile in the world is the estuarine or salt-water crocodile (*Crocodylus porosus*) of Southeast Asia, northern Australia, Papua New Guinea, Malay Archipelago, Vietnam and the Philippines. Adult males average 14–16 ft in length and scale 900–1,150 lb. A specimen 28 ft 4 in long, weighing *c.* 4,400 lb, was reportedly found in the Norman River of Australia in 1957.

Smallest Crocodile

The smallest living crocodilian is Osborn's dwarf crocodile (*Osteolaemus osborni*), found in the upper region of the Congo River, W Africa. It rarely exceeds 3 ft 11 in. in length.

Oldest Crocodilian

The greatest age authenticated for a crocodilian is 66 years for a female American alligator (*Alligator mississipiensis*), which arrived at Adelaide Zoo, Australia, on June 5, 1914 as a 2-year-old, and died there on Sept 26, 1978. Another female of this species at the Maritime Museum Aquarium, Gothenburg, Sweden, died on Feb 10, 1987 aged 65 years after the electricity heating its pool was accidentally cut off.

Rarest Crocodilian

The rarest crocodilian is the protected Chinese alligator (*Alligator sinensis*) of the lower Chang Jiang (Yangtse Kiang) River. The total population is currently estimated at 700-1,000 individuals.

Largest Lizards

The largest of all lizards is the Komodo monitor or Ora (*Varanus*

LARGEST CAPTIVE CROCODILE: This estuarine Siamese hybrid named "Yai" was born June 10, 1972 at a Thailand zoo and has grown to a length of 19 ft 8 in and a weight of 2,465 lb.

komodoensis), a dragon-like reptile found on the Indonesian islands of Komodo, Rintja, Padar and Flores. Adult males average 7 ft 5 in in length and weigh 130 lb. Lengths up to 30 ft (*sic*) have been quoted for this species, but the largest specimen to be accurately measured was a male presented to an American zoologist in 1928 by the Sultan of Bima which taped 10 ft 0.8 in. In 1937 this animal was put on display in the St Louis Zoological Gardens for a short period. It then measured 10 ft 2 in in length and weighed 365 lb.

The longest lizard in the world is the slender Salvadori monitor (*Varanus salvadori*) of New Guinea which has been reliably measured up to 15 ft 7 in long.

Oldest Lizard

The greatest age recorded for a lizard is more than 54 years for a male slowworm (*Anguis fragilis*) kept in the Zoological Museum in Copenhagen, Denmark, from 1892 until 1946.

CHAMELEONS move slowly (5 yd per hour) but they can change color and capture prey this way.

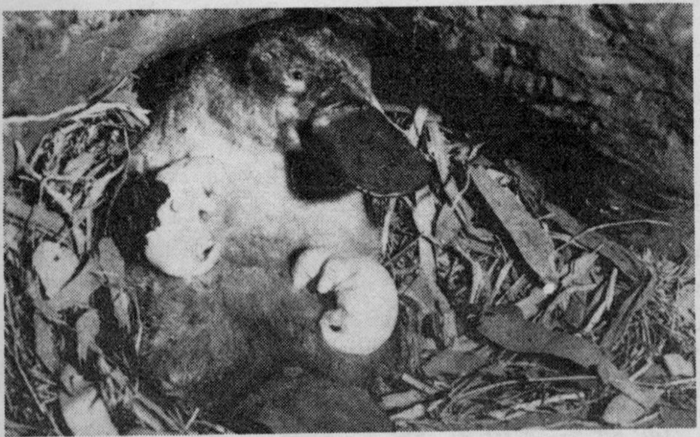

PLATYPUS: With a fleshy bill in duck shape, this aquatic mammal from Australia has dense fur, a broad flattened tail, and lays eggs. It also has the head and feet of a duck, the body of an otter and venomous spurs on its rear ankles (males) and its sensory system, located in its broad flat bill, can pick up electrical charges as small as those caused by the flick of a shrimp's tail.

Largest Chelonians

The largest living chelonian is the Pacific leatherback turtle (*Dermochelys coriacea*). The average adult measures 6–7 ft in overall length (length of carapace 5 ft 5½ in) and weighs up to 1,000 lb. The greatest weight reliably recorded is 1,908 lb for a male captured off Monterey, Calif on Aug 29, 1961. Its length was 8 ft 4 in overall.

The largest living is Marion's tortoise (*Geochelone Testudo gigantea*) of the Indian Ocean islands of Aldabra, Mauritius, and the Seychelles. A male named "Marmaduke" received at the London Zoo in 1951 recorded a peak weight of 616 lb before his death Jan 27, 1963.

Longest-Lived Chelonians

The greatest authentic age is 152+ years for a male Marion's tortoise (*Testudo sumerii*) brought from the Seychelles to Mauritius in 1766, which went blind in 1908, and was accidentally killed in 1918.

The greatest proven age of a continuously observed tortoise is 116+ years for a Mediterranean spur-thighed tortoise (*Testudo graeca*) which died in Paignton Zoo, Devon, England, in 1957.

The oldest turtle on record was an alligator snapping turtle (*Macrochelys temminckii*) at the Philadelphia Zoo, which was accidentally killed on Feb 7, 1949 when it was 58 years 9 months 1 day old.

Slowest-Moving Chelonians

In a recent "speed" test carried out in the Seychelles, in the Indian Ocean, a male giant tortoise (*Geochelone gigantea*) could only cover 5 yd in 43.5 sec (0.23 mph) despite the enticement of a female tortoise.

Deepest Diver

In May 1987 it was reported by Dr Scott Eckert that a leatherback turtle (*Dermochelys coriacea*) fitted with a pressure-sensitive recording device had dived to a depth of 3,973 ft off the Virgin Islands.

Smallest Reptiles

The smallest known species of reptile is believed to be *Sphaerodactylus parthenopion*, a tiny gecko found only on the island of Virgin Gorda, one of the British Virgin Islands in the Caribbean. It is known only from 15 specimens, including some gravid females, found between Aug 10 and 16, 1964. The three largest females measured 0.71 in from snout to vent, with a tail of approximately the same length.

It is possible that another gecko, *Sphaerodactylus elasmorhynchus*, may be even smaller. The only specimen ever discovered was an apparently mature female, with a snout-vent length of 0.67 in and a tail of the same length, found March 15, 1966 among the roots of a tree in the western part of the Massif de la Hotte in Haiti.

Fastest Reptile

The fastest-moving land snake is probably the slender black mamba (*Dendroaspis polylepis*). A speed of 10-12 mph may be possible for short bursts over level ground.

The highest speed measured for any reptile on land is 18 mph by a six-lined race runner (*Cnemidophorus sexlineatus*) pursued by a car near McCormick, SC, in 1941. The highest speed claimed for any reptile in water is 22 mph by a frightened Pacific leatherback turtle (see *Largest Chelonians*).

Rarest and Oldest Snakes

The rarest snake is the keel-sealed boa (*Casarea dussumieri*) of Round Island, western Indian Ocean, which has a total population of 75.

The oldest is a common boa who lived for 40 years 3 months 14 days in the Philadelphia Zoo.

Longest and Heaviest Snakes

The longest of all snakes (average adult length) is the reticulated

LONGEST VENOMOUS SNAKE: The king cobra of Southeast Asia can grow to 18 ft 9 in. *(Photo from Reptile World Serpentarium, Courtesy "Living Snakes of the World in Color" by John M. Mehrtens)* ▲

CRESTED IGUANA of Fiji Islands gets its first view of the outside world. ▼

python (*Python reticulatus*) of Southeast Asia, Indonesia and the Philippines, which regularly exceeds 20 ft 6 in. In 1912 a specimen measuring exactly 32 ft 9½ in was shot near a mining camp on the north coast of Celebes in the Malay archipelago.

The longest (and heaviest) snake ever held in captivity was a female reticulated python (*Python reticulatus*) named "Colossus" who died in Highland Park Zoo, Mifflin, Pa on Apr 15, 1963. She measured 28 ft 6 in and scaled 320 lb at her heaviest.

The heaviest snake is the anaconda (*Eunectes murinus*) of tropical South America, which is nearly twice as heavy as the reticulated python. The greatest authenticated length (and weight) recorded for an anaconda is 27 ft 9 in for a female killed in Brazil *c.* 1960, weighing 500 lb, and with a girth of 44 in.

The heaviest venomous snake is the eastern diamondback rattlesnake (*Crotalus adamanteus*) of the southeastern U.S. One specimen weighed 34 lb and was 7 ft 9 in long.

The longest venomous snake in the world is the king cobra (*Ophiophagus hannah*), also called the hamadryad, of Southeast Asia and the Philippines. A specimen collected near Port Dickson in Malaya in April 1937 grew to 18 ft 9 in in the London Zoo. It was destroyed at the outbreak of war in 1939.

Most Venomous Snakes

The most venomous snake is the sea snake *Hydrophis belcheri* which has a venom 100 times as toxic as that of the Australian taipan (*Oxyuranus scutellatus*). The snake abounds around Ashmore Reef in the Timor Sea, off the coast of northwestern Australia.

The most venomous land snake is the 6-ft-6-in long inland taipan snake (*Oxyuranus microlepidotus*) of the drainage bases of Queensland, Australia, which has a venom 9 times as toxic as that of the tiger snake (*Notechis scutatus*) of Australia and Tasmania. One specimen yielded 0.00385 oz of venom after milking, a quantity sufficient to kill at least 218,000 mice.

More people die of snakebite in Sri Lanka (Ceylon) than any comparable area in the world. An average of 800 people are killed annually on the island by snakes, and 97 per cent of the fatalities are caused by the common krait (*Bungarus ceylonicus*), Russell's viper (*Vipera russelli*) and the Asiatic cobra (*Naja naja*).

Shortest Snakes

The shortest known snake is the thread snake *Leptotyphlops bilineata*, found on the Caribbean islands of Martinique, Barbados and St. Lucia. It has a maximum recorded length of 4.7 in.

The shortest venomous snake is the spotted dwarf adder (*Bitis paucisquamata*) of Little Namaqualand, SW Africa, with adults averaging 9 in in length.

Longest Fangs

The longest fangs of any snake are those of the Gaboon viper (*Bitis gabonica*), of tropical Africa. In a 6-ft-long specimen, the fangs measured 1.96 in. A Gaboon viper bit itself to death on Feb 12, 1963 in the Philadelphia Zoological Gardens. Keepers found the dead snake with its fangs deeply embedded in its own back.

Most Abundant Snake

The sea snake (*Astrotia stokesii*) is found *en masse* from the Arabian Sea to the southwestern Pacific. In May 1929, a coiled mass in the Malacca Straits measured 60 mi.

---

4. AMPHIBIANS (*AMPHIBIA*)

(Salamanders, toads, frogs, newts, caecilians, etc.)

Largest Amphibian

The largest species of amphibian is the Chinese giant salamander (*Andrias davidianus*), which lives in the cold mountain streams and marshy areas of northeastern, central and southern China. The average adult measures 3 ft 9 in in total length and weighs 55–66 lb. One specimen collected in Hunan Province in southern China measured 5 ft 11 in in total length and weighed 143 lb.

Largest Toad

The most massive toad is probably the marine toad (*Bufo marinus*) of tropical South America, which was introduced into Queensland, Australia. An average adult specimen weighs about one pound, but on Nov 19, 1987 a 9½-in female with a 10-in snout vent named "Totally Awesome" at Blank Park Zoo, Des Moines, Iowa, weighed in at 5 lb 1½ oz. She died 5 months later.

Largest Frog

The largest known frog is the rare Goliath frog (*Conrana goliath*) of Cameroon and Equatorial Guinea. A female weighing 7 lb 4.5 oz was caught in the River Mbia, Equatorial Guinea, on Aug 23, 1960. It had a snout-vent length of 13.38 in and measured 32.08 in overall with legs extended.

Largest Tree Frog

The largest species of tree frog is *Hyla vasta*, found only on the island of Hispaniola (Haiti and the Dominican Republic) in the West Indies. The average snout-vent length is about 3.54 in, but a female collected from the San Juan River, Dominican Republic, in March 1928 measured 5.63 in.

Longest-Lived Amphibian

The greatest authentic age recorded for an amphibian is about 55 years for a male Japanese giant salamander (*Andrias japonicus*) which died in the aquarium at Amsterdam Zoological Gardens June 3, 1881. It was brought to Holland in 1829, at which time it was estimated to be 3 years old.

Rarest Amphibian

The rarest amphibian is the Israel painted frog (*Discoglossus

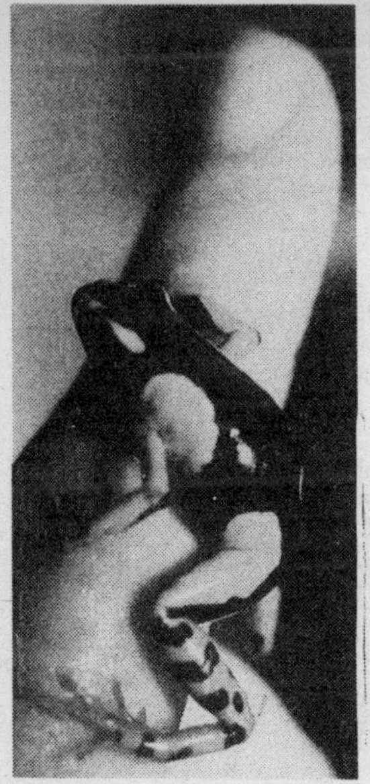

TINY FROG: Despite being only an inch long, this Madagascan long jumper has difficulty hiding from its enemies because of its bright coloration. ◄

LARGEST TOAD: This 9½-in long, 5-lb-1½-oz toad set the record on Nov 19, 1987 about 5 months before her death. *(Doug Landphir, Farmland Insurance Cos.)* ►

MOST VENOMOUS FROG: This 2-toned golden dart-poison frog secretes in its skin the most potent biotoxin known to man. ►

nigriventer), which has only been recorded from the eastern shore of Israel's Lake Huleh (Hula Lake). Since its discovery in 1940 only 5 specimens have been collected.

Smallest Amphibian

The smallest known amphibian is the arrow-poison frog *Sminthillus limbatus*, found only in Cuba. Fully grown specimens have a snout-vent length of 0.44–0.48 in.

Smallest Toad

The smallest toad is the sub-species *Bufo beiranus beiranus*, first discovered *c.* 1906 near Beira, Mozambique, East Africa. Adult specimens have a maximum recorded snout-vent length of 0.94 in.

Highest and Lowest Amphibian

The greatest altitude at which an amphibian has been found is 26,246 ft in the Himalayas for a common toad (*Bufo vulgaris*). This species has also been found at a depth of 1,115 ft in a coal mine.

Most Poisonous Venom

The most active known venom is the batrachotoxin derived from the skin secretions of the golden dart-poison frog (*Phyllobates terribilis*) of western Colombia, South America, which is at least 20 times more toxic than that of any other known dart-poison frog. An average adult specimen contains enough poison to kill 1,500 people.

Longest Frog Jump

The record for the standard three consecutive leaps is 33 ft 5½ in by a female South African sharpnosed frog (*Rana oxyrhynchus*) named "Santjie" at a frog derby held at Lurula Natal Spa, Paulpietersburg, Natal, S Africa May 21, 1977. At the annual Calaveras County Jumping Frog Jubilee at Angels Camp, Calif, the record is 21 ft 5¾ in by "Rosie the Riveter," an American bullfrog (*Rana catesbeiana*), owned and trained by Lee Guidicci of Santa Clara, Calif on May 18, 1986. "Santjie" would have been ineligible at Calaveras because entrants there must measure at least 4 in "stem to stern."

5. FISHES *(AGNATHA, GNATHOSTOMATA)*

Largest Freshwater Fishes

The largest fish which spends its whole life in fresh or brackish water is the rare Pa Beuk or Pla Buk (*Pangasianodon gigas*), a giant catfish found in the deep waters of the Mekong River of Laos and Thailand. Adult males average 8 ft in length and weigh about 360 lb. This size was exceeded by the European catfish or wels (*Silurus glanis*) in earlier times (in the 19th century lengths of up to 15 ft and weights up to 720 lb were reported for Russian specimens from the Dnieper River), but today anything over 6 ft and 200 lb is considered large. The arapaima (*Arapaima glanis*), also called the pirarucu, found in the Amazon and other South American rivers and often claimed to be the largest freshwater fish, averages 6½ ft and 150 lb. The largest "authentically recorded" measured 8 ft 1½ in and weighed 325 lb. It was caught in the Rio Negro, Brazil, in 1836. In Sept 1978 a Nile perch (*Lates niloticus*) weighing 416 lb was netted in the eastern part of Lake Victoria, Kenya.

Largest Sea Fishes

The largest fish is the rare, plankton-feeding whale shark (*Rhincodon typus*) which is found in the warmer areas of the Atlantic, Pacific and Indian Oceans. The longest scientifically measured one on record was a 41½ ft specimen captured off Baba Island near Karachi, Pakistan, on Nov 11, 1949. It measured 23 ft round the thickest part of its body and weighed an estimated 33,600 lb.

The largest carnivorous fish (excluding plankton-eaters) is the comparatively rare great white shark (*Carcharodon carcharias*), also called "the man-eater," which ranges from the tropics to temperate-zone waters. Adult specimens (females are larger than males) average 14–15 ft in length and generally scale 1,150–1,700 lb but larger specimens have been recorded.

The length record is 21 ft for a female caught off Castillo de Cojimar, Cuba, in May 1945. She weighed 7,302 lb.

The longest of the bony or "true" fishes (Pisces) is the oarfish (*Regalecus glesne*), also called the "King of the Herrings," which has a worldwide distribution. In *c.* 1885 a 25-ft-long example weighing 600 lb was caught by fishermen off Pemaquid Point, Maine. Another oarfish, seen swimming off Asbury Park, NJ by a team of scientists from the Sandy Hook Marine Laboratory on July 18, 1963, was estimated to measure 50 ft in length.

The heaviest bony fish in the world is the ocean sunfish (*Mola mola*), which is found in all tropical, subtropical and temperate waters. On Sept 18, 1908 a huge specimen was accidentally struck by the *SS Fiona* off Bird Island about 40 miles from Sydney, NSW, Australia, and towed to Port Jackson. It measured 14 ft between the anal and dorsal fins and weighed 4,927 lb.

Smallest Fishes

The shortest recorded marine fish—and the shortest known vertebrate—is the dwarf goby (*Trimmatom nanus*) of the Chagos Archipelago, central Indian Ocean. In one series of 92 specimens collected by the 1978–9 Joint Services Chagos Research Expedition of the British Armed Forces, the adult males averaged 0.338 in in length and the adult females 0.350 in. The lightest of all vertebrates and the smallest catch possible for any fisherman is the dwarf goby (*Schindleria praematurus*) from Samoa which measures 0.47–0.74 in. Mature specimens have been known to weigh only 2 mg, which is equivalent to 17,750 to the oz.

The smallest commercial fish is the now endangered Sinarapan (*Mistichthys luzonensis*), a goby found only in Lake Buhi, Luzon, Philippines. Adult males measure 0.39–0.51 in in length, and a dried 1-lb fish cake contains about 70,000 of them!

The smallest known shark is the long-faced dwarf shark (*Squaliolus laticaudus*) of the western Pacific which does not exceed 5.9 in.

The shortest and lightest freshwater fish species is the dwarf pygmy goby (*Pandaka pygmaea*), a colorless and nearly transparent species found in streams and lakes on Luzon, the Philippines. Adult males measure only 0.28–0.38 in long and weigh only 4–5 mg (0.00014–0.00017 oz).

Fastest Fishes

The cosmopolitan sailfish (*Istiophorus platypterus*) is generally considered to be the fastest species of fish, although the practical difficulties of measurement make data extremely difficult to secure. A figure of 68 mph (100 yd in 3 sec) has been cited for one off Long Key, Fla. The swordfish (*Xiphias gladius*) has also been credited with very high speeds, but the evidence is based mainly on bills that have been found deeply embedded in ships' timbers. A speed of 50 knots (57.6 mph) has been calculated from a penetration of 22 in by a bill into a piece of timber, but 30–35 knots (35–40 mph) is the most conceded by some experts. A wahoo (*Acanthocybium solandri*) 43 in in length is capable of attaining a speed of 47.8 mph.

Some American fishermen believe that the bluefin tuna (*Thunnus thynnus*) is the fastest fish in the sea, and burst speeds up to 64.62 mph have been claimed for this species, but the highest speed recorded so far is 43.4 mph in a 20-sec dash.

Most Abundant Fish

The most abundant species is probably the 3-in-long deep-sea bristlemouth (*Cyclothone elongata*) which has a worldwide distribution.

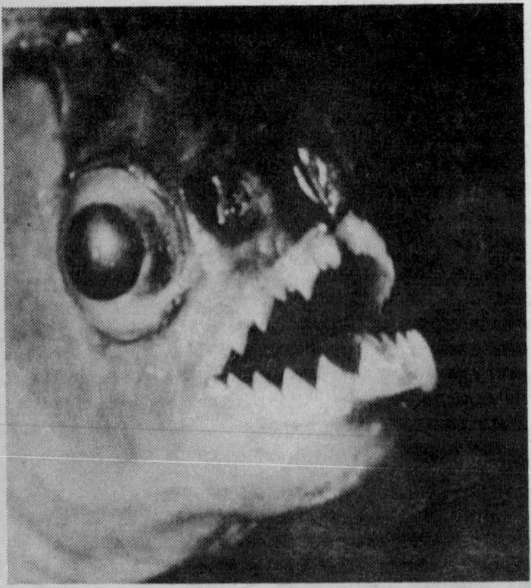

MOST FEROCIOUS FISH: The piranhas with their razor-sharp teeth move about in schools of 1,000 strong. *(Bruce Coleman)*

Deepest Fish

The greatest depth from which a fish has been recovered is 27,230 ft in the Puerto Rico Trench (27,488 ft) in the Atlantic by Dr Gilbert L. Voss of the US research vessel *John Elliott*. The fish was a 6½-in-long *Bassogigas profundissimus* taken in Apr 1970 and was only the fifth such brotulid ever caught.

Longest-Lived Fishes

Aquaria are of too recent origin to be able to establish with certainty which species of fish can fairly be regarded as the longest-lived. Early indications are that it may be the lake sturgeon (*Acipenser fulvescens*) of N America. One specimen found in Lake Winnebago, Wis, lived 82 years, an estimate based on its annuli, 1951–54. In July 1974 a figure of 228 years (*sic*) was attributed by growth ring count to a female Koi fish, a form of fancy carp, named "Hanako" living in a pond in Higashi Shirakawa, Gifu Prefecture, Japan, but the greatest authoritatively accepted age for this species is "more than 50 years."

The death of an 88-year-old female European eel (*Anguilla anguilla*) named "Putte" in the aquarium at Halsingborg Museum, Sweden was reported in 1948. She was allegedly born in the Sargasso Sea of the North Atlantic in 1860, and was caught in a river as a 3-year-old elver (young eel).

Oldest Goldfish

Goldfish (*Carassius auratus*) have been reported to live for over 40 years in China. A specimen named "Fred," owned by A. R. Wilson of Worthing, W Sussex, Eng., died on Aug 1, 1980, aged 41 years.

Shortest-Lived Fishes

The shortest-lived fishes are probably certain species of the suborder Cyprinodontei (killifish) found in Africa and South America which normally live about 8 months in the wild.

Most Venomous Fish

The most venomous fish are the stonefish (Synanceidae) of the tropical waters of the Indo-Pacific, and in particular *Synanceja horrida* which has the largest venom glands of any known fish. Direct contact with the spines of its fins, which contain a strong neurotoxic poison, often proves fatal.

Most Valuable Fish

The most valuable fish is the Russian sturgeon (*Huso huso*). One 2,706-lb female caught in the Tikhaya Sosna River in 1924 yielded 541 lb of best quality caviar, valued at $184,500 in 1986, at the rate of $340 per lb.

Most and Least Fish Eggs

The ocean sunfish (*Mola mola*) produces in a single spawning up to 300 million eggs, each of them measuring about 0.05 in in diameter. The egg yield of the tooth carp *Jordanella floridae* of Florida is only about 20 over a period of several days.

Most Electric Fish

The most powerful electric fish is the electric eel (*Electrophorus electricus*), which is found in the rivers of Brazil, Colombia, Venezuela and Peru. An average-sized specimen can discharge 400 volts at 1 ampere, but measurements up to 650 volts have been recorded.

6. STARFISHES *(ASTEROIDEA)*

Largest and Heaviest Starfishes

The largest of the 1,600 known species of starfish in terms of total arm span is the very fragile brisingid *Midgardia xandaros*. A specimen collected by the Texas A & M University research vessel *Alaminos* in the southern part of the Gulf of Mexico in the late summer of 1968 measured 54.33 in from tip to tip but the diameter of its disc was only 1.02 in. Its dry weight was only 2.46 oz. The heaviest species of starfish is the five-armed *Thromidia catalai* of the western Pacific. One specimen, collected off Ilot Amedee, New Caledonia, Sept 14, 1969, and later deposited in the Noumea Aquarium, weighed an estimated 13.2 lb with a total arm span of 24.8 in.

Smallest Starfish

The smallest known starfish is the asterinid sea star (*Patiriella parvivipara*) discovered by Wolfgang Zeidler on the west coast of the Eyre Peninsula, S Australia, in 1975, which has a maximum radius of 0.18 in and a diameter of 0.35 in.

Most Destructive Starfish

The Crown of Thorns (*Acanthaster planci*) of the Indo-Pacific region and the Red Sea can destroy 46.5–62 sq in of coral in a day.

Deepest Starfish

The greatest depth from which a starfish has been recovered is 24,881 ft for a specimen of *Porcellanaster ivanovi*, collected by the Russian research ship *Vityaz* in the Marianas Trench, in the western Pacific in about 1962.

7. ARACHNIDS *(ARACHNIDA)*

Largest and Heaviest Spiders

The largest known spider is the Goliath bird-eating spider (*Theraphosa blondi*) of the coastal rain forests of northern South America. One female specimen owned by Charles Seiderman of NYC reached a peak weight of 4.35 oz, a body length of 4 in, a leg span of 10½ in, and 1-in-long fangs. It had been captured in Surinam.

LARGEST SPIDER: This huge quarter-pound "Theraphosa blondi" female had a leg span of 10½ in. *(Photo by its owner, Charles J. Seiderman)*

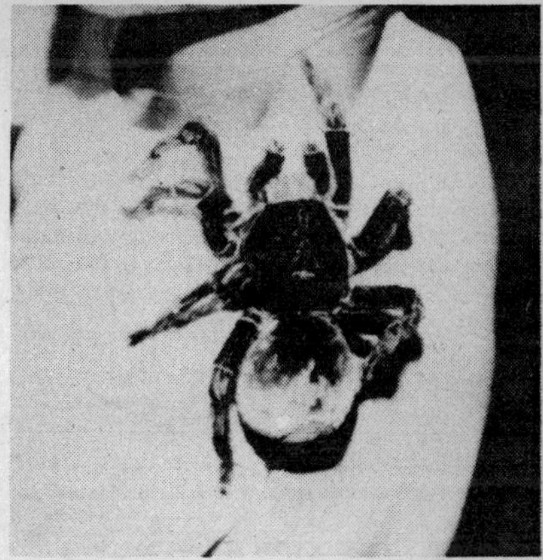

An outsized male example collected in Apr 1965 by an expedition in Venezuela had a leg span of 11.02 in.

Smallest Spider

The smallest known spider is *Patu marplesi* (family Symphytognathidae) of Western Samoa. The type specimen (a male found in moss at *c.* 2,000-ft altitude near Malolelei, Upolu, in Jan 1956) measures 0.016 in overall—half the size of a printed period (.).

Largest and Smallest Webs

The largest webs are the aerial ones spun by the tropical orb weavers of the genus *Nephila*, which have been measured up to 18 ft 9¾ in in circumference. The smallest webs are spun by spiders such as *Glyphesis cottonae*, etc., which are smaller than a postage stamp, covering ¾ of a sq in.

Most Venomous Spiders

The most venomous spiders are the Brazilian wandering spiders of the genus Phoneutria and particularly *P. fera*, which has the most active neurotoxic venom of any living spider. These large and highly aggressive creatures frequently enter human dwellings and hide in clothing or shoes. When disturbed, they bite furiously several times, and hundreds of accidents involving these species are reported annually. Fortunately an effective antivenin is available, and when deaths do occur they are usually among children under the age of 7.

Fastest Spider

The fastest-moving arachnids are the long-legged sun spiders of the genus *Solpuga*, which live in the arid semi-desert regions of Africa and the Middle East. Some species probably have a burst sprint capability of at least 10 mph.

Rarest Spider

The most elusive of all spiders are the rare trapdoor spiders of the genus *Liphistius* which are found in Southeast Asia.

Longest-Lived Spider

The longest-lived of all spiders are the primitive *Mygalomorphae* (tarantulas and allied species). One mature female tarantula, collected at Mazatlan, Mexico, in 1935 and estimated to be 12 years old at the time, was kept in a laboratory for 16 years, making a total of 28 years.

8. CRUSTACEANS

(Crabs, lobsters, shrimps, prawns, crayfish, barnacles, water fleas, fish lice, wood lice, sand hoppers and krill, etc.)

Largest Crustacean

The largest of all crustaceans (although not the heaviest) is the giant spider crab (*Macrocheira kaempferi*), also called the stilt crab, which is found in deep waters off the southeastern coast of Japan. Mature specimens usually have a 12–14-in-wide body and a claw span of 8–9 ft, but unconfirmed measurements up to 19 ft have been reported. A specimen with a claw span of 12 ft 1½ in weighed 41 lb.

Largest Lobster

The largest species of lobster, and the heaviest of all crustaceans, is

SMALLEST CRAB: Only ¼ in long, the pea crab is aptly named. It lives in the mantle cavities of bivalve mollusks. ***(Heather Angel)***

the American or North Atlantic lobster (*Homarus americanus*). The largest lobster, a specimen weighing 44 lb 6 oz measuring 3 ft 6 in from the end of the tail-fan to the tip of the largest claw, was caught off Nova Scotia, Canada, on Feb 11, 1977. It was later sold to Steve Karathanos, owner of a Bayville, NY restaurant.

Smallest Crustaceans

The smallest known crustaceans are water fleas of the genus *Alonella*, which may measure less than 0.0098 in long. They are found in northern European waters.

The smallest known lobster is the Cape lobster (*Homarus capensis*) of South Africa which measures 3.9–4.7 in in total length.

The smallest crabs in the world are the aptly named pea crabs (family Pinnotheridae). Some species have a shell diameter of only 0.25 in, including *Pinnotheres pisum*.

Longest-Lived Crustacean

The longest-lived of all crustaceans is the American lobster (*Homarus americanus*). Very large specimens may be as much as 50 years old.

Deepest Crustacean

The greatest depth from which a crustacean has been recovered is 34,450 ft for *live* amphipods from the Challenger Deep, Marianas Trench, West Pacific by the US research vessel *Thomas Washington* in Nov 1980. Amphipods and isopods have also been collected in the Ecuadoran Andes at a height of 13,300 ft.

---

9. INSECTS

Largest Cockroach

The largest cockroach is the giant burrowing cockroach (*Macropanesthia rhinoceros*) of tropical northern Queensland, Australia. A female measuring 3.11 in in length, 1.49 in across and weighing 0.77 oz was collected at Agnes Water, Queensland, in Dec. 1986.

Longest Insect

The longest insect in the world is the giant stick-insect *Pharnacia serratipes* of Indonesia, females of which have been measured up to 13 in in body length. The longest beetle known (excluding antennae) is the Hercules beetle (*Dynastes hercules*) of Central and South America, which has been measured up to 7.48 in. More than half the length, however, is taken up by the prothoracic horn.

Smallest Insects

The smallest insects recorded so far are the "hairy-winged" beetles of the family Ptiliidae (= Trichopterygidae) and the "battledore-wing fairy flies" (parasitic wasps) of the family Myrmaridae. They are smaller than some of the protozoa (single-celled animals).

The male bloodsucking banded louse (*Enderleinellus zonatus*), ungorged, and the parasitic wasp (*Caraphractus cinctus*) may each weigh as little as 0.005 mg, or 5,670,000 to an oz. The eggs of the latter each weigh 0.0002 mg or 141,750,000 to an oz.

HEAVIEST INSECT: The Goliath beetle (next to a ladybug) weighs as much as 3½ oz and measures 4¼ in.

Heaviest Insects

The heaviest living insects are the Goliath beetles (family Scarabaeidae) of Equatorial Africa. The largest members of the group are *Goliathus regius* and *Goliathus goliathus* (*giganteus*). In one series of fully grown males (females are smaller) the weight ranged from 2.5–3.5 oz.

Toughest Insect

The larva of the chironomid fly *Polypedilum vanderplanki* can tolerate temperatures from −215.6°F to −454°F and is the most advanced organism that can be totally dehydrated.

Rarest

It was estimated by Dr Erwin (US) in 1982 that there may be 30 million species of insect—more than all other classes and phyla put together. Thousands are single holotypes.

Fastest-Flying Insects

Experiments have proved that a widely publicized claim by an American entomologist in 1926 that the deer bot-fly (*Cephenemyia pratti*) could attain a speed of 818 mph at an altitude of 12,000 ft was wildly exaggerated. If true, it would have generated a supersonic "pop." Acceptable modern experiments have now established that the highest maintainable air speed of any insect, including the deer bot-fly, is 24 mph, rising to a maximum of 36 mph for short bursts.

Fastest Moving on Land

The large tropical cockroaches (*Dictyoptera*), specimens measuring about 1.18 in in length, have been timed at 2.68 to 2.90 mph, or 40–43 body lengths per second.

Loudest Insects

The loudest of all insects is the male cicada (family Cicadidae). At 7,400 pulses per min its tymbal (sound) organs produce a noise (officially described by the US Dept of Agriculture as "Tsh-ee-EEEE-e-ou") detectable over a quarter of a mile distance.

Largest Dragonfly

The largest dragonfly is *Megaloprepus caeruleata* of Central and South America, which has been measured up to 7.52 in across the wings and 4.72 in in body length.

Longest-Lived Insects

The longest-lived insects are the splendor beetles (*Buprestidae*), some of which remain in the larvae stage for more than 30 years. On May 27, 1983 a *Buprestis aurulenta* appeared from the staircase timber in the home of Mr W. Euston of Prittlewell, Southend-on-Sea, Eng after 47 years as a larva.

Honey Yield

The greatest amount of wild honey ever extracted from a single hive is 622 lb reported by John R. Clift of Minneapolis for a single hive with 2 queens in 1983.

Largest Flea

The largest known flea is *Hystrichopsylla schefferi*, described from a single specimen taken from the nest of a mountain beaver (*Aplodontia rufa*) at Puyallup, Wash in 1913. Females measure up to 0.31 in in length, which is the diameter of a pencil.

Flea Jumps

The champion jumper among fleas is the common flea (*Pulex irritans*). In one American experiment carried out in 1910 a specimen allowed to leap at will performed a long jump of 13 in and a high jump of 7¾ in. In jumping 130 times its own height a flea subjects itself to a force of 200 g. Siphonapterologists recognize 1,830 varieties of fleas.

Largest Butterflies and Moths

The largest known butterfly is the protected Queen Alexandra birdwing (*Ornithoptera alexandrae*) of Papua New Guinea. Females may have a wing span exceeding 11.02 in and weigh over 0.88 oz.

The largest moth (though not the heaviest) is the Hercules moth (*Coscinoscera hercules*) of tropical Australia and New Guinea. A wing area of up to 40.8 sq in and a wing span of 11 in have been recorded. In 1948 an unconfirmed measurement of 14.17 in was reported for a female captured near the post office at the coastal town of Innisfail, Queensland, Australia. The rare owlet moth (*Thysania agrippina*) of Brazil has been measured up to 12.16 in wing span.

Smallest Butterfly

The smallest known butterfly is the recently discovered *Micropsyche ariana*, which has a wing span of 0.275 in. The type specimen was collected on Mt. Khwajaghar in the Koh-i-Baba range, Afghanistan. The smallest of the estimated 140,000 known species of Lepidoptera are the moths *Johanssonia aceto sae (Stainton)*, found in Great Britain, and *Stigmella ridiculosa* from the Canary Islands, which have a wing span of 0.08 in and a similar body length.

Rarest Butterfly

The birdwing butterfly *Ornithopteria* (= *Troides*) *allottei* of Bougainville, Solomon Islands is known from less than a dozen specimens. A male from the collection of C. Rousseau Decelle was auctioned for £750 (then $2,100) in Paris on Oct 24, 1966.

Largest Butterfly Preserves

Stratford-upon-Avon Butterfly Farm (Eng) has a main flight area of 6,338 sq ft which can accommodate 2,000 exotic butterflies in authentic rain forest conditions. The total of all flight areas at the butterfly farm which opened on June 15, 1985, is 8,789 sq ft.

The enclosed flight space of The Australian Butterfly Sanctuary at Kurunda, Queensland, Australia is 129,250 sq ft.

10. CENTIPEDES (*CHILOPODA*)

Longest and Shortest

The longest known species of centipede is a large variant of the widely distributed *Scolopendra morsitans*, found on the Andaman Islands, Bay of Bengal, India. Specimens have been measured up to 13 in in length and 1½ in in breadth. The shortest recorded centipede is an unidentified species which measures only 0.19 in.

Most Legs

The centipede with the greatest number of legs is *Himantarum gabrielis* of southern Europe which has 171–177 pairs when adult.

Fastest

The fastest centipede is probably *Scutigera coleop trata* of southern Europe which can travel at a rate of 1.1 mph.

11. MILLIPEDES (*DIPLOPODA*)

Longest and Shortest

The longest species of millipede known are the *Graphidostreptus gigas* of Africa and *Scaphistostreptus seychellarum* of the Seychelles Islands in the Indian Ocean, both of which have been measured up to 11.02 in in length and 0.78 in in diameter. The shortest millipede in the world is the British species *Polyxenus lagurus*, which measures 0.082–0.15 in in length.

Most Legs

The greatest number of legs reported for a millipede is 375 pairs (750 legs) for *Illacme plenipes* of Calif.

MILLIPEDES have as many as 750 legs (not 1,000), and this giant from the Seychelles Islands is nearly 1 ft long. (*J. Watson/WWF*)

12. SEGMENTED WORMS (*ANNELIDA*)

Longest and Shortest Earthworms

The longest known species of earthworm is *Microchaetus rappi* (= *M. microchaetus*) of South Africa. In *c.* 1937 a giant earthworm measuring 22 ft in length when naturally extended and 0.78 in in diameter was collected in the Transvaal, S Africa.

The shortest segmented worm known is *Chaetogaster annandalei*, which measures less than 0.019 in in length.

On Feb 2, 1988 an "earthworm" 6 ft in length was reported in Wiltshire, Eng. The specimen was later sent to the British Museum (Natural History) for identification, where it was found to be the intestine of a hedgehog (*Erinaceus europaeus*).

Greatest Size Difference Between Sexes

The largest female marine worms of the species *Bonellia viridis* are at least 100 million times heavier than the smallest males. The female is up to 39.3 in long against the miserable 0.04 in of the male.

Worm Charming

The record for attracting (by vibrations) earthworms to the surface of a one-sq-meter of soil is 149 worms in 15 min on Mar 22, 1986 by a team led by Bob Benn of Dartmouth, Eng.

13. MOLLUSKS

(Squids, octopuses, snails, shellfish, etc.)

Largest Squid

The largest known invertebrate is the Atlantic giant squid *Architeuthis dux*. On Nov 2, 1878 a specimen measuring 55 ft in total length (head and body 20 ft, tentacles 35 ft) was killed after it ran aground in Thimble Tickle Bay, Newfoundland, Canada. It weighed an estimated 4,400 lb. This squid has the largest eye of any animal—15.75 in in diameter. In Oct 1887 another giant squid (*Architeuthis longimanus*) measuring 57 ft in total length was washed up in Lyall Bay, NZ, but 49 ft 3 in of this was tentacle.

LONGEST-LIVED SPECIES: The quahog of the North Atlantic may live for 150 years. *(Heather Angel)*

Largest Octopus

The largest octopus known to science is *Octopus apollyon* of the coastal waters of the N Pacific. One huge individual caught single-handed by skin diver Donald E. Hagen in Lower Hoods Canal, Puget Sound, Wash, on Feb 18, 1973, had a relaxed 23-ft radial spread and weighed 118 lb 10 oz.

Largest Bivalve Shells

The largest of all existing bivalve shells is the marine giant clam *Tridacna gigas*, found on the Indo-Pacific coral reefs. A specimen measuring 43.3 in in length and weighing 734 lb, collected off Ishigaki Island, Okinawa, was found in 1956 but not formally measured until Aug 1984 by Dr Shomei Shirai.

Smallest Shell

The smallest shell is the univalve *Ammonicera rota*, which measures 0.02 in in diameter, found in British waters.

Most Expensive Shell

The value of a seashell does not necessarily depend on its rarity or its prevalence. The most sought-after shell at the moment is probably *Conus lamberti sowerbie* from New Caledonia in the Pacific, which could fetch $10,000 on the open market.

Largest Gastropods

The largest known gastropod is the trumpet or baler conch (*Syrinx aruanus*) of Australia. One outsized specimen collected off W Australia in 1979 and now owned by Don Pisor of San Diego, Calif (who bought it from a Taiwan fisherman in 1979) measures 30.39 in in length and has a maximum girth of 39.37 in. It weighed nearly 40 lb when alive.

The largest known land gastropod is the African giant snail (*Achatina* sp.). A specimen "Gee Geronimo" owned by Christopher Hudson (1955–79) of Hove, E Sussex, Eng, measured 15½ in from snout to tail (shell length 10¾ in) in Dec 1978 and weighed exactly 2 lb. The snail was collected in Sierra Leone, W Africa, in June 1976.

Snail Speed

The fastest-moving species of land snail is probably the common garden snail (*Helix aspersa*). According to tests carried out in the US absolute top speed for this snail is 0.0313 mph (or 55 yd per hour).

---

14. RIBBON WORMS *(NEMERTINA)*

Longest Worm

The longest of the 550 recorded species of ribbon worms, also called nemertines (or nemerteans), is the "boot-lace worm" (*Lineus longissimus*), found in the shallow waters of the North Sea. A specimen washed ashore at St Andrews, Fife, Scotland, in 1864, after a severe storm, measured more than 180 ft in length.

Immolation

Some ribbon worms (nemertines) absorb themselves when food is scarce. One specimen under observation digested 95 per cent of its own body in a few months without apparently suffering any ill effects. As soon as food became available the lost tissue was restored.

15. JELLYFISHES AND CORALS *(CNIDARIA)*

Largest Jellyfish

The largest jellyfish is the Arctic giant jellyfish (*Cyanea capillata arctica*) of the northwestern Atlantic. One specimen washed up in Massachusetts Bay had a bell diameter of 7 ft 6 in and tentacles stretching 120 ft.

Coral

The world's greatest stony coral structure is the Great Barrier Reef off Queensland, northeast Australia. It stretches 1,260 miles and covers 80,000 sq mi. The largest reported discrete coral growth is a stony colony of *Galaxea fascicularis* found in Sakiyama Bay off Irimote Island, Okinawa on Aug 7, 1982 by Dr. Shomei Shirai. It measured more than 52½ ft overall.

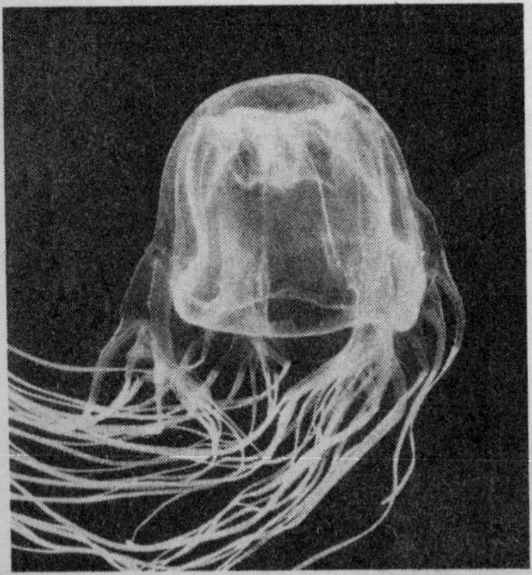

MOST VENOMOUS JELLYFISH: The beautiful but deadly Australian sea wasp has caused the death of 66 people off the coast of Queensland since 1880. Victims die within 3 min. Best protection is wearing pantyhose. *(Neville Coleman/Bruce Coleman Ltd)*

16. SPONGES *(PORIFERA)*

Largest and Smallest

The largest sponge is the barrel-shaped loggerhead sponge (*Spheciospongia vesparium*), found off the islands of the West Indies and off Fla. Single individuals measure up to 3½ ft high and 3 ft in diameter. Neptune's cup or goblet (*Poterion patera*) of Indonesia grows up to 4 ft in height, but it is a less bulky animal. In 1909, a wool sponge (*Hippospongia canaliculatta*) measuring 6 ft in circumference was collected off the Bahama Islands. When first taken from the water it weighed between 80 and 90 lb, but after it had been dried and relieved of all excrescences it scaled 12 lb. (This sponge is now preserved in the US National Museum, Washington, DC.)

The smallest known sponge is the widely distributed *Leucosolenia blanca*, which measures 0.11 in in height when fully grown.

Deepest Sponges

Sponges have been taken from depths of up to 18,500 ft.

17. EXTINCT ANIMALS

In this and future editions, only new discoveries of extinct animals and pictures of them will be published. For a complete section on this subject, see the *1984 Guinness Book of World Records* (Sterling edition).

Birds

The largest known flying bird was the giant teratorn (*Argentavis magnificens*) which lived in Argentina about 6 million years ago. Fossil remains discovered at a site 100 mi west of Buenos Aires, Argentina in 1979 indicate that this gigantic vulture had a wing span of 23–25 ft and weighed about 265 lb.

In 1987 an expedition from the Charleston Museum of S Car discovered the fossil remains of a 30-million-year-old giant sea-bird (*Pseudodontorns sp.*), which was related to the pelicans and cormorants. It had a wing span of 19 ft and weighed about 90 lb.

Dinosaur Deaths

Fossil evidence suggests that dinosaur extinction in western America was a gradual (not sudden) process that began 7 million years before the end of the Cretaceous era. It was not due to the impact of a meteorite 65 million years ago, according to a report from paleontologists from the Univ of Minn writing in *Science*, May 2, 1986.

Earliest Reptile

A 15-in-long insectivore from south central Kentucky, discovered in

1972, was confirmed on Oct 22, 1984 as dating from 310 million years ago.

Largest and Longest Dinosaur

In 1985 the remains of a diplodocide said to be "the largest dinosaur ever known" were excavated from a site near Albuquerque, NM. According to the NM Museum of Natural History this animal, named *Seismosaurus* ("earthshaker"), measured an estimated 100–120 ft in total length and weighed at least 89 tons.

The largest marine reptile, a short-necked pliosaur, may have been 46 ft long, judging by a mandible of 9 ft 10 in found in Oxfordshire, Eng.

The longest dinosaur discovered is the Moroccan brachiosaurid *Breviparopus*. A trackway discovered at Taghabalout was left by an individual measuring 157 ft long.

DINOSAUR JAWS: This ▲ skeleton of a pliosaur that was 42 ft long is at Harvard University.

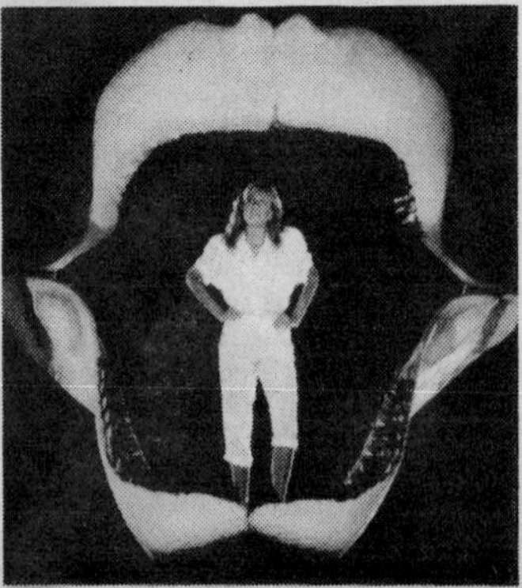

JAWS OF THE LARGEST ► KNOWN FISH: Jonah could have been easily swallowed by this 80-ft shark. *(Seaphot)*

Fastest Dinosaurs

Trackways can be used to estimate dinosaur speeds, and one from the Lower Cretaceous of Texas discovered in 1981 indicated that a carnivorous dinosaur had been moving at 25 mph. Some of the Ornithomimids (ostrich dinosaurs) were even faster, and the 220-lb *Dromiceiomimus* could probably out-sprint an ostrich, which has a top speed of 45 mph.

Smallest Dinosaurs

The smallest dinosaurs so far recorded are the chicken-sized *Compsognathus* ("pretty jaw") of southern W Germany and southeast France, and an undescribed plant-eating fabrosaurid from Colorado, both of which measured 29.5 in from the snout to the tip of the tail and weighed about 15 lb.

PLANT KINGDOM (*PLANTAE*)

The medicinal value of plants was known to Neanderthal man in Iraq *c.* 60,000 BC. The earliest evidence for a garden is a relief of *c.* 3000 BC in Egypt depicting a specimen palm in a protective enclosure amid irrigation or decorative waterways. Though the Romans had gardens in England from AD 43, the earliest surviving garden is at Romsey Abbey, Hampshire laid out *c.* 1092.

Oldest Living Things

"King Clone," the oldest known clone of the creosote plant (*Larria tridentata*) found in southwestern Calif, was estimated in Feb 1980 by Prof Frank C. Vasek to be 11,700 years old.

It is possible that crustose lichens in excess of 19.6 in in diameter may be as old. In 1981 it was estimated that Antarctic lichens of more than 3.9 in in diameter are at least 10,000 years old.

Largest Blossoming Plant

The largest blossoming plant is the giant Chinese wisteria at Sierra Madre, Calif. It was planted in 1892 and now has branches 500 ft long. It covers nearly an acre, weighs 252 tons and has an estimated 1,500,000 blossoms during its blossoming period of five weeks, when up to 30,000 people pay admission to visit.

Rarest Plants

Plants thought to be extinct are rediscovered each year and there are thus many plants of which specimens are known in but a single locality.

Cuttings from a Cafe marron tree *Ramosmania heterophylla*, a single specimen growing on Rodriguez Island, Indian Ocean, reported in Apr 1986 were flown to the Royal Botanical Gardens, Kew, W London, in an attempt to propagate it and preserve the species.

Pennantia baylisiana, a tree found in 1945 on Three Kings Island, off New Zealand, only exists as a female and cannot fruit. In May

1983, it was reported that there was a sole surviving specimen of the lady's slipper orchid (*Cypripedium calceolus*).

Herbs

Herbs are not botanically defined, but consist of plants whose leaves or roots are of culinary or medicinal value. The most heavily consumed is coriander (*Coriandrum sativum*). It is used in curry powder, confectionery, in bread and in gin.

Champion Plant Collector

Dr Julian A. Steyermark of the Herbario Nacional, Caracas, Venezuela had, by Sept 1985 made an unrivalled total of 137,000 collections, of which 132,000 were solo.

Deepest and Densest Roots

The greatest reported depth to which roots have penetrated is a calculated 400 ft in the case of a wild fig tree at Echo Caves, near Ohrigstad, East Transvaal, South Africa. A single winter rye plant (*Secale cereale*) has been shown to produce 387 miles of roots in 1.83 cu ft of earth.

Earliest Flower

The oldest fossil of a flowering plant with palm-like imprints was found in Colorado in 1953 and dated about 65 million years old.

Fastest Growth

The case of a *Hesperogucca whipplei* of the family Liliaceae growing 12 ft in 14 days was reported from Treco Abbey, Isles of Scilly, England, in July 1978.

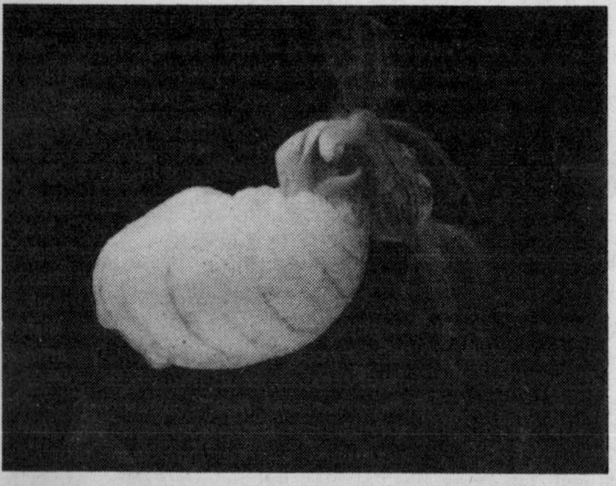

RAREST PLANT: This is probably the sole surviving specimen of the lady's-slipper orchid, found in May, 1983. *(Bruce Coleman)*

FRUITS & VEGETABLES

Most and Least Nutritive Fruits. An analysis of the 38 commonly eaten raw (as opposed to dried) fruits shows that the one with the highest calorific value is the avocado (*Persea americana*) with 741 calories per edible lb. That with the lowest value is cucumber with 73 calories per lb. Avocados probably originated in Central and South America and also contain vitamins A, C, and E and 2.2% protein.

Apple. An apple weighing 3 lb 1 oz was reported by V. Loveridge of Ross-on-Wye, England in 1965. Mr & Mrs Harold Spitler of Arcanum, O, grew 2 Stark® Jumbo apples 17½ in in circumference in 1985.

Artichoke. An 8-lb specimen was reported by A.R. Lawson of Tollerton, N Yorkshire, Eng, in 1964.

Beet. A sugar beet weighing 45½ lb was grown in 1974 by Robert Meyer of Brawley, Calif.

Broccoli. A head of broccoli weighing 28 lb 14¾ oz was grown in 1964 by J. T. Cooke of Funtington, W Sussex, England.

Cabbage. The heaviest cabbage known today, weighing 118 lb, was grown by Mr E Stone of E Woodyates, Wiltshire, Eng in 1987.

In 1865 William Collingwood of The Stalwell, County Durham, England, grew a red cabbage with a circumference of 259 in. It reputedly weighed 123 lb.

Carrot. A carrot weighing 15 lb 7 oz was grown by Miss I. G. Scott of Nelson, NZ, in Oct 1978.

Cauliflower. A record cauliflower weighing 52 lb 11½ oz was also grown by Mr Cooke (see *Broccoli*) in 1966.

Celery. A 35-lb 8-oz bunch was reported grown by E. Stone of E. Woodgates, Eng, in 1986.

Collard. A 35-ft-tall, 59¼-in-wide collard was grown by Bobby Rackley of Rocky Mount, NC, in 1980.

Corn. A cornstalk 31 ft high was grown in 1946 in Washington, Iowa by Don Radda.

Cucumber. Mrs. Eileen Chappel grew a 59 lb monster at Nudgee, Queensland, Australia in Mar 1988.

Eggplant. A 5-lb-5.4-oz eggplant was reported grown in Sept 1984 by brothers John and Jim Charles in Summerville, SC.

Garlic. In 1985, Robert Kirkpatrick of Eureka, Calif, grew an elephant garlic 18½ in in circumference, weighing 2 lb 12 oz.

Gourd. A record gourd of the zucca type measuring 93½ in in length was grown in 1986 by B. W. Saylor of Licking, Mo. The heaviest gourd, weighing 64½ lb, was grown in Milton, Fla by

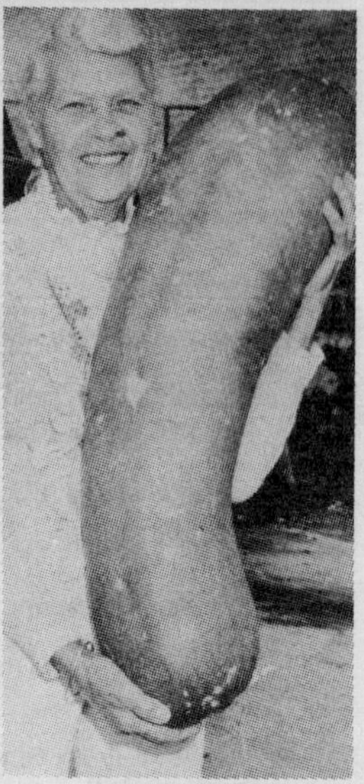

LARGEST VEGETABLES: (Above left) Charles Wilber of Crane Hill, Ala has trouble reaching the top of his 4 hybrid tomato plants which produced 1,368 lb of fruit. *(Joyce M. Rodgers)* (Above right) Mrs. Eileen Chappel of Queensland, Australia, hugs her baby cucumber. This one was 37¼ lb but she grew a larger one of 48½ lb in May, 1986, and a still larger one of 59 lb in Mar 1988. *(Brisbane Telegraph)* (Right) June Rutherford of Hatch, NM, grew this 13½-in-long prize pepper.

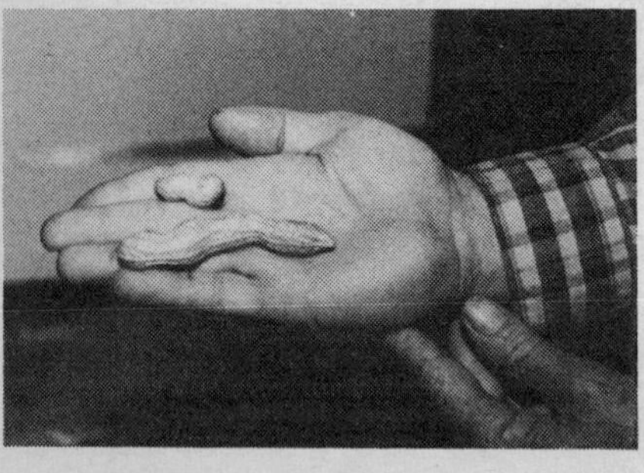

◄ PRIZE PEANUT: Billy Senkbeil of Sylvester, Ga, holds in his palm the 3 11/16 in peanut he grew.

the students of Central High School in 1986.

Grapefruit. A 6-lb-8½- oz grapefruit was weighed for Joshua and Allison Sosnow in Tucson, Ariz on Dec 21, 1984.

Kohlrabi. A kohlrabi weighing 36 lb was grown in 1979 by Emil Krejci of Mt Clemens, Mich.

Lemon. Charlotte and David Knutzen of Whittier, Calif, reported in May 1984 a lemon with a circumference of 29½ in, weighing 8½ lb.

LARGEST ONION: Weighing 8 lb 13½ oz, this was grown in Glamorgan, Wales, by Ivor Mace in 1987.

Lettuce. A head of 25 lb was grown by C. Bowcock of Willaston, England in 1974.

Lima Bean. One bean pod measuring 14 in in length was grown by Norma McCoy of Hubert, NC, in 1979.

Melons. A watermelon weighing 260 lb was reported by Grace's Gardens in Sept 1985. The grower was Jason Bright of Hope, Ark. The largest cantaloupe reported was one of 55 lb grown by Gene Daughtridge of Rocky Mount, NC, in 1982.

Mushrooms. See *Fungi,* p. 123.

Okra Stalk. An okra plant 17 ft 6¼ in tall was grown by Charles H. Wilber of Crane Hill, Ala in 1983. This record was tied by a plant grown by Buddy & Evelyn Crosby of Brooksville, Fla in 1986.

Onion. An onion weighing 8 lb 13½ oz was grown by Ivor Mace of Glamorgan, Wales in 1987.

Orange. The heaviest orange is one weighing 5 lb 8 oz exhibited in Nelspruit, South Africa on June 19, 1981. It was the size of a human head, but was stolen.

Parsnip. A parsnip 142¾ in long was reported by K. Lloyd of Kydwelly, Wales in 1984. The heaviest was 10 lb 8½ oz grown by C. Moore of Peacehaven, W. Sussex, England in 1980.

Peanut. Billy Senkbeil of Sylvester, Ga, grew a 3$^{11}/_{16}$ in peanut in 1987.

Pear. A pear weighing 3.09 lb was harvested on May 10, 1979 by K. and R. Yeomans, Armidale, NSW, Australia.

Pepper. A NuMex Big Jim pepper 13½ in long was grown by June Rutherford of Hatch, NM, in 1975. A bell pepper plant reached a height of 8 ft 1 in and yielded 150 peppers in

TALLEST CORN: To ▲ show the 31-ft-height of his stalk, Don Radda of Washington, Ia, in 1946 had his family dramatize it.

HEAVIEST CABBAGE: ▲ This "monster" grown in Wiltshire, Eng, in 1987 by Mr E. Stone weighed 118 lb. *(Henry Wills)*

►
WHO GREW THIS MONSTER WATERMELON? The boy on the far left did. He is Jason Bright of Hope, Ark. His father, grandfather and little brother are proudly helping him get the weight accurate—260 lb.

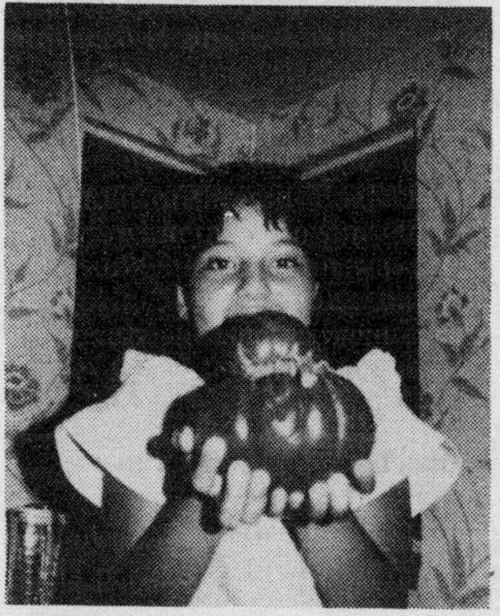

LARGEST GREEN SQUASH (Above left): Ed Gancarz of Jacobstown, NJ, grew this 595½ lb baby in Oct 1986, at the same time his brother Robert grew the BIGGEST PUMPKIN (Above right). It measured 11 ft 11¼ in in circumference and weighed 671 lb. *(Both photos by Marland J. Schmitt)*

HEAVIEST TOMATO: ▲ Gordon Graham of Edmond, Okla, won the Page Seed Co's $1,000 Giant Tomato Contest with this 7 lb 12 oz baby.

► FRUIT VINE: Record bunch of grapes weighing 20 lb 11½ oz grown by Bozzolo y Perut in Santiago, Chile, in 1984.

1987. It was grown by Robert Allen of Gillespie, Ill.

Pineapple. A pineapple weighing 17½ lb was harvested by Dole Philippines, Inc, at South Cotabato, Philippines, in Nov 1984. Pineapples up to 28.6 lb were reported in 1978 from Taranaca, Brazil.

Potato. A potato weighing 18 lb 4 oz was reported dug up by Thomas Seddal in his garden in Chester, England, on Feb 17, 1795. A yield was reported of 515 lb from a 2½-lb parent seed by C. Bowcock of Willaston, England, planted in 1977.

Pumpkin. The largest was grown by Robert Gancarz of Jacobstown, NJ in Oct 1986. It weighed 671 lb, measured 11 ft 11¼ in in circumference, and won the World Pumpkin Federation Contest.

Radish. A radish of 27 lb, 27½ in long, was grown by Ron Whitford in Wollongong, Australia, in Nov 1985.

Squash. A squash weighing 595.5 lb was grown by Edward Gancarz of Jacobstown, NJ in Oct 1986. It measured 11 ft in circumference.

Strawberry. A single berry weighing 8.17 oz was grown in July 1983 by George Anderson of Folkestone, England.

Sweet Potato. A 40¾ lb sweet potato was produced by Ovid Harrison, Kite, Ga on Oct 18, 1982.

Tomato. A 7 lb 12 oz tomato was grown by Gordon Graham of Edmond, Okla in 1986. Mr. Graham also grew the longest tomato plant of 53 ft 6 in in 1985.

A single plant produced 16,897 tomatoes, it was reported at the Tsukuba Science Expo, Japan on Feb 28, 1988.

The greatest weight was 342 lb 2 oz on a hybrid tomato plant grown by Charles H. Wilber of Crane Hill, Ala, in 1985, in a group of 4 plants whose fruit totaled 1,368 lb.

Turnip. A turnip weighing 73 lb was reported in Dec 1768. In modern times the record is 35 lb 4 oz for a turnip grown by C. W. Butler of Nafferton, Humberside, England.
A turnip of 51 lb was reported from Alaska in 1981.

Zucchini. A zucchini that weighed 36 lb 3 oz and was 29½ in long was grown by M. M. Ricci of Montreal, Canada in 1982.

GARDEN FLOWERS & PLANTS

Aspidistra. The aspidistra (*Aspidistra elatior*) was introduced as a parlor palm to Britain from Japan and China in 1822. The largest measured 56 in in 1983.

Begonia. A begonia plant 5 ft 2 in tall was grown by Ralph Wettstein of Islington, Ont, Canada in 1987. A still taller single stalk of a begonia plant measuring 6 ft high was grown indoors by Tom Worrall, 11, of Fort Collins, Colo.

Fourteen-Leafed Clover. A

fourteen-leafed white clover (*Trifolium repens*) grown on one petiole was found by Randy Farland near Sioux Falls, SD, June 16, 1975. However, a more recent discovery of a fourteen-leafed clover was made by Paul Haizlip of Bellevue, Washington, on June 22, 1987.

Dahlia. A 16-ft-5-in dahlia was grown by Sam and Pat Barnes of Chattahoochee, Fla, in 1982. They have also grown a 5-ft-½-in tall chrysanthemum.

Gladiolus. A gladiolus 8 ft 4½ in high was grown in 1981 by A. Breed of Melrose, Scotland.

Hollyhock. The tallest reported hollyhock (*Althaea rosea*) is one of 24 ft 3 in grown by W. P. Walshe of Eastbourne, E. Sussex, England in 1961.

Marigold. An Aztec marigold (*Tagetes erecta*) 8½ ft tall was grown by Germaine Auert-Brown of Palm Beach Gardens, Fla, in Sept 1987.

SMALLEST PLANT: It takes 5,000 of these "Wolffia"-type flowering plants to fill a thimble. *(Wayne P. Armstrong)* ►

LARGEST BLOOM: The stinking corpse lily has a bloom 3 ft across and weighs up to 15 lb. Mottled orange-brown and white, these parasitic plants of southeast Asia attach themselves to vines of the jungle. They got their name from really smelling that way.

◄ TALLEST BEGONIA: This plant grew to a record height of 5 ft 2 in for Ralph Wettstein of Islington, Ont, Canada in 1987.

Petunia. A petunia plant 13 ft 8 in tall was grown by Bert Lawrence of Windham, NY over a 2-year period, 1984–85, indoors in winter and outdoors in summer.

Philodendron. A philodendron 1,114 ft long, and 31 years old, was grown by Prof F. J. Francis of the Univ of Mass. It was dismembered in Dec 1984.

Rhododendron. The largest species of rhododendron is the scarlet *Rhododendron arboreum,* examples of which reach a height of 65 ft on Mt Japfu, Nagaland, India. The cross section of the trunk of a *Rhododendron giganteum,* from Yunnan, China, reputedly 90 ft high, is preserved at Inverewe Garden, Highland, Scotland.

Rose Tree. A "Lady Banks" rose tree at Tombstone, Ariz, has a trunk 40 in thick, stands 9 ft high and covers an area of 5,380 sq ft, supported by 68 posts and several thousand feet of iron piping. This enables 150 people to be seated under the arbor. The original cutting came from Scotland in 1884.

Sunflower. The record height of 24 ft 2½ in was reached by a sunflower grown by Marten Heijms of The Netherlands in 1983.

A sunflower head measuring 32¼ in in diameter was grown by Mrs. Emily Martin of Maple Ridge, BC, Canada in Sept 1983. A fully mature sunflower 2.2 in tall was grown by Michael Lenke of Lake Oswego, Ore in 1985, using a bonsai technique.

Hedges. The tallest hedge is the Meikleour beech hedge in Perthshire, Scotland. It was planted in 1746 and has now attained a trimmed height of 85 ft. It is 600 yd long, and some of its trees now exceed 120 ft.

Vines. The largest recorded grape vine was one planted in 1842 at Carpinteria, Calif. By 1900 it was yielding more than 9 tons of grapes in some years, and averaging 7 tons per year. It died in 1920.

A single bunch of grapes (red Thomson seedless) weighing 20 lb 11½ oz was weighed in Santiago, Chile, in May 1984.

Largest and Slowest Inflorescence

The largest known inflorescence is that of *Puya raimondii,* a rare Bolivian plant with an erect panicle (diameter 8 ft) which emerges to a height of 35 ft. Each of these bears up to 8,000 white blooms. In 1974 the flower-spike of an agave in Berkeley, Calif was measured to be 52 ft long. This is also the slowest flowering plant and the largest of all herbs. The panicle emerges after about 150 years and then dies.

Plants at Highest Altitude

The greatest certain altitude at which any flowering plants have been found is 21,000 ft on Kamet (25,447 ft), India, by N. D. Jayal in 1955. They were *Ermania himalayensis* and *Ranunculus lobatus.*

Most Spreading Plant

The greatest area covered by a single clonal growth is that of the wild box huckleberry (*Gaylussacia brachyera*), a mat-forming evergreen shrub first reported in 1796. A colony covering 8 acres was discovered in 1845 near New Bloomfield, Pa. Another colony, covering about 100 acres, was "discovered" on July 18, 1920, near the Juniata River in Pa. It has been estimated that this colony began 13,000 years ago.

Largest Cactus

The largest of all cacti is the saguaro (*Cereus giganteus* or *Carnegiea gigantea*), found in Ariz, southeastern Calif, and Sonora, Mexico.

The tallest specimen known is 57 ft 11¾ in tall. Located in the Maricopa Mts 11 mi east of Gila Bend, Ariz, it was discovered and measured on Jan 17, 1988 by J.D. and R.M. Fairfield, and R.N. and D.J. Wells.

An armless cactus 78 ft in height was measured in 1978 by Hube Yates in Cave Creek, Ariz. It was toppled in a windstorm in July 1986 at an estimated age of 150 years.

Largest Blooms

The mottled orange-brown and white parasitic stinking corpse lily (*Rafflesia arnoldi*) has the largest of all blooms. These attach themselves to the cissus vines of the jungle in southeast Asia. They measure up to 3 ft across and ¾ in thick, and attain a weight of 15 lb.

The spathe and spadix of the less massive green and purple flower of *Amorphophallies titanum* of Sumatra may attain a length of 5 ft.

Most Valuable Flower

The $10,000 prize offered by the Burpee Co. in 1954 for producing the first all-white marigold was won on Aug 12, 1975 by Alice Vonk of Sully, Iowa.

Smallest Plants

The smallest flowering plant is the floating aquatic duckweed *Wolffia angusta* which is only 1/42nd of an inch in length and 1/85th of an inch in width. It weighs 1/190th of an oz; its fruit, resembling a minuscule fig, weighs 400,000 to the oz.

The smallest "plant" is a unicellular alga and is classified under *Protista*.

Worst Weeds

The most intransigent weed is the mat-forming water weed *Salvinia auriculata*, found in Africa. It was detected on the filling of Kariba Lake, in May 1959 and within 11 months had choked an area of 77 sq mi, rising by 1963 to 387 sq mi. The worst land weeds are regarded as purple nut sedge, Bermuda grass, barnyard grass, jungle rice, goose grass, Johnson grass, Guinea grass, cogon grass and lantana.

Largest Leaves

The largest leaves of any plant belong to the raffia palm (*Raphia ruffia*) of the Mascarene Islands in the Indian Ocean, and the

Amazonian bamboo palm (*R. toedigera*) of South America, whose leaf blades may measure up to 65 ft in length with petioles up to 13 ft.

The largest undivided leaf is that of *Alocasia macrorrhiza*, found in Sabah, East Malaysia. One found in 1966 measured 9 ft 11 in long and 6 ft 3½ in wide, and had an area of 34.2 sq ft on one side.

Seaweed

The longest species of seaweed is the Pacific giant kelp (*Macrocystis pyrifera*), which does not exceed 196 ft in length. It can grow 18 in in a day.

The greatest depth at which plant life has been found is 884 ft by Mark and Diane Littler (US) off San Salvador Island, Bahamas, in Oct 1984. These maroon-colored algae survived though 99.9995% of sunlight was filtered out.

Wreaths and Arrangements

The largest constructed wreath was built by The Farm Stand, wholesale nurserymen of Walworth, NY in Nov 1985 measuring 100 ft 8 in in diameter and weighing 9,840 lb.

The largest arrangement of a single variety of flower was made by Johan Weisz, floral designer of Amsterdam, and 15 assistants at the City Hall, Aalsmeer, Netherlands Sept 23-25, 1986. It consisted of 35,000 "Zurella" roses and measured 71 ft 6 in in length, 25 ft 2 in in width and 24 ft 11 in high.

Seeds

The largest seed is that of the double coconut or Coco de Mer (*Lodoicea seychellarum*), the single-seeded fruit of which may weigh 40 lb. This grows only in the Seychelles Islands in the Indian Ocean. The smallest seeds are those of *epiphytic* orchids, at 35 million to the oz (*cf.* grass pollens at up to 6,000 million grains per oz). A single plant of the American ragweed can generate 8,000 million pollen grains in 5 hours.

The most protracted claim for the viability of seeds is that made for the Arctic lupin (*Lupinus arcticus*) found in frozen silt at Miller Creek in the Yukon, Canada, in July 1954 by Harold Schmidt. The seeds were germinated in 1966 and dated by the radio-carbon method of associated material to at least 8,000 BC and more probably to 13,000 BC.

Largest Orchids

The largest of all orchids is *Grammatophyllum speciosum*, native to Malaysia. Specimens up to 25 ft high have been recorded. The largest orchid flower is that of *Phragmipedium caudatum*, found in tropical areas of America. Its petals grow up to 18 in long, giving it a maximum outstretched diameter of 3 ft. The flower is, however, much less bulky than that of the stinking corpse lily (see *Largest Blooms*).

Galeola foliata, a saprophyte of the vanilla family, has been recorded at a height of 49 ft on decaying rainforest trees in Queensland, Australia. The smallest orchid is *Platystele jungermannoides*, found in Central America. Its flowers are 0.04 in across.

BRIGHTEST CHRISTMAS TREE: ▲ Friendship, Wis, claims that this 45-ft-tall white spruce, decorated with approximately 27,650 Christmas tree lights, has set a world record. The "National Enquirer" 125-ft-tall tree in Lantana, Fla, pictured in the 1987 Guinness Book was taller, but had fewer lights—15,100. *(L. Roger Turner)*

►

TALLEST CACTUS: Standing 57 ft 11 in high, this saguaro in Ariz. was just discovered in Jan. 1988. Note size of the discoverers below. *(Dennis J. Wells, Phoenix)*

Highest-Priced Orchid

The highest price ever paid for an orchid is £1,207.50 (then $6,000), paid by Baron Schröder to Sanders of St Albans for an *Odontoglossum crispum* (variety *pittianum*) at an auction by Protheroe & Morris of Bow Lane, London, England, on March 22, 1906. A cymbidium orchid called "Rosanna Pinkie" was sold in the US for $4,500 in 1952.

Grasses

The world's commonest grass is *Cynodon ductylon* or Bermuda grass. The "Callie" hybrid, selected in 1966, grows as much as 6 in a day and stolons reach 18 ft in length.

Mosses

The smallest of mosses is the pygmy moss (*Ephemerum*), and the longest is the brook moss (*Fontinalis*), which forms streamers up to 3 ft long in flowing water.

Tallest and Fastest-Growing Bamboo

The tallest recorded bamboo was a Thorney bamboo culm (*Bambusa arundinacea*) felled at Pattazhi, Travancore, India, in Nov 1904, which measured 121½ ft. Some species of the 45 genera of bamboo have attained growth rates of up to 36 in per day (0.00002 mph).

Largest and Smallest Ferns

The largest of all the more than 6,000 species of fern is the tree-fern (*Alsophila excelsa*) of Norfolk Island, in the South Pacific, which attains a height of up to 60 ft. The smallest are *Hecistopteris pumila,* found in Central America, and *Azolla caroliniana,* which is native to the US and has fronds as small as ½ in.

TREES

Oldest Tree

The oldest recorded tree was a bristlecone pine (*Pinus longaeva*) designated WPN-114, which grew at 10,750 ft above sea level on the northeast face of Mt Wheeler in eastern Nevada. It was found to be about 5,100 years old, but was cut down with a chain saw. The oldest known *living* tree is the bristlecone pine named Methuselah at 10,000 ft on the Calif side of the White Mts, with a confirmed age of 4,600 years. In March 1974 it was reported that this tree produced 48 live seedlings. Dendrochronologists estimate the *potential* life span of a bristlecone pine at nearly 5,500 years, but that of a "big tree" (*Sequoia giganteum*) at perhaps 6,000 years. No single cell lives more than 30 years.

Largest Forest

The largest afforested areas are the vast coniferous forests of the

MOST MASSIVE LIVING THING: The "General Sherman" tree, a giant sequoia in Calif, stands almost 275 ft tall. It has a girth of 114.6 ft, and has grown for 2,500 years at the slow rate of 1/25th of an inch per year. *(National Park Service)* ►

BONSAI PLANTS live to a ripe old age. This one was 1,000 years old in 1980. ▼

northern USSR, lying between latitude 55° N. and the Arctic Circle. The total wooded areas amount to 2.7 billion acres (25% of the world's forests), of which 38% is Siberian larch. The USSR is 34% afforested.

Earliest Species of Tree

The earliest species of tree still surviving is the maidenhair tree (*Ginkgo biloba*) of Zhekiang, China, which first appeared about 160 million years ago, during the Jurassic era. It was "re-discovered" by Kaempfer (Netherlands) in 1690, and reached England *c.* 1754. It has been grown in Japan since *c.* 1100 where it was known as *ginkyo* (silver apricot) and now called *icho*.

Fastest-Growing Tree

Discounting bamboo, which is not botanically classified as a tree, but as woody grass, the fastest rate of growth recorded is 35 ft 3 in in 13 months by an *Albizzia falcata* planted on June 17, 1974, in Sabah, Malaysia. The youngest recorded age for a tree to reach 100 ft is 64 months for one of the species planted on Feb 24, 1975, also in Sabah.

Tallest Trees

The tallest known species of tree is the coast redwood (*Sequoia*

FASTEST GROWING: Bamboo, botanically a woody grass and not a tree, can reach 100 ft in height in less than 3 months. These are in Hawaii. *(Photo by Alex Hansen)*

sempervirens), growing indigenously near the coast of Calif north of Monterey to the Oregon border.

The tallest tree ever measured was the Ferguson Tree, a mountain ash (*Eucalyptus regnans*) at Watt River, Vic, Australia. It measured 435 ft tall and 18 ft in diameter 5 ft above ground level. It almost certainly measured 470–480 ft originally. A *Eucalyptus amygdalina* at Mt Bawbaw, Victoria, Australia is believed to have measured 470 ft in 1885. According to the researches of Dr A. C. Carder (Canada) the closest measured rivals to these champions have been:

415 ft—Douglas fir, Lynn Valley, B.C., Canada, 1902
393 ft—mineral Douglas fir, Wash State, 1905
380 ft—Nisqually fir, Wash State, 1899
375 ft—Cornthwaite mountain ash, Thorpdale, Victoria, Australia, 1880
367.8 ft—"Tallest Tree" (sequoia) Redwood Creek, Humboldt County, Calif, 1963 (tallest living, crown dying)
*367.6 ft—Coast redwood (sequoia), Guerneville, Calif, 1873.

*Tallest standing tree in the world. It is possible that the "Harry Cole" tree, Humboldt County, Calif, is at least 370 ft tall since it still has a growing top; it measured 367.4 ft in 1964.

Trees of Greatest Girth

El Arbol del Tule tree, in the state of Oaxaca, in Mexico, is a 135-ft-tall Montezuma cypress (*Taxodium mucronatum*) with a girth of 117.6 ft at a height of 5 ft above the ground. A figure of 167 ft in circumference was reported for the pollarded European chestnut (*Castanea sativa*) known as the "Tree of the 100 Horses" on the edge of Mt Etna, Sicily, Italy, in 1972 and measurements up to 180 ft have been attributed to baobab trees (*Adansonia digitata*).

A great banyan tree (*Ficus benghalensis*) in the Indian Botanical Garden, Calcutta, covers an area of approximately 3 acres with its 1,775 prop or supporting roots and a circumference of 1,350 ft. It dates from before 1787.

Heaviest and Lightest Woods

The heaviest of all woods is black ironwood (*Olea laurifolia*), also called South African ironwood, with a specific gravity of up to 1.49, and weighing up to 93 lb per cu ft.

The lightest wood is *Aeschynomene hispida*, found in Cuba, which has a specific gravity of 0.044 and a weight of only 2¾ lb per cu ft. The wood of the balsa tree (*Ochroma pyramidale*) is of very variable density— between 2½ and 24 lb per cu ft. The density of cork is 15 lb per cu ft.

Most Massive Tree

The most massive living thing on earth is a giant sequoia "big tree" (*Sequoiadendron giganteum*) named the "General Sherman," standing 274.9 ft tall, in Sequoia National Park, Calif. It has a true girth of 114.6 ft (at 5 ft above the ground). The "General Sherman" has been estimated to contain the equivalent of 600,120 board ft of timber. The foliage is blue-green, and the reddish brown bark may be up to 24 in thick in parts. The largest known petrified tree is one of this species with a 295-ft trunk near Coaldale, Nev.

The seed of a "big tree" (sequoia) weighs only 1/6,000th oz. Its growth to maturity may therefore represent an increase in weight of 1,300,000 millionfold.

Slowest-Growing Trees

The speed of growth of trees depends largely upon conditions, although some species, such as box and yew, are always slow-growing. The extreme is represented by a specimen of Sitka spruce which required 98 years to grow to 11 in tall, with a diameter of less than 1 in, on the Arctic tree-line. The growing of miniature trees or *bonsai* is an Oriental cult mentioned as early as *c.* 1320.

Tallest Christmas Tree

The tallest cut Christmas tree was a 221-ft Douglas fir erected at Northgate Shopping Center, Seattle, Wash, in Dec 1950.

Remotest Tree

The tree most distant from any other is believed to be one at an oasis in the Ténéré Desert, Niger Republic. There were no other trees within 31 miles. In Feb 1960 it survived being rammed by a truck being backed up by a French driver. The tree was transplanted and is now in the Museum of Niamey, Niger.

A still more remote tree is believed to be a Norwegian spruce, the only one on Campbell Island, Antarctica. Its nearest companion would be over 120 miles away on the Auckland Islands.

Most Expensive Tree

The highest price ever paid for a tree is $51,000 for a single Starkspur golden delicious apple tree from near Yakima, Wash, bought by a nursery in Missouri in 1959.

Forest Fire

What may be the largest forest fire on record burned 13,500 sq mi in East Kalimantan, the Indonesian part of Borneo, continuing from Feb to June, 1983. The area is bigger than the states of Mass and Conn together.

KINGDOM PROTISTA

Protista were first discovered in 1676 by Anton van Leeuwenhoek (1632–1723), a Dutch microscopist. Among Protista are characteristics common to both plants and animals. The more plant-like are termed Protophyta (protophytes), including unicellular algae, and the more animal-like are placed in the phylum Protozoa (protozoans) which includes amoebas and flagellates.

The largest protozoans, in terms of volume, which are known to have existed were calcareous foraminifera (Foraminiferida) belonging to the genus *Nummulites*, a species of which, in the Middle Eocene rocks of Turkey, attained 8.6 in in diameter. The largest existing protozoan, a species of the fan-shaped *Stannophyllum* (Xenophyophorida), can exceed this in length (9.8 in has been recorded) but not in volume.

The smallest of all protophytes is the marine microflagellate alga *Micromonas pusilla*, with a diameter of less than 2 microns or 0.00008 in.

The protozoan *Monas stigmatica* has been measured to move a distance equivalent to 40 times its own length in a sec. No human can cover even seven times his own length in a sec.

The protozoan *Glaucoma*, which reproduces by binary fission, divides as frequently as every 3 hours. Thus in the course of a day it could become a "six greats grandparent" and the progenitor of 510 descendants.

KINGDOM FUNGI

Fungi were once classified in the subkingdom Protophyta of the kingdom Protista.

Martin Mortenson, a science teacher at Dodgeland Jr High, Reeseville, Wis, found a puffball (*Calvatia gigantea*) 76½ in in circumference in 1985.

A 72-lb example of the edible mushroom *Polyporus frondosus* was reported by Joseph Opple near Solon, Ohio, in Sept 1976. A mushroom of "nearly 100 lb" and 20 in in circumference was reported Oct 3, 1985 from Potenza, Italy.

The largest officially recorded tree fungus was a specimen of *Oxyporus* (*Fomes*) *nobilissimus*, measuring 56 in by 37 in and weighing at least 300 lb found by J. Hisey in Wash State in 1946.

Most Poisonous Toadstool

The yellowish-olive death cup (*Amanita phalloides*) is regarded as the world's most poisonous fungus. From 6 to 15 hours after tasting, the effects are vomiting, delirium, collapse and death. Among its victims was Cardinal Giulio de' Medici, Pope Clement VII (1478–1534).

KINGDOM PROCARYOTA

Largest and Smallest Bacteria

Anton van Leeuwenhoek (1632–1723) was the first to observe bacteria, in 1675. The largest of the bacteria is the sulphur bacterium *Beggiatoa mirabilis*, which is from 16 to 45 microns in width and which may form filaments several millimeters long.

The smallest of all free-living organisms are the pleuro-pneumonia-like organisms (PPLO) of the *Mycoplasma*. One of these, *Mycoplasma laidlawii*, first discovered in sewage in 1936, has a diameter during the early part of its life of only 100 millimicrons, or 0.000004 in. Examples of the strain known as H.39 have a maximum diameter of 300 millimicrons and weigh an estimated 1.0×10^{-16} of a gram.

Fastest Bacteria

The rod-shaped bacillus *Bdellovibrio bacteriovoras*, by means of a polar flagellum rotating 100 times/sec, can move 50 times its own length of 2μm per second. This would be the equivalent of a human sprinter reaching 200 mph or a swimmer crossing the English Channel in 6 min.

Highest Bacteria

In Apr 1967 the US National Aeronautics and Space Administration (NASA) reported that bacteria had been discovered at an altitude of 135,000 ft (25.26 miles).

Toughest Bacteria

The bacterium *Micrococcus radiodurans* can withstand atomic radiation of 6,500,000 röntgens or 10,000 times greater than radiation that is fatal to the average man.

In March 1983 John Barras (Univ of Oregon) reported bacteria from sulfurous sea bed vents thriving at 583°F in the East Pacific rise at Lat 21°N.

Largest and Smallest Viruses

Dmitriy Ivanovsky (1864–1920) first reported filterable objects in 1892, but Martinus Willem Beijerink (1851–1931) first confirmed the nature of viruses in 1898. These are now defined as aggregates of two or more types of chemical (including either DNA or RNA) which are infectious and potentially pathogenic. The longest known is the rod-shaped *Citrus tristeza* virus with particles measuring 200 × 10 nm (1 nanometer = 1×10^{-9} m).

The smallest known viruses are the nucleoprotein plant viruses such as the satellite of tobacco *necrosis virus* with spherical particles 17 nm in diameter. A putative new infectious sub-microscopic organism but without nucleic acid, named a "prion," was announced from the Univ of Calif in Feb 1982.

Viroids (RNA cores without protein coating) are much smaller than viruses. They were discovered by Theodor O. Diener (US) in Feb 1972.

Dr Rohwer of Bethesda, Md, stated in Sept 1984 that scrapie-specific protein was smaller than the concept of a "yet-to-be identified prion."

PARKS, ZOOS, AQUARIA AND OCEANARIA

Oceanaria

The first oceanarium, opened in 1938, is Marineland of Florida located 18 miles south of St Augustine. Up to 7 million gallons of sea water are pumped daily through two major tanks, one rectangular (100 ft long by 40 ft wide by 18 ft deep) containing 450,000 gallons and one circular (233 ft in circumference and 12 ft deep) containing 400,000 gallons. The tanks are seascaped, including coral reefs and even a shipwreck.

Largest Aquarium

The world's largest aquarium has been the $40 million Monterey Bay (Calif) Aquarium opened on Oct 20, 1984, with 83 tanks with a capacity of 716,000 gallons. Exhibited are 5,500 specimens of 525 species of fauna and flora. The two biggest tanks hold 335,000 and 326,000 gallons.

Claiming to be larger is the Sydney Aquarium, Australia, holding a total of 875,838 gal of water. It contains fewer fish than Monterey, 5,000, displayed in a variety of habitats including 2 massive floating oceanariums, 21 major aquarium tanks and 29 smaller aquarium tanks.

Largest Park

The largest park is the Wood Buffalo National Park in Alberta, Canada (established 1922), which has an area of 11,172,000 acres (17,560 sq mi).

Zoos

The earliest known collection of animals (not a public zoo) was that set up by Shulgi, a 3rd dynasty ruler of Ur in 2094–2047 BC at Puzurish in southeast Iraq.

Today there are an estimated 500 zoos in the world. The oldest known zoo is that at Schönbrunn, Vienna, Austria, built in 1752 by the Holy Roman Emperor Franz I for his wife Maria Theresa. The oldest privately owned zoo in the world is that of the Zoological Society of London, founded in 1826. Its collection is housed partly in Regent's Park, London (36 acres), and partly at Whipsnade Park, Bedfordshire (541 acres, opened 1931). At the stocktaking on Jan 1, 1987, it was found to house 10,638 specimens—2,628 mammals, 1,916 birds, 664 reptiles and amphibians, an estimated 2,290 fish, and an estimated total of 3,040 invertebrates. Locusts, bees and ants are excluded from these figures.

Chapter 3

The Natural World

STRUCTURE AND DIMENSIONS

The earth is not a true sphere, but flattened at the poles and hence an oblate spheroid. The polar diameter of the earth (7,899.806 miles) is 26.575 miles less than the equatorial diameter (7,926.381 miles). The earth has a pear-shaped asymmetry with the north polar radius being 148 ft longer than the south polar radius. There is also a slight ellipticity of the equator since its long axis (about Longitude 37°W.) is 522 ft greater than the short axis. The greatest departures from the reference ellipsoid are a protuberance of 240 ft in the area of Papua New Guinea, and a depression of 344 ft south of Sri Lanka (Ceylon) in the Indian Ocean.

The greatest circumference of the earth—at the equator—is calculated as 24,901.46 miles, compared with 24,859.73 miles at the meridian. The area of the surface is estimated to be 196,937,400 sq mi. The period of axial rotation, *i.e.* the true sidereal day, is 23 hours 56 min 4.0996 sec, mean time.

Earth's Structure

The earth's mass is 6,585,600,000,000,000,000,000 tons and its density is 5.515 times that of water. The volume is an estimated 259,875,300,000 cu mi. The earth picks up cosmic dust but estimates vary widely with 30,000 metric tons a day being the upper limit. Modern theory is that the earth has an outer shell or lithosphere 50 miles thick, then an outer and inner rock layer or mantle extending 1,745 miles deep, beneath which there is an iron-rich core of radius measuring 2,164 miles. If the iron-rich core theory is correct, iron would be the most abundant element in the earth. At the center of the core the estimated density is 13.09 g/cm^3; the temperature 4,500°C and the pressure 23,600 tons f/sq in.

OCEANS

Largest Ocean

The area of the earth covered by the sea is estimated to be 139,670,000 sq mi, or 70.92% of the total surface. The mean depth of the hydrosphere was at one time estimated to be 12,450 ft, but recent surveys suggest a lower estimate of 11,660 ft. The total weight of the water is estimated as 1.45×10^{18} tons, or 0.022% of the earth's total weight. The volume of the oceans is estimated to be 308,400,000 cu mi, compared with 8,400,000 cu mi of fresh water.

The largest ocean is the Pacific. Excluding adjacent seas, it represents 45.8% of the world's oceans and is 64,186,300 sq mi in area. The average depth is 12,925 ft. From Guayaquil, Ecuador, on the east, to Bangkok, Thailand, on the west, the Pacific could be said to stretch 10,905 miles in the shortest straight navigable line.

Deepest Depths in the Ocean

The deepest part of the ocean was first pin-pointed in 1951 by the British Survey Ship *Challenger* in the Marianas Trench in the Pacific Ocean. The depth was measured by sounding and by echo-sounder and published as 5,960 fathoms (35,760 ft). Subsequent visits have resulted in slightly deeper measurements by multi-beam sonar now refined to 5,940 fathoms (35,640 ft) or 6.85 mi made by the Soviet research ship *Vityaz* in 1959. On Jan 23, 1960 the US Navy bathyscaphe *Trieste* descended to the bottom, which is 35,820 ft.

A metal object, say a pound ball of steel, dropped into water above this trench would take nearly 64 min to fall to the sea bed 6.79 miles below, where hydrostatic pressure is over 18,000 lb per sq in.

Largest Gulf

The largest gulf in the world is the Gulf of Mexico, with an area of 580,000 sq mi and a shoreline of 3,100 miles from Cape Sable, Fla, to Cabo Catoche, Mexico.

Largest Bay

The largest bay measured by shoreline length is Hudson Bay in northern Canada with a shoreline of 7,623 miles and an area of 317,500 sq mi. The area of the Bay of Bengal however is bigger—839,000 sq mi.

Highest Sea-Mountain

The highest known submarine mountain or sea-mountain was one discovered in 1953 near the Tonga Trench between Samoa and New Zealand. It rises 28,500 ft from the sea bed, with its summit 1,200 ft below the surface.

Clearest Sea

The Weddell Sea just off Antarctica has been deemed by scientists to have the clearest water of any sea. Dutch researchers from the

German Alfred Wegener Institute, on finding a "Secchi" disc visible at a depth of 262 ft on Oct 13, 1986, ascertained that the clarity corresponded to that of distilled water.

Greatest Tides

The greatest tides in the world occur in the Bay of Fundy, which separates the peninsula of Nova Scotia from Maine and the Canadian province of New Brunswick. Burncoat Head in the Minas Basin, Nova Scotia, has the greatest mean spring range with 47.5 ft. A unique figure of 54½ ft was recorded at springs in 1953 at nearby Leaf Basin.

Tahiti experiences virtually no tide.

The normal interval between tides is 12 hours 25 min.

LONGEST FJORD IN LAND OF FJORDS: In Norway, the Sogne Fjord is only 3 mi wide at its widest, but it extends 113.7 mi inland from the sea, through spectacular highlands.

Longest Fjords

The longest "fjord" is the Nordvest Fjord arm of the Scoresby Sund in eastern Greenland, which extends inland 195 mi from the sea. The longest of Norwegian fjords is the Sogne Fjord, which extends 113.7 mi inland from Sygnefest to the head of the Lusterfjord arm at Skjolden. It averages barely 3 mi in width and has a deepest point of 4,085 ft.

Greatest and Strongest Currents

The world's strongest currents are the Nakwakto Rapids, Slingsby Channel, British Columbia, Canada (Lat. 51° 05′N., Long. 127° 30′W.) where the flow rate may reach 16.0 knots (18.4 mph).

Highest Waves

The highest officially recorded sea wave was measured by Lt Frederic Margraff, USN from the USS *Ramapo* proceeding from Manila, Philippines, to San Diego, Calif, on the night of Feb 6–7, 1933 during a 68-knot (78.3 mph) hurricane. The wave was computed to be 112 ft from trough to crest.

A landslip on July 9, 1958 caused a 100-mph wave to wash 1,720 ft high along the fjord-like Lituya Bay, Alaska.

Highest Seismic Wave

The highest recorded seismic sea wave, or *tsunami*, (often mistakenly called a "tidal wave") was one of an estimated 278 ft, which appeared off Ishigaki Island, Ryukyu Chain, Apr 24, 1771. It tossed an 850-ton block of coral more than 1.3 miles. *Tsunami* (a Japanese word meaning: *tsu*, overflowing; *nami*, a wave) have been observed to travel at 490 mph.

Icebergs

The largest iceberg on record was an Antarctic tabular iceberg of over 12,000 sq mi (208 miles long and 60 miles wide) sighted 150 miles west of Scott Island, in the South Pacific Ocean, by the USS *Glacier* Nov 12, 1956. This iceberg was larger than Belgium.

The 200-ft-thick Arctic ice island T.1 (140 sq mi), discovered in 1946, was tracked for 17 years.

The tallest iceberg measured was one of 550 ft reported off western Greenland by the USCG icebreaker *East Wind* in 1958.

Straits

The longest straits in the world are the Tatarskiy Proliv or Tartar Straits between Sakhalin Island and the USSR mainland, running 497 miles from the Sea of Japan to Sakhalinsky Zaliv. This distance is marginally longer than the Malacca Straits, which extend 485 miles.

The broadest named straits are the Davis Straits between Greenland and Baffin Island, which at one point narrow to 210 miles. The Drake Passage between the Diego Ramírez Islands, Chile, and the South Shetland Islands, is 710 miles across.

The narrowest navigable straits are those between the Aegean island of Euboea and the mainland of Greece. The gap is only 45 yd wide at Khalkis. The Seil Sound, Strathclyde, Scotland, narrows to a point only 20 ft wide where a bridge joins the island of Seil to the mainland and is thus said by the islanders to span the Atlantic.

LAND

There is satisfactory evidence that at one time the earth's land surface comprised a single primeval continent of 80 million sq mi, now termed Pangaea, and that this split about 190 million years ago, during the Jurassic period, into two super-continents, termed Laurasia (Eurasia, Greenland and North America) and Gondwanaland (comprising Africa, Arabia, India, South America, Oceania and Antarctica), named after Gondwana, India, which itself split 120 million years ago. The South Pole was apparently in the area of the Sahara as recently as the Ordovician period of *c*. 450 million years ago.

Rocks

The age of the earth is generally considered to be within the range 4,430 ± 20 million years, by analogy with directly measured ages of meteorites and of the moon. However, no rocks of this great age have yet been found on earth. Geological processes have presumably destroyed them.

The greatest reported age for any scientifically dated rock is 6 billion years in the case of 10 small diamonds found in Zaire, Apr 6, 1988 and assessed by Japanese scientists.

The world's highest rock pinnacle is Ball's Pyramid near Lord Howe Island in the Pacific, which is 1,843 ft high, but has a base axis of only 220 yd. It was first scaled in 1965.

The largest exposed isolated monolith is the 1,237-ft-high Mt Augustus (3,627 ft above sea level), discovered June 3, 1858 about 200 miles east of Carnarvon, Western Australia. It is an up-faulted monoclinal gritty conglomerate 5 miles long and 2 miles across and thus twice the size of the celebrated monolithic arkose Ayer's Rock (1,100 ft), 250 miles southwest of Alice Springs, in Northern Territory, Australia.

It was estimated in 1940 that La Gran Piedra, a volcanic plug in the Sierra Maestra, Cuba, weighs 68,718 tons.

Largest Balanced Rock

Balanced 3,937 ft high at the very edge of a cliff, this sacred rock in Kyaik-tiyo (southeast Burma) seems to be in danger of toppling any moment and crashing down the cliff. Legend has it that the pagoda on top of the rock contains a hair of the Gautama Buddha and that this hair with its divine power keeps the rock balanced. Every faithful Burmese tries to visit this sacred place at least once a year, bringing gold leaf to cover a piece of the rock. The pilgrimage is the supreme goal of the faithful. Those who make the pilgrimage three times are supposed to be rewarded with eternal good fortune and immeasurable wealth.

Sheerest Wall

Mount Rakaposhi (25,498 ft) rises 19,652 vertical ft from the Hunza Valley, Pakistan, with an overall gradient of 31° over a horizontal distance of 32,808 ft.

The 3,200-ft-wide northwest face of Half Dome, Yosemite, Calif, is 2,200 ft high, but nowhere departs more than 7° from the vertical. It was first climbed (Class VI) in 5 days in July 1957 by Royal Robbins, Jerry Gallwas, and Mike Sherrick.

LARGEST ROCK PINNACLE: Off the southeast coast of Australia is Lord Howe Island where this pyramid-like rock juts up 1,843 ft near the shore.

Largest Peninsula

The world's largest peninsula is Arabia, with an area of about 1,250,000 sq mi.

Largest and Smallest Continents

Of the earth's surface 41.25% or 81,200,000 sq mi is covered by continental masses and shelves of which only about two-thirds of 29.08% of the earth's surface (57,270,000 sq mi) is land above water, with a mean height of 2,480 ft above sea level. The Eurasian land mass is the largest, with an area (including islands) of 20,733,000 sq mi. The Afro-Eurasian land mass, separated artificially only by the Suez Canal, covers an area of 32,233,000 sq mi or 56.2% of the earth's land mass.

The smallest is the Australian mainland, with an area of about 2,941,526 sq mi, which, together with Tasmania, New Zealand, New Guinea and the Pacific Islands, is described as Oceania.

Largest Islands

Discounting Australia, which is usually regarded as a continental land mass, the largest island is Greenland (renamed Kalaallit Nunaat, May 1, 1979), with an area of about 840,000 sq mi. There is some evidence that Greenland is in fact several islands overlaid by an ice-cap without which it would have an area of 650,000 sq mi.

Remotest Island

The remotest inhabited island in the world is Tristan da Cunha, discovered in the South Atlantic by Tristão da Cunha, a Portuguese admiral, in Mar 1506. It has an area of 38 sq mi (habitable area 12 sq mi) and was annexed by the United Kingdom Aug 14, 1816. After evacuation in 1961 (due to volcanic activity), 198 islanders returned in Nov 1963. The nearest inhabited land is the island of St Helena, 1,320 miles to the northeast. The nearest continent, Africa, is 1,700 miles away.

Newest Island

The newest island is the lava islet of Fukuto Kuokanoba near Iwo Jima in the Pacific reported in Jan 1986. It measures 2,132 × 1,476 ft (1/10 of a sq mi) and is 40 ft above sea level.

> The largest island in a lake is Manitoulin Island (1,068 sq mi) in the Canadian (Ontario) section of Lake Huron. The island itself has a lake of 41.09 sq mi on it, called Manitou Lake, which is the world's largest lake within a lake, and in that lake are a number of islands.

Largest Atolls

The largest atoll is Kwajalein in the Marshall Islands, in the central Pacific. Its slender 176-mile-long coral reef encloses a lagoon of 1,100 sq mi.

The atoll with the largest land area is Christmas Atoll, in the Line Islands, in the central Pacific Ocean. It has an area of 248 sq mi. Its principal settlement, London, is only 2½ miles distant from Paris, its other settlement.

Greatest Archipelago

The greatest archipelago is the 3,500-mile-long crescent of over 13,000 islands that form Indonesia.

Longest Reef

The longest reef is the Great Barrier Reef off Queensland, north-eastern Australia, which is 1,260 statute miles in length. Between 1959 and 1971 a large section between Cooktown and Townsville was destroyed by the proliferation of the Crown of Thorns starfish (*Acanthaster planci*).

Highest Mountains

The mountain whose summit is farthest from the earth's center is the Andean peak of Chimborazo (20,702 ft), 98 miles south of the equator in Ecuador. Its summit is 7,057 ft farther from the earth's center than the summit of Mt Everest. The highest mountain on the equator is Volcán Cayambe (18,996 ft), Ecuador, at Longitude 77° 58′ W. A mountaineer atop the summit would be moving at 1,038 mph relative to the earth's center due to the earth's rotation.

The world's tallest mountain measured from its submarine base (3,280 fathoms) in the Hawaiian Trough to peak is Mauna Kea

(Mountain White) on the island of Hawaii, with a combined height of 33,476 ft, of which 13,796 ft are above sea level. Another mountain whose dimensions, but not height, exceed those of Mt Everest and K2 is the volcanic Hawaiian peak of Mauna Loa (Mountain Long) at 13,680 ft. The axes of its elliptical base, 16,322 ft below sea level, have been estimated at 74 mi and 53 mi. It should be noted that Cerro Aconcagua (22,834 ft) is more than 38,800 ft above the 16,000-ft-deep Pacific abyssal plain or 42,834 ft above the Peru-Chile Trench, which is 180 mi distant in the South Pacific.

MT EVEREST was restored as the highest peak after being measured by satellite transit surveyor at 29,078 ft high, compared to 28,238 ft for K-2.

Mount Everest's status as the tallest mountain at 29,028 ft high, recognized for 135 years (1852–1987) was finally challenged by K2 (formerly Goduen-Austin), also known as Chogori, in Pakistan in an announcement on Mar 6, 1987 by the US K2 Expedition. Their satellite transit surveyor yielded altitudes of between 29,064 and 29,228 ft as against the hitherto official 19th century figure for K2 of 28,250 ft and the 20th century proposed height of 28,740 ft. These compare with Everest's latest altitude of 29,029 ft announced by the Chinese on July 25, 1973.

However, the Research Council in Rome announced on Oct 23, 1987 that new satellite measurements restored Everest to primacy, at 29,078 ft, and put K2 down to 28,238 ft.

Unclimbed Mountain

The highest unclimbed mountain is now only the 31st highest—Zemu Gap Peak (25,526 ft) in the Sikkim Himalaya.

Greatest Mountain Ranges

The greatest land mountain range is the Himalaya-Karakoram, which contains 96 of the world's 109 peaks of over 24,000 ft. The greatest of all mountain ranges is, however, the submarine Indian-East Pacific Oceans Cordillera, extending 19,200 miles from the Gulf of Aden to the Gulf of California by way of the seabed between Australia and Antarctica, with an average height of 8,000 ft above the base ocean depth. The longest mountain range above ground is the Andes of S America at about 5,000 mi.

Longest Lines of Sight

Alaska's Mt McKinley (20,320 ft) has been sighted from Mt Sanford (16,237 ft) 230 mi away. McKinley, so named in 1896, was called Denali (Great One) in the Athabascan language. Vatnajokull (6,952 ft) on the eastern coast of Iceland, has been seen by refracted light from the Faeroe Islands 340 mi distant.

Highest Halites

Along the northern shores of the Gulf of Mexico for 725 miles there exist 330 subterranean "mountains" of salt, some of which rise more than 60,000 ft from bedrock and appear as the low salt domes first discovered in 1862.

Greatest Plateau

The most extensive high plateau is the Tibetan Plateau in Central Asia. The average altitude is 16,000 ft and the area is 77,000 sq mi.

Sand Dunes

The highest measured sand dunes are those in the Saharan sand sea of Isaouane-n-Tifernine of east central Algeria at Lat. 26° 42′ N., Long. 6° 43′ E. They have a wave-length of nearly 3 miles and attain a height of 1,410 ft.

Deepest and Largest Depressions

The deepest depression so far discovered is the bed rock in the Bentley sub-glacial trench, Antarctica, at 8,326 ft below sea level.

The deepest exposed depression on land is the shore surrounding the Dead Sea, now 1,312 ft below sea level. The deepest point on the bed of this saltiest of all lakes is 2,388 ft below the Mediterranean. The deepest part of the bed of Lake Baykal in Siberia, USSR, is 4,872 ft below sea level.

The greatest submarine depression is a large area of the floor of the northwest Pacific which has an average depth of 15,000 ft.

The largest exposed depression in the world is the Caspian Sea basin in the Azerbaydzhani, Russian, Kazakh, and Turkmen republics of the USSR and northern Iran. It is more than 200,000 sq mi, of which 143,550 sq mi is lake area. The preponderant land area of the depression is the Prikaspiyskaya Nizmennost', lying around the northern third of the lake and stretching inland for a distance of up to 280 miles.

Longest and Shortest Rivers

The two longest rivers are the Amazon (*Amazonas*), flowing into the South Atlantic, and the Nile (*Bahr-el-Nil*) flowing into the Mediterranean. Which is the longer is more a matter of definition than of simple measurement.

Not until 1971 was the true source of the Amazon discovered by Loren McIntyre (US) in the snow-covered Andes of southern Peru. His expedition was sponsored by the Interamerican Geodetic Survey and the National Geographic Society. The Amazon begins with snowbound lakes and brooks that converge to form the Apurimac, a torrent in a deep canyon. The Apurimac joins other streams to become the Ene, the Tambo, then the Ucayali. From the confluence of the Ucayali and Maranon above Iquitos, Peru, the river is called Amazon for its final 2,300 miles as it flows eastward through Brazil into the Atlantic Ocean. Some of its tributaries—particularly the Rio Negro and the Rio Madeira—are themselves among the dozen largest rivers in the world. The Amazon has several mouths that widen toward the sea; thus the exact point of the river's end is uncertain. If the Para River estuary, the most distant mouth, is counted, the Amazon length is approximately 4,195 miles. Because of seasonal flooding and changes in channels, geographers tend to round off the length at 4,000 miles.

The first explorer to paddle the full length of the Amazon was Piotr Chmielinski (b 1953, Poland) who had been one of the expedition traversing the Colca Canyon (see page 92). Joe Kane (b 1953, San Francisco) walked 200 mi at the start and then joined in the paddling to Belem. Kayaks were used almost the whole way but a raft was needed over some rough rapids, where other members of the party joined in the paddling. The trip took 174 days, from Aug 29, 1985 to Feb 19, 1986, and was sponsored by Canoandes Expeditions, Inc (Wyoming).

The length of the Nile watercourse, as surveyed by M. Devroey (Belgium) before the loss of a few miles of meanders due to the formation of Lake Nasser, behind the Aswan High Dam, was 4,145 miles. This course is the hydrologically acceptable one from the source in Burundi of the Luvironza branch of the Kagera feeder of the Victoria Nyanza *via* the White Nile (*Bahr-el-Jebel*) to the delta.

The world's shortest named river is the Roe River in Montana, which flows into the Missouri River, and is 201 ft long.

Largest Basin and Longest Tributaries

The largest river basin is that drained by the Amazon (4,007 miles). It covers about 2,720,000 sq mi, has about 15,000 tributaries and sub-tributaries, of which four are more than 1,000 miles long. This includes the longest of all tributaries, the Madeira, with a length of 2,100 miles, which is surpassed by only 14 rivers in the whole world.

The longest sub-tributary is the Pilcomayo (1,000 miles long) in South America. It is a tributary of the Paraguay River (1,500 miles long), which is itself a tributary of the Paraná (2,500 miles).

Greatest Flow

The greatest flow of any river is that of the Amazon, which discharges an average of 4,200,000 cu ft of water per sec into the

Atlantic Ocean, rising to more than 7 million "cusecs" in full flood. The lower 900 miles of the Amazon average 50–60 ft and in some places reach 300 ft in depth.

The flow of the Amazon exceeds the flow of the next 8 largest rivers, is 60 times greater than that of the Nile, and its 8 trillion gallons a day would furnish 20 times the daily water need of the US for drinking, industry, farming and electric power.

Longest Estuary

The longest estuary is that of the often-frozen Ob', in the northern USSR, at 550 miles. It is up to 50 miles wide.

Longest and Fastest-Moving Glaciers

It is estimated that 6,020,000 sq mi, or about 10.5% of the earth's land surface, is permanently glaciated. The longest glacier known is the Lambert Glacier, discovered by an Australian aircraft crew in Australian Antarctic Territory in 1956–57. It is up to 40 miles wide and, with its upper section known as the Mellor Glacier, it measures at least 250 miles in length. With the Fisher Glacier limb, the Lambert forms a continuous ice passage about 320 miles long. The longest Himalayan glacier is the Siachen (47 miles) in the Karakoram range, though the Hispar and Biafo combine to form an ice passage 76 miles long. The fastest-moving major glacier is the Quarayaq in Greenland which flows 65–80 ft per day.

WHERE THE BLACK WATERS MEET THE BROWN: The point in the Amazon River near Manaos, Brazil, where the Rio Negro churns its black waters into the muddier waters of the main Amazon stream. The waters travel several miles downstream before merging. The first explorers to travel the full length of the world's longest river were the men in these boats, Piotr Chmielinski and Joe Kane.

Greatest Avalanches

The greatest avalanches, though rarely observed, occur in the Himalayas, but no estimate of their volume has been published. It was estimated that 120 million cu ft of snow fell in an avalanche in the Italian Alps in 1885. (See also *Disasters.*)

The 250-mph avalanche triggered by the Mt St Helens eruption in Wash May 18, 1979 was estimated to measure 96 billion cu ft (see pages 96 and 97).

Greatest Waterfall Flow

On the basis of the average annual flow, the greatest waterfalls are the Boyoma (formerly Stanley) Falls in Zaïre with 600,000 cusec (cu ft/sec). The Guaira (Salto das Sete Quedas) on the Alto Paraná river between Brazil and Paraguay at times attained a peak flow rate of 1,750,000 cusec (cu ft/sec). The completion of the Itaipu dam in 1982 ended this claim to fame.

It has been calculated that, when some 5½ million years ago the Mediterranean basins began to be filled from the Atlantic through the Straits of Gibraltar, a waterfall was formed 26 times greater than the Guaira and perhaps 2,625 ft high.

Highest Waterfall

The highest waterfall (as opposed to a vaporized "Bridal Veil") is the Salto Angel (Angel Falls), in Venezuela, on a branch of the Carrao River, an upper tributary of the Caroní, with a total drop of 3,212 ft and the longest single drop 2,648 ft. It was rediscovered in 1935 by a US pilot named Jimmy Angel (d Dec 8, 1956). He later crashed nearby on Oct 9, 1937. The fall, known by the Indians as Cherun-Meru, was first reported by Ernesto Sanchez La Cruz in 1910.

Widest Waterfalls

The widest waterfalls are Khône Falls (50–70 ft high) in Laos, with a width of 6.7 miles and a flood flow of 1,500,000 cu ft per sec.

The widest waterfall in the Americas is the spectacular Iguazú near the Argentina-Brazil-Paraguay intersect which is 2½ mi wide and 237 ft high, with a volume about twice that of Niagara (although this varies greatly—in 1975 it dried up for 4 days).

Largest Lakes

The largest inland sea or lake is the Kaspiskoye More (Caspian Sea) between southern USSR and Iran. It is 760 miles long and its total area is 139,000 sq mi. Of the total area, 55,280 sq mi (38.6%) are in Iran, where the lake is named the Darya-ye-Khazar. Its maximum depth is 3,360 ft and its surface is 93 ft below sea level. Its estimated volume is 21,500 cu mi of saline water. Its surface has varied between 105 ft below sea level (11th century) and 72 ft (early 19th century).

The fresh-water lake with the greatest surface area is Lake Superior, one of the Great Lakes. The total area is about 31,800 sq mi, of which 20,700 sq mi are in the US (Minn, Wis and Mich) and 11,100 sq mi in Ontario, Canada. It is 600 ft above sea level. The fresh-water lake with the greatest volume is Baykal with an estimated volume of 5,520 cu mi.

Underground Lake

Reputedly the largest underground lake is the Lost Sea, which lies 300 ft underground in the Craighead Caverns, Sweetwater, Tenn. Discovered in 1905, it covers an area of 4½ acres.

Largest Lagoon

The largest is Lagoa dos Patos in southern Brazil. It is 158 mi long and extends over 4,110 sq mi.

Highest Lake

The highest steam-navigated lake is Lake Titicaca (maximum depth 1,214 ft), with an area of about 3,200 sq mi (1,850 sq mi in Peru, 1,350 sq mi in Bolivia), in South America. It is 130 mi long and is situated at 12,506 ft above sea level.

There is an unnamed glacial lake near Mt Everest at 19,300 ft. Tibet's largest lake, Nam Tso (772 sq mi), lies at an elevation of 15,060 ft.

Deepest Lake

The deepest lake is Ozero (Lake) Baykal in central Siberia, USSR. It is 385 miles long and between 20 and 46 miles wide. In 1957 the lake's Olkhon Crevice was measured to be 6,365 ft deep and hence 4,872 ft below sea level.

Natural Bridge (Arch)

The longest natural bridge in the world is the Landscape Arch in the Arches National Park 42 miles north of Moab, Utah. This natural

HIGHEST NAVIGABLE LAKE: Lake Titicaca in the Andes on the border between Peru and Bolivia is 12,506 ft high and 130 mi long. Though there are steamships on the lake, the natives prefer their light balsa sailboats.

sandstone arch spans 291 ft and is set about 100 ft above the canyon floor. In one place erosion has narrowed its section to 6 ft.

Larger in mass, however, is the Rainbow Bridge, Utah, discovered on Aug 14, 1909, which has a span of 278 ft but is over 22 ft wide.

The highest natural arch is the sandstone arch 25 miles west-northwest of K'ashih, Sinkiang, China, estimated in 1947 to be nearly 1,000 ft tall, with a span of about 150 ft.

Longest and Largest Cave and Cavern

The most extensive cave system is under the Mammoth Cave National Park, Ky, first discovered in 1799. On Sept 9, 1972 an exploration group led by Dr John P. Wilcox completed a connection, pioneered by Mrs Patricia Crowther, on Aug 30, between the Flint Ridge Cave system and the Mammoth Cave system, so making a combined system with a total mapped passageway which is now over 330 mi.

The largest cave chamber is the Sarawak Chamber, Lobang Nasip Bagus, in the Gunung Mulu National Park, Sarawak, discovered and surveyed by the 1980 British-Malayasian Mulu Expedition. Its length is 2,300 ft; its average width is 980 ft and it is nowhere less than 230 ft high. It could garage 7,500 buses; Yankee Stadium would fit into one end.

DEEPEST CAVES BY COUNTRIES

These depths are subject to continuous revisions.

Depth in Ft		
5,036	Réseau Jean Bernard	France
4,619	Puerta de Illamina	Spain
4,495	Snieznaja Piezcziera	USSR
4,439	Sistema Huautla	Mexico
3,999	Schwersystem	Austria
3,986	Complesso Fighiera Corchia	Italy
3,802	Anou Ifflis	Algeria
3,346	Slebenhengste system	Switzerland
2,943	Jama u Vjetrena brda	Yugoslavia
2,917	Nettlebed system	New Zealand
2,569	Jaskinia Sniezna	Poland
2,464	Ghar Parau, Zagros	Iran

Tallest Stalagmite

The tallest known stalagmite is La Grande Stalagmite in the Aven Armand cave, Lozère, France, which has attained a height of 98 ft from the cave floor. It was found in Sept 1897.

Longest Stalactite

The longest known stalactite is a wall-supported column extending 195 ft from roof to floor in the Cueva de Nerja, near Málaga, Spain. Probably the longest free-hanging stalactite is one of 23 ft in the Poll, an Ionian cave in County Clare, Ireland.

The tallest cave column is probably the 128-ft high Flying Dragon Pillar in the Nine Dragons Cave (Daji Dong), Guizhou, China.

Largest and Deepest Gorges

The largest land gorge is the Grand Canyon on the Colorado River in north-central Ariz. It extends from Marble Gorge to the Grand Wash Cliffs, over a distance of 217 miles, varies in width from 4 to 13 miles and is up to 5,300 ft deep.

The deepest land gorge is the Colca River Canyon in southern Peru, where the sides rise to a maximum of 14,339 ft on one side and about 10,607 ft on the other. It was first traversed by a Polish kayak team called CANOANDES from the Univ of Krakow, May 12–June 14, 1981.

The submarine Labrador Basin Canyon is *c.* 2,150 miles long.

The deepest canyon in low relief territory is Hell's Canyon, dividing Oregon and Idaho. It plunges 7,900 ft from the Devil Mountain down to the Snake River.

A stretch of the Kali River in central Nepal flows 18,000 ft below its flanking summits of the Dhaulagiri and Annapurna groups.

The deepest submarine canyon yet discovered is one 25 miles south of Esperance, Western Australia, which is 6,000 ft deep and 20 miles wide.

Largest Swamp

The largest is in the basin of the Pripet or Pripyat River, a tributary of the Dnieper in the USSR. These swamps cover an estimated area of 18,125 sq mi.

Largest Desert

Nearly an eighth of the world's land surface is arid with an annual rainfall of less than 9.8 in. The Sahara in North Africa is the largest in the world. At its greatest length, it is 3,200 miles from east to west. From north to south it is between 800 and 1,400 miles. The area covered by the desert is about 3,250,000 sq mi. The land level varies from 436 ft below sea level in the Qattara Depression, Egypt, to the mountain Emi Koussi (11,204 ft) in Chad. The diurnal temperature range in the western Sahara may be more than 80°F.

Sea Cliffs

The highest sea cliffs yet pinpointed anywhere in the world are those on the north coast of east Molokai, Hawaii, near Umilehi Point, which descend 3,300 ft to the sea at an average gradient of more than 55°.

WEATHER*

The meteorological records given here necessarily relate largely to the last 140 to 160 years, since data before that time are both sparse and often unreliable. Reliable registering thermometers were introduced as recently as c. 1820.

It is believed that 1.2 million years ago the world's air temperature averaged 95°F.

The longest continuous observations have been maintained at the Radcliffe Observatory, Oxford, England since 1815, though discontinuous records have enabled the Chinese to assert that 903 BC was a very bad winter.

Greatest Temperature Ranges

The highest *shade* temperature ever recorded was 136.4°F at Al' Aziziyah (El Azizia), Libya, on Sept 13, 1922.

The lowest *screen* temperature ever recorded was −128.6°F at Vostok (11,220 ft above sea level), Antarctica on July 22, 1983. A platinum thermometer was used. The coldest permanently inhabited place is the Siberian village of Oymyakon (pop. 600) in the USSR, where the temperature reached −96°F in 1964.

The greatest temperature variation recorded in a 24-hr period is 100°F (a fall from 44°F to −56°F) at Browning, Mont, Jan 23–24, 1916. The most freakish rise was 49°F in 2 min at Spearfish, SD, from −4°F at 7:30 a.m. to 45°F at 7:32 a.m. Jan 22, 1943.

The greatest recorded temperature ranges in the world are around the Siberian "cold pole" in the eastern USSR. Temperatures in Verkhoyansk (67°33′N, 133°23′E) have ranged 192°F from −94°F (unofficial) to –98°F.

Humidity and Discomfort

Human discomfort depends not merely on temperature but on the combination of temperature, humidity, radiation and wind speed. The US Weather Service uses a Temperature-Humidity Index, which equals two-fifths of the sum of the dry and wet bulb thermometer readings plus 15. A THI reading of 98.2 has been recorded twice in Death Valley, Calif—on July 27, 1966 (119°F, 31% humidity) and on Aug 12, 1970 (117°F, 37% humidity). A person driving at 45 mph in a car without a windshield in a temperature of −45°F would, by the chill factor, experience the equivalent of −125°F, which is within 3.5°F of the world record.

Most Equable Temperature

The location with the most equable recorded temperature over a short period is Garapan, on Saipan, in the Mariana Islands, Pacific Ocean. During the nine years 1927–35, inclusive, the lowest temper-

*For more specialized weather records, see "Weather Facts and Feats." (2nd edition) a Guinness Superlatives Book (Sterling).

ature recorded was 67.3°F Jan 30, 1934, and the highest was 88.5°F Sept 9, 1931, giving an extreme range of 21.2°F.

Upper Atmosphere

The lowest temperature ever recorded in the atmosphere is −225.4°F at an altitude of about 50 to 60 miles, during noctilucent cloud research above Kronogard, Sweden, July 27–Aug 7, 1963.

A jet stream moving at 408 mph at 154,200 ft (29.2 miles) was recorded by Skua rocket above South Uist, Outer Hebrides, Scotland, on Dec 13, 1967.

Thickest Ice

The greatest recorded thickness of ice on the earth's surface is 2.97 miles (15,670 ft) measured by radio echo soundings from a US Antarctic Research aircraft at 69° 9′ 38″ S, 135° 20′ 25″ E in Wilkes Land on Jan 4, 1975.

HAIL PILED HIGH: ▲ During a furious summer thunderstorm in Cheyenne, Wyo, Aug 2, 1985, a 3-ft cover of hailstones fell, along with 6 in of rain in 4 hours. "It was like someone opened a faucet overhead," said the mayor. Sudden floods followed that killed a dozen people.

◄ HOTTEST STREAK: Death Valley, Calif, had 43 consecutive days of 120°F heat in 1917.

Waterspouts

The highest waterspout of which there is reliable record was one observed May 16, 1898, off Eden, NSW, Australia. A theodolite reading from the shore gave its height as 5,014 ft. It was about 10 ft in diameter.

Lightning

The visible length of lightning strokes varies greatly. In mountainous regions, when clouds are very low, the flash may be less than 300 ft long. In flat country with very high clouds, a cloud-to-earth flash may measure 4 miles, though in the most extreme cases such flashes have been measured at 20 miles. The intensely bright central core of the lightning channel is extremely narrow. Some authorities suggest that its diameter is as little as half an inch. This core is surrounded by a "corona envelope" (glow discharge) which may be 10–20 feet wide.

The speed of a lightning discharge varies from 100 to 1,000 miles per sec for the downward leader track, and reaches up to 87,000 miles per sec (nearly half the speed of light) for the powerful return stroke.

Every few million strokes there is a giant discharge, in which the cloud-to-earth and the return lightning strokes flash from and to the top of the thunder clouds.

In these "positive giants" energy of up to 3,000 million joules (3×10^{16} ergs) has been recorded. The temperature reaches about 30,000°C, which is more than five times greater than that of the surface of the sun.

Deepest Permafrost

The deepest recorded permafrost is more than 4,500 ft, reported from the upper reaches of the Viluy River, Siberia, USSR, in Feb 1982.

Hurricane Damage

The hurricane named Frederic in 1979 caused the most damage along the US coastline, according to the National Hurricane Center. $2.3 *billion* is estimated. The big hurricane, Alicia, in 1983 did $300 million less damage.

Most Intense Rainfall

Difficulties attend rainfall readings for very short periods but the figure of 1.50 in in 1 min at Barst, Guadeloupe, Nov 26, 1970, is regarded as the most intense recorded in modern times.

Longest-Lasting Rainbow

A rainbow lasting for over 3 hours was reported from North Wales on Aug 14, 1979.

NOCTILUCENT CLOUDS retain sunlight after sunset due to their extreme height—50 mi. Seen here over Antarctica, they are thought to contain ice crystals or meteoric dust. This phenomenon is being observed from 15 stations in northern Europe where it occurs irregularly—43 nights in 1979 and only 15 in 1970. (*Science Photo Library*)

OTHER WEATHER RECORDS

Hottest Place (Annual mean): Dallol, Ethiopia, 94°*F*, *1960–66*. In Death Valley, Calif, 120°F or more was recorded on 43 consecutive days, July 6–Aug 17, 1917. At Marble Bar, W Australia (maximum 121°F) maximums over 100°F for 160 consecutive days Oct 31, 1923–Apr 7, 1924. Wyndham, W Australia had 333 days in 1946 when temperature reached 90°F.

Greatest Snowfall (24 hours): 76 in, Silver Lake, Colo, Apr 14–15, 1921. (12 months): 1,224.5 in, Paradise, Mt Rainier, Wash, Feb 19, 1971–Feb 18, 1972. (Single storm): 189 in, Mt Shasta Ski Bowl, Calif. (Greatest depth of snow on ground): 27.7 in at Helen Lake, Mt. Lassen, Calif Apr 1983.

Wettest Place (Annual mean): Tutunendo, Colombia, average 463.4 in.

Coldest Place (Extrapolated annual mean): Polus Nedostupnosti, Pole of Cold (78°S, 96°E), Antarctica, −72°F (16°F lower than Pole). (Coldest measured mean): Plateau Station, Antarctica −70°F.

Maximum Sunshine 97% (over 4,300 hours a year), eastern Sahara. St Petersburg, Fla, had 768 consecutive days, Feb 9, 1967–March 17, 1969.

Minimum Sunshine: Nil at North Pole—for winter stretches of 186 days.

Greatest Rainfall (24 hours): 73.62 in, Cilaos, La Réunion, Indian Ocean, March 15–16, 1952. (Calendar month): 366.14 in, Cherrapunji, Meghalaya, India, July, 1861. (12 months): 1,041.78 in, Cherrapunji, Meghalaya, Aug 1, 1860–July 31, 1861.

Highest Surface Wind-speed: 231 mph, Mt Washington (6,288 ft), NH, Apr 12, 1934. 280 mph in a tornado at Wichita Falls, Tex, Apr 2, 1958.

Barometric Pressure (Highest): 1,083.8 mb (32 in), Agata, Siberia, USSR (alt. 862 ft) Dec 31, 1968. (Lowest): 870 mb (25.69 in), 300 miles west of Guam in the Pacific Ocean on Oct 12, 1979 by the US Air Weather Service. The USS *Repose*, a hospital ship, recorded 856 mb (25.55 in) in the eye of a typhoon off Okinawa on Sept 16, 1945.

Largest Hailstones: 2¼ lb reported to have killed 92 people in Bangladesh April 14, 1986. A stone weighing 1.67 lb fell in Coffeyville, Kans on Sept 3, 1970. It measured 7½ in diameter (could have been 8 in when it fell) and 17½ in in circumference.

Thunder Days (Year): 322 days, Bogor (formerly Buitenzorg), Java, Indonesia (average, 1916–19). Between Lat 35° N and 35° S there are some 3,200 thunderstorms each 12 nighttime hours, some of which can be heard at a range of 18 miles.

Windiest Place: The Commonwealth Bay, George V Coast, Antarctica, where gales reach 200 mph.

Driest Place: Desierto de Atacama, near Calama, Chile, almost rainless for about 400 years to 1971, although several times a century a squall may strike a small area of it.

Longest Sea Level Fogs (Visibility less than 1,000 yd): Fogs persist on the Grand Banks, Newfoundland, Canada, where the average is more than 120 days per year.

Most Rainy Days (Year): Mt Waialeale (5,148 ft) Kauai, Hawaii, up to 350 days per year.

EARTHQUAKES

It is estimated that each year there are some 500,000 detectable seismic or micro-seismic disturbances of which 100,000 can be felt and 1,000 cause damage. The deepest recorded hypocenters are of 447 miles in Indonesia in 1933, 1934 and 1943.

Worst Death Toll

The greatest loss of life occurred in the earthquake which rocked every city of the Near East and eastern Mediterranean *c.* July 1201.

Contemporary accounts estimate the loss of life at 1.1 million. Less uncertain is the figure of 830,000 fatalities in the prolonged quake (*ti chen*) in the Shensi, Shansi and Honan provinces of China, of 1556 Feb 2 (New Style) (Jan 23 Old Style). The highest death toll in modern times has been in the Tangshan earthquake (magnitude 8.2) in eastern China on 1976 July 27 (local time was 3:00 a.m. on July 28). A first figure published Jan 4, 1977 revealed 655,237 killed, later adjusted to 750,000. On Nov 22, 1979, the New China News Agency unaccountably reduced the death toll to 242,000. As late as Jan 1982, the site of the city was still a prohibited area.

The greatest material damage was in the earthquake on the Kwanto plain, Japan, at 11:58 a.m. of 1923 Sept 1 (magnitude 8.2, epicenter in Latitude 35° 15′N., Longitude 139° 30′E.). In Sagami Bay, the sea bottom in one area sank 1,310 ft. The official total of persons killed and missing in this earthquake, called the *Shinsai* or Great Quake, and the resultant fires was 142,807. In Tokyo and Yokohama 575,000 dwellings were destroyed. The cost of the damage was estimated at $2.8 billion. It has however been estimated that a 7.5-magnitude shock (G-R scale) 30 miles north of Los Angeles would result in damage estimated at $75 billion.

VOLCANOES

The total number of known active volcanoes is 850 of which many are submarine. The greatest concentration is in Indonesia, where 77 of its 167 volcanoes have erupted within historic times. The name "volcano" was first applied to the now dormant Vulcano Island in the Aeolian group in the Mediterranean, and that name derives from Vulcan, Roman god of destructive fire.

Highest Volcanoes

The highest extinct volcano in the world is Cerro Aconcagua (Stone Sentinel), 22,588 ft high, on the Argentine side of the Andes. It was first climbed on Jan 14, 1897 by Mathias Zurbriggen, and was the highest mountain climbed anywhere until June 12, 1907.

The highest dormant volcano is Ojos del Salado, Argentina (22,588 ft). It has a small steaming crater below the summit at about 21,325 ft which makes it the highest active volcano as well.

Longest Lava Flow

The longest lava flow, known as *pahoehoe* (twisted cord-like solidifications), is that from the eruption of Laki in southeast Iceland, which flowed 40½–43½ miles in 1783. The largest known prehistoric flow is the Roza basalt flow in North America, *c.* 15 million years ago, which had an unsurpassed length (300 miles), area (15,400 sq mi) and volume (300 cu mi).

Largest Crater

The world's largest *caldera* or volcano crater is that of Toba, north-central Sumatra, Indonesia, covering 685 sq mi.

GREATEST AVALANCHE: The volcanic eruption of Mt St Helens in Wash State on May 18, 1980 produced a 250-mph avalanche, destroying 100 sq mi of forests and leaving 66 persons dead or missing. (*Robert Harding Picture Library*) ◄

LARGEST ERUPTION IN US HISTORY: This was a forest of green fir trees before the eruption of Mt St Helens in 1980. (*AP Laserphoto*) ▼

Greatest Eruption

The total volume of matter discharged in the eruption of Tambora, a volcano on the island of Sumbawa, in Indonesia, Apr 5–7, 1815, has been estimated as 36.4 cu mi. The energy of this 1,395-mph eruption, which lowered the height of the island from 13,450 ft to 9,350 ft, was 8.4×10^{19} joules. The volcano thus lost 4,100 ft in height and a crater 7 mi in diameter was formed. This compares with a probable 15 cu mi ejected by Santorini and 4.3 cu mi ejected by Krakatoa. The internal pressure causing the Tambora eruption has been estimated at 46,500,000 lb per sq in.

LARGEST ACTIVE VOLCANO: On the Big Island of Hawaii, high up at 13,677 ft, is the peak of Mauna Loa, which erupted as recently as Apr 1984, and at all times its molten lava can be seen. (*Colorific*)

The ejecta in the Taupo eruption in New Zealand *c.* 130 AD has been estimated at 33,000 million tons of pumice moving at one time at 400 mph. It flattened 6,180 sq mi (over 26 times the devastated area of Mt St Helens). Less than 20% of the 15.4 × 10^9 tons of pumice ejected in this most violent of all documented volcanic events fell within 125 miles of the vent.

Largest Active Volcano

The world's largest active volcano is Mauna Loa (13,677 ft), Hawaii, which erupted in 1975 and in Apr 1984. It has a dome 75 mi long and 64 mi wide with a lava flow that occupies more than 2,000 sq mi of the island. Its pit crater measures 4 sq mi and is 500–600 ft deep. It has averaged one eruption every 3½ years since 1832.

Largest Eruption in US

Mt St Helens, located in the Cascade Range in Wash State, about 50 miles northeast of Portland, Ore, had lain dormant for 123 years when it began to show signs of becoming active and violent in Mar 1980. By early May a bulge about 330 ft high was noticeable, and on May 18 a blast 500 times greater than the 20 kiloton atomic bomb that fell on Hiroshima broke out the whole north side of the mountain. Lava flowed out at a speed of 250 mph.

Greatest Explosion

The greatest explosion (possibly since Santoríní in the Aegean Sea *c.* 1628 BC) occurred *c.* 10:00 a.m. (local time), or 3:00 a.m. G.M.T., on Aug 27, 1883 with an eruption of Krakatoa, an island (then 18 sq mi) in the Sunda Strait between Sumatra and Java, in Indonesia. A total of 163 villages were wiped out, and 36,380 people killed by the wave it caused. Rocks were thrown 34 miles high, and dust fell 10 days later at a distance of 3,313 miles. The explosion was recorded 4 hours later on the island of Rodrigues, 2,968 miles away, as "the roar of heavy guns" and was heard over 1/13th part of the surface of the globe. This explosion has been estimated to have had about 26 times the power of the greatest H-bomb test detonation, but was still only a fifth of the size of the Santoríní cataclysm.

Mirages

The largest mirage on record was that sighted in the Arctic at 83°N., 103°W. by Donald B. MacMillan in 1913. This type of mirage, known as the Fata Morgana, appeared as the same "hills, valleys, snow-capped peaks extending through at least 120 degrees of the horizon" that Peary had misidentified as Crocker Land 6 years earlier.

On July 17, 1939, a mirage of Snaefell Jokull glacier (4,715 ft) on Iceland was seen from the sea at a distance of 335–350 miles.

GEYSERS

Tallest Geyser

The Waimangu ("black water" in the Maori language) geyser, in New Zealand, erupted to a height in excess of 1,500 ft in 1904, but has not been active since it erupted violently at 6:20 a.m. Apr 1, 1917, killing 4 people.

Currently the world's tallest active geyser is the US National Park Service Steamboat Geyser, in Yellowstone National Park, Wyo, which erupted at intervals ranging from 5 days to 10 months between 1962 and 1969 to a height of 250–380 ft.

The *Geysir* ("gusher") near Mt Hekla in south-central Iceland, from which all others have been named, spurts, on occasion, to 180 ft, while the adjacent Strokkur, reactivated by drilling in 1963, spurts at 10–15 min intervals.

Greatest Geyser Discharge

The greatest measured water discharge from a geyser has been 990,000 gallons by the Giant Geyser in Yellowstone National Park, Wyo, which has been dormant since 1955.

Chapter 4

The Universe & Space

Light-Year

That distance traveled by light at the speed 186,282.397 miles per sec, or 670,616,629.2 mph *in vacuo*, in one tropical (or solar) year (365.24219878 mean solar days at Jan 0, 12 hours Ephemeris time in 1900 AD) is 5,878,499,814,000 miles. The unit was first used in March 1888, and fixed at this constant in Oct 1983.

Magnitude

A measure of stellar brightness such that the light of a star of any magnitude bears a ratio of 2.511886 to that of a star of the next magnitude. Thus a fifth magnitude star is 2.511886 times as bright, while one of the first magnitude is exactly 100 (or 2.511886^5) times as bright, as a sixth magnitude star. In the case of such exceptionally bright bodies as Sirius, Venus, the moon (magnitude −12.71) or the sun (magnitude −26.8), the magnitude is expressed as a minus quantity.

Proper Motion

That component of a star's motion in space which, at right angles to the line of sight, constitutes an apparent change of position of the star in the celestial sphere.

The universe is the entirety of space, matter and antimatter. An appreciation of its magnitude is best grasped by working outward from the earth, through the solar system which is revolving around the center of the Milky Way galaxy, once in each 237,000,000 years at a speed of 492,000 mph and has a velocity of 44,700 mph relative to stars in our immediate region and then on to the remotest extra-galactic nebulae and quasars.

Meteor Shower

Meteoroids are mostly of cometary or asteroidal origin. A meteor is the light phenomenon caused by entry of a meteoroid into earth's atmosphere. The greatest meteor "shower" on record occurred on the night of Nov 16–17, 1966, when the Leonid meteors (which recur every 33¼ years) were visible between western North America and eastern USSR. It was calculated that meteors passed over Arizona at a rate of 2,300 per min for a period of 20 min from 5 a.m. Nov 17, 1966.

Oldest and Largest Meteorites

The oldest dated meteorites are from the Allende Fall over Chihuahua, Mexico, Feb 8, 1969, dating back 4,610 million years.

It was reported in Aug 1978 that dust grains in the Murchison meteorite which fell in Australia in Sept 1969 predate the formation of the solar system 4,600 million years ago.

When a meteoroid penetrates to the earth's surface, the remnant, which could be either aerolite (stony) or siderite (metallic), is described as a meteorite. This occurs about 150 times per year over the whole land surface of the earth. Although the chances of being struck are deemed negligible, the most anxious time of day for meteorophobes is 3 p.m. In historic times, the only recorded person injured by a meteorite has been Mrs E. H. Hodges of Sylacauga, Alabama, on Nov 30, 1954, when a 9-lb stone went through her roof.

The largest known meteorite is one found in 1920 at Hoba West, near Grootfontein in southwest Africa. This is a block 9 ft long by 8 ft broad, weighing 132,000 lb.

The largest meteorite exhibited by any museum is the "Tent" meteorite, weighing 68,085 lb, found in 1897 near Cape York, on the west coast of Greenland, by the expedition of Commander (later Rear Admiral) Robert Edwin Peary (1856–1920). It was known to the Eskimos as the Abnighito and is now exhibited in the Hayden Planetarium in NYC.

The largest piece of stony meteorite recovered is a piece of 3,902 lb which was part of a shower that struck Jilin (formerly Kirin), China, March 8, 1976.

There was a mysterious explosion of 12½ megatons at Lat. 60° 55′ N., Long. 101° 57′ E., in the basin of the Podkamennaya Tunguska River, 40 miles north of Vanavar, in Siberia, USSR at 00 hrs 17 min 11 sec UT June 30, 1908. The cause was variously attributed to a meteorite (1927), a comet (1930), a nuclear explosion (1961) and to antimatter (1965). This devastated an area of about 1,500 sq mi, and the shock was felt more than 600 miles away.

The theory is now favored that this was the terminal flare of stony debris from a comet, possibly Encke's comet, at altitude of less than 20,000 ft. A similar event may have occurred over the Isle of Axeholm, Lincolnshire, Eng, a few thousand years before. A stony meteorite with a diameter of 6.2 miles striking the earth at 55,925 mph would generate an explosive energy equivalent to 100 million megatons. Such events should not be expected to recur more than once in 75 million years.

Largest Craters

It has been estimated that some 2,000 asteroid-earth collisions have occurred in the last 600 million years. A total of 102 collision sites or astroblemes has been recognized. A crater 150 miles across and a half mile deep has been postulated in Wilkes Land, Antarctica, since 1962. It would have been caused by a 14,560 million-ton meteorite striking at 44,000 mph. In Dec 1970 USSR scientists reported an astrobleme in the basin of the Popigai River with a 60-mile diameter and a maximum depth of 1,300 ft. There is a possible crater-like formation or astrobleme 275 miles in diameter on the eastern shore of Hudson Bay, where the Nastapoka Islands are just off the coast.

The largest proven crater is the Coon Butte or Barringer Crater, discovered in 1891 near Canyon Diablo, Winslow, northern Ariz. It is 4,150 ft in diameter and now about 575 ft deep, with a parapet rising 130–155 ft above the surrounding plain. It has been estimated that an iron-nickel mass with a diameter of 200–260 ft, and weighing about 2,240,000 tons, gouged this crater *c.* 25,000 BC.

The New Quebec (formerly the Chubb) "Crater," first sighted June 20, 1943, in northern Ungava, Canada, is 1,325 ft deep and measures 6.8 miles around its rim.

Fireball

The brightest fireball ever recorded photographically was one observed over Sumava, Czechoslovakia, Dec 4, 1974, by Dr Zdeněk Ceplecha, which had a momentary magnitude of −22, or 10,000 times brighter than a full moon.

Tektites

The largest tektite of which details have been published was one of 7.04 lb found in 1932 at Muong Nong, Saravane Province, Laos, and now in the Paris Museum.

THE MOON

The earth's closest neighbor in space and only natural satellite is the moon, at a mean distance of 238,855 statute miles center-to-center or 233,812 miles surface-to-surface. In the present century the closest approach (smallest perigee) was 216,398 miles surface-to-surface or 221,441 miles center-to-center on Jan 4, 1912, and the farthest distance (largest apogee) was 247,675 miles surface-to-surface or 252,718 miles center-to-center on Mar 2, 1984.

The moon was only a few earth radii distant during the "Gerstenkorn period" 3,900 million years ago. It has a diameter of 2,159.3 miles and has a mass of 7.35×10^{19} metric tonnes with a mean density of 3.344. The average orbital speed is 2,287 mph.

The first direct hit on the moon was achieved at 2 min 24 sec after midnight (Moscow time) Sept 14, 1959, by the Soviet space probe *Luna II* near the *Mare Serenitatis*. The first photographic images of the hidden side were collected by the USSR's *Luna III* from 6:30 a.m. Oct 7, 1959, from a range of up to 43,750 miles, and transmitted to the earth from a distance of 292,000 miles.

Highest Moon Mountains

As there is no sea level on the moon, the heights of lunar mountains can be measured only in relation to an adopted reference sphere with a radius of 1,079.943 miles. Thus the greatest elevation attained on this basis by any of the 12 US astronauts has been 25,688 ft, on the Descartes Highlands, by Capt John Watts Young, USN, and Major Charles M. Duke, Jr, Apr 27, 1972.

Moon Samples

The age attributed to the oldest of the moon material brought back to earth by the *Apollo* program crews has been soil dated to 4,720 million years.

Temperature Extremes on the Moon

When the sun is overhead, the temperature on the lunar equator reaches 243° F (31° F above the boiling point of water). By sunset the temperature is 58° F, but after nightfall it sinks to −261° F.

Largest and Deepest Craters

Only 59% of the moon's surface is directly visible from the earth because it is in "captured rotation," *i.e.*, the period of rotation is equal to the period of orbit. The largest wholly visible crater is the walled plain Bailly, toward the moon's South Pole, which is 183 miles across, with walls rising to 14,000 ft. Partly on the averted side, the Orientale Basin measures more than 600 miles in diameter.

The deepest crater is the moon's Newton crater, with a floor estimated to be between 23,000 and 29,000 ft below its rim and 14,000 ft below the level of the plain outside. The brightest directly visible spot on the moon is *Aristarchus*.

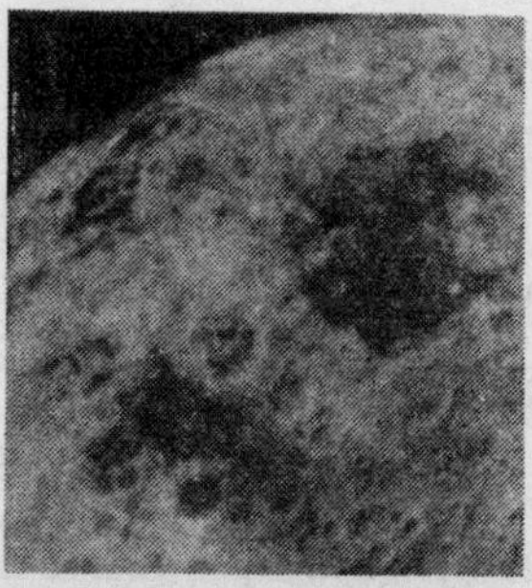

CRATERS ON THE FAR SIDE OF THE MOON: Never seen on earth, the hidden side was first photographed by a Soviet space probe in 1959.

FAMOUS FOOTSTEP: The first step onto the moon left this print in the dust. Neil Armstrong, astronaut, had a quote prepared: "That's one small step for man, one giant leap for mankind." (*NASA*)

THE SUN

The earth's 66,620 mph orbit of 584,017,800 miles around the sun is elliptical; hence our distance from the sun varies. The orbital speed varies between 65,520 mph (minimum) and 67,750 mph. The average distance of the sun is 1.000000230 astronomical units or 92,955,829 miles. The closest approach (perihelion) is 91,402,000 miles, and the farthest departure (aphelion) is 94,510,000 miles.

Sun's Temperature and Dimensions

The sun has a central temperature of about 15,400,000K (K stands for the Kelvin absolute scale of temperatures), a core pressure of 1,650,000,000 tons per sq in (25.4 PPa) and uses up nearly 4½ million tons of hydrogen per sec, thus providing a luminosity of 3×10^{27} candlepower, with an intensity of 1½ million candles per sq in. The sun has the stellar classification of a "yellow dwarf" and, although its density is only 1.407 times that of water, its mass is 332,946 times as much as that of the earth. It has a mean diameter of 865,270 miles. The sun with a mass of $1,958 \times 10^{27}$ metric tonnes represents more than 99% of the total mass of the solar system, but will exhaust its energy in 10 billion years.

Largest and Most Frequent Sunspots

To be visible to the *protected* naked eye, a sunspot must cover about one two-thousandth part of the sun's disc and thus have an area of about 500 million sq mi. The largest sunspot occurred in the sun's southern hemisphere on Apr 8, 1947. Its area was about 7 billion sq mi, with an extreme longitude of 187,000 miles and an extreme latitude of 90,000 miles. Sunspots appear darker because they are more than 1,500° C cooler than the rest of the sun's surface temperature of 5,525° C. The largest observed solar prominence was one protruding 365,000 miles, photographed on Dec 19, 1973 during the third and final Skylab mission.

On Oct 1957 a smoothed sunspot count showed 263, the highest recorded index since records started in 1755 (*cf.* previous record of 239 in May 1778). In 1943 a sunspot lasted for 200 days from June to Dec.

Longest Eclipse Duration

The maximum possible duration of an eclipse of the sun is 7 min 31 sec. The longest actually *measured* was June 20, 1955 (7 min 8 sec), seen from the Philippines. That of July 16, 2186 in the mid-Atlantic should last 7 min 29 sec. This will be the longest for 1,469 years. Durations can be extended by observers being airborne, as on June 30, 1973 when an eclipse was "extended" to 72 min for observers aboard a *Concorde* jet. An annular eclipse may last for 12 min 24 sec. The longest totality of any lunar eclipse is 104 min. This has occurred many times.

Most and Least Frequent Eclipses

The highest number of eclipses possible in a year is 7, as in 1935, when there were 5 solar and 2 lunar eclipses; or 4 solar and 3 lunar eclipses, as occurred in 1982. The lowest possible number in a year is 2, both of which must be solar, as in 1944 and 1969.

Earliest Recorded Eclipses

For the Middle East, lunar eclipses have been extrapolated to 3450 BC and solar eclipses to 4200 BC.

Comets

The earliest records of comets date from the 7th century BC. The speeds of the estimated 2,000,000 comets vary from 700 mph in outer space to 1,250,000 mph when near the sun.

The successive appearances of Halley's Comet have been traced back to 467 BC. It was first depicted in the Nuremberg Chronicle of 684 AD. The first prediction of its return by Edmund Halley (1656–1742) proved true on Christmas Day, 1758, 16 years after his death.

The European satellite *Giotto* (launched July 2, 1985) penetrated to within 335 mi of the nucleus of Halley's Comet, Mar 13–14, 1986, to discover that it was 9.3 mi in length and velvet black in color.

Closest Comet Approach to Earth

On July 1, 1770 Lexell's Comet, traveling at a speed of 23.9 miles per sec (relative to the sun), came within 745,000 miles of the earth. However, the earth is believed to have passed through the tail of Halley's Comet, most recently on May 19, 1910.

Largest Comets

The tail of the Great Comet of 1843 trailed for 205 million miles. The bow shock of Holmes' Comet of 1892 once measured 1½ million mi in diameter.

Shortest and Longest Comet Period

Of all the recorded periodic comets (these are members of the solar system), the one which most frequently returns is Encke's Comet, first identified in 1786. Its period of 1,206 days (3.3 years) is the shortest established. Not one of its 53 returns (to the end of 1983) has been missed by astronomers. Now increasingly faint, it is expected to "die" by Feb 1994. The most frequently observed comets are Schwassmann-Wachmann I, Kopff and Oterma, which can be observed every year between Mars and Jupiter.

At the other extreme is Delavan's Comet of 1914, whose path has not been accurately determined. It is not expected to return for perhaps 24 million years.

PLANETS

The nine major planets (including the earth) are bodies within the solar system which revolve around the sun in definite orbits. The search for Planet X continues.

Mars Meteorites

Eight SNC meteorites named after their find sites at Shergotty, India; Nakla, Egypt and Chassigny, France, are believed to have emanated from Mars. Mars, known since 1965 to be cratered, has temperatures ranging from 85°F to −190°F.

Planet Features

By far the highest and most spectacular surface feature is Olympus Mons (formerly Nix Olympica) in the Tharsis region of Mars, with a diameter of 310–370 miles and a height of 75,450–95,150 ft above the surrounding plain. Venus has a canyon 4 mi deep and 250 mi long 1,000 mi south of Venusian equator. The ice cliff on the Uranian moon Miranda is 65,000 ft high.

Viewed from earth, by far the brightest of the five planets visible to the naked eye is Venus, with a maximum magnitude of −4.4. The faintest is Pluto, with a magnitude of 15. Uranus at magnitude 5.5 is only marginally visible.

Earth is the densest planet with an average figure of 5.515 times that of water, while Saturn has an average density only about one-eighth of this value or 0.687 times that of water.

The most dramatic recorded conjunction (coming together) of the seven principal members of the solar system besides the earth (sun, moon, Mercury, Venus, Mars, Jupiter and Saturn) occurred on Feb 5, 1962, when 16° covered all seven during an eclipse. It is possible that the seven-fold conjunction of Sept 1186 spanned only 12°. The next notable conjunction will take place May 5, 2000.

Largest, Fastest and Hottest Planets

Jupiter, with an equatorial diameter of 88,846 miles and a polar diameter of 83,082 miles, is the largest of the 9 major planets, with a mass 317.83 times and a volume 1,321.4 times that of the earth. It also has the shortest period of rotation, with a "day" of only 9 hours 50 min 30.003 sec in its equatorial zone.

Mercury, which orbits the sun at an average distance of 35,983,100 miles, has a period of revolution of 87.9686 days, so giving the highest average speed in orbit of 107,030 mph.

A surface temperature of 864°F has been estimated from measurements made from Venus by the USSR probes *Venera* and US *Pioneer* Cytherean surface probes.

Brightest Star

Sirius A (*Alpha Canis Majoris*), also known as the Dog Star, is apparently the brightest star of the 5,776 stars visible in the heavens, with an apparent magnitude of −1.46. It is in the constellation *Canis Major* and is visible in the winter months of the northern hemisphere, being due south at midnight on the last day of the year. The Sirius system is 8.64 light-years distant and has a luminosity 26 times as much as that of the sun. It has a diameter of 1,450,000 miles and a mass of 4.20×10^{27} metric tons. The faint white dwarf companion star Sirius B has a diameter of only 6,000 miles but is 350,000 times heavier than the earth. Sirius will reach a maximum magnitude of −1.67 in *c.* 61,000 AD.

Most and Least Luminous Stars

If all the stars could be viewed at the same distance the most luminous would be *Eta Carinae* (see *Most Massive Star*) which now has a total luminosity 6,500,000 times greater than that of the sun, but at its peak brightness in 1843 was at least 10 times more luminous than this. The visually brightest star is the hypergiant *Cygnus* OB2 No. 12, which is 5,900 light-years distant from our own galaxy and which has an absolute visual magnitude of −9.9 and is therefore visually 810,000 times brighter than our sun. This brightness may be matched by the supergiant IV b 59 in the nearby galaxy Messier 101, but this depends on the distance adopted for this galaxy (estimates vary between 15,600,000 and 19,700,000 light-years). The variable π *Carinae* in *c.* 1840 had an absolute luminosity 4 million times that of the sun. The faintest star detected is the recently discovered RG 0058.8-2807 (see *Lightest Star*) which has a total luminosity only 0.00021 that of the sun and an absolute visual magnitude of 20.2, so that the visual brightness is less than one millionth that of the sun.

Brightest and Latest Super-Nova

The brightest star seen by man is believed to be the super-nova SN 1006 in Apr 1006 near *Beta Lupi* which flared for 2 years and attained a magnitude of −9 to −10. The remnant is believed to be the radio source G.327.6 + 14.5, nearly 3,000 light-years distant. Others have occurred in 1054, 1604, 1885 and most recently on Feb 23, 1987 when Ian Shelton sighted that designated −69,202 in the Large Magellanic Cloud 170,000 light years distant.

Black Holes

This term for a star that has undergone complete gravitational collapse was first used by Prof John Archibald Wheeler at an Institute for Space Studies meeting in NYC on Dec 29, 1967.

The first tentative identification of a Black Hole was announced in Dec 1972 in the binary-star X-ray source Cygnus X-1. The best candidate is LMC X-3 of 10 solar masses, 180,000 light-years distant, reported in Jan 1983. The critical size has been estimated to be as low as a diameter of 3.67 miles. One at the center of the Seyfert galaxy, NGC 4151 in *Canes Venatici*, was estimated by Michael Preston (GB) in Oct 1983 to be of between 50–100 million solar masses.

Longest Name

The longest name for any star is *Shurnarkabtishashutu*, the Arabic for "under the southern horn of the bull."

Aurorae

Polar lights, known since 1560 as Aurora Borealis or Northern Lights in the northern hemisphere and since 1773 as Aurora Australis in the southern hemisphere, are caused by electrical solar discharges in the upper atmosphere and occur most frequently in high latitudes. Aurorae are visible at some time on *every* clear dark night in the polar areas within 20° latitude of the magnetic poles.

The extreme height of aurorae has been measured at 620 miles, while the lowest may descend to 45 miles.

Reliable figures exist only from 1952 since when the record high and low number of nights of auroral displays in Shetland (geomagnetic Lat. 63°) has been 203 (1957) and 58 (1965). The most recent great display in northwest Europe was that of Sept 4–5, 1958. Extreme cases of displays in very low latitudes were those reported at Cuzco, Peru (Aug 2, 1744); Honolulu, Hawaii (Sept 1, 1859); and, questionably, Singapore (Sept 25, 1909).

NORTHERN LIGHTS, a display caused by solar electrical discharges in the upper atmosphere, occur most often in the polar areas. *(Jim Grace/Science Photo Library)*

THE UNIVERSE

Outside the Milky Way galaxy, which is part of the so-called Local Group of galaxies moving at a speed of 1,400,000 mph relative to the microwave background radiation in a direction offset 44° from the center of the Virgo cluster, there exist 10,000 million other galaxies.

The largest discrete object in the universe is a filamentary arrangement of Abell clusters stretching across the South Galactic Cap and measuring 1,000 million light-years, 5.88×10^{21} mi in length, announced by Jack O. Burns and David Batuski of the Univ of NM, Albuquerque, in May 1984 measuring 730 million light-years.

Farthest Visible Object

The most remote heavenly body visible to the naked eye is the Great Galaxy in *Andromeda* (Mag. 3.47) known as Messier 31. This is a rotating nebula of spiral form, its distance from the earth about 2,150,000 light-years, or about 12,600,000,000,000,000,000 miles, and it is moving toward us.

It is just possible, however, that, under ideal seeing conditions, Messier 33, the Spiral in Triangulum (Mag. 5.79), can be glimpsed by the naked eye of keen-sighted people at a distance of 2,360,000 light-years.

Quasars

An occultation of 3C-273, observed from Australia on Aug 5, 1962, enabled the existence of quasi-stellar radio sources ("quasars" or QSO's) to be announced by Maarten Schmidt (b Netherlands 1929). The red shift proved to be $z = 0.158$. Quasars have immensely high luminosity for bodies so distant and of such small diameter. In May 1983, it was announced that the quasar S5 0014+21 had a luminosity 1.1×10^{15} times greater than that of the sun. The first double quasar (0957 + 56) among the 1,500 known quasars was announced in May 1980.

Pulsars

The earliest observation of a pulsating radio source of "pulsar" CP 1919 (now PSR 1919 + 21) by Dr Jocelyn Bell Burnell was announced from the Mullard Radio Astronomy Observatory, Cambridgeshire, England, on Feb 24, 1968. It had been detected on Nov 28, 1967.

The fastest spinning is pulsar 1937 + 214 which is in the region of the minor constellation *Vulpecula* (the Fox), 16,000 light-years distant. It has a pulse period of 1.557806449 milli-sec and a spindown rate of 1.0511×10^{-19} sec/sec. However, the most accurate stellar clock is the pulsar, PSR 1955+09, which has a spindown rate of only 2.1×10^{-20} sec/sec.

Remotest Object

Both the interpretation of very large red shifts exhibited by quasars and the estimation of equivalent distances remain controversial. The record red shift of z = 4.43 for quasar 0051-279 was announced by Stephen Warren *et al* in November, 1987 from analyses from plates from the UK Schmidt Telescope, Siding Spring, NSW, Australia. Assuming an "observable horizon" of 14 billion light-years, this quasar would be more than 13.1 billion light-years distant. The 3K background radiation or primordial hiss discovered in 1965 by Arno Penzias and Robert Wilson of Bell Laboratories appears to be moving at a velocity of 99.9998% of the speed of light.

Age of the Universe

For the age of the universe a value of 16.3 ± 2 eons or gigayears (an eon or gigayear being 1 billion years) is obtained from cosmochronology and nucleochronology. Based on the presently accepted Friedman models of the universe, with zero cosmological constant, then the equivalent Hubble ratio is about 60 km/sec Mpc, which compares to the most likely experimental value of 80 km s^{-1} Mpc^{-1}. In 1973 an *ex nihilo* creation was postulated by Edward P. Tryon (US). Modified versions of the Inflationary Model, originally introduced by Alan Guth (US) in 1981, now rival the "Big Bang" theory of creation.

ROCKETRY AND MISSILES

War rockets, propelled by a charcoal-saltpeter-sulphur gunpowder, were described by Tsen Kung Liang of China in 1042. These early rockets became known in Europe by 1258.

The first launching of a liquid-fueled rocket (patented July 14, 1914) was by Dr Robert Hutchings Goddard (1882–1945) (US) at Auburn, Mass, March 16, 1926, when his rocket reached an altitude of 41 ft and traveled a distance of 184 ft. The USSR's earliest rocket was the semi-liquid-fueled GIRD-IX tested Aug 17, 1933.

Longest Ranges

On March 16, 1962 Nikita Khrushchev, then Premier of the USSR, claimed in Moscow that the USSR possessed a "global rocket" with a range of about 19,000 miles (more than half the earth's circumference), capable of hitting any target in the world from either direction.

Most Powerful Rocket

It has been suggested that the USSR lunar booster which blew up at Tyuratam in the summer (July 3) of 1969 had a thrust of 10–14 million lb.

The most powerful rocket is the USSR's *Energia* launched on May 15, 1987 from the Baikonur Cosmodrome. Weighing 2,205 tons and with a thrust of 4,410 tons it is capable of placing 143 tons into low Earth orbit. It measures 196.8 ft tall with a maximum diameter of 52.5 ft and comprises a core stage powered by 4 liquid oxygen and liquid hydrogen engines—the first cryogenic units flown by the Russians. There are also 4 strap-on boosters powered by single RD 170 engines burning liquid oxygen and kerosene. An 8-strap version with an upper stage could place up to 237 tons into low Earth orbit, 35 tons to the Moon and 29 tons to Venus or Mars.

Closest Approach to the Sun by a Rocket

The research spacecraft *Helios B* approached within 27 million miles of the sun on Apr 16, 1976. It was carrying both US and West German instrumentation.

Remotest Man-Made Object

Pioneer 10 launched from Kennedy Space Center, Cape Canaveral, Fla, crossed the mean orbit of Pluto on Oct 17, 1986, being then at a distance of 3,670 million mi. It will be beyond the furthest extension of Pluto's orbit by April 1989 and will continue into space at *30,450 mph*. In 34,593 AD it will make its nearest approach to the *Star Ross* 248,103 light-years distant. Before 1991, *Voyager I*, travelling faster, will surpass *Pioneer 10* in remoteness from the earth.

If an alien body should encounter *Pioneer 10*, it will find a map on board giving earth's location in relation to 14 radio beacon stars and an engraving of two earthlings, one male, one female. *Pioneer 10* in 5 billion years, if not intercepted, may cross the rim of our galaxy. By that time, however, both sun and earth will no doubt be dead!

First Artificial Satellite

The first artificial satellite was successfully put into orbit at an altitude of 142/588 miles and a velocity of more than 17,750 mph from Tyuratam, a site located 170 miles east of the Aral Sea, on the night of Oct 4, 1957. This spherical satellite, *Sputnik 1* ("Fellow Traveler") officially designated "Satellite 1957 Alpha 2," weighed 184.3 lb, with a diameter of 22.8 in, and its lifetime is believed to have been 92 days, ending on Jan 4, 1958. It was designed under the direction of former Gulag prisoner, Dr Sergey Pavlovich Korolyov (1907–66).

The physical laws controlling the flight of artificial satellites were first propounded by Sir Isaac Newton (1642–1727) in his *Philosophiae Naturalis Principia Mathematica* ('Mathematical Principles of Natural Philosophy'), begun in March 1686 and first published in the summer of 1687.

Earliest Successful Manned Satellites

The first successful manned space flight began at 9:07 a.m. (Moscow time), or 6:07 a.m. G.M.T., Apr 12, 1961. Flight Major (later Colonel) Yuriy Alekseyevich Gagarin (1934–68) completed a single orbit of the earth in 108 min in the USSR's space vehicle *Vostok* ("East") *1* (10,416 lb). The maximum speed was 17,560 mph and the maximum altitude 203.2 miles in a flight of 25,394.5 miles.

The explosion of the *Challenger S1L* space shuttle on Jan 28, 1986, the worst human disaster in space history, when 7 were killed, has caused NASA to delay further manned space exploration. The number killed in launcher explosions in the USSR has never been revealed.

Heaviest and Largest Space Object

The heaviest object orbited is the Saturn V third stage with *Apollo 15* (spacecraft) which, prior to trans-lunar injection in parking orbit weighed 154.88 tons. The 442-lb US RAE (Radio Astronomy Explorer) B or *Explorer 49* launched on June 10, 1973 had, however, antennae 1,500 ft from tip to tip.

Most Expensive Project

The total cost of the US manned space program up to and including the lunar mission of *Apollo 17* has been estimated to be $25,541,400,000. The first 15 years of the USSR space programme from 1958 to Sept 1973 has been estimated to have cost $45 billion. The cost of the NASA Shuttle program was $9.9 billion to the launch of *Columbia* on Apr 12, 1981.

First Extra-Terrestrial Vehicle

The first wheeled vehicle landed on the moon was *Lunakhod I* which began its earth-controlled travels on Nov 17, 1970. It moved a total of 6.54 miles on gradients up to 30° in the Mare Imbrium.

LONGEST MANNED FLIGHT: Col Romanenko (USSR) with 2 partners stayed in space 326 days of 1987, traveling 98.1 million miles.

Astronauts

Earliest
Col Yuriy Gagarin
(b Mar 9, 1934) (USSR)
Vostok 1 Apr 12, 1961

First Woman
Lt-Col Valentina
Vladinirovna Tereshkova
(USSR) (48 orbits)
(b Mar 6, 1937)
Vostok 6 June 16, 1963

First Space Walk
Lt-Col Aleksey A. Leonov
(b May 20, 1934) (USSR)
Voskhod 2 Mar 18, 1965

First Undisputed Fatality
Col Vladimir Komarov
(b Mar 16, 1927) (USSR)
Soyuz 1 Apr 23, 1967

First on Moon
Neil A. Armstrong
(b Aug 5, 1930) (US)
Apollo XI July 21, 1969

Longest on Moon
Capt Eugene A. Cernan (USN)
(b Mar 14, 1934) (US)
Dr Harrison H. Schmitt
(b July 3, 1935) (US)
74 hours 59 min
Apollo 17 Dec 7–19, 1972

Youngest
Col Gherman S. Titov (USSR)
(b Sept 11, 1935)
(25 yrs 329 days)
Vostok 2 Aug 6, 1961

Oldest
Karl G. Henize (US)
(58 years)
19th Space Shuttle July 29, 1985

First Untethered "Float" in Space
(wearing a Manned
Maneuvering Unit)
Man: Capt Bruce McCandless
(USN) (b 1938)
Challenger Feb 7, 1984

Woman: Dr Kathryn Sullivan
(b 1952) (US)
Challenger Oct 11, 1984

First Feminine Space Walk
Mme Svetlana
Savitskaya-Khatkovsky
Salyut 7 (USSR) July 25, 1984

Longest Manned Flight
326 days
Col Yuri Romanenko, 43
Alexandr Alexandrov,
and Anatoly Levchenko
(USSR) 98.1 million miles
Soyuz TM-3 Feb 5–Dec 29, 1987
Valeriy Ryumin (USSR)
3 flights aggregating 326 days

Most Journeys
Capt John Watts Young
(USN) (b 1930)
6 space flights to Dec 8, 1983
Total 34 days
19 hours 42 min 13 sec

Largest Crew
8, aboard *Challenger 9* (US),
launched Oct 30, 1986 and
lasting 7 days 44 min 51 sec.

Chapter 5

The Scientific World

ELEMENTS

All known matter in, on, and beyond the earth is made up of chemical elements. It is estimated that there are 10^{87} electrons in the known universe. The total of naturally occurring elements is 94, comprising, at ordinary temperature, 2 liquids, 11 gases and 81 solids. The so-called "fourth state" of matter is plasma, when negatively charged electrons and positively charged ions are in flux.

Lightest and Heaviest Sub-Nuclear Particles

By Apr 1986, the existence was accepted of 29 "stable" particles, 56 meson resonance multiplets *and* 48 baryon resonance multiplets representing the eventual discovery of 224 particles and an equal number of anti-particles. The heaviest "stable" particle fully accepted is the neutral weak gauge boson, the Z°, of mass 92.9 ± 1.6 GeV which was first detected in May 1983 by the UA1 Collaboration, CERN, Geneva, Switzerland using the 540 GeV Super Proton Synchrotron proton-antiproton beam collider. The heaviest hadron accepted is the upsilon (6S) meson resonance of mass 11.02 GeV and lifetime 8.3×10^{-24} sec, which consists of a bottom or beauty quark and its anti-quark, and which was first identified in Oct 1984 by two groups using the electron storage ring facilities at Cornell Univ, Ithaca, NY. Sub-atomic concepts require that the masses of the graviton, photon, and neutrino should all be zero. Based on the sensitivities of various cosmological theories, upper limits for the masses of these particles are 7.6×10^{-67} g for the graviton; 3.0×10^{-53} g for the photon and 1.4×10^{-32} g for the neutrino (*cf.* 9.10939×10^{-28} g for the mass of an electron).

Newest Particles

The discovery in July 1984 by the Crystal Ball Collaboration, Hamburg, W Germany, of a particle of mass 8.32 GeV known as the "zeta," and which was associated with the existence of the important theoretical particle known as the Higgs boson, has not been confirmed.

Most and Least Stable Particles

Experiments from 1982 to 1984 have confirmed that the proton has a lifetime in excess of 1×10^{30} years compared to theoretical predictions based on the "grand unified theory," which suggests that the lifetime may be less than 1×10^{34} years. The least stable or shortest-lived particles are the two baryon resonances N(2220) and N(2600), both 1.6×10^{-24} sec, although the *predicted* lifetimes of both the weak gauge bosons, the $W \pm$ and Z°, are 2.4×10^{-25} sec.

Most Absorbent Substance

The US Dept of Agriculture Research Service announced on Aug 18, 1974 that "H-span" or Super Slurper, composed of one half starch derivative and one fourth each of acrylamide and acrylic acid, can, when treated with iron, retain water 1,300 times its own weight.

Smelliest Substance

The most evil-smelling substance, of the 17,000 smells so far classified, must be a matter of opinion, but ethyl mercaptan (C_2H_5SH) and butyl seleno- mercaptan (C_4H_9SeH) are powerful claimants, each with a smell reminiscent of a combination of rotting cabbage, garlic, onions and sewer gas.

Most Expensive Perfume

The retail prices of the most expensive perfumes tend to be fixed with an eye to public relations rather than levels solely dictated by the cost of ingredients and packaging. The Chicago-based firm Jōvan marketed from Mar 1984 a cologne called Andron which contains a trace of the attractant pheromone androstenol which had a cost of $2,750 per oz.

Perfume Shower

Some 198 gallons of jasmine essence perfume were sprayed over 140,000 people who attended a local carnival in Rio de Janeiro, Brazil, on Feb 9, 1986, as arranged by Carlos Norberto Varaldo of Chiero da Terra Perfumes.

Most Potent Poison

The rickettsial disease, Q-fever, can be instituted by a *single* organism but is only fatal in 1 in 1,000 cases. About 10 organisms of *Francisella tularenesis* (formerly known as *Pasteurella tularenesis*) can institute tularemia, variously called alkali disease, Francis disease or deerfly fever, and this is fatal in upwards of 10 cases in 1,000.

The most lethal man-made chemical is TCDD (2,3,7,8-tetrachlorodibenzo-p-dioxin) utilized in herbicides, discovered in 1872. It is said to be 150,000 times more deadly than cyanide at 3.1×10^{-9} moles/kg.

Most Powerful Nerve Gas

VX, 300 times more toxic than phosgene ($COCl_2$) used in World War I, was developed at the Chemical Defence Experimental Establishment, Porton Down, Wiltshire, England in 1952. Patents applied for in 1962 and published in Feb 1974, show it to be Ethyl S-2-diisopropylamimoethylphosphonothiolate. The lethal dosage is 10 mg-minute/m^3 airborne or 0.3 mg orally.

Most Powerful Drugs

The most powerful commonly available drug is d-Lysergic Acid Diethylamide tartrate (LSD-25, $C_{20}H_{25}N_3O$) first produced in 1938 for common cold research and as a hallucinogen by Dr Albert Hoffmann (Swiss) Apr 16–19, 1943.

The most potent analgesic drug is the morphine-like R33799, confirmed in 1978 to have almost 12,000 times the potency of morphine.

Interferon was reportedly available for $10 per millionth of a microgram.

Most Prescribed Drug

The top-selling prescription drug in the world is the anti-ulcer drug Zantac, manufactured by Glaxo Holdings PLC. Worldwide sales in 1986 exceeded $1 billion.

Finest Powder

The ultimate in fine powder is solid helium, which was first postulated to be a monatomic powder as early as 1964.

DRINK

Most Alcoholic Liquor

The strength of liquor is expressed by degrees proof. In the US, proof is double the actual percentage of alcohol (C_2H_5OH) by volume at 60°F in a liquor. Pure or absolute alcohol is thus 200 degrees proof. A "hangover" is said to be aggravated by the presence of toxic congenerics such as amyl alcohol ($C_5H_{11}OH$).

During independence (1918–40) the Estonian Liquor Monopoly marketed 196 proof potato alcohol. In 31 US states *Everclear* (190 proof or 95% alcohol) is marketed by the American Distilling Co, "primarily as a base for homemade cordials."

Most Expensive Wine

Record prices paid for single bottles *usually* arise when two or more self-promoters are seeking publicity. They bear little relation to the market value.

The highest price paid for any bottle has been £105,000 ($157,500) for a 1787 Chateau Lafite claret sold to Christopher Forbes (US) at Christie's London on Dec 5, 1985. The price was affected by the bottle having been initialed by Thomas Jefferson. In Nov 1986 its cork, dried out by exhibition lights, slipped thus making the wine undrinkable.

Oldest Vintage Wine

The oldest datable wine ever found were two bottles from Xinyang, Hunan, China in 1980 from a tomb dated to 1300 BC. A wine jar recovered in Rome bears the label "Q. Lutatio C. Mario Cos," meaning that it was produced in the consulship of 102 BC. A bottle of

1748 Rudesheimer Rosewein was auctioned at Christie's of London, for £260 ($570) Dec 6, 1979.

Greatest Wine Auction and Tasting

The largest single sale of wine was conducted by Christie's of London, July 10–11, 1974 at Quaglino's Ballroom when 2,325 lots containing 432,000 bottles realized £962,190 (then $2,309,256).

The largest wine-tasting ever reported was that staged by the Wine Institute at St Francis Hotel, San Francisco, on July 17, 1980 with 125 pourers, 90 openers and a consumption of 3,000 bottles.

Strongest and Weakest Beer

The strongest beer as measured by original gravity is Samichlaus Dark 1987 brewed by Brauerei Hürlimann of Zürich, Switzerland. It has an original gravity of 1228° and is 14.93 per cent alcohol by volume at 20°C.

The most alcoholic beer in the world is Domesday Ale brewed by the Cornish Brewery Company Ltd, Redruth, Cornwall, with an alcohol content of 15.86 per cent by volume. It has an original gravity of 1143.5°.

The weakest liquid ever marketed as beer was a sweet ersatz beer which was brewed in Germany by Sunner, Colne-Kalk, in 1918. It had an original gravity of 1000.96°, with less than 0.2% alcohol.

Largest and Smallest Bottles

The largest bottles normally used in the wine and spirit trade are the Jeroboam (equal to 4 bottles of champagne or, rarely, of brandy, and from 5 to 6½ bottles of claret, depending on whether the bottle was blown or molded) and the double magnum (equal, since *c*. 1934, to 4

LARGE WINE BOTTLE: Equal in volume to 35 ordinary wine bottles this 26-liter champagne bottle is called a "Sovereign" by Taittinger, the producer. Here, the French ambassador in Norway is unveiling the new-size bottle for the launching of the Norwegian passenger liner "Sovereign of the Sea" in Jan 1988.

PROOF OF THE LONGEST NEGATIVE: Photographer Bob Paluzzi shows a contact print of his 200° super-wide landscape shot of the skyline of Las Vegas, Nev. With a 16-in camera, he took it all in a single shot.

bottles of claret or, more rarely, red burgundy). A complete set of champagne bottles would consist of the ¼ bottle, ½ bottle, bottle, magnum, Jeroboam, Rehoboam, Methuselah, Salmanazer, Balthazar and the Nebuchadnezzar, which has a capacity of 16 liters (33.8 pints), and is equivalent to 20 bottles.

On the occasion of the launching of the passenger liner *Sovereign of the Sea* in Jan 1988, a bottle was provided by the champagne producers, Taittinger, equal in volume to 35 whole wine bottles, or 26 liters. It was suggested that this be known as a 'Sovereign'.

In May 1958 a 5-ft-tall sherry bottle with a capacity of 20½ Imperial gallons (24.6 US gallons) was blown in Stoke-on-Trent, Staffordshire, England. This bottle, with the capacity of 131 normal bottles, was named an "Adelaide."

The smallest bottles of liquor now sold are White Horse bottles of Scotch whisky containing 1.3 milliliters (about 4/100ths of an ounce) for about 50 cents per bottle in "cases" of 12.

Champagne Cork Flight

The longest distance for a champagne cork to fly from an untreated and unheated bottle 4 ft from level ground is 109 ft 6 in by Capt Michael Hill at Kennington, Eng on Nov 3, 1987.

PHOTOGRAPHY

Earliest Cameras

The earliest veiled reference to a photograph on glass taken in a camera was in a letter from Joseph Nicéphore Niepce (1765–1833), a

French physician and scientist, dated July 19, 1822. It was a photograph of a copper engraving of Pope Pius VII taken at Gras, near Chalon-sur-Saône.

One of the earliest photographs taken was one of a diamond-paned window in Lacock Abbey, Wiltshire, England, taken in Aug 1835 by William Henry Fox Talbot (1800–1877), the inventor of the negative-positive process.

Largest and Smallest Cameras

The largest and most expensive industrial camera ever built is the 30-ton Rolls-Royce camera now owned by BPCC Graphics Ltd of Derby, England, completed in 1956. It measures 8 ft 10 in high, 8 ft 3 in wide and 46 ft long. The lens is a 63-in-f/16 Cooke Apochromatic. It is still in full use.

Apart from cameras built for intra-cardiac surgery and espionage, the smallest camera marketed has been the circular Japanese "Petal" camera with a diameter of 1.14 in and a thickness of 0.65 in. It has a focal length of 0.47 in (12 mm).

Fastest Camera

A camera built for research into high-power lasers by the Blackett Laboratory of Imperial College of Science and Technology, London, registers images at the rate of 33 billion per sec.

Most Expensive Cameras and Equipment

The most expensive complete range of camera equipment is that of Nikon of Tokyo, Japan who marketed a range of 24 cameras with 172 lenses and 553 accessories in 1987. The total cost of the range would be $249,750.

The highest auction price for an antique camera was £21,000

($42,000) for a J. B. Dancer stereo camera patented in 1856 and sold at Christie's, London, on Oct 12, 1977.

Longest Negative

Using a 16-in Century Cirkut camera, Robert J. Paluzzi captured a 200° view of Las Vegas, Nev, in a single shot on June 22, 1985. The resulting negative measured 9 ft by 16 in.

TELESCOPES

Earliest Telescope

Although there is evidence that early Arabian scientists understood something of the magnifying power of lenses, the first known use of lenses to form a telescope has been attributed to Roger Bacon (*c.*1214–92) in England. The prototype of modern refracting telescopes was completed by Johannes Lippershey for the Netherlands government on Oct 2, 1608.

Largest Reflector

The largest telescope is the alt-azimuth mounted, 236.2-inch telescope sited on Mt Semirodriki, near Zelenchukskaya in the Caucasus Mts, USSR, at an altitude of 6,830 ft. Work on the mirror, weighing 78 tons, was not completed until the summer of 1974. Regular observations were begun on Feb 7, 1976, after 16 years' work. The weight of the 138-ft-high assembly is 946 tons. Being the most powerful of all telescopes, its range, which includes the location of objects down to the 25th magnitude, represents the limits of the observable universe. Its light-gathering power would enable it to detect the light from a candle at a distance of 15,000 miles.

Work started on Sept 15, 1985, on the $70 million Keck 393.7-in reflector comprising 36 independently controlled fitting hexagonal mirrors for Caltech and the Univ of California. It is sited on Mt Mauna Kea, Hawaii and due to be completed by 1989.

Note: The attachment of an electronic charge-coupled-device (CCD) increases the "light-grasp" of a telescope by a factor up to 100 fold. Thus a 200-in telescope achieves the light-gathering capacity of a 1,000-in telescope.

Largest Refractor

The largest refracting (*i.e.* magnification by lenses) telescope in the world is the 62-ft-long, 40-in telescope completed in 1897 at the Yerkes Observatory, Williams Bay, Wis, belonging to the University of Chicago. In 1900, a 49.2-in refractor 180 ft in length was built for the Paris Exposition, but its optical performance was too poor to justify attempts to use it.

Oldest and Highest Observatories

The oldest astronomical observatory building extant is the "Tower of the Winds'' used by Andronichus of Cyrrhos in Athens, Greece, *c.* 70 BC. It is equipped with sundials and a water clock.

The highest-altitude observatory in the world is the University of Denver's High Altitude Observatory at an altitude of 14,100 ft, opened in 1973, on Mt Evans, Colo. The principal instrument is a 24-in Ealing Beck reflecting telescope.

Largest Radio Telescope

The largest radio-telescope installation is the US National Science Foundation VLA (Very Large Array). It is Y-shaped with each arm 13 miles long with 27 mobile antennae (each 82 ft in diameter) on rails. It is 50 miles west of Socorro in the Plains of San Augustin, NM and was dedicated on Oct 10, 1980 at a cost of $78 million.

A computer-linked very long base-line array of 82-ft radio telescopes stretched over 2,600 miles on Lat 49.3°N has been planned by the Canadian Astronomical Society.

Largest Dish Telescopes

Radio waves of extraterrestrial origin were first detected by Karl Jansky of Bell Telephone Laboratories, Holmdel, NJ, using a 100-ft-long shortwave rotatable antenna in 1932. The largest trainable dish-type radio telescope is the 328-ft-diameter, 3,360-ton assembly at the Max Planck Institute for Radio Astronomy of Bonn in the Effelsberger Valley, W Germany; it became operative in May 1971. The cost of the installation, begun in Nov 1967, was DM36,920,000 ($14,760,000).

The world's largest dish-type radio telescope is the partially-steerable ionospheric assembly built over a natural bowl at Arecibo, Puerto Rico, completed in Nov 1963 at a cost of about $9 million. It has a diameter of 1,000 ft and the dish covers 18½ acres. Its sensitivity was raised by a factor of 1,000 and its range to the edge of the observable universe at some 15,000 million light-years by the fitting of new aluminum plates at a cost of $8,800,000. Rededication was on Nov 16, 1974.

Space Telescope

The first space observatory was the US Orbiting Solar observatory 0504 launched on Oct 18, 1967. The largest will be the $1.2 billion NASA Space Telescope of 12.32 tons and 43 ft in overall length with a 94.5 inch reflector eventually to be placed in orbit at *c* 300 mi altitude aboard a US Space Shuttle.

Planetaria

The ancestor of the planetarium is the rotatable Gottorp Globe, built by Andreas Busch in Denmark between 1654 and 1664 to the orders of Olearius, court mathematician to Duke Frederick III of Holstein. It is 34.6 ft in circumference, weighs 4 tons and is now preserved in Leningrad, USSR. The stars were painted on the inside.

The earliest optical installation was not until 1923 in the Deutsches Museum, Munich, by Zeiss of Jena, Germany.

The world's largest planetarium, with a diameter of 82½ ft, is in Moscow.

GEMS

Rarest and Commonest Minerals

The rarest mineral cannot be certainly established. The total known amount of scotlandite ($PbSO_3$) comprises only a few tens of milligrams. Though probably found in the 19th century in Leadhills, Strathclyde, Scotland this first naturally occurring yellowish sulphite was only certainly identified in 1978 by Dr R. S. W. Braithwaite. The world's commonest mineral is silicate of calcium, iron magnesium and manganese collectively known as olivine.

Hardest Gems

The hardest of all gems, and hardest known naturally occurring substance, is diamond, which is, chemically, pure carbon. Diamond has 5 times the indentation hardness of the next hardest mineral, corundum (Al_2O_3). Hardnesses are compared on Mohs' scale, on which talc is 1, a fingernail is 2½, window glass 5, topaz 8, corundum 9, and diamond 10.

Smallest Brilliant Cut Diamond

A diamond weighing 0.00063 of a carat, 0.02 in in size, is owned by Gebroedeus van den Wouwer of Antwerp, Belgium.

Largest Crystals

An 187-ton beryl ($Be_3Al_2Si_6O_{18}$) measuring 59 ft long and 11½ ft in diameter was recorded at Malakialina, Madagascar (formerly Malagasy Republic) in 1976.

A 520,000-carat (229-lb) aquamarine, [Be_3Al_2 $(SiO_3)_6$] found near Marambaia, Brazil in 1910, yielded over 200,000 carats of gem-quality cut stones.

Most Valuable Emerald

The highest price paid at auction (Apr 2, 1987 at Sotheby's, Geneva, Switzerland) for an emerald is $2,126,646 for a rectangular step-cut emerald with cut corners weighing 19.77 carats. It was mounted in 1936 by Cartier, London, as an engagement ring of (then King) Edward VIII for his bride, Wallis Warfield Simpson (later, the Duchess of Windsor), within a stylized leaf border set with brilliant-cut diamonds. The stone itself, valued at the highest per-carat rate for an emerald, was remounted in its present setting by Cartier, Paris, in1958.

Biggest Find

A 1,905-carat uncut star sapphire was found in a display of cheap stones in Nov 1986 in a Tucson, Ariz show by Roy Whetstine, a Kilgore, Texas dealer, who paid $10 for the stone that is worth $2 million.

A 599-carat diamond was found in July 1986 by a worker in the Premier Mine, near Pretoria, S Africa. But its discovery was kept secret until March 11, 1988, when Julian Ogilvie Thompson, chairman of the De Beers Co, named it the Centenary Diamond in honor of the company's birthday. In cut form the diamond will weigh about 350 carats and be worth $30 million.

Densest Gem Mineral

The densest of all gem minerals is stibiotantalite $[(SbO)_2(Ta,Nb)_2O_6]$, a rare brownish-yellow mineral found in San Diego County, Calif with a density of 7.46 grams per cc. The alloy platiniridium has a density of more than 22.0.

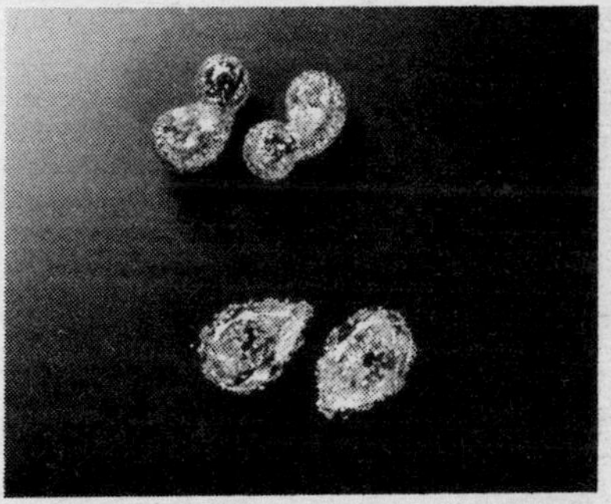

$2,273,311 for a pair of CANARY YELLOW DIAMOND LAPEL CLIPS (above) by Harry Winston—from the Duchess of Windsor's jewelry collection sold at Sotheby's, Geneva, Apr 1987. In this lot were earclips (below) that sold for less than record amounts.

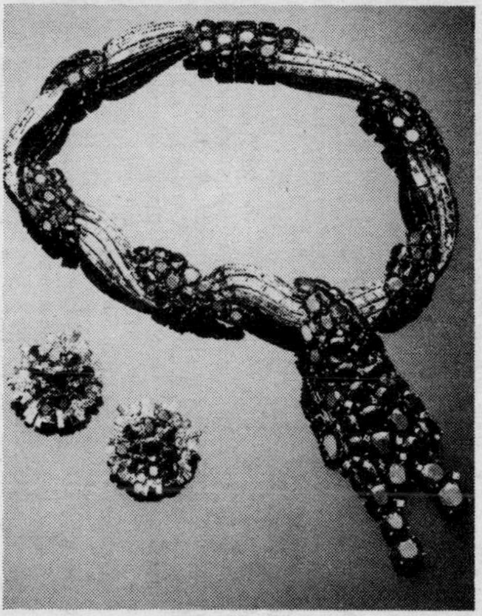

$2,603,308 RUBY AND DIAMOND NECKLACE: This record piece was auctioned in the sale of the Duchess of Windsor's collection at Sotheby's Geneva, Apr 1987.

PRECIOUS STONE RECORDS

The carat was standardized at 205 mg (0.007054 oz) in 1877. The metric carat of 200 mg was introduced in 1914.

Largest	*Largest Cut Stone*	*Other Records*
Diamond (pure crystallized carbon) 3,106 metric carats (over 1¼ lb)—*The Cullinan*, found by Mr Gray, Jan 25, 1905, in the Premier Mine, Pretoria, South Africa. Named after mine's discoverer Sir Thomas Cullinan. Presented to King Edward VII in 1907. The first synthetic diamonds were produced by Prof H. T. Hall at the General Electric Research Laboratories, on Dec 16, 1954. In Feb 1984 a Tass report from Leningrad, USSR, announced that the Institute of High Frequency Currents had produced an artificial diamond weighing 4½ lb.	530.2 metric carats. 74 facets, pear-shaped. Cleaved from *The Cullinan* in 1908 in Amsterdam by Jak Asscher and polished by Henri Koe. Known as *The Star of Africa* No. 1 and now in the British Royal Sceptre. The *Cullinan II* is 317.40 carats. Third on the list of the 55 diamonds of more than 100 carats is the Great Mogul of 280 old carats lost in the sack of Delhi in 1739 and arguably the most valuable object ever lost. In Nov 1984 the Zale Corporation of NYC announced that it may be feasible to cut their pale yellow 890-carat uncut stone from Africa into the world's largest cut stone, one of 550–600 carats.	Diamond is the hardest-known naturally occurring substance, with 5 times the indentation hardness of the next hardest mineral, corundum. The peak hardness on the Knoop scale is 8,400 compared with an average diamond of 7,000. The rarest color for diamond is blood red. The largest example is a flawless 5.05-carat stone found in 1927 in Lichtenberg, South Africa now in a private collection in the US. The world record price per carat was set at $926,000 when a red diamond was sold at Christie's NYC, Apr 28, 1987. The 42.92 carat Terestchenko blue diamond was auctioned at Christie's, Geneva, Switz, Nov 14, 1984 for $4,580,000. The largest blue diamond is the 45.85 carat Copenhagen Blue. The Argyle field of W Australia yielded 6.2 million carats in 1983 and 5.7 million in 1984, and is now the most prolific in the world.
Emerald (green beryl) [$Be_3Al_2(SiO_3)_6$]	86,136-carat natural beryl Gleim emerald. Found in Carnaiba, Brazil, Aug 1974. Carved by Richard Chan (Hong Kong). Appraised at	An 18.35-carat ring was sold for $520,000 at Sotheby Parke Bernet, NYC, in Apr 1977.

Sapphire (corundum, any color but red) (Al_2O_3) 2,302- carat stone found at Anakie, Queensland, Australia, in *c.* 1935, now a 1,318-carat head of President Abraham Lincoln (1809–65)	1,444-carat black star stone carved from a 2,097-carat stone in 1953–55 into a bust of Pres-Gen Dwight David Eisenhower (1890–1969). 1,905-carat star bought for $10 by Texas dealer, worth $2½ million.	*Note:* Both the sapphire busts are in the custody of the Kazanjian Foundation of Los Angeles. Auction record for a single stone was set by a step-cut sapphire of 66.03 carats at £579,300 (about $1,332,400) from the Rockefeller Collection at Sotheby's, Zurich May 8, 1980.
Ruby (red corundum) (Al_2O_3) 8,500-carat semi-translucent to opaque natural ruby exhibited in Smithsonian, now cut in shape of Liberty Bell, 5½ in tall, exhibited in jeweler Kazanjian's window, Beverly Hills, Calif.	Largest star ruby is 2,475- carat Rajarathna, India, animated star of 6 lines, cut as a cabochon. Largest double star is 1,370-carat Neelanjahl cabochon cut stone displaying 12 star lines, 3 in high, 2 in diameter. Owned by G. Vidyaraj of Bangalore, India.	The highest price a ruby sold for was $100,639 per carat at Christie's sale in Geneva in Nov 1979 in the case of a 4.12-carat caspian-shaped ruby. The ability to make corundum prisms for laser technology up to over 12 in in length seems to have little bearing on the market for natural gems.

RECORDS FOR OTHER PRECIOUS MATERIALS

Largest	*Where Found*	*Notes on Present Location, etc.*
Pearl (Molluscan consecretion) 14 lb 1 oz 9½ in long × 5½ in in diameter—*Pearl of Lao-tze*	At Palawan, Philippines, May 7, 1934, in shell of giant clam	The property of Wilburn Dowell Cobb, from 1936 until his death, valued at $4,080,000 in July 1971, sold on May 15, 1980 at auction in San Francisco by his estate for $200,000 to Peter Hoffmann, jeweler of Beverly Hills, Calif. In May 1982, an appraisal for the owners (Hoffmann and Victor Barbish) by the San Francisco Gem Laboratory suggested a value of $32,640,000. Largest known gem quality abalone pearl ever found is now in the collection of Lowell Jones of St. Louis. Weighing 349.41 carats, this beautiful pearl exhibits a fine range of color.

(*continued*)

Black Pearl 0.71 in diameter	Namarai Bay, Fiji Islands	Found by Yasuhiro Tokito on Jan 26, 1984.
Opal (SiO_2 NH_2O) 220 troy oz (yellow-orange)	Coober Pedy, Australia	The Olympic Australis (17,700 carats), found in Aug 1956, owned by Altmann & Cherny Pty Ltd is on public display in Melbourne and is valued at $1.8 million (US). An opal containing much "potch" (colorless material) named the Desert Flame was found at Andamooka, South Australia. The 34.215-carat mass first reported in Sept 1969 was broken up and auctioned off on Aug 29, 1978.
Rock Crystal (Quartz) (SiO_2) Ball: 106¾ lb 12⅞ in in diameter, the *Warner* sphere	Burma (originally a 1,000-lb piece)	US National Museum, Washington, DC
Topaz $Al_2SiO_4(F, OH)_2$ *Brazilian Princess* 21,327 carats, 221 facets (light blue)	Light blue, from Brazil	Amer Museum of Natural History, NYC, from Dec 10, 1985. Valued at $1,066,350 or $50 per carat. Cut from a 75-lb crystal. World's largest faceted stone.
Amber (coniferous fossil resin) 33 lb 10 oz	Reputedly from Burma, acquired in 1860	Bought by John Charles Bowing (d 1893) for £300 in Canton, China. Natural History Museum, London, since 1940
Nephrite Jade $Ca_2(Mgte)_5(Si_4O_{11})_2(OH)_2$ Boulder of 157.65 tons (315,315 lb), 21,300 cu ft	Reported in China, Sept 17, 1978	Jadeite can be virtually any color except red or blue. The largest-known example is a block from Burma weighing 36.96 tons.
Marble (Metamorphosed $CaCO_3$) 100.8 tons (single slab)	Quarried at Yule, Colo	A piece of over 50 tons was dressed from this slab for the coping stone of the Tomb of the Unknown Soldier in Arlington National Cemetery, Va
Nuggets—Gold (Au) 7,560 oz (472½ lb) (reef gold) *Holtermann Nugget*	Beyers & Holtermann Star of Hope Gold Mining Co, Hill End, NSW, Australia Oct 19, 1872	The purest large nugget was the Holtermann nugget, found at Moliagul, Victoria, Australia, which yielded 220 lb of pure gold from a 630-lb slab of slate. The largest nugget was the *Welcome Stranger*, found at Moliagul, Victoria, Australia in 1869, which yielded 2,248 troy oz of pure gold from 2,280¼ oz.
Silver (Ag) 2,750 lb troy	Sonora, Mexico	Appropriated by the Spanish Government before 1821

ABALONE PEARL: This ► baroque gem quality pearl is the largest known. In the collection of Lowell Jones of St Louis, it weighs 349.41 carats and is for sale at $3½ million. (*ZAN, NYC*)

LARGEST FACETED ▲ STONE: The light blue topaz called the "Brazilian Princess," weighing 21,327 carats, has 221 facets and was cut from a 75-lb crystal. Now in NYC's American Museum of Natural History, it is valued at about $50 per carat—total $1,066,350.

$1,292,000 EMERALD, found in Brazil in this form in 1974, was, after carving, said to be worth this much. ◄

SMALLEST DIAMOND to be brilliant cut with 57 facets. This feat was achieved by D. Drucker & Zohn of Amsterdam, The Netherlands, from a stone with a diameter of only 2.2 mm (0.0009 of an inch). Its weight after faceting was 0.0012 carats. Bar in photo is one inch long (1 13/16 in here). ▼

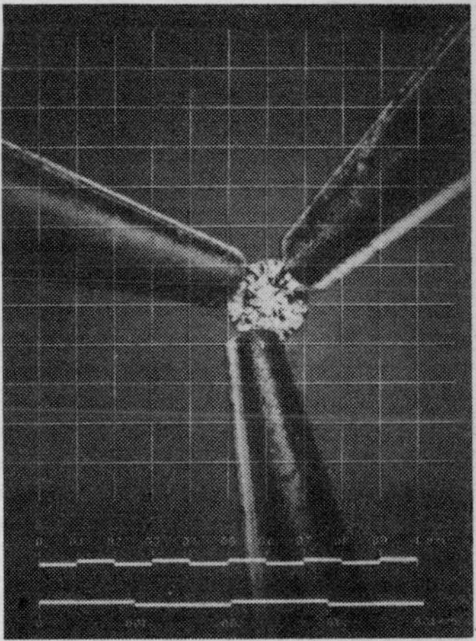

$1,026,656 SAPPHIRE AND DIAMOND BRACELET (left) from the Duchess of Windsor's jewelry collection sold at Sotheby's, Geneva, Apr 1987. The other jewel in this photo was not a record.

$6,380,000 DIAMOND (right): This pear-shaped gem weighs 64.83 carats and measures 2 in long by 1 in wide by ½ in deep. Classed as "D Flawless," it has extraordinary whiteness. *(Christie's NYC)*

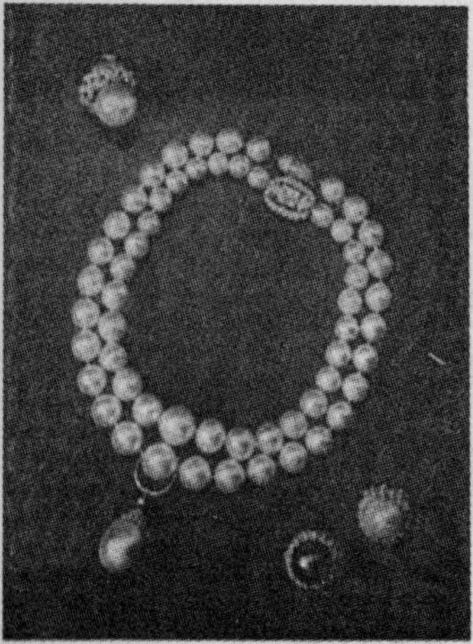

$773,326 NATURAL PEARL NECKLACE (left) from the Duchess of Windsor's collection sold at Sotheby's Geneva, Apr 1987.

$467,123 PEARL (right): This 133.20-grain pearl, La Pelegrina, sold for this record price in May 1987 at Christie's Geneva, Switzerland.

Newest Gemstones

Tanzanite was discovered in Tanzania in 1969. It reached $1,200 per carat in 1977. The deep purple Royal Lavalite found in Hotazel, South Africa by Randy Polk of Phoenix, Ariz reached $1,300 per carat in 1982.

Most Precious Diamond

An extremely rare unmounted, circular-cut fancy purplish-red diamond of 0.95 carats sold for $880,000, at Christie's, NYC, on Apr 28, 1987, establishing a record of $926,000 per carat. The price was more than seven times the former record of $127,000 per carat, set at Christie's, Geneva, in 1980 by a pink diamond of 7.27 cts. The diamond has a diameter of approximately 6½ millimeters, the size of a small pea.

Largest Pearl from US

The abalone pearl found in 1985 by divers off the S Calif coast weighs 349.41 carats and is valued at $3½ million by its present owner, Lowell Jones of St Louis, Mo. It is said to be the largest natural pearl from US waters.

NUMERALS

In dealing with large numbers, scientists use the notation of 10 raised to various powers, to eliminate a profusion of zeros. Example: 19,160,000,000,000 miles would be written 1.916×10^{13} miles. A very small number is treated similarly—for example, 0.0000154324 of a gram, would be written 1.54324×10^{-5} gram (g). Of the prefixes used before numbers the smallest is "tredo" from the Danish "tredyvo" for 30, indicating 10^{-30} of a unit. The highest is "dea" (Greek *deca,* ten) symbol D, indicating 10 groups of 3 zeros (10^{30}) or a nonillion.

Prime Numbers

A prime number is any positive integer (excluding 1) having no integral factors other than itself and unity, *e.g.* 2, 3, 5, 7, or 11. The lowest prime number is thus 2. The highest known prime number is $2^{216,091}-1$ discovered in Sept 1985 by analysts using a Cray X-MP/24 computer at Chevron Geosciences Co in Houston, Tex. It is the 30th known Marsenne prime, and contains 65,050 digits. The lowest non-prime or composite number (excluding 1) is 4.

Perfect Numbers

A number is said to be perfect if it is equal to the sum of its divisors other than itself, *e.g.* $1+2+4+7+14=28$. The lowest perfect number is 6 ($1+2+3$). The highest known, and the 30th so far discovered, is $(2^{216,091}-1) \times 2^{216,090}$. It is a consequence of the highest known prime (see above).

Highest Numbers

The highest lexicographically accepted named number in the system of successive powers of ten is the centillion, first recorded in 1852. It is the hundredth power of a million, or one followed by 600 zeros. The highest named number outside the decimal notation is the Buddhist *asankhyeya*, which is equal to 10^{140}.

The number 10^{100} is designated a Googol, a term devised by Dr Edward Kasner of the US (d 1955). Ten raised to the power of a Googol is described as a Googolplex. Some conception of the magnitude of such numbers can be gained when it is said that the number of electrons in some models of the observable universe probably does not exceed 10^{87}.

The highest number ever used in a mathematical proof is a bounding value published in 1977 and known as Graham's number. It concerns bichromatic hypercubes and is inexpressible without the special "arrow" notation, devised by Knuth in 1976, extended to 64 layers. Mr Candelaria ("the only man infinity fears") of Loma Linda, Calif has devised a Large Number Denomination System concluding with a milli-decilli-fiveillionillion.

Most Accurate and Inaccurate Versions of "Pi"

The greatest number of decimal places to which *pi* (π) has been calculated is 133,554,000 by Yasumasu Kanada (Japan) Jan 13, 1987, at the NEC Fuchu Factory, Tokyo. The printout was almost 20,000 pages long.

In 1897, the General Assembly of Indiana enacted in House Bill No. 246 that *pi* was *de jure* 4, for the most inaccurate version.

Longest and Shortest Time Measure

The longest measure of time is the *kalpa* in Hindu chronology. It is equivalent to 4.32 billion years. In astronomy a cosmic year is the period of rotation of the sun around the center of the Milky Way galaxy, *i.e.* 225,000,000 years. In the Late Cretaceous Period of *c.* 85 million years ago, the earth rotated faster so resulting in 370.3 days per year, while in Cambrian times, some 600 million years ago, there is evidence that the year extended over 425 days.

Owing to variations in the length of a day, which is estimated to be increasing irregularly at the average rate of about a millisecond per century, due to the moon's tidal drag, the second has been redefined. Instead of being 1/86,400th part of a mean solar day, it has since 1960 been reckoned as 1/31,556,925.9747th part of the solar (or tropical) year at 1900 AD, Jan 0 less 12 hours, Ephemeris time. In 1958 the second of Ephemeris time was computed to be equivalent to 9,192,631,770 ± 20 cycles of the radiation corresponding to the transition of a cesium 133 atom when unperturbed by exterior fields. The greatest diurnal change recorded has been 10 milliseconds on Aug 8, 1972, due to the most violent solar storm recorded in 370 years of observation.

The accuracy of the cesium beam frequency standard approaches 8 parts in 10^{14} compared to 2 parts in 10^{13} for the methane-stabilized helium-neon laser and 6 parts in 10^{13} for the hydrogen maser.

Most-Proven Theorem

A book published in 1940 contained 370 different proofs of Pythagoras's Theorem including one by President James Garfield (US)

Longest Proof

The longest mathematical proof is the proof of the classification of all finite simple groups. It is spread over more than 14,000 pages in nearly 500 papers in mathematical journals contributed by more than 100 mathematicians over a period of more than 35 years.

Oldest Mathematical Puzzle

As I was going to St Ives
I met a man with seven wives.
Every wife had seven sacks,
and every sack had seven cats.
Kitten, cats, sacks and wives,
how many were going to St Ives?

PHYSICAL EXTREMES (TERRESTRIAL)

Finest Balance

The most accurate balance is the Sartorius Model 4108, manufactured in Göttingen, W Germany, which can weigh objects of up to 0.5 grams (about .018 oz) to an accuracy of 0.01 μg or 0.00000001 g, which is equivalent to little more than one-sixtieth of the weight of the ink on a period dot (.).

Largest Barometer

A water barometer 39 ft in height was constructed by Bert Bolle, Curator of the Barometer Museum, Maartensdijk, Netherlands where the instrument is situated.

Largest Bubble Chamber

The largest bubble chamber is the $7 million installation completed in Oct 1973, at Weston, Ill. It is 15 ft in diameter and contains 7,259 gallons of liquid hydrogen at a temperature of −247°C (−412.6°F) with a superconducting magnet of 3 tesla.

Fastest Centrifuge

Ultra-centrifuges were invented by Theodor Svedberg (b Aug 30, 1884) (Sweden) in 1923.

The highest man-made rotary speed ever achieved and the fastest speed of any earth-bound object is 4,500 mph by a swirling tapered 6-in carbon fiber rod in a vacuum at Birmingham University, England, reported Jan 24, 1975.

Finest Cut

The $13 million Large Optics Diamond Turning Machine at the

Lawrence Livermore National Laboratory in Calif was reported in June 1983 to be able to sever a human hair 3,000 times lengthwise.

Longest Echo

The longest recorded echo in any building is one of 15 sec following the closing of the door of the Chapel of the Mausoleum, Hamilton, Lanc, Eng built 1840–55.

Most Powerful Electric Current

The most powerful electric current generated is that from the Zeus capacitor at the Los Alamos Scientific Laboratory, NM. If fired simultaneously the 4,032 capacitors would produce for a few micro seconds twice as much current as that generated elsewhere on earth.

Hottest Flame

The hottest flame that can be produced is from carbon subnitride (C_4N_2) which at one atmosphere pressure is calculated to reach 5,261 K.

Highest Measured Frequency

The highest *directly* measured frequency is a visible yellow-green light at 520.2068085 terahertz (a terahertz being a million million hertz or cycles per second) for the o-component of the 17-1 P(62) transition line of iodine 127. The highest measured frequency determined by precision metrology is a green light at 582.491703 terahertz for the b_{21} component of the R(15) 43-0 transition line of iodine 127. However with the decision on Oct 20, 1983 by the *Conférence Générale des Poids et Mesures* (CGPM) to define exactly the meter (m) in terms of the velocity of light (c) such that "the meter is the length of the path traveled by light in vacuum during a time interval of 1/299,792,458 of a second" then frequency (f) and wavelength (λ) are exactly interchangeable through the relationship $f\lambda = c$.

Lowest Friction

The lowest coefficient of static and dynamic friction of any solid is 0.02, in the case of polytetrafluoroethylene ($[C_2F_4]_n$), called PTFE—equivalent to wet ice on wet ice. It was first manufactured in quantity by E. I. du Pont de Nemours & Co Inc in 1943, and is marketed as Teflon.

In the centrifuge at the University of Virginia a 30-lb rotor magnetically supported has been spun at 1,000 revolutions per sec in a vacuum of 10^{-6} mm of mercury pressure. It loses only one revolution per sec per day, thus spinning for years.

Smallest Hole

A hole of 40 A° (4×10^{-9} mm) was shown visually, using a JEM 100 C electron microscope and Quantel Electronics devices at the Dept of Metallurgy, Oxford, England, on Oct 28, 1979. To find such a hole is equivalent to finding a pinhead in a haystack measuring 1.2 miles × 1.2 miles.

An electron microscope beam on a sample of sodium beta-alumina

FUMIGATION: During the restoration of the Mission Inn complex in Riverside, Calif, June 28–July 1, 1987, this was the scene as 350 tarpaulins were used in ridding the building of termites. *(Fume Masters Inc)*

MOST POWERFUL LIGHT BEAM: This 2-mi-long Linear Accelerator at Stanford, Calif, runs through the Santa Cruz Mountains and produces a record light beam through a 4x½-in. slit. A more powerful version, a Linear Collider or "atom smasher," costing $115 million to begin operation soon may "change the shape of particle physics."*(Science Photo Library)*

at the Univ of Illinois in May 1983 bored a hole 2×10^{-9} m in diameter accidentally.

Most Powerful Laser Beams

The first illumination of another celestial body was achieved May 9, 1962, when a beam of light was successfully reflected from the moon by the use of a laser (light amplification by stimulated emission of radiation) attached to a 48-in telescope at MIT, Cambridge, Mass. The spot was estimated to be 4 miles in diameter on the moon. The device was propounded in 1958 by Dr Charles Hard Townes (b US 1915) of Bell Telephone Laboratories. Such a flash for 1/5,000th sec can bore a hole through a diamond by vaporization at 10,000°C, produced by 2×10^{23} photons.

The "Shiva" laser was reported at the Lawrence Livermore Laboratory, Calif to be concentrating 2.6×10^{13} watts into a pinhead-sized target for 9.5×10^{-11} sec in a test on May 18, 1978.

Most Durable Light

The average bulb lasts for 750–1,000 hours. There is some evidence that a 5-watt carbide filament bulb made by the Shelby Electric Co and presented by Mr Bernell in the Fire Department, Livermore, Calif was first shedding light in 1901, and is still burning when lit.

Shortest Light Pulse

Charles Z. Shank and colleagues of the AT & T Laboratories in NJ achieved a light pulse of 8 femtoseconds (8×10^{-15} sec) announced in 1985.

The pulse comprised only 4 or 5 wavelengths of visible light or 2.4 micrometers long.

Brightest Light

The brightest steady artificial light sources are laser beams, generated at the Los Alamos National Laboratory, NM, announced in Mar 1987 by Dr Robert Graham. An ultraviolet flash lasting 1 picosecond (1×10^{-12} sec) is intensified by an energy of 5×10^{15} watts.

Of continuously burning sources, the most power- ful is a 313-kW high pressure argon arc lamp of 1,200,000 candle power, completed by Vortek Industries, Inc of Vancouver, BC, Canada, in Mar 1984.

The most powerful searchlight ever developed was one produced during the 1939–45 war by the General Electric Company Ltd at the Hirst Research Centre in Wembley, Greater London, England. It had a consumption of 600 kW and gave an arc luminance of 300,000 candles per sq in and a maximum beam intensity of 2.7 billion candles from its parabolic mirror (diameter 10 ft).

Heaviest Magnet

The heaviest magnet is one measuring 196 ft in diameter, with a weight of 40,000 tons, for the 10 GeV synchrophasotron in the Joint Institute for Nuclear Research at Dubna, near Moscow.

Weakest and Strongest Magnetic Fields

The weakest magnetic field ever measured is one of 8×10^{-15} tesla in the heavily shielded room at the Francis Bitter National Magnet Laboratory at MIT, Cambridge, Mass. It is used by Dr David Cohen for research into the very weak magnetic fields generated in the heart and brain.

The strongest continuous magnetic field strength has been one of 33.6 teslas achieved at the same laboratory on Mar 20, 1986, using a hybrid magnet with holmium pole pieces which enhanced the central field.

Smallest Microphone

A microphone for a new technique of pressure measurement in fluid flow was developed in 1967 by Prof Ibrahim Kavrak of Bogazici Univ, Istanbul, Turkey. It has a frequency response of 10 Hz to 10 KHz and measures 0.06 × 0.03 in.

Most Powerful Microscopes

The most powerful microscope is the scanning tunneling microscope invented at the IBM Zurich, Switz, research laboratory in 1981. It has the magnifying ability of 100 million and is capable of resolving down to 1/100th the diameter of an atom (3×10^{-10}).

By using field ion microscopy the tips of probes of scanning tunneling microscopes have been shaped to end in a single atom—the last three layers constituting the world's smallest man-made pyramid consisting of 7, 3 and 1 atoms. It was announced in July 1986 from AT & T Bell Laboratories, Murray Hill, NJ that they had successfully deposited a single atom (probably of germanium) from the tungsten tip of a scanning tunneling microscope back on to a germanium surface.

Loudest Noise

The loudest noise created in a laboratory is 210 decibels or 400,000 acoustic watts reported by NASA in Oct 1965. The noise came from a 48-ft steel and concrete test bed with 60-ft-deep foundations at Huntsville, Ala. Holes can be bored in solid material by this means and the audible range has been put at 100 mi.

Highest Note

The highest note yet attained is 60 gigahertz (60,000 million vibrations per sec), generated by a laser beam striking a sapphire crystal at MIT, Cambridge, Mass, in Sept 1964.

Most Powerful Particle Accelerator

The 6,562-ft diameter proton synchrotron at the Fermi National Accelerator Laboratory east of Batavia, Ill, is the highest-energy atom-smasher in the world. On May 14, 1976 an energy of 500 giga electron volts (5×10^{11}) was achieved for the first time. On Oct 13, 1985 a center of mass energy of 1.6 tera electron volts (1.6×10^{12} electron volts) was achieved by colliding beams of protons and antiprotons. This involves 1,000 superconducting magnets maintained at a temperature of −452°F by means of the world's largest helium liquefying plant, which produces 990 gallons per hour and began operating Apr 18, 1980.

The aim of CERN (*Conseil Européen pour la Recherche*) to collide

QUIETEST PLACE: An echoless test chamber at Bell Labs in Murray Hill, NJ, is used to study reverberation, the problem that sometimes occurs during telephone conference calls, when it sounds as if one of the speakers is talking into a barrel.

beams of protons and antiprotons in their Super Proton Synchrotron (SPS) near Geneva, Switzerland, at 270 GeV × 2 = 540 GeV was achieved at 4:55 a.m. on July 10, 1981. This is the equivalent of striking a fixed target with protons at 150 TeV or 150,000 GeV.

The US Dept of Energy set up a study for a $6 billion Super Superconductivity Collider (SSC) 1995 with two 20 Te V proton and antiproton colliding beams on Aug 16, 1983 with a diameter of 52 mi.

Highest Pressures

The highest sustained laboratory pressures yet reported are of 1.70 megabars (12,320 tons force per sq in) achieved in the giant hydraulic diamond-faced press at the Carnegie Institution's Geophysical Laboratory in Washington, DC, reported in June 1978. This laboratory announced solid hydrogen achieved at 57 kilobars pressure on March 2, 1979. If created, metallic hydrogen is expected to be silvery white but soft, with a density of 1.1 g/cc. The pressure required for this transition is estimated by H. K. Mao and P. M. Bell to be 1 megabar at 25°C. Using dynamic methods and impact speeds of up to 18,000 mph, momentary pressures of 75 million atmospheres (548,000 tons per sq in) were reported from the US in 1958.

Sharpest Objects and Smallest Tubes

The sharpest objects yet made are glass micropipette tubes used in intracellular work on living cells. Techniques developed and applied by Prof Kenneth T. Brown and Dale G. Flaming of the Dept of Physiology, Univ of Calif, achieved by 1,977 beveled tips with an outer diameter of 0.02 μm and 0.01 μm inner diameter. The latter is smaller than the smallest known nickel tubing by a factor of 340 and is 6,500 times thinner than human hair.

Highest Temperatures

The highest man-made temperatures yet attained are those produced in the center of a thermonuclear fusion bomb, which are of the order of 300 million–400 million°C. Of controllable temperatures, the highest effective laboratory figure reported is 230 million°C achieved in the Tokamak Fusion Test Reactor at the Princeton Plasma Physics Laboratory, NJ, in June 1986. A figure of 3000 million°C was reportedly achieved in the USSR with Ogra injection-mirror equipment in *c* 1962.

Lowest Temperatures

The lowest temperature reached is 3×10^{-8} Kelvin above absolute zero attained in a two-stage nuclear demagnetization cryostat at Espoo, Finland, by the team led by Prof Olli V. Lounasmaa (b 1930) and announced in June 1984. Absolute or thermodynamic temperatures are defined in terms of ratios rather than as differences reckoned from the unattainable absolute zero, which on the Kelvin scale is −273.15°C or −459.67°F. Thus the lowest temperature ever attained is 1 in 9.1×10^9 of the melting point of ice (0°C or 273.15K or 32°F).

Tokyo University's Institute of Solid State Physics announced on Feb 15, 1983 that a team led by Prof. Kazuo Ono had attained a temperature within 0.00003 of a degree of absolute zero at which molecular motion ceases.

Smallest Thermometer

Dr. Frederich Sachs, a biophysicist at the State Univ of NY at Buffalo, has developed an ultra-microthermometer for measuring the temperature of single living cells. The tip is one micron in diameter, about 1/50th the diameter of a human hair.

Highest Vacuum

The highest or "hardest" vacuums obtained in scientific research are of the order of 10^{-14} torr, achieved at the IBM Thomas J. Watson Research Center, Yorktown Heights, NY in Oct 1976 in a cryogenic system with temperatures down to −269°C (−452°F). This is equivalent to depopulating baseball-sized molecules from 1 yard apart to 50 miles apart.

Highest Velocity

The highest velocity at which any solid visible object has been projected is 335,000 mph in the case of a plastic disc at the Naval Research Laboratory, Wash DC, reported in Aug 1980.

Lowest Viscosity

The California Institute of Technology announced on Dec 1, 1957, that there was no measurable viscosity, *i.e.* perfect flow, in liquid helium II, which exists only at temperatures close to absolute zero (−273.15°C or −459.67°F).

Highest Voltage

The highest potential difference ever obtained in a laboratory has been 32 ± 1.5 million volts by the National Electrostatics Corporation at Oak Ridge, Tenn, on May 17, 1979.

Chapter 6

The Arts & Entertainment

1. PAINTING

Earliest Art

Evidence of Paleolithic art was first found in 1833 at Veyrier near Geneva, Switz, when Francois Mayor (1779–1854) found two harpoon-like objects decorated with geometric figures. The oldest known dated examples come from La Ferrassie, near Les Eyzies in the Périgord, France, in layers dated to *c*. 25,000 BC. Blocks of stone were found with engraved animals and female symbols; some of the blocks also had symbols painted in red ochre. Pieces of ochre with ground facets have been found at Lake Mungo, NSW, Australia, in a context *ante* 30,000 BC but there is no evidence whether these were used for body-painting or art.

Largest Paintings

Kimiko Hibino (b 1942) completed what is now the world's largest painting, showing over 800 species of the Animal Kingdom on a canvas 1.86 miles long and 7.2 ft wide (70,709 sq ft) on Oct 27, 1985. It was unveiled with the help of 3,000 volunteers along the bank of the Tamagawa River in Tokyo.

The largest "Old Master" is *Il Paradiso*, painted between 1587 and 1590 by Jacopo Robusti, *alias* Tintoretto (1518–94), and his son Domenico on the east wall of the Sala del Maggior Consiglio in the Palazzo Ducale (Doge's Palace) in Venice, Italy. The work is 72 ft 2 in long and 22 ft 11½ in high and contains some 350 human figures.

Most Valuable Painting

The "Mona Lisa" (*La Gioconda*) by Leonardo da Vinci (1452–1519) in the Louvre, Paris, was assessed for insurance purposes at the highest figure ever at $100 million for its move for exhibition in Washington, DC and NYC from Dec 14, 1962, to March 12, 1963. However, insurance was not concluded because the cost of the closest security precautions was less than that of the premiums. It was painted in *c*. 1503–07 and measures 30.5 × 20.9 in. It is believed to portray

MOST EXPENSIVE PAINTING: "Irises" by Vincent Van Gogh (b Mar 30, 1853, Zundert, The Netherlands—d July 29, 1890, Auvers-sur-Oise, France) was sold for a record $53.9 million (including buyer's premium) at Sotheby's NYC on Nov 11, 1987. It took less than 4 minutes to sell the 28 in × 36⅝ in canvas which Van Gogh had painted in 1889 while a voluntary patient at the Saint-Remy Mental Asylum in Provence, France.

Mona (short for Madonna) Lisa Gherardini, the wife of Francesco del Giocondo of Florence, or Constanza d'Avalos, coincidentally nicknamed La Gioconda, mistress of Giuliano de Medici. Francis I, King of France, in 1517 bought the painting for his bathroom for 4,000 gold florins or 492 oz of gold now worth $330,000.

Highest Auction Prices

The highest price ever paid in a public auction for any painting was $53.9 million for Vincent Van Gogh's *Irises* at Sotheby's NYC on Nov 11, 1987. The seller was philanthropist and art collector John Whitney Payson and the winning bidder was "a European agent for an unidentified collector." *Irises*, an oil on canvas measuring 28 × 36⅝ in, was painted by Van Gogh (1853–90) in May 1889 soon after his arrival in St.-Remy, France. It was seen most recently at the NY Metropolitan Museum's 1987 exhibition "Van Gogh in Saint-Remy and Auvers."

The highest total realizations for a single session fine arts auction came to $110,022,000 at Sotheby's NYC the same day Van Gogh's *Irises* was sold. Also included were Claude Monet's *Le Jardin Fleuri* which sold for $5,830,000 and two other Monets that sold for more than $2 million as well as Braque's *Le Violin* which fetched $3,300,000.

The record bid at auction for a 20th century painting is $4 million for Jackson Pollock's (1912–56) *Search*, spatter-painted in 1955 and sold at Sotheby's NYC on May 4, 1988. It was sold from the estate of Andy Warhol (1927–87).

The highest price ever paid for a painting by a female artist is $1,100,000, at Christie's, NYC on May 17, 1983, for *Reading Le Figaro* by Mary Cassatt (US) (1844–1926). She worked mainly from Paris.

The auction record for an abstract painting is $5.06 million for *Composition in a Square with Red Corner* painted by the Dutch modernist Piet Mondrian (1872–1944), in 1938 and sold at Sotheby's NY on Nov 18, 1986 to an anonymous Japanese businessman.

Living Artist

The highest price paid at auction for a work by a living artist is $4.18 million for "Divers" (1962) by Jasper Johns at Christie's NYC on May 2, 1988.

Miniature Portrait

The highest price ever paid for a portrait miniature is $172,500 by an anonymous buyer at a sale held by Sotheby's, London, Mar 24, 1980, for a miniature of Jane Broughton, age 21, painted on vellum by Nicholas Hilliard (1547–1619) in 1574. The painted surface measures 1.65 in in diameter.

Highest-Priced Drawing

The highest price ever paid for any drawing is £3,546,000 ($4,539,800) for a study of an apostle's head and hand for *The Transfiguration* in the Vatican by Raphael (Raffaello Santi 1483–1520) and sold for the 11th Duke of Devonshire (b 1920) at Christie's, London, July 3, 1984.

Most Prolific Painters

Pablo Picasso (1881–1973), born in Spain, was the most prolific of all painters. During a career that lasted for 78 years, it has been estimated that he produced about 13,500 paintings or designs, 100,000 prints or engravings, 34,000 book illustrations, and 300 sculptures and ceramics plus drawings and tapestries. His lifetime work has been valued at $750,000,000.

Morris Katz (b 1932) of Greenwich Village, NYC, is the most prolific painter of saleable works in the world. His total sold, as of July 1, 1988, was 181,818. Described now as a "realistic, impressionistic" modern artist, Katz appears regularly on cable TV on the "Instant Art Show." He paints with palette knife and crushed pads of toilet paper, and sells his paintings "cheap and often." He also set other records— painting a 12 × 16-in canvas of a child in the snow in 30 sec at the Roma Pizza Guinness Record Holders Convention in NYC, May 9, 1988, and painting for 12 hours non-stop (except for rest breaks) at the Penta Hotel, NYC, on July 15, 1987, during which time he made 103 paintings and sold 55 on the spot, donating the proceeds to the Boy Scouts of America.

Most Repetitious Painter

Copying his own painting as many as 5,000 times is the record set

MOST PROLIFIC ART TEACHER: Constance G. Gordon (Mrs Robert Asch) (b New Britain, Conn) first devised a 4-step system of teaching painting in 1944–45. On Aug 16, 1965 she conducted the longest-ever art class (for Tupperware) in Orlando, Fl, taking the "pain" out of painting for 2,500 "first-time" artists. Through the medium of large movie screens, TV series and 17 art books she has subsequently taught uncountable millions.

FASTEST MURAL: In 20 min 44 sec, Morris Katz painted this 8 ft long by 48 in high wall of the Cadillac Bar in midtown NYC on May 10, 1988, using oil paints, palette knife and crumpled toilet paper. *(Anne Marie Battica)*

by William A. Bixler (1876–1961) who painted *Old Swimmin' Hole*, 1912–18 and sold the copies to raise funds to erect a statue of poet James Whitcomb Riley in Greenfield, Ind. Riley's poem of the same name was the inspiration for the painting.

Youngest Exhibitor

Lewis Melville "Gino" Lyons (b Apr 30, 1962) painted his *Trees and Monkeys* on June 4, 1965, submitted it to the Royal Academy of Arts, England, on March 17, 1967, for its Annual Summer Exhibition, and it was exhibited on Apr 29, 1967.

Oldest and Largest Museums

The oldest museum in the world is the Ashmolean Museum in Oxford, England, built in 1679–83. Since 1924 it has housed an exhibition of scientific instruments.

The largest single museum is the American Museum of Natural History between 77th and 81st Sts on Central Park West, NYC. Founded in 1874, it comprises 22 interconnected buildings with 1.5 million sq ft of floor space.

The largest complex of museums is Washington, D.C.'s Smithsonian Institution, comprising 15 museums with 6,000 employees. It contains more than 134 million items. The most popular museum in numbers of visitors is the Smithsonian Air and Space Museum, which opened in July 1976. On one day in 1984 the doors had to be closed when 118,437 people crowded in. The total attendance at the Smithsonian is about 24 million per year.

Largest Galleries

The largest gallery showing modern art is located in Place Beaubourg, Paris, on the top floors of the Georges Pompidou National Center for Art and Culture. Named after the French president who first had the idea and who authorized the spending (some say foolishly) of many millions of francs, this museum is unusual on the outside. Looking more like an ocean liner or an ultramodern factory because of its escalator appendages, this art museum and library has changing exhibits on the lower floors, showing the latest in international art and design. Opened in 1977, it has a deluxe restaurant on its roof and a world record total of 183,000 sq ft of floor space.

The world's largest art gallery is the Winter Palace and the neighboring Hermitage in Leningrad, USSR. One has to walk 15 miles to visit each of the 322 galleries, which house nearly 3 million works of art and objects of archeological interest.

The most heavily endowed gallery is the J. Paul Getty Museum, Malibu, Calif, with $1,600,000,000 in Jan 1974 plus $187 million per year for acquisitions. It has 38 galleries.

Finest Brush

The finest standard brush sold is the 000 in Series 7 by Winsor and Newton, known as the "triple goose." It is made of 150–200 Kolinsky sable hairs weighing 0.000529 oz.

Largest and Highest-Priced Poster

The largest recorded poster was one measuring 328 × 328 ft

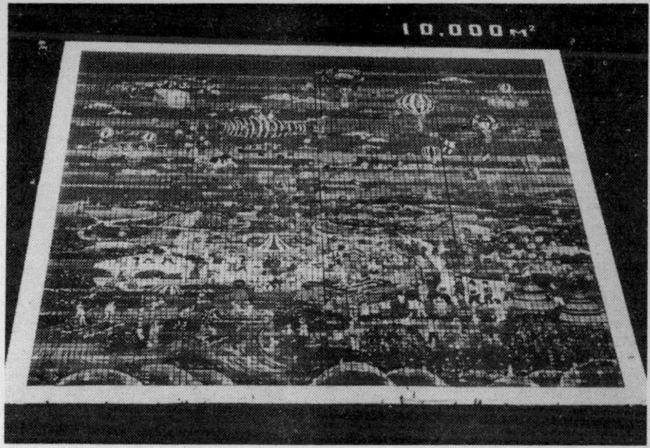

LARGEST POSTER: Made in Hokkaido, Japan by 10,000 citizens for the Obihiro Festival, this poster measured 328 × 328 ft (10,000 sq meters).

LARGEST BANNER: Hung from the roof edge of the Reunion Arena, Dallas, Tex, was this vinyl banner 350 ft long and 18 ft tall announcing the arrival of the Ringling Bros Barnum & Bailey Circus, June 29, 1988.

(107,584 sq ft) made by 10,000 citizens of Obihiri, Hokkaido, Japan on July 26, 1987 for the Green Frontier Festival.

The record price is £62,000 ($93,000) for a poster advertising the 1902 Vienna Exhibition, designed by Koloman Moser (b Vienna, Mar 30, 1868, d Oct 18, 1918) sold at Christie's London on Apr 1, 1985.

Earliest Mural

The earliest known murals on man-made walls are the clay relief leopards at Catal Hüyük in southern Anatolia, Turkey, discovered by James Malaart at level VII in 1961 and dating from *c.* 6200 BC.

Largest Mural

Claims for murals are difficult to compare. One 95,442-sq-ft face of the 23-story Vegas World Hotel in Las Vegas, Nev, is covered in part by a wall painting which is broken up by strips of windows.

The largest "mural" was unveiled in 44 colors on the 30-story Villa Regina condominium, Biscayne Bay, Miami, Fla, on Mar 14, 1984 covering 300,000 sq ft. *Entries for this category are being assessed on overall area only.*

Stained Glass

The oldest stained glass in the world represents the Prophets in a window of the cathedral of Augsburg, Bavaria, Germany, dating from *c.* 1050.

The largest stained glass window is the complete mural of The Resurrection Mausoleum, Justice, Ill, measuring 22,381 sq ft, in 2,448 panels completed in 1971. The back-lit stained glass mural installed in 1979 in the atrium of the Ramada Hotel, Dubai, United Arab Emirates, is 135 ft high.

Largest Mosaic

The largest mosaic is on the walls of the central library of the Universidad Nacional Autónoma de México, Mexico City. There are four walls, the two largest measuring 12,949 sq ft each, representing the pre-Hispanic past.

---

2. SCULPTURES

Earliest Sculptures

The earliest known example of sculpture is a 2½- in-long figure of a horse carved from mammoth ivory dated to *c.* 28,000 BC, and found in the Vogelherd cave in W Germany. A piece of ox rib found in 1973 at Pech de l'Aze, Dordogne, France, in an early Middle Paleolithic layer of the Riss glaciation *c.*105,000 BC appears to have several possibly intentionally engraved lines on one side. A churingo or curved ivory plaque rubbed with red ochre from the Middle Paleolithic Mousterian site at Tata, Hungary, has been dated to 100,000 BC by the thorium/uranium method.

Largest Sculptures

The largest sculptures are the mounted figures of Jefferson Davis (1808–89), Gen Robert Edward Lee (1807–70) and Gen Thomas Jonathan ("Stonewall") Jackson (1824–63), covering 1.33 acres on the face of Stone Mountain, near Atlanta, Ga. They are 90 ft high. Roy Faulkner was on the mountain face for 8 years 174 days with a thermo-jet torch, working with the sculptor Walker Kirtland Hancock and other helpers from Sept 12, 1963 to March 3, 1972.

The world's largest sculpture will probably not be completed for many years due to the death in 1982 of the sculptor who conceived the idea and spent 35 of his 74 years on the site at Thunderhead Mt in the southern Black Hills of South Dakota near Mt Rushmore. The sculptor, Korczak Ziolkowski, started blasting away at the first of 7 million tons of granite June 3, 1948. By 1982 he had the rough outline of the sculpture showing the Sioux Indian, Tashunca-Uitco, known as Chief Crazy Horse (*c.* 1849–77) mounted on his stallion carved and visible to passersby in the distance. Ziolkowski left enough funds (he had raised $4 million) so his wife and 10 children, along with the Crazy Horse Memorial Foundation, could continue the work. When and if completed the carving will measure 563 ft by 641 ft.

In 1984, another 200,000 tons of granite were blasted off the mountain face, bringing the total to 7.8 million tons.

Most Expensive Sculptures

The highest price ever paid for a sculpture is $3,900,000 paid by private treaty in London in early 1977 by the J. Paul Getty Museum, Malibu, Calif for the 4th-century BC bronze statue of a youth attributed to the school of Lysippus. It was found by fishermen on the seabed off Faro, Italy in 1963.

The highest price paid *at auction* is $3,630,000 for Alberto Giacometti's (Switz, 1901–66) 1960 bronze *Large Female Standing II*, 107 in high, at Christie's NYC on May 12, 1987. Two other Giacometti bronzes of female figures were sold in the same auction.

The three figures, part of a series of six, were originally part of a monumental city-scape for the Chase Manhattan Plaza, NYC, that was later abandoned.

The highest price paid for the work of a living sculptor is $1,265,000 given at Sotheby Parke Bernet Galleries, NYC, May 21, 1982, for the 75-in-long elmwood *Reclining Figure* by Henry Moore (b Cas-tleford, W Yorkshire, England, July 30, 1898).

Ground and Hill Figures

In the Nazca Desert 185 mi south of Lima, Peru there are straight lines (one more than 7 miles long), geometric shapes and shapes of plants and animals drawn on the ground sometime between 100 BC and 600 AD for an uncertain but probably religious, astonomical or even economic purpose by a not precisely identified civilization. They were first detected from the air *c.* 1928 and can only be recognized as artwork from the air.

In Aug 1968 a 330-ft-tall figure was found on a hill above Tarapacá, Chile.

Most Massive Mobile

The most massive mobile is *White Cascade* weighing more than 8 tons and measuring 100 ft from top to bottom installed on May 24–25, 1976 at the Federal Reserve Bank of Philadelphia. It was designed by Alexander Calder (1898–1976), whose first mobiles were exhibited in Paris in 1932, and whose *Big Crinkley* sold for a record $700,000 at Sotheby's NYC on May 10, 1984.

MOST MASSIVE MOBILE: Alexander Calder's "White Cascade" can be seen in a bank in Philadelphia. *(Edw. J. Bonner)*

3. LANGUAGE AND LITERATURE

Earliest Language

The ability to speak is believed to be dependent upon physiological changes in the height of the larynx between *Homo erectus* and *Homo sapiens sapiens,* as developed *c* 45,000 BC.

The earliest written language discovered has been on Yangshao culture pottery from Paa-t'o, near Xi'an (Sian) in the Shanxi (Shensi) province of China found in 1962. This bears proto-characters for the numbers 5, 7 and 8 and has been dated to 5000–4000 BC.

The earliest dated pictographs are on clay tablets from Nippur, southern Iraq, from a level equivalent to Uruk V/VI and dated in 1979 to *c.* 3400 BC.

Tokens or tallies from Tepe Asiab and Ganji-I- Dareh Tepe in Iran have however been dated to 8500 BC.

Oldest Language

The written language with the longest continuous history is Chinese, extending over more than 6,000 years from the Yangshao culture. (*See above*.)

Oldest Words in English

It was first suggested in 1979 that languages ancestral to English and to Latvian (both Indo-European) split *c.* 3500 BC.

Shortly to be published research indicates that about 40 words of a pre-Indo-European substrate survive in English, including apple (apal), bad (bad), gold (gol), and tin (tin).

The earliest known piece of English writing (*c* 630 AD) is a fragment of Irish uncial script in an ecclesiastical history sold for $100,000 by the Folger Shakespeare Library, Wash, DC, to the British Rail Pension Fund at Sotheby's, London on June 25, 1985.

Commonest Language

Today's world total of languages and dialects still spoken is about 5,000 of which some 845 come from India. The language spoken by more people than any other is Northern Chinese, or Mandarin, by an estimated 68% of the population, hence 709 million people in 1985. The so-called national language (*Guóyŭ*) is a standardized form of Northern Chinese (*Bĕifanghuà*) as spoken in the Peking area. This was alphabetized into *zhùyīn fùhào* of 37 letters in 1913. On Feb 11, 1938, the *Hanya-Pinyin-Fang'an* system, which is a phonetic pronunciation guide, was introduced.

The next most commonly spoken language and the most widespread is English, by an estimated 400 million in mid-1986. English is spoken by 10% or more of the population in 45 sovereign countries. In Great Britain and Ireland, there are 6 indigenous tongues: English, Cornish, Scots, Gaelic, Irish Gaelic, Welsh, as well as Romany (gypsy).

Largest Vocabulary

The English language contains about 490,000 words, plus another 300,000 technical terms, the most in any language, but it is doubtful if any individual uses more than 60,000. Those in Great Britain who have undergone a full 16 years of education use perhaps 5,000 words in speech and up to 10,000 words in written communications. The members of the International Society for Philosophical Enquiry (no admission for IQ's below 148) have an average vocabulary of 36,320 words. Shakespeare employed a vocabulary of about 33,000 words.

Greatest Linguist

The most multilingual living person in the world is Georges Henri Schmidt (b Strasbourg, France, Dec 28, 1914), who served as Chief of the UN Terminology Section 1965–71. In the 1975 edition of *Who's Who in the United Nations* he listed "only" 19 languages because he was then unable to find the time to "revive" his former fluency in 12 others.

Powell Alexander Janulus (b 1939) has worked with 41 languages in the Provincial Court of British Columbia, Vancouver, Canada.

Oldest Letter and Alphabet

The oldest letter is "O," unchanged in shape since its adoption in the Phoenician alphabet *c.* 1300 BC. The newest letters added to the English alphabet are "j" and "v," which are of post-Shakespearean use, *c*. 1630. Formerly they were used only as variants of "i" and "u." There are now some 65 alphabets in use.

Longest Words

Lengthy concatenations and some compound or agglutinative words or nonce words are or have been written in the closed-up style of a single word.

The longest word ever to appear in literature occurs in *The Ecclesiazusae*, a comedy by Aristophanes (448–380 BC). In the Greek it is 170 letters long but transliterates into 182 letters in English, thus: lopadotemachoselachogaleokranioleipsanodrimhypotrimmatosilphioparaomelitokatakechymenokichlepikossyphophattoperisteralektryonoptekephalliokigklopeleiolagoiosiraiobaphetraganopterygon. The term describes a fricassee of 17 sweet and sour ingredients, including mullet, brains, honey, vinegar, pickles, marrow (the vegetable) and ouzo (a Greek drink laced with anisette).

The longest word in the Oxford English Dictionary is floccipaucinihilipilification (alternatively spelt in hyphenated form with "n" in seventh place), with 29 letters, meaning "the action of estimating as worthless," first used in 1741, and later by Sir Walter Scott (1771–1832). Webster's Third International Dictionary lists among its 450,000 entries pneumonoultramicroscopicsilicovolcanoconiosises (47 letters), the plural of a lung disease contracted by some miners.

The longest regularly formed English word is praetertranssubstantiationalistically (37 letters), used by Mark McShane in his novel *Untimely Ripped,* published in 1963. The medical term hepaticocholangiocholecystenterostomies (39 letters) refers to the surgical creations of new communications between gall bladders and hepatic ducts and between intestines and gall bladders. The longest in common use are disproportionableness and incomprehensibilities (21 letters). Interdenominationalism (22 letters) is found in Webster's and hence perhaps interdenominationalistically (28 letters) is permissible.

Most Meanings

The most overworked word in English is the word "set" which has 58 noun uses, 126 verbal uses and 10 as a participial adjective.

Longest Palindromic Words

The longest known palindromic word (same spelling backwards as forwards) is *saippuakivikauppias* (19 letters), the Finnish word for a dealer in lye. The longest in the English language is *redivider* (9 letters). The 9-letter word, *Malayalam,* is a proper noun given to the language of the Malayali people in Kerala, southern India, while *Kanakanak* near Dellingham, Alaska, is a 9-letter palindromic place name. The contrived chemical term *detartrated* has 11 letters. In American English the word *releveler* is also a 9-letter palindrome, though in England it is spelled *releveller* and hence is not palindromic.

Commonest Words and Letters

In written English, the most frequently used words are, in order: the, of, and, to, a, in, that, is, I, it, for *and* as. The most used in conversation is I. The commonest letter is "e" and the commonest initial letter is "T."

Shortest Pangram

Pangrammists who try to produce meaningful sentences of minimal length utilizing all the letters in the alphabet have now attained the ultimate of 26-letter brevity. Michael Jones of Chicago compiled in 1984 the sentence to describe the situation in which a wryneck woodpecker from the grasslands of Africa climbed up the side of a male bovid which is grazing on sacred Muslim-owned land, viz: "Veldt jynx grimps waqf zho buck."

Most Synonyms

The condition of being inebriated has more synonyms than any other condition or object. Delacorte Press has published a selection of 1,224 from 2,241 compiled by Paul Dickson of Garrett Park, Md.

Worst Tongue-Twisters

The most difficult tongue-twister is deemed by Ken Parkin of Teesside, England, to be "The sixth sick sheik's sixth sheep's sick"—especially when spoken quickly.

Longest Abbreviation

The 55-letter full name of Los Angeles (El Pueblo de Nuestra Señora la Reina de los Angeles de Porciuncula) is abbreviated to LA, or 3.63% of its length.

Longest Anagrams

The longest non-scientific English words which can form anagrams are the 18-letter transpositions "conservationalists" and "conversationalists." The longest scientific transposals are "hydroxydesoxycorticosterone" and "hydroxydeoxycorticosterones," each with 27 letters.

Smallest Letters

The 16 letters MOLECULAR DEVICES have been etched into a salt crystal by an electron beam so that the strokes are only 2 to 3 nm wide—the width of 20 hydrogen atoms. This was done by Michael Isaacson at Cornell University in Feb 1982.

Longest Place Names

The official name for Bangkok, capital of Thailand, is Krungthep Mahanakhon. The full name is, however: Krungthep Mahanakhon Bovorn Ratanakosin Mahintharayutthaya Mahadilok pop Noparatratchathani Burirom Udomratchanivetmahasathan Amornpiman Avatarnsathit Sakkathattiyavisnukarmprasit (167 letters) which, in the most scholarly transliteration, emerges with 175 letters.

Shortest Place Names

The shortest place names in the world are the French village of Y (population 143), so named since 1241, the Danish village Å on the island Fyn, the Norwegian village of Å (pronounced "Aw"), the Swedish place Å in Vikholandet, U in the Caroline Islands of the Pacific, and the Japanese town of Sosei which is alternatively called Aioi or O. There was once a 6 in West Virginia. Today in the US, there are 10 two-lettered place names, including 7 in Kentucky: Ed, Uz, Oz, Ep, and Or, among them.

Longest First Name

The longest name appearing on a birth certificate is that of Rhoshandiatellyneshiaunneveshenk Koyaanfsquatsiuty Williams born to Mr and Mrs James L. Williams in Beaumont, Tex, on Sept 12, 1984. On Oct 5, 1984, the father filed an amendment which expanded his daughter's first name to 1,019 letters and the middle name to 36 letters.

The longest Christian or given name on record is one of 622 letters given by Mr Scott Roaul Sör-Lökken of Missoula, Mont to his daughter Miss S. Ellen Georgianna Sör-Lökken (b 1979). The "S" stands for a 598-letter name designed to throw a monkey wrench into the computers of federal bureaucracy. She is known as "Snow Owl" for short or "Oli" for shorter.

Most Christian Names

The great-great-grandson of Carlos III of Spain, Don Alfonso de Borbón y Borbón (1866–1934), had 94 Christian names, of which several were lengthened by hyphenation.

Most Popular Personal Names

According to NYC birth registrations in 1987 the 10 most popular girl's names are Jessica, Jennifer, Stephanie, Melissa, Christina, Nicole, Amanda, Ashley, Tiffany and Samantha, in that order. The 10 most popular boy's names are Michael, Christopher, Jonathan, Daniel, David, Anthony, Joseph, Matthew, John and Andrew, in that order. Spellings vary.

In England the most popular girl's names were Sarah, Claire and Emma, and for boys Christopher, Matthew and David.

Shortest Personal Name

The commonest single-letter surname is O, prevalent in Korea, but with 52 examples in US phone books (1973–81) and 12 in Belgium. This name causes the most distress to those concerned with the prevention of cruelty to computers. Every other letter, except Q, has been traced in US phone books (used as a surname) by A. Ross Eckler. There are two one-letter Burmese names: E (calm), pronounced "aye," and U (egg), pronounced "oo." U used before the name means "uncle."

There exist among the 47,000,000 names on the Dept. of Health & Social Security index 6 examples of a one-lettered surname.

Commonest Family Names

The commonest family name in the world is the Chinese name Chang (Zhang) which is borne, according to estimates, by between 9.7% and 12.1% of the Chinese population, so indicating even on the lower estimate that there are at least some 104 million Changs—more than the entire population of all but 7 of the 170 other sovereign countries of the world.

The commonest surname in the English-speaking world is Smith. The most recent published count showed 659,050 nationally insured Smiths in Great Britain, of whom 10,102 are plain John Smith, and another 19,502 are John plus one or more given-name Smiths. Including uninsured persons, there are over 800,000 Smiths in England and Wales alone. There are an estimated 2,382,509 Smiths in the US.

Most Versions of a Family Name

Edward A. Nedelcov of Regina, Saskatchewan, Canada, has collected 990 versions of the spelling of his family name since Jan 1960. Mzilikazi of Zululand (b *c.* 1795) had his name chronicled in 325 spellings, according to researches by Dr R. Kent Rasmussen.

Last Word

In the US, the determination to derive commercial or other benefit from being the last listing in the local telephone book has resulted in self-given names starting with up to 9 z's—the extreme example being Mr Zachary Zzzzzzzzzzra in the San Francisco book. Last in the book for North Hollywood, LA, however, is Mr B. Zzzzygot.

The last name in the 1985 London telephone book is the Zzzzzz Coffee Shop in Gray's Inn Road.

Oldest Mechanically Printed Book

It is generally accepted that the earliest mechanically printed full-length book was a "42-line" Gutenberg Bible, printed in Mainz, Germany, *c.* 1454 by Johann Henne zum Gensfleisch zur Laden, called "zu Gutenberg" (*c.* 1398–*c.* 1468). Work on water-marks published in 1967 indicates a copy of a surviving printed "Donatus" Latin grammar was made from paper made in *c.* 1450. The earliest exactly dated printed work is the Psalter completed Aug 14, 1457, by Johann Fust (*c.* 1400–1466) and Peter Schöffer (1425–1502), who had been Gutenberg's chief assistant. The earliest printing by William Caxton, though undated, would appear to be *The Recuyel of the Historyes of Troye* in Cologne in late 1473 to spring 1474.

A complete two-volume edition of the Gutenberg Bible, 1450–56, was sold for $2.2 million at Christie's, NYC, on April 7, 1978. One of only 21 extant complete copies, the Gutenberg was sold for the General Theological Seminary, NYC to the Stuttgart (W Germany) State Library.

Manuscript

The highest price ever paid for a complete manuscript is £2.2 million ($5 million) by Armand Hammer at Christie's, London on Dec 12, 1980 for Leonardo da Vinci's 36-page Codex Leicester illustrated manuscript on cosmology compiled in *c* 1507.

Scientific Manuscript

The highest price paid for a scientific manuscript was $1,160,000 for a 72-page document by Albert Einstein, written in black ink and pencil around 1912, auctioned at Sotheby's, NYC, Dec 2, 1987. On this page Einstein laid out his "special" theory of relativity, and in one spot wrote the equation $EL = mc^2$ (L was a value that turned out to be 1) and then changed it to his famous $E = mc^2$ (energy equals mass times the speed of light squared). The document is a rarity because Einstein discarded most of his manuscripts after they were published. In this case, publication was delayed by the advent of World War I. In the meantime, Einstein put aside the work and began to incorporate its central ideas into a "general" theory of relativity. The manuscript was sold to an "anonymous collector."

Musical Manuscript

The highest price paid was $4,394,500 for a manuscript containing 9 symphonies by Wolfgang Amadeus Mozart (1756–91) at Sotheby's London, on May 22, 1987. The manuscript contains Symphonies Nos.

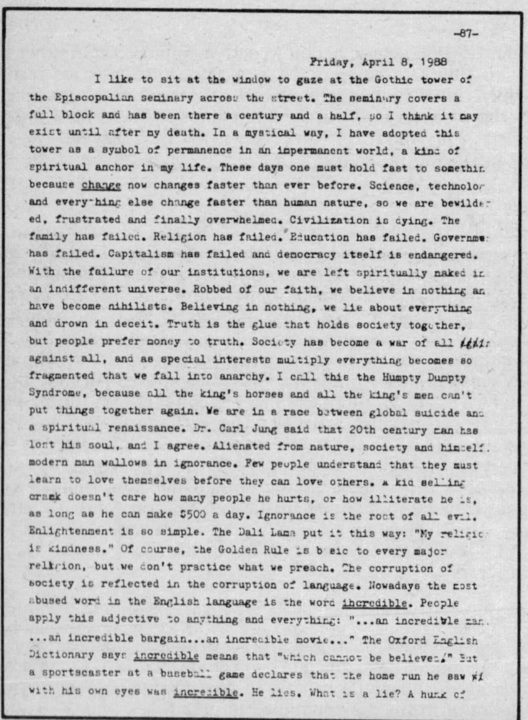

-87-

Friday, April 8, 1988

I like to sit at the window to gaze at the Gothic tower of the Episcopalian seminary across the street. The seminary covers a full block and has been there a century and a half, so I think it may exist until after my death. In a mystical way, I have adopted this tower as a symbol of permanence in an impermanent world, a kind of spiritual anchor in my life. These days one must hold fast to somethin because change now changes faster than ever before. Science, technolog and every thing else change faster than human nature, so we are bewilder ed, frustrated and finally overwhelmed. Civilization is dying. The family has failed. Religion has failed. Education has failed. Governme has failed. Capitalism has failed and democracy itself is endangered. With the failure of our institutions, we are left spiritually naked in an indifferent universe. Robbed of our faith, we believe in nothing an have become nihilists. Believing in nothing, we lie about everything and drown in deceit. Truth is the glue that holds society together, but people prefer money to truth. Society has become a war of all against all, and as special interests multiply everything becomes so fragmented that we fall into anarchy. I call this the Humpty Dumpty Syndrome, because all the king's horses and all the king's men can't put things together again. We are in a race between global suicide and a spiritual renaissance. Dr. Carl Jung said that 20th century man has lost his soul, and I agree. Alienated from nature, society and himself, modern man wallows in ignorance. Few people understand that they must learn to love themselves before they can love others. A kid selling crack doesn't care how many people he hurts, or how illiterate he is, as long as he can make $500 a day. Ignorance is the root of all evil. Enlightenment is so simple. The Dali Lama put it this way: "My religio is kindness." Of course, the Golden Rule is basic to every major religion, but we don't practice what we preach. The corruption of society is reflected in the corruption of language. Nowadays the most abused word in the English language is the word incredible. People apply this adjective to anything and everything: "...an incredible man. ...an incredible bargain...an incredible movie..." The Oxford English Dictionary says incredible means that "which cannot be believed." But a sportscaster at a baseball game declares that the home run he saw with his own eyes was incredible. He lies. What is a lie? A hunk of

PAGE FROM LARGEST DIARY: 18 million words are contained in the diary kept by Edward Robb Ellis since 1927.

22 through 30, all probably composed in Salzburg, Austria, in 1773 and 1774, when Mozart was still in his teens. The anonymous purchaser offered the manuscript for display to the Pierpont Morgan Library in NYC.

Smallest Book

The smallest marketed bound printed book with cursive material is one printed on 22 gsm paper measuring 1 mm × 1 mm (1/25 × 1/25 in), comprising the children's story "Old King Cole!" and published in 85 copies in Mar 1985 by The Gleniffer Press of Paisley, Scotland. The pages can only be turned (with care) by the use of a needle.

Largest and Longest Diaries

Col Ernest Loftus (GB) of Harare, Zimbabwe began his daily diary on May 4, 1896 at the age of 12 and has thus completed 91 years.

George C. Edler (1889–1987) of Kensington, Md, kept a diary from Jan 1, 1910, a total of 78 years.

Edward Robb Ellis (b 1911) of NYC began his diary in 1927, and in May 1988 had compiled 18 million words in 60 volumes.

Longest Index

The Tenth Collective Index of *Chemical Abstracts,* completed in June 1983, contains 23,948,253 entries in 131,445 pages in 75 volumes, and weighs 380 lb.

Most Expensive Paged Work

The highest price paid for any book was $11.9 million for the 226-leaf manuscript "The Gospel Book of Henry the Lion, Duke of Saxony" at Sotheby's London on Dec 6, 1983. The book, 13½ × 10 in, was illuminated by the monk Herimann in *c.* 1170 at Helmershansen Abbey with 41 full-page illustrations, and was bought by the W German government for display at two German museums.

The highest price ever paid for a printed book is $5,390,000 for a single volume of the Gutenberg Bible containing the Old Testament from Genesis to the Psalms, printed in 1455 in Mainz, Ger. It was bought by the Maruzen Co Ltd, a Tokyo book dealer, at an auction held by Christie's, NYC on Oct 23, 1987.

The most expensive book in print is *The Birds of America,* containing a full set of reproductions by John James Audubon (1785–1851) of ornithological prints, published by the Abbeville Press, NYC, to sell for $15,000.

Largest Dictionary

The largest English language dictionary is the 12-volume Royal quarto *Oxford English Dictionary* of 15,487 pages published between 1884 and 1928 with a first supplement of 963 pages in 1933 and a further 4-volume supplement, edited by R. W. Burchfield. The final volume (Se-Z and the bibliography) was published in 1986. The work contains 414,825 word listings, 1,827,306 illustrative quotations and reputedly 227,779,589 letters and figures, 63.8 times more than the Bible. The greatest outside contributor was Marghanita Laski (1915–88) with 175,000 quotations from 1958 until her death.

Deutsches Wörterbuch started by Jacob and Wilhelm Grimm in 1854 was completed in 34,519 pages and 33 volumes in 1971. Today's price is DM5,456.97 (now $3,000).

The *Grove's Dictionary of Music and Musicians* (edited by Stanley Sadie, b 1930) published in 20 volumes by Macmillan's in Feb 1981 contains over 22 million words and 4,500 illustrations and is the largest specialist dictionary. The price is $480.

Earliest and Largest Encyclopaediae

The earliest known encyclopaedia was compiled in Athens by Speusippus (*post* 408–*c.* 338 BC) in *c.* 370 BC. He was a nephew of Plato.

The largest encyclopaedia is *La Enciclopedia Universal Ilustrada Europeo-American* (J. Espasa & Sons, Madrid and Barcelona) totaling 105,000 pages in 104 volumes with 10 appendices and an annual supplement since 1935 comprising 165,200,000 words. The price is $2,325.

Most Comprehensive Encyclopaedia

The most comprehensive English language encyclopaedia is the *New Encyclopaedia Britannica*, first published in Edinburgh, Scotland, in Dec 1768–1771. A group of booksellers in the US acquired reprint rights in 1898 and complete ownership in 1899. The current 32-volume 15th edition contains 32,330 pages and 44 million words from more than 4,000 contributors. It is now edited in Chicago.

Highest-Priced Printed Document

A newly discovered copy of the Declaration of Independence, the 22nd copy known to exist, printed in 1776 by Samuel T. Freeman & Co, was auctioned to the Chapin Library, Williams College on Apr 22, 1983, at Christie's, NYC, for $412,500, setting a record for printed documents.

The highest price paid at auction for a rare copy of the first printing in 1789 of the US Constitution was $110,000 at Sotheby's, NYC on May 13, 1987.

Largest Publication

The largest publication in the world is the 1,112- volume set of *British Parliamentary Papers* of 1800–1900 published by the Irish University Press in 1968–1972. A complete set weighs 3.64 tons, cost $74,900 in mid-1985 and would take 6 years to read at 10 hours per day. The production and leather binding required the skins of 34,000 Indian goats and the use of $22,000 worth of gold ingots. The total print run was 500 sets, and the price per set in 1984 was $54,600.

Oldest Bibles

The oldest known bible is the *Codex Vaticanus* written in Greek *ante* 350 AD and preserved in the Vatican Museum, Rome.

The oldest Dead Sea Scrolls date from *c.* 225–200 BC. Made of leather and papyrus and comprising fragments of Exodus and Samuel I, they were discovered in Cave 4 near Qumran, Jordan in 1952.

The earliest complete Bible *printed* in English was one edited by Miles Coverdale, Bishop of Exeter (*c.* 1488–1569), while living in Antwerp, and printed in 1535. William Tyndale's New Testament in English had, however, been printed in Cologne and in Worms, Germany in 1525 while John Wycliffe's first manuscript translation dates from 1382.

Hand-Written Bible

The Bible Society of Maine is in possession of a hand-written Bible produced in 1924 by 1,607 people. It weighs 88½ lb and measures 23 × 29 × 4½ in thick.

Maps

The oldest known map of any kind is a clay tablet depicting the Euphrates River flowing through northern Mesopotamia (Iraq), dated *c.* 3800 BC. The earliest printed map in the world is one of western China dated to 1115 AD.

The largest is a giant relief map of California, by Reuben Hall displayed in the Ferry Building, San Francisco, from 1924 to 1962, now in storage at Hamilton Air Force Base, Novato, Calif, which measures 450 × 18 ft and weighs 43 tons. Known as *Paradise in Panorama* it required 29 man-years and $147,000 to build.

Highest-Priced Atlas

The highest price paid for an atlas is $700,000 for a Gerardus Mercator atlas of *c.* 1571 Europe sold at auction at Sotheby's, London, March 13, 1979.

Longest Novel

The longest important novel ever published is *Les hommes de bonne volonté* by Louis Henri Jean Farigoule (1885–1972), *alias* Jules Romains, of France, in 27 volumes in 1932–46. The English version, *Men of Good Will,* was published in 14 volumes in 1933–46 as a "novel-cycle." The 4,959-page edition published by Peter Davies Ltd has an estimated 2,070,000 words, excluding a 100-page index. The novel *Tokuga-Wa Ieyasu* by Sohachi Yamaoka has been serialized in Japanese daily newspapers since 1951. Now completed, it required 40 volumes in book form.

Familiar Quotes

John Bartlett's book of Familiar Quotations began when the young man of 16 found a job, in 1836, at the Harvard University bookstore. In the 13 years it took him to save enough money to buy the bookstore, he read almost every book in it. In 1855, using printers from the university, he himself published 1,000 copies of his book of quotes, a now-famous literary institution.

Most Prolific Writers

After receiving a probable record 743 rejection slips, the British novelist John Creasey (1908–73), under his own name and 25 *noms de plume*, had 564 books totaling more than 40 million words published from 1932 to his death on June 9, 1973.

The writer with the longest series of books is Margaret Farrar, whose crossword puzzle books first published Apr 10, 1924 reached a total of 133 by the time of her death in June 1984.

Top-Selling Authors

Currently the top-selling authoress is Barbara Cartland with global sales of over 500 million copies for 470 titles in 24 languages. She has averaged 23 titles per year for the last decade.

The all-time sales estimate of books by Erle Stanley Gardner (1889–1970) (US) to Jan 1, 1986, is 319,034,707 copies in 37 languages. The top-selling woman crime writer has been Dame Agatha Christie (*née* Agatha Mary Clarissa Miller), later Lady Mallowan (formerly Mrs Archibald Christie) (1890–1976). Her 87 crime novels have sold an estimated 300 million copies in 103 languages. *Sleeping Murder* was published posthumously in 1977.

It was announced on March 13, 1953, that 672,058,000 copies of the works of Marshal Josef Vissarionovich Dzhugashvili, also known as Stalin (1879–1953), had been sold or distributed in 101 languages.

DANIELLE STEEL, from Dec 1981 (381 consecutive weeks) to July 1988, has had at least one book written by her on a major best-seller list and on the NY Times hardcover or paperback lists. *(Roger Ressmeyer)*

Best Sellers

Excluding versions of the Bible, the world's all-time best selling copyright book is the *Guinness Book of World Records* first published from London in Sept 1955 by the Guinness Brewery to settle arguments in Britain's pubs and edited by Norris Dewar McWhirter (b

Aug 12, 1925) and his twin Alan Ross McWhirter (killed Nov 27, 1975). Its cumulative sale in 26 languages to mid-1988 is in excess of 60 million copies.

It is believed that the 1879 edition of *The McGuffey Reader*, compiled by Henry Vail and published for school distribution in the US by Van Antwerp Bragg and Co, sold 60 million copies in the pre-copyright era.

The novel with the highest sales has been *Valley of the Dolls* (first published March 1966) by Jacqueline Susann (Mrs Irving Mansfield) (1921–74) with a worldwide total of 29,104,000 to May 26, 1988. In the first 6 months Bantam sold 6.8 million.

Greatest Advance

The greatest advance royalty paid for any book is $5,000,000 paid for *Whirlwind* by James Clavell at an auction in NYC won by William Morrow & Co and its affiliated company, Avon Books, both of NYC. Mary Higgins Clark (US) signed a contract for $10,100,000 for 4 novels and a book of short stories, on May 5, 1988.

Slowest Seller

The accolade for the world's slowest-selling book (known in publishing as slooow-sellers) probably belongs to David Wilkins' translation of the New Testament from Coptic into Latin, published by Oxford University Press in 1716 with 500 copies. Selling an average of one each 139 days, it remained in print for 191 years.

Oldest Authoress

The oldest authoress was Mrs Alice Pollock (*née* Wykeham-Martin) (1868–1971) of Haslemere, Surrey, England, whose book *Portrait of My Victorian Youth* (Johnson Publications) was published in March 1971 when she was aged 102 years 8 months.

Youngest Authoress

The youngest recorded commercially published author is Dorothy Straight (b May 25, 1958) of Washington, DC, who wrote *How the World Began* in 1962, aged 4. It was published in Aug 1964 by Pantheon Books.

Most Rejections of a Best Seller

The record for rejections before publication (and best-sellerdom) is *Zen and the Art of Motorcycle Maintenance* by Robert M. Pirsig which was rejected by 121 publishers before William Morrow & Co. accepted it in 1974. After hardcover publications it was paperbacked by Bantam for 7 years and the license was renewed in 1984 "for $500,000 which was almost double the amount paid for its initial license," the author told *Guinness*.

Highest-Paid Writer

In 1958, a Mrs Deborah Schneider of Minneapolis wrote 25 words to complete a sentence in a competition for the best blurb for Plymouth cars. She won from about 1,400,000 entrants the prize of $500 every month for life. On normal life expectations she would collect $12,000 per word. No known anthology includes Mrs Schneider's deathless prose.

Longest Biography

The longest biography in publishing history is that of Sir Winston Churchill by his son Randolph (4,832 pages) and Martin Gilbert (13,830 pages) to date comprising some 8,214,000 words.

Georges Simenon (b Feb 13, 1903, Liege, Belgium) wrote 22 autobiographical books from 1972 to date.

Fastest and Slowest Publishing

The fastest time in which a book has been published is less than 24 hours by Corgi Books (Eng) from receipt of final manuscript to finished copies, in the case of John Lisners' *The House of Horrors*, a 223-page paperback on the mass murderer in North London, Dennis Nilsen sentenced to life imprisonment at 4:23 PM on Nov 4, 1983.

The fastest time in which a hardback book has been published is 43 hours 15 min in the case of *The ITN Book of the Royal Wedding*, published by Michael O'Mara. Typesetting began at 2:00 PM on July 24, 1986 and the books were on sale at 9:15 AM two days later.

The slowest was the German dictionary *Deutsche Worterbuch*, begun by the brothers Grimm in 1854 and finished in 1971.

Slowest proofreading record goes to Oxford Univ Press who sent out proofs of *Constable's Presentment to the Dugdale Society* in Dec 1949 and received them back 35 years later, in Dec 1984.

Highest Printings

The world's most widely distributed book is the Bible, which has been translated into 303 languages and portions of it into a further 1,581 languages. This compares with 222 languages for *Lenin*. It has been estimated that between 1815 and 1975 some 2,500,000,000 copies were printed of which 1,500,000,000 were handled by Bible Societies.

It has been reported that 800 million copies of the red-covered booklet *Quotations from the Works of Mao Tse-tung* were sold or distributed between June 1966, when possession became virtually mandatory in China, and Sept 1971, when their promoter, Marshal Lin Piao, died in an air crash.

The total disposal through non-commercial channels by Jehovah's Witnesses of *The Truth That Leads to Eternal Life*, published by the Watchtower Bible and Tract Society of Brooklyn, NYC (1968), reached 106,486,735 in 116 languages by May 1, 1987.

Largest Printers

The largest printers in the world are R. R. Donnelley & Co of Chicago. The company, founded in 1864, has plants in 24 main centers, and has turned out $2,482 million worth of work per year. More than 1,927 million tons of paper and board are consumed every year.

The largest printer under one roof is the US Government Printing Office in Washington, DC, founded in 1860. The Superintendent of Documents sells almost $60 million worth of US governmental

MOST WIDELY-READ COLUMNIST: Ann Landers gives advice in 1,200 daily and weekly newspapers to an estimated 90 million readers.

publications every year, has had as many as 20,000 (now 17,200) titles in print, and receives 6,500 mail orders each day.

Longest-Lived Comic Strip

The most durable newspaper comic strip has been the Katzenjammer Kids (Hans and Fritz) created by Rudolph Dirks, first published in the *New York Journal* on Dec 12, 1897, and carried on by his son.

The earliest strip was *The Yellow Kid* which first appeared in the *New York Journal* on Oct 18, 1896. The most widely syndicated is "Peanuts"® by Charles Schulz, which is syndicated by United Features Syndicate in 26 languages in 2,012 newspapers in 68 countries with an estimated circulation of 78½ million daily. It began in Oct 1950. In 1986, the income from his comic strip brought Schulz an estimated $1 million per month.

Most Widely Syndicated Columnist

The most widely syndicated columnist is Ann Landers (*née* Eppie Lederer) (b July 14, 1918) whose words now appear in 1,200 newspapers with an estimated readership of 90 million. In Feb 1987 she switched after 32 years from the *Chicago Sun-Times* to the *Chicago Tribune*.

Ranan R. Lurie (b May 26, 1932) is the most widely syndicated political cartoonist in the world. His work is published in 51 countries in 400 newspapers with a circulation of 62 million copies.

Ramon Coffman (b July 24, 1896) wrote a children's box called "Uncle Ray's Corner" that ran in US, Canadian and overseas newspapers for 62 years (1925–87).

Most Expensive Autographs

The highest price ever paid on the open market for a single autograph letter signed is $360,000 paid on Oct 29, 1986 at Sotheby's,

NY for a letter by Thomas Jefferson condemning prejudice against Jews in 1818. It was sold by Charles Rosenbloom of Pittsburgh.

The highest price ever for a single letter is $110,000 ($100,000 to the seller plus $10,000 commission to the auction gallery) paid on Oct 18, 1979 at the Hamilton Galleries, NYC, for a tiny note—actually a receipt—signed by Button Gwinnett (1732–77) of Georgia, one of the lesser known signers of the Declaration of Independence.

The highest price for the autograph of a living person was $12,500 (plus 10%) paid at the Hamilton Galleries on Jan 22, 1981, for a letter from President Ronald Reagan praising Frank Sinatra.

A record $4,675 (plus 10%) was paid at a Hamilton sale on Aug 12, 1982 by Barry D Hoffman for the signed portrait of Al Capone (1899–1947).

Most Expensive Expense Account

An expense account by Paul Revere, dated Jan 3, 1774 and signed by John Hancock, was auctioned for $70,000 at Sotheby Parke Bernet, NYC, April 26, 1978.

Most Valuable Autographs

Only one example of the signature of Christopher Marlowe (1565–93) is known. It is in the Kent County Archives, England, on a will of 1583. It is estimated that a seventh Shakespearean signature would realize at least $1.5 million at auction.

Most Autographs

Dong Kingman, well-known Chinese-American watercolor artist, signed personally 10,000 each of 12 of his lithographed paintings (making 120,000 in all) in Hong Kong in 12 days of continuous sitting, May 8–19, 1980, for Rocky Aoki's Benihana Collection.

Bond Signing

The greatest feat of autographing was performed by Arne Aaaser of Den Norske Creditbank, Oslo, Norway. He signed 20,000 bonds in 16 hours 2 min 50 sec, March 4–5, 1982.

Poets Laureate

The youngest Poet Laureate was Laurence Eusden (1688–1730), who at the age of 30 years 3 months on Dec 24, 1718, was appointed. The greatest age at which a poet has succeeded is 73 in the case of William Wordsworth (1770–1850) on Apr 6, 1843. The longest-lived Laureate was John Masefield, who died on May 12, 1967, aged 88 years 345 days. The longest which any poet has worn the laurel is 41 years 322 days, in the case of Alfred (later the 1st Lord) Tennyson (1809–92), who was appointed Nov 19, 1850, and died in office Oct 6, 1892.

Most Successful Poem

If by Joseph Rudyard Kipling (1865–1936), first published in 1910, has been translated into 27 languages and according to Kipling was "anthologized to weariness."

Christmas Cards

The greatest number of personal Christmas cards sent out is believed to be 62,824 by Werner Erhard of San Francisco, founder of est, in Dec 1975.

Longest Letter

The longest personal letter based on word count is one of 1,402,344 words, mailed by Alan Foreman of Erith, Kent, Eng, to his wife Janet on Jan 25, 1984.

Most Love Letters

The Rev Canon Bill Cook and his fiancée, later wife, Helen, of Norfolk, Eng, exchanged 6,000 love letters during their 4½-year wartime separation Mar 1942–May 1946.

Letters to the Editor

The *Upper Dauphin Sentinel*, Pa, published a letter of 25,513 words over 8 issues from Aug to Nov 1979, written by John Sultzbaugh of nearby Lykens, Pa.

The shortest literary correspondence on record was that between Victor Marie Hugo (1802–85) and his publisher, Hurst and Blackett, in 1862. The author was on holiday and anxious to know how his new novel *Les Misérables* was selling. He wrote "?". The reply was "!".

Largest Libraries

The largest library is the Library of Congress (founded Apr 24, 1800), on Capitol Hill, Washington, DC. By 1988, it contained 86 million items, including 22 million books and pamphlets. The buildings contain 64.6 acres of floor space and 532 miles of book shelves.

The largest non-statutory library is the New York Public Library (founded 1895) on Fifth Avenue, NYC, with a floor area of 525,276 sq ft and 88 miles of shelving. Including 82 branch libraries, its collection embraces 11,952,450 volumes, 14,466,478 manuscripts, and 363,679 maps.

Overdue Books

The most overdue (US) book taken out by a known borrower was a book on febrile diseases (London, 1805, by Dr J. Currie) checked out in 1823 from the University of Cincinnati Medical Library and reported returned Dec 7, 1968, by the borrower's great-grandson Richard Dodd. The fine was calculated as $2,264, but waived.

A German book was borrowed from a Cambridge Univ library by Col Robert Walpole in 1667–68 and found and returned in 1955, some 288 years later.

Most Personal Mail

The highest confirmed count of letters received by any private citizen in a year is 900,000 letters by baseball star Henry Aaron, reported by the US Postal Department in June 1974 the year that he surpassed Babe Ruth's career home run record. About a third of them were letters of hate.

Oldest Newspapers

A copy has survived of a news pamphlet published in Cologne, Germany in 1470.

The oldest existing newspaper in the world is the Swedish official journal *Post och Inrikes Tidningar*, founded in 1645. It is published by the Royal Swedish Academy of Letters.

Most Newspapers

The US had 1,645 general circulation daily newspapers in Sept 1987. They had a combined net paid circulation of 62.8 million copies per day. The peak year for US newspapers was 1910 when there were 2,202. The leading newspaper readers in the world are the people of Sweden, where 580 newspapers were sold per each 1,000 persons in 1985.

Largest and Smallest Newspaper Issue

The most massive single issue of a newspaper was *The New York Times* of Sunday, Oct 17, 1965. It comprised 15 sections with a total of 946 pages, including about 1,200,000 lines of advertising. Each copy weighed 7½ lb and sold for 50 cents locally. With advertising sections added, the paper in Aug 1987 weighed 14 lb.

The largest page size ever used has been 51 in × 35 in for *The Constellation*, printed in 1859 by George Roberts as part of the Fourth of July celebrations in NYC.

The smallest original page size has been 3 × 3¾ in of the *Daily Banner* (25 cents per month) of Roseberg, Ore, issues of which, dated Feb 1 and 2, 1876, survive.

Highest Newspaper Circulation

The highest circulation for any newspaper is that for the *Yomiuri Shimbun* (founded 1874) of Japan which attained a figure of 14,474,573 on Apr 1, 1988. This has been achieved by totaling the figures for editions published in various centers with a morning circulation of 9,456,625 and an evening circulation of 5,017,948. It has a staff of 10,205.

Trud, the Soviet trade union daily, is printed in 53 cities in 15.4 million copies of which only 70,000 are bought at newsstands.

Largest Circulation Periodicals

The largest circulation of any weekly periodical is that of *TV Guide*, which, in 1974, became the first magazine in history to sell a billion copies in a year. The weekly average for Jan to July 1988 was 17.2 million.

In its 39 basic international editions the *Reader's Digest* (established Feb 1922) circulates 28,000,000 copies monthly, in 15 languages, including a US edition of 16,250,000 copies guaranteed.

Parade, the syndicated Sunday newspaper color magazine supplement, is distributed with 312 newspapers every Sunday. The circulation as of Aug 7, 1988 was 32,590,000.

Advertising Rates

The highest price ever for a single page of advertising is $408,900 for a four-color back cover of *Parade* on Aug 7, 1988. The record for a four-color inside page is $355,600 in *Parade* on Aug 7, 1988. The advertising revenue from the Nov 1982 US edition of *Reader's Digest* was a peak $14,716,551.

The highest expenditure ever incurred on a single advertisement in a periodical is $3,200,000 by Gulf and Western Industries for insertions in the Feb 5, 1979 *Time* magazine (US and selected overseas editions).

Crossword Puzzles

The earliest known crossword was a 9 × 9 Double Diamond published in *St. Nicholas* magazine for children for Sept 1875 in NYC. However, a 25-letter acrostic of Roman provenance was discovered on a wall in Cirencester, England in 1868.

The largest published crossword has been one compiled by Robert Trucot of Québec, Canada. It comprised 82,951 squares, 12,489 clues across and 13,125 down and covered 38.28 sq ft.

4. MUSIC

Earliest Instruments

Whistles and flutes made from perforated phalange bones have been found at Upper Paleolithic sites of the Aurignacian Period (*c.* 25,000–22,000 BC), *e.g.* at Istallóskö, Hungary, and in Molodova, USSR.

Pianos

The earliest pianoforte in existence is one built in Florence, Italy, in 1720, by Bartolommeo Cristofori (1655–1731) of Padua, and now preserved in the Metropolitan Museum of Art, NY.

The grandest grand piano built was one weighing 1⅓ tons and measuring 11 ft 8 in long, made by Chas. H. Challen & Son Ltd of London in 1935. The longest bass string measured 9 ft 11 in and the tensile stress on the 726-lb frame was 33.6 tons.

The highest price ever paid for a piano is $390,000 for a Steinway grand of *c.* 1888 sold at Sotheby Parke Bernet, NYC on March 26, 1980 for the Martin Beck Theatre and bought by a non-pianist.

The smallest playable piano is a one-eighth scale model of a 1910 Knabe measuring 7½ × 3⅜ × 6½ in, built by Emil J. Cost.

Organs

The largest and loudest musical instrument ever constructed and now only partly functional is the Auditorium Organ in Atlantic City, NJ. Completed in 1930, this heroic instrument has two consoles (one with seven manuals and another movable one with five), 1,477 stop controls and 33,112 pipes ranging in tone from 3/16 in to the 64-ft tone. It had the volume of 25 brass bands, with a range of 7 octaves. It also had the loudest organ stop, operated by a pressure of 100 in of water (3½ lb/sq in) which created a pure trumpet note of ear-splitting volume, more than six times the volume of the loudest locomotive whistles.

The largest fully functional organ today is the six-manual 30,067-pipe Grand Court Organ in the John Wanamaker main store in Philadelphia, installed in 1911 and enlarged before 1930. It has a 64-ft tone *gravissima* pipe.

The largest church organ is in Passau Cathedral, Germany. It was completed in 1928 by D. F. Steinmeyer & Co. It has 16,000 pipes and five manuals. The most powerful electronic organ is the 5,000-watt Royal V. Rodgers organ, designed by Virgil Fox with 465 speakers, installed by Orient Shoji Co in Chuo-Ku, Tokyo, Japan in June 1983.

The chapel organ at the US Military Academy at West Point, NY, has, since 1911, been expanded from 2,406 to 18,200 pipes.

Largest Natural Musical Instrument

In Luray Caverns, Virginia, stalactites covering an area of 3 acres are connected to and activated by keys on a console organ. When struck by electronically controlled rubber-tipped hammers or plungers, the organ produces music of concert quality. The natural pipes have been ground and tuned to vibrate to create the notes of the musical scale.

Double Bass Viol

The largest double bass ever constructed was 14 ft tall, built in 1924

LARGEST NATURAL MUSICAL INSTRUMENT: Luray Caverns in Virginia has this organ on which a musician plays concert-quality music by electronically hitting stalactites with rubber hammers. The music can be heard throughout the caves.

in Ironia, NJ by Arthur K. Ferris, allegedly on orders from the Archangel Gabriel. It weighed 1,300 lb with a sound box 8 ft across, and had leathern strings totaling 104 ft. Its low notes could be felt rather than heard.

Most Valuable Musical Instrument

The highest price paid at auction for any musical instrument is $1,227,600 at Sotheby's, London on June 22, 1988 for a Stradivarius violoncello known as "The Cholmondeley," made in Cremona, Italy *c.* 1698.

Most Durable Musicians

Elise Maude Stanley Hall (1877–1976) gave piano recitals for 90 years, giving her final concert in Rustenburg, Transvaal, S Africa aged 97. Charles Bridgeman (1779–1873) of All Saints Parish Church, Hertford, Eng, who was appointed organist in 1792, was still playing 81 years later in 1873. Norwegian pianist Reidar Thommesen (b June 7, 1889) played over 30 hours a week in theatre cafés when he was in his 90's.

Most Valuable Violin

At an auction for the Lady Blunt Stradivarius violin of 1721, the asking price was £820,000 ($1,148,000) at Sotheby's London on Nov 14, 1985, but bids failed to reach that level.

The highest price ever *paid* at auction for a violin or any musical instrument is $889,240 for a 1709 Stradivarius played by the celebrated English concert violinist, Marie Hall (1884–1956), auctioned at Sotheby's, London, Eng, on Mar 31, 1988. The violin, acquired by Hall in 1905, was bought by an unidentified South American dealer. The instrument had last been auctioned in 1968, when it sold for $52,600—a record at the time.

Most Durable Fiddlers

Rolland S. Tapley retired as a violinist from the Boston Symphony Orchestra after playing for a reputedly unrivaled 58 years from Feb 1920 to Aug 27, 1978. Otto E. Funk, 62, walked 4,165 miles from NYC to San Francisco, playing his Hopf violin every step of the way westward. He arrived June 16, 1929, after 183 days on the road.

Largest and Most Expensive Guitars

The largest and presumably also the loudest playable guitar is one 14 ft 3¼ in tall and 309 lb, built by Joe Kovacic of Lado Musical, Inc., Scarborough, Ont, Canada.

The most expensive standard-sized guitar is the German chittara battente, built by Jacob Stadler (dated 1624), which sold for £10,500 ($25,200) at Christie's, London, June 12, 1974.

Largest Harp

What is probably the world's largest true playable harp was built in 1982 in Santa Fe, N Mex. Standing 13 ft 4 in high and measuring 7½ ft in width and 48 in in depth, it is built to scale 2½ times as large as a concert harp. The work of Wave Roark Barron with Kristin

LARGEST CLASSICAL CONCERT CROWD: As part of the Miss Liberty Weekend celebration in NYC the NY Philharmonic Orchestra attracted an estimated 800,000 people to Central Park on July 5, 1986. This shot was taken from a helicopter in the early evening. *(Newsday)*

SMALLEST PLAYABLE VIOLIN is the record claimed by Craig B. Dill of Chester, Calif, whose violin measures $^{15}/_{16}$ of an inch. But does it play music? It's on display at the Chester Museum and this couldn't be verified. ▼

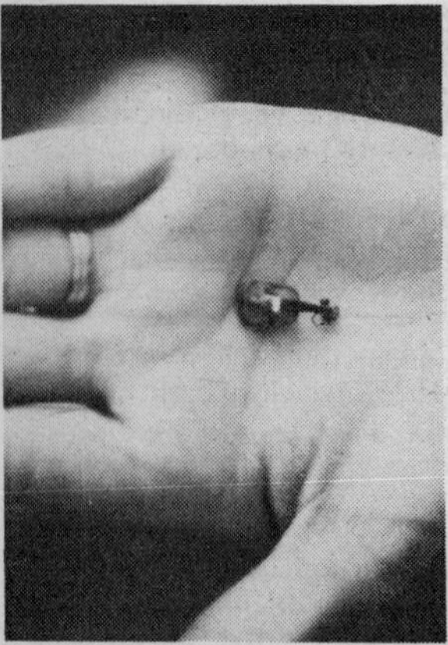

LARGEST GUITAR: Standing 14 ft 3¼ in high, this non-electric instrument, built by Jack Kovacic, weighs 309 lb. ▲

Novaswan and Lee Barron, it has an enclosed sound box, a harmonic curve, 41 stainless steel aircraft cable strings, brushed steel revolving base, hand molded redwood trunk seat for two, and can be plucked by hand or played by wind. Sale price: $15,000.

Largest Brass Instrument

The largest recorded brass instrument is a tuba standing 7½ ft tall, with 39 ft of tubing and a bell 3 ft 4 in across. This contrabass tuba was constructed for a world tour by the band of John Philip Sousa (1854–1932), the "March King," *c.* 1896–98, and is still in use. This instrument is now owned by a circus promoter in South Africa.

Longest Alphorn

The longest alphorn measuring 118 ft long with a 24½ in diameter barrel was made of spruce wood by Swiss-born Peter Wutherich, 68, of Boise, Idaho, and shown on KBCI-TV on Feb 20, 1987. It took 754 hours of labor over a year and a half to complete.

Largest Drum

The largest drum ever constructed was one 13 ft in diameter, built by the Supreme Drum Co, and played at the Royal Festival Hall, London on May 31, 1987.

Easiest and Most Difficult Instruments

The American Music Conference announced in Sept 1977 that the easiest instrument is the ukelele and the most difficult are the French horn and the oboe. The latter has been described as "the ill woodwind that no one blows good."

Stringed Instruments

The largest moveable stringed instrument ever constructed was a pantaleon with 270 strings stretched over 50 sq ft, used by George Noel in 1767.

The greatest number of musicians required to operate a single instrument was the 6 needed to play the gigantic orchestrion, known as the Appolonican, built in 1816 and played until 1840.

Largest Choir

Excluding "sing-alongs" by stadium crowds, the largest choir was one of 60,000 which sang in unison as a finale of a choral contest among 160,000 participants in Breslau, Germany on Aug 2, 1937.

Largest Bands

The most massive band ever assembled was one of 20,100 at the Ullevaal Stadium, Oslo, June 28, 1964, made up of Norges Musikkorps Forbund bands from all over Norway.

Greatest Classical Concert Attendance

The greatest attendance at any classical concert was an estimated 800,000 at a free open-air concert by the NY Philharmonic on the Great Lawn of Central Park, NYC, on July 5, 1986, as part of the

Statue of Liberty Weekend. A record number of police—22,000—kept order and "fostered a friendly mood" for the entire weekend in Manhattan.

Pop Concert Attendance

Estimating the size of audiences at open-air events where no one pays admission is often left to police departments, newspaper and television reporters, city officials, concert promoters and the featured players' publicity agents. Although the crowds are enormous in Central Park, NYC, on the Washington Mall and elsewhere, estimates vary widely and there is no way to check accuracy.

The best claims are: 400,000 at an Elton John concert in Central Park on Sept 13, 1980; 500,000 (?) at a Simon and Garfunkel reunion concert also in Central Park a year later, and 725,000 for Steve Wozniak's 1983 US Festival in San Bernardino, Calif. Diana Ross is said to have drawn 800,000 to her Central Park concert that was rained out on July 21, 1983.

A claim of 600,000 was made for a rock festival ("Summer Jam") at Watkins Glen, NY July 29, 1973. Of those attending, only 150,000 actually paid for admission. There were 12 "sound towers."

Most Prolific Composers

The most prolific composer of all time was probably Georg Philipp Telemann (1681–1767) of Germany. He composed 12 complete sets of services (one cantata every Sunday) for a year, 78 services for special occasions, 40 operas, 600 to 700 orchestral suites, 44 Passions, plus concertos and chamber music.

The most prolific symphonist was Johann Melchior Molter (*c.* 1695–1765) of Germany, who wrote 165. Joseph Haydn (1732–1809) of Austria wrote 104 numbered symphonies, some of which are regularly played today.

Among classical composers the most prolific and rapid was Wolfgang Amadeus Mozart (1756–91) of Austria, who wrote *c.* 1,000 operas, operettas, symphonies, violin sonatas, divertimenti, serenades, motets, concertos for piano and many other instruments, string quartets, other chamber music, masses and litanies, of which only 70 were published before he died, aged 35. His opera *The Clemency of Titus* (1791) was written in 18 days and three symphonic masterpieces, *Symphony No. 39 in E flat major, Symphony No. 40 in G minor* and the *"Jupiter" Symphony No. 41 in C major,* were reputedly written in the space of 42 days in 1788. His overture to *Don Giovanni* was written in full score at one sitting in Prague in 1787 and finished on the day of its opening performance.

Longest Symphony

The longest of all single classical symphonies is the orchestral *Symphony No. 3 in D minor* by Gustav Mahler (1860–1911) of Austria. This work, composed in 1896, requires a contralto, a women's and a boys' choir, in addition to a full orchestra. A full performance requires 1 hour 40 min, of which the first movement alone takes between 30 and 36 min.

The *Symphony No. 2* (the Gothic) composed in 1919–22 by Havergal Brian (1876–1972) was played by over 800 performers (4 brass bands) in the Victoria Hall, Hanley, Staffordshire, England on May 21, 1978, conducted by Trevor Stokes. A recent broadcast required 1 hour 45½ min. Brian wrote an even vaster work based on Shelley's *Prometheus Unbound* lasting 4 hours 11 min but the full score has been missing since 1961.

The symphony *Victory at Sea* written by Richard Rodgers and arranged by Robert Russell Bennett for NBC-TV in 1952 lasted 13 hours.

Marching Bands

The largest marching band was assembled by the Los Angeles Dodgers at Dodger Stadium on Apr 15, 1985. It consisted of 3,182 musicians and 1,342 majorettes, flag bearers, drill team members and directors for a total of 4,524 students from 52 high schools in the area. They played 3 tunes as well as the National Anthem under the directorship of Danny Kaye (1913–87). The longest recorded musical march by a marching band is one of 37.9 miles from Lillehammer to Hamar, Norway, in 15 hours when, on May 10, 1980, 26 of 35 members of the Trondheim Brass Band survived the playing of 135 marches.

Longest Piano Compositions

The longest continuous non-repetitious piece for piano ever specifically composed for the piano has been "The Well-Tuned Piano" by La Monte Young first presented by the Dia Art Foundation at the Concert Hall, Harrison St, NYC on Feb 28, 1980. The piece lasted 4 hours 12 min 10 sec.

Symphonic Variations, composed in the 1930's by Kaikhosru Shapurji Sorabji (b 1892) into 500 pages of close manuscript in 3 volumes would last for 6 hours at the prescribed tempo.

Greatest Span

The pianist Sergei Vassilievitch Rachmaninov (1873–1943) had a span of 12 white notes and could play a left-hand chord of C, E flat, G, C, G.

Highest-Paid Pianist

The highest-paid classical concert pianist was Ignace Jan Paderewski (1860–1941), Prime Minister of Poland (1919–21), who accumulated a fortune estimated at $5 million of which $500,000 was earned in a single season in 1922–23. The *nouveau riche* wife of a US industrialist once required him to play in her house behind a curtain.

Wladziu Valentino Liberace (1917–87) earned more than $2 million per 26-week season with a peak of $138,000 for a single night's performance at Madison Square Garden, NYC, in 1954.

Between 1937 and 1976, Artur Rubinstein (1887–1982) commanded 70 percent of the gross takings at his concerts.

Highest-Paid Singers

Of great fortunes earned by singers, the highest on record are those of Enrico Caruso (1873–1921), the Italian tenor, whose estate was about $9 million, and the Italian-Spanish coloratura soprano Amelita Galli-Curci (1889–1963), who received about $3 million. In 1850, up to $653 was paid for a single seat at the concerts given in the US by Johanna ("Jenny") Maria Lind (1820–87), later Mrs Otto Goldschmidt, the "Swedish Nightingale." She had a range of nearly three octaves, of which the middle register is still regarded as unrivaled.

The tenor "Count" John Francis McCormack (1884–1945) of Ireland gave 10 concerts to capacity audiences in a single season in Carnegie Hall, NYC.

David Bowie drew a fee of $1.5 million for a single show at the US Festival in Glen Helen Regional Park, San Bernardino County, Calif on May 26, 1983. The 4-man Van Halen rock singing group attracted a matching fee.

Surpassing the $81 million grossed by Michael Jackson's "Victory Tour" July–Dec 1984, is the tour which Bruce Springsteen made beginning in Apr 1984 that grossed an estimated $117 million. It ended with 4 nights in the LA Coliseum (capacity 85,000) when $5,800,000 was grossed.

Longest and Shortest Operas

The longest of commonly performed operas is *Die Meistersinger von Nürnberg* by Wilhelm Richard Wagner (1813–83) of Germany. A normal uncut performance of this opera as performed by the Sadler's Wells company between Aug 24 and Sept 19, 1968 entailed 5 hours 15 min of music. *The Heretics* by Gabriel von Wayditch, a Hungarian-American, is orchestrated for 110 pieces and lasts 8½ hours.

The shortest published was *Deliverance of Theseus* by Darius Milhaud (b Sept 4, 1892) first performed in 1928, which lasts for 7 min 27 sec.

Longest Aria

The longest single aria, in the sense of an operatic solo, is Brünnhilde's Immolation Scene in Wagner's *Götterdämmerung*. A well-known recording has been precisely timed at 14 min 46 sec.

Longest Operatic Encore

The longest listed in the *Concise Oxford Dictionary of Opera* was of the entire opera of Cimarosa's called *Il Matrimonio Segreto* at its premiere in 1792. This was at the command of Austro-Hungarian Emperor Leopold II (1790–92).

Curtain Calls

Luciano Pavarotti, singer, set a world record with 165 curtain calls at the W Berlin Opera, Germany, on Mar 3, 1988. The audience of 2,000 stood and cheered for 67 min.

Opera Houses

The largest is the Metropolitan Opera House, Lincoln Center, NYC, completed in Sept 1966, at a cost of $45,700,000. It has a capacity of

3,800 seats in an auditorium 451 ft deep. The stage is 234 ft in width and 146 ft deep. The tallest opera house is one housed in a 42-story building on Wacker Drive in Chicago.

The Teatro della Scala (La Scala) in Milan, Italy, shares with the Bolshoi Theatre in Moscow the distinction of having the greatest number of tiers. Each has 6 with the topmost being nicknamed the *Galiorka* by Russians.

Youngest and Oldest Opera Singers

The youngest opera singer in the world has been Jeanette Gloria (Ginetta) La Bianca, (b Buffalo, NY May 12, 1934) who made her official debut as Rosina in *The Barber of Seville* at the Teatro dell'Opera, Rome, May 8, 1950, aged 15 years 361 days, but who appeared as Gilda in *Rigoletto* at Velletri, Italy, 45 days earlier. Miss La Bianca was taught by Lucia Carlino and managed by Angelo Carlino.

The tenor Giovanni Martinelli sang Emperor Altoum in *Turandot* in Seattle, Wash Feb 4, 1967, when aged 81.

Danshi Toyotake (b Aug 1, 1891) has been singing *Gidayu* in Japan for 91 years.

Oldest Songs

The oldest known song is the *shaduf* chant, which has been sung since time immemorial by irrigation workers on the man-powered pivoted-rod bucket raisers of the Nile water mills (or *saqiyas*) in Egypt. The oldest known harmonized music is the English song *Sumer is icumen in* which dates from *c.* 1240.

Top Songs of All Time

The most frequently sung songs in English are *Happy Birthday to You* (based on the original *Good Morning to All,* by Mildred and Patty S. Hill of New York, published in 1935 and in copyright until 2010); *For He's a Jolly Good Fellow* (originally the French *Malbrouk*), known at least as early as 1781, and *Auld Lang Syne* (originally the Strathspey *I fee'd a Lad at Michaelmas*), some words of which were written by Robert Burns (1759–96). *Happy Birthday* was sung in space by the Apollo IX astronauts March 8, 1969.

Top Selling Sheet Music

Sales of three non-copyright pieces are known to have exceeded 20 million copies, namely *The Old Folks at Home* by Stephen Foster (1855), *Listen to the Mocking Bird* (1855) and *The Blue Danube* (1867). Of copyright material, the two top-sellers are *Let Me Call You Sweetheart* (1910, by Whitson and Friedman) and *Till We Meet Again* (1918, by Egan and Whiting), each with some 6 million by 1967. Other huge sellers have been *St Louis Blues*, *Stardust* and *Tea for Two*.

Most Successful Songwriters

The songwriters responsible for the most No. 1 singles are John Lennon and Paul McCartney. In America McCartney is credited as writer on 32 No. 1 hits, 6 more than Lennon. In Britain Lennon authored 27 number one's, McCartney 26. In both countries 23 of their No. 1's were jointly written. Barry Gibb of the Bee Gees has written or co-written 16 No. 1's. The most successful female songwriter in America is Carole King with 8 No. 1's—in Britain it is Madonna with 4.

National Anthems

The oldest national anthem is the *Kimigayo* of Japan, in which the words date from the 9th century. The anthem of Greece constitutes the first four verses of the Solomos poem, which has 158 verses. The shortest anthems are those of Japan, Jordan and San Marino, each with only four lines. Of the 11 wordless national anthems, the oldest is that of Spain, dating from 1770.

Longest Rendering of an Anthem

"God Save the King" was played non-stop 16 or 17 times by a German military band on the platform of Rathenau Railway Station, Brandenburg, on the morning of Feb 9, 1909. The reason was that King Edward VII was struggling inside the train to get into his German Field-Marshal uniform before he could emerge.

---

5. THEATRE

Theatre as we know it has its origins in Greek drama performed in honor of a god, usually Dionysus. The earliest amphitheatres date from the 5th century BC. The first stone-built theatre in Rome (erected in 55 BC) could accommodate 40,000 spectators. A theatre in Epidauros, Greece, built by Polycleitos in the 4th century BC is an extremely well-preserved amphitheatre.

Oldest Theatre

The oldest indoor theatre is the Teatro Olimpico in Vicenza, Italy. Designed in the Roman style by Andrea di Pietro, *alias* Palladio (1508–80), it was begun three months before his death and finished in 1583 by his pupil Vincenzo Scamozzi (1552–1616).

Largest and Smallest Theatres

The largest building used for theatre is the National People's Congress Building (*Ren min da hui tang*) on the west side of Tian An Men Square, Peking, China. It was completed in 1959 and covers an area of 12.9 acres. The theatre seats 10,000 and is only occasionally used as such, as in 1964 for the play "The East Is Red."

The highest capacity purpose-built theatre is the Perth Entertainment Centre in Western Australia, completed at a cost in Australian dollars of $8.3 million in Nov 1976, with a capacity of 8,003 seats. The stage area is 12,000 sq ft.

The smallest regularly operated professional theatre is the Piccolo in Juliusstrasse, Hamburg, W Germany. It was founded in 1970 and has a maximum capacity of 30 seats.

Largest Theatre Show Room

The largest is in the Ziegfeld Room, Reno, Nev with a 176-ft passerelle, 3 main elevators capable of lifting 1,200 show girls, two 62½-ft-circumference turntables and 800 spotlights.

Largest Amphitheatre

The largest amphitheatre ever built is the Flavian amphitheatre or Colosseum of Rome, Italy, completed in 80 AD. Covering 5 acres and with a capacity of 87,000, it has a maximum length of 612 ft and maximum width of 515 ft.

Longest Runs

Plays

The longest continuous run of any show is of *The Mousetrap* by Agatha Christie (Lady Mallowan) (1890–1976). This thriller opened at the Ambassadors Theatre (capacity 453), London, Nov 25, 1952 and moved after 8,862 performances "down the road" to St Martin's Theatre, London, March 25, 1974. The 30th Anniversary performance on Nov 25, 1982 was the 12,481st and the total in Mar 1988 is 14,693.

The Vicksburg Theatre Guild of Vicksburg, Miss, has been playing the melodrama *Gold in the Hills* by J. Frank Davis discontinuously but every season since 1936.

Revues

The greatest number of performances of any theatrical presentation is 47,250 in the case of *The Golden Horseshoe Revue*—a show staged at Disneyland Park, Anaheim, Calif. The show was started on July 16, 1955, closed on Oct 12, 1986, and was seen by 16 million people. The three main performers were, Dick Hardwick (formerly it was Wally Boag), Fulton Burley, and Betty Taylor, who played as many as five houses a day in a routine lasting 45 min.

Broadway and Off-Broadway

The long-run record for a "Broadway" show of any type was set on Sept 29, 1983, when *A Chorus Line* had its 3,389th performance at the Shubert Theatre. It is estimated that 23 million people worldwide saw it since it opened on July 25, 1975, and paid $260 million to the box office.

The Broadway record for the longest run of a drama (rather than a musical) is 3,224 performances (including benefits, etc.) by *Life With Father*, written by Howard Lindsay and Russel Crouse. The play opened at the Empire Theatre on Nov 8, 1939, and closed July 12, 1947, at the Alvin Theatre.

Longer running off-Broadway (i.e. in Boston) is an audience-participation comedy/murder-mystery called "Shear Madness" that reached its 3,225th performance on Nov 16, 1987 after having opened on Jan 29, 1980. It has been running continuously (still going) at the Charles Playhouse Stage II, and other companies have presented it in Chicago, St Louis, Phila, Wash DC, Montreal and Barcelona.

Longer running still was the London show, *No Sex Please, We're British* which finally ended its run after 6,761 performances on Sept 5, 1987 after almost 17 years.

Musicals

The longest-running musical is the off-Broadway show *The Fantasticks* by Tom Jones and Harvey Schmidt which reached its 10,864th performance on June 8, 1986, after 26 years. *The Fantasticks* was scheduled to close on that date, but the closing announcement stirred up so much new demand for tickets, that the musical play has had to stay open indefinitely. The show set a record by playing 11,740 performances to July 14, 1988. On May 3, 1988 it started its 29th year in the same theatre, the Sullivan Street Playhouse, Greenwich Village, NYC.

LONGEST RUN: For the ▲ finale of performance No. 3,389 of "A Chorus Line" on Sept 29, 1983 which broke the record for a Broadway show, 332 players who had appeared during the run in all roles were invited and appeared on stage. In mid-1988, the play was still running, and 23 million people worldwide had seen it on stage. (*Photo © 1983 Martha Swope. Courtesy of Merle Debuskey & Associates*)

► "FANTASTICK" THEATRE OWNER: Jules Field in front of the Sullivan St Playhouse in Greenwich Village, where the longest running off-Broadway musical began its 29th year in 1988.

One-Man Shows

The longest run of one-man shows is 849 by Victor Borge (b Copenhagen Jan 3, 1909) in his *Comedy in Music* from Oct 2, 1953, to Jan 21, 1956, at the Golden Theatre, NYC.

The world aggregate record for one-man shows is 1,700 performances of *Brief Lives* by Roy Dotrice (b Guernsey, England, May 26, 1923) including 400 straight at the Mayfair Theatre, London, ending July 20, 1974. He was on stage for more than 2½ hours per performance of this 17th century monologue, and required 3 hours for makeup and 1 hour for removal, thus aggregating 40 weeks in the chair as well.

Most Durable Leading Actors

Kanzaburo Nakamura, of Tokyo, Japan, has played 803 leading roles on stage in Kabuki theatre, Nov 1926–Jan 1987, an estimated total of 20,150 performances.

Dame Anna Neagle (1904–86) played the lead in *Charlie Girl* at the Adelphi Theatre, London, England, for 2,062 of 2,202 performances between Dec 15, 1965 and March 27, 1971. She played the same rôle a further 327 times in 327 performances in Australasia.

Marian Seldes did not miss a single performance in Ira Levin's long-running Broadway hit *Deathtrap* from the show's opening on Feb 26, 1978, to its close on June 27, 1982. She portrayed the character Myra Bruhl in 1,793 consecutive performances.

Most Ardent Theatregoer

Dr H. Howard Hughes (b 1902) of Fort Worth, Tex, professor emeritus at Texas Wesleyan University, attended 5,720 shows in the period 1956–1986.

Edward Sutro (1900–78) in England saw 3,000 first-night productions from 1916 to 1956, and possibly more than 5,000 shows in his 60 years of theatre-going.

Irate Playwright

Eugene O'Neill was expelled from Princeton for throwing a beer bottle through the college president's window. The president, by the way, was Woodrow Wilson, the only US President ever to possess a Ph.D.

Shakespeare

The longest play is *Hamlet*, with 4,042 lines and 29,551 words, 1,242 words longer than *Richard III*. Of Shakespeare's 1,277 speaking parts, the longest is the title role in *Hamlet* with 11,610 words.

Youngest Broadway Producer

Margo Feiden (Margo Eden) (b NY, Dec 1944) produced the musical *Peter Pan*, which opened Apr 3, 1961, when she was 16 years 5 months old. She wrote *Out Brief Candle*, which opened Aug 18, 1962, and is now a leading art dealer.

Longest Play

The longest recorded theatrical production has been "The Acting Life" staged in the Tom Mann Theatre, Sydney, Australia on Mar 17–18, 1984 with a cast of 10. The production required 19½ hours (21 hours with intermissions).

Shortest Criticism

The shortest dramatic criticism in theatrical history was that attributed to Wolcott Gibbs (1902–58), writing about the farce *Wham!* He wrote the single word "Ouch!"

An even shorter criticism came from TV film critic Leonard Maltin whose review of the movie "Isn't It Romantic?" was simply "No."

Highest-Paid Entertainers

The highest-paid entertainer, Dolly Parton, earns $400,000 for a live concert. Johnny Carson's fee for the non-televised Sears Roebuck Centenary in Oct 1984 was set at $1 million.

Longest Professional Chorus Line

The longest chorus line in theatre history was up to 120 in some of the early *Ziegfeld Follies*. In the finale of *A Chorus Line* on the night of Sept 29, 1983, when it broke the record as the longest-running Broadway show ever, 332 top-hatted "strutters" appeared on the stage. The Rockettes at Radio City Music Hall, NYC, regularly have 36 precision-timed dancers.

No off-stage record claims will be considered.

Shortest Runs

The shortest run on record was that of *The Intimate Revue* at the Duchess Theatre, London, March 11, 1930. Anything which could go wrong did. With scene changes taking up to 20 minutes apiece, the management scrapped seven scenes to get the finale on before midnight. The run was described as "half a performance."

A number of Broadway productions open and close the same night. There were 11 such "turkeys" in the 1978–79 season.

The most spectacular was the Royal Shakespeare Company's musical *Carrie* which closed after 5 performances at the Virginia Theatre, Broadway, on May 17, 1988 with a loss of $7.5 million.

Most Rôles

The greatest recorded number of theatrical, film, advertising and television rôles is 3,382 from 1951 to Mar 1988 by Jan Leighton (US).

Fashion Shows

The most prolific producer and most durable commentator of fashion shows is Adalene Ross of San Francisco, with over 4,711 in both categories to mid-1988.

Ice Shows

Holiday on Ice Productions Inc, founded by Morris Chalfen in

1945, stages the world's most costly live entertainment with up to seven productions playing simultaneously in several of 75 countries drawing 20 million spectators paying $40 million in a year. The total number of skaters and other personnel exceeds 900. By Mar 1988, 250 million had seen the show.

Wrestling Shows

The wrestler who has received most for a single bout has been Kanii Antonio Inoki of Japan on June 26, 1976. He received $2 million for the wrestler vs. boxer bout against Muhammad Ali in the Budokan Arena, Tokyo, Japan which ended in a "draw."

6. RADIO BROADCASTING

Earliest Broadcast

The first advertised broadcast was made on Dec 24, 1906, by Canadian-born Prof Reginald Aubrey Fessenden (1868–1932) from the 420-ft mast of the National Electric Signaling Company at Brant Rock, Mass. The transmission included Handel's *Largo*. Fessenden had achieved the broadcast of speech as early as Nov 1900, but this was highly distorted.

Transatlantic Transmissions

The earliest claims to have received wireless signals (the letter S in Morse Code) across the Atlantic were received by Guglielmo Marconi (1874–1937), George Stephen Kemp and Percy Paget from a 10-kilowatt station at Poldhu, Cornwall, England, at Signal Hill, St John's, Newfoundland, Canada, at 12:30 p.m. Dec 12, 1901. Human speech was first heard across the Atlantic in Nov 1915, when a transmission from the US Navy station at Arlington, Va, was received by US radio-telephone engineers up on the Eiffel Tower, Paris.

Earliest Radio-Microphone

The first radio-microphone, which was in essence also the first "bug," was devised by Reg Moores (GB) in 1947, and first used on 76 MHz in the ice show *Aladdin* at Brighton Sports Stadium, England, in Sept 1949.

Smallest Set

The Toshiba AM-FM RP=1070 with built-in loudspeaker measures 3.5 × 2.1 × 0.05 in, and with battery weighs 2½ oz.

Most Heard Broadcaster

Larry King has broadcast on network for 27½ hours a week since Jan 30, 1978 from Wash DC on Mutual Broadcasting Systems to all 50 states (now on 272 stations).

Most Durable Radio Program*

CKNW's "Roving Mike" program with Bill Hughes has been broadcast 6 days a week in New Westminster, BC, Canada since 1944. On Oct 8, 1987, the program celebrated its 13,000th consecutive broadcast.

Highest Radio Listener Response

The highest recorded response to a radio show occurred Nov 27, 1974, when on a 5-hour talk show on WCAU, Philadelphia, Howard Sheldon, the astrologist, registered a total of 388,299 calls on the "Bill Corsair Show."

Topmost Prize on Radio

Mary Buchanan, 15, on WKRQ, Cincinnati, won a prize of $25,000 a year for 40 years ($1 million) on Nov 21, 1980.

Most Assiduous Radio Ham

Richard C. Spenceley (d July 30, 1982) of KV4AA at St. Thomas, US Virgin Islands built his contacts (QSO's) to a record level of 48,100 in 365 days in 1978.

---

7. TELEVISION

The invention of television, the instantaneous viewing of distant objects by electrical transmissions, was not an act but a process of successive and interdependent discoveries. The first commercial cathode-ray tube was introduced in 1897 by Karl Ferdinand Braun (1850–1918), but was not linked to "electric vision" until 1907 by Boris Rosing of Russia in St Petersburg (now Leningrad). A. A. Campbell Swinton (GB 1863–1930) published the fundamentals of television transmission June 18, 1908 in a brief letter to *Nature* entitled "Distant Electric Vision." The earliest public demonstration of television was given on Jan 27, 1926, by John Logie Baird (1888–1946) of Scotland, using a development of the mechanical scanning system suggested by Paul Gottlieb Nipkow (1860–1940) on Jan 6, 1884. He had achieved the transmission of a Maltese Cross over 10 ft in Hastings, East Sussex, England, in Feb 1924, and the first facial image (of William Taynton, 15) on Oct 30, 1925. Taynton had to be bribed with 2 shillings sixpence. A patent application for the Iconoscope had been filed Dec 29, 1923, by Dr Vladimir Kosma Zworykin (born in Russia 1889, became a US citizen in 1924, d 1982). It was not issued until Dec 20, 1938.

Kenjiro Takayanagi (b Jan 20, 1899) succeeded in transmitting a 40-line electronic picture on Dec 25, 1926 with a Braun cathode-ray tube and a Nipkow disc at Hamamatsu Technical College, Japan. Baird launched his first television "service" via a BBC transmitter on Sept 30, 1929 and marketed the first sets, The Baird Televisions, in

*Also see television for records that began on radio.

May 1930. Public transmissions on 30 lines were made from Aug 22, 1932 until Sept 11, 1935.

In 1987, some 1,550 million tapes were rented from more than 26,000 video rental stores in the US, compared with 26 million tapes from 2,500 stores in 1980, according to Tim Baskerville, the publisher of Video Marketing Newsletter in LA.

Video Tape Recording

Alexander M. Poniatoff first demonstrated video tape recording, known as Ampex (his initials plus "ex" for excellence) in 1956.

The earliest demonstration of a home video recorder was on June 24, 1963, at the BBC News Studio at Alexandra Palace, London, of the Telcan developed by Norman Rutherford and Michael Turner of the Nottingham Electronic Valve Co.

Greatest TV Audience

It has been estimated that nearly one-third of the world's population (1.6 billion people) watched the "Live Aid" telethon concerts on July 13–14, 1985 to raise funds for Ethiopia, including stations hooked up by a record 12 satellites. This was the most successful appeal ever made on TV.

The greatest estimated number of viewers worldwide for a pre-scheduled event is 2.5 billion for the live and recorded transmissions of the XXIIIrd Olympic Games in LA July 27-Aug 13, 1984. ABC-TV aired 187½ hours on 56 cameras.

The serial which attracted the highest viewership was the final first-run episode of M*A*S*H on Feb 28, 1983, on CBS-TV which drew an estimated total audience of 125 million people in the US, with a 60.3 rating and a 77% share of the viewing audience.

Television Viewing

The US had by Jan 1987 89.13 million TV households, with 42.82 million having cable TV. The number of homes with color sets reached 82,680,000 (91%).

In 1987, there were more than 500 million homes with TV sets in the world, of which 89.13 million were in the US, with 8,250 TV stations worldwide, of which 1,194 were in the US.

The National Coalition on TV Violence published an estimate in June 1985 that by his 16th birthday the *average* US child will have seen 50,000 TV murders or attempted murders and 200,000 acts of violence. Between ages 2 and 11, the average viewing time is 28 hours per week.

Iceland has a TV-free day on Thursday to reduce disruption of family life. Otherwise transmissions are normally limited to between 8 and 11 p.m. July 1982 was declared a TV-free month. Upper Volta had only one set for each 1,000 inhabitants by 1974.

Transatlantic Transmission

The earliest transatlantic satellite transmission was achieved at 1 a.m. July 11, 1962, *via* the active satellite *Telstar I* from Andover, Maine, to Pleumeur Bodou, France. The picture was of Frederick R.

HIGHEST PAID TV PERFORMER: Bill Cosby (seen here with his TV wife, Phylicia Ayers-Allen Rashad) was reported to have earned at least $57 million in 1987 from TV and his other entertainment activities. (*Rex Features*) ◄

HIGHEST PAY for a single ► taping of TV was $2 million to singer Kenny Rogers in Feb 1983 by HBO.

DICK CLARK GETS GUINNESS AWARD for his "American Bandstand," the longest running musical show on national TV. Left to right: Julio Iglesias, David A. Boehm (editor of "Guinness Book of World Records"), Dick Clark (holding Award cup) and Dionne Warwick.

Kappell, chairman of the American Telephone and Telegraph Company, which owned the satellite. The first "live" broadcast was made July 23, 1962, and the first woman to appear was the *haute couturière* Ginette Spanier, directrice of Balmain, Paris, the next day.

On Feb 9, 1928 the image of J. L. Baird (see above) and of a Mrs Howe was transmitted from Station 2 KZ at Coulsdon, Surrey, Eng to Station 2 CVJ, Hartsdale, NY.

Largest Contracts

The highest-paid television performer currently is Bill Cosby, who was reported in Sept 1987 to have earned $57 million in 1987 for his TV shows, concerts, albums, and endorsements.

The highest rate for any TV contract ever signed was one for $7 million for 7 hours of transmission with NBC by Marie Osmond, announced on Mar 9, 1981. This includes talent and production costs.

John William Carson (b Oct 23, 1925), host of *The Tonight Show,* has a contract reportedly calling for annual payment of $5 million for the one-hour show he hosts 4 times weekly.

The highest-paid current affairs or news performer is Dan Rather of CBS who reportedly signed for $2.5 million per year beginning in 1986.

Most Expensive Production

The Winds of War, a 7-part Paramount World War II saga, aired by ABC in 1983 cost $42 million over 14 months of shooting. Its final episode had a rating of 41 and a 56% share (of the sets turned on).

Longest Program

The longest pre-scheduled telecast on record was one of 163 hours 18 min by GTV 9 of Melbourne, Australia, covering the Apollo XI moon mission July 19–26, 1969.

The longest continuous TV transmission under a single director was the York student television production "Breaker 88" transmitted Jan 29–30, 1988 for 28 hours 2 min under the direction of Keith Hide-Smith. The program's producer was Lawrence De'Ath and the technical co-ordinator John Mills.

Most Durable Radio-TV Shows and Performances

The most durable show is NBC's *Meet the Press,* first transmitted Nov 6, 1947 and weekly since Sept 12, 1948. It was originated by Lawrence E. Spivak, who until 1975 appeared weekly as either moderator or panel member.

Joe Franklin started in 1951 on ABC-TV NY with his show and in 1965 switched to WWOR-TV. He hosted his 22,954th broadcast on July 20, 1988 after a total of 37 consecutive years.

Over a period of 43 years, Hugh Downs appeared on camera on network television 10,032½ hours to July 1988.

The longest-running musical show on national TV is Dick Clark's "American Bandstand," which reached its 35th anniversary on Sept 15, 1987, and is continuing.

"Guiding Light," the soap-opera sponsored by Procter & Gamble, began airing on radio in Jan 1937 and moved to television in June 1952. It has been running continuously 5 days a week for more than

MOST PROLIFIC PRODUCER: Aaron Spelling, producer of "Dynasty," and many other TV shows, has put on 1,770 TV episodes since 1956. To view all of his produced work would take a full 3½ months. (*Rex Features*)

50 years. To July 1, 1988 it has had 12,670 episodes, of which 8,790 have been on television.

Highest TV Advertising Rates

The highest fee paid for a 30-second commercial is $1.5 million paid by Japanese TV in Dec 1985 to Boy George for promoting gin.

NBC announced that its rate for advertising on the 1987 Super Bowl XXI broadcast was $600,000 per half minute, in a game watched by 127 million.

Largest and Smallest Sets

The largest is the Sony Jumbo Tron color TV screen at the Tsukuba International Exposition '85 near Tokyo, in Mar 1985, which measured 80 ft × 150 ft.

The Seiko TV-Wrist Watch launched on Dec 23, 1982 in Japan has a 1.2 in screen and weighs only 2.8 oz. Together with the receiver unit and the headphone set the entire black-and-white system, costing 108,000 yen (then $463), weighs only 11.3 oz. The smallest single-piece TV set is the Casio-Keisanki TV-10 weighing 11.9 oz with a 2.7 in screen.

The smallest color TV set is the liquid crystal display (LCD) Japanese Epson launched in 1985 with dimensions of 3 × 6¾ × 1⅛ in, weighing, with batteries and its 52,800 crystals, only 16 oz.

Most Prolific Producer

The most prolific TV producer is Aaron Spelling (b 1928) who, in the years from 1956 to mid-1987, produced more than 1,770 episodes totaling 2,250 hours of air time as well as 207½ hours of movies and

8 feature films. The total hours equals 13.7 million feet of film, which, if projected 24 hours a day, would take over 3½ months to screen.

Most Prolific Scriptwriter

The most prolific television writer is the Rt. Hon. Lord Willis (b Jan 13, 1918), known as Ted Willis, who in the period 1949–87 has created 35 series, 30 stage plays, and 38 feature films. He had 24 plays produced. His total output since 1942 can be estimated at 19 million words.

---

8. MOTION PICTURES

The earliest motion pictures ever taken were by Louis Aimé Augustin Le Prince (1842?–90). He reportedly achieved dim moving outlines on a white-washed wall at the Institute for the Deaf, Washington Heights, NYC, as early as 1885–87. The earliest surviving film (2⅛-in-wide paper roll) is from his camera patented in Britain taken in early Oct 1888 of the garden of his father-in-law Joseph Whitley in Rounday, Leeds, W Yorkshire, at 10 to 12 frames per sec.

The first commercial presentation of motion pictures was at Holland Bros Kinetoscope Parlor at 1155 Broadway, NYC, on Apr 14, 1894. Viewers could see 5 films for 25 cents or 10 for 50 cents from a double row of Kinetoscopes developed by William Kennedy Laurie Dickson (1860–1935), assistant to Thomas Alva Edison (1847–1931).

The earliest publicly presented film on a screen was *La Sortie des Ouvriers de l'Usine Lumière* probably shot in Aug or Sept 1894 in Lyon, France. It was exhibited at 44 Rue de Rennes, Paris, on Mar 22, 1895, by the Lumière brothers, Auguste Marie Louis Nicholas (1862–1954) and Louis Jean (1864–1948).

Earliest Sound Movie ("Talkie")

The earliest sound-on-film motion picture was achieved by Eugene Augustin Lauste (1857–1935) who patented his process Aug 11, 1906 and produced a workable system using a string galvanometer in 1910 at Benedict Road, Stockwell, London.

The earliest public presentation of sound on film was by the Tri-ergon process at the Alhambra cinema, Berlin, Germany on Sept 17, 1922.

Dr Lee de Forest (1873–1961) was responsible for the screening in the US of the first sound picture before a paying audience at the Rialto Theatre, NYC, Apr 15, 1923. The first all-talking picture was Warner Bros' *Lights of New York*, shown at the Strand Theatre, NYC, July 6, 1928.

Movie Theatres

The largest theatre that has facilities to show movies and formerly did show them is the Radio City Music Hall, NYC, opened on Dec 27, 1932, with 5,945 seats (now 5,882). The Roxy, opened in NYC on Mar 11, 1927, had 6,214 seats (later 5,869) but was closed Mar 29, 1960. The largest movie theatre now is the 5,041-seat Fox Theatre in

Detroit, Mich. Originally opened in 1928, the Fox is principally a live entertainment theatre but still shows films occasionally. The largest drive-in cinema is Loew's Open Air at Lynn, Mass, with a capacity for 5,000 cars.

Saudi Arabia (population 8.4 million) has no cinemas. San Marino has a total of 7, one for every 3,190 inhabitants. The US has the most cinemas with one for every 11,000 inhabitants.

Biggest Screen

The permanently installed cinema screen with the largest area is one 92 ft 9 in × 70 ft 6 in, installed in the Keong Emas Imax Theatre, Taman Mini Park, Jakarta, Indonesia, opened Apr 20, 1984. It was made by Harkness Screens Ltd of Hertfordshire, England.

A temporary screen 297 × 33 ft (9,801 sq ft) was used at the 1937 Paris Exposition. A TV screen 80 × 150 ft (12,000 sq ft) was set up at the Tsukuba International Exposition in Tokyo in Mar 1985.

Most and Least Expensive Films

The most expensive film ever made is believed to be *Superman,* of which the negative cost is estimated by *Variety* to have been $55 million. Estimates in excess of $60 million have been made for *Superman II,* but *Variety* quotes $54 million.

The least expensive film was Cecil Hepworth's highly successful release of *Rescued by Rover* in 1905 in England which cost $37.40.

Film Rights

The highest price ever paid for film rights is $9,500,000 announced on Jan 20, 1978 by Columbia for *Annie,* the Broadway musical by Charles Strouse, based on the comic strip *Little Orphan Annie*.

Highest Box Office Gross

The box office gross championship for films is highly vulnerable to inflated ticket prices. *Gone With the Wind* with Clark Gable (1901–1960) and Vivien Leigh (1913–1967) released in 1939 is undoubtedly the highest in box office gross.

Highest Film Rentals

Variety, the trade publication that is highly respected for its accuracy, lists *E.T.* as tops for rentals with $228,379,346 through Dec 31, 1987, and no new releases joining the top 10 of all time since 1985. *Star Wars* remains #2, followed by 2 George Lucas productions. *Beverly Hills Cop II* led the 1987 new films with $80,857,776 in rentals.

Movie-Going

The Chinese Ministry of Culture reported in Sept 1984 that there were 27 billion cinema attendances in 1983—or nearly 27 per person per year. The Soviet Union claims to have the most movie theatres in the world, with 163,400 in 1974, but this includes buildings merely equipped with even 16-mm projectors. The US has 20,200 actual movie theatres.

Longest Film

The longest film ever premiered was the 48-hour-long *The Longest Most Meaningless Movie in the World* in 1970. It was British-made and later cut to 90 min.

Longest-Running Film

Emmanuelle opened on June 26, 1974 at the Paramount City, Paris, and closed on Feb 26, 1985—the longest continuous run of any one film at one cinema.

Highest Earnings by an Actor

The highest rate of pay in cinema history is that paid to Sylvester Stallone (b July 6, 1946). He received $12 million for *Cobra* and the same for *Over the Top* before breaking his own record with a reported $16 million for *Rocky IV*. The highest paid actresses are Meryl Streep (b Summit, NJ, 1949) with $4 million for *Out of Africa* and the same for *Heartburn*, and Barbra Streisand with $5 million for *Nuts*.

Most Portrayed Character

The character most frequently recurring on the screen is Sherlock Holmes, created by Sir Arthur Conan Doyle (1859–1930). Sixty-nine actors portrayed Holmes in 194 films between 1900 and 1988.

In horror films, the character most often portrayed is Count Dracula created by the Irish writer Bram Stoker (1847–1912). The Count or his

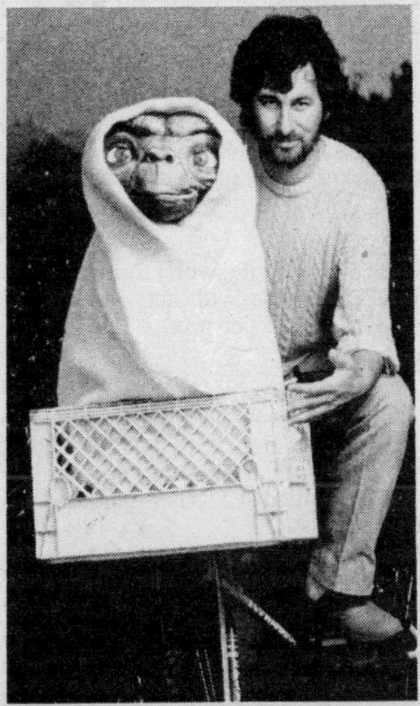

HIGHEST FILM RENTALS: "E.T.: The Extra-Terrestrial" set the record with over $228 million. The little charmer is seen here with his producer, Steven Spielberg. (*Courtesy Universal Pictures and Mr Spielberg*)

immediate family were represented 155 times compared to the 108 times his closest rival, Frankenstein's monster, has appeared.

Largest Number of Costumes

The largest number of costumes for any one film was 32,000 for the 1951 film *Quo Vadis*.

Most Costume Changes by One Person

Elizabeth Taylor changed costume 65 times in *Cleopatra* (1963). The costumes were designed by Irene Sharaff and cost $130,000.

The most expensive costume worn in a film was Constance Bennett's sable coat in *Madam X*. It was valued at $50,000. The most expensive costume designed and made specially for a film was Edith Head's mink and sequins dance costume worn by Ginger Rogers in *Lady in the Dark*. It cost Paramount $35,000.

Largest Loss

It was reported on Nov 20, 1980 that United Artists had withdrawn Michael Cimino's production of *Heaven's Gate* because its total cost including distribution and studio overheads had reached $44,000,000.

Stuntman Earnings

Dar Robinson was paid $100,000 for the 1,100-ft-high leap he made from the CN Tower in Toronto in Nov 1979 for *High Point*. His parachute opened at only 300 ft above the ground. He died in a motorcycle stunt during movie-making in Page, Ariz, on Nov 21, 1986, aged 39.

Most Films Seen

Albert E. Van Schmus (b 1921) saw 16,945 films in 33 years (1949–1982) as a rater for Motion Picture Association of America Inc.

Most Violent Movie

A study on the portrayal of violence showed the worst film on record was *Red Dawn*, released in the US in 1984, with acts of violence occurring at the rate of 134 per hour or 2.23 per min.

Most Oscars

Walter (Walt) Elias Disney (1901–66) won more "Oscars"—the awards of the Academy of Motion Picture Arts and Sciences, instituted on May 16, 1929, for 1927–28—than any other person. The physical count comprises 20 statuettes and 12 other plaques and certificates, including posthumous awards.

The only performer to win four Oscars for her starring rôles has been Katharine Hepburn (b Hartford, Conn, Nov 9, 1909), in *Morning Glory* (1933), *Guess Who's Coming to Dinner* (1967), *The Lion in Winter* (1968) and *On Golden Pond* (1981). She was nominated 12 times. Her college career ended when she was expelled from Bryn Mawr for smoking a cigarette.

Only 4 other actors have won 2 Oscars in starring roles—Fredric

Longest Oscar Speech

Greer Garson (b Sept 1908, N Ireland) in 1942 took over 1½ hours to say "Thank you" for her *Mrs. Miniver* award. (Some say the speech was only 6 min but seemed longer.) With the ceremony now on TV, acceptances are supposed to be limited to 45 sec.

March in 1932, 1946; Spencer Tracy in 1937, 1938; Gary Cooper in 1941, 1952; and Marlon Brando in 1954, 1972.

Edith Head (d. 1981) won 8 individual awards for costume design.

The youngest person ever to win an Oscar was Shirley Temple (b Apr 23, 1928) with her 1934 honorary award at age 5, and the oldest is George Burns (b Jan 20, 1896) at age 80 for *The Sunshine Boys.*

The film with most awards has been *Ben Hur* (1959) with 11. The film with the highest number of nominations was *All About Eve* (1950) with 14. It won 6.

Oscars are said to have been named after Oscar Pierce of Texas. When the figurines were first delivered to the executive offices of the Academy of Motion Picture Arts and Sciences, the executive secretary exclaimed, "Why, they look just like my Uncle Oscar." And the name stuck.

9. RECORDED SOUND

The phonograph was first *conceived* by Charles Cros (1842–88), a French poet and scientist who described his idea in sealed papers deposited in the French Academy of Sciences Apr 30, 1877. The first practical device was realized by Thomas Alva Edison (1847–1931), who gained his first patent Feb 19, 1878 for a wax cylinder machine constructed by his mechanic, John Kruesi. It was first demonstrated on Dec 7, 1877, and patented on Feb 19, 1878. The horizontal disc was introduced by Emile Berliner (1851–1929).

Oldest Voice Recorded

Lajos Kossuth (b Sept 9, 1802), former governor of Hungary, made a speech in Turin, Italy, on Sept 20, 1890 which is preserved on a wax cylinder in the National Library in Budapest.

Tape Recordings

Magnetic recording was invented by Valdemar Poulsen (1869–1942) of Denmark with his steel wire Telegraphone in 1898 (US Patent No. 661619). Fritz Pfleumer (German patent 500900) introduced tape in 1928. Plastic tapes were devised by BASF of Germany in 1932–35, but were not marketed until 1950 by Recording Associates of NYC. In Apr 1983, Olympic Optical Industry Co of Japan marketed a micro-cassette recorder 4.2 in × 2 in × 0.55 in weighing 4.4 oz.

Most Successful Solo Recording Artists

On June 9, 1960 the Hollywood Chamber of Commerce presented Harry Lillis (*alias* Bing) Crosby, Jr (1904–77) with a platinum disc to commemorate the alleged sale of 200 million from 2,600 singles and 125 albums he had recorded. On Sept 15, 1970 he received a second platinum disc when Decca Records claimed a sale of 300,650,000 discs. No independently audited figures of his global lifetime sales from his royalty reports have ever been published, and experts regard figures so high as this, before the industry became highly developed, as exaggerated.

No independently audited figures have ever been published for Elvis Aaron Presley (b Tupelo, Miss, 1935–77). In view of Presley's worldwide tally of over 170 major hits on singles and over 80 top-selling albums from 1956 and continuing after his death, it may be assumed that it was he who succeeded Crosby as the top-selling solo artist of all time.

CBS Records reported in Aug 1983 that sales of albums by Julio Iglesias (b 1943) in 6 languages had surpassed the 100 million mark.

Most Successful Group

The singers with the greatest sales of any group have been The Beatles. This group from Liverpool, England, comprised George Harrison (b Feb 25, 1943), John Ono (formerly John Winston) Lennon (b Oct 9, 1940; d Dec 8, 1980), James Paul McCartney (b June 18, 1942) and Richard Starkey, *alias* Ringo Starr (b July 7, 1940). The all-time Beatles sales by May 1985 were estimated by EMI at over 1,000 million discs and tapes.

Oldest Records

The oldest records in the BBC library are white wax cylinders dating from 1888. The earliest commercial disc recording was manufactured in 1895. The BBC library, the world's largest, contains over 1 million records, including 5,250 with no known matrix.

The earliest jazz record made was *Indiana* and *The Dark Town Strutters Ball*, recorded for the Columbia label in NYC on or about Jan 30, 1917 by the Original Dixieland Jazz Band, led by Dominick (Nick) James La Rocca (1889–1961). This was released May 31, 1917. The first jazz record to be released was the ODJB's *Livery Stable Blues* (recorded Feb 24), backed by *The Dixie Jass Band One-Step* (recorded Feb 26), released by Victor on March 7, 1917.

Earliest Golden Discs

The earliest recording eventually to aggregate a total sale of a million copies were performances by Enrico Caruso (b Naples, Italy, 1873, d 1921) of the aria *Vesti la giubba* (*On with the Motley*) from the opera *I Pagliacci* by Ruggiero Leoncavallo (1858–1919), the earliest version of which was recorded on Nov 12, 1902.

The first single recording to surpass the million mark was Alma Gluck's rendition of *Carry Me Back to Old Virginny* on the Red Seal Victor label on a 12-in single-faced (later backed) record (No. 74420).

The first actual golden disc was one sprayed by RCA Victor for presentation to Alton "Glenn" Miller (1904–44) for his *Chattanooga Choo Choo* on Feb 10, 1942.

Biggest Sellers

The greatest seller of any record to date is *White Christmas* by Irving Berlin (b Israel Bailin, at Tyumen, Russia, May 11, 1888), as recorded by Bing Crosby on May 29, 1942. It was announced on Christmas Eve 1987 that North American sales alone reached 170,884,207 copies in all versions by June 30, 1987.

MOST SUCCESSFUL CONCERT TOUR: Recording artist Bruce Springsteen made a tour beginning in Apr 1984 which grossed an estimated $117 million, the last 4 nights alone at the LA Coliseum (85,000 audience) making a gross $5.8 million. *(LFI)*

WOMEN'S ALBUM BEST SELLER: Whitney Houston's 1985 debut album sold 14 million worldwide in 2 years.

The highest claim for any "pop" record is an unaudited 43 million for *Rock Around the Clock,* copyrighted in 1953 by the late Max Freedman and James E. Myers, under the name of Jimmy De Knight, and recorded Apr 12, 1954 by Bill Haley and the Comets.

The single record *Do They Know It's Christmas?,* written and produced by Bob Geldof (Eire) and Midge Ure (UK) played by an all-star ensemble of British musicians under the name Band Aid, sold 3.6 million copies on discs and cassettes by May 1987 in the UK and 8.1 million more worldwide.

The best-selling album of all time is *Thriller* by Michael Jackson (b Gary, Ind, Aug 29, 1958) with global sales of 40 million copies by May 1988.

The best-selling album by a group is Fleetwood Mac's *Rumours* with over 20 million sales to May 1987.

The best-selling album by a woman is *Whitney Houston* by Whitney Houston released in 1985. It had sold over 14 million copies by May 1987, including over 9 million in America, one million in the UK, and a further million in Canada. This is also the "best-selling debut album of all time."

The first classical long-player to sell a million was a performance featuring the pianist Harvey Lavan (Van) Cliburn, Jr (b Kilgore, Tex, July 12, 1934) of the *Piano Concerto No. 1* by Pyotr Ilyich Tchaikovsky (1840–93) of Russia. This recording was made in 1958 and sales reached 1 million by 1961, 2 million by 1965 and about 2,500,000 by Jan 1970.

Best-Seller Chart Records

Singles record charts were first published by *Billboard* on July 20, 1940, when the No. 1 record was *I'll Never Smile Again* by Tommy Dorsey (b Nov 19, 1905, d Nov 26, 1956). Three discs have stayed at the top for a record 13 consecutive weeks—*Frenesi* by Artie Shaw from Dec 1940; *I've Heard that Song Before* by Harry James from Feb 1943; and *Goodnight Irene* by Gordon Jenkins and the Weavers from Aug 1950. *Tainted Love* by Soft Cell stayed on the chart for 43 consecutive weeks from Jan 1982. The Beatles have had the most No 1 records (20), Conway Twitty the most Country No 1's (35) and Aretha Franklin the most Black No 1's (20). Aretha Franklin is also the female solo artist with the most million-selling singles with 14 between 1967 and 1973. Elvis Presley has had the most hit singles on *Billboard's Hot 100–149* from 1956 to May 1987.

Billboard first published an album chart on March 15, 1945, when the No. 1 record was *King Cole Trio* featuring Nat "King" Cole (b March 17, 1919, d Feb 15, 1965). *South Pacific* was No. 1 for 69 weeks (non-consecutive) from May 1949. *Dark Side of the Moon* by Pink Floyd enjoyed its 674th week on the charts in May 1987 (over 19.5 million sold).

The Beatles had the most No. 1's (15), Elvis Presley was the most successful male soloist (9), and Simon and Garfunkel the top duo with 3. Elvis Presley had the most hit albums (93 from 1956–May 1987). Barbra Streisand has the most No. 1 albums (6), most hit albums in total (39 between 1963 and June 1987), 29 of which have been certified gold (500,000 sales), or platinum (1 million sales) by the RIAA, making Streisand the best-selling female singer of all time.

Most Golden Discs

The only *audited* measure of gold, platinum and multiplatinum singles and albums within the US is certification by the Recording Industry Association of America introduced Mar 14, 1958. Out of the 2,582 RIAA awards made to Jan 1, 1985, The Beatles with 47 (plus one with Billy Preston) have most for a group. Paul McCartney has an additional 27 awards outside the group, and with Wings (including one with Stevie Wonder and one with Michael Jackson).

The most awards to an individual is 51 to Elvis Presley, spanning 1958 to Jan 1, 1986. Globally, however, Presley's total of million-selling singles has been authoritatively put at "approaching 80."

Compact Discs

Announced by Philips in 1978, and introduced by the same company in 1982, the Compact Disc (CD) increasingly challenges the LP and cassette as a recording medium. By 1986 the CD represented 7 percent of all albums sold in the UK, 10 percent in America and 20 percent in Japan. The first CD to sell a million copies worldwide was Dire Straits' *Brothers in Arms* in 1986.

Most Recordings

Miss Lata Mangeshker (b 1928) has reportedly recorded between 1948 and 1984 not less than 30,000 solo, duet and chorus-backed songs in 20 Indian languages. She frequently has 5 sessions in a day and has "backed" 2,000 films.

Grammy Awards

The record number of Grammy awards in a year is 8 by Michael Jackson in 1984. The all-time record is 25 since 1958 by the orchestral conductor Sir Georg Solti (GB) (b Budapest, Hungary, Oct 21, 1912).

Phonographic Identification

Dr Arthur B. Lintgen (b 1932) of Rydal, Pa, has unique and proven ability to identify the music on phonograph records purely by visual inspection without hearing a note.

Chapter 7

The World's Structures

EARLIEST STRUCTURES

The earliest known human structure is a rough circle of loosely piled lava blocks found in 1960 on the lowest cultural level at the Lower Paleolithic site at Olduvai Gorge in Tanzania, revealed by Dr Mary Leakey in Jan 1960. The structure was associated with artifacts and bones on a work-floor, dating to *circa* 1,700,000 BC.

The earliest evidence of *buildings* yet discovered is that of 21 huts with hearths or pebble-lined pits and delimited by stake holes, found in Oct 1965 at the Terra Amata site in Nice, France, thought to belong to the Acheulián culture of 120,000 years ago. Excavation carried out between June 28 and July 5, 1966 revealed one hut with palisaded walls having axes of 49 and 20 ft.

The oldest free-standing structures, described in 1647, are now believed to be the megalithic temples at Mgarr and Skorba in Malta and Ggantija in Gozo, dating from *c.* 3250 BC.

The remains of a stone tower 20 ft high built into the walls of Jericho have been excavated, and dated to 5000 BC, the foundation of the walls to as early as 8350 BC.

1. BUILDINGS FOR WORKING

Largest Industrial Building

The largest industrial plant in the world is the Nizhniy Tagil Railroad Car and Tank Plant, USSR, which has 204.3 acres of floor space. It has an annual capacity to produce 2,500 T-72 tanks.

Largest Commercial Buildings

The greatest ground area covered by any building under one roof is the flower auction building of the cooperative VBA (Verenigde Bloemenveilingen Aalsmeer), The Netherlands, which measures 2,546 × 1,794 ft with a floor surface of 84.82 acres. A new extension to 91.05 acres was built in 1986.

The building with the largest cubic capacity is the Boeing Compa-

TALLEST OFFICE BUILDING: The Sears Tower dominates the Chicago skyline with its 110 stories, 16,000 windows, and height of 1,454 ft (1,559 ft counting TV towers). In gross area, however, the Sears Tower contains only 4,400,000 sq ft compared to the World Trade Center's total of 8,740,000 sq ft.

MONUMENT TO ENGINEERING: This 66-ton "geometry set" built in Jeddah, Saudi Arabia, is said to be a reminder of the importance of engineering and planning in the development taking place in that nation. The top of the compass stands 122 ft 2½ in above the ground. *(Al Maktaba Stones)*

ny's main assembly plant at Everett, Wash, completed in 1968. The building, constructed for the manufacture of Boeing 747 jet airliners, has a maximum height of 115 ft and has a capacity of 200 million cu ft.

Largest Scientific Building

The most capacious scientific building is the Vehicle Assembly Building (VAB) at Complex 39, the selected site for the final assembly and launching of the Apollo moon spacecraft on the Saturn V rocket, at the John F. Kennedy Space Center (KSC) on Merritt Island near Cape Canaveral, Fla. It is a steel-framed building measuring 716 ft in length, 518 ft in width and 525 ft in height. The building contains four bays, each with its own door 460 ft high. Construction began in Apr 1963 by the Ursum Consortium. Its floor area is 343,500 sq ft (7.87 acres) and its capacity is 129,482,000 cu ft. The building was "topped out" on Apr 14, 1965 at a cost of $108,700,000.

Largest Administrative Building

The largest ground area covered by any office building is that of the Pentagon, in Arlington, Va. Built to house the US Defense Department's offices, it was completed Jan 15, 1943 and cost about $83 million. Each of the outermost sides of the Pentagon is 921 ft long and the perimeter of the building is about 1,500 yd. The 5 stories of the building enclose a floor area of 6½ million sq ft. During the day 29,000 people work in the building. The telephone system of the building has more than 44,000 telephones connected by 160,000 miles of cable and its 220 staff members handle 280,000 calls a day. Two restaurants, 6 cafeterias and 10 snack bars and a staff of 675 form the catering department of the building. The corridors measure 17 miles in length and there are 7,748 windows to be cleaned.

Largest and Tallest Office Buildings

The largest office buildings with the largest rentable space are the twin towers comprising the World Trade Center in NYC, with a total of 4,370,000 sq ft (100.32 acres) in each. The taller tower (Tower Two) is 1,362 ft 3¼ in high. The tip of the TV antenna on Tower One is 1,710 ft above street level, and is thus 151 ft taller than the antenna of the Sears Tower (see below).

The *tallest* office building is the Sears Tower, the national headquarters of Sears Roebuck & Co on Wacker Drive, Chicago, with 110 stories, rising to 1,454 ft and completed in 1974. Its *gross* area is 4,400,000 sq ft (101.0 acres). It was "topped out" on May 4, 1973, surpassing the World Trade Center in New York in height, at 2:35 p.m. Mar 6, 1973 with the first steel column reaching to the 104th story. The addition of two TV antennae brought the total height to 1,559 ft. The building's population is 16,700, served by 103 elevators and 18 escalators. It has 16,000 windows.

Tentative plans for a 169-story 2,300-ft-tall building, projected to cost $1,250,000,000, for the Chicago Loop, were published on Oct 27, 1981. Plans for a 150-story, 1,670-ft-tall tower, on the upper West Side of NYC, entitled Television City, were unveiled by Donald Trump on Nov 15, 1985.

Largest Garages and Parking Lots

The largest car park is the West Edmonton Mall in Edmonton, Alberta, Canada, which has covered garaging for 20,000 vehicles, and overflow facilities for 10,000 more cars. The largest private garage ever built was one for the Sultan of Brunei (see page 248).

The largest multistoried garage is the KMB Overhaul Centre operated by the Kowloon Motors Bus Co Ltd, Hong Kong. Built for double-decker buses, its 4 floors occupy more than 11.6 acres.

Largest Hangars

The largest hangar is Hangar 375 ("Big Texas") at Kelly Air Force Base, San Antonio. The high bay area measures 2,000 × 300 × 90 ft, with 4 doors each 250 ft wide and 60 ft high, weighing 657 tons. It is surrounded by a 44-acre concrete apron.

Delta Air Lines' jet base, on a 140-acre site at Hartsfield International Airport, Atlanta, Ga has 36 acres under its roof.

Air-Supported Structure

The largest air-supported roof is the roof of the 80,600-seat octagonal Pontiac Silverdome Stadium, Mich measuring 522 ft wide and 722 ft long. Air pressure of 5 lb per sq in supports the 10-acre translucent fiberglass roofing. The structural engineers were Geiger-Berger Associates of NYC. It caved in during a snowstorm and gale in 1984 and the damage cost was estimated at $5 million, according to *The Detroit News*. The largest standard-size air hall was a temporary military structure in Lima, Ohio, which was 860 ft long, 140 ft wide and 65 ft high made by Irvin Industries of Stamford, Conn.

Wooden Buildings

The largest all-wood buildings are the two US Navy airship hangars built in 1942–43 at Tillamook, Ore. Now worth $6 million, they are used by the Louisiana-Pacific Corp as a sawmill. They measure 1,000 ft long, 170 ft high at the crown and 296 ft wide at the base.

Grain Elevator

The largest single-unit grain elevator is that operated by the C-G-F Grain Company at Wichita, Kans. Consisting of a triple row of storage tanks, 123 on each side of the central loading tower or "head house," the unit is 2,717 ft long and 100 ft wide. Each tank is 120 ft high, with an inside diameter of 30 ft, giving a total storage capacity of 20 million bushels of wheat. The largest collection of elevators is at Thunder Bay, Ontario, Canada, on Lake Superior, with a total capacity of 103.9 million bushels.

Largest Embassy

The largest embassy is the USSR embassy on Bei Xiao Jie, Peking, China, in the northeastern corner of the walled city. The whole 45-acre area of the old Orthodox Church mission (established 1728), now known as the *Bei guan*, was handed over to the USSR in 1949.

2. BUILDINGS FOR LIVING

Castles and Forts

Fortifications existed in all the great early civilizations, including that of ancient Egypt from 3000 BC. Fortified castles in the more accepted sense only existed much later. The oldest in the world is that at Gomdan, Yemen, which originally had 20 stories and dates from before 100 AD.

The largest inhabited castle is the British Royal residence of Windsor Castle, Berkshire. It is primarily of 12th-century construction and is in the form of a waisted parallelogram, 1,890 ft × 540 ft.

The total area of Dover Castle (England), however, covers 34 acres with a width of 1,100 ft and a curtain wall of 1,800 ft, or, if underground works are taken in, 2,300 ft.

The largest ancient castle is Hradcany Castle, Prague, Czechoslovakia, built in the 9th century. It is a very oblong, irregular polygon with an axis of 1,870 ft and an average traverse diameter of 420 ft, with a surface area of 18 acres.

The walls of Ur (now Muquyyar in Iraq), destroyed in 2006 BC were 88½ ft in thickness.

Largest Palaces

The largest palace is the Imperial Palace (*Gu gong*) in the center of Peking (*Beijing*, northern capital), China, which covers a rectangle 1,050 yd × 820 yd, an area of 177.9 acres. The outline survives from the construction of the third Ming emperor Yung-lo of 1402–24, but due to constant rearrangements most of the intramural buildings are 18th century. These consist of 5 halls and 17 palaces of which the last occupied by the last Empress was the Palace of Accumulated Elegance (*Chu xia gong*) until 1924.

The Palace of Versailles, 14 mi southwest of Paris, has a facade with 375 windows, 634 yd in length. The building, completed in 1682 for Louis XIV, required over 30,000 workmen.

Brunei, a former British protectorate on the island of Borneo, newly independent (1984), completed in Jan 1984 the largest residential palace currently in use. Built for the Sultan, it reportedly cost $422 million, has its own mosque and heliport, 1,788 rooms, a garage for the Sultan's 110 cars and space for 800 vehicles in all, and 2 mi of air conditioning. The whole of Brunei has only 500 mi of roads.

The world's largest moats are those which surround the Imperial Palace in Peking. From plans drawn by French sources they appear to measure 54 yd wide and have a total length of 3,600 yd. The city's moats total 23½ miles in all.

Apartment Houses

The tallest block of apartments is Lake Point Towers of 70 stories, 645 ft high in Chicago.

The newly constructed condominium Metropolitan Tower on W 57 St, NYC, overlooking Central Park, is higher—716 ft in all—but is not entirely devoted to apartments. Just 48 of its 78 stories are residential and the lower floors are sold to commercial enterprises. Builder-developer is the Harry Maclowe Real Estate Co.

The Cudecom Building, an 8-story apartment block in Bogota, Colombia, weighing 8,470 tons was moved intact 95 ft on Oct 6, 1974 to make way for a road.

TALLEST APARTMENT HOUSE: From the 78th floor of the new Metropolitan Tower, 57th St., NYC, the tenant gets this view, with Fifth Ave on the right and Central Park West on the left.

LARGEST PALACE: The Sultan of Brunei lives in this capital city on the island of Borneo in a $422 million residence of 1,788 rooms and 257 lavatories with its own mosque and heliport, an underground garage for his 110 cars, and 2 mi of air-conditioning.

Largest Hotels

The Hilton Hotel in Las Vegas (built 1974–81) with 3,174 bedrooms claims to be the largest hotel, although it has fewer bedrooms than the Hotel Rossiya in Moscow with 3,200 bedrooms. The Hilton also has 13 international restaurants, 125,000 sq ft of convention space, a 48,000 sq ft pillar-free ballroom, and a 10-acre rooftop recreation deck. Over 3,600 are employed.

This compares with the 12-story Hotel Rossiya in Moscow, with 3,200 rooms providing accommodation for 6,000 guests, opened in 1967.

The Izmailovo Hotel complex, opened July 1980 for the XXIInd Olympic Games in Moscow, was designed to accommodate 9,500 people.

Tallest Hotels

The tallest new hotel, measured from the street level of its main entrance to the top, is the 741.9-ft-tall 73-story Westin Stamford Hotel in Raffles City, Singapore, "topped out" in Mar 1985. The $235 million hotel is operated by Westin Hotel Co. Their Detroit Plaza Hotel in Detroit (almost a duplicate of their Peachtree Center Plaza Hotel in Atlanta, Ga) is slightly taller. This hotel, opened in early 1977, is 748 ft tall starting from its lower street level, when measured from its back entrance to the top.

Most Expensive Homes

The highest asking price for a residence is $52 million for the 22½-acre former home of banker Otto H. Kahn, called Oheka Castle, in Cold Spring Hills, LI, NY. Built in the style of the French chateaux, it has 164 rooms, including 39 fireplaces, and cost $11 million when it was built in 1920.

The most expensive private house ever built is the Hearst Ranch at San Simeon, Calif. It was built 1922–39 for William Randolph Hearst (1863–1951), at a total cost of more than $30 million. It has more than 100 rooms, a 104-ft-long heated swimming pool, an 83-ft-long assembly hall and a garage for 25 limousines. The house would require 60 servants to maintain it.

The largest private house (now open to tourists) is 250-room Biltmore House in Asheville, NC. It is owned by George and William Cecil, grandsons of George Washington Vanderbilt II (1862–1914). The house was built between 1890 and 1895 on an estate of 119,000 acres, at a cost of $4,100,000, and is now valued at $55 million with 12,000 acres.

Longest Continuous Home Construction

Winchester House in San Jose, Calif, with 160 rooms, has been under construction for 38 years. The original house was an 8-room farmhouse with unattached barn on the 161-acre estate that belonged to Oliver Winchester, who did not invent the Winchester rifle, but owned the patent on it. Sarah Winchester, widowed in 1886, consulted a psychic in Boston who told her that she alone could balance the ledger for those killed by Winchester firearms by never stopping construction on the estate. She took her $20 million to Calif to build a weird castle with 13 bathrooms, 52 skylights, 47 fireplaces, 10,000 windows, 40 staircases, 2,000 doorways and closets opening to blank walls, secret passageways, trap doors, three $10,000 elevators, and more. No expense was spared. Fine lumber was purchased, some imported. The house remodeling is intended to confuse the ghosts that inhabit the house. Still incomplete and being worked on, it is now a tourist attraction.

Most Expensive Hotel Suite

The costliest hotel accommodation is the roof-top Royal Suite at $3,000 per day for a minimum term of 3 months in the Marbella Dinamar Hotel, Spain. It has 2 halls, 2 dining rooms, 5 double bedrooms, 7 bathrooms, a kitchen, a service area, a study/library/office, a lounge, an 8-meter heated swimming pool with a massage system, 2 solariums, a sauna and an 18 hole putting green.

Spas

The largest spa measured by number of available hotel rooms is Vichy, Allier, France, with 14,000 rooms. Spas are named after the watering place called Spa in the Liège province of Belgium where hydropathy was developed from 1626. The highest French spa is Barèges, Hautes-Pyrénées, at 4,068 ft above sea level.

---

3. STRUCTURES FOR ENTERTAINMENT

Largest Circus

The largest permanent circus is Circus Circus, Las Vegas, Nev, opened Oct 18, 1968 at a cost of $15 million. It covers an area of 129,000 sq ft capped by a 90-ft-high tent-shaped flexiglass roof. (Circus Stunt records are in Chapter 11.)

The largest traveling circus is the Circus Vargas in the US which can accommodate 5,000 people under its Big Top.

Night Clubs

The oldest night club (*boîte de nuit*) was "Le Bal des Anglais" at 6 Rue des Anglais, Paris 5, France. Founded in 1843, it closed *c.* 1960.

The largest night club in the world is Gilley's Club (formerly Shelly's) built in 1955 and extended in 1971 on Spencer Highway, Houston, Tex. It has a seating capacity of 6,000 under one roof covering 4 acres.

In the more classical sense the largest night club is "The Mikado" in the Akasaka district of Tokyo, Japan, with a seating capacity of 2,000. It is "manned" by 1,250 hostesses. Binoculars are essential to an appreciation of the floor show.

The lowest night club is the "Minus 206" in Tiberias, Israel, on the shores of the Sea of Galilee. It is 676 ft below sea level. An alternative candidate is "Outer Limits," opposite the Cow Palace, San Francisco, which was raided for the 151st time on Aug 1, 1971. It has been called both "The Most Busted Joint" and "The Slowest to Get the Message."

Restaurants

The earliest restaurant was opened in 1725 in Calle de Cuchilleras 17, Madrid. The painter Goya was a dishwasher there in 1765 when he was 19.

The highest restaurant in the world is at the Chacaltaya ski resort, Bolivia at 17,519 ft.

> The biggest restaurant reported is the Tump Nak Thai in Bangkok, Thailand, which consists of 65 adjoining houses built on 10 acres, with 1,000 waiters to serve 3,000 potential customers.

Largest Harem

The world's most capacious harem is the Winter Harem of the Grand Seraglio at Topkapi, Istanbul, Turkey completed in 1589 with 400 rooms. By the time of the deposing of Abdul Hamid II in 1909 the number of *carge* (those who serve) had dwindled from 1,200 to 370 odalisques with 127 eunuchs.

Largest Stadiums

The largest stadium is the open Strahov Stadium in Prague, Czechoslovakia. It was completed in 1934 and can easily accommodate 240,000 spectators for mass displays of up to 40,000 Sokol gymnasts or aerobic devotees.

The largest football (soccer) stadium is the Maracaña Municipal Stadium in Rio de Janeiro, Brazil, which has a normal capacity of 205,000, of whom 155,000 may be seated. A crowd of 199,854 was accommodated for the World Cup final between Brazil and Uruguay on July 16, 1950. A dry moat, 7 ft wide and over 5 ft deep, protects players from spectators and *vice versa*.

The largest covered stadium in the world is the Azteca Stadium, Mexico City, opened in 1968, which has a capacity of 107,000, of whom nearly all are under cover.

The largest retractable roof is being constructed to cover the 60,000-capacity Toronto Blue Jays' new stadium near the CN Tower for completion by Aug 1988. The diameter will be 679 ft.

Largest One-Piece Roof

The transparent acrylic glass "tent" roof over the Munich Olympic Stadium, W Germany, measures 914,940 sq ft in area. It rests on a steel net supported by masts. The roof of longest span is the 680-ft diameter of the Louisiana Superdome. The major axis of the elliptical Texas Stadium, Irving, Tex, completed in 1971 is, however, 787 ft 4 in.

Largest Indoor Arena

The largest indoor stadium is the 13-acre $173-million 273-ft-tall Superdome in New Orleans, La, completed in May 1975. Its maximum seating capacity for conventions is 97,365 or 76,791 for football. Box suites rent for $35,000, excluding the price of admission. A gondola with six 312-in TV screens produces instant replay.

Largest Amusement Park

The largest amusement resort is Disney World on 28,000 acres of Orange and Osceola Counties, 20 miles southwest of Orlando in central Florida. It was opened on Oct 1, 1971. This $400 million investment attracted 10,700,000 visitors in its first year, and well above 20 million each year thereafter.

The $900 million Epcot Center (Experimental Prototype Community of Tomorrow) next to Disney World near Orlando was opened in Oct 1982. Peak days see 120,000 at Epcot and Magic Kingdom, the two parks in Orlando.

The most attended resort in the world is Disneyland, Anaheim, Calif (opened 1955) where the total number of visitors reached 250 million on Aug 24, 1985. The greatest attendance on one day was 82,516 on Aug 16, 1969.

Largest Carousel

The *Columbia*, located in Marriott's Great America in Santa Clara, Calif, is a gilded double-decker carousel 100 ft or 10 stories high from base to pinnacle, and 27½ ft in circumference. It can carry 115 passengers. On board are 103 carousel animals (including on the lower level 36 "jumping" horses, 6 standing horses, a 50-year-old horse, a camel, giraffe, lion, tiger, dragon, deer, sea horse, 2 ostriches, pigs, cats and rabbits) and 2 chariots. On the upper level are 45 more "jumping" horses and another chariot. This merry-go-round runs at a speed of 7 revolutions per min. Construction cost was $1.8 million.

AMUSEMENT PARK RESTAURANT: Gargantua sits 114 ft above the Mirapolis Park outside Paris.

Fairs

The earliest major international fair was the Great Exhibition of 1851 in the Crystal Palace, Hyde Park, London, which in 141 days attracted 6,039,195 admissions.

The largest International Fair site was that for the St Louis-Louisiana Purchase Exposition, which covered 1,271.76 acres and drew an attendance of 19,694,855. It also staged the 1904 Olympic Games.

The record attendance for any fair was 64,218,770 for Expo '70 held on an 815-acre site at Osaka, Japan, from March to Sept 13, 1970. It made a profit of 19,439,402,017 yen (over $45 million).

Ferris Wheel

The original Ferris Wheel, named after its constructor, George W. Ferris (1859–96), was erected in 1893 at the Midway, Chicago, at a cost of $385,000. The wheel was 250 ft in diameter, 790 ft in circumference, weighed 1,198 tons, and carried 36 cars each seating 60 people, making a total of 2,160 passengers. The structure was removed in 1904 to St Louis, and was eventually sold as scrap for $1,800.

In 1897, a Ferris Wheel with a diameter of 284 ft was erected for the Earl's Court Exhibition, London. It had 10 1st-class and 30 2nd-class cars.

The largest wheels now operating are "Giant Peter" at Himeji Central Park, Himeji City, Hyogo, and one at the city of Tsukuba, both in Japan, and with a height of 278 ft 10 in. The latter has 46 cars with capacity for 384 riders.

Longest Slide

The longest slide in the world is the Bromley Alpine Slide on Route 11 in Peru, Vt. This has a length of 4,600 ft (0.87 mile) and a vertical drop of 820 ft.

Largest Pleasure Beach

The largest pleasure beach is Virginia Beach, Va. It has 28 miles of beach front on the Atlantic and 10 miles of estuary frontage. The area which embraces 255 sq mi, contains 134 hotels and motels.

Pleasure Piers

The longest pleasure pier is Southend Pier at Southend-on-Sea in Essex, England. It is 1.34 miles in length, and was first opened in Aug 1889, with final extensions made in 1929. A railway on the pier closed in Oct 1978, but reopened on May 2, 1986. In 1949–50, the pier had 5,750,000 visitors.

The resort with most piers is Atlantic City, NJ, with 6 existing pre-World War II and 5 currently.

Roller Coasters

The maximum speeds claimed for roller coasters have in the past been exaggerated for commercial reasons. The twin-track, triple-helix American Eagle at Marriott's Great America, Gurnee, Ill, opened on

May 23, 1981, has a vertical drop of 147.4 ft on which a speed of 66.31 mph is reportedly reached. The longest roller coaster in the world is *The Beast* at King's Island near Cincinnati, Ohio. Scientific tests at the base of its 141-ft-high drop returned a speed of 64.77 mph on Apr 5, 1980. The total track length of 7,400 ft incorporates 800 ft of tunnels, a 540° banked double turn.

The tallest is the 246-ft-high *Moonsault Scramble* at Fujikyu Highland Park, Japan, opened June 24, 1983. Its speed is 65.2 mph.

Bars

The largest beer-selling establishment is the Mathäser, Bayerstrasse 5, Munich, W Germany, where the daily sale reaches 100,000 pints.

LONGEST ROLLER COASTER: ▲ With a "stimulating" drop of 141 ft, "The Beast" at King's Island, near Cincinnati, O, runs at a top speed of 64.77 mph over 7,400 ft of track, including 800 ft of tunnel and a 540° banked double turn. *(Rick Norton, King's Island)*

► LARGEST CAROUSEL: Of the 120 carousels left in the US (at one time there were 2,000) the tallest is the "Columbia" at Marriott's Great America, Santa Clara, Calif. This double-decker gilded merry-go-round designed by R. Duell & Associates is 100 feet high and can carry 115 passengers.

It was established in 1829, was demolished in World War II, rebuilt by 1955, and now seats 5,500 people. Consumption at the Dube beer halls in the Bantu township of Soweto, Johannesburg, South Africa, may, however, be higher on some Saturdays when the average of 6,000 gallons is far exceeded.

The longest permanent bar is the 340-ft-long bar in Lulu's Roadhouse, Kitchener, Ontario, Canada opened on Apr 3, 1984. Temporary bars have been erected of greater length.

The bar at Erickson's on Burnside Street, Portland, Ore in its heyday (1883–1920) ran continuously around and across the main saloon, measuring 684 ft. The chief bouncer, Edward "Spider" Johnson, had a chief assistant named "Jumbo" Reilly who weighed 320 pounds and was said to resemble "an ill-natured orangutan." Beer was 5 cents for 16 fluid ounces.

Ballroom

The largest dance floor, 256 ft long, is one used for championships at Earl's Court Exhibition Hall, Kensington, London.

4. TOWERS AND MASTS

Tallest Structure

The tallest structure is the guyed Warszawa Radio mast at Konstantynow 60 miles northwest of Warsaw, Poland, which is 2;120 ft 8 in tall, or more than four-tenths of a mile. The mast was completed July 18, 1974 and put into operation July 22, 1974. Work began on the tubular steel construction, with its 15 steel guy ropes, in 1970. It was designed by Jan Polak and weighs 615 tons. The mast is so high that anyone falling off the top would reach terminal velocity, and hence cease to be accelerating, before hitting the ground.

Tallest Tower

The tallest self-supporting tower (as opposed to a guyed mast) is the $44 million CN Tower in Metro Centre, Toronto, Canada. It rises to 1,822 ft 1 in. Excavation began Feb 12, 1973, for the 145,000-ton structure of reinforced, lost-tensioned concrete, and it was "topped out" Apr 2, 1975. A 416-seat restaurant revolves in the 7-floor Sky Pod at 1,140 ft, from which the visibility extends to hills 74½ miles distant. Lightning strikes the top about 200 times (in 30 storms) each year.

The tallest tower built before the era of television masts is the Tour Eiffel (Eiffel Tower), in Paris, designed by Alexandre Gustave Eiffel (1832–1923) for the Paris Exhibition and completed on March 31, 1889. It was 985 ft 11 in tall, now extended by a TV antenna to 1,052 ft 4 in, and weighs 8,091 tons. The maximum sway in high winds is 5 in. The whole iron edifice, which has 1,792 steps, took 2 years, 2 months, and 2 days to build and cost 7,799,401 francs 31 centimes.

5. BRIDGES

Oldest

Arch construction was understood by the Sumerians as early as 3200 BC and a reference exists to a Nile bridge in 2650 BC. The oldest surviving datable bridge is the slab stone single arch bridge over the River Meles in Smyrna (now Izmir), Turkey, which dates from *c.* 850 BC.

Longest Suspension Bridge

The longest bridge span is the main span of the Humber Estuary Bridge in England, at 4,626 ft. Work began on July 27, 1972. The towers are 533 ft 1⅝ in tall from datum and are 1⅜ inches out of parallel, to allow for the curvature of the earth. Including the Hessle and Barton side spans, the bridge stretches 1.37 miles. The bridge was structurally completed on July 18, 1980 at a cost of £91 million (about $185 million) and was opened by HM the Queen on July 17, 1981. Tolls ranging from 60 pence for motorcycles to £8 for heavy vehicles, operative from May 4, 1981, are the highest in Britain.

The Mackinac Straits Bridge between Mackinaw City and St Ignace, Mich is the longest suspension bridge measured between anchorages (1.58 miles) and has an overall length, including viaducts of the bridge proper measured between abutment faces, of 3.63 miles.

The double-deck road-railroad Akashi-Kaikyo suspension bridge linking Honshu and Shikoku, Japan, is scheduled to be completed in 1988. The main span will be 6,496 ft in length with an overall suspended length with side spans totaling 11,680 ft.

The Seto-Ohashi double-deck road and rail bridge linking Kojima, Honshu with Sakaide, Shikoku, Japan opened on Apr 10, 1988 at a cost of $8.820 billion and 17 lives. The toll for cars is $43 each way for the 7.9 mi on spans and viaducts.

Work on the Messina Bridge linking Sicily with the Italian mainland is due to start in 1989. The single span will be the world's largest by far at 10,892 ft. The cost of such a project was estimated by 1982 to have passed the $20 billion mark.

Widest and Narrowest Bridges

The widest long-span bridge is the 1,650-ft-long Sydney Harbour Bridge, Australia, which is 160 ft wide. It carries 2 electric overhead railroad tracks, 8 lanes of roadway and a cycleway and footway. It was officially opened March 19, 1932. The Crawford Street Bridge in Providence, RI, has a width of 1,147 ft. However, the river is being diverted and the bridge replaced in 1988.

The Somerset drawbridge in Bermuda has in the center an 18-in-wide wooden flap that opens to allow the masts of sailboats to pass through.

Covered Bridge

The longest covered bridge is that at Hartland, New Brunswick, Canada, measuring 1,282 ft overall, completed in 1899.

Railroad Bridges

The longest railroad bridge in the world is the Huey P. Long Bridge, Metairie, La, with a railroad section 22,996 ft (4.35 miles) long. It was completed Dec 16, 1935, with a longest span of 790 ft.

The Yangtse River Bridge completed in 1968 in Nanking, China, is the longest combined highway and railroad bridge. The rail deck is 4.20 miles and the road deck an additional 2.85 miles.

Floating Bridge

The longest floating bridge is the Second Lake Washington Bridge in Seattle, Wash. Its total length is 12,596 ft and its floating section measures 7,518 ft (1.42 miles). It was built at a cost of $15 million, and completed in Aug 1963.

Highest Bridges

The highest bridge is the suspension bridge over the Royal Gorge of the Arkansas River in Colorado. It is 1,053 ft above the water level. It has a main span of 880 ft and was constructed in 6 months, ending on Dec 6, 1929. The highest railroad bridge in the world is at Fades, outside Clermont-Ferrand, France. It was built 1901–09 with a span of 472 ft and is 435 ft above the River Sioule. The highest road bridge is at an altitude of 18,380 ft near Khardungla, Ladakh, India, built by the Indian army in Aug 1982. Called the Bailey Bridge, it is only 98.4 ft long.

NARROWEST DRAWBRIDGE: To let sailboats with tall masts go through, the Somerset Bridge in Bermuda has an 18-in-wide wooden flap in the center.

Largest Aqueducts

The greatest of ancient aqueducts was the Aqueduct of Carthage in Tunisia, which ran 87.6 miles from the springs of Zaghouan to Djebel Djougar. It was built by the Romans during the reign of Publius Aelius Hadrianus (117–138 AD). By 1895, 344 arches still survived. Its original capacity has been calculated at 8,400,000 gallons per day. The triple-tiered aqueduct Pont du Gard, built in 19 AD near Nîmes, France, is 160 ft high. The tallest of the 14 arches of the Aguas Livres Aqueduct, built in Lisbon, Portugal, in 1784, is 213 ft 3 in.

The longest aqueduct, in the modern sense of a water conduit as opposed to an irrigation canal, is the California State Water Project aqueduct, completed in 1974 to a length of 826 miles, of which 385 miles is canalized.

6. CANALS

Relics of the oldest canals in the world, dated by archeologists to *c.* 4000 BC, were discovered near Mandali, Iraq, early in 1968.

Longest Canals

The longest canalized system is the Volga-Baltic Canal opened in Apr 1965. It runs 1,850 miles from Astrakhan up the Volga, *via* Kuybyshev, Gorkiy and Lake Ladoga, to Leningrad, USSR. The longest canal of the ancient world was the Grand Canal of China from Peking to Hangchou. It was begun in 540 BC and not completed until 1327 AD by which time it extended for 1,107 miles. The estimated work force *c.* 600 AD reached 5 million on the Pien section. By 1950 the silt had piled up to the point that it was, in no place, more than 6 ft deep. It is now, however, opened up and plied by ships of up to 2,240 tons.

The longest big ship canal is the Suez Canal, linking the Red and Mediterranean Seas, opened Nov 16, 1869, but inoperative from June 1967 to June 1975. The canal was planned by the French diplomat Ferdinand de Lesseps (1805–1894) and work began Apr 25, 1859. It is 100.6 miles in length from Port Said lighthouse to Suez Roads, 197 ft wide. The work force was 8,213 men and 368 camels. The USS *Shreveport* transited southbound Aug 15–16, 1984 in a record 7 hours 45 min. A vessel with a beam of 188.1 ft and a length of 1,103.3 ft, a dwt of 322,446 tonnes, named *S S Settebello*, was the largest vessel to transit the Suez. (The Panama Canal width is more than 50 ft narrower.)

Busiest Canal

The busiest big ship canal is the Kiel Canal linking the North Sea with the Baltic Sea in W Germany with over 45,000 transits recorded in 1987. Next comes the Suez Canal with over 20,000 transits and third the Panama Canal with over 10,000 transits. Busiest in terms of tonnage of shipping using it is the Suez Canal with nearly 440,000,000 grt.

The lowest toll for use of the Panama Canal was 36 cents for the swimmer Richard Halliburton in 1928.

Seaway

The longest artificial seaway is the St Lawrence Seaway (189 miles long) along the NY State-Ontario border from Montreal to Lake Ontario, which enables ships up to 728 ft long and 26.2 ft draught, some of which are of 29,000 tons, to sail 2,342 miles from the North Atlantic, up the St Lawrence Estuary and across the Great Lakes to Duluth, Minn, on Lake Superior (602 ft above sea level). The project cost $470 million and was opened Apr 25, 1959.

Irrigation Canal

The longest irrigation canal is the Karakumskiy Kanal, stretching 528 miles from Haun-Khan to Ashkhabad, Turkmenistan, USSR. In Sept 1971 the navigable length was reported to have reached 280 miles. The length of the $925 million project will eventually reach 930 miles.

LONGEST SHIP CANAL: A satellite view from space of the 100.6-mi-long Suez Canal looking south near the point where it enters the Red Sea. Egypt is to the right and Saudi Arabia to the distant left. *(Daily Telegraph)*

Largest and Deepest Locks

The largest single lock is the sea lock at Zeebrugge, Belgium, measuring 1640 × 187 × 75.4 ft giving a volume of 857,066 cu yd. The Berendrecht Lock, Antwerp, Belgium, has the same length but a width of 223 ft and a depth of 70.5 ft giving a volume of 956,000 cu yd.

The deepest lock is the John Day Dam lock on the Columbia River, Ore and Wash, completed in 1963. It can raise or lower barges 113 ft and is served by a 1,100-ton gate.

The highest lock elevator overcomes a head of 225 ft at Ronquières on the Charleroi-Brussels Canal in Belgium. Two 236-wheeled caissons, each able to carry 1,512 tons, take 22 min to cover the 4,698-ft-long ramp.

---

7. DAMS

The earliest known dams were those uncovered by the British School of Archeology in Jerusalem in 1974 at Jawa in Jordan. These stone-faced earth dams are dated to *c.* 3200 BC.

Most Massive Dam

Measured by volume, the largest dam in the world is the earth-and-rock-fill Pati Dam on the Pavana River, Argentina with a volume of 311,527,000 cu yd. It is 108.6 mi in length and 118 ft high. The Chapetón Dam also on the Pavana is planned to have a volume of 387,400,000 cu yd and a crest length of 139 mi. Both will be surpassed in volume by the Syncrude Tailings Dam in Canada with 706,000,000 cu yd.

Highest Dam

The highest dam will be the Rogunsky earthfill dam in the USSR which will have a final height of 1,098 ft across the Vakhsh River, Tadjikistan, with a crest length of only 1,975 ft. Building since 1973, completion date is still unconfirmed. Meanwhile, the tallest is the 984-ft-high Narek dam in the USSR.

Largest Concrete Dam

The largest concrete dam, and the largest concrete structure, is Grand Coulee Dam on the Columbia River, Wash. Work on the dam was begun in 1933, it began working on Mar 22, 1941 and was completed in 1942 at a cost of $56 million. It has a crest length of 4,173 ft and is 550 ft high. It contains 10,585,000 cu yd of concrete and weighs about 19,285,000 tons. The hydroelectric power plant (now being extended) will have a capacity of 9,780,000 kW.

Longest River Dam and Sea Dam

The longest river dam is the 44.7-mi-long 134.5-ft-high Yacyreta-Apipe dam completed in 1983 across the Paraná on the Paraguay–Argentina border.

In the early 17th century, an impounding dam of moderate height was built in Lake Hungtze, Kiangsu, China, to a reputed length of 62 miles.

The longest sea dam is the Afsluitdijk stretching 20.195 miles across the mouth of the Zuider Zee in two sections of 1.553 miles (mainland of North Holland to the Isle of Wieringen) and 18.641 miles (Wieringen to Friesland). It has a sea-level width of 293 ft and a height of 24 ft 7 in.

Strongest Structure

The world's strongest structure will be the 793-ft-high Sayano-Shusenskaya dam on the Yenisey River, USSR. Under construction, it is designed to bear a load of 20,160,000 tons from a fully filled reservoir of 41,000 million cu yd capacity.

Largest Reservoirs and Man-Made Lake

The most voluminous man-made reservoir is the Kahkovskaya Reservoir, USSR, with a volume of 147,550,000 acre-ft.

The largest artificial lake measured by surface area is Lake Volta, Ghana, formed by the Akosombo dam, completed in 1965. By 1969, the lake had filled an area of 3,275 sq mi with a shoreline 4,500 miles in length.

The completion in 1954 of the Owen Falls Dam near Jinja, Uganda, across the northern exit of the White Nile River from the lake Victoria Nyanza, marginally raised the level of that *natural* lake by adding 218.9 million acre-ft, and technically turned it into a reservoir with a surface area of 17,169,920 acres (26,828 sq mi).

The $4 billion Tacurai Dam converted the Tocantins River in Brazil into a 1,180-mile-long chain of lakes in 1984.

Largest Polder (Reclaimed Land)

The largest of the five great polders in the old Zuider Zee, The Netherlands, will be the 149,000-acre (232.8-sq-mi) Markerwaard. Work on the 66-mi-long surrounding dike was begun in 1957. The water area remaining after the erection of the 1927–32 dam (20 mi in length) is called IJssel Meer, which will have a final area of 487.5 sq mi.

Largest Levees

The most massive levees ever carried out are the Mississippi levees begun in 1717 and vastly augmented by the US Government after the disastrous floods of 1927. These extend for 1,732 miles along the main river from Cape Girardeau, Mo, to the Gulf of Mexico and comprise more than 1,000 million cu yd of earthworks. Levees on the tributaries comprise an additional 2,000 miles. The 650-mile segment from Pine Bluff, Ark, to Venice, La, is continuous.

8. TUNNELS

Longest Tunnel

The longest tunnel of any kind is the NYC-W Delaware water supply tunnel begun in 1937 and completed in 1944. It has a diameter of 13 ft 6 in and runs for 105 miles from the Rondout Reservoir in the Catskill Mountains into the Hillview Reservoir, on the border line of NYC and Yonkers.

Road Tunnel

The longest road tunnel is the 10.14-mile-long two-lane St Gotthard Road Tunnel from Goschenen to Airolo, Switzerland, opened to traffic on Sept 5, 1980. Nineteen lives were lost during the construction, which cost almost $400 million since 1969.

The largest-diameter road tunnel was blasted through Yerba Buena Island in San Francisco Bay. It is 76 ft wide, 58 ft high and 540 ft long. More than 80 million vehicles cross on its two decks every year.

Excavation of the projected $9.6 billion Euro-tunnel under the English Channel between Folkestone, Kent, Eng and Calais, France, began in July 1987 and is to be completed by 1993. The length of the twin rail tunnels of 24 ft 11 in diameter will be 31.03 miles.

Railroad Tunnel

The longest railroad tunnel is the Seikan Rail Tunnel (33.46 miles), 787 ft beneath sea level and 328 ft below the sea bed of the Tsugaru Strait between Tappi Saki, Honshu, and Fukushima, Hokkaido, Japan. Tests started on the sub-aqueous section of 14½ mi in 1964, construction began in June 1972, the tunnel was holed through on Jan 27, 1973 (after a loss of 34 lives) and in Mar 1985 the tunneling was finished after 20 years 10 months. The cost was about $3,750,000,000.

Bridge-Tunnel

The longest bridge-tunnel system is the Chesapeake Bay Bridge-Tunnel, extending 17.65 miles from Virginia's eastern shore to Virginia Beach, Va. It cost $200 million, took 42 months to complete, and opened on Apr 15, 1964. The longest bridged section is Trestle C (4.56 miles long) and the longest tunnel is the Thimble Shoal Channel Tunnel (1.09 miles).

Canal-Tunnel

The longest canal-tunnel is that on the Rove Canal between the port of Marseilles, France and the Rhône River, built 1912–27. It is 4.53 mi long, 72 ft wide and 37 ft high. Built to be navigated by sea-going ships, it was closed in 1963 following a collapse of the structure and has not been reopened.

Subway Tunnel

The longest continuous vehicular tunnel is the Moscow Metro

underground railroad line from Belyaevo to Medvedkovo. It runs 19.07 mi and was completed in 1978–79.

Irrigation, Hydroelectric and Sewerage Tunnels

The longest irrigation tunnel is the 51.5-mile-long Orange-Fish Rivers Tunnel, South Africa, begun in 1967, at an estimated cost of $150 million. The boring was completed in Apr 1973. The lining to a minimum thickness of 9 in will give a completed diameter of 17 ft 6 in.

The Majes project in Peru involves 60.9 miles of tunnels for hydroelectric and water supply purposes. The dam is at 13,780 ft altitude.

The Chicago TARP (Tunnels and Reservoir Plan) involves 120 miles of sewerage tunneling.

Tunneling

The longest unsupported example of a machine-bored tunnel is the Three Rivers Water Tunnel driven 30,769 linear ft with a 10.5-ft-diameter for the City of Atlanta, Ga from Apr 1980 to Feb 1982. S & M Constructors Inc of Cleveland, Ohio, achieved 179 ft in a day through the granite, schist and gneiss.

Wind Tunnels

The largest wind tunnel is a low-speed tunnel with a closed test section measuring 40 × 80 ft, built in 1944, at Ames Research Center, Moffett Field, Calif. The tunnel encloses 900 tons of air and cost approximately $7 million. The maximum volume of air that can be moved is 60 million cu ft per min. On July 30, 1974, NASA announced an intention to increase it in size to 80 × 120 ft for 345-mph speeds with a 135,000 hp system.

The most powerful is the 216,000-hp installation at the Arnold Engineering Test Center at Tullahoma, Tenn, opened in Sept 1956. The highest Mach number attained with air is Mach 27 at the plant of the Boeing Company, Seattle, Wash. For periods of microseconds, shock Mach numbers of the order of 30 (22,830 mph) have been attained in impulse tubes at Cornell University, Ithaca, NY.

---

9. SPECIALIZED STRUCTURES

Advertising Signs

The largest neon advertising sign measures 210 × 55 ft, built for Marlboro cigarettes at Kowloon, Hong Kong, in May 1986. It contains 35,000 ft of neon tubing and weighs 126½ tons.

Broadway's largest billboard has been 11,426 sq ft in area—equivalent to 107 ft × 107 ft. Broadway's largest working sign in Times Square, NYC, in 1966, showed two 42½-ft-tall "bottles" of Haig Scotch Whisky and an 80-ft-long "bottle" of Gordon's Gin being "poured" into a frosted glass.

The largest sign advertising an American city is the 370-ft-wide

LARGEST RADIO-TELESCOPE INSTALLATION: With each arm 13 miles long, this VLA (Very Large Array), costing $78 million in 1980, stands on the Plains of San Augustin, New Mexico.

HOLLYWOOD sign in the hills above Los Angeles, placed by the Hollywood Chamber of Commerce. The letters (30 × 45 ft) were crumbling, and to obtain funds for their restoration, Hugh Hefner, publisher of *Playboy*, held a party in the spring of 1979, the proceeds of which amounted to $45,000.

The most conspicuous sign ever erected was the electric Citroën sign on the Eiffel Tower, Paris. It was switched on on July 4, 1925 and could be seen 24 miles away. It was in six colors with 250,000 lamps and 56 miles of electric cables. The letter "N" which terminated the name "Citroën" between the second and third levels measured 68 ft 5 in in height. The whole apparatus was taken down after 11 years in 1936.

An interior-lit fascia advertising sign in Clearwater, Fla, completed by Adco Sign Corp in Apr 1983 measures 1,168 ft 6½ in in length.

The most massive animated sign today is reputed to be outside the Circus Circus Hotel, Reno, Nev, named Topsy the Clown. It is 127 ft tall and weighs 44.8 tons with 1.4 miles of neon tubing. The clown's smile measures 14 ft across.

The highest advertising signs are the four Bank of Montreal logos atop the 72-story 935-ft-tall First Canadian Place Building in Toronto. Each sign, built by Claude Neon Industries Ltd measures 20 ft × 22 ft, and was lifted into place by helicopter.

Longest Breakwater

The longest breakwater protects the port of Galveston, Texas. The granite South Breakwater is 6.74 miles long.

Cemetery

The world's largest cemetery is one in Leningrad, USSR, which contains over 500,000 of the 1,300,000 victims of the German army's siege of 1941–42.

The world's largest crematorium is at the Nikolo-Arkhangelskoye Cemetery, East Moscow, completed in March 1972. It has 7 twin furnaces and several Halls of Farewell for atheists.

Tallest Columns

The tallest columns (as opposed to obelisks) are the 36 fluted pillars of Vermont marble in the colonnade of the Education Building, Albany, NY. Each one measures 90 ft tall and 6½ ft in base diameter.

The tallest load-bearing stone columns are those measuring 69 ft in the Hall of Columns of the Temple of Amun at Karnak, opposite Thebes on the Nile, the ancient capital of Upper Egypt. They were built in the 19th dynasty in the reign of Rameses II in *c.* 1270 BC.

Largest Dome

The world's largest dome is the Louisiana Superdome in New Orleans. It has an outside diameter of 680 ft. (For more details, see *Largest Indoor Arena.*) The largest dome of ancient architecture is that of the Pantheon, built in Rome in 112 AD, with a diameter of 142½ ft.

Doors

The largest doors are the 4 in the Vehicle Assembly Building near Cape Canaveral, Fla with a height of 460 ft. (See *Largest Scientific Building.*)

The world's heaviest door is that leading to the laser target room at Lawrence Livermore National Laboratory, Calif. It weighs 360 tons, is up to 8 ft thick and was installed by Overly.

Largest Drydock

The largest drydock is Okopo No 1 at Choje Island in S Korea, with a maximum shipbuilding capacity of 1,200,000 tons deadweight. It measures 1,722.4 ft long × 430 ft wide, and was completed in 1979.

Longest and Highest Fences

The longest fence is the dingo-proof fence enclosing the main sheep areas of Australia. The wire fence is 6 ft high, goes 1 ft underground, and stretches for 3,437 miles, more than the distance from Seattle to NY. The Queensland State Government discontinued full maintenance in 1982, but 310 mi is now being repaired.

The tallest fences are security screens 65.6 ft high built by Harrop-Allin of Pretoria to keep out Soviet RP67 rocket missiles from fuel depots and refineries in South Africa.

Tallest Flagpole

The tallest flagpole ever erected was outside the Oregon Building at the 1915 Panama-Pacific International Exposition in San Francisco. Trimmed from a Douglas fir, it stood 299 ft 7 in in height.

The tallest unsupported flagpole is the 282-ft tall steel pole weighing

120,000 lb, erected on Aug 22, 1985 at the Canadian Expo '86 in Vancouver, Brit Columbia. It supports a gigantic hockey stick 205 ft long.

Tallest Fountain

The tallest fountain is at Fountain Hills, Ariz built at a cost of $1½ million for McCulloch Properties Inc. At full pressure of 375 lb/sq in and at a rate of 7,000 gallons/min, the 560-ft column of water weighs more than 9 tons. The nozzle speed achieved by the three 600 hp pumps is 146.7 mph.

Tallest Ice Palace

The largest single ice construction project was an ice palace built in January 1986 in St. Paul, Minn, during its Winter Carnival. Designed by Ellerbe Associates, Inc. and built by 750 unionized construction volunteers, it used 9 thousand 700-lb blocks of ice and stood 128 ft 9 in high, the height of a 13-story building.

However, as Robert Arthur Olsen, historian of the St Paul Winter Carnival points out, the 1889 palace may have been 130 ft tall, but it was not surveyed, only measured from photos.

A snow palace, called Galliber's Dream Castle, was unveiled on Feb 7, 1987 at the Asahikawa Winter Festival at Asahikawa City, Hokkaido, Japan. Measuring 312.9 ft wide, 9 ft high and 98.4 ft deep, it was one of 4 such structures which altogether spanned a width of 702.7 ft and which took 6,500 people to construct.

Longest Jetty

The longest deep-water jetty is the Quai Hermann du Pasquier at Le Havre, France with a length of 5,000 ft. Part of an enclosed basin, it has a constant depth of water of 32 ft on both sides.

Largest Kitchen

The largest kitchen ever set up has been the Indian Government field kitchen set up in Apr 1973 at Ahmadnagar, Maharashtra, in the famine area. The kitchen daily provided 1.2 million subsistence meals.

Tallest Lampposts

The tallest lighting columns ever erected are four 208 ft 4 in high made in France and installed by a British company at Sultan Qaboos Sports Complex, Muscat, Oman.

Lighthouses

The $23 million 328-ft-tall rock lighthouse built in 1983–85, 24.8 mi southwest of L'Ile d'Ouessant, Brittany, France, is visible at 40 nautical mi. With reflective clouds at optimal altitude the loom is detectable in Isles of Scilly 105 mi distant.

The lights with the greatest visible range are those 1,092 ft above the ground on the Empire State Building, NYC. Each of the four-arc mercury bulbs has a rated candlepower of 450 million, visible 80 miles away on the ground and 300 miles away from aircraft. They were switched on on March 31, 1956.

The tallest lighthouse is the steel tower 348 ft tall near Yamashita

Park in Yokohama, Japan. It has a power of 600,000 candles and is visible 20 mi away.

Largest Maze

The largest maze is Il Labirinto at Villa Pisani, Stra, Italy with 4 mi of paths. Napoleon was "lost" in it in 1807. The oldest dateable representation of a labyrinth is that on a clay tablet from Pylos, Greece, from *c.* 1200 BC.

The largest hedge maze is at Longleat, Wiltshire, Eng with 1.69 mi of paths flanked by 16,180 yew trees. It was opened on June 6, 1978 and measures 381 × 187 ft.

Tallest Monuments

The tallest monument is the stainless steel Gateway to the West Arch in St Louis, completed Oct 28, 1965, to commemorate the westward expansion after the Louisiana Purchase of 1803. It is a sweeping arch, spanning 630 ft and rising to a height of 630 ft, which cost $29 million. It was designed in 1947 by Eero Saarinen (d 1961).

The tallest monumental column commemorates the battle of San Jacinto (Apr 21, 1836), on the bank of the San Jacinto River near Houston, Tex. General Sam Houston (1793–1863) and his force of 743 Texan troops killed 630 Mexicans (out of a total force of 1,600) and captured 700 others, with the loss of 9 men killed and 30 wounded. Constructed in 1936–39, at a cost of $1½ million, the tapering column is 570 ft tall, 47 ft square at the base, and 30 ft square at the observation tower, which is surmounted by a star weighing 220 tons. It is built of concrete, faced with buff limestone, and weighs 35,150 tons.

TALLEST MONUMENT: The stainless steel Gateway to the West Arch on the bank of the Mississippi in St Louis is 630 ft high and 630 ft wide. (*Daily Telegraph*)

LARGEST LEGO STATUE: This sculpture of the Indian chief Sitting Bull at the Legoland Park, Billund, Denmark, measures 25 ft to the top of the feather. The largest statue ever constructed from Lego, it required 1,500,000 bricks, individually glued together to withstand the weather.

ICE PALACE: The largest ice construction is this 9,000-ice-block, 128-ft-9-in high twin tower in St Paul, Minn made for the 1986 Winter Carnival.

BIGGEST SCAFFOLDING: For the workers to repair the statue of Miss Liberty in NY Harbor 1984–86, this massive scaffolding, 315 ft high to the top of the torch, had to be built. *(Fred R. Tannery)*

Largest Prehistoric Monument

The largest trilithons exist at Stonehenge, to the south of Salisbury Plain, Wiltshire, with single sarsen blocks weighing over 50 tons and requiring over 550 men to drag them up a 9° gradient. The earliest stage in the construction of the ditch has been dated to 2800 BC. Whether Stonehenge was a lunar calendar, a temple, a navigation school, or an eclipse-predictor is still debated.

Naturist Resorts

The oldest naturist resort (the term "nudist camp" is deplored by naturists) is Der Freilichtpark, Klingberg, W Germany, established in 1903. The largest is the Beau Valley Country Club, Warmbaths, South Africa, extending over 988 acres with up to 20,000 visitors a year. However, 100,000 people visit the smaller Centre Helio-Marin at Cap d'Agde, southern France, which covers 222 acres.

Obelisks

The largest standing obelisk (of Tuthmosis III's day) was 118.1 ft tall when brought from Aswan, Egypt, by Emperor Constantine in 357 AD. It was repositioned in the Piazza San Giovanni in Laterane, Rome, on Aug 3, 1588. It now stands 107.6 ft tall and weighs 502.3 tons.

A heavier but unfinished and not standing obelisk remains at Aswan, probably commissioned by Queen Hatshepsut *c.* 1490 BC. It is 136.8 ft in length and weighs 1,289.5 tons.

The longest an obelisk has remained *in situ* is that still at Heliopolis, near Cairo, Egypt, erected by Senusret I *c.* 1750 BC.

Longest Pier

The longest pier is the Dammam Pier, Saudi Arabia, on the Persian Gulf with an overall length of 6.79 miles. The work was begun in July 1948 and completed March 15, 1950. The area was subsequently developed into the King Abdul Aziz Port with 39 deep-water berths.

Largest and Oldest Pyramids

The largest pyramid, and the largest monument ever constructed, is the Quetzalcóatl at Cholula de Rivadabia, 63 miles southeast of Mexico City. It is 177 ft tall and its base covers an area of nearly 45 acres. Its total volume has been estimated at 4.3 million cu yd, compared with 3,360,000 cu yd for the Pyramid of Cheops. The pyramid-building era here was between the 2nd and 6th centuries AD.

The oldest known pyramid is the Djoser step pyramid at Saqqâra, Egypt, constructed by Imhotep to a height of 204 ft, originally with a Tura limestone casing, *c.* 2650 BC. The largest known single block came from the Third Pyramid of Mycerinus and weighs 319.2 tons. The oldest New World pyramid is that on the island of La Venta in southeastern Mexico built by the Olmec people *c.* 800 BC. It is 100 ft tall with a base dimension of 420 ft.

Most Massive Scaffolding

The 152-ft-high Statue of Liberty on a 150-ft-high pedestal in NY Harbor, a gift from France in 1886, in going through a period of renovation (1984–86) had scaffolding surrounding it that was the largest free-standing scaffolding in the world. Designed and installed by Universal Builders Supply Inc. of Mount Vernon, NY, the structure consisted of over 6,000 aluminum components, weighed 160,000 lb, and was proportioned to withstand hurricane wind gusts of 100 mph. The 420-ft-long access ramp, together with the internal and external scaffolds, was constructed by an average of 22 very proud workers, battling winter conditions. The crane, from the top of its 315-ft corner tower, lowered Miss Liberty's rusting flame and torch to the ground on July 4, 1984.

Largest Scarecrow

The largest scarecrow was built by Stephen Speers and family of Paris, Ont, Canada on Sept 5, 1987. "Stretch" measured 73 ft 5¾ in in height and 39 ft in width.

Sewage Works

The largest single full treatment sewage works is the West-Southwest Treatment Plant, opened in 1940 on a site of 501 acres in Chicago. It serves an area containing 2,940,000 people. It treated an average of 835,000,000 gal of waste per day in 1973. The capacity of its sedimentation and aeration tanks is 1.6 million cu yd.

Largest Snow Construction

The largest snowman ever constructed was one 63½ ft tall in Anchorage, Alaska, made from Feb 20 to Mar 5, 1988 by Myron L. Ace and his group of 8. "Super Frosty" got built despite a 70 mph dust storm and 40° temperature, but he couldn't stay white. The 8-ft-sq cubes of snow were lifted into place by a crane.

BLACK SNOWMAN: A 70-mph dust storm covered "Super Frosty," the 63½-ft-tall snowman made in Anchorage, Alaska in Mar 1988.

Longest Stairs

The longest is the service staircase for the Niesenbahn funicular which rises to 7,759 ft near Spiez, Switzerland. It has 11,674 steps and a banister. The T'ai Chan temple stairs of 6,600 stone-cut steps in the Shantung Mts, China, ascend 4,700 ft in 5 miles.

The longest spiral staircase is one 1,103 ft deep with 1,520 steps, installed in the Mapco-White County Coal Mine, Carmi, Ill, by Systems Control Inc in 1981.

Tallest Statue

The tallest full-figure statue is that of the "Motherland," an enormous prestressed concrete female figure on Mamayev Hill, outside Volgograd, USSR, designed in 1967 by Yevgenyi Vuchetich, to commemorate victory in the Battle of Stalingrad (1942–43). The statue from its base to the tip of a sword clenched in her right hand measures 270 ft.

Tallest Swing

The tallest swing is a glider swing 30 ft high, constructed by Kenneth R. Mack, Langenburg, Sask, Canada for Uncle Herb's Amusements. The swing is capable of taking its 4 sides 25 ft off the ground.

Largest Tomb

The largest tomb yet discovered is the Mount Li tomb, belonging to Zheng, the first Emperor of China. It dates to 221 BC and is situated 25 miles east of Xianyang. The two walls surrounding the grave measure 7,129 × 3,195 ft and 2,247 × 1,896 ft. Several pits in the tomb contained a vast army of an estimated 8,000 life-size terracotta soldiers.

Tallest Totem Pole

The tallest totem pole is 173 ft tall raised on June 6, 1973 at Alert Bay, British Columbia, Canada. It tells the story of the Kwakiutl and took 36 man-weeks to carve.

Largest Tent

The largest tent ever erected was one covering an area of 188,368 sq ft (4.32 acres) put up by the firm of Deuter from Augsburg, W Germany, for the 1958 "Welcome Expo" in Brussels, Belgium.

Largest Trash Dump

Located at Fresh Kills, Staten Island, NYC, covering more than 3,000 acres, this landfill receives 22,000 tons of trash daily and employs more than 600 who labor in shifts around the clock. Nearly 300 pieces of heavy equipment, including bulldozers, vacuum trucks, compactors, huge trash wagons, and the "princes" of heavy metal machinery, 90-foot cranes with gargantuan shovels, move the piles of trash.

At the present rate of growth, the trash pile, which stood at 130 ft high at the beginning of 1988, will reach 505 feet within the next decade—which would make it the highest point on the Eastern Seaboard south of Maine. When at that height, the Fresh Kills landfill will no longer be used as a dumping ground—NYC plans to turn it into a ski slope.

Longest Wall

The Great Wall of China, completed during the Ch'in dynasty, reign of Shih Huang-ti (246–210 BC), has a main-line length of 2,150 miles with a further 1,780 miles of branches and spurs, with a height of from 15 to 39 ft and up to 32 ft thick. It runs from Shanhaikuan, on the Gulf of Pohai, to Yümên-kuan and Yang-kuan and was kept in repair up to the 16th century. Some 32 miles of the Wall have been destroyed since 1966. Part of the Wall was blown up to make way for a dam in July 1979. On Mar 6, 1985 a report from China stated that a 5-year-long survey proved that the total length had been 6,200 mi.

Water Tower

The tallest is in Union, NJ, built in 1965 to a height of 210 ft, with a capacity of 250,000 gal.

Waterwheel

The largest waterwheel is the Mohammadieh Noria wheel at Hama in Syria, with a diameter of 131 ft. It dates from Roman times.

LARGEST WATERWHEEL: Built in Roman times, the wheel in northern Syria on the River Orontes is 131 ft in diameter. *(Robert Harding)*

Largest Windows

The largest sheet of glass ever manufactured was one of 538.2 sq ft, or 65 ft 7 in × 8 ft 2½ in, exhibited by the Saint Gobain Company in France at the *Journées Internationales de Miroiterie* in March 1958. The largest single windows are those in the Palace of Industry and Technology at Rondpoint de la Défense, Paris, with an extreme width of 715.2 ft and a maximum height of 164 ft.

Wine Cellar

The largest wine cellars are at Paarl, those of the Ko-operative Wijnbouwers Vereeniging (K.W.V.), near Capetown, in the center of the wine district of South Africa. They cover an area of 25 acres and have a capacity of 36 million gallons.

The Cienega Winery of the Almaden Vineyards in Hollister, Calif covers 4 acres and can house 37,300 oak barrels containing 1.83 million gallons of wine.

Ziggurat (Stage or Temple Tower)

The largest surviving ziggurat (from the verb *zaqaru*, Babylonian, to build high) is the Ziggurat of Ur (now Muquyyar, Iraq) with a base 200 ft × 150 ft built to at least 3 stories of which only the first and part of the second now survive to a height of 60 ft. It has been dated between *c.* 2113 BC and *c.* 2096 BC.

The largest ziggurat ever built was by the Elamite King Untash *c.* 1250 BC, known as the Ziggurat of Choga Zanbil, 18.6 mi from Haft Tepe, Iran. The outer base was 344 ft and the fifth "box" 91.8 ft nearly 164 ft above.

Largest Building Demolished by Explosives

The largest was the 21-story Traymore Hotel, Atlantic City, NJ on May 26, 1972. The 600-room hotel had a cubic capacity of 6,495,500 cu ft. Controlled Demolition Inc of Towson, Md did the job.

The tallest chimney ever demolished by explosives was the Matla Power Station chimney, Kriel, South Africa, on July 19, 1981. It stood 902 ft high and was brought down by Dykon, Inc. of Tulsa, Okla for the Electrical Supply Commission of Johannesburg, S Africa.

10. BORINGS AND MINES

Man's deepest penetration into the earth's crust is a geological exploratory drilling in the Kola peninsula, USSR, begun in 1970. By 1987, 42,650 ft or 8.07 mi was reached. Progress has understandably greatly slowed to 1,640 ft per year as the eventual target of 49,212 ft, in 1989–90 is neared. The drill bit is mounted on a turbine driven by a mud pump. The temperature at 6.83 mi was already 392°F.

The W German government announced that an 8.75-mi deep hole will be drilled into the earth's crust by 1995 at an estimated cost of $150 million. The super hole will be drilled starting in 1988, either in the Black Forest or northeastern Bavaria.

The deepest recorded drilling into the sea bed is by the *Glomar Challenger* of the US Deep Sea Drilling Project to 5,709 ft off northwestern Spain in 1976. The deepest site is now 23,077 ft below the surface on the western wall of the Marianas Trench in May 1978.

Mines

A table giving full information appeared in all annual editions of the *Guinness Book* through 1988.

Largest Gas Deposits

The largest gas deposit in the world is at Urengoi, USSR, with an eventual production of 200,000 million cu meters per year through 6 pipelines, from proved reserves of 7 million cu meters. The trillionth cu meter was produced on Apr 23, 1986.

Largest Gas Tank

The largest gas holder or tank is that at Fontaine l'Eveque, Belgium, where disused mines have been adapted to store up to 17,650 million cu ft of gas at ordinary pressure. Probably the largest conventional gas tank is that at Wien-Semmering, Vienna, Austria, completed in 1968, with a height of 274 ft 8 in and a capacity of 10.59 million cu ft.

Oil Fields

The largest oil field is the Ghawar Field, Saudi Arabia, developed by ARAMCO, which measures 150 miles by 22 miles.

Greatest Gusher

The greatest ever recorded blew at Alborz No 5 well near Qum, Iran on Aug 26, 1956. The uncontrolled oil gushed to a height of 170 ft at 120,000 barrels per day. It was closed after 90 days' work by B. Mostofi and Myron Kinley of Texas.

The Lake View No. 1 gusher in Calif on Mar 15, 1910 may have yielded 125,000 barrels in its first 24 hours.

Greatest Flare

The greatest gas fire ever burnt was at Gassi Touil in the Algerian Sahara from noon on Nov 13, 1961 to 9:30 a.m. on Apr 28, 1962. The pillar of flame rose 450 ft and the smoke 600 ft. It was eventually extinguished by Paul Neal ("Red") Adair (b 1932), of Houston, Tex, using 550 lb of dynamite. His fee was understood to be about $1 million.

Wells

The deepest water well is the Stensvad Water Well 11-W1 7,320 ft deep, drilled by the Great Northern Drilling Co Inc in Rosebud County, Mont in Oct–Nov 1961.

The Thermal Power Co geothermal steam well begun in Sonoma County, Calif in 1955 is now down to 9,029 ft.

Greatest Oil Spill

The slick from the Mexican marine blow-out beneath the drilling rig

Ixtoc I in the Bay of Campeche, Gulf of Mexico on June 3, 1979 reached 400 miles by Aug 5, 1979. It eventually was capped on Mar 24, 1980, after a loss of 3 million barrels.

The worst oil spill in history was 260,000 tons of oil from the super-tankers *Atlantic Empress* and *Aegean Captain* when they collided off Tobago on July 19, 1979.

Oil Platforms

The world's most massive oil platform is the *Stratfjord B* Concrete Gravity-base platform built at Stavanger, Norway, and operated by Mobil Exploration Norway Inc until Dec 31, 1986. Tow-out to its permanent field began on Aug 1, 1981, and it was the heaviest object ever moved—899,360 tons ballasted weight. She was towed by 8 tugs with a combined power of 115,000 hp. The height of the concrete structure is 670 ft and the overall height 890 ft. It thus weighs almost three times the weight of each of the towers of the World Trade Center (321,800 tons).

The tallest production platform is the 1,132-ft-tall Shell Cognac platform built in 1976 and placed outside the Mississippi River (La) delta.

GOLD RUSH: Like ants in an anthill, thousands of Brazilians go down into the pits along the Amazon and climb out with wet soil to check for gold content.

Chapter 8

The Mechanical World

1. SHIPS

Aborigines are thought to have been able to cross the Torres Strait from New Guinea to Australia, then at least 43½ miles across, as early as 40,000 BC. They are believed to have used double canoes. An 18-in paddle found at Star Carr, North Yorkshire, England, has been dated to *c.* 7600 BC.

The earliest surviving "vessel" is a pinewood dugout found in Pesse, Netherlands, now in the Provincial Museum, Assen, dated to *c.* 6315 BC ± 275.

The oldest surviving boat is the 27-ft-long, 2½-ft-wide wooden eel-catching canoe discovered at Tybrind Vig on the Baltic island of Funen which dates back to *c.* 4490 BC.

The oldest shipwreck ever found is one of a Cycladic trading vessel located off the islet of Dhokos, near the Greek island of Hydra, reported in May 1975 and dated to 2450 BC ± 250.

Earliest Power Vessels

Propulsion by steam engine was first achieved when in 1783 the Marquis Jouffroy d'Abbans ascended a reach of the Saône River near Lyons, France in the 180-ton paddle steamer *Pyroscaphe*.

The tug *Charlotte Dundas* was the first successful power-driven vessel. She was a stern paddle-wheel steamer built for the Forth and Clyde Canal, Scotland, in 1801–02 by William Symington (1763–1831), using a double-acting condensing engine constructed by James Watt (1736–1819).

The screw propeller was invented and patented by the Kent, England, farmer Sir Francis Pettit Smith (1808–71) in 1836.

Oldest Vessels Afloat

The oldest active steam ship is the *Skibladner,* which has plied Lake Mjøsa, Norway, since 1856. Originally built in Motala, Sweden, she has had two major refittings.

The oldest mechanically propelled boat of certain date is the 48-ton Bristol steam-driven dredger or drag-boat *Bertha* of 50 ft, designed by I. K. Brunel (1806–59) in 1844 and afloat in the custody of the Exeter Maritime Museum, Devon, England.

G. H. Pattinson's 40-ft steam launch *Dolly*, raised after 67 years from Ullswater, England in 1962, and now on Lake Windermere, also probably dates from the 1840's.

Sailing Ships

The largest sailing vessel ever built was the *France II* (5,806 gross tons), launched at Bordeaux in 1911. The *France II* was a steel-hulled, 5-masted barque (square-rigged on 4 masts and fore-and-aft rigged on the aftermost mast). Her hull measured 418 ft overall. Although principally designed as a sailing vessel with a stump topgallant rig, she was also fitted with two steam engines. She was wrecked off New Caledonia in 1922.

The only 7-masted sailing vessel ever built was the 375.6-ft-long *Thomas W. Lawson* (5,218 gross tons), built at Quincy, Mass in 1902. She was lost off the Isles of Scilly on Dec 15, 1907.

Largest Sails and Sailing Vessel

Sails are known to have been used for marine propulsion since 3500 BC. The largest spars ever carried were those in the British Royal Navy battleship *Temeraire*, completed at Chatham, Kent, on Aug 31, 1877. She was broken up in 1921. The fore and main yards measured 115 ft in length. The foresail contained 5,100 sq ft of canvas, weighing 2 tons, and the total sail area was 25,000 sq ft. H M Battleship *Sultan* was ship-rigged when completed at Chatham, Kent, Eng, on Oct 10, 1871 and carried 34,100 sq ft of sails plus 15,300 sq ft of stunsails. She was not finally broken up until 1946.

The largest sailing vessel in service is the 342-ft *Kruzenshtern*, built *c*. 1933 and now used by the USSR marine schools of Kaliningrad and Murmansk.

Longest Day's Run Under Sail

The longest day's run calculated for any commercial vessel was one of 462 nautical miles (532.0 statute miles) by the clipper ship *Champion of the Seas* (2,722 registered tons) of the Liverpool Black Ball Line running before a northwesterly gale in the south Indian Ocean under the command of Capt. Alex Newlands in 1854. The elapsed time between the fixes was 23 hours 17 min giving an average of 19.97 knots.

Fastest Circumnavigation, Solo

Philippe Monet (France) set a speed record of 129 days 19 hours 17 min, sailing alone, around the world from Brest, France, via Cape Town, back to Brest, in his 77-ft trimaran *Kriter Brut de Brut*, 1986–87.

Dodge Morgan (US) in the 60-ft-long Bermudan sloop, *American Promise*, sailed non-stop W–E via Cape Horn from Bermuda on Nov 12, 1985 and traversed 25,671 mi in 150 days 1 hour 6 min at the rate of 171.1 mi/day, returning to Bermuda Apr 11, 1986.

Largest Human-Powered Ships

The largest human-powered ship was the giant *Tessarakonteres* 3-banked catamaran galley with 4,000 rowers built for Ptolemy IV *c*.

210 BC in Alexandria, Egypt. It measured 420 ft with up to 8 men to an oar of 38 cubits (57 ft) in length.

The longest canoe is the 117-ft-long, 20-ton Kauri wood Maori war canoe *Nga Toki Matawhaorua,* built with adzes at Kerikeri Inlet, New Zealand in 1940 to hold a crew of 70 or more. The "Snake Boat" *Nadubhagom* 135 ft long from Kerala, southern India has a crew of 109 rowers and 9 "encouragers."

Largest Wooden Ships

The heaviest wooden ship ever built was the *Richelieu,* 333 ft 8 in long and of 9,558 tons, launched in Toulon, France, on Dec 3, 1873. The longest modern wooden ship ever built was the New York-built *Rochambeau* (1867–72), formerly *Dunderberg*. She measured 377 ft 4 in overall. It should be noted that the biblical length of Noah's Ark was 300 cubits or, at 18 in to a cubit, 450 ft (but see *Largest Junks*).

Tallest Mast

The *Astra*, a Class J sailing vessel built about 1938, has been refitted with the tallest mast in the world. At 164 ft in length and constructed of extruded aluminum this weighs 2.8 tons and can support a sail area of 16,140 sq ft.

Largest Junks

The largest junk on record was the seagoing *Cheng Ho,* flagship of Admiral Cheng Ho's 62 treasure ships, of *c.* 1420, with a displacement of 3,100 tons and a length variously estimated up to 538 ft and believed to have had 9 masts.

FASTEST PACIFIC CROSSING: The containership "Sea-Lane Commerce" set a record in 1973 of just over 6 days (4,840 nautical miles) from Yokohama to Calif, which has yet to be surpassed.

A river junk 361 ft long, with treadmill-operated paddle wheels, was recorded in 1161 AD. A floating fortress 600 ft square, built by Wang Chun on the Yangtze, took part in the Chin-Wu river war, *c.* 280 AD. Present-day junks do not, even in the case of the Chiangsu traders, exceed 170 ft in length.

Earliest Turbine

The first turbine ship was the *Turbinia,* built in 1894, at Wallsend-on-Tyne, England, to the design of Charles Algernon Parsons (1854–1931). The *Turbinia* was 100 ft long and of 44½ tons displacement with machinery consisting of three steam turbines totaling about 2,000 shaft hp. At her first public demonstration in 1897 she reached a speed of 34.5 knots (39.7 mph).

Fastest Atlantic Crossing

A 65-ft powerboat, the *Virgin Atlantic Challenger II*, sailed by Richard Branson, a 35-year-old US businessman and his crew of 6, set a world record in June 1986 for all types of boats, by taking only 3 days 8 hours 31 min from NYC to Bishop's Rock off the coast of Eng. This beat the record held by the 51,988 gross ton transatlantic liner *United States* by 2 hours 11 min.

Fastest Pacific Crossing

The fastest crossing of the Pacific Ocean (4,840 nautical miles) was 6 days 1 hour 27 min by the containership *Sea-Land Commerce* (50,315 tons) from Yokohama, Japan to Long Beach, Calif, June 30–July 6, 1973, at an average speed of 33.27 knots (38.31 mph). Master of the ship was Felton Ross Worthy of Huntsville, Ala.

Longest Sailboat

The longest is the 440-ft-long French-built *Wind Song* with 4 aluminum masts each 204 ft high. The polyester sails are computer-controlled. It is operated as a Pacific cruise vessel for 150 passengers by Windstar Sail Cruises.

Largest Passenger Liner

The world's largest passenger ship (by tonnage) is the 73,219 gross ton Norwegian cruise ship *Sovereign of the Seas*. Built at the French shipyard Chantiers de l'Atlantique at St Nazaire, she entered service from Miami in Jan 1988.

The largest liner afloat and longest liner ever built is the *Norway* of 70,202.19 gross tons and 1,035 ft 7½ in in length. She was built as the *France* in 1961 and renamed after purchase in June 1979 by Knut Kloster of Norway. Her second maiden voyage was from Southampton on May 7, 1980.

The *Queen Elizabeth II*, of 67,140 gross tons with an overall length of 963 ft, set a "turn-around" record of 5 hours 47 min in NYC on Nov 21, 1983. Her 96-day 1986 world cruise cost $146,895 per person in the penthouse suite. Her original steam-turbine machinery was replaced with diesel electric units in Apr 1987.

The original *Queen Elizabeth,* no longer afloat, was the heaviest ship ever built with 83,673 gross tons originally (later 82,998), but a length of 1,031 ft, some 4 ft shorter than the *Norway*. Her last passenger voyage ended on Nov 15, 1968. In 1970 she was removed to Hong Kong to serve as a floating marine university and renamed *Seawise University*. On Jan 9, 1972 she was set on fire by 3 simultaneous outbreaks. The gutted hull was cut up and removed by 1978. (*Seawise* was a pun on the new owner's initials—C. Y. Tung (1911–1982).)

Largest Battleships

The largest battleship now is the USS *New Jersey,* with a full-load displacement of 65,000 tons and an overall length of 887 ft 7 in, exactly 4 in longer than its sister ships, the *Iowa,* the *Missouri,* and the *Wisconsin,* which at the time of commissioning in 1943–44 all displaced 45,000 tons. She was on active service last (with her nine 16-inch guns, capable of firing projectiles of 2,700 lb a distance of 23 mi) off the Lebanon coast, Dec 14, 1983–Feb 26, 1984. The USS *Iowa* was reactivated in May 1984 at a cost of $405 million.

The Japanese battleships *Yamato* (completed on Dec 16, 1941 and sunk southwest of Kyushu by US planes on Apr 7, 1945) and *Musashi* (sunk in the Philippine Sea by 11 bombs and 16 torpedoes on Oct 24, 1944) were the largest battleships ever commissioned, each with a full-load displacement of 72,809 tons. With overall length of 863 ft, a beam of 127 ft and a full-load draught of 35½ ft, they mounted nine 18.1-in guns in three triple turrets. Each gun weighed 162 tons and was 75 ft in length, firing a 3,200-lb projectile.

Largest Aircraft Carriers

The warships with the largest full-load displacement in the world are the Nimitz class US Navy aircraft carriers USS *Nimitz*, *Theodore Roosevelt, Dwight D. Eisenhower, Abraham Lincoln,* and *Carl Vinson* at 91,487 tons. They are 1,092 ft in length overall and have a speed well in excess of 30 knots (35 mph) with their nuclear-powered 260,000 shaft hp geared steam turbines. They have to be refueled after about 900,000 miles steaming. Their complement is 6,300. The total cost of the *Abraham Lincoln,* laid down at Newport News, in Dec 1984 will exceed (together with the *George Washington*) $3¼ billion, excluding the 90-plus aircraft carried. The USS *Enterprise* is, however, 1,102 ft long and thus still the longest warship ever built.

Most Carrier Landings

The greatest number of plane landings on an aircraft carrier in one day was 602 achieved by Marine Air Group 6 of the US Pacific Fleet Air Force aboard the USS *Matanikou* on May 25, 1945 between 8 A.M. and 5 P.M.

MOST DANGEROUS NUCLEAR SUBMARINE: This USSR Typhoon class sub is one of 3 of the largest known. Secretly built at a covered shipyard, this 28,000-ton sub can carry 20 SS NX 20 missiles, each with 7 independently targeted warheads. It was caught on the surface by a British photographer. With its power, it alone can obliterate any country within 5,000 mi of it.

FASTEST WARSHIP is this hovercraft, the USN SES-100B, a 78-ft 112-ton test vehicle that sped 105.8 mph on Chesapeake Bay in 1980.

Fastest Destroyer

The highest speed attained by a destroyer was 45.25 knots (51.84 mph) by the 3,120-ton French destroyer *Le Terrible* in 1935. She was built in Blainville and powered by four Yarrow small-tube boilers and two Rateau geared turbines giving 100,000 shaft hp. She was removed from the active list in 1957.

Longest, Fastest and Deepest Submarines

The largest submarines are of the USSR Typhoon class code-named Oscar. The launch of the first at the secret covered shipyard at Severodvinsk on the White Sea was announced by NATO on Sept 23, 1980. It is believed to have a dived displacement of 28,000 tons, and measure 557.6 ft overall and be armed with 20 SS NX 20 missiles with a 5,000-nautical-mile range, each with 7 warheads. By 1987, two others being built in Leningrad will also be operational, each deploying 140 warheads.

The Russian Alfa-class nuclear-powered submarines have a reported maximum speed of 42 knots (about 48 mph). With use of titanium steel they are believed to be able to dive to 2,500 ft. A US spy satellite over Leningrad's naval yard on June 8, 1983 showed they were being lengthened and are now 260.1 ft long.

The two US Navy vessels able to descend 12,000 ft are the 3-man *Trieste II* (DSV 1) of 303 tons, recommissioned in Nov 1973 and the DSV 2 (deep submergence vessel) USS *Alvin*. The *Trieste II* was reconstructed from the record-breaking bathyscaphe *Trieste*, but without the Krupp-built sphere, which enabled it to descend to 35,820 ft.

Largest Cargo Vessel

The largest vessel capable of carrying dry cargo is the 365,000-dwt ore carrier *Berge Stahl*, built in Korea for the Norwegian owner Sig Bergesen Dy. It has a length of 1,125 ft, a beam measuring 208 ft and was launched on Nov 5, 1986.

Largest Tanker

The largest tanker and ship of any kind was the 624,038 ton-deadweight *Seawise Giant* converted for C. Y. Tung in 1979. (The name is a pun on the owner's initials.) She was 1,504 ft (more than ¼ mi) long with a beam of 225 ft 11 in, had a draught of 80 ft 9 in. She was attacked Oct 5, 1987 and destroyed May 14, 1988 by Iraqi *Mirage* jets in the Persian Gulf.

Largest Hydrofoil

The largest naval hydrofoil is the 212-ft-long *Plainview* (347 tons full load), launched by Lockheed Shipbuilding and Construction Company at Seattle, Wash June 28, 1965. She has a service speed of 50 knots (57 mph).

Three 165-ton Supramar PTS 150 Mk. III hydrofoils, carrying 250 passengers at 40 knots, ply the Malmö-Copenhagen crossing between Sweden and Denmark. They were built by Westermoen Hydrofoil Ltd of Mandal, Norway.

A 500-ton wing ground effect vehicle capable of carrying 900 tons has been reported in the USSR.

Containerships

Shipborne containerization began in 1955 when the tanker *Ideal X* was converted by Malcolm McLean (US). She carried containers only on deck.

The largest containerships are the 12 built by US Lines in Korea in 1984–85. They are capable of carrying 4,482 TEU (the equivalent of 20 ft containers) and have a gross tonnage of 57,075.

Largest Barges

Four RoRo (roll-on roll-off) barges, of the *El Rey* class of 16,700 tons and 580-ft length each, built by FMC Corp of Portland, Ore and operated by the Crowley Maritime Corp of San Francisco are currently the largest. They carry up to 376 trailer trucks each with tri-level loading, between Florida and Puerto Rico.

Largest Whale Factory

The largest whale factory ship is the USSR's *Sovietskaya Ukraina* (32,034 gross tons), with a summer deadweight of 51,520 tons completed in Oct 1959. She has a 714½ ft length and 84 ft 7 in beam.

Most Powerful Tug

The most powerful is *Smit Singapore* commissioned in Apr 1984 by Smit Tak International, of 22,000 hp and 189 tons bollard pull at full power. She is 246.7 ft long and 51.5 ft wide.

Garbage Scow Goes Begging for 155 Days

The entire world has problems disposing of refuse. The worst dilemma was faced by the garbage barge *Mobro*. Loaded with 3,168 tons of trash, mostly from Islip, NY, it was towed out of a harbor on the Long Island coast for what was supposed to be a routine voyage on Mar 22, 1987. The destination was North Carolina where it was to be sold for the production of methane gas.

Unfortunately, while the barge was at sea, the deal was declared null and void, and in sheer desperation the barge continued to chug its way south while its owners tried to get ports in Louisiana, the Bahamas, Mexico and Belize to take the trash—but all flatly refused.

By the end of April the *Mobro* was slowly schlepping its rancid cargo back to New York. After a voyage of more than 4,000 mi, which attracted daily headlines in the international press, the *Mobro* finally arrived in Gravesend Harbor outside Brooklyn. No NYC official (from the mayor down) wanted anything to do with the trash. The *Mobro* remained at anchor.

The courts finally decided in July to allow the *Mobro* to unload its trash into the Brooklyn incinerator, provided the 400 tons of resulting ash would be trucked back to Islip. However, legal challenges delayed the unloading until Aug 24, ending the *Mobro's* tortuous sea odyssey at 155 days.

Largest Propeller

The largest ship propeller is the triple-bladed screw of 36 ft 1 in diameter made by Kawasaki Heavy Industries Ltd on Mar 17, 1982 for the 208,000-ton bulk-ore tanker *Hoei Maru*.

Most Powerful Dredger

The most powerful dredger is the 468.4-ft-long *Prins der Nederlanden* of 10,586 grt. Using two suction tubes, she can dredge 22,400 tons of sand from a depth of 115 ft in less than one hour.

Most Powerful Icebreaker

A 61,000-ton nuclear-powered barge-carrying merchantman designed for work along the USSR's Arctic coast was completed in early 1982 and is known to be designed to break ice.

The longest purpose-built icebreaker is the 25,000-ton 460-ft-long

Rossiya, powered by 75,000 hp nuclear engines built in Leningrad and completed in 1985. A new $(CAN) 500 million, 100,000 hp, 636-ft-long icebreaker of the Polar Class 8 was ordered by the Canadian government in Oct 1985.

The largest *converted* icebreaker has been the 1,007-ft-long SS *Manhattan* (43,000 shp), which was converted by the Humble Oil Co. into a 150,000-ton icebreaker with an armored prow 69 ft 2 in long. She made a double voyage through the North-West Passage in Arctic Canada from Aug 24 to Nov 12, 1969. The North-West Passage was first navigated by Roald Amundsen (Norway) in the sealing sloop *Gjöa* on July 11, 1906.

Largest and Fastest Car Ferry

The largest car and passenger ferry is the 37,800-gross-ton M/S *Mariella* which entered service across the Baltic Sea between Helsinki and Stockholm in May 1985. Built in Turku, Finland for the Viking Line, she is 581 ft long, 95 ft in the beam and can carry 2,500 passengers and 580 cars.

The fastest car and passenger ferry is the 24,065 gross-ton gas turbine-powered *Finnjet.* Built in 1977, she operates in the Baltic between Helsinki and Travemunde, W Germany and is capable of exceeding 30 knots.

Most Expensive Yacht

On Dec 17, 1987, Donald Trump, the NYC real-estate tycoon, purchased from the Sultan of Brunei the 282-ft yacht, called the *Nabila,* which he renamed *Trump Princess,* for $30 million. It was estimated that the 5-story vessel, refitted, including gold-plated bathroom fixtures and a marble-floored disco had cost some $29 million.

Fastest Building of a Ship

The fastest-ever building time for a major ship was 4 days 15 hours in the case of the 10,920-ton displacement *Robert E. Peary* at Kaiser's Yard, Portland, Ore, from Nov 8 (keel laid) to launch on Nov 12, 1942. She was operational on Nov 15 and was No 440 of the fleet of 2,742 11.6-knot Liberty Ships built in 18 US shipyards from Sept 27, 1941.

Largest River Boat

The largest inland river boat is the 382-ft-long *Mississippi Queen,* designed by James Gardner of London. The vessel was commissioned on July 25, 1976 in Cincinnati, O, and is now in service on the Mississippi River.

Largest Collision

The closest approach to an irresistible force striking an immovable object occurred on Dec 16, 1977, 22 miles off the coast of southern Africa, when the tanker *Venoil* (330,954 dwt) struck her sister ship *Venpet* (330,869 dwt).

LARGEST HOVERCRAFT: This ACV (air cushion vehicle) is used regularly on crossings of the English Channel. Built by the British Hovercraft Corp, it can cruise at 75 mph on a calm day. (*BHC*)

RIVERBOAT RACE: Each year two paddlewheel steamboats race 1,039 mi upriver from New Orleans to St. Louis. Here the "Mississippi Queen" (top) (382 ft long) is trying to pass the "Delta Queen" in the 8 mi sprint at the end of the full race, and not succeeding, although she did win the overall race. The record run was made in 1870 when the "Robert E. Lee," famed in song, made the course in 3 days, 18 hours, 14 min, a time never equaled in 118 years.

Survival after Shipwreck

The longest recorded survival alone on a raft is 133 days (4½ months) by Second Steward Poon Lim (b Hong Kong) of the UK Merchant Navy, whose ship, the SS *Ben Lomond*, was torpedoed in the Atlantic 565 miles west of St Paul's Rocks at Lat 00° 30′ N and Long 38° 45′ W at 11:45 A.M. on Nov 23, 1942. He was picked up by a Brazilian fishing boat off Salinópolis, Brazil, Apr 5, 1943, and was able to walk ashore. In July 1943 he was awarded the British Empire Medal, and now lives in NYC.

Maurice and Maralyn Bailey survived 118⅔ days in an inflatable dinghy 4½ ft in diameter in the northeast Pacific from March 4 to June 30, 1973.

Largest Wreck

Energy Determination is the largest ship ever wrecked. Weighing 312,186 dwt this VLCC (Very Large Crude Carrier) blew up and broke in two in the Straits of Hormuz on Dec 12, 1979. Her full value was $58 million. The largest wreck removal was carried out in 1979 by Smit Tak International, who removed the remains of the 139,900-ton French tanker *Betelguese* from Bantry Bay, Ireland, within 20 months.

Hovercraft (Skirted Air-Cushion Vehicle)

The ACV (air-cushion vehicle) was first made a practical proposition by Sir Christopher Sydney Cockerell (b June 4, 1910), a British engineer who had the idea in 1954, published his Ripplecraft report 1/55 on Oct 25, 1955, and patented it on Dec 12, 1955. The earliest patent relating to air-cushion craft was applied for in 1877 by John I. Thornycroft (1843–1928) of Chiswick, London and the Finn, Toivo Kaario, developed the idea in 1935.

The first flight by a hovercraft was by the 4½-ton Saunders Roe SR-N1 at Cowes, Isle of Wight, on May 30, 1959. With a 1,500-lb-thrust Viper turbojet engine, this craft reached 68 knots in June 1961.

The longest hovercraft journey was one of 5,000 mi through 8 West African countries between Oct 15, 1969 and Jan 3, 1970 by the British Trans-African Hovercraft Expedition.

The largest civil hovercraft is the 342-ton British built SRN 4 MK III with a capacity of 418 passengers and 60 cars. It is 185 ft in length, powered by 4 Siddeley Marine Proteus engines which give a maximum speed in excess of the permitted cross-Channel operating speed of 65 knots.

The 3,000-ton US Navy Large Surface Effect Ship (LSES) was built by Bell Aerospace under contract from the Department of Defense in 1977–81.

The greatest altitude a hovercraft is operating at is on Lake Titicaca, Peru, where since 1975 an HM2 Hoverferry has been hovering 12,506 ft above sea level.

2. ROAD VEHICLES

CARS

Most Cars

As of Jan 1987, there were 380,836,904 passenger cars in the world, 132,347,200 (or 34.75 percent of them) in the US.

The US people purchased 11,453,705 foreign and domestically made cars in 1986, more for a single year than any country in history.

Earliest Automobiles

The earliest car of which there is record is a 2-ft-long steam-powered model, constructed by Ferdinand Verbiest (d 1687), a Belgian Jesuit priest, which he described in his *Astronomia Europaea*. His 1668 model was possibly inspired either by Giovanni Branca's description of a steam turbine published in 1629, or by writings on "fire carts" during the Chu dynasty (*c*. 800 BC).

The earliest full-scale automobile was the first of two military steam tractors completed at the Paris Arsenal in 1769 by Nicolas-Joseph Cugnot (1725–1804). This vehicle reached about 2¼ mph. His second, larger tractor, completed in 1771, today survives in the *Conservatoire national des arts et métiers* in Paris.

The first passenger-carrying automobile was a steam-powered road vehicle carrying 8 passengers built by Richard Trevithick (1771–1833). It first ran on Dec 24, 1801 in Cornwall, Eng.

The Swiss Isaac de Rivaz (d 1828) built a carriage powered by his "explosion engine" in 1805.

The first practical internal-combustion-engined vehicle was built by a Londoner, Samuel Brown (patented Apr 25, 1826) whose 4-hp 2-cylinder atmospheric-gas 88-liter engined carriage climbed Shooters Hill, Blackheath, Kent, England in May 1826.

Earliest Gasoline-Driven Cars

The first successful gasoline-driven car, the Motorwagen, built by Karl-Friedrich Benz (1844–1929) of Karlsruhe, ran at Mannheim, Germany in late 1885. It was a 560-lb 3-wheeler reaching 8–10 mph. Its single-cylinder 4-stroke chain-drive engine (bore 91.4 mm, stroke 160 mm) delivered 0.85 hp at 200 rpm. It was patented on Jan 29, 1886. Its first 1-km road test was reported in the local newspaper of June 4, 1886, under the news heading "Miscellaneous." Two were built in 1885 of which one has been preserved in "running order" at the Deutsches Museum, Munich.

Earliest Registrations

The world's first plates were probably introduced by the Parisian police in France in 1893. The first American plates were in 1901 in NY. Registration plates were introduced in Britain in 1903. The original A1 plate was secured by the 2nd Earl Russell (1865–1931) for his 12-hp Napier. This plate, willed to Trevor Laker of Leicester, was sold in Aug 1959, for £2,500 (then $7,000) in aid of charity. License plate No. 3 was reported sold at a Hong Kong government auction for US $131,600 in Jan 1984.

Fastest Road Cars

Various detuned track cars have been licensed for road use but are not purchasable production models. Manufacturers of very fast and very expensive models understandably limit speed tests to stipulated engine revs. The fastest current manufacturer's *claim* (as opposed to independent road tests) for any road car is the Jaguar £100,000 ($180,000) 205-mph two-door coupe being developed at their Engineering Design Centre, Coventry, Eng, May 25, 1988. Ferrari claimed a speed of 201 mph for their $250,000 F40 in July 1987.

The highest road-tested acceleration reported is 0–60 mph in 4.1 sec. for an MG Metro 6R4 International Rally Car in 1986.

Largest Cars

Of cars produced for private road use, the largest has been the Bugatti "Royale" Type 41, known as the "Golden Bugatti," of

EXHIBIT LIMOUSINE: This 60-ft-long, 20,000-lb car, called "The American Dream," has 16 wheels, 2 Cadillac front-wheel-drive engines, a swimming pool, a hot tub, a water bed, a helicopter landing pad, a crystal chandelier and living quarters including 3 color TV's, one giant screen, a microwave oven, video-cassette recorder, 10-speaker stereo, 10 telephones in all, mirrored ceiling, cocktail table and hardwood flooring. The car has 8 steerable axles, one engine mounted up front which drives 3 of them and a second engine in the rear driving the other 5. The limo requires 2 drivers communicating by radio through headsets, and is operated like a hook-and-ladder fire engine in going around corners. While it is not allowed on normal streets, it is operable, but is mostly used for automotive shows and movies. In this picture, it is on the dock at Long Beach, Calif, alongside the Hotel Queen Mary. It is owned by Jay Ohrbeg of Hollywood, Calif, and is for sale at $2 million. Fifty people can crowd into it at one time.

FASTEST CARS

Category	*mph*	*Car*	*Driver*	*Place*	*Date*
Jet-Engined (*official*)	633.468	Thrust 2	Richard Noble (GB)	Black Rock Desert, Nevada	Oct 4, 1983
Rocket-Engined (*official*)	622.287	Blue Flame	Gary Gabelich	Bonneville, Utah	Oct 23, 1970
Wheel-Driven (*turbine*)	429.311	Bluebird	Donald Campbell (UK)	Lake Eyre, Australia	July 17, 1964
Wheel-Driven (*multi-piston-engine*)	418.504	Goldenrod	Robert Summers	Bonneville, Utah	Nov 12, 1965
Wheel-Driven (*single-piston-engine*)	357.391	Herda-Knapp-Milodon	Bob Herda	Bonneville, Utah	Nov 2, 1967
Rocket-Engined (*unofficial*)*	739.666	Budweiser Rocket	Stan Barrett	Edwards Air Force Base, California	Dec 17, 1979

* This published speed of Mach 1.0106 is *not* officially sanctioned by the USAF whose Digital Instrumented Radar was not calibrated or certified. The radar information was *not* generated by the vehicle directly but by an operator aiming the dish by means of a TV screen. To claim a speed to 6 significant figures appears quite unsustainable.

which only 6 (not 7) were made at Molsheim, France by the Italian, Ettore Bugatti, and all survive. First built in 1927, this car has an 8-cylinder engine of 12.7 liter capacity, and measures over 22 ft in length. The hood is over 7 ft long.

Of custom-built cars the longest is a 16-wheeled 60-ft-long Cadillac called "The American Dream" (see photo and caption on page 289).

Fastest Diesel-Engined Car

The diesel-engined prototype 230-hp 3-liter Mercedes C 111/3 attained 203.3 mph in tests on the Nardo Circuit, Italy, Oct 5–15, 1978, and in Apr 1978 averaged 195.398 mph for 12 hours, so covering a world record 2,399.76 mi.

Most Expensive Special Cars

The most expensive car to build was the Presidential 1969 Lincoln Continental Executive delivered to the US Secret Service on Oct 14, 1968. It has an overall length of 21 ft 6.3 in with a 13-ft-4-in wheelbase and, with the addition of 2 tons of armor plate, weighs 12,000 lb. The cost for research, development and manufacture was estimated at $500,000, but it is rented for a mere $5,000 per annum. Even if all four tires were to be shot out it can travel at 50 mph on inner rubber-edged steel discs.

Carriage House Motor Cars Ltd of NYC in March 1978 completed 4 years' work on converting a 1973 Rolls-Royce, including lengthening it by 30 in. The price tag was $500,000.

Most Expensive Standard Cars

The most expensive British standard car is the Rolls-Royce 8-cylinder 6,750 cc Phantom VI quoted in 1987 at £195,596 (incl tax) ($312,953). More expensive are custom-built models. Jack Barclay Ltd of Berkeley Square, London, quotes £350,000 ($560,000) for an armor-plated version.

The unrivaled collector of Rolls-Royces was Bhagwan Shri Rajneesh (b 1931), the Indian mystic of Rajneeshpuram, Oregon. His disciples bestowed 93 of these upon him before his deportation in Nov 1985.

Most Expensive Used Cars

The greatest price paid for a used car is $9,845,000 for a 1931 Bugatti Royale (one of only 6 produced) by Nicholas Harley, a London vintage car dealer, at Christie's London on Nov 19, 1987.

Ettore Bugatti, the noted Italian auto designer, and members of his family owned the car for the first 20 years of its life—and then in 1951 it was sold to Briggs Cunningham, US racing driver and America's Cup yachtsman, who featured the Bugatti at his Costa Mesa, Calif, Automotive Museum for the next 36 years.

Longest in Production

The longest any car has been in mass production is 49 years (1938 to date), including wartime interruptions, in the case of the Volkswagen "Beetle" series, originally designed by Ferdinand Porsche. The 20-millionth car came off the final production line in Mexico on May

15, 1981 and more than 21 million had been built by Jan 1, 1987. Residual production continues in South America.

Most Inexpensive

The cheapest car of all time was the 1922 Red Bug Buckboard, built by Briggs and Stratton Co of Milwaukee, Wis listed at $150–$125. It had a 62-in wheelbase and weighed 245 lb. The early models of the King Midget cars were sold in kit form for self-assembly for as little as $100 as late as 1948.

Largest Engines

The most powerful piston-engine car is "Quad A1." It was designed and built in 1964 by Jim Lytle and was first shown in May 1965 at the Los Angeles Sports Arena. The car features 4 Allison V–12 aircraft engines with a total of 6,840 cu in (112,087 cc) displacement and 12,000 hp. The car has 4-wheel drive, 8 wheels and tires, and dual 6-disc clutch assemblies. The wheelbase is 160 in. It weighs 5,860 lb and has 96 spark plugs and 96 exhaust pipes.

The largest car ever used was the "White Triplex," sponsored by J. H. White of Philadelphia. Completed early in 1928, after 2 years' work, the car weighed about 4½ tons and was powered by three Liberty V12 aircraft engines with a total capacity of 81,188 cc developing 1,500 bhp at 2,000 rpm. It was used to break the world speed record, but crashed at Daytona, Fla on March 13, 1929.

Currently, the most powerful car on the road is the 6-wheeled Jameson-Merlin powered by a 27,000-cc 1,760-hp Rolls-Royce V12 Merlin aero-engine, governed down to a maximum speed of 185 mph. It has a range of 300 miles with tanks of 72-gallon capacity. The vehicle weighs 2.96 tons overall.

Largest Production-Car Engine

The highest engine capacity of a production car was 13½ liters (824 cu in), in the case of the Pierce-Arrow 6-66 Raceabout of 1912–18, the Peerless 6-60 of 1912–14 and the Fageol of 1918. The most powerful current production car is the Lamborghini Countach 5000 S quattrovalvole with a 5,167-cc V12 engine developing 455 bhp.

Most Durable Car

The highest recorded mileage for a car was 1,184,880 authenticated miles by Aug 1978 for a 1957 Mercedes 180D owned by Robert O'Reilly of Olympia, Wash. Its subsequent fate is unknown.

R. L. Bender of Madison, Wis claimed 1,020,000 mi for his car in Dec 1983. Bender's car reached 1,021,041 mi on June 9, 1984. He has been driving it since 1958.

Longest Fuel Range

The greatest distance driven without refueling on a tank full of fuel (19.41 gals) is 1,150.3 mi by an Audi 100 turbo-diesel driven by Stuart Bladon with his son Bruce (navigator) and Bob Proctor (RAC observer) across Eng from Land's End to John O'Groats and back to West Falkirk in 22 hours 28 min in July 1984. The average speed was 51.17 mph giving 59.27 mpg.

Gasoline Consumption

At the Silverstone racetrack in Eng on July 1, 1988, Wasaki Oka of Japan driving for Team 1200 Honda covered a distance of 6,409 mi on one Imp gallon.

Go-Karting

The highest mileage recorded in 24 hours on a closed twisting circuit was 1,018 laps of a mile each for a 4-man team (Owen Nimmo, Gary Ruddock, Jim Timmins, and Danny Upshaw) on Sept 4–5, 1983 at Erbsville Kartway, Waterloo, Ont, Canada. The kart was 5 hp 140 cc Honda-engined.

Two-Wheel Driving (Wheelies)

Gilbert Bataille of Paris drove a Leyland T45 Road Runner Truck on two side wheels for 2.864 mi at the British Truck Grand Prix, Silverstone, Eng, on Aug 17, 1986.

Steve Murty drove a Multi-Part Skytrain truck on its rear wheels for 1,049 ft at the same track on Aug 17, 1986. The 60-ton truck was powered by a 500-bhp Cummins turbo-charged 14-litre engine and had a ZF-Ecomat hp 600 5-speed automatic gearbox.

A speed of 83.8 mph was achieved in a standard Volvo 760 at Anderstrop, Sweden, on May 18, 1986 by Goran Eliason of Boras, Sweden.

Long-Distance Driving

The fastest circumnavigation embracing more than an equator's length of driving (24,901.47 road miles) is one in 74 days 1 hour 11 min by Garry Sowerby (driver) and Ken Langley (navigator) of Canada from Sept 6 to Nov 19, 1980 in a Volvo 245 westward from Toronto through 4 continents and 23 countries. The distance covered was 26,738 miles.

The folk-singers Manfred Müller and Paul-Ernst Luhrs drove around the world covering 78 countries and 174,000 mi between Mar 30, 1964 and Apr 23, 1984. They started and finished in Bremerhaven, W Germany.

Starting at the southern tip of S America, Garry Sowerby (see above) and his co-driver Tim Cahill (of Canada) drove 14,642 mi to the northern edge of Alaska in under 24 days from Sept 29–Oct 22, 1987 in a virtually stock 1988 GMC Sierra 6.2 L diesel pickup truck utilizing Stanadyne fuel system components and fuel conditioners. Where no road existed in the thickest jungle area of Panama, Sowerby and Cahill drove to the tip of a peninsula, then back to the nearest port, took their truck on a boat and landed at the nearest port to connect to a road again.

The first traverse of the world's greatest land mass (Afro-Eurasia) was achieved by Richard Pape, who, driving south, left the North Cape of Norway in an Austin A90 on July 28 and arrived in Cape Town, S Africa, on Oct 22, 1955 with the milometer recording 17,500 mi after 86 days. The speed record for the same route was set by Ken Langley and Garry Sowerby of Canada (see above) driving north in 28 days 13 hours 10 min for 12,531 mi Apr 4–May 2, 1984.

Solar-Powered Vehicle

The highest speed attained under IHPVA (International Human Powered Vehicle Association) rules by a solely solar-powered vehicle is 24.74 mph at Bellflower, Calif, on July 1, 1984 by *Sunrunner*, designed by Joel Davidson and Greg Johanson of Photovoltaic Power Systems.

Steam Cars

On Aug 19, 1985 Robert E. Barber broke the 79-year-old steam-car record, driving no. 744, *Steamin' Demon*, at 145.607 mph on the Bonneville Salt Flats, Utah. It was built by the Barber-Nichols Engineering Co.

Longest Skid Marks

The longest recorded skid marks on a public road were 950 ft long, left by a Jaguar car involved in an accident on the M.1 near Luton, Bedfordshire, England June 30, 1960. Evidence given in the High Court case *Hurlock v. Inglis and others* indicated a speed "in excess of 100 mph" before the application of the brakes.

The skid marks made by the jet-powered *Spirit of America*, driven by Craig Breedlove, after the car went out of control at Bonneville Salt Flats, Utah Oct 15, 1964, were nearly 6 miles long.

BUILT TO DRIVE BACKWARDS: This 1929 Ford Model A roadster may look funny with its headlights in the rear, but it carried its owners, Charles Creighton and James Hargis 7,180 miles from NYC to LA and back entirely in reverse gear in just 42 days.

LONGEST DRIVE SOUTH-TO-NORTH: Garry Sowerby and Tim Cahill (Canadians both) drove this car from the southern tip of S America to the northern edge of Alaska (with one detour by water) in less than 24 days, Sept 29 to Oct 22, 1987.

Driving in Reverse

Charles Creighton (1908–70) and James Hargis of Maplewood, Mo drove their Ford Model A 1929 roadster in reverse from NYC to Los Angeles (3,340 miles), July 26–Aug 13, 1930 *without* stopping the engine once. They arrived back in NY on Sept 5, again in reverse, thus completing 7,180 miles in 42 days.

The highest average speed attained in any non-stop reverse drive exceeding 500 miles was achieved by Gerald Hoagland, who drove a 1969 Chevrolet Impala 501 miles non-stop in 17 hours 38 min at Chemung Speed Drome, NY July 9–10, 1976 to average 28.41 mph.

Brian "Cub" Keene and James "Wilbur" Wright drove their Chevrolet Blazer 9,031 mi in 37 days (Aug 1–Sept 6, 1984) through 16 US states and Canada. Though it was prominently named "Stuck in Reverse," law enforcement in Okla refused to believe it and insisted they drive in reverse reverse, i.e. forwards, out of the state.

Longest Tow

The longest tow on record was one of 4,759 miles from Halifax, Nova Scotia to Canada's Pacific coast, when Frank J. Elliott and George A. Scott of Amherst, Nova Scotia persuaded 168 passing motorists in 89 days to tow their Model T Ford (in fact, engine-less) to win a $1,000 bet on Oct 15, 1927.

Taxis

The largest taxi fleet is that in Mexico City, with 60,000 "normal" taxis, plus minibuses (*pesaros*) (communal "fixed route" taxis) and *settas* (airport taxis) in mid-1984.

The longest fare on record is one of 7,533 miles through 10 countries from Marble Arch, London, England, from Sept 19 to Oct 18, 1981. The trip was sponsored for charity and the driver was Stephen Tillyer.

Francis Edward Kenyon (b 1904) was continuously licensed as a cab driver in Manchester, Eng, for 57 years 36 days, 1924–1981.

Largest Vehicles and Windshield Wipers

The most massive vehicle ever constructed is the Marion 8-caterpillar crawler used for conveying *Saturn V* rockets to their launching pads at the John F. Kennedy Space Center, Cape Canaveral, Fla. It measures 131 ft 4 in by 114 ft and two of them built at the same time cost $12,300,000. The loaded train weight is 9,000 tons. Its windshield wipers with 42-in blades are the world's largest.

The most massive automotive land vehicle is "Big Muskie," the 10,700-ton mechanical shovel built by Bucyrus-Erie for the Musk mine. It is 487 ft long, 151 ft wide and 222 ft high with a grab capacity of 325 tons.

The longest vehicle ever built is the Arctic Snow Train now owned by the world-famous wire-walker Steve McPeak (see Chapter 11). This 54-wheeled 572-ft-long vehicle was built by R G Le Tourneau, Inc of Longview, Tex for the US Army. Its gross train weight is 400 tons with a top speed of 20 mph and it was driven by a crew of 6 when used as an "Overland Train" for the military. McPeak repaired it and every punctured tire lone-handed in often sub-zero temperatures in Alaska. It generates 4,680 shp and has a capacity of 7,826 gallons.

Largest Ambulance

The largest ambulances are the 59-ft-0½-in-long articulated Alligator Jumbulances Mark VI, VII, VIII and IX, operated by The Across Trust to convey the sick and handicapped on holidays and pilgrimages from Britain to Continental Europe. They are built by Van Hool of Belgium with Fiat engines, cost £200,000 ($360,000) and convey 44 patients and staff.

Buses

The first municipal motor bus service was inaugurated on Apr 12, 1903, between the Eastbourne railway station and Meads, East Sussex, in England. A steam-powered bus named *Royal Patent* ran between Gloucester and Cheltenham, England, for 4 months in 1831.

The longest regularly scheduled bus route is by "Across Australia Coach Lines," which inaugurated a regularly scheduled service between Perth and Brisbane on Apr 9, 1980. The route is 3,389 miles and takes 75 hours 55 min.

The longest buses are the 12-ton, 76-ft-long articulated buses, with 121 passenger seats and room for an additional 66 "strap-hangers," built by the Wayne Corp of Richmond, Ind for use in the Middle East.

The largest bus fleet consists of 6,580 single-deck buses in Rio de Janeiro, Brazil in 1983.

Largest Dump Truck

The largest dump truck is the Terex Titan 33-19 manufactured by the Terex Division of the General Motors Corp. It has a loaded weight of 604.7 tons and a capacity of 350 tons. When unloading, its height is 56 ft. The 16-cylinder engine delivers 3,300 hp and the fuel tank holds 1,560 gallons. It went into service in Nov 1974.

Largest Tires

The largest tires are manufactured in Topeka, Kans by the Goodyear Co for giant dump trucks. They are 12 ft in diameter, weigh 12,500 lb and cost $74,000. A tire 17 ft in diameter is believed to be the practical upper limit.

Largest Load

On July 14–15, 1984, John Brown Engineers & Contractors BV (Eng) moved the Conoco Kotter Field production deck with a roll-out weight of 4,193 tons for the Continental Netherlands Oil Company of Leidsenhage, Netherlands.

Largest and Most Powerful Tractor

The largest tractor is the $459,000 22-ton US Dept of Agriculture Wide Tractive Frame Vehicle completed by Ag West of Sacramento, Calif in June 1982. It measures 33 ft between its wheels which are designed to run on permanent paths, and weighs 24.1 tons. The sport of tractor-pulling was put on a national US championship basis in 1967 at Bowling Green, Ohio where the winner was "The Purple Monster" built and driven by Roger E. Varns. Today there are 12 classes ranging up to "12,200 lb unlimited."

LARGEST AMBULANCE: This 59-ft-long articulated vehicle is one of 4 Alligator Jumbulances, built in Belgium to transport 44 patients and staff at a time of holidays and pilgrimages across Europe.

MOST ► ILLUMINATED TRUCK: "Midnight Bandit," the creation of Todd Pellegrini of Hummelstown, Pa, has 1,900 lights, connected by over 5,000 ft of wire and 45 toggle switches to three 50-amp alternators and five 12-volt batteries. It took over 5 years to fully equip this 1971-F250 Ford Explorer camper truck.

MOST POWERFUL TRUCK: This 1987 Ford L&L 9000 truck has achieved 210.2 mph. Owned and driven by Ken Warby of Cincinnati, O, it weighs 44.1 tons and is equipped with a General Electric J79, tuned to produce 20,000 ft of thrust.

Lawn Mowers

The widest gang mower on record is the 5.6-ton 60-ft-wide 27-unit Big Green Machine, used by the sod farmer Jay Edgar Frick of Monroe, Ohio. It mows an acre in 60 sec.

The longest lawn mower ride was made by Ben Garcia of Old Orchard Beach, Maine, a distance of 2,801 mi from Maine to LA, Sept 14–Dec 4, 1986.

Largest Earth Mover

The largest wheeled loader is 55.1 ft long, with the world's largest tires, 11½ ft in diameter, and a bucket of 671 cu ft capacity. Weighing 198.5 tons, it was developed for open-air coal mining in Australia, by SMEC, a consortium of 11 manufacturers in Tokyo, Japan.

Most Powerful Fire Engine

The most powerful fire appliance is the 860-hp 8-wheel Oshkosh fire truck used for aircraft fires. It can discharge 49,920 gallons of foam through 2 turrets in just 150 sec. It weighs 66 tons.

The fastest is the Jaguar XJ12 "Chubb Firefighter," which in Nov 1982 attained a speed of 130.57 mph in servicing the *Thrust 2* land speed record trials.

Most Powerful Wrecker

The most powerful wrecker is the Twin City Garage and Body Shop 2.35-ton 36-ft-long 969 International M6-23 "Hulk," stationed in Scott City, Mo, which can lift more than 336 tons on its short boom.

Amphibious Vehicle Circumnavigation

The only circumnavigation of the world by an amphibious vehicle was achieved by Ben Carlin (Australia) (d Mar 7, 1981) in an amphibious jeep "Half-Safe." He completed the last leg of the Atlantic crossing (the English Channel) on Aug 24, 1951. He arrived back in Montreal, Canada on May 8, 1958 having completed a circumnavigation of 39,000 miles over land and 9,600 miles by sea and river. He was accompanied on the transatlantic stage by his ex-wife Elinore (US) and on the long transpacific stage (Tokyo to Anchorage) by Broye Lafayette De Mente (b Missouri, 1928).

Longest Motor Trip

The longest continuous trailer tour was one of 143,716 miles by Harry B. Coleman and Peggy Larson in a Volkswagen Camper from Aug 20, 1976 to Apr 20, 1978 through 113 countries. Saburo Ouchi (b Feb 7, 1942) of Tokyo, Japan, drove 167,770 miles in 91 countries from Dec 2, 1969 to Feb 10, 1978.

Rocket-Powered Ice Sled

The highest speed recorded is 247.93 mph by *Oxygen* driven by Sammy Miller (b Apr 15, 1945) on Lake George, NY, on Feb 15, 1981.

LONGEST LAWN MOWER RIDE: Ben Garcia of Old Orchard Beach, Maine, rode 2,201 mi from there to LA in 1986 on his "Woofmobile." It took almost 3 months.

LARGEST EARTH MOVER: This Japanese-made giant loader uses the world's largest tires, 11½ ft in diameter (note size of man alongside), and weighs almost 200 tons. The bucket's capacity is 671 cu ft. It is used for open-air coal mining in Australia.

FARTHEST ON A SNOWMOBILE: 7,211 miles in 60 days is the record set by Tony Lenzini of Duluth, Minn, on this 1986 Arctic Cat Cougar.

Snowmobiles

Tony Lenzini of Duluth, Minn with his 1986 Arctic Cat Cougar snowmobile drove a total of 7,211 miles in 60 riding days between Dec 28, 1985 and Mar 20, 1986.

Richard and Raymond Moore and Loren Matthews drove their snowmobile 5,876 mi from Fairbanks, Alaska to Fenton, Mich, in 39 days from Feb 3–Mar 13, 1980.

The record speed for a snowmobile is 158.53 mph, set by Marv Jorgenson of Minneapolis at the St Paul Winter Festival at Lake Phelan, Minn, on Feb 3, 1985.

MOTORCYCLES

Earliest

The earliest internal-combustion-engined motorized bicycle was a wooden-framed machine built during October–November 1885 by Gottlieb Daimler (1834–1900) of Germany at Bad Cannstatt and first ridden by Wilhelm Maybach (1846–1929). It had a top speed of 12

FASTEST ROAD MACHINE: This 115-bhp Japanese Honda V65 Magna has a design speed of 176 mph. With a liquid-cooled, in-line V4, 16-valve DoHC engine, it has 1098-cc capacity. ◄

MOST ► EXPENSIVE MOTORCYCLE: A 4-stroke 45-degree V-Twin engine of 1340 cu in capacity propels this 2-tone Harley Davidson FLHTC Electra Glide Classic costing more than $14,000. It has a sound system with handlebar controls, 3-position rider floorboards and a seat with "floating" backrest.

mph and developed one-half of one hp from its single-cylinder 264-cc 4-stroke engine at 700 rpm. Known as the "Einspur," it was lost in a fire in 1903. The earliest factory which made motorcycles in quantity was opened in 1894 by Heinrich and Wilhelm Hildebrand and Alois Wolfmüller at Munich, Germany. In its first 2 years this factory produced over 1,000 machines, each having a water-cooled 1,488-cc twin-cylinder 4-stroke engine developing about 2.5 bhp at 600 rpm—the highest capacity motorcycle engine ever put into production.

Fastest Track Motorcycle

There is no satisfactory answer to the identity of the fastest track machine, other than to say that the current Kawasaki, Suzuki and Yamaha machines have all been geared to attain speeds marginally in excess of 186.4 mph under race conditions.

Duration

The longest time a solo motorcycle has been kept in non-stop motion is 560 hours by Norberto Naummi, Foppiani Maurizio, and Roberto Ghillani, who covered 18,000 mi at an average speed of 33.69 mph in Varano de Melegani, Italy, Aug 16–Sept 8, 1986.

Fastest Road Motorcycle

The 115-bhp Japanese Honda V65 Magna with a liquid-cooled, in-line V4, 16-valve DoHC engine of 1,098-cc capacity has a design speed of 173 mph.

BICYCLES AND UNICYCLES

The first design for a machine propelled by cranks and pedals, with connecting rods, has been attributed to Leonardo da Vinci (1452–1519) or one of his pupils, dated *c.* 1493. The earliest such design actually built was in 1839–40 by Kirkpatrick Macmillan (1810–78) of Dumfries, Scotland. It is now in the Science Museum, London.

Smallest Bicycle

The world's smallest wheeled *rideable* bicycle is one with 1-in diameter gold-plated wheels, with a wheelbase of 2¾ in, a seat 7 in from the floor and pedals of ¾ in, built and ridden by Charly Charles in his act at Circus Circus Hotels in Reno and Las Vegas, Nev.

With slightly smaller wheels (1.37 in), weighing 24.6 oz, a bicycle with more leg room was built and ridden by Jacques Puyoou of Pau, France in 1983. He has also built a tandem bike 14.1 in long to accommodate Mme Puyoou.

Charly Charles has also built a tandem bike with wheels 2½ in in diameter and the rear seat 10 in off the ground, where his wife, Kathryn, sits during their act.

Largest Bicycle

A classic Ordinary bicycle with a 65¼-in front wheel and an 18-inch back wheel was constructed by the Coventry Machinists Co in 1881.

TALL UNICYCLE: "Large ▲ Marge" is the name given this 66-in wheel, being ridden by Steve Gordon, one of its constructors.

DOUBLE-DECKER ▲ TANDEM BIKE: From the ground to the upper story handlebars is 11.1 ft. Built by Kesaichiro Tagawa of Osaka, Japan, this two-seater is 16.4 ft long.

◄ SMALLEST RIDEABLE BIKE: Charly Charles of Las Vegas aboard the 7-in-high seat on his 14k gold-plated wheeled bicycle with diamond-studded pedals. His bike collection includes a slightly bigger bike with silver-dollar wheels, another with 50-cent-piece wheels, and a tandem bike with 2½-in wheels and a 10-in-high seat for his wife.

It is now owned by Paul Foulkes-Halbard of Crowborough, Sussex, Eng.

A bicycle with an 8-ft-2½-in front wheel with pedal extenders was built in 1878 for circus demonstrations.

Longest Bicycle

The longest true tandem bicycle ever built (*i.e.* without a third stabilizing wheel) is one of 66 ft 11 in for 35 riders built by the Pedaalstompers Westmalle of Belgium. They rode *c.* 195 ft in practice on Apr 20, 1979. The machine weighs 2,425 lb.

Fastest Cycle Riding

The speed records for human-powered vehicles are 61.94 mph (single rider) by John Seibert at La Garita, Colo, Oct 27, 1980, and 62.92 mph (multiple riders) by Dave Grylls and Leigh Barczewski at the Ontario Speedway, Calif, May 4, 1980. (Also see Chapter 12—*Cycling*.)

Unicycles

The tallest unicycle ever mastered is one 101 ft 9 in tall ridden by Steve McPeak (with a safety wire or mechanic suspended to an overhead crane) for a distance of 376 ft in Las Vegas Oct 19, 1980. The free-style riding of ever taller unicycles (that is, without any safety harness) must inevitably lead to serious injury or fatality.

Hanspeter Beck of Jindabyne, S Australia unicycled 3,876.08 mi in 51 days, 23 hours, 25 min, June 30–Aug 20, 1985, going from W Australia to Melbourne. Brian Davis of Tillicoultry, Scotland rode 901 mi from Land's End to John O'Groats May 16–June 4, 1980 in 19 days 1¾ hours. Takayuki Koike of Kanagawa, Japan set a record for 100 mi in 6 hours 44 min 21.84 sec on Aug 9, 1987. The sprint record from a standing start over 100 meters is 13.71 sec by John Foss of Westbury, NY in Tokyo, Japan, on Aug 1, 1987. Deepak Lele of Maharashtra, India, unicycled 3,963 mi from NYC to LA, but took 111 days, June 6–Sept 25, 1984.

A unicycle nicknamed "Large Marge" with a 66-in wheel was constructed by Dave Moore, Michael Leebolt, and Steve Gordon, of Moorpark, Calif. Gordon first rode it on Oct 17, 1986.

3. RAILROADS

Earliest

Wagons running on wooden rails were used for mining as early as 1550 at Leberthal, Alsace, near the French-German border, and at the Broseley Colliery, Shropshire, England in Oct 1605. Richard Trevithick (1771–1833), built his first steam locomotive for the 3-ft-gauge iron plateway at Coalbrookdale, Shropshire, in 1803, but there is no evidence that it ran. The first known to have *run* was his second locomotive, which drew wagons with men riding on them in a demonstration run at Penydarren, Wales, on Feb 22, 1804, but it broke the plate rails.

Fastest Rail Speed

The world's fastest rail speed with passengers is 252 mph by W Germany's Intercity Experimental train in a test run on May 1, 1988 between Wurzburg and Fulda.

The highest speed recorded on any national rail system is 236 mph by the French SNCF high-speed train TGV-PSE on trial near Tonnerre Feb 26, 1981. The TGV (Train à Grande Vitesse), inaugurated in 1981, two years later reduced its scheduled time for the Paris–Lyon run of 264 miles from 2 hours 14 min to 2 hours exactly, so averaging 132 mph. The peak speed attained was 168 mph.

> The highest speed attained by a railed vehicle is 6,121 mph or Mach 8 by an unmanned rocket sled over the 9½-mile-long rail track at White Sands Missile Range, NM on Oct 5, 1982.

Most Powerful Locomotive

The most powerful steam locomotive, measured by tractive effort, was No. 700, a triple-articulated or triplex 2–8–8–8–4–6-cylinder engine which the Baldwin Locomotive Co built in 1916 for the Virginian Railroad. It had a tractive force of 166,300 lb working compound and 199,560 lb working simple.

Probably the heaviest train ever hauled by a single engine was one of 17,100 tons made up of 250 freight cars stretching 1.6 miles by the *Matt H. Shay* (No. 5014), a 2–8–8–8–2 engine which ran on the Erie Railroad from May 1914 until 1929.

Greatest Load

The heaviest single pieces of freight ever conveyed by rail are limited by the capacity of the rolling stock. The world's strongest and only rail carrier, with a capacity of 889.7 tons, is the 370.4-ton, 36-axle, 301-ft-10-in-long "Schnabel," built for a US railway by Krupp, W Germany in Mar 1981.

The heaviest load ever moved on rails was the Church of the Virgin Mary built in 1548 at Most, Czechoslovakia, weighing nearly 12,000 tons, moved in Oct-Nov 1975 because it was in the way of mining for coal deposits. It was moved 800 yd at 0.0013 mph over a period of 4 weeks at a cost of $15,300,000.

Most Traveling

The record number of countries traveled through entirely by train in 24 hours is 10 by Aaron Kitchen Feb 16–17, 1987. His route started in Yugoslavia and continued through Austria, Italy, Liechtenstein, Switzerland, France, Luxembourg, Belgium, Netherlands, arriving in W Germany 22 hours 42 min later.

Using Amtrak's "All Aboard America" $299 ticket, valid for a month, James J. Brady of Wilmington, O, traveled through 442 (out of 498) stations over 21,485 unduplicated mi of track (out of 23,000) Feb 11–Mar 11, 1984.

John E. Ballenger of Dunedin, Fla has logged 76,485 mi of unduplicated rail routes in North and South America in his lifetime.

Handpumped Railcars

The fastest time (20.008 mph) in the now annual races at Port Moody, BC, Canada, over 300 meters (985 ft) by a 5-man team (1 pusher, 4 pumpers) was 33.54 sec set on June 27, 1982.

Waiting Rooms

The largest waiting rooms are the four in Peking Station, Chang'an Boulevard, Peking, China, opened in Sept 1959, with a total standing capacity of 14,000.

Stations

The biggest railroad station is Grand Central Terminal, NYC, built 1903–13. It covers 48 acres on 2 levels with 41 tracks on the upper level and 26 on the lower. On average, more than 550 trains and 180,000 people per day use it, with a peak of 252,288 on July 3, 1947.

The highest station is Condor, Bolivia, at 15,705 ft on the

WIDE GAUGE RAILS: A train station in Madrid, Spain shows the 5-ft-6-in width used in Spain, Portugal, Argentina, Chile and the countries around India. The narrowest gauge track is a mere 10½ in for a track in Norfolk, Eng. *(Photo Incafo)*

meter-gauge Rio Mulato-to-Potosí line. The oldest station in the world is Liverpool Road Station, Manchester, England, first used in 1830. It is now part of a museum.

Steepest Grade

The steepest standard gauge gradient by adhesion is 1:11 between Chedde and Servoz on the meter gauge electric SNCF Chamonix line, France.

Widest and Narrowest Gauges

The widest gauge in standard use is 5 ft 6 in. This width is used in Spain, Portugal, India, Pakistan, Bangladesh, Sri Lanka, Argentina and Chile. In 1885, there was a lumber railway in Oregon with a gauge of 8 ft.

The narrowest gauge on which public services are operated is 10¼ in on the Wells Harbour (0.7 mi) and the Wells-Walsingham Railways (4 mi) in Eng.

Longest Line

The longest run is one of 5,864¼ miles on the Trans-Siberian Line between Moscow and Nakhodka in the Soviet Far East. There are 97 stops on the journey, which takes 8 days 4 hours 25 min. The 1,927.5-mi Baykal-Amur Magistral (BAM) northern line, begun with forced labor in 1938, was restarted in 1974 and put into service on Oct 27, 1984. It will cut 310 miles off the route around the southern end of Lake Baykal. A total of 13.5 billion cu ft of earth (8 billion lb) was removed and 3,901 bridges built in this $10 billion project.

Longest Straight Length

The longest straight is on the Commonwealth Railways Trans-Australian line over the Nullarbor Plain from Mile 496 between Nurina and Loongana, Western Australia, to Mile 793 between Ooldea and Watson, South Australia, 297 miles dead straight although not level.

Platforms

The longest railroad platform is the Khargpur platform in West Bengal, India, which measures 2,733 ft in length. The State Street Center subway platform in "The Loop" in Chicago measures 3,500 ft in length.

The two platforms comprising the New Nisato railway station on the Musashino line, Saitama, Japan, are 984 ft 3 in apart and are connected by a bridge.

Subways

The earliest (first section opened Jan 10, 1863) and one of the most extensive underground railway or rapid transit systems of the 67 in the world is that of the London Underground, with 254 miles of route, of which 85 miles is bored tunnel and 20 miles is "cut and cover." This whole system is now operated by a staff of 22,000 serving 273 stations. The 457 trains comprising 3,875 cars carried 759 million passengers in 1986–87.

The subway with most stations is operated by the NYC Transit Authority (first section opened on Oct 27, 1904) with a total of 231.73 route miles of track and a record 1,096,006,529 passengers in 1979. The stations are close set and total 458. The record for traveling the whole system was 21 hours 8½ min by Mayer Wiesen and Charles Emerson, Oct 8, 1973.

The busiest subway system is that in Greater Moscow with as many as 6½ million passengers per day. At mid-1985, it had 123 stations and 123 mi of track.

Busiest Rail System

The most crowded rail system is the Japanese National Railways, which in 1986 carried 19,017,419 passengers daily. Professional pushers are employed to squeeze in passengers before the doors can be closed. Among articles reported lost in the crush in 1986 were 572,700 umbrellas, 285,092 clothing items, 217,968 books and stationery items, 5,913 accessories and 201,170 purses.

BIGGEST PORTABLE MODEL TRAIN SET: Lionel Corp produced a movable 65-ft-long platform with this miniature town with overhead railway, besides on-the-ground track.

LOCOMOTIVE in a nutshell. On this electrical model railway, this engine, made to fit on a 6.5 mm-(¼-inch) track, has run 477 mi in 1,219 hours in one year.

Longest Freight Train

The longest and heaviest freight train on record was one about 4 miles in length consisting of 500 coal cars with three 3600 hp diesels pulling and three more in the middle, on the Iaeger, West Virginia, to Portsmouth, Ohio stretch of 157 miles on the Norfolk and Western Railway on Nov 15, 1967. The total weight was nearly 47,250 tons.

Model Railways

The non-stop duration record for a model train (locomotive plus 6 coaches) is 864 hours 30 min from June 1 to July 7, 1978, covering 678 miles, organized by Roy Catton at "Pastimes" Toy Store, Mexborough, S. Yorkshire, England.

The longest recorded run by a model *steam* locomotive is 144 miles in 27 hours 18 min by the 7¼-in gauge "Winifred" built in 1974 by Wilf Grove at Thames Ditton, Surrey, England on Sept 8–9, 1979. "Winifred" works on 80 lb/sq-in pressure and is coal-fired with a 2⅛-in bore cylinder and a 3⅛-in stroke.

The most miniature model railway ever built is one of 1:1000 scale by Jean Damery (b 1923) of Paris. The engine ran on a 4½-volt battery and measures 5⁄16ths of an in overall.

4. AIRCRAFT

Note: The use of the Mach scale for aircraft speeds was introduced by Prof Ackeret of Zurich, Switzerland. The Mach number is the ratio of the velocity of a moving body to the local velocity of sound. This was first employed by Dr Ernst Mach (1838–1916) of Austria in 1887. Thus Mach 1.0 equals 760.98 mph at sea level at 15° C (59°F) and is assumed, for convenience, to fall to a constant 659.78 mph in the stratosphere, *i.e.* above 11,000 m (36,089 ft).

Earliest Flights

The first controlled and sustained power-driven flight occurred near Kill Devil Hill, Kitty Hawk, NC at 10:35 a.m. on Dec 17, 1903, when Orville Wright (1871–1948) flew the 12-hp chain-driven *Flyer I* for a distance of 120 ft, at an airspeed of 30 mph, a ground speed of 6.8 mph and an altitude of 8–12 ft for about 12 sec, watched by his brother Wilbur (1867–1912), 4 men and a boy. Both brothers, from Dayton, Ohio, were bachelors because, as Orville put it, they had not the means to "support a wife as well as an airplane." The *Flyer* is now in the National Air and Space Museum of the Smithsonian Institution, Washington, DC.

The first hop by a man-carrying airplane entirely under its own power was made when Clément Ader (1841–1925) of France flew in his *Eole* for about 164 ft at Armainvilliers, France, on Oct 9, 1890. It was powered by a lightweight steam engine of his own design which developed about 20 hp (15 kW).

The earliest "rational design" for a flying machine (according to the British Royal Aeronautical Society) was published by Emanuel Swedenborg (1688–1772) in Sweden in 1717.

Transatlantic Flights

The first crossing of the North Atlantic by air was made by Lt-Cdr (later Rear Admiral) Albert C. Read (1887–1967) and his crew (Stone, Hinton, Rodd, Rhoads and Breese) in an 84-knot Curtiss flying boat NC-4 of the US Navy from Trepassy Harbour, Newfoundland, Canada *via* the Azores, to Lisbon, Portugal, May 16 to 27, 1919. The whole flight of 4,717 miles originating from Rockaway Air Station, Long Island, NY, on May 8, required 53 hours 58 min terminating at Plymouth, England on May 31. The Newfoundland-Azores leg (1,200 miles) took 15 hours 18 min at 81.7 knots.

FIRST TO FLY: Were it not for these men, the Wright brothers, Wilbur and Orville, air flight might not have been possible. Here they are on the way to making their historic flight dressed in stiff collars and ties. The takeoff in 1903 came after a ground speed of 6.8 mph was reached. The plane flew for 12 sec at a height of 8–12 ft. (*Air & Space Museum, Washington*) ◄

LANDING IN KREMLIN SQUARE: ► After a 540-mi flight from Finland, during which he flew through Soviet-defended zones, Mathias Rust (W Ger, b 1968) piloted his Cessna 172B right into the heart of Moscow. He now resides in a Russian jail for his "stunt."

The first non-stop transatlantic flight was achieved 18 days later, from 4:13 p.m. GMT on June 14, 1919 from Lester's Field, St John's, Newfoundland, 1,960 miles to Derrygimla bog near Clifden, Co Galway, Ireland, at 8:40 a.m. GMT June 15, when the pilot Capt John William Alcock (1892–1919), and Lt Arthur Whitten Brown (1886–1948) flew across in a Vickers *Vimy*, powered by two 360-hp Rolls-Royce *Eagle VIII* engines.

The 79th man to complete a transatlantic trip but the first to fly alone was Capt (later Col and Brig Gen) Charles A. Lindbergh (1902–74), who took off in his 220-hp Ryan monoplane *Spirit of St Louis* at 12:52 p.m. GMT on May 20, 1927 from Roosevelt Field, Long Island, NY. He landed at 10:21 p.m. GMT on May 21, 1927 at Le Bourget airfield, Paris, France. His flight of 3,610 miles lasted 33 hours 29½ min and he won a prize of $25,000.

The transatlantic flight speed record is 1 hour 54 min 56.4 sec by Maj James V. Sullivan, 37, and Maj Noel F. Widdifield, 33, flying a Lockheed SR-71A eastwards on Sept 1, 1974. The average speed, slowed by refueling by a KC-135 tanker aircraft, for the NY-London stage of 3,461.53 miles was 1,806.963 mph. The solo record (Gander to Gatwick) is 8 hours 47 min 32 sec by Capt John J. A. Smith in a Rockwell 685 on March 12, 1978.

Transpacific Flight

The first non-stop Pacific flight was by Maj Clyde Pangborn and Hugh Herndon in the Bellanca cabin plane *Miss Veedol* from Sabishiro Beach, Japan, 4,558 miles to Wenatchee, Wash in 41 hours 13 min on Oct 3–5, 1931. (For earliest crossing see 1924 flight below.)

Circumnavigational Flights

A strict circumnavigation of the earth requires passing through two antipodal points and is thus a minimum distance of 24,859.75 miles. (The FAI permits flights which exceed the length of the Tropic of Cancer or Capricorn, namely 22,858.754 miles, to be called round-the-world.)

The earliest such flight (26,345 miles) was made by two US Army Douglas DWC amphibians in 57 "hops." The *Chicago* was piloted by Lt Lowell H. Smith and Lt Leslie P. Arnold and the *New Orleans* was piloted by Lt Erik H. Nelson and Lt John Harding. The planes took off from Seattle, Wash on Apr 6, 1924 and landed back there on Sept 28, 1924.

The earliest solo claim was by Wiley Hardemann Post (1898–1935) (US) in the Lockheed Vega *Winnie Mae*, starting and finishing at Floyd Bennett Field, NYC July 15–22, 1933, in 10 "hops." His distance of 15,596 miles with a flying time of 115 hours 36 min was, however, at too high a latitude to qualify.

The first non-stop round-the-world flight was completed on Mar 2, 1949, by the USAF's Boeing B-50 Superfortress *Lucky Lady II*, piloted by Capt James Gallagher from Carswell AFB, Tex in 94 hours 1 min. The aircraft was refueled 4 times on its 23,452-mile flight.

The fastest flight has been an easterly flight of 36 hours 54 min 15 sec by the Boeing 747 SP "Friendship One" (Capt Clay Lacy) from Seattle, Wash with 141 passengers Jan 28-30, 1988. The plane reached 803 mph over the Atlantic and refueled only in Athens and Taipei.

The smallest aircraft to complete a circumnavigation is a 20-ft-11-in single-engined 180-hp Thorp T-18, built in his garage by its pilot Donald P. Taylor of Sage, Calif. His 26,190-mile flight in 37 stages took 176 flying hours, ending in Oshkosh, Wis on Sept 30, 1976.

Jet-Engine Flight

Proposals for jet propulsion date back to 1909, by Capt Marconnet of France and Henri Coanda (1886–1972) of Rumania, and to the turbojet proposals of Maxime Guillaume in 1921. The earliest tested run was that of the British Power Jets Ltd's experimental WU (Whittle Unit) on Apr 12, 1937, invented by Flying Officer Frank Whittle who had applied for a patent on jet propulsion in 1930.

The first flight by an airplane powered by a turbojet engine was made by the Heinkel He 178, piloted by Flugkapitän Erich Warsitz, at Marienehe, Germany Aug 27, 1939. It was powered by a Heinkel He S3b engine (834-lb as installed with long tailpipe) designed by Dr Hans "Pabst" von Ohain and first tested in Aug 1937.

Circum-Polar Flights

In a so-called "Flight of the Arctic Tern," from Paris to Paris over the North and South Poles, flying a Piper Malibu (PA-46-310P) single-engine plane, Richard Norton, American airline captain, and Calin Rosetti, head of satellite navigation systems at the European Space Agency, traveled 34,342 statute miles in 185 hours 41 min. They also set 16 other point-to-point records.

The first circum-polar flight was flown solo by Capt Elgen M. Long, 44, in a Piper Navajo, Nov 5 to Dec 3, 1971. He covered 38,896 miles in 215 flying hours. The cabin temperature sank to −40°F over Antarctica.

Supersonic Flight

The first supersonic flight was achieved Oct 14, 1947 by Capt (later Brig-Gen) Charles ("Chuck") Elwood Yeager, USAF retired (b Feb 13, 1923), over Edwards Air Force Base, Muroc, Calif in a US Bell XS-1 rocket plane (*Glamorous Glennis*), with Mach 1.015 (670 mph) at an altitude of 42,000 ft. In Feb 1986, Yeager was still breaking records. He flew from Burbank, Calif to LaGuardia Airport, NYC, in 5 hours, 23 min in a Piper-Cheyenne 400-LS, a record for a business turboprop plane of less than 13,000 lb.

The first woman to fly faster than the speed of sound was Jacqueline Cochran (US), who on May 18, 1953, flew a North American F-86 Sabre at 652 mph.

Heaviest and Smallest Planes

The highest recorded gross takeoff weight of an aircraft has been 892,872 lb in the case of an Antonov An-124. This aircraft lifted a payload of 377,473 lb to a height of 35,269 ft on July 26, 1985. A Boeing 747-300 operated by the manufacturer took off at a weight of 871,000 lb during noise-level certification flights from Glasgow, Montana, on July 19, 1987.

AROUND THE WORLD WITHOUT REFUELING: The "Voyager," a light plane weighing only 8,934 lb, carrying 1,240 gal of fuel, circumnavigated the earth from Edwards Air Force Base, Calif, Dec 14–23, 1986 in 216 hours 3 min 44 sec. "Voyager" averaged 115.8 mph in flying 25,012 mi. Its wing span is 110.8 ft. ◄

CONSTRUCTORS AND PILOTS: Dick Rutan, 48, and Jeana Yeager, 34, flew the "Voyager" from a tiny cockpit which only one could enter at a time. The plane, which was designed by Dick's brother, Burt Rutan, took 2 years (22,000 man-hours) to construct. ▼

A Boeing 747 (Capt Eric Moody) became the "world's heaviest glider" when all 4 engines stopped at 37,000 ft up, due to volcanic ash from Mt Galunggung, Indonesia on June 24, 1982 on Flight BA 009 with 263 aboard. The crew got the engines restarted after 13 min and landed the plane at Jakarta.

The $34 million Piasecki Helistat, comprising a framework of light-alloy and composite materials to mount 4 Sikorsky SH-34J helicopters and the envelope of a Goodyear ZPG-2 patrol airship, was exhibited on Jan 26, 1984 at Lakehurst, NJ. Designed for use by the US Forest Service and designated Model 94-37J Logger, it has an overall length of 343 ft and is intended to carry a payload of 24 tons.

Three planes vie for the record as the world's smallest. The "Sky Baby" designed by Ray Stits of Riverside, Calif and first flown by the co-builder Robert H. Starr of Tempe, Ariz, May 26, 1952, weighs 452 lb empty, is 9 ft 10 in long, with wing span of 7 ft 2 in, and has top air speed of 185 mph. Another record smallest plane was designed and built by Starr and first flown by him in Ariz on Jan 28, 1984. Called the "Bumble Bee," it weighs more (756 lb) but is shorter, 9 ft 4 in long, with a wing span of 6 ft 6 in, and a top air speed of 180 mph. Both planes use Continental C-85 engines. A third plane with the smallest wing span (6 ft 3 in) and lightest in weight (252 lb empty) is the "Baby Bird" built by Donald R. Stits. It is longer (11 ft), is powered by a 55-hp 2-cylinder Hirth engine, and was first flown by Harold Nemer on Aug 4, 1984 at a top speed of 110 mph at Camarillo, Calif.

The smallest jet is the 280-mph *Silver Bullet* built by Bob Bishop (with Corky Fornof, partner) with a 17-ft wing span and weighing 432 lb.

Ultralight Plane

On Aug 3, 1985, Anthony A. Cafaro (b Nov 30, 1951) flew a ULA single-seater *Gypsy Skycycle,* having a maximum weight of 245 lb, a maximum speed of 65 mph, and a capacity of 5 gal for 7 hours 31 min at Dart Field, Mayville, NY. Nine fuel pickups were completed during the flight.

Solar-Powered Flight

The solar-powered *Solar Challenger,* designed by a team led by Dr Paul MacCready, was flown for the first time entirely under solar power on Nov 20, 1980. On July 7, 1981, piloted by Steve Ptacek (US), the *Solar Challenger* became the first aircraft of this category to achieve a crossing of the English Channel. Taking off from Pontois-Cormeilles, Paris, the 163-mi journey to Manston, Kent, Eng, was completed in 5 hr 23 min at a maximum altitude of 11,000 ft. The aircraft has a wing span of 47 ft.

Largest and Fastest Airliners

The highest-capacity jet airliner is the Boeing 747 jumbo jet, first flown on Feb 9, 1969. It has a capacity of from 385 to more than 500 passengers with a maximum speed of 602 mph. Its wing span is 195.7 ft and its length, 231.8 ft. It entered service on Jan 22, 1970. Its range 8,000 mi or more, the first 747-400 was rolled out on Jan 26, 1988 for service with Northwest Airlines with a wing span of 213 ft, and it has capacity for 422 passengers.

The greatest passenger load on a commercial airliner was 674 people—306 adults, 328 children and 40 babies—from the cyclone-devastated Darwin to Sydney, Australia on Dec 29, 1974.

The supersonic BAC/Aerospatiale *Concorde,* first flown on March 2, 1969, with a capacity of 128 passengers, cruises at up to Mach 2.2 (1,450 mph). It became the first supersonic airliner used for passenger service on Jan 21, 1976. The NY-London record time is 2 hours 55 min 15 sec set Feb 6, 1988, average of 1,215 mph.

Heaviest and Fastest Bombers

The heaviest bomber is the 8-jet swept-wing Boeing B-52H *Stratofortress,* which has a maximum takeoff weight of 488,000 lb. It has a wing span of 185 ft and is 157 ft 6¾ in in length, with a speed of over 650 mph. The B-52 can carry 12 SRAM thermonuclear short-range attack missiles or 24 750-lb bombs under its wings and 8 more SRAMs or 84 500-lb bombs in the fuselage.

The fastest operational bombers are the French Dassault Mirage IV, which can fly at Mach 2.2 (1,450 mph) at 36,000 ft; the General Dynamics FB-111A, with a maximum speed of Mach 2.5; and the Soviet swing-wing Tupolev Tu-26 known as "Backfire," which has an estimated over-target speed of Mach 2.0 to 2.5 and a combat radius of 3,570 miles.

Highest Air Speed

The official air speed record is 2,193.167 mph by Capt Eldon W. Joersz and Maj George T. Morgan, Jr, in a Lockheed SR-71A near Beale Air Force Base, Calif on July 28, 1976 over a 9.3–15.5-mi course.

The fastest fixed-wing craft was a North American Aviation X-15A-2, which flew for the first time (after modification from X-15A) on June 25, 1964, powered by a liquid oxygen and ammonia rocket propulsion system. Ablative materials on the airframe enabled a temperature of 3,000°F to be withstood. The landing speed was 210 knots (242 mph) momentarily. The highest speed attained was 4,520 mph (Mach 6.72) when piloted by Maj William J. Knight, USAF (b 1930) on Oct 3, 1967. An earlier version piloted by Joseph A. Walker (1920–66) reached 354,200 ft (67.08 miles) over Edwards Air Force Base, Calif on Aug 22, 1963. The program was suspended after the final flight of Oct 24, 1968.

The US NASA Rockwell International Space Shuttle Orbiter *Columbia* was launched from the Kennedy Space Center, Cape Canaveral, Fla, commanded by Commander John W. Young USN and piloted by Robert L. Crippen on Apr 12, 1981 after the expenditure of $9,900 million since 1972. *Columbia* broke all records for space by a fixed-wing craft with 16,600 mph at main engine cut-off. After re-entry from 400,000 ft, experiencing temperatures of 3,920°F, she glided home weighing 108 tons with the highest ever landing speed of 216 mph on Rogers Dry Lake, Calif on Apr 14, 1981. Under a new FAI category P for aerospacecraft, the *Columbia* is holder of the current absolute world record for duration of 8 days 00 hr 4 min 45 sec, with 2 astronauts, but *Challenger* (launched June 18, 1983) has since set a duration record of 6 days 2 hr 23 min 59 sec with 5 astronauts including Sally K. Ride, the first female space shuttle astronaut, and on a previous mission it set a new record altitude of 206.36 miles.

Columbia also holds the current absolute world record for the greatest mass lifted to altitude, a figure of 235,634 lb.

Fastest Jet

The fastest jet aircraft is the USAF Lockheed SR- 71A reconnaissance aircraft which first flew on Dec 22, 1964 and attained a speed of 2,193.167 mph July 28, 1976 (official record). In the same hour, the "Concorde" would have traveled 1,335 mi and a Boeing 747 "jumbo" 600 mi. The "Voyager" would have covered 122 mi. The SR-71A has a wing span of 55.6 ft, a length of 107.4 ft and weighs 170,000 lb at takeoff. Its reported range is 2,982 miles at Mach 3 at 78,750 ft. It can attain an altitude of 100,000 ft.

It was reported on Jan 15, 1988 that the US Air Force was developing secretly a Mach 5 3,800-mph high-altitude (above 100,000 ft) *Stealth* aircraft.

The fastest combat aircraft in service is the USSR Mikoyan MIG-25 fighter (code name "Foxbat"). The reconnaissance "Foxbat-B" has been tracked by radar at about Mach 3.2 (2,110 mph). When armed with 4 large underwing air-to-air missiles known to NATO as "Acrid," the fighter "Foxbat-A" is limited to Mach 2.8 (1,845 mph). The single-seat "Foxbat-A" spans 45 ft 9 in, is 78 ft 2 in long, and has a maximum takeoff weight of 82,500 lb.

Most Capacious Aircraft

The Aero Spacelines Super Guppy has a cargo hold with a usable volume of 49,790 cu ft and a maximum takeoff weight of 87.5 tons. Wing span is 156.3 ft, length 141 ft 10 in. Its cargo compartment measures 108 ft 10 in in length with a cylindrical section of 25 ft in diameter, making it the only airbus big enough to transport parts of other airbuses.

Fastest Piston-Engined Aircraft

The fastest speed at which a piston-engined plane has ever been measured was for a cut-down privately owned Hawker *Sea Fury* which attained 520 mph in level flight over Texas in Aug 1966, piloted by Mike Carroll (k 1969) of Los Angeles.

The FAI accredited record for a piston-engined aircraft is 517.055 mph over Mojave, Calif by Frank Taylor (US) in a modified North American P-51D *Mustang* powered by a 3,000-hp Packard Merlin, over a 15–25 km course, on July 30, 1983.

Fastest Biplane

The fastest recorded biplane was the Italian Fiat C. R. 42B, with a 1,010-hp Daimler-Benz DB601 A engine, which attained 323 mph in 1941. Only one was built.

Largest Wing Span

The "Spruce Goose," the wooden flying boat with the world's

LARGEST WING SPAN: This mammoth wooden flying boat, the "Spruce Goose," is being moved to a land location as it can't fly (never could, except for one 1,000-yd flight in 1947). The men standing on the wing (319 ft 11 in across) give you an idea of its size. Howard Hughes had it built; it had been at anchor in Long Beach (Calif) Harbor from 1947 to 1980, when it was sold to entrepreneur Jack Wrather who made it into a walk-through museum next to the "Queen Mary," a dockside museum too. In the boat watching the maneuver along with hundreds on shore is (then) Governor Jerry Brown. *(Dean Moon)*

LARGEST CAPACITY: The Super Guppy holds a cargo of 49,790 cu ft. *(Aero Spacelines)*

largest wing span—319 ft 11 in—but which could not fly for more than a thousand yards, was moved by giant cranes in 1982 6 mi across the harbor in Long Beach (Calif) to rest in a 700-ft-diameter dome to become a walk-through museum. Alongside is the *Queen Mary* which from 1936 to 1940 was the world's largest ocean liner. Now at Pier J in Long Beach, one can within a few hours and a few yards examine both record holders.

The "Spruce Goose" was piloted on its test run by the man who had it built, Howard R. Hughes (1905–76), who later became the fabulous multimillionaire recluse. On Nov 2, 1947, he revved up the 8 propeller-driven engines and taxied the 213-ton craft across the water and up to a height of 70 ft. For 1,000 yards, it stayed up and then it set down into the harbor and never flew again. Hughes had spent $40 million on it.

Among current aircraft, the Soviet Antonov An-124 has a span of 240 ft 5¾ in and the Boeing 747-400 one of 213 ft.

Fastest Propeller-Driven Aircraft

The Soviet Tu-114 turboprop transport recorded a speed of 545.076 mph carrying heavy payloads over measured circuits. It is developed from the Tupolev Tu-95 bomber, known in the West as the "Bear," and has four 14,795-hp* engines. The turboprop-powered Republic XF-84H prototype US Navy fighter which flew on July 22, 1955 had a top design speed of 670 mph, but was abandoned.

Largest Aircraft Propeller

The largest aircraft propeller ever used was the 22-ft-7½-in diameter Garuda propeller, fitted to the Linke-Hofmann R II built in Wroclaw, Poland, which flew in 1919. It was driven by four 260-hp Mercedes engines and turned at only 545 rpm.

Flight Duration

The flight duration record is 64 days, 22 hours, 19 min and 5 sec, set by Robert Timm and John Cook in a Cessna 172 "Hacienda." They took off from McCarran Airfield, Las Vegas, Nev just before 3:53 PM local time on Dec 4, 1958 and landed at the same airfield just before 2:12 p.m. on Feb 7, 1959. They covered a distance equivalent to 6 times around the world with continued refueling without landing.

Youngest and Oldest Pilots

The youngest age at which anyone has ever qualified as a military pilot is 15 years 5 months in the case of Sgt Thomas Dobney (b May 6, 1926) of the British Royal Air Force. He had overstated his age (14 years) on induction.

The oldest pilot is Ed McCarty (b Sept 18, 1885) of Kimberly, Idaho who in 1979 was flying his rebuilt 30-year-old Ercoupe at the age of 94.

Percival Spencer (b Apr 30, 1897) made his first solo flight on Apr 2, 1911 and is still flying, his latest flight being on Oct 4, 1987, when he was 90 years old. He holds the longest active flight record, according to the "Early Birds of America."

Greatest Altitude

The official altitude record by an aircraft taking off from the ground under its own power is 123,524 ft (23.39 miles) by Aleksandr Fedotov (USSR) in a Mikoyan E-266M (MIG-25) aircraft, powered by two 30,865-lb thrust turbojet engines on Aug 31, 1977.

In the same aircraft he established the fastest climb record on May 17, 1975 reaching 30,000 m (98,425 ft) in 4 min 11.7 sec after takeoff.

Most Flying Hours

Max Conrad (1903–79) (US) logged 52,929 hours 40 min of flight time, a total of more than 6 years airborne, between 1928 and mid-1974. He completed 150 transatlantic crossings in light aircraft.

The record supersonic passenger is Fred Finn who made 604 Concorde crossings by June 1986.

Most Takeoffs and Landings from Airports

Al Yates and Bob Phoenix of Texas made 193 takeoffs and daylight landings at unduplicated airfields in 14 hours 57 min in a Piper Seminole on June 15, 1979.

LONGEST HUMAN-POWERED (FOOT-PEDALED) FLIGHTS: This 90-ft craft flew 37.2 mi on Jan 22, 1987 at Edwards Air Force Base, Calif, taking 2 hours 13 min 14 sec as it averaged 16.7 mph. Another Daedalus 88 flew 74 mi over the Aegean Sea on Apr 23, 1988, averaging 18.5 mph, but crash-landed after 3½ hours.

ELECTRIC PLANE: This plane, with a wing span of 39 ft 4 in, a length of 23 ft and a weight of 882 lb is the first electrically propelled aircraft. Its Bosch 8-kW motor of 10.7 hp is powered by Varta nickel-cadmium batteries. Designed by model aircraft constructor Fred Militky (US), it had its maiden flight on Oct 21, 1973. *(K.J.A. Brookes)*

Longest and Shortest Scheduled Flights

The longest scheduled non-stop flight is the United Airlines and Qantas flight from LA to Sydney covering 7,487 mi. It takes 14 hours 50 min in a Boeing 747 SP (Special Performance) plane.

The longest non-stop flight was one of 7,950 statute mi from Melbourne, Aust to LA by Pan Am Clipper Flight 816 on July 2, 1984 when the scheduled stop in Sydney was cancelled because of a strike. The pilot was Capt David Riggs and the flight took 13 hours 59 min.

The longest delivery flight by a commercial jet is 8,936 nautical miles or 10,290 statute miles from Seattle, Wash to Cape Town, South Africa by South African Airway's Boeing 747 SP *Matroosberg*. She made the 17-hour-22½-min flight loaded with 196.5 tons of pre-cooled fuel March 23–29, 1976.

The shortest scheduled flight is made by Loganair between the Orkney Islands (Scotland) of Westray and Papa Westray, which has been flown with twin-engined 10-seat Britten-Norman Islander transports since Sept 1967. Though scheduled for 2 minutes, in favorable wind conditions it has been accomplished in 58 sec by Capt Andrew D. Alsop.

United Airlines provides the shortest scheduled flight by Boeing 727 jet between San Francisco and Oakland, Calif. There are three flights daily and return, the flight time averaging 5 minutes for the 12 mi journey.

Gary W. Rovetto of Island Air on Mar 21, 1980 flew on the scheduled flight from Center Island to Decatur Island, Wash in 41 sec.

Air Safety

Experiments at Langley Air Force Base in Virginia include hurling dead chickens at airplanes traveling 700 mph to see how jets can avoid hitting birds that cause accidents. The "chicken gun" is a converted 20-ft cannon that shoots 4-lb chickens at engines, windshields and landing gear.

Largest Airports

The largest airport is the $2,625 million King Khalid International Airport outside Riyadh, Saudi Arabia, covering an area of 86 sq mi, opened on Nov 14, 1983. It has the world's largest control tower 243 ft in height.

The Hajj Terminal at the $2,940 million King Abdul-Aziz airport near Jeddah is the world's largest roofed structure covering 370 acres.

The present 6 runways and 5 terminal buildings of the Dallas/Fort Worth Airport, Tex are planned to be extended to 9 runways and 13 terminals with 260 gates with an ultimate capacity for 150 million passengers annually.

The largest airport terminal is Hartsfield Atlanta International Airport opened Sept 21, 1980, with floor space covering 50.5 acres. It has 138 gates handling nearly 50 million passengers annually but has a capacity for 75 million.

Highest and Lowest Airports

The highest airport in the world is La Sa (Lhasa) Airport in Tibet at 14,315 ft. The highest landing ever made by a fixed-wing plane was at 19,947 ft on Dhaulagiri, Himalaya, by a Pilatus Porter, named *Yeti*, supplying the 1960 Swiss Expedition. The lowest landing field is El Lisan on the east shore of the Dead Sea, 1,180 ft below sea level, but during World War II BOAC short C-class flying boats operated from the surface of the Dead Sea 1,292 ft below sea level. The lowest international airport is Schiphol, at Amsterdam, Holland at 13 ft below sea level. Although not an international airport, the one nearby at Rotterdam at 15 ft below sea level is lower.

AIRPORT NEAREST TO CITY: Gibraltar is favored with an airport only half a mile from the center of the city. The runway is seen here with Spain in the background. *(Ace Photo Agency)*

LARGEST HELICOPTER: Weighing 115 tons, the Soviet's Mil Mi-12 (V-12) helicopter, known as "Homer," has a rotor span of 219 ft 10 in and a length of 121 ft 4½ in. *(K. J. A. Brookes)*

Busiest Airport

The busiest airport is the Chicago O'Hare International Airport, with a total of 795,026 movements and 54,770,673 passengers in 1986. This represents a takeoff or landing every 39.66 sec around the clock. Heathrow Airport outside London handles more *international* traffic than any other.

The busiest landing area ever has been Bien Hoa Air Base, South Vietnam, which handled more than one million takeoffs and landings in 1970. The largest "helipad" was An Khe, South Vietnam.

The heliport at Morgan City, La., one of a string used by helicopters flying energy-related offshore operations into the Gulf of Mexico, has pads for 46 helicopters.

Airport Distance to City Centers

The airport farthest from the city center it allegedly serves is Viracopos, Brazil, which is 60 miles from São Paulo. The Gibraltar airport is 880 yd from the center.

Longest Runway

The longest runway is 7 miles in length (of which 15,000 ft is concreted) at Edwards Air Force Base on the bed of Rogers Dry Lake at Muroc, Calif. The whole test center airfield extends over 65 sq mi. In an emergency, an auxiliary 12-mile strip is available along the bed of the Dry Lake.

The longest civil airport runway is one of 16,076 ft (3.04 miles) at Pierre van Ryneveld Airport, Upington, South Africa, constructed in 5 months, Aug 1975–Jan 1976. A paved runway 20,500 ft long (3.88 mi) appears on maps of Jordan at Abu Husayn.

Round-the-World by Helicopter

H. Ross Perot and Jay Coburn, both of Dallas, Tex, made the first helicopter circumnavigation of the globe in "Spirit of Texas" Sept 1–30, 1982. The first solo round-the-world flight in a helicopter was completed by Dick Smith (Australia) on July 22, 1983. Flown from and to the Bell Helicopter facility at Fort Worth, Tex, in a Bell Model 206L *Long Ranger III*, his unhurried flight began on Aug 5, 1982 and covered a distance of 35,258 miles.

Largest and Strongest Helicopters

The largest helicopter is the Soviet Mil Mi-12 ("Homer"), also known as the V-12. It is powered by four 6,500-hp turboshaft engines, and has a span of 219 ft 10 in over its rotor tips with a fuselage length of 121 ft 4½ in and weighs 115.7 tons.

On Feb 3, 1982, at Podmoscovno in the Soviet Union, a Mil Mi-26 heavy-lift helicopter, crewed by G. V. Alfeurov and L. A. Indeev (co-pilot), lifted a total mass of 125,153.8 lb to a height of 6,560 ft.

Highest Helicopters

The altitude record for helicopters is 40,820 ft by an Aerospatiale SA 315 B *Lama* over France on June 21, 1972. The highest recorded landing has been at 23,000 ft, below the southeast face of Everest, in a rescue sortie in May 1971. The World Trade Center Helipad is 1,385 ft above street level in NYC, on the South Tower.

Fastest Helicopter

Trevor Eggington, 53, averaged 249.10 mph over Somerset, Eng, on Aug 11, 1986 in a Westland Lynx Company demonstrator helicopter.

Autogyros

The autogyro or gyroplane, a rotorcraft with an unpowered rotor turned by the airflow in flight, preceded the practical helicopter with engine-driven rotor. Juan de la Cierva (Spain) made the first successful autogyro flight with his model C.4 (commercially named an *Autogiro*) at Getafe, Spain, on Jan 9, 1923.

Wing Cdr Kenneth H. Wallis (GB) holds the straight-line distance record of 543.27 miles, set in his WA-116F autogyro on Sept 28, 1975 non-stop from Lydd, England to Wick, Scotland. Wallis flew his WA-116, with 72-hp McCulloch engine, to a record speed of 120.5 mph over a 1.86-mi straight course on Sept 18, 1986. On July 20, 1982, he established a new autogyro altitude record of 18,516 ft in his WA-121/Mc.

It was reported that on Apr 8, 1931, Amelia Earhart (US) reached a height in excess of 19,000 ft at Pitcairn Aviation Field, Pa.

Flying Boats

The fastest flying boat ever built has been the Martin XP6M-1 Seamaster, the US Navy 4-jet-engined minelayer, flown in 1955–59 with a top speed of 646 mph. In Sept 1946, the Martin JRM-2 Mars flying boat set a payload record of 68,327 lb.

The official flying-boat speed record is 566.69 mph, set by Nikolai Andrievsky and a crew of 2 in a Soviet Beriev M-10, powered by 2 AL-7 turbojets, over a 10–15 mile course on Aug 7, 1961. The M-10 holds all 12 records listed for jet-powered flying boats, including an altitude of 49,088 ft set by Georgiy Buryanov and crew over the Sea of Azov Sept 9, 1961.

Ballooning

I. William Deiches (b 1934) of Brentwood, Essex, Eng, has adduced that the "mace-head" of the Scorpion King *c.*3100 BC found at Hierakonpolis, Egypt is in reality a depiction of a paneled hot-air balloon of papyrus construction.

The earliest recorded ascent was by a model hot-air balloon invented by Father Bartolomeu de Gusmâo (*né* Lourenço) (b Santos, Brazil, 1685), which was flown indoors at the Casa da India, Terreiro do Paço, Portugal on Aug 8, 1709.

The record distance (great-circle distance between takeoff and first landing point) traveled by a balloon is 5,208.68 miles by the Raven experimental helium-filled balloon *Double Eagle V,* with a capacity 399,053 cu ft, Nov 9–12, 1981, from Nagashima, Japan, to Covello, Calif. The crew for this first manned balloon crossing of the Pacific Ocean was Ben L. Abruzzo, Rocky Aoki, Ron Clark and Larry M. Newman.

The first balloon crossing of the North Atlantic had been made

HOT-AIR BALLOON WORLD CHAMPIONSHIPS: In 1984 all these balloons gathered in Albuquerque, New Mexico, in a modern revival of the craft that began in the US in 1961. This has become an annual event. (*Split Second*)

during Aug 12–17, 1978 in the gas balloon *Double Eagle II* crewed by Ben L. Abruzzo, Maxie L. Anderson and Larry M. Newman.

The first solo crossing of the North Atlantic was by ex-USAF Col Joe Kittinger (see *Parachuting*) who flew in the 3,000-sq-meter helium-filled balloon *Rosie O'Grady* approx 3,543 mi from Caribou, Maine to Montenotte, Italy in 86 hours, Sept 14–18, 1984.

The first hot-air balloon to cross the North Atlantic, Maine to Ireland, was the 21-story-high "Virginia Atlantic Flyer," which flew 2,789.6 mi in late June–early July 1987. The pilots, Richard Bramson, 36, a British millionaire, and Per Lindstrand, 38 (Sweden), touched down only briefly in Ireland, then tried to proceed across the North Channel of the Irish Sea to Scotland, but the balloon could not quite make it. The men jumped from the gondola into the water offshore, were rescued, and the balloon crashed into the sea an hour later.

The first crossing of the US was by the helium-filled balloon *Super Chicken III* (pilots Fred Gorell and John Shoecraft) from Costa Mesa, Calif, 2,515 mi to Blackbeard's Island, Ga Oct 9–12, 1981.

The FAI endurance and distance record for a gas and hot-air balloon is 96 hours 24 min and 2074.817 miles by *Zanussi* crewed by Donald Allan Cameron (GB) and Major Christopher Davey which failed by only 103 miles to achieve the first balloon crossing of the Atlantic on July 30, 1978.

Highest Manned and Unmanned Balloons

The highest altitude attained by an unmanned balloon was 170,000 ft, by a Winzen Research balloon of 47,800,000 cu ft, launched at Chico, Calif, in Oct 1972.

The greatest altitude reached in a manned balloon is an unofficial 123,800 ft (23.45 miles) by Nicholas Piantanida (1933–66) of Bricktown, NJ, from Sioux Falls, SD on Feb 1, 1966. He landed in a cornfield in Iowa but did not survive.

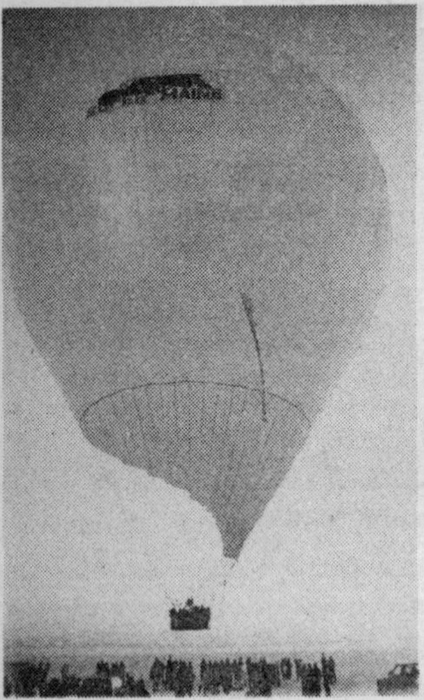

"SUPER MAINE," a hot-air balloon of 2.6 million cu ft, rose 50 ft, carrying 61 passengers at Portland, Maine, on Feb 19, 1988. Its envelope reached 220 ft above the ground. *(Barb Cooper/LSP Promotions)* ◄

GIANT BALLOON: The "Financial Times," London, celebrated its 100th anniversary by launching its front page in the form of a 39-ft-high 90,000-cu-ft balloon on June 8, 1988, in front of Tower Bridge across the Thames. ►

The official record for a manned balloon is 113,740 ft by Cdr Malcolm D. Ross, USNR, and the late Lt-Cdr Victor E. Prother, USN, in an ascent from the deck of USS *Antietam* on May 4, 1961 over the Gulf of Mexico.

The altitude record for a hot-air balloon was set by Julian Nott (GB), who, on Oct 31, 1980, attained an altitude, which has been ratified by the FAI, of 55,137 ft, taking off from Longmont, near Denver, Colo, in the Cameron-built ICI balloon *Innovation*.

The record altitude in an open basket is 53,000 ft by Chauncey Dunn (US) on Aug 1, 1979. He wore a pressure suit.

Largest Balloons

The largest balloons built have an inflatable volume of 70 million cu ft, stand 1,000 ft tall, and fly unmanned. They are made by Winzen Research Inc, Minn.

"Super Maine," with an envelope that reached 220 ft above the ground, took off and rose 50 ft carrying 2.6 million cu ft of hot air and 61 passengers in Portland, Maine, 6:34 AM on Feb 19, 1988. It was the creation of Tom Handcock of Portland, Maine, a commercial balloonist for 9 years, and 18 assistants. The envelope was made of spun-bonded olifin with 112 gores. Computation of the capacity of the balloon was by "ice cream cone" formula, named for a sphere on top of a cone.

Airships

The earliest flight of an airship was by Henri Giffard from Paris in his steam-powered coal-gas 88,300-cu ft 144-ft-long rigid airship Sept 24, 1852.

The largest non-rigid airships ever constructed were the US Navy ZPG 3-Ws. Four were built with a capacity of 1,516,300 cu ft, were 403.4 ft long and 85.1 ft in diameter, with a crew of 21. The first one flew on July 21, 1958, but crashed into the sea in June 1960.

The largest rigid airship (except for her sister ship, the *Hindenburg*, which was 5.6 ft longer) was the 236-ton German *Graf Zeppelin II* (LZ130), with a length of 803.8 ft and a capacity of 7,062,100 cu ft. She made her maiden flight on Sept 14, 1938 and in May and August 1939 made radar spying missions in British air space. She was dismantled in April 1940.

The most people ever carried in an airship were 207 in the US Navy *Akron* in 1931. The transatlantic record is 117 by the German *Hindenburg* in 1937.

The FAI accredited distance record for airships is 3,967.1 miles, set by the German *Graf Zeppelin*, captained by Dr Hugo Eckener between Oct 29 and Nov 1, 1928. The German Zeppelin L59 flew from Yambol, Bulgaria to south of Khartoum, Sudan and returned Nov 21–25, 1917 to cover a minimum of 4,500 mi.

The longest recorded flight by a non-rigid airship (without refueling) is 264 hours 12 min by a US Navy Goodyear-built ZPG-2 class ship (Cdr J. R. Hunt, USN) from the S Weymouth, Mass Naval Air Station March 4, 1957 and landing back at Key West, Fla March 15 after having flown 9,448 miles.

The world altitude, duration and distance records, of 10,365 ft, 1 hr 26 min 52 sec, and 23.03 miles, respectively, are held by the Cameron D-38 *hot-air* airship flown at Cunderdin, W. Australia on Aug 27, 1982 by R. W. Taafe (Australia).

Model Aircraft

The record for altitude is 26,929 ft by Maynard L. Hill (US) on Sept 6, 1970, using a radio-controlled model and on July 4, 1983 set a closed-circuit distance record of 1,231 mi. The free-flight speed record is 213.70 mph by V. Goukoune and V. Myakinin (both USSR) with a radio-controlled model at Klementyeva, USSR, on Sept 21, 1971. The record duration flight is one of 32 hours 7 min 40 sec by Eduard Svoboda (Czechoslovakia) flying a radio-controlled glider Aug 23–24, 1980. An indoor model with a rubber motor, designed by J. Richmond (US), set a duration record, 52 min 14 sec, Aug 31, 1979.

The smallest model aircraft to fly is one weighing 0.004 oz powered by attaching a horsefly and designed by the insectonaut Don Emmick of Seattle, Wash on July 24, 1979. One flew for 5 min at Kirkland, Wash.

Paper Airplane

The flight duration record for a paper aircraft over level ground is 17.20 sec by Ken Blackburn at the Mecca, Milwaukee, Wis, July 28, 1987. A paper plane was witnessed in Aug 1933 to have flown 1¼ miles after a throw by "Chick" C. O. Reinhart from a 10th-story office window at 60 Beaver Street, NYC across the East River. It was helped by a hot updraft from a coffee-roasting plant.

The indoor record with a 12 ft ceiling is 1 min 33 sec set in the Fuji TV studios, Tokyo, Japan on Sept 21, 1980. An indoor distance record of 196 ft 2 in was set by Tony Felch of Rockland, Wis at the Mecca, Milwaukee, Wis, on July 28, 1987.

The largest flying paper airplane was constructed on Apr 26, 1986 by Grahame Foster, David Broom and Andrew Barnes at the Old Warden Aerodrome, Bedfordshire, Eng. It was launched from a platform at a height of 10 ft and flew for 54 ft.

---

5. POWER PRODUCERS

Earliest and Largest Windmills

The earliest recorded windmills are those used for grinding corn in Iran (Persia) in the 7th century AD.

The largest Dutch windmill is the Dijkpolder, in Maasland, built in 1718. The sails measure 95¾ ft from tip to tip. The tallest windmill still standing is the 9-story Sutton mill, Norfolk, Eng, built in 1853 which, before being struck by lightning in 1941, had sails 73 ft in diameter with 216 shutters.

The most powerful wind generator is the 3,000-kW 492-ft-tall turbine, built by Grosse Wind energie-Anlage, which was set up in 1982 on the Friesian coast of W Germany. A £10.5-million ($16.8 million) 3,000-kW aero generator with 196 ft 10 in blades on Burgar Hill, Evie, Orkney Islands, by Taylor Woodrow was switched on in a gale on Nov 10, 1987. It should yield 9 million kW/hours per year.

The largest conventional windmill is the $14.2 million GEC MOD-5A installation on the north shore of Oahu, Hawaii, which will

SOLAR ONE: What looks like a field of mirrors is actually a field of mirrors. To create a solar power plant that yields 10 million watts, 1,818 mirrors had to be strategically placed to reflect the Calif sun. Total cost: $141 million. *(Franklin Berger)*

NEW GIANT POWER STATION: The Itaipu plant on the Brazil-Paraguay border will begin generating a record 12,600,000 kW from 18 turbines in 1988–89.

produce 7,300 kW when the wind reaches 32 mph with 400-ft rotors. Installation started in Mar 1984.

Atomic Power

The first atomic pile was built in an abandoned squash court at the University of Chicago. It "went critical" at 3:25 p.m. on Dec 2, 1942. The largest atomic power station is the one in Fukushima, Japan, having 10 reactors giving 9,096 MW.

The largest single nuclear reactor is the 1,450-MW (net) reactor at the Ignalina station, Lithuania, USSR, put on full power in Jan 1984. The largest under construction is the CHOOZ-B1 reactor in France which is scheduled for operation in 1991 and will have a net capacity of 1,457 MW.

Tokamak-7, the prototype thermonuclear reactor was declared in January 1982 by USSR academician Velikhov to be operating "reliably for months on end."

Largest Power Plant

Currently, the most powerful installed power station is the Grand Coulee, Wash, with 9.7 million kilowatt hours (ultimately 10,080 MW), which began operating in 1942.

The $11-billion Itaipu project on the Paraná River on the Brazil-Paraguay border began generating power formally on Oct 25, 1984 and will by 1988–89 attain 12,600,000 kW from 18 turbines. Construction began in 1975 with a force reaching 28,000 workers.

A 20,000-MW power station project on the Tunguska River, USSR, was announced in Feb 1982.

The largest coal-fired power complex at Ekibastuz, Kazakhstan, USSR, began generating in May 1982.

Solar Power Plant

The largest solar furnace is the $141-million 10-MW "Solar I," 12 miles southeast of Barstow, Calif, first tested in Apr 1982. It comprises 1,818 mirrors in concentric circles focused on a boiler atop a 255-ft high tower. Sunlight from 222 heliostats is concentrated on a target 114 ft up in the power tower.

The $30-million thermal solar energy system at Pakerland Packing Co, Green Bay, Wis, completed in Jan 1984, comprises 9,750 4 × 8 ft collectors covering 7.16 acres. It will yield up to 8 billion BTU's a month.

Largest Generator

Generators in the 2,000,000 kW (or 2,000 MW) range are now in the planning stages both in the UK and the US. The largest operational turbo-generator is 1,450 MW being installed at the Ignalina Atomic Power Station in Lithuania and is now in operation.

Tidal Power Station

The first major tidal power station is the *Usine marèmotrice de la Rance*, officially opened on Nov 26, 1966 at the Rance estuary in the Golfe de St Malo, Brittany, France. Built in 5 years, at a cost of

$75,600,000, it has a net annual output of 544 million kW/h. The 880-yd barrage contains 24 turbo-alternators.

A $46 million pilot Annapolis River project for the Bay of Fundy, Nova Scotia, Canada, was begun in 1981.

The $1 billion Passamaquoddy project for the Bay of Fundy, Maine and New Brunswick remains a project.

Biggest Blackout

The greatest power failure in history struck 7 northeastern US states and Ontario, Canada, Nov 9–10, 1965. About 30 million people in 80,000 sq mi were plunged into darkness. Two people were killed. In NYC the power failed at 5:27 PM on Nov 9, and was not fully restored for 13½ hours. The total losses resulting from another NYC power failure, on July 13, 1977, which lasted for 52 min, but as long as 25 hours in some areas, have been estimated at $1 billion, including losses due to looting.

Biggest Boiler

The largest boilers ever designed are those ordered in the US from the Babcock & Wilcox Co with a capacity of 1,330 MW, so involving the evaporation of 9,330,000 lb of steam per hour.

Longest-Lasting Battery

The zinc foil and sulfur dry pile batteries made by Watlin and Hill of London in 1840 have powered ceaseless tintinnabulation inside a bell jar at the Clarendon Laboratory, Oxford since that year.

Largest Turbines

The largest hydraulic turbines are those rated at 815,000 kW (equivalent to 1.1 million hp), 32 ft in diameter, with a 449-ton runner and a 350-ton shaft, installed by Allis-Chalmers at the Grand Coulee "Third Powerplant" in Wash.

The largest reversible pump-turbine is that made by Allis-Chalmers for the Bath County Project, Va. It has a maximum rating of 457 MW as a turbine and maximum operating head of 1,289 ft. The impeller/runner diameter is 20 ft 9 in with a synchronous speed of 257.1 rpm.

The largest gas turbine is type GT 13 E from BBC Brown Boveri AG with a maximum output of 140 MW. The first machine is being installed in Holland in order to increase the general output of a 500 MW steam-powered plant (Hemweg 7) by more than 46 percent.

6. ENGINEERING

The earliest machinery still in use is the *dâlu*—a water-raising instrument known to have been in use in the Sumerian civilization which originated *c.* 3500 BC in Lower Iraq—even earlier than the *Saqiyas* of the Nile.

Largest Blast Furnace

The largest blast furnace is one with an inner volume of 179,040 cu ft and a 48-ft 6½-in diameter hearth at the Oita Works, Kyushu, Japan, completed in Oct 1976, with an annual capacity of 4,905,600 tons.

Highest Cable Cars

The highest and longest aerial ropeway is the Teleférico Mérida (Mérida téléphérique) in Venezuela, from Mérida City (5,379 ft) to the summit of Pico Espejo (15,629 ft), a rise of 10,250 ft. The ropeway is in four sections, involving 3 car changes in the 8-mile ascent in one hour. The fourth span is 10,070 ft in length. The two cars work on the pendulum system—the carrier rope is locked and the cars are hauled by means of three pull ropes powered by a 230-hp motor. They have a maximum capacity of 45 persons and travel at 32 ft per sec (21.8 mph).

The longest single-span ropeway is the 13,500-ft-long span from the Coachella Valley to Mt San Jacinto (10,821 ft), Calif opened Sept 12, 1963.

HIGHEST CABLE ROPEWAY: The Teleferico Merida in Venezuela is also the longest. It rises 5,379 ft to the summit of Pico Espejo at 15,629 ft above sea level. The cable car ride takes an hour. *(South American Pictures)*

Largest Cat Cracker

The largest catalytic cracker is the Exxon Co's Bayway Refinery plant at Linden, NJ with a fresh feed rate of 5,040,000 gallons per day.

Longest Conveyor Belt

The longest single-flight conveyor belt is one of 18 miles in W Australia by Cable Belt Ltd of England.

The longest multi-flight conveyor is one of 62 miles between the phosphate mine near Bucraa and the Atlantic port of El Aaiun, Morocco, built by Krupp and completed in 1972. It has 11 flights of between 5.6 and 6.8 miles in length and was driven at 10.06 mph, but has been closed down due to Polisario Front guerilla activity.

Most Powerful Cranes

The most powerful cranes are those aboard the semi-submersible vessel *Balder* operated by Heerema Marine Contractors, Switzerland. It has one 3,000- and one 2,000-ton capacity crane which, working in tandem, can raise a 5,000-ton piece. Its capacity has now been raised to close to 6,600 tons.

Brown & Root (US) announced the building of a 150,000-ton crane-ship with lifting capacity of more than 7,000 tons in Dec 1983.

The 92.3-ft-wide Rahco (R. A. Hanson Disc Ltd.) gantry crane at the Grand Coulee Dam Third Powerplant was tested to lift a load of 2,500 tons in 1975. It successfully lowered a 3,944,000-lb generator rotor with an accuracy of 1/32 in.

The tallest mobile crane is the 890-ton Rosenkranz K10001 with a lifting capacity of 1,100 tons and a combined boom and jib height of 663 ft. It is carried on 10 trucks, each limited to 75 ft 8 in and an axle weight of 130 tons. It can lift 33.6 tons to a height of 525 ft.

Dragline Excavators

The Ural Engineering Works at Ordzhonikdze, USSR, completed in March 1962, has a dragline known as the ES-25(100) with a boom of 328 ft and a bucket with a capacity of 31.5 cu yd. The largest walking dragline (and also the largest automotive land vehicle) is "Big Muskie," the Bucyrus-Erie 4,250W with an all-up weight of 13,440 tons and a bucket capacity of 220 cu yd on a 310-ft boom. This, the largest mobile land machine, is now operating on the Central Ohio Coal Co's Muskingum site in Ohio.

Fastest Passenger Elevators

The fastest domestic passenger elevators are the express elevators to the 60th floor of the 787.4-ft-tall "Sunshine 60" building, Ikebukuro, Tokyo, Japan, completed Apr 5, 1978. They were built by Mitsubishi Corp and operate at a speed of 2,000 ft per min, or 22.72 mph.

Much higher speeds are achieved in the winding cages of mine shafts. A hoisting shaft 6,800 ft deep, owned by Western Deep Levels Ltd in South Africa, winds at speeds of up to 40.9 mph (3,595 ft per min). Descending at a speed of even 10 mph causes "otisitis" (popping of the ears).

Graham Coates (UK) established an involuntary duration record when trapped in an elevator for 62 hours in Brighton, Eng, May 24–26, 1986.

Largest Excavator

The largest excavator is the 14,325-ton bucket wheel excavator being assembled at the open-cast lignite mine of Hambach, W Germany with a rating of 260,000 cu yd per 20-hour working day. It

MOVING STAIRWAY TO THE STARS: (Left) In 4 stages outdoors at Ocean Park, Hong Kong, this escalator has an overall length of 745 ft, rising 377 ft from bottom to top. (Above) The luxurious covered stairs can carry 4,000 passengers in either direction at the same time, making it the longest and largest escalator ride ever built.

is 690 ft in length and 269 ft tall. The wheel is 222 ft in circumference with 6.5-cu-yd buckets.

First and Longest Escalators

The name "escalator" was registered in the US on May 28, 1900, but the earliest "Inclined Elevator" was installed by Jesse W. Reno on the pier at Coney Island, NYC in 1896.

The longest escalators on the Leningrad Underground, USSR, at Lenin Square, have 729 steps and a vertical rise of 195 ft 9½ in.

The longest "moving sidewalks" are those installed in 1970 in the Neue Messe Centre, Düsseldorf, W Germany, which measure 738 ft between comb plates.

Largest Forging

The largest forging on record is a generator shaft 55 ft long weighing 450,600 lb forged by Bethlehem Steel in Oct 1973 for Japan.

Largest Fork-Lift Truck

Kalmar LMV of Sweden manufactured in 1985 10 counter-balanced fork-lift trucks capable of lifting loads up to 88.4 tons at a load center of 90.5 in. They were built to handle the large diameter pipeline in the Libyan "Great Man-Made River Project."

Largest Lathe

The largest lathe is the 126-ft long 458.6-ton giant lathe built by Waldrich Siegen of Germany in 1973 for the South African Electricity Supply Commission at Rosherville. It has a capacity for 330-ton work pieces and a swing-over bed 16 ft 5 in in diameter.

Greatest Lifting Operation

The heaviest lifting operation in engineering history was the raising of the entire 0.745 mi long Ekofisk complex in the North Sea owing to the sinking of the sea bed. The complex consists of 8 platforms weighing some 44,100 tons. It was raised 21 ft 4 in by 122 hydraulic jacks Aug 17–18, 1987. Hydraudyne Systems & Engineering bv of Boxtel, Netherlands developed and supplied the computer-controlled hydraulic system.

Slowest Machine

A nuclear environmental machine for testing stress corrosion has been developed by Nene Instruments of Wellingborough, Eng, that can be controlled at a speed as slow as one million millionth of a millimetre per minute, or 3.28 ft in about 2,000 million years.

Largest Nuts

The largest nuts ever made weigh 11,713.5 lb each and have an outside diameter of 52 in and a 25-in thread. Known as "Pilgrim Nuts," they are manufactured by Doncasters Moorside Ltd of Oldham, England, for use on the columns of a large forging press.

Largest Oil Tanks

The largest oil tanks ever constructed are the five Aramco 1½ million-barrel capacity storage tanks at Ju'aymah, Saudi Arabia. The tanks are 72 ft tall with a diameter of 386 ft and were completed Mar 1980.

Longest Pipelines

The longest crude oil pipeline is the Interprovincial Pipe Line Co's installation from Edmonton, Alberta, Canada, to Buffalo, NY, a distance of 1,775 miles. Along the length of the pipe 13 pumping stations maintain a flow of 8,280,000 gallons of oil per day.

The eventual length of the Trans-Siberian Pipeline will be 2,319 miles, running from Tuimazy through Omsk and Novosibirsk to Irkutsk. The first 30-mile section was opened in July 1957.

The world's most expensive pipeline is the Alaska Pipeline running 798 miles from Prudhoe Bay to Valdez. By completion of the first phase in 1977 it had cost at least $6 billion. The pipe is 48 in in diameter and will eventually carry up to 2 million barrels of crude oil per day.

The longest submarine pipeline is that of 264 miles for natural gas from the Union Oil Platform to Rayong, Thailand, opened on Sept 12, 1981.

The longest natural gas pipeline is the Trans-Canada Pipeline which by 1974 had 5,654 miles of pipe up to 42 in in diameter. The Tyumen-Chelyabinsk-Moscow-Brandenburg gasline stretches 2,690 miles.

The longest water pipeline runs a distance of 350 miles to the Kalgoorlie gold fields from near Perth, W Australia. Engineered in 1903, the system has since been extended five-fold by branches.

The large caliber Urengoi-Uzhgovod line to W Europe begun in Nov 1982 stretched 2,765 mi when completed on July 25, 1983. It has a capacity of 42,000 million cu yd per year.

Largest Press

The two most powerful production machines are forging presses in the US. The Loewy closed-die forging press, in a plant leased from the US Air Force by the Wyman-Gordon Co at North Grafton, Mass weighs 10,600 tons and stands 114 ft 2 in high, of which 66 ft is sunk below the operating floor. It has a rated capacity of 50,000 tons, and went into operation in Oct 1955. The other similar press is at the Aluminum Company of America in Cleveland.

In Jan 1986 ASEA's QUINTUS Dept delivered a sheet metal forming press to BMW, Munich, W Germany. This press, which is the largest in the world in terms of forming pressure and press force is a QUINTUS Fluid Cell Press with a press force of 106,000 tonnes.

There has been a report of a press in the USSR with a capacity of 83,025 tons at Novo Kramatorsk. The Bêché and Grohs counterblow forging hammer, manufactured in W Germany, is rated at 66,000 tons.

Fastest Printer or Typesetting Machine

The fastest printer is the Radiation Inc electro-sensitive system at the Lawrence Radiation Laboratory, Livermore, Calif. High speed recording of up to 30,000 lines per min, each containing 120 alphanumeric characters, is attained by controlling electronic pulses through chemically impregnated recording paper which is rapidly moving under closely spaced fixed styli. It can thus print the wordage of the whole Bible (773,692 words) in 65 sec—3,333 times as fast as the world's fastest human typist.

Largest Radar Installations

The largest of the three installations in the US Ballistic Missile Early

Warning System (BMEWS) is the one near Thule, Kalaatdlet Nunaat (Greenland) 931 miles from the North Pole, completed in 1960 at a cost of $500 million. Its sister stations are at Cape Clear, Alaska, completed in July 1961, and a $115 million installation at Fylingdales Moor, North Yorkshire, Eng completed in June 1963. The largest scientific radar installation is the 21-acre ground array at Jicamarca, Peru.

Largest Shovel

With a reach of 236.75 ft and a dumping height of 153 ft, the Marion Power Shovel Co's 6360 has a scooping capacity of 1,620 cu ft. It weighs 24,250,000 lb and uses 20 electric motors that generate 45,000 hp to operate its 220.5-ft-long boom arm.

Largest Transformer

The largest single-phase transformers are rated at 1,500,000 kV of which 8 are in service with the American Electric Power Service Corporation. Of these, 5 step down from 765 to 345 kV.

Longest and Highest Transmission Lines

The longest span between pylons of any power line is that across the Sogne Fjord, Norway, between Rabnaberg and Fatlaberg. Erected in 1955 by the Whitecross Co Ltd of Warrington, England as part of the high-tension power cable from Refsdal power station at Vik, it has a span of 16,040 ft and a weight of 13 tons. In 1967, two further high-tensile steel/aluminum lines 16,006 ft long, and weighing 37 tons, manufactured by Whitecross and British Insulated Callender's Cables Ltd, were erected here.

The highest power lines are those across the Straits of Messina, with towers of 675 ft (Sicily side) and 735 ft (Calabria) and 11,900 ft apart.

The highest voltages now carried are 1,330,000 volts on the DC Pacific Inter-tie in the US for a distance of 1,224 miles. The Ekibastuz DC transmission lines in Kazakhstan, USSR, are planned to be 1,490 miles long with a 1,500,000-volt capacity.

Largest Valve

The largest valve is the 32-ft diameter 190-ton butterfly valve designed by Boving & Co Ltd of London for use at the Arnold Air Force Base engine test facility in Tennessee.

Largest Wind Tunnel

The largest wind tunnel is one at NASA-Ames Research Center in Mountain View, Palo Alto, Calif, reopened on Dec 11, 1987 with a 40 × 80 ft tunnel powered by six 22,500 hp motors, enabling a best speed of 345 mph.

Longest and Strongest Wire Rope

The longest wire ropes are the 4 made at British Ropes Ltd, Wallsend, Tyneside, England, each measuring 14.9 miles. The ropes are 35 mm in diameter, weigh 120 tons each and were ordered for use in the construction of the 2,000 MW cross-Channel power cable.

The thickest ever made are spliced crane strops 11¼ in thick, made of 2,392 individual wires in March 1979 by British Ropes at Willington Quay, Tyneside, England, designed to lift loads of 3,000 tons.

The heaviest wire ropes (4 in number) are each of 130 metric tons, made for the twin-shaft system of Western Deep Levels Gold Mine, S Africa.

TIMEPIECES

Oldest Clocks

The earliest mechanical clock, that is, one with an escapement, was completed in China in 725 AD by I Hsing and Liang Ling-tsan.

The oldest surviving working clock is the faceless clock dating from 1386, or possibly earlier, at Salisbury Cathedral, Wiltshire, England, which was restored in 1956 having struck the hours for 498 years and ticked more than 500 million times. Earlier dates, ranging back to *c.* 1335, have been attributed to the weight-driven clock in Wells Cathedral, Somerset, England, but only the iron frame is original. A model of Giovanni de Dondi's heptagonal astronomical clock of 1348–64 was completed in 1962.

Public Clocks

The largest four-faced clock is that on the building of the Allen-

LARGEST CLOCK: "Timepiece," the clock that hangs 5 stories high in the atrium of the International Square Building in Wash, DC, measures 51 ft in each direction. It is computer-driven and is accurate to within 1/100th of a second.

Bradley Co of Milwaukee, Wis. Each face has a diameter of 40 ft 3½ in with a minute hand 20 ft in overall length.

The largest single-faced clock was the octagonal Colgate clock on the Hudson River shore in Jersey City, NJ, which had a 50-ft diameter and a minute hand 27 ft 3 in in length. It is now dismantled.

The tallest four-faced clock is on the Williamsburgh Savings Bank, Brooklyn, NYC. It is 430 ft above street level.

Most Accurate Time Measurer

The most accurate time-keeping devices are the twin atomic hydrogen masers installed in 1964 in the US Naval Research Laboratory, Washington, DC. They are based on the frequency of the hydrogen atom's transition period of 1,420,450,751,694 cycles per sec. This enables an accuracy to within one sec in 1,700,000 years.

Largest Clock

The largest clock, called "Timepiece," is 51 ft × 51 ft × 51 ft, and hangs in the International Square Building, Wash, DC, suspended 5 stories above the atrium.

The Su Sung clock, built in China at K'aifeng in 1088–92, had a 22-ton bronze armillary sphere for 1⅔ tons of water. It was removed to Peking in 1126 and was last known to be working in its 40-ft-high tower in 1136.

The largest clock face is in the floral clock at Tokachigaoka Park, Otofuke, Japan, completed on Aug 1, 1982 with a diameter of 59 ft 0⅝ in.

Most Expensive Clock

The Thomas Tompion (1639–1713) English-made bracket clock, which sold at auction at Christie's, London, for £110,000 on June 2, 1980, was bought by the British Museum in a private sale for £500,000 (approx. $750,000) on July 15, 1982.

Longest Pendulum

The longest pendulum is 73 ft 9¾ in on the water-mill clock installed by Hattori Tokeiten Co. in the Shinjuku NS Building, Tokyo, Japan, in 1983.

Most Accurate Clock

The most accurate and complicated clockwork is the Olsen clock, installed in the Copenhagen Town Hall, Denmark. The clock, which has more than 14,000 units, took 10 years to make and the mechanism of the clock functions in 570,000 different ways. The celestial pole motion of the clock will take 25,753 years to complete a full circle, the slowest moving designed mechanism in the world. The clock is accurate to 0.5 sec in 300 years—50 times more accurate than the previous record.

Largest Sundial

The largest is the Samrat Yantra in Jaipur, India, built in 1724. It has a gnomon (column) height of 88.5 ft and a vertical height of 118 ft.

LONGEST PENDULUM: This watermill clock has a pendulum 73 ft 9¾ in long. The lock was installed by Hattori Tokeiten Co in the Shinjuku NS building in Tokyo, Japan.

LARGE CUCKOO CLOCK: Topped by reindeer horns and displaying animals from the Black Forest on its sides, this cuckoo clock is in Wiesbaden, Germany.

Oldest Watch

The oldest watch (portable clockwork timekeeper) is one made of iron by Peter Henlein in Nürnberg, Bavaria, Germany, *c.* 1504. The earliest wristwatches were those of Jacquet-Droz and Leschot of Geneva, Switzerland, dating from 1790.

Longest and Heaviest Watches

A facsimile "Swatch" watch was made for demonstration and draped from the roof of the Bank of Bilbao in Madrid, Spain, Dec 7–12, 1985. It was 531 ft 6 in long, and 65 ft in diameter.

The "Eta" watch on the Swiss Pavilion at Expo 86 in Vancouver, BC, Canada, from May–Oct 1986, weighed 38½ tons and stood 80 ft high.

Smallest and Thinnest Watch

The smallest watches are produced by Jaeger Le Coultre of Switzerland. Equipped with a 15-jeweled movement, they measure just over ½ in in length and 3/16th in in width. The movement, with its case, weighs under ¼ oz.

The thinnest wristwatch is the Swiss Concord Delirium IV which measures 0.039 in (0.98 mm) in thickness and retailed for $16,000 in June 1980 with an 18-carat gold bracelet.

Most Expensive Watches

Excluding watches with jeweled cases, the most expensive standard men's pocket watch is the Swiss *Grande Complication* by Audemars-Piguet, which retailed for $336,000 in Mar 1987, up from $100,000 a few years ago.

The record price for an antique watch is $1,005,375 paid at Christie's, Geneva, Switzerland on May 13, 1986 by a European collector for a gold-enameled and diamond-set pocket watch with a movement from *c.* 1650, by the Parisian maker Jehan Cremfdorff. At the same auction, $153,750 was paid for a 1955 Patek Philippe wristwatch, one of only three. It includes a perpetual calendar and records the phases of the moon.

Computers

In May 1988 NEC (Nippon Electric Co) announced a $2,880 million research program for a fifth generation computer able to read handwriting and understand speech in many languages and incorporating super-conduction and Josephson functions.

A geared calculator dated *c.* 80 BC was found in the sea near Antikythera Island off northwest Crete in April 1900.

The earliest programmable electronic computer was the 1,500-valve Colossus. It was run in Dec 1943 at Bletchley Park, England, to break the German coding machine Enigma. It arose from a concept published in 1936 by Dr Alan Mathison Turing (1912–54). It was declassified on Oct 25, 1975.

The first stored-program computer was the Manchester University Mark I which incorporated the Williams storage cathode-ray tube (pat. Dec 11, 1946). It ran its first program written by Prof Tom Kilburn (b 1921) for 52 min on June 21, 1948.

Computers were greatly advanced by the invention of the point-contact transistor by John Bardeen and Walter Brattain announced in July 1948, and the junction transistor by R. L. Wallace, Morgan Sparks and Dr William Shockley in early 1951.

The concept of the integrated circuit, which has enabled micro-miniaturization, was first published on May 7, 1952 by Geoffrey W. A. Dummer (b 1909) in Wash DC. The microcomputer was achieved in 1969–73 by M. E. Hoff Jr of Intel Corporation with the production of the microprocessor silicon chip "4004."

Most Powerful and Fastest Computer

The world's most powerful and fastest computer is the liquid-cooled Cray-2, named after Seymour R. Cray of Cray Research, Inc., Minneapolis. Its memory has a capacity of 256 million 64-bit words, resulting in a capacity of 32 million bytes of main memory. It attains speeds of 250 million floating point operations per sec. The cost of a mid-range system was quoted in Oct 1985 at $17 million.

Smallest Word Processor

The world's smallest word processor, the Easi-Text 1350, was introduced by Minimicro of Huntington, Eng, in Apr 1986. It is based on the Sharp PC-1350 computer which measures 7.2 × 2.8 × 0.6 in and the entire system including an A4 size Epson P-80 printer fits into an executive briefcase.

Megabits

The megabit barrier was broken in Feb 1984, with the manufacture of a 1024K bit integrated circuit, the size of a drawing pin head and as thin as a human hair, by 4 Japanese companies, Hitachi, NEC, NTT Atsugi Electrical Communications and Toshiba. Toshiba announced that manufacture of an 80 picosecond LSI (large scale integration) chip of gallium arsenide would start in 1985–86.

Fastest Transistor

A transistor capable of switching 230,000 million times per sec was announced by Illinois State University on Oct 5, 1986.

Chapter 9

The Business World

In this chapter, the pound sterling has been converted, unless otherwise noted, at an average exchange rate of £1 = $2.20 for 1979, $2.30 for 1980, $1.80 for 1981, $1.56 for 1982, $1.50 for 1983, $1.40 for 1984 and early 1985, $1.50 for late 1985 and early 1986, $1.60 for late 1986 and early 1987, $1.80 for late 1987 and early 1988, and at the prevailing exchange rates for earlier years.

1. COMMERCE

Greatest Assets

The business with the greatest amount in physical assets has been the Bell System, which comprised the American Telephone and Telegraph Company, and its subsidiaries. The Bell System's total assets on the consolidated balance sheet at the time of its divestiture and breakup into 8 companies on Dec 31, 1983 reached $149,529 million. The plant included more than 142 million telephones. The number of employees was 1,036,000. The company's market value of $47,989 million was held among 3,055,000 shareholders. A total of 20,109 shareholders had attended the Annual Meeting in Apr 1961, thereby setting a world record.

Currently the largest assets of any corporation are $74,042 million by the Exxon Corporation, the world's largest oil company, on Jan 1, 1988. It has 100,000 employees. The first company to have assets in excess of $1 billion was the United States Steel Corporation with $1,400 million at the time of its creation by merger in 1917.

Greatest Sales

The first company to surpass $1 billion in annual sales was the US Steel Corporation in 1917. Now there are 570 corporations with sales exceeding $1 billion including 272 from the US. The *Fortune 500 List* of Apr 1987 is headed by General Motors Corp of Detroit with $102,813.7 million for 1986.

The largest single company in sales is Cargill Inc, the Minneapolis, Minnesota grain-trading company, with sales of $32,000 million in 1985–86.

Greatest Profit and Loss

The greatest net profit made by any corporation in 12 months is $7,647 million by American Telephone and Telegraph Co, Oct 1, 1981–Sept 30, 1982.

The greatest loss ever recorded is also by AT&T, which lost $4,900 million in the fourth quarter of 1983 immediately after the breakup of the monopoly, when losses had to be taken on a one-time basis.

The Argentine government-owned Petroleum Company (YPF) is reported to have lost $4,643,995,000 in 1983.

Greatest Bankruptcy

William G. Stern (b Hungary, 1936), of Golders Green, north London, England, a US citizen since 1957, who set up Wilstar Group Holding Co in the London property market in 1971, was declared bankrupt for $229,480,345 in Feb 1979. This figure rose to $314,875,000 by Feb 1983. He was discharged for $600,000, suspended for 2½ years on Mar 28, 1983.

Esal Commodities declared it was in debt for a record £170 million ($238 million) in London on Jan 18, 1985. In connection with this, Rajendra Sethia (b 1950) was arrested in New Delhi, India, on Mar 2, 1985, on charges including criminal conspiracy and forgery and was declared bankrupt as well by the High Court in London. His personal debts were estimated at £140 million ($196 million).

Largest Employer

The world's largest employer is Indian Railways with 1,613,280 staff in 1985–86.

Corporate Seal Was a Potato

A £700 million corporation was set up in 36 hours in Eng and with no time to get a company seal, the banker, Samuel Montagu of London, cut a potato in half, carved the necessary words in reverse, dipped the smooth-cut face of the potato in ink and sealed the document with that.

Largest Jury Award

A Texas jury on Dec 10, 1985 awarded the Pennzoil Company of Texas $11.12 billion in a suit against Texaco, headquartered in White Plains, NY, for improperly enticing the Getty Oil Co to back out of a merger with Texaco in 1984.

Greatest Barter Deal

The biggest barter in trading history was 36 million barrels of oil valued at $10,800,000,000 given by the Royal Saudi Airline for 10 Boeing 747 airliners in July 1984.

Largest Take-Overs

The largest corporate take-over agreement in commercial history is by Chevron (formerly Standard Oil Co. of California) which on June 15, 1984 bought Gulf Oil Corp for $13,231,253,000. The fees of the financial intermediaries were estimated by *Fortune* to be $63.9 million.

The greatest auction in the corporate world was the purchase of Hughes Aircraft Co by General Motors Corp for $5 billion on June 5, 1985.

Accountants

The largest firm of accountants worldwide is that resulting from the merger of Peat Marwick International and Klynveld Main Goerdeler of the Netherlands announced on Sept 3, 1986 with a combined annual revenue of $2,700 million and a total of 58,000 employees.

Advertising Agency

The largest advertising agency is Saatchi & Saatchi/Compton Ltd of London, following their acquisition of the US agency, Ted Bates Worldwide, announced on May 12, 1986. *Advertising Age* lists the group's billings for 1987 at about $11,360 million.

Biggest Advertiser

The biggest advertiser is Sears Roebuck and Co with $1,165.1 million spent in 1987, excluding its catalogue.

Aerospace Company

The largest aerospace company is Boeing with 1987 sales of $15,355 million and a work force of 118,500.

Cessna Aircraft Co of Wichita, Kans had total sales of $469 million in 1987. The company holds the record for producing more than 177,000 aircraft since Clyde Cessna's first was built in 1911.

Largest Airlines

The largest airline is the USSR State airline "Aeroflot," so named since 1932. This was instituted on Feb 9, 1923, with the title of Civil Air Fleet of the Council of Ministers of the USSR, abbreviated to "Dobrolet." It operates 1,650 aircraft over more than 620,000 mi of routes, employs 500,000 people and carried 119 million passengers and 3 million tons of freight in 1987.

The commercial airline carrying the greatest number of passengers was United Airlines, based in Chicago, which carried its peak passenger load of 41,273,000 in 1984. The line in 1986 had 319 planes operating, and 47,900 employees.

Aluminum Producer

The largest producer of primary aluminum is Alcan Aluminium Ltd of Montreal, Canada with its affiliated companies. It had an output of 2,422,000 metric tons in 1987.

Auctioneering

The largest and oldest firm of art auctioneers is the Sotheby Group of London and New York, founded in 1744. The turnover in 1987 was $1.4 billion.

The highest gross realization for a single-session fine arts auction was $63,596,500 recorded by Sotheby's, NYC on May 11, 1987. The sale consisted of modern and impressionist paintings and sculpture.

The largest jewelry auction sale brought $50,231,887 for the benefit of the Institut Pasteur when the jewels of the Duchess of Windsor (1896–1986) were sold at Sotheby's, Geneva, Switz, Apr 2–3, 1987.

Bicycle Manufacturers

The world's biggest manufacturer of bicycles is Hero Cycles of Ladhiana, Punjab, India founded in 1956 by the Munjal brothers. In 1986 they turned out 2,220,000 units. China is estimated to have 210 million bicycles.

Bookstores

The bookshop with the most titles and the longest shelving (30 miles of it) is W. & G. Foyle Ltd of London. First established in 1904 in a small shop in Islington, the company is now at 119–125 Charing Cross Road. On one site, the area is 75,825 sq ft.

The most capacious individual bookstore measured by square footage is Barnes & Noble Bookstore on Fifth Avenue at 18th Street, NYC, with 154,250 sq ft and 12.87 miles of shelving.

Breweries

The largest single brewing organization is Anheuser-Busch, Inc based in St Louis, with 12 breweries in the US. In 1986 the company sold 76,000,000 US barrels, the greatest annual volume ever produced by a brewing company. The company's St Louis plant covers 100 acres and after completion of current modernization will have an annual capacity in excess of 13,000,000 US barrels.

The largest brewery on a single site is Adolph Coors Co of Golden, Colo, where 15,658,000 barrels were sold in 1987.

Car Manufacturers

In 1980, Japan with 11,043,000 vehicles overtook the US as the world's No. 1 motor car manufacturer.

The largest car manufacturer and largest manufacturing company in the world is General Motors Corp of Detroit. During the year 1987, worldwide sales totaled $101,781,900,000. Its assets on Dec 31, 1987, were valued at $87,421,900,000, and there were 813,000 employees.

The largest single automobile plant is the Volkswagenwerk, Wolfsburg, W Germany, with 60,000 employees and a capacity of 4,000 vehicles daily. The surface area of the factory buildings is 371 acres and that of the whole plant, with 43.5 miles of rail sidings, is 4,892 acres.

Chain Store

F. W. Woolworth, which celebrated its centenary year in 1979, now operates the largest chain—6,799 stores worldwide. Frank W. Woolworth, with an idea that he could sell merchandise for a nickel, rented a counter in an already existent Watertown, NY, general store in 1878. Then he opened his first "Five Cent Store" in Utica, NY on Feb 22, 1879. This failed after 6 months. Next he opened a "Five Cent Store" in Lancaster, Pa, which soon became a "5¢-&-10¢ Store." This succeeded. The 1987 income from continuing operations was $251 million.

Chocolate Factory

The largest chocolate and confectionary factory is that built by Hershey Foods Corp of Hershey, Pa in 1903–05. It now has 2 million sq ft of floor space.

Computer Company

The largest computer firm is International Business Machines Corp (IBM) which had assets in Dec 1987 of $63,688 million and gross income of $54,217 million. In 1979 it made the largest borrowing in corporate history with $1 billion. Its worldwide employees numbered 389,348. There are about 787,988 shareholders.

Largest Department Store

The largest single store is R. H. Macy & Co Inc at Broadway and 34th St, NYC. It has a floor space of 2,151,000 sq. ft., and in 1987 had 14,000 employees who handle 400,000 items.

The department store with the fastest-moving merchandise is the Marks & Spencer store at Marble Arch, London, where £1,500 ($2,700) worth of goods per sq ft of selling space per year is believed to be an understatement.

Distillery

The largest distilling company is The Seagram Company Ltd of Canada. Its sales in the year ending Jan 31, 1988 totaled US $3,815,480,000. The group employs about 13,400, including about 3,690 in the U.S.

The largest Scotch establishment for blending and bottling is the United Distillers' Shieldhall plant in Glasgow, where the capacity is 234 million bottles a year.

Fishery

With a single throw of the net, 120 million fish were caught by the Norwegian boat M/S *Flomann* in the Barents Sea, Aug 28, 1982. The catch weighed 2,724 tons.

General Merchandise at Retail

The largest retailing firm is Sears Roebuck and Co of Chicago (founded by Richard Warren Sears in the North Redwood railroad station in Minnesota in 1886). Worldwide revenues, including its consumer and financial subsidiaries, were $28.09 billion in the year ending Dec 31, 1987. It had 813 retail stores and 2,801 catalogue merchants. The corporation's total assets were valued at $23.82 million.

Grocery Store Chain

The largest grocery chain is The Kroger Co, based in Cincinnati, O, with sales in 1987 amounting to $17.7 billion and assets of $2.37 billion. Kroger operates 1,320 supermarkets and 800 convenience stores. It employs 170,000.

Hotels

The top revenue-earning hotel business is Holiday Inns hotel system with 1987 revenues of $5 billion from 1,600 hotels (320,000 rooms) in 53 countries at Dec 31, 1987.

The business was founded by Charles Kemmons Wilson with his first Holiday Inn on Summer Ave, Memphis, Tenn in 1952.

Insurance Policies and Claims

The largest life insurance policy ever written was one for $44 million for a Calgary land developer, Victor T. Uy, in Feb 1982 by Transamerica Occidental Life Insurance Co of California. The salesman was local manager Lorenzo F. Reyes.

Linda Mullendore, wife of a murdered Oklahoma rancher, received some $18 million as of Nov 14, 1970, the largest pay-out on a single life. Her husband had paid $300,000 in premiums in 1969.

Insurance Companies and Losses

The company with the highest volume of insurance in force is the Prudential Insurance Company of America of Newark, NJ with $702.8 billion at Dec 31, 1987. Consolidated assets are $104.9 billion.

The largest single association is the Blue Cross and Blue Shield Association, the medical insurance organization, with a membership of about 76.8 million in 1987. Benefits paid out in 1987 totaled $44,500 million.

The largest marine insurance loss was $82 million for the self-propelled semi-submersible drilling platform *Ocean Ranger* (14,914 tons gross) built for Ocean Drilling & Exploration Co of New Orleans in 1976. On Feb 15, 1982 she was lost with 84 lives in the Hibernia Field, off Newfoundland.

The largest sum claimed for consequential losses is $1,700 million against owning, operating and building corporations, and Claude Phillips, resulting from the 66-million-gallon oil spill from M. T. *Amoco Cadiz* on the Brittany coast on Mar 16, 1978.

Mineral Water

The largest mineral water firm is Source Perrier, near Nimes, France with an annual production of more than 2.5 billion bottles, of which 1.5 billion now come from Perrier and Contrexeville. The French drink about 60 liters (63½ qts) of mineral water per person per year.

Oil Refinery

The world's largest refinery has been the Amerada Hess refinery at St Croix, Virgin Islands, producing 345,000 barrels a day in 1987.

Paper Company

The largest company in paper, fiber and wood products is Georgia-Pacific of Atlanta, with 1987 sales of $8,603 million, and 42,000 workers.

Pharmaceutical Company

The largest company marketing pharmaceuticals and health care products, Johnson & Johnson of New Brunswick, NJ, had sales of $8,012 million in 1987.

Photographic Store

The photographic store with the largest selling area is Jessop of Leicester Ltd's Photo Centre, Hinckley Road, Leicester, England which opened in June 1979 with an area of 27,000 sq ft.

Public Relations

The largest public relations firm is Burson-Marsteller of NYC, a unit of Young & Rubicam, whose net fee income for 1987 was $137,214,000. Hill & Knowlton Inc have most offices worldwide with 56, and 1,800 employees, including one office in Beijing, China.

Publishing

The publishing company generating most net revenue is Time Inc of NYC, with $4,193 million in 1987. The largest .educational book publishing concern in the world is the Book Division of McGraw-Hill Inc of NYC, with sales of $487.7 million in 1986, with 2,000 new books and educational products.

Restaurants

The largest restaurant chain is McDonald's Corp in Oakbrook, Ill, founded Apr 15, 1955, in Des Plaines, a suburb of Chicago, by Ray A. Kroc (1903–84), BH (Bachelor of Hamburgerology). By Apr 6, 1988, the number of restaurants licensed and owned in 47 countries and territories reached 10,000 with an aggregate annual output of 65 billion 100% beef hamburgers. Sales systemwide in 1987 surpassed $14.3 billion. The company serves 22 million customers every day.

By purchasing the Kentucky Fried Chicken chain of 6,500 restaurants, Pepsico Inc, which already owned the Pizza Hut and Taco Bell chains, is the conglomerate with most restaurants—14,000.

Shipbuilding

In 1987, the gross tonnage of ships completed throughout the world fell short of the record 18,156,526 gross tons in 1985. The figures for the USSR, Rumania and the People's Republic of China are incomplete. Japan completed 8,177,953 gross tons (48.55% of the world's total).

The leading shipbuilding firm in 1986, the peak year, was Hyundai of S Korea which completed 43 vessels of 1,925,882 gross tons.

Shipping Line

The largest shipping owners and operators are the Exxon Corporation, whose fleets of owned/managed and chartered tankers in 1987 totaled a daily average of 9,200,000 deadweight tons.

Shopping Centers

The largest shopping center is the $1.2 billion W Edmonton Mall, Alberta, Canada, first opened on Sept 15, 1981 and completed 4 years later. It covers 5.2 million sq ft on 110 acres, encompasses 828 stores and services, as well as 6 major department stores. Parking is provided for 20,000 vehicles for more than 500,000 shoppers per week.

The world's first shopping center was Roland Park Shopping Center in Baltimore, Md, built in 1896.

The world's largest wholesale merchandise market is the Dallas Market Center, located on Stemmons Freeway, Dallas, Tex, with nearly 9.3 million sq ft in 8 buildings. The complex covers 150 acres with some 3,400 permanent showrooms displaying merchandise of more than 26,000 manufacturers. The center attracts 600,000 buyers each year to its 38 annual markets and trade shows.

Soft Drink Producer

The world's most popular soft drink is Coca-Cola with over 301 million sold per day by early 1985 in more than 155 countries. "Coke" was invented by Dr John S. Pemberton of Atlanta, Ga in 1886, the company was formed in 1892, and its famous bottle was patented in 1915. The secret "7X" formula was unchanged until 1985 when Coca-Cola had 21.7% of the $28 billion market to Pepsico's 18.8%.

Pepsico's overall 1986 sales of $9.3 billion were $600 million higher than Coca-Cola's in 1986.

Steel Company

The largest producer of steel in the non-Communist world has been Nippon Steel of Tokyo, which produced 26,030,000 tons of steel and steel products in 1987. This was 240,000 tons less than in 1986.

Sugar Mill

The highest recorded output for any sugar mill was set in 1966–67 by Ingenio de San Cristobal y Anexas, S.A. of Veracruz, Mexico, with 273,310 tons refined from 3,181,897 tons of cane ground.

The largest cane sugar plant is the California & Hawaii Sugar Co plant founded in 1906 at Crockett, Calif with an output of 8 million lb per day.

Tobacco Company

The largest tobacco company is the group of subsidiaries and affiliates of B.A.T. Industries (British-American Tobacco Co Ltd, founded in London in 1902). They operate 120 tobacco factories in 50 countries. Consolidated turnover in 1986 was $30,667.2 million and total assets were $14,984 million Dec 31, 1986. The Group's sales in 1986 topped 577 billion cigarettes.

The largest and most automated cigarette plant is the $1 billion

RESTAURANT SCHOOL: Hamburger U or Moo U in Elk Grove Village, Ill, is owned and operated by McDonald's, the world's largest single chain of restaurants, with 10,000 shops. The students (2,000 at a time) learn everything about fast-food cooking, serving and management, so they can get Golden Chef's hats. ►

SHOPPING MALL DRAGON: Suspended over the Metroplex Mall in Kuala Lumpur, Malaysia, this 388-ft-11-in long "fire dragon" not only celebrates the Year of the Dragon but "brings prosperity day after day." ▼

Reynolds Tobacco Co plant at Tobaccoville, NC, opened in Sept 1986, which produces more than 110 billion cigarettes per year.

Toy Store

The biggest toy store is Hamley's of Regent Street Ltd, founded in London in 1760 in the Holborn area, and moved to Regent Street in 1901. It has selling space of 45,000 sq ft on 6 floors with over 300 employees during the Christmas season.

Undertaker (or Mortician)

The world's largest undertaking business is the SCI (Service Corporation International, based in Houston, Tex) with 454 funeral homes and 73 flower shops and limousine fleets with associated cemeteries. Their annual revenue in this most recession-proof of industries was $386,632,000 in the year ending Apr 30, 1987.

LONGEST SOFT TOY: This plush pink caterpillar is 250 ft long, has 1,000 legs, and weighs 300 lb. Made in Taiwan, and called "Lots-a-Lots-a-Leggggggs," it was originated for Commonwealth Toy & Novelty Co. of NYC by Brooke Keith, a US toy designer. Smaller versions in pink and other colors are sold by Commonwealth, who hold the copyright.

FINANCE

The oldest Stock Exchange of the 138 listed in the world is said to be that in Amsterdam, The Netherlands, founded in 1602.

The largest in trading volume in 1987 was Tokyo with $1,750 billion, moving ahead of the NYSE, which had a volume of $1,590 billion.

Largest Investment House

The largest securities company and once the world's largest partnership (124 partners before becoming a corporation in 1959), is Merrill Lynch, Pierce, Fenner & Smith, Inc of NYC (founded Jan 6, 1914). Its parent, Merrill Lynch & Co, has assets of $55 billion, 44,000 employees, more than 1,000 offices around the world, and 5 million customer accounts.

Highest Value Stock

The highest price quoted for a share of F. Hoffmann-La Roche of Basel, Switzerland, was 101,000 Swiss Fr (then $38,486) on Apr 23, 1976.

New York Stock Exchange (NYSE) Records

New records in 1986 and 1987 have been set almost daily to the point where an annual book of this kind cannot do more than publish the most unusual. Daily and weekly newspapers must be consulted for latest records.

The record for a day's trading is 302,469,040 shares on Jan 23, 1987.

The record-setting daily increase was set on Apr 3, 1986 when the Dow Jones index increased 69.89 points.

Largest Reverse Stock Split

On June 7, 1982, Madison National Life Insurance Co of Middleton, Wis split its stock selling over-the-counter 20,000 to 1, specifically reducing authorized shares from 1,500,000 to 75 shares total.

Largest New Issue

The largest security offering in history was one of $1,375 million in American Telephone and Telegraph Co stock in a rights offer on 27,500,000 shares of convertible preferred stock on June 2, 1971.

Greatest Personal Loss and Gain

The highest recorded personal paper losses on stock values have been those of Ray A. Kroc, chairman of McDonald's Corp with $64,901,718 on July 8, 1974 and Edwin H. Land, president of Polaroid Corp with $59,397,355 May 28–29, 1974, when Polaroid stock closed down $12.12 on that day.

An investor who paid $375 in the morning of Dec 10, 1985 for an option on Pennzoil could have cashed it at the end of the same day for $10,250, for the fastest gain in history. The stock jumped from 19¾ to 83 that day.

Largest Bank

The International Bank for Reconstruction and Development (founded Dec 27, 1945), the "World Bank" (a UN specialized agency) at 1818 H Street NW, Wash, DC, had an authorized share capital of $169.7 billion on Apr 27, 1988. There were 151 members with a subscribed capital of $87.4 billion on Dec 31, 1986. The International Monetary Fund in Wash, DC, had 151 members with total quotas of SDR 89,987.6 million ($114,068.28 million) as of Apr 1987.

The biggest commercial bank is Dai-Ichi Kango Bank Ltd of Japan with assets in July 1987 of $275,300 million. The 10 largest banks in the world are Japanese. Citibank, the largest in the US, is 28th.

The bank with the most branches is the State Bank of India which had 11,171 branches on Jan 1, 1987, with assets of $26,340 million.

LAND

The world's largest landowner is the United States Government, with a holding of 727 million acres (1,135,937 sq mi), which is more than the area of the 8th largest country, Argentina, and 12 times larger than the UK. The world's largest private landowner is reputed to be International Paper Co, with 9 million acres.

Land Values

Currently the most expensive land is in the central Ginza district of Tokyo, where the site of the Crown nightclub was bought on Oct 28, 1985 for $18,300 per sq ft.

The price for a grave site with excellent *Fung Shui* in Hong Kong may cost US $33,800 for a 4 × 10 ft plot. The China Square Inch Land Ltd at a charity auction on Dec 2, 1977 sold 1 sq cm (0.155 sq in) of land at Sha Tau Kok for HK $2,000 (the equivalent of US $17,405,833,737 per acre).

Greatest Urban Land Sale

The 3 square blocks of land under Rockefeller Center, NYC, were sold by Columbia Univ to Rockefeller Center for $400 million in Mar 1985.

Highest and Lowest Rent

The highest rentals in the world for prime sites in May 1988 were in Tokyo, Japan ($166.16 per sq ft) and London ($108.00), before taxes and service charges. Tokyo, after the extra charges, is $184.05.

> The rent for a 3-room apartment in the Fuggerei in Augsburg, W Germany, since it was built by Jacob Fugger in 1519, has been 1 Rhine guilder (now DM 1.72 or less than $1) per month. Fugger was the extremely wealthy philanthropist who pioneered social welfare.

Greatest Land Auction

The greatest auction ever was that at Anchorage, Alaska, on Sept 11, 1969, for 179 tracts of 450,858 acres of the oil-bearing North Slope, Alaska. An all-time record bid of $72,277,133 for a 2,560-acre lease was made by the Amerada Hess Corporation-Getty Oil consortium. The bid indicated a price of $28,233 per acre.

2. MANUFACTURED ARTICLES

Antique

The largest antique ever sold has been the London Bridge in March 1968. The sale was made by Ivan F. Luckin of the Court of Common Council of the Corporation of London to the McCulloch Oil Corp of Los Angeles for $2,460,000. Over 10,000 tons of facade stonework were reassembled at a cost of $6.9 million at Lake Havasu City, Ariz, and "rededicated" Oct 10, 1971.

Auction

The highest amount ever paid at auction for a paged work was $11.9 million for a 12th-century illuminated manuscript "The Gospels of Henry the Lion" at Sotheby's, London Dec 6, 1983. (See page 205.)

Basket

The biggest basket ever made was 15 ft tall, woven by Nineteenth Century Basket Co, Warren, Ohio in 1986.

Bathtub

A bathtub made entirely of gold, with an appraised value of $5 million, was reported in Lagos, Nigeria in Jan 1984. Owned by a former high-ranking official of the ousted government, it was taken into his vacation home in England. The underwriters called to insure the house agreed to insure everything but the tub, and suggested it best be left in a bank.

Beds

The bed made in 1984 for Stephen King's "Cat's Eye" movie set a new record 40 ft 9 in long, 20 ft 9 in wide, with headboard 21 ft 1½ in high, and footboard 15 ft 8¼ in high. The pillows measured 12 ft by 8 ft.

The heaviest bed is a waterbed 12 ft wide and 15 ft 4 in long, made in Nov 1986 by Atlantic Waterbeds of Yarmouth, Nova Scotia. It holds 1,050 gallons of water, weighing over 5 tons.

Blankets

The largest blanket ever made measured 70 × 152 ft (10,640 sq ft). It was the work of the employees of the Adolph Coors Co, Golden, Colo, who contributed 1,100 woolen squares that were knitted together.

Candle

A candle 80 ft high and 8½ ft in diameter was exhibited at the 1897 Stockholm Exhibition by the firm of Lindahls. The overall height was 127 ft.

Currently the largest candle is made by the Atletiek-en Trimvereniging Tegelen Sportsclub of Tegelen, The Netherlands, on June 1, 1986. It stands 89 ft 1 in high.

LARGEST BLANKET: Thirty people across can be covered by the 10,640-sq-ft (70 by 152 ft) blanket made in Golden, Colo, from 1,100 squares knitted together by the employees of the Adolph Coors Company.

Carpets and Rugs

A 52,225-sq-ft 28-ton red carpet was laid along the Avenue of the Americas from Radio City Music Hall to the NY Hilton Feb 13, 1982, by the Allied Corp for the "Night of 100 Stars" show in NYC.

The most magnificent carpet ever made was the Spring carpet of Khusraw made for the audience hall of the Sassanian palace at Ctesiphon, Iraq. It was about 7,000 sq ft of silk and gold thread, encrusted with emeralds. It was cut up as booty by military looters in 635 AD and from the known realization value of the pieces, must have had an original value of some $2,400 million.

The most finely woven old carpet known is one having more than 2,600 knots per sq in produced in Mar 1985 by the Bikaner Woollen Mills of Varanasi, Uttar Pradesh, India. The carpet was displayed at the 1986 *Heimtextil* International Trade Fair in Frankfurt, W. Germany, where a consensus of expert opinion declared the "knottage" to be close to 3,000 per sq in.

Chair

The largest chair is 41 ft 8½ in tall and 23 ft 9½ in wide. The deck chair was constructed by Luigi Bernasconi & Co, Mendrisio, Switzerland, and was exhibited Apr 11–13, 1987.

Chandeliers

The largest chandeliers were a set of 10 built for the palace of the Sultan of Brunei in 1983. (See page 248).

The largest chandelier in Britain (and possibly in the world) is the 30-ft-diameter chandelier in the Chinese Room at the Royal Pavilion, Brighton, which was made in 1818 and weighs 2,200 lb.

Cigars

The largest cigar ever made measures 16 ft 8½ in, weighs 577 lb 9 oz, and contains 3,330 tobacco leaves wrapped around a core of cardboard. It took Tinus Vinke and Jan Weijmer 243 hours to make and is now in the Tobacco Museum in Kampen, The Netherlands.

The largest marketed cigar in the world is the 14-in Valdez Emperado by San Andres Cigars.

The most expensive standard cigar, the 9¼-in-long Montecristo "A" retails at $21.50.

Cigarettes

World production in 1985 was 9,873 billion cigarettes. The people of China were estimated to have consumed 1,180 million in 1985.

Cigarette Lighter

The most expensive table cigarette lighter is the 18-carat gold Leader Lighthouse table lighter, in the shape of a lighthouse, set on an island base of amethyst. It weighs 35.28 lb and the base weighs 112 lb. The windows of the lighthouse are amethyst. Priced at $56,000 it was offered in 1985 at Alfred Dunhill, London.

Curtains

The largest functional curtain is one 550 ft long × 65 ft high in the Brabazon hangar at British Aerospace Filton, Bristol, used to enclose aircraft in the paint-spraying bay. It is electrically drawn.

The largest curtain ever built was the bright orange-red 4½-ton 185-ft-high curtain suspended 1,350 ft above and across the Rifle Gap, Grand Hogback, Colo, by the Bulgarian-born sculptor Christo (*né* Javacheff), 36, on Aug 10, 1971. It blew apart in a 50-mph gust of wind 27 hours later. The total cost of displaying this work of art was $750,000.

Dolls

The most outsize girl doll ever paraded was made by the Belgian student body KSA on May 15, 1983 in Ostend. It measured 167 ft 6 in overall. The most massive boy doll built was one 62 ft 4 in high by the Fermain Youth Club, Macclesfield, Eng, on Nov 5, 1983.

A rag doll 38.8 ft long and properly proportioned was made at Linvilla Orchards, Media, Pa in Sept 1983.

Dress

The largest "dress" ever made was one 100 ft long made of 2,500 yd of aqua and pink dacron weighing 1,000 lb for the "engagement" between Miss Liberty (US) and Christopher Columbus (Spain). It was created by Antoni Miraldi in Oct 1986.

The EVA suits for extra-vehicular activity worn by space shuttle crews from 1982 had a unit cost of $2.3 million.

The dress with the highest price tag ever exhibited was one designed by Serge Lepage, and exhibited in the Schiaparelli spring/summer collection in Paris on Jan 23, 1977. Called "The Birth of Venus" and studded with 512 diamonds, it carried a record price tag of 7.5 million francs (then $1.5 million).

FLAGS IN LIGHT OVER MANHATTAN: All 4 sides of the top floors of the Citicorp Building in midtown were lit up in full color to celebrate July 4, 1988. ▼

LARGEST "DRESS": 100 ft ▲ long, made from 2,500 yds of dacron, weighing 1,000 lbs, this was created by Antoni Miraldi in Oct 1986 for the "engagement" of Miss Liberty and Christopher Columbus. *(Marta Sentis)*

LARGEST DUCK DECOY: Made of fiberglass over a metal framework and painted with urethane paint, this giant loon duck decoy measures 20 ft in length, 10 ft in height, and 7½ ft in width. It swims in Silver Lake, Virginia, Minn in summer as a symbol of the Loon Area Ethnic Arts & Crafts Festival.

Emperor Field Marshal Jean-Bédel Bokassa's coronation robe, with a 39-ft-long train, was encrusted with 785,000 pearls and 1,220,000 crystal beads by Guiselin of Paris for $144,500 for use at Bangui, Central African Empire (now Republic) in Dec 1977.

A platinum bikini valued at $9,500 was made by Mappin and Webb Jewelers, London. It was worn by Miss United Kingdom in the 1977 Miss World beauty pageant.

Fabrics

The most expensive fabric is Vicuña cloth manufactured by Fuji Keori Ltd of Osaka, Japan, at $3,235 per meter in July 1983.

The most expensive wool cloth is Shatoosh (or Shatusa), a brown-gray cloth from the throat hair of Indian goats. It was sold for $1,000 per yard by Neiman-Marcus.

The oldest surviving fabric discovered from Level VI A at Çátal Hüyük, Turkey, has been radio-carbon dated to 5900 BC.

The most expensive evening-wear fabric was one 37½ in wide, hand embroidered, in a series of designs on pure silk grounds, with as many as 155,000 hand-sewn tiny sequins and pearls per sq yd, designed by Alan Hershman of London; it cost $975 per meter.

Fireworks

The largest firework ever produced was *Universe I* exploded for the Lake Toya Festival, Hokkaido, Japan on Aug 28, 1983. The 928-lb shell was 42.5 in in diameter and burst to a diameter of 2,830 ft, with a 5-color display.

The longest firecracker display was produced by the Hyatt Regency Hotel, the President Hotel and the Department of Tourism in Macao, near Hong Kong, June 27, 1987. The total length of the display was 13,084 ft and consisted of 2,788,000 firecrackers. It burned for 6 hours 45 min.

Flags

The oldest known flag is one dating to *c.* 3000 BC, found in 1972 at Khablis, Iran. Made of metal, it measures 9 × 9 in, and depicts an eagle, lions and goddesses.

The largest flag made, "The Great American Flag," was first displayed in Evansville, Ind on Mar 22, 1980 (in 1981, in front of the Washington Monument in Washington, DC and on Flag Day 1983 on the Ellipse south of the White House). It weighs 7.7 tons and measures 411 × 210 ft. The project is the brainchild of Len Silverfine, who has donated it to the White House.

The largest flag *flown* from a flagstaff is a Brazilian national flag measuring 229 ft 8 in × 328 ft 1 in in the capital, Brasilia. The study of flags is known as vexillology.

Floats

The largest float was the 155-ft-long, 24-ft-wide "Merry Christmas America" float bearing 3 double arches, a 17-ft Christmas tree, two 15-ft peppermint candy sticks and 5,380 sq ft of wrapping paper used at the 40th annual Christmas parade, Baton Rouge, La, on Dec 5, 1986.

Furniture

The largest item of furniture is the wooden bench in Green Park, Obiharo, Hokkaido, Japan, which seats more than 1,400 people and measures 1,512 ft long. It was completed by a team of 800 on Mar 9, 1987. (Also see *Sofa*.)

Glass

The most priceless example of the art of glass-making is usually regarded as the Portland Vase which dates from late in the 1st century BC or 1st century AD. It was made in Italy and was in the possession of the Barberini family in Rome from at least 1642. It was eventually bought by the Duchess of Portland in 1792, but smashed while in the British Museum on Feb 7, 1845.

The thinnest glass, type D263, has a minimum thickness of 0.00137 in. It is made by Deutsche Spezialglas AG, Grünenplan, W Ger for use in electronic and medical equipment.

Gold

The gold coffin of the 14th century BC Pharaoh Tutankhamun discovered by Howard Carter on Feb 16, 1923 in the Valley of the Kings, western Thebes, Egypt weighed 243 lb. It is on exhibit in the Cairo Museum.

Grill

A 328.7-ft-long grill was made for a barbecue at Barcelona, Spain, on Sept 22, 1986. A single *butifarra* (sausage) 5,917 ft in length was cooked on it.

Jig-Saw Puzzles

The largest jig-saw puzzle was 84 ft 10½ in × 55 ft 2½ in with 15,520 pieces, constructed by the Monadnock United Way of Keene, NH at the Keene College gym, Sept 21–23, 1985.

Fujisankei Communications Group of Japan commissioned Yanoman Co to produce a puzzle 10.63 × 19.29 ft with 61,752 pieces. Each piece was sold for charity.

Custom-made Stave puzzles made by Steve Richardson of Vermont, of 2,640 pieces cost $5,620 in Mar 1988.

Knife

The penknife with the greatest number of blades is the Year Knife made by the cutlers Joseph Rodgers & Sons Ltd, of Sheffield, England, whose trademark was granted in 1682. The knife was made in 1822 with 1,822 blades, and was designed to match the year of the Christian era until 2000 AD, but had to halt at 1,973 because there was no more space for blades.

Needles

The earliest needles were made of bone. The largest recorded needle is one 6 ft 1 in long made by George Davies of Thomas Somerfield, Eng, for stitching on mattress buttons lengthways. One is preserved in the National Needle Museum, Forge Mill, Redditch, Eng.

Nylon

The lowest denier nylon yarn ever produced is the 6 denier used for stockings exhibited at the Nylon Fair in London in Feb 1956. The sheerest stockings normally available are 9 denier. An indication of the thinness is that a hair from the average human head is about 50 denier.

Pens

The highest price ever paid for a fountain pen was reported as 1.3 million French francs ($2,340,000). Bought by a Japanese collector in Feb 1988, the "Anemone" pen, made by Reden in France, was encrusted with 600 precious stones including emeralds, rubies, amethysts, sapphires, and onyx. It took over a year for skilled craftsmen to complete.

The most expensive writing pens were 18-carat pairs of pens (one fiber-tipped and one ballpoint) capped by diamonds of 3.88 carats sold by Alfred Dunhill Ltd, London, for £9,943 ($17,900) the pair.

Pipe

A very large meerschaum pipe with a bowl fashioned into a portrayal of Antony and Cleopatra had been priced at $15,000 by Racine and Laramie of San Diego, Calif, in Feb 1982.

Pistol

The pistol with the largest magazine capacity is the .22LR M.100P with 103 rounds of continuous firepower, manufactured by Calico, Bakersfield, Calif.

Post Cards

Deltiology is claimed to be the third largest collecting hobby next only to stamps and coins. Austria issued the first cards in 1869 followed by Britain in 1872.

The highest price paid for a post card was $4,400 for one of 5 known Mucha Waverly Cycle post cards. It was sold by Susan Brown Nicholson of Lisle, Ill, in Sept 1984.

Quilt

The largest quilt is one made by 7,000 citizens of North Dakota in the shape of that state with each county a replica of the county's shape, including landmarks and historical places. Overall size is 85 x 134 ft, totaling 11,390 sq ft. It was constructed under the eye of Leona Tennyson (known as the Betsy Ross of the Prairie) who spent 2 years directing the project for the 1989 centennial of North Dakota.

Ropes

The largest rope ever made was a coir fiber launching rope with a circumference of 47 in made in 1858 for the British liner *Great Eastern* by John and Edwin Wright. It consisted of four strands, each of 3,780 yarns.

The longest fiber rope ever made without a splice was one of 10,000

JEWELED FOUNTAIN PEN: Encrusted with 600 precious stones, this "Anemone" pen, made in France, sold to a Japanese collector for what is said to be $2,340,000. (*Gamma*)

◄

LARGEST SHOE: It took the skins of 2 cows to make this 158-lb, 4¼-ft-long giant shoe. It was cobbled in Madrid, Spain, by Alonso de la Prieta. ▲

fathoms (11.36 miles) of 6½-in circumference manila by Frost Brothers (now British Ropes Ltd) in London in 1874.

Scarf

The longest scarf ever knitted measured an amazing 20 miles 13 ft long. It was knitted by residents of Abbeyfield Houses for the Abbeyfield Society, Eng, and was completed on May 29, 1988.

Shoes

Emperor Bokassa of the Central African Empire (now Republic) commissioned pearl-studded shoes from the House of Berluti, Paris for his self-coronation in Dec 1977 at a cost of $85,000.

The most expensive sports shoes obtainable are the mink-lined golf shoes with 18-carat gold embellishments and ruby-tipped gold spikes by Stylo Matchmakers International Ltd of Northampton, England, which retail for $17,000 per pair.

James Smith, founder of James Southall & Co of Norwich, England, introduced sized shoes in 1792.

The largest shoes ever sold, excluding those made for cases of elephantiasis, are a pair of size 42 built for the giant Harley Davidson of Avon Park, Fla. The largest shoes normally available are size 14.

For advertising and display purposes facsimiles of shoes and boots weighing up to 1½ tons have been constructed.

Silver

The largest single pieces of silver are the pair of water jugs of 10,408 troy oz (867.3 troy lb) made in 1902 for the Maharaja of Jaipur (1861–1922). They are 5 ft 3 in tall with a circumference of 8 ft 1½ in and have a capacity of 1,800 Imperial gallons (2,162 US gallons). They are now in the City Palace, Jaipur. The silversmith was Gorind Narain.

Sofa

The longest standard sofa manufactured for market is the Augustus Rex Sofa, 12 ft 3 in in length made by Dodge & Son of Sherborne, Eng. Barton Grange Hotel, near Preston, Lancashire, Eng bought a 14-ft-long pink leather settee for £3,250 ($3,900) on Oct 4, 1984.

Table

The longest table was set up from La Punta to The Terramar, Sitges, Spain on Oct 4, 1986. It was 2,636.2 yds in length and was used to seat 6,400 people.

Tablecloth

The world's largest tablecloth is one 219 yd long × 2 yd wide double damask, made by John S. Brown & Sons Ltd of Belfast, N Ireland, and shipped to a royal palace in the Middle East. There was also an order for matching napkins for 450 places.

Tapestries

The earliest known examples of tapestry-woven linen are three

LARGEST QUILT: 7,000 citizens of North Dakota contributed quilts to make one gigantic replica of the state, 85 x 134 ft, totaling 11,390 sq ft. Each county's quilt included landmarks and historical places. Don't be concerned: Those people walking on the quilt are in their stocking feet. *(Dave Wallace, Fargo)*

SALAD BOWL CHANDELIER: To serve his Caesar salad to 458 people, George Moore, restauranteur of Ocala, Fla, had this 6-ft-7-in-diameter bowl constructed. First filled with salad on Mar 29, 1988, it weighs 720 lb, is made of 184 individual pieces of wood, and has 262 lights installed around its rim. When it isn't used for salad, it can be hung upside down in the restaurant as a chandelier.

pieces from the tomb of Thutmose IV, the Egyptian pharaoh, dating from 1483 to 1411 BC.

The largest tapestry ever woven is the "History of Irak," with an area of 13,370.7 sq ft. Designed by the Yugoslavian artist Frane Delale and completed in 1986, it adorns the wall of an amphitheatre in Baghdad.

Time Capsule

The largest time capsule is the Tropico Time Tunnel measuring 10,000 cu ft in a cave in Rosamond, Calif, sealed by the Kern Antelope Historical Society on Nov 20, 1966, and intended for opening in the year 2866.

> Located beneath the campus of Oglethorpe College in Atlanta, Ga, is the Crypt of Civilization, the first successful attempt to bury a record of this culture for any future inhabitants or visitors to the planet Earth. Conceived in 1935 by the college's president, Thornwell Jacobs, the swimming-pool-sized crypt was begun in 1938, completed and sealed in 1940, and is scheduled to be opened in 8113 A.D. The crypt is filled with writings, newsreels, recordings, and samples from the world of 1940. Included are a quart of beer, a set of Lincoln logs, a Donald Duck doll, an electric "toastolater," and a baby's pacifier. Also included is a device designed to teach English to the crypt's finders.

Typewriters

The first patent for a typewriter was by Henry Mill in 1714, but the earliest known working machine was made by Pellegrine Turri (Italy) in 1808.

Vase

The largest vase on record is one 8 ft high, weighing 650 lb, thrown by Sebastiano Maglio at Haeger Potteries of Dundee, Ill (founded 1872) during Aug 1976.

The Chinese ceramic authority, Chingwah Lee of San Francisco, was reported in Aug 1978 to have appraised a unique 39-in K'ang Hsi 4-sided vase, then in a bank vault in Phoenix, Ariz, at $60 million.

Wallet

The most expensive wallet ever made is a platinum-cornered, diamond-studded crocodile creation by Louis Quatorze of Paris and Mikimoto of Tokyo selling at £56,000 ($72,000) in Sept 1984.

Zipper

The largest zip-fastener is 2,074 ft long, with 119,007 nylon teeth. It seals the covers of aquatic cables by RIRI, Mendrisio, Switzerland.

COLLECTIONS

BOTTLES (MINIATURE). George E. Terren of Southboro, Mass, has a collection of 29,508 miniature distilled spirit and liquor bottles as of Mar 1, 1988.

BOTTLE CAPS. The largest collection of bottle caps is probably the collection of Helge Friholm of Soborg, Denmark, which consists of 44,217 different undamaged caps from 149 countries as of June 18, 1987.

CARS. The greatest collection of vintage cars was the William F. Harrah collection in Reno, Nev. of 1,700, estimated in 1984 to be worth more than $4 million. All but 300 of the collection have been sold since Mr. Harrah died, and one car sold in 1987 for $6.5 million.

CIGAR BANDS. Joseph Hruby of Lyndhurst, Ohio, has the largest known collection of cigar bands with 170,146 different examples, dating from *c.* 1895.

CIGARETTES. The largest collection of cigarettes is that of Robert E. Kaufman, MD, of NYC. In Apr 1988, he had 8,200 different brands of cigarettes with 43 kinds of tips made in 172 countries. The oldest brand represented is "Lone Jack," made in the US *c.* 1885.

CIGARETTE CARDS. The earliest known tobacco card is "Vanity Fair" dated 1876 issued by Wm S. Kimball & Co of Rochester, NY. The largest known collection is that of Edward Wharton-Tigar (b 1913) of London with a collection of more than 1 million cigarette cards in about 45,000 sets.

The most valuable card is one of 30 known "Sweet Caporal" baseball series cards of Honus Wagner, who was a non-smoker, which was sold for $100,000 in Jan 1988 to a hobbyist in the Midwest who wishes to remain anonymous.

CIGARETTE LIGHTERS. Since 1970 Bent Hansen of Praesto, Denmark, has collected 7,060 cigarette lighters from all over the world.

CREDIT CARD COLLECTION. The largest collection of valid credit cards, as of Apr 1987, is one of 1,199 all different, by Walter Cavanagh (b 1943) of Santa Clara, Calif (known as "Mr Plastic Fantastic"). The cost of acquisition was nil, and he keeps them in the world's longest wallet, 250 ft long, weighing 35 lb, worth more than $1.4 million in credit.

KEYS. Harley O. (Rowdy) Yates of Tahoe, Calif, has collected 41,281 different keys from 16 countries and about 300 companies in 54 years.

MATCHBOX LABELS. Collectors of labels are phillumenists. The oldest match label of accepted provenance is that of Samuel Jones *c.* 1830. The finest collection of trademark labels (excluding any bar or other advertising labels) is some 280,000 pieces collected by Robert Jones of Indianapolis.

POSTAGE STAMPS. See page 419.

POSTCARDS. A 12-year-old, Mario Morby, of Streetly, W Midlands, Eng, has a collection of 1,000,265 postcards.

SALT AND PEPPER SHAKERS. The largest collection consists of 12,746 sets, stored in two buildings in Traer, Iowa. It belongs to Mrs. Ruth Rasmussen, who has been collecting since 1946.

MINIATURE RECORDS:

In this photo are 26 tiny working tools. The hammer is 27.4 mm tall (25.4 mm equal 1 in), the hand drill 33.9 mm and the miter box 33.2 mm. Included also are 3 drill bits, a level, and nails.

Small mosaic over 100 years old: this picture of the Colosseum in Rome contains over 2,500 pieces and measures 34 mm x 21 mm.

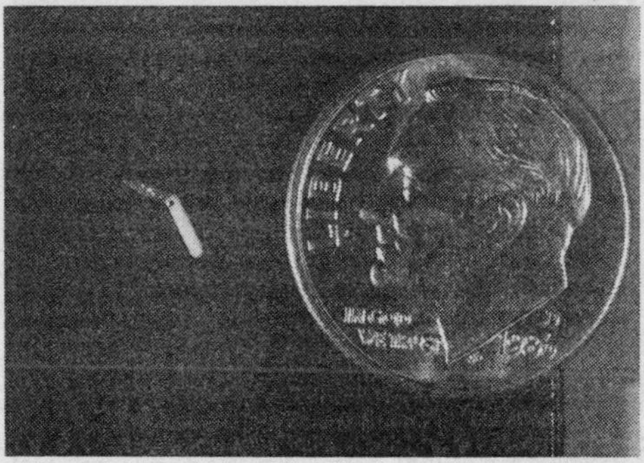

Smallest pocketknife only 5.9 mm long with its 2.6 mm blade extended. All these are on display at Mott Miniatures, Knott's Berry Farm, Buena Park, Calif.

SOAPS. A claim for the largest soap collection from 65 nations comprising 8,000 different bars has been made by Laval Lev Malachi of Phoenix, Ariz.

SPIRITS & LIQUEURS. The largest reported collection of distilled spirits or liqueurs in any bar is 1,722 unduplicated labels collected by Ian Boasman at Bistro French, Preston, Lancashire, Eng, audited in May 1986. The greatest collection of whisky bottles is one of 3,100 unduplicated labels assembled by Sig Edward Giaccone at his Whiskyteca, Salo, Lake Garda, Italy.

TEETH. Brother Giovanni Battista Orsenigo of the Ospedale Fatebenefratelli, Rome, Italy, also a dentist, conserved all the teeth he extracted. In 1903, the number was counted and found to be 2,000,744 teeth, indicating an average of 185 a day. (Also see p. 30.)

WATCHES. Robert Walker of Yakima, Wash, has a collection of 1,920 pocket and wrist watches, saved over 20 years as a hobby, according to Leonard Katz of the "National Enquirer." More watches (the more valuable ones) are in a vault and were not counted with the others in May 1987.

ANTIQUE SALES AT AUCTION

ART COLLECTION. The collection of Robert von Hirsch (1883–1977), German industrialist, which included early medieval sculptures, madonnas, paintings of the masters and modern artists, was sold over a period of 7 days for the highest total ever—$34,110,950 at Sotheby's London in the summer of 1978.

ART NOUVEAU. The highest auction price for any piece of *art nouveau* is $360,000 for a spider-web leaded glass mosaic and bronze table lamp by L. C. Tiffany at Christie's, NYC on Apr 8, 1980.

BABE RUTH MEMORABILIA. A brass circular locker tag, 2⅛ in in diameter, *c.* 1930, inscribed on obverse "Babe Ruth 3," was sold at auction for $7,150, against only a $400 estimate, at Phillips NYC, Nov 7, 1987, auction. The reverse inscription reads, "Yankee Stadium, The Bronx, New York, Locker 3."

BED. A 1930 black lacquer king-size bed made by Jean Durand was auctioned at Christie's, NYC on Oct 2, 1983 for $75,000.

BLANKET. The most expensive blanket was a Navajo Churro handspun serape of *c.* 1852 sold for $115,500 (including premium) at Sotheby's, NYC on Oct 22, 1983.

BOTTLES: The highest price paid at auction for a colored medicine bottle was $13,000 for a sarsaparilla bottle, *c.* 1850, embossed "Wynkoops Sarsaparilla For The Blood ½ Gallon New York," at Harmer Rooke Galleries, NYC on Mar 24, 1988. (See photo.)

CAROUSEL ART. The highest price ever paid at auction for a carousel animal is $35,200 for a large outside row tiger by Charles Looff, Brooklyn, N.Y., *c.* 1900, at Phillips, New York, May 3, 1986. The tiger, 47 in high and 89 in long, has a snarling expression and wears jeweled fancy straps. He had been exhibited at the John and Mable Ringling Museum of Art.

CARPET. In 1946 the Metropolitan Museum of Art, NYC privately

FOUR OF ANDY WARHOL'S COOKIE JARS from the American artist's collection: In all, 175 cookie jars sold for a record $247,000, Apr 16-May 3, 1988 at Sotheby's NYC. The entire 16-session Warhol sale, consisting of more than 2,500 lots of fine arts objects, grossed $25,333,368. An unprecedented 27 experts of Sotheby's were required to catalogue the acquisitions.

HIGHEST PRICE BOTTLE: $13,000 ▲ was paid for this 19th century colored sarsaparilla medicine bottle (the one on the far right) which was found in an old Connecticut farmhouse and sold at auction at Harmer Rooke Galleries, NYC, Mar 24, 1988. It measures 13 in high, 4 5/8 in wide and 2 3/4 in deep. *(Harmer Rooke)*

GLASS FIRE CHIEF'S TRUMPET: This rare cranberry glass, New England-type trumpet sold at auction for $14,300, Mar 5, 1988. *(Robert Skinner Galleries)* ◄

paid $1 million for the 26.5 × 13.6 ft Anhalt Medallion carpet made in Tabriz or Kashan, Persia *c.* 1590. The highest price ever paid at auction for a carpet is £231,000 ($360,000) for a 17th century "Polonaise" silk and metal thread carpet at Sotheby's, London on Oct 13, 1982.

CERAMICS. The Greek urn painted by Euphronios and thrown by Euxitheos in *c.* 530 was bought by private treaty by the Metropolitan Museum of Art, NYC, for $1.3 million in Aug 1972.

CHESS SET. The highest price paid at auction for a chess set (believed to be unique) is $44,000 for a bronze set of 32 playing pieces, ranging in height from 2¾ to 5 in, executed in about 1950 by the noted Italian sculptor Alberto Giacometti (1901–66) at Sotheby's, NYC, May 12, 1987.

CIGARETTE CARDS. The most expensive set was auctioned at Phillips, London for £17,050 ($30,690) on July 30, 1987. It was a complete set of 20 Taddy's Clowns.

CORKSCREW. A 19th-century English-style bronze corkscrew was sold for £4,620 ($6,468) at Sotheby's London on May 29, 1985.

DOLL. The highest price paid at auction for a doll is £67,100 ($107,360) for a rare William and Mary period wooden doll, English, *c.* 1690, 14½ in high at Sotheby's, London, March 24, 1987. It was purchased by Mme Didi Vierny for a planned doll museum in Paris.

DOLLHOUSE. The highest price ever paid for a dollhouse is $256,500 for "Titania's Palace," consisting of 16 rooms, measuring 6 ft high, 12 ft wide and 8 ft deep, at Christie's, London, Jan 10, 1978. This magnificent dollhouse is the work of British miniaturist Sir Neville Wilkinson, who required 15 years to complete the project (1907–22). "Titania's Palace" is lavishly furnished, containing 2,000 miniature works of art, ranging from an array of tiny paintings to a guest book signed by Shirley Temple, Charlie Chaplin and W. B. Yeats. The buyer was "Legoland," the giant family theme park in Billund, Denmark, where the dollhouse may be seen.

DUCK DECOY. The highest price paid at auction for a wooden duck decoy is $319,000 for an A. Elmer Crowell "Preening Pin Tail Drake," *c.* 1915, overall length 18 in, at Richard W. Oliver Galleries, Kennebunk, Maine, July 5, 1986.

EARRINGS. Sotheby's at a 1981 sale sold a pair of diamond ear pendants for $6,647,000.

EMBROIDERED NEEDLEWORK SAMPLER. The highest price paid at auction for an embroidered needlework sampler was $198,000 for a 9 × 10½ in specimen crafted in 1788 by 10-year-old Ruthy Rogers of Marblehead, Mass, at Robert W. Skinner Galleries, Bolton, Mass, on June 6, 1987. Bearing the young artist's name at the bottom, it shows an elaborately clad woman standing beside a fruit tree along with birds and potted flowers.

FIRE BUCKET. The highest price paid at auction for a fire bucket is $9,350 for a painted leather type, 12½ in high, 2-gallon capacity, eastern US, dated 1822, at Robert W. Skinner Galleries, Bolton, Mass., Oct 31, 1987. (See photo.)

FURNITURE. The highest price ever paid for a single piece of furniture is $2,750,000 at Sotheby's, NY on Jan 31, 1987 for a Chippendale carved mahogany wing armchair, *c.* 1770, made by Philadelphia cabinetmaker Thomas Affleck for General John Cadwalader by NY dealer Leigh Keno.

HIGHEST PRICE JEWEL: The highest price paid at auction for any jewel is $7,480,000 paid by a private Saudi Arabian collector, for a 52.59-carat D flawless emerald-cut white diamond at Christie's NYC, on Apr 20, 1988.

HIGHEST PRICED NEEDLEWORK SAMPLER: This embroidered American needlework sampler crafted by a ten-year-old girl in 1788 sold for $198,000 at Robert W. Skinner Galleries, Bolton, Mass, on June 6, 1987.

$9,350 FIRE BUCKET: Sold at a 1987 auction, this 1822 leather 2-gallon bucket features a flaming-house vignette with firemen watching. The handle has been broken off. *(Robert W. Skinner, Inc)*

HIGHEST PRICE SHOES: $165,000 was paid at auction for these "Ruby Slippers" worn by Judy Garland in "The Wizard of Oz" in 1938. The sequined size-6B shoes, created by Gilbert Adrian and produced by the Innes Shoe Co, LA, were sold to an anonymous collector at Christie's East, NYC, June 21, 1988 after a furious 6-min bidding battle. *(Christie's)*

GLASS. The record is £520,000 ($1,040,000) plus premium for a Roman glass cage-cup of *c.* 300 AD measuring 7 in in diameter and 4 in in height, sold at Sotheby's, London, on June 4, 1979 to Robin Symes. It was the highest price paid for any antiquity.

The highest price for a fire chief's trumpet is $14,300 for an extremely rare ornamental cranberry glass type, New England, *c.* 1880, 16¼ inches high, paid at auction at the Robert W. Skinner Galleries, Bolton, Mass, Mar 5, 1988.

HAT. The highest price ever paid for a hat is $66,000 by the Alaska State Museum at a NYC auction in Nov 1981 for a Tlingit Kiksadi ceremonial frog helmet from *c.* 1600.

JADE. The highest price ever paid for an item in jade is $396,000 (including premium) at Sotheby's, NYC on Dec 6, 1983 for a mottled brownish-yellow belt-hook and pendant mask of the Warring States Period of Chinese history.

MECHANICAL TOY. The auction record is £25,500 ($35,700) for a model train set of Stephenson's *Rocket* made by Marklin of Germany in tin plate in 1909 sold at Sotheby's, London on May 29, 1984.

MIRRORS. Twin Chippendale mirrors were sold for £280,000 ($420,000) to Roy Miles, a London dealer, at Christie's, London, on Apr 10, 1986.

MUSICAL BOX. The highest price paid at auction for a musical box is $37,620 (with premium) for a Swiss-made example made for a Persian prince in 1901, sold at Sotheby's, London on Jan 23, 1985.

PAPERWEIGHT. The highest price ever paid for a glass paperweight is $143,000 (including premium) at Sotheby's, NYC on Dec 2, 1983 for a blue glass weight made at Pantin, Paris *post* 1850.

PHOTOGRAPH. The highest price ever paid at auction for a photograph is $104,500 for a signed photo of Abraham Lincoln and son Tad at Sotheby's, Mar 27, 1985 by Malcolm Forbes, Jr.

PISTOL. The highest price paid at auction for a pistol is $242,000 at Christie's NYC on May 14, 1987 for a .45 calibre Colt single-action army revolver, Serial No. 1 for 1873.

PLAYING CARDS. The highest price paid for a deck of playing cards is $143,352 (including premium) by the Metropolitan Museum of Art, NYC, at Sotheby's, London on Dec 6, 1983.

PORCELAIN AND POTTERY. The highest auction price for any ceramic or any Chinese work of art is $2,087,655 (£1,159,864) for a rare copper-red Ming made in the reign of the Chinese Emperor Hongwu between 1368 and 1398. It was bought by an anonymous bidder at Sotheby's Hong Kong on May 17, 1988.

SHOES. The highest price paid at auction for a pair of shoes was $165,000 for the "Ruby Slippers" worn by Judy Garland in the 1939 MGM film "The Wizard of Oz," at Christie's East, NYC, June 21, 1988.

SILVER. The highest price ever paid for a single piece of English silver is £770,000 ($1,232,000) for an *epergne* by de Lamerie sold at Christie's London, by the Earl of Portarlington and bought by Jacques Koopman on Dec 17, 1986. The 100-piece Paul de Lamerie service made for the 7th Earl of Thanet *c.* 1745 was sold by Lord Hothfield at Sotheby's, London on Nov 22, 1984 for £825,000 ($1,031,250).

STAINED GLASS. The largest price paid at auction for any work in stained glass was $528,000 for a 79½-in-high "Magnolia" floor type Tiffany lamp, *c.* 1910, at Christie's, NYC, Dec 15, 1984.

SWORD. The highest price paid for a sword is the £823,045 ($1,316,872) for the Duke of Windsor's Royal Navy Officer's sword (presented to him by King George V in 1913) at Sotheby's, Geneva, Apr 2–3, 1987.

TABLE. A Philadelphia tea table was auctioned at Christie's, NYC, on Jan 25, 1986 for $1,045,000, the highest price ever paid for a piece of American furniture.

> Eric deWilde, a Hollywood, Fla schoolboy, found a bag of diamonds on a railroad track in Mar 1983, partly crushed by train wheels. At Christie's, NYC, on June 20–21, 1984, the found jewels were auctioned off for $350,000. The highest single item was a man's 5.9 carat diamond ring that brought $27,000. DeWilde received all the proceeds from his discovery which came about when he was searching with a flashlight for his missing bicycle.

TAPESTRY. The highest price paid for a tapestry is £550,000 ($1,155,000) for a Swiss medieval tapestry frieze in two parts dated 1468–76 at Sotheby's, Geneva, Switzerland, Apr 10, 1981, by the Basle Historische Museum.

TEDDY BEAR. The highest price paid at auction for a teddy bear is $15,840 (£8,800) for a rare white (actually tan) plush German-made Steiff muzzled teddy bear, *c.* 1913, 20 in high, at Sotheby's London, May 15, 1987. A similar, smaller muzzled Steiff, 18 in high, also broke the previous world teddy bear auction record ($9,152) at Sotheby's by drawing a winning bid of $10,890.

TOY SOLDIERS. The highest price paid for a single toy soldier is £1,200 ($2,160) for an extremely rare 70 mm scale figure of the Colonel-in-Chief, the Welsh Guards at Phillips London on Sept 9, 1987.

TYPEWRITER. The highest price paid for an antique machine is £3,000 ($6,450) for an 1886 Daw and Tait machine auctioned at Sotheby's, London on Dec 12, 1980.

WALKING STICK AND HAT. The highest auction price has been

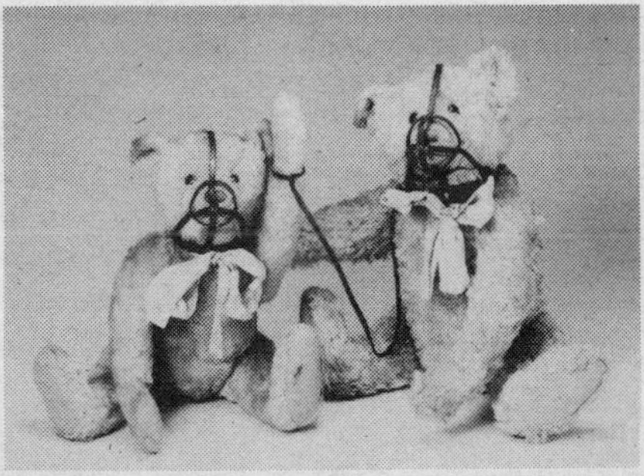

TEDDY BEARS: The bear on the right sold for £8,800 ($15,840 approx) at Sotheby's London, May 15, 1987. At the same auction his little brother (left) sold for £6,050 ($10,890 approx). Both are rare "white" plush Steiff (German-made) teddys, 20 and 18 in tall, respectively.

$151,800 for Charlie Chaplin's cane and hat at Christie's London, Dec 11, 1987.

WEATHERVANE. The highest price paid at auction for a weathervane is $203,500 for a rare locomotive and tender copper weathervane, American, *c.* 1882, at Robert W. Skinner Galleries, Bolton, Mass, Mar 21, 1987. The locomotive, reproduced in fine detail, is mounted on a track with two ball finials at track's end, and attached ball counterweight. The weathervane's overall dimensions are: 17 in high, 61 in long and 8 in deep. This weathervane, installed in 1882 on the Dept Building of the Providence and Worcester Railway in Woonsocket, Rhode Island, was a town landmark until it was removed in the late 1960s, when the building was sold.

3. AGRICULTURE

Origins

It has been estimated that only 21% of the world's land surface is cultivable and that only 7.6% is actually under cultivation. Evidence adduced in 1971 from Nok Nok Tha and Spirit Cave, Thailand tends to confirm plant cultivation and animal domestication were part of the culture *c.* 11,000 BC. Goats were herded on Mt Carmel, Palestine (now Israel) as early as 16,000 BC, and were domesticated at Asiab, Iran by *c.* 8050 BC. Dogs were domesticated at Star Carr, Yorkshire, Eng by *c.* 7700 BC. The earliest definite date for sheep is *c.* 7200 BC at Argissa-Magula, Thessaly, Greece, and for pig and cattle *c.* 7000 BC at the same site. The earliest date certain for horse is *c.* 4350 BC from Dereivka, Ukraine, USSR.

Farms

The largest farms are collective farms in the USSR. These have been reduced in number from 235,500 in 1940 to only 18,000 in 1980, and have been increased in size so that units of over 60,000 acres are not uncommon.

The pioneer farm of Laucidio Coelho near Campo Grande, Mato Grosso, Brazil, *c.* 1901 was 3,358 sq mi (2,150,000 acres) with 250,000 head of cattle at the time of his death in 1975.

Largest Chicken Ranch

The largest chicken ranch is the Croton Egg Farm, Croton, Ohio, which has 4.8 million hens laying some 3.7 million eggs daily.

Largest Turkey Farm

The largest turkey farm is that of Bernard Matthews Ltd, centered at Great Witchingham, Norfolk, Eng, with 2,500 workers tending 8,000,000 turkeys.

Largest Cattle Station

The largest cattle station is the Anna Creek station of 11,626.8 sq mi, S Australia, owned by the Kidman family. The biggest component is Strangway at 5,449 sq mi. Until 1915 the Victoria River Downs Station, Northern Territory, was over three times larger, with an area of 22,400,000 acres (35,000 sq mi).

Largest Sheep Station

The largest sheep station in area is Commonwealth Hill, in the northwest of South Australia. It grazes between 60,000 and 70,000 sheep, about 700 cattle and 54,000 *uninvited* kangaroos, in an area of 4,080 sq mi.

The head count on Sir William Stevenson's 30,000-acre Lochinver Station in New Zealand was 117,500 on Jan 1, 1983 on 21,000 acres.

The largest sheep move on record occurred when 27 horsemen moved a mob of 43,000 sheep 40 miles from Barcaldine to Beaconsfield Station, Queensland, Australia, in 1886.

Largest Community Garden

The largest community garden project is that operated by the City Beautiful Council and the Benjamin Wegerzyn Garden Center at Dayton, O. It comprises 1,173 allotments each of 812 sq ft.

Largest Piggery

The largest piggery is at the Sljeme pig unit in Yugoslavia, which is able to process 300,000 pigs in a year.

Mushroom Farm

The largest mushroom farm is Moonlight Mushrooms, Inc, founded in 1937 in a disused limestone mine near West Winfield, Pa. It has over 900 employees working underground, in a maze of galleries 110 miles long, producing 23,000 tons of mushrooms per year.

Multiple Births (Livestock)

A cow named "Lyubik" gave birth to 7 calves at Mogilev, USSR, it was reported on Apr 25, 1964. Five live and one dead calf were recorded from a Friesian at Te Puke, New Zealand, July 27, 1980, but none survived. A case of 5 live calves at one birth was reported in 1928 by T. G. Yarwood of Manchester, England. The lifetime prolificacy record is 39 by "Big Bertha," owned by Jerome O'Leary of Blackwaterbridge, Co Kerry, Ireland. A Danish black and white bull named "Soender Jylland's Jens" left 220,000 surviving progeny by artificial insemination when put to sleep aged 11 in Copenhagen in Sept 1978.

The highest recorded number of piglets in one litter is 36 of which only one was lost at the age of one month and 35 survived to adulthood. A 3-year-old sow named "Old Faithful" on the farm of Lloyd Hofmeyer, south of Sanborn, Iowa, farrowed the litter Apr 17–20, 1965. It was her 4th litter, and she weighed 1,000 lb just before giving birth.

A case of 8 lambs at a birth was reported by D. T. Jones of Priory Farm, Gwent, Wales, in June 1956, and by Ken Towse of Buckton, Eng, in Mar 1981 but none lived. A case of a sheep living to 26 years was recorded in flock book records by H. Poole, Wexford, Ireland. Many cases of sextuplet lambs have been reported.

Egg-Laying

The highest authenticated rate of egg-laying is by a white leghorn chicken hen, # 2988 at the College of Agriculture, Univ of Missouri, with 371 eggs in 364 days in an official test, conducted by Prof Harold V. Biellier, ending on Aug 29, 1979.

The heaviest egg *reported* is one of 16 oz with double yolk and double shell, laid by a white leghorn at Vineland, NJ, Feb 25, 1956. The largest *recorded* was one of "nearly 12 oz" for a 5-yolked egg 12¼ in around the long axis and 9 in around the shorter axis laid by a Black Minorca at Mr Stafford's Damsteads Farm, Mellor, Lancashire, England in 1896.

The highest claim for the number of yolks in a chicken's egg is 9 reported by Mrs Diane Hainsworth of Hainsworth Poultry Farms, Mt Morris, NY, in July 1971 and also from a hen in Kirghizia, USSR in Aug 1977.

The white goose "Speckle" owned by Donny Brandenberg of Goshen, Ohio, on May 3, 1977 laid a 24-oz egg measuring 13½ × 9½ in in circumferences.

An Aylesbury duck laid 457 eggs in 463 days including an unbroken run of 375 in 375 days before dying on Feb 7, 1986. The duck belonged to Annette and Angela Butler of Princes Risborough, Bucks, Eng.

Crop Yields

A yield of 370 bushels of corn from an acre, was achieved by Herman Warsaw of Saybrook, Ill (McLean County) in 1985, according to the Farm Journal.

The highest recorded yield for sugar beet is 62.4 tons per acre by Andy Christensen and Jon Giannini in the Salinas Valley, California.

The greatest number of US barrels of potatoes picked in a 9½ hr day is 235 by Walter Sirois (b 1917) of Caribou, Maine, on Sept 30, 1950.

Plowing in 24 Hours

The greatest recorded acreage plowed in 24 hours is 156.74 acres achieved with a 6-furrow plow to a depth of 9 in. The plower was C.M. van den Heever in Potgietersrus, S Africa, Jan 8–9, 1988. He used a 158-hp Fiat 160/90 DT tractor.

Milk Yields

The highest recorded world lifetime yield of cows' milk is 465,224 lb by the cow named #289, a Holstein Friesian (b Sept 6, 1964) (d May 1, 1984), owned by Manuel Maciel & Son, Hanford, Calif.

The greatest recorded yield for one lactation (365 days) is 55,661 lb by the Holstein "Beecher Arlinda Ellen" owned by Mr and Mrs Harold L. Beecher of Rochester, Ind in 1975. The highest reported milk yield in a day is 241 lb by "Urbe Blanca" in Cuba on or about Jan 23, 1982.

The record for hand milking was set by Andy Faust at Collinsville, Okla, in 1937 when he achieved 120 gallons in 12 hr.

The highest recorded milk yield for any goat is 7,714 lb in 365 days

WILD BOAR RACE: "Kloten-Joe II," the winner of the 100-meter pig sprint set a record of 11 sec in Hamburg, W Germany, Apr, 29, 1984. His trainer, Willi Seiker is encouraging him to stay in the lane, as 4,000 spectators also cheer the animals on.

by "Osory Snow-Goose" owned by Mr and Mrs G. Jameson of Leppington, NSW, Australia in 1977. A 15-year-old goat owned by Mrs Nanbui Meghani of Bhuj, Gujarat, India, was reported in Nov 1984 to have lactated continuously for 12 years.

Butter Fat Yield

The world record lifetime yield is 16,370 lb by the US Holstein "Breezewood Patsy Bar Pontiac" in 3,979 days. Her lactation record for 365 days of 2,230 lb was reported on Oct 8, 1976.

Cheese

The most active cheese-eaters are the people of France, with an annual average in 1983 of 43.6 lb per person. The biggest producer is the US with a factory production of 4,773,500,000 lb in 1980.

The largest cheese ever made was a cheddar of 34,591 lb, made in 43 hours, Jan 20–22, 1964, for the Wisconsin Cheese Foundation by Steve Siudzinski of Langes Corners, Wis, for exhibition at the NY World's Fair. It was transported in a specially designed 45-ft-long refrigerated tractor trailer "Cheese-Mobile."

Heaviest Cattle, Pigs, Sheep, and Goats

Of heavyweight cattle the heaviest on record was a Holstein-Durham cross named "Mount Katahdin" exhibited by A. S. Rand of Maine, 1906–10 and frequently weighed at an even 5,000 lb. He was 6 ft 2 in at the shoulder with a 13 ft girth and died in a barn fire *c.* 1923.

The highest recorded birthweight for a calf is 225 lb from a British Friesian cow at Rockhouse Farm, Swansea, Wales, in 1961. A calf of 270 lb was born dead from a Holstein who gave birth by Caesarean section on May 28, 1986 at Simitar Farms, Henryetta, Okla, belonging to Mrs. Sherlene O'Brien.

The heaviest hog recorded was the Poland-China hog "Big Bill" of 2,552 lb measuring 9 ft long with a belly on the ground, owned by Burford Butler of Jackson, Tenn, and chloroformed in 1933. Raised by W. J. Chappall, he was mounted and displayed in Weakely County, Tenn until 1946.

The highest recorded birthweight for a lamb is 38 lb at Clearwater, Sedgwick County, Kansas, in 1975, but neither this lamb nor the ewe survived. A lamb of the same weight was born on Apr 7, 1975 in Howard, SD, but died soon after. The heaviest sheep ever recorded was an old Leicester (Eng) Longwool ram which scaled 472 lb.

The largest goat ever recorded was a British Saanen named "Mostyn Moorcock," owned by Pat Robinson of Ewyas Harold, Herefordshire, Eng, which reached a weight of 400 lb (shoulder height 44 in and overall length 66 in). He died in 1977 aged 4 years. Some pygmy goats only weigh 33–44 lb.

Sheep Shearing

The highest recorded speed for sheep shearing in a working day was that of John Fagan, who machine-sheared 804 lambs (average 89.3 per hour) in 9 hours at Hantoru Rd, Pio Pio, New Zealand, on Dec 8, 1980. The hand-shearing (solo blade) record for a 9-hour day is 353 lambs by Peter Casserly of Christchurch, New Zealand, Feb 13, 1976.

In a shearing marathon, 4 men machine-sheared 2,519 sheep in 24 hours at Stewarts Trust, Waikia, Southland, New Zealand, on Feb 11, 1982.

Mr Lavor Taylor (b Feb 27, 1896) of Ephraim, Utah claims to have sheared 515,000 sheep to May 1984.

Turkey Plucking

Vincent Pilkington of Cootehill, County Cavan, Ireland, killed and plucked 100 turkeys in 7 hours 32 min on Dec 15, 1978. His record for a single turkey is 1 min 30 sec on RTE Television in Dublin on Nov 17, 1980.

Joe Glaub (US) killed 7,300 turkeys in a "working" day on May 23, 1983. Mrs Madge Colenso gutted 94 turkeys in 60 min at Rivington Farm, Burstow, Surrey, Eng, on Dec 20, 1984.

Chicken Plucking

The record time for plucking chickens clean was set in the 1976 championship contest at Masaryktown, Fla, Oct 9, when a team of 4 women (Doreena Cary, Diane Grieb, Kathy Roads and Dorothy McCarthy) plucked 12 birds naked in 32.9 sec.

Ernest Hausen (1877–1955) of Fort Atkinson, Wisc, died undefeated after 33 years as a champion. On Jan 19, 1939 he was timed for one chicken at 4.4 sec, and reportedly twice did 3.5 sec a few years later.

Leaving a single feather produces the cry "Fowl!"

Largest Vineyard

The largest vineyard extends over the Mediterra-nean façade between the Rhone and the Pyrenees in the départements (provinces) of Aude, Hérault, Gard and Pyrénées-Orientales. It has an area of 2,075,685 acres of which 52.3% is *monoculture viticole*.

Largest Rice Farm

The largest contiguous wild rice (*Zizania aquatica*) farm is Clearwater Rice Inc at Clearbrook, Minn with 2,000 acres. In 1986 it yielded 577,000 lb.

Largest Wheat Field

The largest single fenced field sown with wheat was one of 35,000 acres, sown in 1951 near Lethbridge, Alberta, Canada.

Largest Hop Field

The largest hop field is one of 1,912 acres near Toppenish, Wash, owned by John I. Haas, Inc, the world's largest hop growers, with hop farms in Calif, Ida, Ore and Wash with a total area of 4,199 acres.

LIVESTOCK SALES RECORDS

Note: Some exceptionally high livestock auction sales are believed to result from collusion. Others are marketing and publicity exercises with little relation to true market prices.

Bull

The highest price ever paid for a bull is $2,500,000 for the beefalo (a ⅜ bison, ⅜ charolais, ¼ Hereford) "Joe's Pride" sold by D. C. Basolo of Burlingame, Calif to the Beefalo Cattle Co of Canada, of Calgary, Alberta, on Sept 9, 1974.

Cow

The highest price ever paid for a cow is $1.3 million for the Holstein "Mist," purchased by a syndicate at an auction in E Montpelier, Vt, on July 13, 1985. She had had 14 pregnancies.

Sheep

The highest price ever paid for a ram is $A79,000 (about $73,500) by the Gnowangerup Animal Breeding Centre, Western Australia for a Merino ram from the Colinsvale Stud, Mount Bryan, South Australia, at the Royal Adelaide Show on Sept 10, 1981.

The highest price ever paid for wool is $A320 per kg greasy for a bale of Tasmania superfine at the wool auction in Tasmania, Australia on Feb 25, 1988 by Fujii Keori Ltd of Osaka, Japan, top bidders since 1973.

Pig

The highest price ever paid for a pig is $56,000 for a cross-bred barrow named "Bud," owned by Jeffrey Roemisch of Hermleigh, Tex, and bought by E. A. "Bud" Olson and Phil Bonzio on Mar 5, 1985.

Horse

The highest price for a draught horse is $47,500 paid for the 7-year-old Belgian stallion "Farceur" by E. G. Good at Cedar Falls, Iowa Oct 16, 1917.

Goat

An angora goat was sold for £14,700 ($26,460) at a sale at Longhope, Gloucestershire, Eng on May 23, 1987.

Chapter 10

The Human World

1. POLITICAL AND SOCIAL

The land area of the earth is estimated at about 57,267,400 sq mi (including inland waters), or 29.08% of the world's surface area.

Largest Political Division

The British Commonwealth of Nations, a free association of 49 sovereign independent states and 27 non-sovereign states and dependencies, covers an area of 13,095,000 sq mi with a population which in 1980 surpassed 1,000 million.

COUNTRIES

The world comprises 170 sovereign countries and 59 separately administered non-sovereign territories, making 229. The United Nations still list the *de jure* territories of East Timor (now incorporated into Indonesia), Western Sahara (now in Morocco) and the uninhabited Canton and Enderbury Islands (now disputed between the US and Kiribati) but do not list the three Baltic States of Estonia, Latvia and Lithuania though their forcible incorporation into the USSR in 1940 has never been internationally recognized. Neither do they list the *de facto* territories of Taiwan, Mayotte or Spanish North Africa, the 4 Antarctic Territories or the Australian Territory of Coral Sea Islands and Heard and McDonald Islands.

Largest Country

The country with the greatest area is the Union of Soviet Socialist Republics (the Soviet Union), comprising 15 Union (constituent) Republics with a total area of 8,648,500 sq mi, or 15% of the world's total land area, and a total coastline (including islands) of 66,090 miles. The country measures 5,580 miles from east to west and 2,790 miles from north to south. Its population on Jan 1, 1987 was 281,700,000.

Smallest Country

The smallest independent country is the State of the Vatican City,

SMALLEST MARITIME SOVEREIGN NATION is Monaco, to the south of France, crowded with buildings, piers and 38,179 people per sq mi but with only 3½ mi of shoreline.

which was made an enclave within the city of Rome, Feb 11, 1929. The enclave has an area of 108.7 acres (0.17 sq mi).

The maritime sovereign country with the shortest coastline is Monaco with 3.49 miles excluding piers and breakwaters.

The world's smallest republic is Nauru, less than 1 degree south of the equator in the Western Pacific. It became independent on Jan 31, 1968, has an area of 5,263 acres (8.2 sq mi) and a population of 8,100 (latest estimate, mid-1986).

The smallest colony in the world is Gibraltar (since 1969, the City of Gibraltar), with an area of 2½ sq mi. However, Pitcairn Island, the only inhabited (55 people at Dec 31, 1986) island of a group of 4 (total area 18½ sq mi), has an area of 1½ sq mi, or 960 acres.

The official residence, since 1834, of the Grand Master of the Order of the Knights of Malta, totaling 3 acres and comprising the Villa del Priorato di Malta on the lowest of Rome's seven hills (the 151-ft Aventine) retains certain diplomatic privileges as does 68 Via Condotti. The order has accredited representatives to foreign governments. Hence, it is sometimes cited as the smallest "state" in the world.

Flattest and Most Elevated Countries

The country with the lowest highest point is the Republic of the Maldives, which attains 8 ft above sea level. The country with the highest lowest point is Lesotho. The egress of the Senqu (Orange) riverbed is 4,530 ft above sea level.

Frontiers

The country with the most land frontiers is China, with 13—Mongolia, USSR, N Korea, Hong Kong, Macau, Vietnam, Laos,

Burma, India, Bhutan, Nepal, Pakistan, and Afghanistan. These extend for 14,900 mi. France, if all her *Départements d'outre-mer* are included, may, if her territorial waters are extended, have 20 frontiers.

The longest *continuous* frontier is between Canada and the US, which (including the Great Lakes boundaries) extends for 3,987 miles (excluding 1,538 miles with Alaska).

The frontier which is crossed most frequently is that between the US and Mexico. It extends for 1,933 miles and has more than 120 million crossings every year. The Sino-Soviet frontier, broken by the Sino-Mongolian border, extends for 4,500 miles with no reported figures of crossings.

The "frontier" of the Holy See (Vatican City) in Rome measures 2.53 miles. The land frontier between Gibraltar and Spain at La Linea, closed in June 1969 and reopened at midnight, Feb 4–5, 1985, measures 1,672 yd. Zambia, Zimbabwe, Botswana and Namibia (South West Africa) almost merge.

Most Impenetrable Boundary

The 858-mile-long "Iron Curtain," dividing the Federal Republican (West) and the Democratic Republican (East) parts of Germany, utilizes 2,230,000 land mines and 50,000 miles of barbed wire, in addition to many watchtowers containing detection devices. The whole 270-yd-wide strip occupies 133 sq mi of E German territory and costs an estimated $7 billion to build and maintain. It reduced the westward flow from more than 200,000 in 1961 to a trickle of 30 (including 8 guards in 1985). The death toll has been 184 since 1962. Construction of the second wall began in E Berlin in Mar 1984.

Most Populous Country

The largest population of any country is that of China, which in *pinyin* is written Zhongguo (central land). The census of July 1982 was 1,008,175,288 (excluding Taiwan, Hong Kong and Macau), while the 1984 population stood at 1,036,004,000. The rate of natural increase in the People's Republic of China is now estimated to be 38,700 a day or 14.1 million per year. The mid-year 1987 estimate is 1,053.7 million. The census required 5,100,000 enumerators to work for 10 days. India is set to overtake China during the next century.

Least Populous State

The independent state with the smallest population is the Vatican City or the Holy See (see *Smallest Country*), with 750 inhabitants in mid-1986, and a zero birth rate.

Most Densely Populated Places

The most densely populated territory is the Portuguese province of Macau (or Macao), on the southern coast of China. It has an estimated population of 342,000 (mid-1985) in an area of 6.2 sq mi, giving a density of 63,225 per sq mi.

Of countries over 1,000 sq mi, the most densely populated is Bangladesh with a population of 103,200,000 (1986) living in 55,126 sq mi at a density of 1,882 per sq mi.

The Indonesian island of Java (with an area of 48,763 sq mi) had a population of 91,271,000 (1986) giving a density of 1,871 per sq mi.

Of territories with an area of approximately 400 sq mi, Hong Kong (400.5 sq mi) contains 5,533,000 people (1986) giving the territory a density of 13,390 per sq mi. Hong Kong is now the most populous of all colonies. The name "Hong Kong" is the transcription of the local pronunciation of the Peking dialect version of Xiang gang (a port for incense). The 1976 by-census showed that the west area of the urban district of Mong Kok on the Kowloon Peninsula had a density of 652,910 people per sq mi. In 1959, at the peak of the housing crisis in Hong Kong, it was reported that in one house designed for 12 people the number of occupants was 459, including 104 in one room and 4 living on the roof.

Populations

The daily increase in the world's population is 237,400, or 158 per minute. For past, present and future estimates, see table.

WORLD POPULATION—PROGRESSIVE ESTIMATES

Date	*Millions*	*Date*	*Millions*
10000 BC	*c.* 5	1960	3,049
1 AD	*c.* 200	1970	3,704
1000	*c.* 275	1975	4,033
1250	375	1980	4,432
1500	420	1981	4,508
1650	550–600	1982	4,586
1700	615	1983	4,465
1750	720	1984	4,763
1800	900	1985	4,837
1900	1,625	1986	4,917
1920	1,862	1987(*mid*)	5,000*
1930	2,070	2000	6,122
1940	2,295	2025	8,206
1950	2,513	2100	10,500

NOTE: The UN publication "State of World Population, 1984" forecast that the world population will not stabilize until 2095 at *c.* 10,500 million but will reach 6,100 million by Dec 31, 2000.

The all-time peak annual increase of 2.0% *c.* 1958–1962 had declined to 1.73% by 1975–1980. By 1990 this should decline to 1.5%. This, however, produces an annual increment of 83 million peaking to 90 million in the 1990's. The French demographer Biraben has calculated that 58,800 million people died between 40,000 BC and 1980 AD. This indicates that there have thus been some 63,700 million specimens of *Homo sapiens sapiens* who have ever lived.

*Population Institute of Wash, DC, declared its landmark was reached on July 7, 1986, whereas the UN "medium" prediction was for Mar 1987.

Most Sparsely Populated Territory

Antarctica became permanently occupied by relays of scientists as of Oct 1956. The population varies seasonally and reaches 2,000 at times.

The least populated territory, apart from Antarctica, is Kalaallit Nunaat (formerly Greenland), with a population of 53,406 (1986) in an area of 840,000 sq mi, giving a density of one person to every 15.12 sq mi. Some 84.3% of the island comprises an ice cap.

CITIES

Most Populous City

The most populous "urban agglomeration" in the world is the Tokyo-Yokohama Metropolitan Area, of 1,081 sq mi, containing an estimated 29,002,000 people in 1981. The municipal population of Tokyo in 1985 was 11,903,900. The population of the metropolitan area of Greater Mexico City in 1985 was published as 17,321,800 with the city proper at 10,499,000 (1984 est).

Oldest City

The oldest known walled town is Jericho (Ariha), about 5 miles north of the Dead Sea. Radio-carbon dating on specimens from the lowest levels reached by archeologists indicate habitation there by perhaps 3,000 people as early as 7800 BC. The settlement of Dolni Vestonice, Czechoslovakia has been dated to the Gravettian culture *c.* 27,000 BC. The oldest capital city in the world is Dimashq (Damascus), capital of Syria. It has been continuously inhabited since *c.* 2500 BC.

Elevations of Cities, Capitals and Dwellings

The highest capital city, before the domination of Tibet by China, was Lhasa, at an elevation of 12,087 ft above sea level. La Paz, the administrative and *de facto* capital of Bolivia, stands at an altitude of 11,916 ft above sea level. Its El Alto airport is at 13,385 ft. The city was founded in 1548 by Capt Alonso de Mendoza on the site of an Indian village named Chuquiapu. It was originally called Ciudad de Nuestra Señora de La Paz (City of Our Lady of Peace), but in 1825 was renamed La Paz de Ayacucho, its present official name. Sucre, the legal capital of Bolivia, stands at 9,301 ft above sea level.

The new town of Wenchuan, founded in 1955 on the Chinghai-Tibet road, north of the Tangla Range, is the highest at 16,732 ft above sea level.

The settlement of Ein Bokek, which has a synagogue on the shores of the Dead Sea, is the lowest town in the world at 1,291 ft below sea level.

Largest Town in Area

The largest town in area is Mount Isa, Queensland, Australia. The area administered by the City Council is 15,822 sq mi.

Most Remote Town from Sea

The town most remote from the sea is Urumqi (formerly Tihwa,

Sinkiang), capital of the Uighur Autonomous Region of China, at a distance of about 1,400 miles from the nearest coastline. Its population was estimated to be 320,000 in 1974.

HIGHEST CAPITAL CITY: La Paz, the administrative capital of Bolivia, is 11,916 ft up in the Andes, and its airport is 1,469 ft still higher up. The highest lake in the world, Titicaca, is only 30 mi away. *(Tony Morrison)*

Emigration

More people emigrate from Mexico than from any other country. An estimated 800,000 emigrated illegally into the US in 1976 alone. The Soviet invasion of Afghanistan in Dec 1979 caused an influx of 2,725,000 refugees mainly into Pakistan.

The most patient "refusenik" was a USSR citizen who had waited 20½ years for an exit visa. Benjamin Bogomolny (b Apr 7, 1946) first applied in 1966. He arrived in Vienna on Oct 14, 1986. Vladimar Stefak (b Oct 29, 1927) is the new champion, having waited since June 1970.

Immigration

The country which regularly receives the most legal immigrants is the US. It has been estimated that in the period 1820–1985, the US received 52,520,358 *official* immigrants. One immigrant in every 24 in the US is, however, an *illegal* immigrant. In 1986, US patrols on the Mexican border arrested 629,000 aliens.

Birth Rate

The highest estimated by the UN is 55.1 per 1,000 for Kenya in 1980–85. The rate for the whole world was 29.0 per 1,000 in 1984. A worldwide survey published in July 1985 showed no country with a rising birth rate, the last being Nepal in 1981. Excluding Vatican City, where the rate is negligible, the lowest recorded rate is 9.3 per 1,000 (1985) for San Marino.

Death Rate

The rate for the whole world was 11.0 per 1,000 in 1984. The highest of the latest available recorded death rates is 40 deaths per 1,000 of the population in Kampuchea (Cambodia) (1975–80). The lowest of the latest available recorded rates is 3 deaths per 1,000 in Tonga in 1853.

Natural Increase

The rate of natural increase for the whole world is estimated to be 29.0 − 11.0 = 18.0 per 1,000 in 1984, compared with a peak 22 per 1,000 in 1965. The highest of the latest available recorded rates is 55.1 − 14.0 = 41.1 in Kenya in 1980–85.

The lowest rate of natural increase in any major independent country is W Germany with a negative figure of − 1.9 per 1,000 for 1985 (9.6 births and 11.5 deaths).

Sex Ratio

There were estimated to be 1,006.7 men in the world for every 1,000 women (1981). The country with the largest recorded shortage of males is the USSR, with 1,132.1 females to every 1,000 males (1985 census). The country with the largest recorded woman shortage is Pakistan, with 906 to every 1,000 males in 1981. The figures are, however, probably under-enumerated due to *purdah*, a policy that keeps women from appearing in public.

Marriage Ages

The country with the lowest average age for marriage is India, with 20.0 years for males and 14.5 for females. At the other extreme is Ireland, with 26.8 for males and 24.7 for females. In the People's Republic of China, the *recommended* age for marriage for men has been 28 and for women 25.

Divorces

The country with the most divorces is the US with a total of 1,187,000 in 1985—a rate of 48.94% of the then current annual total of marriages. The all-time high was reached in 1981—1,213,000 or 49.75%.

Infant Mortality

Based on deaths before one year of age, the lowest of the latest available recorded rates is 5.0 deaths per 1,000 live births in Tonga in 1985. The world rate in 1987 was 80 per 1,000 live births.

The highest infant mortality rate recently estimated is *c*. 200 per 1,000 for Djibouti.

In Ethiopia the infant mortality rate was unofficially estimated to be nearly 550 per 1,000 live births in 1969.

Life Expectation

World expectation of life is rising from 47.4 years (1950–55) to 64.5 years (1995–2000). There is evidence that life expectation in Britain in the 5th century AD was 33 years for males and 27 years for females. In the decade 1890–1900 the expectation of life among the population of India was 23.7 years.

Based on the latest available data, the highest recorded expectation of life at age 12 months is 74.54 years for males in Japan and 80.18 years for females (1985).

The lowest recorded expectation of life at birth is 36.6 for males and 37.3 for females in Afghanistan.

STANDARDS OF LIVING

Housing

For comparison, a dwelling unit is defined as a structurally separated room or rooms occupied by private households of one or more persons and having separate access or a common passageway to the street. The country with the greatest recorded number of occupied dwelling units was India, which had 100,251,000 in 1972 and 142,954,921 in 1981.

Hospitals

The largest hospital is the Pilgrim State Hospital, a mental hospital at West Brentwood, LI, NY, with 3,618 beds. It formerly contained 14,200 beds.

The busiest maternity hospital in the world has been the Mama Yemo Hospital in Kinshasa, Zaïre, with 41,930 deliveries in 1976.

The record "birthquake" occurred on one day in May 1976 with 175 babies born. It had 599 beds.

The largest psychiatric institute is at UCLA.

The longest stay in a hospital occurred when Martha Nelson was admitted to the Columbus State Institute for the Feeble-Minded in Ohio in 1875, and stayed until she died in Jan 1975, aged 103 years 6 months, in the Orient State Institution, Ohio, spending more than 99 years in institutions.

Physicians

The country with the most physicians is the USSR, with 831,300, or one to every 307 persons. China had an estimated 1.4 million paramedical personnel known as "barefoot doctors" by 1981.

Nine children (4 sons and 5 daughters) of Dr Antonio B Vicencio of Los Angeles qualified as physicians, 1964–82. Henry Lewis Lutterloh and Elizabeth Grantham of Chatham County, NC, were the grandparents of 19 medical doctors. From 1850 to 1962 they practiced a total of 704 man-years.

Psychiatrists and Psychologists

The country with the most psychiatrists is the US. The registered membership of the American Psychiatric Association (inst. 1894) was 32,000 in 1985. The membership of the American Psychological Association (inst. 1892) was 60,000 in 1986.

Dentists

The country with the most dentists is the US, where 140,000 were registered members of the American Dental Association in 1986.

GOVERNMENT

Oldest Ruling House

The Emperor of Japan, Hirohito (b Apr 29, 1901), is the 124th in line from the first Emperor, Jimmu Tenno or Zinmu, whose reign was traditionally from 660 to 581 BC, but probably from *c.* 40 to *c.* 10 BC. He has been Emperor since Dec 25, 1926, and is currently the world's longest reigning and oldest monarch.

Longest Reigns

The longest recorded reign of any monarch is that of Pepi (Phiops) II, a Sixth Dynasty Pharaoh of ancient Egypt. His reign began in *c.* 2281 BC when he was aged 6, and is believed to have lasted *c.* 94 years.

Minhti, king of Arakan (Burma) is reputed to have reigned for 95 years between 1279 and 1374.

Musoma Kanijo, chief of the Nzega district of western Tanganyika (now part of Tanzania), reputedly reigned for more than 98 years from 1864, when aged 8, until his death on Feb 2, 1963.

The longest reign of any European monarch was that of Afonso I Henrigues of Portugal. He ascended the throne first as a count and then as king on Apr 30, 1112 and died on Dec 6, 1185 after a reign of 73 years 220 days.

Shortest Reign

The Crown Prince Luis Filipe of Portugal was mortally wounded at the time that his father was killed by a bullet, which severed his carotid artery, in the streets of Lisbon on Feb 1, 1908. He was thus technically King of Portugal (Dom Luis III) for about 20 minutes.

Youngest King and Queen

The youngest king is King Mswati III of Swaziland, who was crowned on Apr 25, 1986, age 18. He was the 67th son of King Subhusa II. The youngest queen is Margrethe II of Denmark (b Apr 16, 1940).

Most Prolific Monarchs

The most prolific monogamous "royals" have been Prince Hartmann of Liechtenstein (1613–86) who had 24 children, of whom 21 were born alive, by Countess Elisabeth zu Salm-Reifferscheidt (1623–88). HRH Duke Roberto I of Parma (1848–1907) also had 24 children, but by two wives.

British Royalty

The longest reign was that of Queen Victoria (reigned 1837–1901), 63 years 216 days. She lived 81 years 243 days. King George III (reigned 1760–1820) was the longest reigning king, 59 years 96 days.

The shortest reign was 13 days, July 6–19, 1553, by Jane (Lady Jane Grey) who was beheaded soon after at the age of 17. She is known as the "9-day Queen" because she delayed her acceptance of the allegiance of the Lords of the Council until July 9 and wasn't actually proclaimed queen until July 10, 1553.

The king with the most legitimate children was Edward I (reigned 1272–1307), known as Longshanks, who had 18. King Henry I (b 1068–d 1135), in addition to having 1 (possibly 2) legitimate son(s) and a daughter, had at least 20 bastard children (9 sons, 11 daughters) and possibly 22 by 6 mistresses. Queen Anne (b 1665–d 1714) had 17 pregnancies, but produced only 5 live births.

The most married ruler was Henry VIII (reigned 1509–47) who married 6 times.

For the period Oct 30, 1683 to Feb 6, 1685, there were 7 English monarchs living simultaneously. George II had just been born, Charles II was still alive, as were James II, William and Mary, Anne, George I, and also Richard Cromwell, who had been Head of State 1658–59, and who lived under the alias John Clarke until 1712.

Highest-Paid Legislators

The most highly paid of all the world's legislators are members of the US Congress, who from Jan 1, 1986 receive $75,000 in salary, plus honoraria of $20,940. In addition, up to $1,021,167 per year is allowed for office help, with a salary limit of $50,000 for any one staff member per year (limited to 16). Besides, Senators are authorized up to $143,000 per year, depending on the state, for an Official Office Expense Account from which are paid official travel expenses, telegrams, long-distance telephone calls, air-mail postage, stationery, subscriptions to newspapers, and office expenses in the home state.

When abroad they have access to "counterpart funds." They also are entitled to very low charges for filming, speech and radio transcriptions, and beauty treatments (females only).

The President of the US has a salary of $200,000 taxable plus $170,000 non-taxable for travel or entertainment and a lifetime pension of $69,630 per annum.

Largest Legislature

The largest legislative assembly is the National People's Congress of the People's Republic of China. The Congress which convened in June 1983 had 2,978 members.

Constitutions

The world's oldest constitution is that of the US ratified by the necessary Ninth State (New Hampshire) on June 21, 1788 and declared to be in effect on Mar 4, 1789. The only countries without one-document constitutions are Israel, Libya, New Zealand, Oman, and the United Kingdom.

Longest UN Speech

The longest speech made in the UN was one of 4 hours 29 min by the president of Cuba, Fidel Castro Ruz (b Aug 13, 1927) on Sept 26, 1960.

Most Roll Calls Attended

Senator William Proxmire (Democrat, Wis) since Apr 1966 did not miss a single one of the 9,695 roll calls to Aug 27, 1987, whereas the average Senator missed 950.

Filibusters

The longest continuous speech in the history of the US Senate was that of Senator Wayne Morse of Oregon, Apr 24–25, 1953, when he spoke on the Tidelands Oil Bill for 22 hours 26 min without resuming his seat. Senator Strom Thurmond, Democrat (SC), spoke against the Civil Rights Bill for 24 hours 19 min, Aug 28–29, 1957, interrupted only briefly by the swearing-in of a new Senator.

The record for a filibuster in any US legislature is 43 hours by Texas State Senator Bill Meier from Euless, who spoke against nondisclosure of industrial accidents in May 1977.

Oldest Treaty

The Anglo-Portuguese Treaty of Alliance was signed in London 614 years ago on June 16, 1373. The text was confirmed "with my usual flourish" by John de Banketre, Clerk.

First Female Elected Head of State

President Vigdis Finnbogadottir (b 1930) of Iceland became the first democratically elected female head of state on June 30, 1980 and took office on Aug 1, 1980.

LARGEST ELECTION: 379 million people voted in 1984 in India at 480,000 polling places, choosing from among 5,301 candidates. *(Rex Feature)*

First to Allow Female Vote

Wyoming, while still a Territory in 1869, allowed women suffrage. New Zealand allowed women to vote in 1893.

Longest Term of Office

The longest serving current prime minister is Lee Kuan Yew (b Sept 16, 1923) of Singapore who started his 28th year in office on June 5, 1986.

As minister for non-ferrous metallurgy in the USSR, Pyotr Lomako (b 1904) served for 46 years from 1940 to 1986. He was relieved of his post on Nov 1, 1986, aged 82, having served on the Central Committee of the CPSU Union since 1952.

The longest span as a legislator was 83 years by József Madarász (1814–1915). He first attended the Hungarian Parliament in 1832–6 as *oblegatus absentium* (*i.e.* on behalf of an absent deputy). He was a full member in 1848–50 and from 1861 until his death on Jan 31, 1915.

Largest Elections

The largest elections were those beginning on Dec 24, 1984 for the 542-seat Indian *Lok Sabha* (House of the People) in which 379 million eligible voters chose from among 5,301 candidates at 480,000 polling places manned by a 2½ million staff.

The most candidates for one office were 301 to represent Belguum City in the State Assembly in Karnataka, India, on Mar 5, 1985.

Closest Elections

The ultimate in close general elections occurred in Zanzibar (now part of Tanzania) on Jan 18, 1961, when the Afro-Shirazi Party won by a single seat, after the seat of Chake-Chake on Pemba Island had been gained by a single vote.

The narrowest recorded percentage win in an election would seem to be for the office of Southern District highway commissioner in Mississippi on Aug 7, 1979. Robert E. Joiner was declared winner over W. H. Pyron with 133,587 votes to 133,582. The loser got more than 49.9999% of the votes.

Most Defeated Persistent Candidate

Now 80 years old, Harold Stassen, 3-time governor of Minnesota in 1938–40–42, is running for US President in 1988. He has been defeated 17 times striving for high office, starting in 1948 when he lost the Republican Presidential nomination to Thomas Dewey.

Most One-Sided Elections

North Korea recorded a 100% turn-out of electors and a 100% vote for the Workers' Party of Korea in the general election of Oct 8, 1962.

The next closest approach was in Albania on Nov 14, 1982 when a single voter spoiled national unanimity for the official (and only) Communist candidates, who thus obtained only 99.99993 percent of the poll in a 100 percent turn out of 1,627,968.

The highest personal majority won by any politician has been 424,545 votes from a total electorate of 625,179 achieved by Ram Bilas Paswan, the Janata candidate for Jajipur in Bihar, India, in Mar 1977.

In the Liberian presidential election of 1927 President Charles D. B. King (1875–1961) was returned with a majority over his opponent, Mr Thomas J. R. Faulkner of the People's Party, officially announced as 234,000. President King thus claimed a "majority" more than 15½ times greater than the entire electorate.

---

2. MILITARY AND DEFENSE

WAR

Longest War

The longest of history's countless wars was the "Hundred Years' War" between England and France, which lasted from 1338 to 1453 (115 years), although it may be said that the nine Crusades from the First (1096–1104) to the Ninth (1271–91), extending over 195 years, comprised a single Holy War.

The Swiss Jean Jacques Babel estimated that since *c.* 3500 BC there have only been 292 years without recorded warfare.

Shortest War

The shortest war on record was that between the UK and Zanzibar (now part of Tanzania) from 9:02 to 9:40 a.m. on Aug 27, 1896. The UK battle fleet under Rear-Adm Harry Holdsworth Rawson (1843–1910) delivered an ultimatum to the self-appointed Sultan Sa'id

Khalid to evacuate his palace and surrender. This was not forthcoming until after 38 min of bombardment. Admiral Rawson received the Brilliant Star of Zanzibar (first class) from the new Sultan Hamud ibn Muhammad. It was proposed at one time that elements of the local populace should be compelled to defray the cost of the ammunition used.

Largest Armed Forces

Numerically the largest regular armed force in the world is that of the USSR with 5,130,000 (1986). China's People's Liberation Army's strength in 1986 was 2,100,000 with reductions continuing. Her reserves number 5.25 million and her paramilitary forces of armed and unarmed militias are estimated by the International Institute of Strategic Studies at "some 12 million." The US military manpower is 2,143,000.

Largest Navies

The largest navy in terms of manpower is the US Navy, with 570,973 sailors and 196,275 Marines in mid-1986. The active strength in 1985 included 5 nuclear-powered with 10 other aircraft carriers, 3 battleships, 93 nuclear attack submarines and 4 diesel attack submarines, 31 cruisers, 68 destroyers, 106 frigates, and 60 amphibious warfare ships.

The USSR Navy has a larger submarine fleet of 374 vessels (118 nuclear, 256 diesel). It has 5 aircraft carriers, 36 cruisers and 61 destroyers.

Largest Air Force

The greatest air force of all time was the US Army Air Corps (now called the US Air Force), which had 79,908 aircraft in July 1944, and 2,411,294 personnel in March 1944. The US Air Force, including strategic air forces, had 605,805 personnel and 4,887 combat aircraft in mid-1986. The USSR Air Force had 453,000 men in mid-1986. It had 5,150 combat aircraft, and the Offensive Strategic Rocket Forces had about 298,000 operational personnel in mid-1986.

Oldest Army

The oldest army is the 83-strong Swiss Guard in the Vatican City, with a regular foundation dating back to Jan 21, 1506. Its origins, however, extend back before 1400.

Largest Catapults

The largest military catapults, or onagers, could throw a missile weighing 60 lb a distance of 500 yd.

Tallest and Youngest Soldiers

The tallest soldier of all time was Väinö Myllyrinne (1909–63) who was inducted into the Finnish Army when he was 7 ft 3 in and later grew to 8 ft 3 in. The youngest, Marshal Duke of Caxias (b Aug 25, 1803–d May 7, 1880) entered an infantry regiment of the Brazilian army at the age of 5 in 1808, and became a military hero and statesman.

"Star Wars"

The first reported successful "high frontier" interception test in outer space by the US Strategic Defense Initiative occurred over the Pacific on June 10, 1984.

Longest Marches

The longest march in military history was the famous Long March by the Chinese Communists in 1934–5. In 368 days, of which 268 days were days of movement, from Oct to Oct, their force of 90,000 covered 6,000 miles from Kiangsi to Yenan in Shensi *via* Yünnan. They crossed 18 mountain ranges and six major rivers and lost all but 22,000 of their force in continual rear-guard actions against Nationalist Kuo-min-tang (KMT) forces.

The record road march (11 men with 40 lb packs) over a marathon (26 miles 385 yds) was 4 hours 35 min 47.28 sec by a team of 29 British commandos on Nov 1, 1987 in Plymouth, Eng.

Largest Cannon

The highest caliber cannon ever constructed is the *Tsar Puchka* (King of Cannons), now housed in the Kremlin, Moscow. It was built in the 16th century with a bore of 920 mm (36.2 in) and a barrel 10 ft 5 in long. It weighs 44 tons.

Heaviest and Fastest Tanks

The heaviest tank ever constructed was the German Panzer Kampfwagen Maus II, which weighed 212 tons. By 1945 it had reached only the experimental stage and was not proceeded with.

The heaviest operational tank used by any army was the 91.3-ton 13-man French Char de Rupture 2C bis of 1923. It carried a 155-mm howitzer and had two 250-hp engines giving a maximum speed of 8 mph. The most heavily armed tank since 1972 has been the Soviet T-72 with a 125-mm high velocity gun.

The world's fastest tank is the British Scorpion AFV which can reach 50 mph, with 75% payload.

Largest Guns

The two most massive guns ever constructed were used by the Germans in the siege of Sevastapol on the Eastern Front in World War II. They were of a caliber of 800 mm (31.5 in) with barrels 94 ft 8½ in long, and named Dore and Gustav. Their remains were discovered, one near Metzenhof, Bavaria in Aug 1945 and the other in the Soviet zone of Germany. They were built by Krupp as railway guns, carried on 24 cars, two of which had 40 wheels each. The whole assembly of the gun was 141 ft long and weighed 1,482 tons, requiring a crew of 1,500 men. The range for a 9¼-ton projectile was 29 miles.

Greatest Range

The greatest range ever attained by a gun is by the HARP (High

Altitude Research Project) consisting of two 16-in/50-caliber barrels in tandem, 119.4 ft long and weighing 165 tons, at Yuma, Ariz. On Nov 19, 1966, a 185-lb projectile was fired to an altitude of 111.8 miles (590,550 ft). The static V3 underground firing tubes built by the Germans in 50° shafts at Mimoyecques, near Calais, France to bombard London were never operative, due to RAF bombing.

Mortars

The largest mortars ever constructed were Mallets mortar (Woolwich Arsenal, London, 1857), and the "Little David" of World War II, made in the US. Each had a caliber of 920 mm (36¼ in), but neither was ever used in action.

The heaviest mortar used was the tracked German 600-mm (23.6-in) siege piece known as "Karl" used against Stalingrad.

Atomic Bombs

The two atom bombs dropped on Japan by the US in 1945 each had an explosive power equivalent to that of 12,500 tons (12.5 kilotons) of trinitrotoluene, called TNT. The one dropped 1,670 ft above Hiroshima, code-named "Little Boy," was 10 ft long and weighed 9,000 lb.

The most powerful thermonuclear device so far tested is one with a power equivalent to 57 million tons of TNT, or 57 megatons, detonated by the USSR in the Novaya Zemlya area at 8:33 a.m. GMT on Oct 30, 1961. The shock wave was detected to have circled the world three times, taking 36 hours 27 min for the first circuit. Some estimates put the power of this device at between 62 and 90 megatons.

GUN WITH GREATEST RANGE: The HARP can shoot two 16-in/50-caliber barrels, one after the other, each 119.4 ft long and 165 tons in weight. A 185-lb projectile was fired to a height of 590,550 ft in a test in Ariz in 1966.

The largest US H-bomb tested was the 18–22 megaton "Bravo" at Bikini Atoll, Marshall Islands, Mar 1, 1954.

Largest Nuclear Weapons

The most powerful ICBMs are the USSR's SS–18s (Model 5) believed to be armed with ten 750-kiloton MIRVs (multiple independently-targetable re-entry vehicles). Models 1 and 3 have a single 20-megaton warhead.

The US Titan II carrying a W-53 warhead was rated at 5 to 9 megatons but is now withdrawn, leaving the 1–2 megaton W-56 as the most powerful US weapon.

Nuclear Delivery Vehicles

As of mid-1986 the USSR deployed 2,502 strategic nuclear delivery vehicles or 252 above the SALT II contractual ceiling. The USA on the same date deployed 1,910 vehicles or 340 below the 2250 SALT II limit. The comparative number of warheads has been estimated by the International Institute for Strategic Studies at USSR 10,716 and USA 12,846.

---

3. JUDICIAL

LITIGATION

Longest Trial

The longest jury trial in legal history is *Kemner et al* v. *Monsanto Company* which started on Feb 6, 1984. It was still in trial after 556 court days at St Clair County Court House, Belleville, Ill in Apr 1987. There were 49 plaintiffs and 138 witnesses who testified before the Circuit Judge Hon. Richard P. Goldenhersh. The case concerned an alleged toxic spill in Sturgeon, Ill in 1979.

Best-Attended Trial

The greatest attendance at any trial was at that of Major Jesús Sosa Blanco, aged 51, for an alleged 108 murders. At one point in the 12½-hour trial (5:30 p.m. to 6 a.m., Jan 22–23, 1959), 17,000 people were present in the Havana Sports Palace, Cuba. Blanco was executed on Feb 18, 1959.

Highest Bail

The highest bail ever ordered was $1 billion each on May 14, 1986 for two suspected illicit drug dealers in Suffolk County, Long Island, NY. Judge Louis L. Ohlig of the District Court was the judge, who said, "They're not going to be handled with kid gloves any more." The suspects were alleged to be part of a ring that smuggled $24 million of cocaine per month into the US.

Hassen Ebtehaj, later Chairman of the Iranian Bank in Teheran, was granted bail in 1967 in excess of $50 million.

Breach of Contract

The greatest damages ever awarded for a breach of contract were £610,392 ($1,709,000), awarded July 16, 1930, to the Bank of Portugal against the printers Waterlow & Sons Ltd of London, arising from their unauthorized printing of 580,000 five-hundred escudo notes in 1925. This award was upheld in the House of Lords on Apr 28, 1932. One of the perpetrators, Arthur Virgilio Alves Reis, served 16 years (1930–46) in jail.

Greatest Personal Injury Damages

The greatest personal injury damages ever awarded were to an unnamed boy born during a complicated 45-min birth at the US Army's Letterman General Hospital in 1979. If the child, which had "total cerebral palsy," lives out his expected years, the potential US government payment could amount to $70 million.

A Bronx Supreme Court jury on July 18, 1986 awarded $65,086,000 to Mrs Agnes Mae Whitaker against the New York Health and Hospitals Corporation for medical malpractice.

On Nov 24, 1983 a jury in Corpus Christi, Tex, awarded punitive damages of $106 million against Ford Motor Co for alleged design faults in the Ford Mustang II in which Bevary Durrill, 20, died in 1974. An appeal is pending.

Greatest Compensation for Wrongful Imprisonment and Death

Isadore Zimmerman (1917–83) of NY spent 24 years in prison before his conviction for murdering a cop was overturned because of new evidence. On his release at age 66 he was awarded $1 million, which is equivalent to $42,000 for each year he spent in prison. But, after legal fees and expenses, he ended up with only 60 percent of the million. Zimmerman decided not to appeal the award, and died a little more than a year later.

A jury in Volusia county, Florida, on Apr 25, 1984 awarded $200,150,000 to the mother of a 20-year-old high school girl who was one of the 41 victims of the confessed murderer, Gerald Stano. The killer, who must pay this sum, is in prison for life awaiting a number of death sentences.

Alimony and Divorce Settlement

Belgian-born Sheika Dena Al-Fassi, 23, filed the highest ever alimony claim of $3 billion against her former husband Sheik Mohammed Al-Fassi, 28, of the Saudi Arabia royal family, in LA, Calif, in Feb 1982. Explaining the size of the settlement claim, lawyer Marvin Mitchelson alluded to the Sheik's wealth which included 14 homes in Florida alone and numerous private aircraft. When in 1983 she was awarded $81 million she declared herself "very very happy" if she was able to collect.

The reported divorce settlement achieved by the lawyers of Soraya Khashóggi was £500 million ($800 million) plus property from her husband Adnan. Mrs Anne Bass, former wife of Sid Bass of Texas was reported to have rejected $535 million as inadequate to live in the style to which she had been made accustomed.

Defamation Suits

A sum of $16.8 million was awarded to Dr John J. Wild, 58, at the Hennepin District Court of Minnesota on Nov 30, 1972, against the Minnesota Foundation and others for defamation, bad-faith termination of a contract, and interference with professional business relationships, plus $10.8 million in punitive damages. The Supreme Court of Minnesota reduced the award to $1.5 million on Jan 10, 1975, but allowed Dr. Wild the option of a new trial. There was a no-disclosure clause in the settlement.

The $39.6 million awarded in Columbus, O, on Mar 1, 1980, to plaintiff Robert Guccione, publisher of *Penthouse*, for defamation against Larry Flynt, publisher of *Hustler*, was reduced by Judge Craig Wright to $4 million on Apr 17, 1980. The hearing ended in May 1982 with *Penthouse* being cleared of libel in a countersuit.

A $640-million libel suit was brought by the Calif resort La Costa against *Penthouse* in Mar 1975. In May 1982 a jury found for the magazine. In July their verdict was set aside by a Calif judge, who was then removed from the case. Costs exceed $10 million to date.

Heaviest Fine

The Securities and Exchange Commission on Nov 14, 1986 fined Ivan Boesky, 49, the New York arbitrageur, $100 million for breaching their regulations on insider trading.

Longest Lease

The longest lease on record is for 10 million years for a plot for a sewage tank adjoining Columb Barracks, Ireland, signed on Dec 3, 1888.

Shortest and Longest Wills

The shortest valid will in the world is "Vse zene," the Czech for "All to wife," written and dated Jan 19, 1967, by Herr Karl Tausch of Langen, Hesse, Germany. The shortest will contested but subsequently admitted to probate in English law was the case of *Thorne v. Dickens* in 1906. It consisted of the three words "All for Mother" in which "mother" was not his mother but his wife.

The longest will on record was that of Mrs Frederica Evelyn Stilwell Cook (US), proved on Nov 2, 1925 at Somerset House, London. It consisted of four bound volumes containing 95,940 words.

Patent Case

On Mar 13, 1986 Hughes Tool Co of Houston, Tex, was awarded $205,381,259.40 in a suit involving Smith International Inc over an infringement of their patent for the "O" Ring seal used in drilling. The inventor was Edward M. Galle.

Youngest Judges

No collated records on the ages of judicial appointments exist. However, David Elmer Ward had to await the legal age of 21 before taking office after nomination in 1932 as Judge of the County Court at Fort Myers, Fla.

Mass Killing

The best estimate of the number of Jewish victims of the Holocaust or the genocidal "Final Solution" ordered by Adolf Hitler (1889–1945) in Apr 1941 and continued into May 1945 is 5.8 million.

During the regime of Mao Tse-tung (1949–65), 26,300,000 Chinese were said by the USSR to have been killed by government forces. The estimate by the US Senate Judiciary Committee is 32.25 to 61.7 million.

Saving of Life

The greatest number of people saved from extinction by one man is an estimated 90,000 Jews in Budapest, Hungary, from July 1944 to Jan 1945 by the Swedish diplomat Raoul Wallenberg (b Aug 4, 1912). After escaping an assassination attempt by the Nazis, he was imprisoned without trial by the Soviet Union. On Feb 6, 1957 Deputy Foreign Minister Andrei Gromyko said Prisoner "Walenberg" had died in a cell in Lubyanka jail, Moscow, July 16, 1947. Sighting reports within the Gulag system have persisted for 41 years after his disappearance. He was made an Honorary Citizen of the US on Oct 5, 1981 and, on May 7, 1987, a statue to him was unveiled to replace an earlier one also in Budapest.

Largest Criminal Organization

The largest syndicate of organized crime is the Mafia (derived from an Arabic expression connoting beauty, excellence allied with bravery) or La Cosa Nostra ("our thing") which is said to have infiltrated the executive, judiciary and legislative branches of the US Government and others.

The largest criminal trial began in Nov 1987 after 21 months of hearings when a jury in Palermo, Sicily, considered charges against 466 Italian defendants. There are 1,314 witnesses prepared to testify.

The biggest Mafia killing took place Sept 11–13, 1931, following the murder in NYC of the topmost man, Salvatore Maranzano, *Il Capo di Tutti Capi*, when 40 allies were liquidated.

Murder Rates

The country with the highest recorded murder rate is Brazil with 104 registered homicides per 100,000 of the population in 1983, or 370 per day.

A total of 592 deaths was attributed to one Colombian bandit leader, Teófilo ("Sparks") Rojas, aged 27, between 1948 and his death in an ambush near Armenia on Jan 22, 1963. Some sources attribute 3,500 slayings to him, 1945–62.

The highest homicide rates recorded in NYC have been 58 in a week in July 1972, and 13 in a day in Aug 1972. In 1973, the total for Detroit (population then 1,500,000) was 751. The Chicago Crime Commission in Mar 1983 published a list of 1,081 unsolved gang slayings since 1919.

The country with the lowest officially recorded rate in the world is the Maldives (islands in the Indian Ocean, pop. 100,833 in 1966) with a nil rate among its nationals since its independence in July 1965. In the Indian state of Sikkim, in the Himalayas, murder is practically unknown, while in the Hunza area of Kashmir, in the Karakoram, only one definite case by a Hunzarwal has been recorded since 1900.

Suicide

The estimated daily rate of suicides throughout the world surpassed 1,000 in 1965. The country with the highest recorded suicide rate is Denmark with 28.6 per 100,000 of the population in 1986. The number in Japan rose to 69.9 per day in 1986. The country with the lowest recorded rate is Jordan, with a single case in 1970 and hence a rate of 0.04 per 100,000.

The final total number of victims of the mass cyanide poisoning of the Peoples Temple cult near Port Kaituma, Guyana, Nov 18, 1978 was 913. The leader was the paranoid "Rev" Jim Jones of San Francisco, who had deposited millions of dollars overseas.

The volcanic crater of Mt Mihara on an island in Sagami Bay, south of Yokohama, Japan was the scene of more than 1,000 suicides in 1933–36.

Largest Hangings

The most people hanged from one gallows were 38 Sioux Indians by William J. Duly outside Mankato, Minn, for the murder of unarmed citizens on Dec 26, 1862.

The Nazi Feldkommandant simultaneously hanged 50 Greek resistance men as a reprisal in Athens on July 22, 1944.

Longest Prison Sentences

A 10,000-year sentence was imposed on Deuel Wilhelm Davies, 40, on Dec 4, 1981, in Tuscaloosa, Ala, for a triple murder (including his mother-in-law) in 1976. A sentence of 384,912 years was *demanded* at the prosecution of Gabriel March Grandos, 22, at Palma de Mallorca, Spain, March 11, 1972, for failing to deliver 42,768 letters, a sentence of 9 years per letter.

Juan Corona, a Mexican-American, was sentenced on Feb 5, 1973, at Fairfield, Calif, to 25 consecutive life terms for murdering 25 migrant farm workers he had hired, killed and buried in 1970–71 near Feather River, Yuba City, Calif.

Longest Time Served

Paul Geidel (b Apr 21, 1894) was convicted of 2nd degree murder on Sept 5, 1911 as a 17-year-old porter in a NYC hotel. He was released from the Fishkill Correctional Facility, Beacon, NY, aged 85, on May 7, 1980, having served 68 years 8 months 2 days—the longest recorded term in US history. He had first refused parole in 1974.

Rudolph Hess (b Apr 26, 1894), formerly Hitler's deputy, was captured at Eaglesham, Eng, on May 10, 1941 and died in 1987 in his 47th year in prison.

Greatest Mass Arrest

The greatest mass arrest reported in a democratic country was of more than 13,000 people in an antiwar demonstration designed to block rush-hour traffic in Wash, DC, May 3–5, 1971.

THEFT: When Imelda Marcos left her 3,000 pairs (later revised to 1,060 pairs) of shoes in the Philippines palace, she and her husband were accused of "salting away" between $5 and $10 billion out of government funds. (*AP Wirephoto*)

Most Secure Prison

After it became a maximum security Federal prison in 1934, no convict was known to have lived to tell of a successful escape from the prison on Alcatraz Island in San Francisco Bay. A total of 23 men attempted it, but 12 were recaptured, 5 shot dead, one drowned and 5 presumed drowned. On Dec 16, 1962, three months before the prison was closed, one man reached the mainland alive, only to be recaptured on the spot. John Chase was imprisoned for a record 26 years on Alcatraz.

Robbery

The greatest robbery on record was that of the Reichsbank following Germany's collapse in Apr/May 1945. The Pentagon described the event first published in the *Guinness Book* in 1957 as "an unverified allegation." *Nazi Gold,* a book by Ian Sayer and Douglas Botting published in 1984, revealed full details and estimated the total haul at current values as £2,500 million ($3 billion).

The greatest amount lost in a small robbery was on Nov 26, 1983 when £26,369,778 ($36,000,000) worth of gold and platinum in the form of 6,800 bars, together with diamonds and travelers checks, in 76 boxes were removed by 6 masked men from a warehouse vault of Brinks Mat Ltd at Heathrow, England. Michael McAvoy, 32, of East Dulwich, and Brian Robinson, 41, of Lewisham, were each sentenced to 25 years at the Old Bailey on Dec 3, 1984.

An equal amount (est. $36 million) was lost in a haul from 352 safe deposit boxes in Banca Nazionale del Lavoro, Italy, during June 29–July 2, 1984.

Theft

The government of the Philippines announced on Apr 23, 1986 that it had succeeded in identifying $860.8 million that had been "salted away" by former president Ferdinand Edralin Marcos (b Sept 11, 1917) and his wife Imelda. The total stolen, it was asserted, since Nov 1965, was believed to be between $5 and $10 billion.

Art Theft

Since a price for the *Mona Lisa* at the time of its theft from the Louvre on Aug 21, 1911, cannot be established, it has to be considered the highest-priced painting ever stolen. It was recovered in Italy in 1913 when Vincenzo Perruggia was charged with its theft. On Oct 27, 1985 paintings valued at 100 million francs ($14 million) were removed from the Mermotte Museum, Paris.

In a theft from the National Anthropology and History Institute, Mexico City, on Dec 25, 1985, some 140 "priceless" gold, jade and obsidian artifacts were taken.

Bank Robbery

During the extreme civil disorder prior to Jan 22, 1976, in Beirut, Lebanon, a guerrilla force blasted the vaults of the British Bank of the Middle East in Bab Idriss and cleared out safe deposit boxes with contents valued by former Finance Minister Lucien Dahadah at $50 million, and by another source at an "absolute minimum" of $20 million.

Jewel Robbery

The greatest recorded theft of jewels was from the bedroom of the "well-guarded" villa of Prince Abdel Aziz Ben Ahmed Al-Thani near Cannes, France, July 24, 1980, valued at $16 million.

Train Robbery

The greatest recorded train robbery occurred between 3:03 a.m. and 3:27 a.m. on Aug 8, 1963, when a General Post Office mail train from Glasgow, Scotland was ambushed at Sears Crossing and robbed at Bridego Bridge near Mentmore, Buckinghamshire, England. The gang escaped with about 120 mailbags containing £2,631,784 ($6,053,103) worth of bank notes being taken to London for pulping. Only £343,448 ($961,654) was recovered.

Maritime Fraud

A cargo of 198,000 tons of Kuwaiti crude oil on the supertanker *Salem* at Durban was sold without title to the South African government in Dec 1979. The ship mysteriously sank off Senegal on Jan 17, 1980 leaving the government to pay $305 million to Shell International who owned the shipment.

Greatest Kidnapping Ransom

Historically, the greatest ransom paid was that for their chief, Atahualpa, by the Incas to the Spanish conquistador Francisco Pizarro, in 1532–33 at Cajamarca, Peru, which included a hall full of gold and silver, worth in modern money some $170 million.

The greatest ransom ever extorted is $60 million for the release of two businessmen, the brothers Jorge Born, 40, and Juan Born, 39, of Argentina, paid to the left-wing urban guerrilla group Montoneros in Buenos Aires, June 20, 1975.

The youngest person ever kidnapped has been Carolyn Wharton, who was born at 12:46 p.m., March 19, 1955, in the Baptist Hospital, Beaumont, Tex, and kidnapped by a woman disguised as a nurse at 1:15 p.m., when the baby was aged 29 min.

Greatest Hijack Ransom

The highest amount ever paid to aircraft hijackers has been $6 million by the Japanese government in the case of a JAL DC-8 held at Dacca airport, Bangladesh on Oct 2, 1977 with 38 hostages. Six convicted criminals were also exchanged. The Bangladesh government had refused to sanction any retaliatory action.

Computer Fraud

Between 1964 and 1973, some 64,000 fake insurance policies were created on the computer of the Equity Funding Corp involving $2 billion.

Stanley Mark Rifkin (b 1946) was arrested in Carlsbad, Calif, by the FBI on Nov 6, 1978, charged with defrauding a Los Angeles bank of $10.2 million by manipulation of a computer system. In June 1980 he was sentenced to 8 years.

---

4. ECONOMIC

MONETARY AND FINANCE

Highest Tax Rates

The country with the most confiscatory taxation is Norway where in Jan 1974 the Labor Party and Socialist Alliance abolished the 80% top limit. Some 2,000 citizens were then listed in the *Lignings Boka* as paying more than 100% of their taxable income. The shipping magnate Hilmer Reksten was assessed at 491%.

Highest Tax Demand

The highest recorded personal tax demand is one for $336 million for 70% of the estate of Howard Hughes.

Least Taxed People

The lowest income tax is paid by the citizens of Bahrain, Kuwait, Brunei and Qatar, where the rate, regardless of income, is zero.

Wealth Per Capita

The richest nation, measured by average income per capita of population, is United Arab Emirates with $19,120 in 1985. The US, which had taken the lead in 1910, was 3rd, behind Brunei.

In the US, Conn enjoys the highest per capita income level at 130.5% of the national average, followed by NJ at 121.6% and NY at 109%.

Gold Reserves

The country with the greatest monetary gold reserve is the US, whose Treasury had 263.90 million fine oz of the world's 949.86 million fine oz on hand in Mar 1987. Valued at $400 per fine oz, these amounts translate to $105,560 million and $379,944 million, respectively. The US Bullion Depository at Fort Knox, 30 miles southwest of Louisville, Ky, has been the principal depository of US gold since 1936.

Worst Inflation

The world's worst inflation occurred in Hungary in June 1946, when the 1931 gold pengö was valued at 130 quintillion (1.3×10^{21}) paper pengös. Notes were issued for "Egymillard" billion (1 followed by 21 zeros or 10^{21}) pengös on June 3 and withdrawn on July 11, 1946. Notes for 1 sextillion or 10^{27} pengös were issued for tax payments only.

In Germany, on Nov 6, 1923, the circulation of Reichsbank marks reached 400,338,326,350,700,000,000, a level of inflation 755,700 million times the 1913 levels.

Currency

Paper money is an invention of the Chinese, first tried in 812 AD and prevalent by 970 AD. The world's earliest bank notes (*banco-sedlar*) were issued in Stockholm, Sweden, in July 1661, the oldest survivor being one for 5 dalers dated Dec 6, 1662.

The largest paper money ever issued was the one kwan note of the Chinese Ming dynasty issue of 1368–99, which measured 9 × 13 in and was printed on mulberry-bark paper. Three of them were sold at auction for a total of $1,000 in London on Oct 7, 1983. The smallest note ever issued by a bank was the 10 bani note of the Ministry of Finance of Rumania, issued in 1917. It measured (printed area) 1.09 × 1.49 in.

Of German *notgeld* (emergency notes) the smallest were the 1-3 pfennig of Passau (1920–21) measuring 0.70 × 0.72 in. A 200-billion-mark note of the 1920's was auctioned in London Oct 7, 1983 for $255.

Largest Government-Issued Gold Coin

The largest known government-issued gold coin is the 1000-mohur denomination struck in 1613 at Agra, India, by the Moghul Emperor Shah Jahangir of Hindustan. This immense gold piece, the size of a saucer, is 7 ⅞ inches in diameter and weighs just over 350 troy ounces, making it equal to about 355 US $20 gold pieces with a face value of $7,100 and a sheer bullion value of nearly $265,000. The designs on both sides of the coin consist of elaborate Persian legends. This coin came to light only recently and was placed on the public auction block by Habsburg-Feldman, S.A. in Geneva, Switz, on Nov 9, 1987 when floor-bidding reached the $8 million level. However, the coin was withdrawn from the sale and returned to its owner when no bidder chose to top the $8.5 million "protective reserve."

Highest and Lowest Denomination Currency

The highest denomination notes in circulation are US Federal Reserve Bank notes for $10,000. They bear the head of Salmon Portland Chase (1808–73), Secretary of the Treasury during Civil War days. None have been printed since July 1944 and the US Treasury announced in 1969 that no further notes higher than $100 would be issued. Only 348 of the $10,000 bills remain in circulation or are unretired.

The lowest denomination legal tender bank note is the 1 sen (or 1/100th of a rupiah) Indonesian note. Its exchange value is 252 to the US penny.

Greatest Coin Collections

The highest price ever paid was $25,235,360 for the Garrett family collection of US and colonial coins which was donated to Johns Hopkins University. The sales were made at a series of 4 auctions held Nov 28–29, 1979 and Mar 25–28, 1981 at the Bowers & Ruddy Galleries in Wolfeboro, NH. The collection had been put together by members of the Garrett family from 1860–1942.

The most valuable coin collection formed by a single individual to be sold at public auction was the Louis Eliasberg Collection of US gold coins. The collection, grouped into 1,074 lots, was sold by Bowers & Ruddy Galleries in NYC Oct 27–29, 1982 for $12.4 million. This is also the highest total realization for a single coin auction. Eliasberg was a prominent Baltimore banker.

Virgil M. Brand (1862–1926), Chicago brewing magnate, is reputed to have once assembled the world's largest and most valuable private collection of rare coins. In 40 years of collecting, he gathered together nearly 375,000 coins, from ancient to modern, including more than 50,000 gold coins. He had a particular penchant for great rarities, and managed to acquire two 1787 Brasher "Doubloons" (see below), the most valuable US gold piece, along with numerous unique specimens.

Shortly after Brand's death, his heirs began dispersing the collection through private treaty and auction sales, a process requiring nearly 60 years to complete. Several major Brand coin auctions took place in the early 1980s. Numismatic experts say that the Brand holdings contained so many great rarities that if the collection were intact today it would easily yield over $250 million.

The most valuable coin collection still in private hands, according to *Fortune* magazine, is owned by the two "billionaire" Hunt brothers of Houston, Tex—Nelson Bunker Hunt and Herbert Hunt. Their collection, which contains everything from the rarest of Greek and roman coins to modern gold pieces, is reputed to be worth in excess of $50 million.

The highest price paid at auction for a single coin is $725,000 for an extremely rare US 1787 Brasher "Doubloon" at Bowers & Ruddy Galleries, NYC, Nov 29, 1979. This storied gold piece, weighing some 408 grains, was produced by Ephraim Brasher, a New York goldsmith, to equal the value of a Spanish doubloon (about $16.00). Only about six specimens are known to be extant.

A $1 million set of 1804 US coins (including the rare silver dollar) was presented to the King of Spain by dealer Lester Merkin in 1979.

Most Massive Coins

The holed stone discs used for money on the Yap Islands are the most massive coins ever known. Yap, a 38.7-sq-mile group of islands in the western Pacific is part of the US Trust Territory. The stone discs vary in size from "small change" of less than 9 in in diameter to cartwheel-size stones 12 ft across. Even a medium-sized stone coin is valuable enough to be traded for an 18-ft canoe or one wife!

Copper, cast in the form of a cross, is still used to purchase brides among the peoples of isolated northern Rhodesia (now Zimbabwe). Stones are not the only unusual items that have been used as coins. Teas cast into bricks were used for 900 years or more as currency in China, Tibet and other Asian countries. They were stamped with the value and name of the issuing bank. North American Indians made "wampum" (money) out of strings of beads to trade with colonists and among themselves. The Chinese also made spade-shaped coins of bronze, and round copper coins with square center holes which they called "cash."

World's Biggest Loss

An unnamed Italian industrialist was reported to have lost $1,920,000 in five hours at roulette in Monte Carlo, Monaco, on March 6, 1974. A Saudi Arabian prince was reported to have lost more than $1 million in a single session at the Metro Club, Las Vegas, Nev, in Dec 1974.

COINS

Oldest	*c.* 670 BC: electrum staters of King Gyges of Lydia, Turkey[1]
Earliest Dated	MCCXXXIIII (1234): Bishop of Roskilde coins, Denmark (6 known)
Heaviest	43 lb 7¼ oz: Swedish 10 daler copper plate, 1644. See Million Dollar Gold Piece, p. 405
Lightest and Smallest	0.002 g or 14,000 to the oz: Nepalese silver ¼ Jawa, *c.* 1740
Rarest	Many "singletons" known: for example, only 700 Axumite coins are known, of which only one was made of bronze and gold of Kaleb I *c.* 500 AD

[1]Chinese uninscribed "spade" money of the Chou dynasty has been dated to *c.* 770 BC

SIX CAN PLAY SIMULTANEOUSLY on this gigantic slot machine called "Queens Machine" at the Four Queens in Las Vegas.

Largest Slot Machine

The world's largest slot machine (or one-armed bandit), named "Queens Machine," is 9 ft 8 in high, 18 ft long and 8 ft 10 in wide. Six can play at the same time. It supplants Super Bertha, the 555 cu ft monster at Four Queens Hotel & Casino, Las Vegas, Nev.

Million Dollar Gold Piece

The largest souvenir coin was one single piece issued on Mar 21, 1986 for the World Exposition '86 in Vancouver, BC, Canada—a $1 million gold piece, 37½ in in diameter, ¾ in thick, weighing 365 lb avoirdupois (3,123 troy oz of 14-carat gold). The gold was rented from Leach & Garner Co., of Attleboro, Mass, the coin was minted by them, and, on return from Vancouver, was melted down.

Largest Mint

The largest mint is the US Mint built in 1965–69 on Independence Mall, Philadelphia, covering 500,000 sq ft (11½ acres) with an annual capacity on a 3-shift 7-day-a-week production of 8,000 million coins.

A single stamping machine can produce coins at a rate of 10,000 per hour.

Largest Coin Line

A 10-mi-5-ft-7-in-long line of 662,353 quarters was laid edge-to-edge by 100 volunteers in Atlanta working on Mar 16, 1985 for the National Kidney Foundation of Georgia under the sponsorship of WFOX radio and the Women of Georgia Power. It was the longest and also the most valuable amassed collection, worth $165,788.25.

Largest Treasure Troves

The greatest discovery of treasure is the estimated $2 billion of gold coins and platinum ingots from the sunken Tsarist battleship *Admiral Nakhimov* of 8,524 tons 200 ft down off the Japanese island of Tsushima. She was sunk during the Russo-Japanese War, May 27, 1905.

The highest price paid for a hoard has been $7,300,000 for 407,000 US silver dollars from the La Vere Redfield estate in a courtroom auction in Reno, Nev on Jan 27, 1976 by Steven C. Markoff of A-Mark Coin Co, Inc of Beverly Hills, Calif.

A figure of $2 billion of bullion has also been ascribed to the *San Jose* which sank in 700–1,200 ft of water off Colombia in 1708. Diving began in Aug 1984.

The Irish High Court ruled on Dec 10, 1986, that Michael Webb, farmer of Clonmel, Tipperary, have a hoard discovered by him in 1980 returned by the National Museum or be paid £5,225,000 in lieu.

On July 20, 1985, two sons of Mel Fisher found the main cargo of the Spanish *Nuestra Senhora de Atocha* sunk off Key West, Florida in 1622. The value of the cargo already recovered was $80 million, but is now expected to attain close to $400 million mainly in silver bars.

LABOR

Trade Unions

The largest union is Solidarnos (Solidarity) in Poland, founded in Nov 1980, which by Oct 1981 was reported to have 8 million members at the time it was outlawed. The union with the longest name is probably the International Association of Marble, Slate and Stone Polishers, Rubbers and Sawyers, Tile and Marble Setters' Helpers and Marble Mosaic and Terrazzo Workers' Helpers (Wash DC).

Labor Disputes

A labor dispute concerning monotony of diet and working conditions was recorded in 1153 BC in Thebes, Egypt. The earliest recorded strike was one by an orchestra leader from Greece named Aristos in Rome *c.* 309 BC. The cause was meal breaks.

The longest recorded strike ended on Jan 4, 1961, after 33 years. It concerned the employment of barbers' assistants in Copenhagen, Denmark. The longest recorded major strike was one at the plumbing fixtures factory of the Kohler Co in Sheboygan, Wis between Apr 1954 and Oct 1962. The strike is alleged to have cost the United Automobile Workers union about $12 million to sustain.

Working Careers

The longest working life has been 98 years by Mr Izumi of Japan (see page 14) who started work goading draft animals at a sugar mill at Asan, Tokunoshima, Japan in 1872. He became a sugar cane farmer and retired in 1970, aged 105. He died in 1986, aged 120.

Susan O'Hagan (1802–1909) was in domestic service with 3 generations of the Hall family of Lisburn, near Belfast, Northern Ireland, for 97 years from the age of 10 to light duties at 107.

The longest recorded industrial career in one job was that of Miss Polly Gadsby who started at the age of 9 and worked 86 years wrapping elastic for the same company in Leicester, England until she died in 1932 at the age of 95.

FOOD AND DRINK

Prohibition

The longest-lasting imposition of prohibition against consumption of alcoholic beverages has been 26 years in Iceland (1908–34). Other prohibitions have been in Russia, later the USSR (1914–24), and the US (1920–33). The Faroe Islands have had a public (as opposed to private licensed) prohibition since 1918.

Most Expensive Food

The most expensively priced food (as opposed to spice) is First Choice Black Perigord truffles which retail at $13.20 per 0.44 oz can.

However, in Jan 1985 in the Hafr El-Baten market, Riyadh, Saudi Arabia local truffles sold for SR 5000 for 3 kg, equivalent to $60 per 0.44 oz.

Spices

Prices for wild ginseng (root of *Panax quinquefolius*), from the Chan Pak Mt area of China, thought to have aphrodisiacal quality, were reported in Nov 1977 to be as high as $23,000 per oz in Hong Kong. Total shipments from Jilin province do not exceed 141 oz per year. The leading medical journal in the US has likened its effects to "corticosteroid poisoning."

The world's rarest and most prized condiment is Cà Cuong, a secretion recovered in minute amounts from beetles in northern Vietnam. Owing to war conditions, the price rose to $100 per ounce before supplies virtually ceased in 1975.

The hottest of all spices is claimed to be Siling labuyo from the Philippines. The chili pepper or Capsicum known as Tepin from southwestern US comes in pods ⅜ in in diameter. A single dried gram will produce detectable "heat" in 68.3 lb of bland sauce.

Candy

The top-selling candies are Life Savers, with 33,431,236,300 rolls sold between 1913 and May 1987. A tunnel formed by the holes in the middle placed end to end would stretch to the moon and back more than 3 times. Thomas Syta of Van Nuys, Calif made one last 7 hours 10 min (with hole intact) on Jan 15, 1983.

Biggest Barbecues

Three claimants are contesting for the largest barbecue. At the Iowa State Fairgrounds, Des Moines, on June 12, 1988, the turnstiles registered 35,072 attending a barbecue where 20,000 lb of pork (from 122 hogs) were served and consumed in 5 hours. At the Sertoma Club Barbecue, New Port Richey, Fla, 21,112 lb of beef were consumed Mar 7–9, 1986. At Iolani School, Honolulu, Hawaii, 46,386 barbecued chicken halves were consumed by 15,000 people on Jan 31, 1981.

Largest Breads

The longest continuous loaf of bread was measured at 2,356 ft 10 in in length. It was baked in a charcoal-filled trench lined with a pan of silver foil on Nov 3, 1987, by the Northland Job Corps, Vergennes, Vt. About 200 people worked on preparing the baking for 12 hours, although the actual baking took no more than 90 min.

The largest pan loaf baked was one of 3,051 lb 4 oz measuring 9 ft × 5 ft by the Calgary Italian Bakery and Southern Alberta Bakers' Association on July 7, 1986 at Calgary, Alberta.

Largest Cakes

The largest cake ever created was a 90,000-lb 8,800-sq-ft "Duncan Hines" cake that used 31,026 boxes of a yellow cake mix, 20,000 layers of 3 lb each, topped with 30,000 lb of vanilla icing. It took 24 hours to assemble under the direction of Chef Franz Eichenauer after 32 hours of baking in Austin, Tex on Feb 20, 1986 to celebrate the 150th anniversary of the founding of Texas. To cut the cake at the City Coliseum, Prince Charles of Great Britain was on hand. The cake was big enough to feed 300,000 people.

The tallest recorded free-standing cake is one of 83 tiers, 70 ft 4½ in, completed by a team of 20 chefs at the Collins Hotel, Melbourne, Australia on June 18, 1987.

Largest Crepe

Serving over 100 people, the world's largest known crepe was 8 ft in diameter, contained 72 eggs, was filled with strawberries, covered with raspberry sauce and doused with Grand Marnier. It was made by well-known chefs on Apr 9, 1988 in Snowmass, Colo, as part of the Chefs Race National Championships.

Largest Chocolate

The heaviest chocolate Easter egg ever made was one weighing 7,561 lb 13½ oz, measuring 10 ft high, made by Siegfried Berndt at "Macopa" Patisserie, Leicester, England, and completed on Apr 7, 1982. A chocolate egg 18 ft 11½ in tall was constructed by Tobler Suchard of Bedford, Eng on Apr 10, 1987.

The largest chocolate "model" was one measuring 32 ft 9½ in × 16 ft 4.6 in × 28.7 in high of the 1992 Olympic Center in Barcelona, Spain, by the Gremi Provincial de Pastigeria Confiteria School in Nov 1985.

Largest Hamburger

The largest hamburger on record was one of 5,005 lb 13.8 oz made on Oct 13, 1985 by Spur Steak Ranches (Pty) Ltd at Anchor Bay, Cape Town, S Africa. The burger had a diameter of 23 ft 3½ in and was cut into over 15,750 portions after grilling.

TALLEST ► GINGERBREAD HOUSE: It stands 36½ feet high and took 454 hours to build. Using 1,750 lb of flour and sugar, 400 lb of honey, 370 eggs, 68 gallons of egg whites, milk and piping gel, and 120 lb of butter and spices, this house was the creation of the Hyatt Regency Hotel (Houston, Tex) culinary and engineering staff.

LARGEST CREPE: 8 ft wide, this Crepe Suzette contained 72 eggs, was filled with strawberries, covered with raspberry sauce and doused with Grand Marnier. ▼

Largest Jelly

The largest was in a tank filled with 7,700 gallons of watermelon-flavored pink jelly made by Paul Squires and Geoff Ross worth $14,000 at Roma Street Forum, Brisbane, Australia, on Feb 5, 1981.

Largest Milk Shake

The largest was one of 174 gallons that started out (before mixing) with 117½ gallons of vanilla ice cream, 60 gallons of milk, and 17 gallons of strawberry flavoring. It was made in a 198-gallon acrylic shake cup on July 3, 1988, at the Grindstone Festival in Berea, Ohio. It was consumed by the crowd witnessing the shake.

Longest Noodles

The longest continuous cooked noodle (939 ft 11 in) was made in Louisville, Colo, by 4 families who joined recipes and noodles for 8 hours on Sept 1, 1985, built a special 20 × 5-ft cooker, and used 230 lb of charcoal, along with 50 lb of flour and 36 eggs.

Mark Pi at his China Gate Restaurant in Columbus, O, set a record by making 2,048 noodle strips in 34.5 sec on Feb 12, 1982, each strip exceeding 5 ft in length.

Largest Omelets

The largest omelet was one made of 54,763 eggs with 531 lb of cheese in a skillet 30 ft in diameter. It was cooked by Michael McGowan, assisted by his staff and the Sunrise Jaycees of Las Vegas, Nev, on Oct 25, 1986.

A Spanish omelet weighing 660 lb was made by Jose Antonio Rivera Casal at Caracacia, Spain on May 17, 1987 and consisted of 5,000 eggs, 1,102 lb of potatoes, 176 lb of red peppers, 22 lb of salt and 33 gal of oil.

Largest Pancake

A crew representing Birkett Mills baked and flipped a buckwheat pancake 28 ft 1 in in diameter and 2 in deep at Penn Yan, NY on Sept 27, 1987. The pancake contained 810 lb buckwheat flour, 2,025 lb of Puritan mix, was topped with 15 gal of syrup and 68 lb of butter, and weighed, in total, 4,238 lb.

Longest Pastry

The longest pastry in the world is the "record" pastry 1,683 ft 2½ in in length made by chefs at the Hyatt Regency Ravinia, Atlanta, Ga. on July 26, 1986.

Largest Paella

The largest paella measured 52.48 ft in diameter and was made by Josep (Pepitu) Gruges on Aug 25, 1987 in the Playa de Aro, Gerona, Spain. The ingredients included 8,140 lb of rice, 6,600 lb of meat, 3,300 lb of mussels, 1,540 lb each of beans and peppers, 440 lb of garlic and 88 gal of oil. The paella was eaten by 40,000 people who washed it all down with 8,000 bottles of Catalan champagne.

Largest Pies

The largest apple pie ever baked was that by a TV Chef, Glynn Christian, in a 40 ft × 23 ft dish at Hewitts Farm, Chelsfield, Kent, England on Aug 25–27, 1982. Over 600 bushels of apples were included in the pie which weighed 30,115 lb.

The largest cherry pie was one weighing a total of 14.16 tons and containing 25,890 lb of cherry filling. It measured 17 ft 6 in in diameter, 26 in in depth, and was baked by Chef Pierre Bakeries in conjunction with the Michigan Cherry Committee in Traverse City, Mich, on July 25, 1987.

The largest meat pie ever baked was called "The Chuck Wagon Gang's Chili Meat Pie" and weighed 13,362.9 lb. It was baked on Oct 17, 1986 at Odessa, Tex, in a half cylinder 20 ft long and 4 ft in diameter. Its crust alone weighed a ton.

The largest mince pie was one of 2,260 lb, measuring 20 × 5 ft, baked at Ashby-de-la-Zouch, Leicestershire, England, Oct 15, 1932.

A pecan pie 24 ft in diameter, 4 in thick and weighing 13,463 lb, including 1,059½ lb of pecans, was baked in Okmulgee, Okla by students of Okla State U, at the annual Pecan Festival. Cut by the governor of the state, it was served to 8,000 people.

The largest custard pie was one of 448 lb made in the kitchen of Jury's Hotel, Dublin, Ireland under the supervision of Derek McLoughlin and John Clancy on Feb 6, 1987.

The largest key lime pie, 15 ft 7 in in diameter, 4 in deep, weighing 2,138 lb, was made and exhibited on Sept 19, 1987 by chefs at South Seas Plantation, Captiva Island, Fla.

LARGEST PIZZA: It may look like a goalpost on a football field, but it's actually a flagpole in the center of a 100-ft-1-in pizza pie made in Havana, Fla, on Oct 11, 1987, by Lorenzo Amato in cooperation with Roma Food Enterprises.

Largest Pizza

The largest pizza ever baked was one measuring 100 ft 1 in in diameter, made by Lorenzo Amato of Cafe di Lorenzo, Tallahassee, Fla, in cooperation with Louis Piancone, president of Roma Food Enterprises, Inc. The pizza was cut into 94,248 slices and consumed by the 30,000 spectators at the baking in Havana, Fla.

Largest Popsicle®

The largest iced lollipop on a stick was one of 5,750 lb, constructed for the Westside Assembly of God Church, Davenport, Iowa, Sept 7, 1975.

Largest Potato Chip

Charles Chip Inc of Mountville, Pa, produced chips 4 × 7 in from outsize potatoes in Feb 1977.

Mashed Potatoes

A single serving of mashed potatoes weighing 18,260 lb was prepared from instant mashed potato flakes and water in a ready-mix concrete truck and poured into a platform 16 ft by 16 ft (256 sq ft) in Grand Forks, N Dakota before a Potato Bowl football game on Sept 4, 1982. *(No further claims in this category will be considered.)*

Largest Salad

A 114,885-lb salad was tossed together on May 20, 1988 by the King City (Calif) Young Farmers at the Salinas Fair. A true mixed salad, it was made of 17 ingredients, including iceberg lettuce (47,250 heads, or 100,840 lb), mixed lettuce (7,252 lb), celery (1,700 lb), cucumbers (800 lb), cauliflower (600 lb), tomatoes (500 lb), yellow onions (450 lb) and on down to dill (130 lb) and cilantro (25 lb). The salad was topped with 125 gal of dressing and mixed in a 40 × 24 ft "bowl" 6 ft high. It took 8 hours 15 min to prepare it.

Largest Salami

The longest salami on record was one 58 ft 9 in long with a circumference of 20¾ in, weighing 863.5 lb, made by Kutztown Bologna Co, Kutztown, Pa, on August 21, 1986.

Longest Sausage

The longest continuous sausage ever made was one of 9.89 miles prepared by Messrs Dewhurst in 21 hours 17 min on June 17–18, 1987 and transported to Hyde Park, London and cooked by scouts on June 20, 1987. Nearly 100,000 portions weighing 5 tons were served as part of the St John Ambulance Brigade Centenary.

A single sausage 5,917 ft in length was cooked on a grill in Barcelona, Spain on Sept 22, 1986. (See page 358.)

Longest Banana Split

The longest banana split ever made was one 4.39 mi in length made by Princeton Univ students on Apr 25, 1987.

MOST GIGANTIC ICE CREAM SUNDAE: This ice cream sundae weighing 33,616¾ lb was "constructed" by the Knudsen Corp (LA) and Smucker's (Ohio and LA). It took 50 people over 7 hours to build it, while dry ice kept it from melting.

HEAVIEST STRAWBERRY "BOWL": With many competitors due to an abundant 1988 Spring strawberry crop, Goodberry's Restaurant in Arvada, Colo got a record 2,255 lb of berries into this gigantic "bowl."

Heaviest Strawberry Bowl

A "bowl" containing 2,255 lb of strawberries was filled by Goodberry's Restaurant, Arvada, Colo, surpassing many other large bowls to set a new record on June 4, 1988.

Largest Sundae

The most gigantic ice cream sundae, weighing 33,616.75 lb, was constructed July 28, 1985 by the Knudsen Corp of LA and Smucker's of Ohio at the Disneyland Hotel in Anaheim, Calif. The 10-ft-tall, 30-million-calorie sundae included 26,020 lb of ice cream, 7,521.75 lb of topping, and 75 lb of whipped cream. The topping included 2,287 lb of chocolate fudge, 1,706 lb of butterscotch, 1,732 lb of caramel, as well as strawberry, pineapple and cherry syrup. Fork lifts and ladders were used to stack the ice cream blocks.

Largest Dish

The largest single dish is roasted camel, prepared occasionally for Bedouin wedding feasts. Cooked eggs are stuffed in fish, the fish stuffed in cooked chicken, the chickens stuffed into a roasted sheep carcass and the sheep stuffed into a whole camel.

TRANSPORTATION AND MASS COMMUNICATIONS

Merchant Shipping

The world total of merchant shipping (excluding vessels of less than 100 tons gross, sailing vessels and barges) was 75,240 vessels of 403,498,122 gross tonnage on July 1, 1987. The largest merchant fleet in the world at mid-1987 was that under the flag of Liberia with 1,574 ships of 51,412,029 gross tonnage. All the 1987 figures were lower than those of 1985.

Largest and Busiest Ports

Physically, the largest port is the Port of NY and NJ. The port has a navigable waterfront of 755 miles (460 miles in NY State and 295 miles in NJ) stretching over 92 sq mi. A total of 261 general cargo berths and 130 other piers gives a total berthing capacity of 391 ships at one time. The total warehousing floor space is 18,400,000 sq ft (422.4 acres).

The world's busiest port and largest artificial harbor is the Rotterdam-Europoort in The Netherlands, which covers 38 sq mi with 76 mi of quays. It handled 22,600 seagoing vessels carrying a total of 255 million metric tons of seagoing cargo, and about 182,000 barges, in 1986. It is able to handle 310 seagoing vessels simultaneously, of up to 318,000 metric tons and 72 ft draught.

Airlines

The country with the busiest airlines system is the US, where 277,182,916,000 revenue passenger miles were flown on the larger US certified air carriers in domestic operations in 1985. This was equivalent to an annual trip of 1,168 miles for every inhabitant of the US.

> The longest airline ticket was one 39 ft 4½ in long issued for $4,500 to M Bruno Leunen of Brussels, Belgium in Dec 1984 for a 53,203-mi air trip on 80 airlines involving 109 stopovers.

Railroads

The country with the greatest length of railroad is the US, with 184,235 miles of track.

Roads and Traffic

The country with the greatest length of road is the US (50 states), with 3,879,539 mi of graded roads on Dec 31, 1986.

The highest traffic volume of any point is at East Los Angeles, where there is an interchange of the Santa Ana, Pomona, Golden State, Hollywood, San Bernardino and Santa Monica Freeways with a 24-hour average on weekdays of 522,020 vehicles in 1986—363 per min. The most heavily traveled stretch of road is Route 101 at its junction with Route 405 near Encino, Calif, with a weekday volume of 288,000 vehicles.

The place with the highest traffic density is Hong Kong. By Jan 1, 1984, there were 302,118 motor vehicles on 778.9 mi of serviceable roads giving a density of 4.53 yd per vehicle.

> The world's narrowest street is in the village of Ripatransone in the Marche region of Italy. It is called Vico della Virilità (Virility Alley) and is 16.9 in wide.

Widest, Narrowest and Shortest Streets

The widest street is the Monumental Axis, running for 1½ miles from the Municipal Plaza to the Plaza of the Three Powers in Brasilia, the capital of Brazil. The 6-lane boulevard was opened in Apr 1960 and is 273.4 yd wide.

The Bay Bridge Toll Plaza has 23 lanes (17 westbound) serving San Francisco and Oakland.

The title of "The Shortest Street in the World" has been claimed since 1907 by McKinley St in Bellefontaine, Ohio, which is built of vitrified brick and measures 30 ft in length. This title has been disputed by Bacup, Lancashire, Eng where "Elgin Street" by the old market measures 17 ft. 0 in, but is not "carriagable."

Steepest and Crookedest Streets

The steepest streets are Filbert St, Russian Hill and 22nd St, Dolores

WIDEST STREET: Brasilia, the capital of Brazil, built in 1960, has streets laid out with room to spare. The widest is the Monumental Axis, which has 6 lanes, 3 going in one direction and 200 yards away 3 parallel lanes going in the opposite direction. In between are official buildings, parks and loops leading to crossroads as seen here. *(Duncan Rabin/Daily Telegraph)*

Heights, San Francisco, with gradients of 31.5° or a rise of 1 ft for every 3.17 ft.

Lombard Street in San Francisco between Hyde and Leavenworth has 8 consecutive 90-degree turns of 20-ft radius as it descends steeply one way.

First Traffic Light

The *Deseret News* in Salt Lake City, Utah, claims that the first electric red-green traffic light was installed in that city in 1912 at the intersection of 2nd South and Main Sts. The invention of Lester Farnsworth Wire, a SLC traffic cop, it was a 20-in square box resembling a birdhouse. It was not hung high but stood on a pole in the intersection and was operated manually from the curb. This installation preceded the red-green traffic light set up in Aug 1914 in Cleveland, Ohio, at Euclid Ave and E 105 St, which hung 15 ft above the ground and also had a buzzer to warn pedestrians. The first semaphore-type traffic signal was used in London, Eng, in 1868 and used red-green gas lamps at night.

Longest Highways

The longest motorable road is the Pan-American Highway which stretches from northwest Alaska to Santiago, Chile, thence goes eastward to Buenos Aires, Argentina and terminates in Brasilia, Brazil. There remains a gap of 250 miles, known as the Tapon del Darién in Panama, and the Atrato Swamp in Colombia.

CROOKEDEST STREET: San Francisco has plenty of steep hills, but none is as crooked and steep as Lombard. It has 8 consecutive 90-degree turns of 20-ft radius on the way down. Yes, it's one-way.

The longest Interstate Highway in the US is Route 90 which goes 3,087.65 mi from Boston to Seattle.

Lowest Road

The lowest road is that along the Israeli shores of the Dead Sea, 1,290 ft below sea level. The lowest pass is the Rock Reef Pass in Everglades National Park, Fla, which is 3 ft above sea level.

Drivers' Licenses

Regular drivers' licenses are issuable as young as 15 and without a driver education course only in Hawaii and Mississippi. Thirteen US states issue restricted juvenile licenses at 14.

The easiest test for a driver's license is given in Egypt, where the ability to drive 6 meters (19.7 ft) forward and 6 meters in reverse has been deemed sufficient. In 1979 it was reported that accurate reversing between 2 rubber traffic cones had been added, but this soon led to the substitution of white lines when too many cones were destroyed.

Most Parking Tickets

The Los Angeles Dept of Transportation has "captured" a scofflaw car that it believes has accumulated a record number of unpaid parking violations—201 tickets worth $11,598. The 1983 white Mazda sedan was found parked *legally* on Mar 4, 1988. The car's retail value is $2,000, or $9,000 less than the unpaid fines.

Worst Drivers

It was reported that a 75-year-old *male* driver received 10 traffic tickets, drove on the wrong side of the road four times, committed four hit-and-run offenses and caused six accidents, all within 20 minutes, in McKinney, Tex, on Oct 15, 1966.

A record for arrests was set by Tommy Johns in Brisbane, Australia, on Sept 9, 1982 when he faced his 2,000th conviction for drunkenness since 1957.

Oldest Driver

Roy M. Rawlins (b July 10, 1870) of Stockton, Calif, was warned for driving at 95 mph in a 55-mph zone in June 1974. On Aug 25, 1974, he was awarded a Calif State license valid until 1978, but he died on July 9, 1975, one day short of his 105th birthday. Mrs Maude Tull of Inglewood, Calif, who began driving after her husband's death, when she was aged 91, was issued a renewal of her license on Feb 5, 1976, then aged 104.

Walter Herbert Weake of England drove for 75 years without ever having an accident. He began driving in 1894 and drove daily until his death, at age 91, in 1969.

Most Durable Driver

The Goodyear Tire and Rubber Co test driver Weldon C. Kocich drove 3,031,577 mi from Feb 5, 1953 to July 20, 1984, so averaging 96,345 mi per year.

POSTAGE STAMPS

EARLIEST	Put on sale in London May 1, 1840	1 penny Black of Great Britain, Queen Victoria, 68,158,080 printed. Available for pre-payment of postage on May 6, 1840.
HIGHEST PRICE (TENDER)	$1 million	5 cent Blue Alexandria US cover, Nov 25, 1846 by Georg Normann *via* David Feldmans of Geneva on May 9, 1981.
HIGHEST PRICE (AUCTION)	$850,000 $935,000 (with buyer's premium)	British Guiana 1¢ black on magenta provisional postmarked '4 Ap., 1856' by Irwin R. Weinberg syndicate to anonymous collector at Waldorf-Astoria, NYC Apr 5, 1980.
HIGHEST PRICE (ERROR)	$864,386	First issue (1851) of German state of Baden, 9 Kreuzer, printed in error on blue-green paper intended for 6 Kreuzer, instead of dull rose. Only 3 examples known. One sold at auction for $864,386 on Mar 16, 1985 in Wiesbaden, W Germany.
LARGEST PHILATELIC PURCHASE	$11,000,000	Marc Haas collection of 3,000 US postal and pre-postal covers to 1869 by Stanley Gibbons International Ltd of London in Aug 1979.
LARGEST (SPECIAL PURPOSE)	9¾ × 2¾ in	Express Delivery of China, 1913.
(STANDARD POSTAGE)	6.3 × 4.33 in	Marshall Islands 75 cents issued Oct 30, 1979.
SMALLEST	0.31 × 0.37 in	10 cent and 1 peso Colombian State of Bolivar, 1863–6.
HIGHEST DENOMINATION	£100 (then $500)	Red and black, George V, of Kenya, 1925–7.
LOWEST DENOMINATION	3,000 pengö of Hungary	Issued 1946 when 150 million million pengö = 1p 1.5×10^{14} = 1 US penny.
RAREST	Unique examples include	British Guiana (now Guyana) 1 cent black on magenta of 1856 (see above); Swedish 3 skilling banco yellow color error of 1855. Gold Coast provisional of 1885 and US postmaster stamps from Boscawen, New Hampshire, and Lockport, NY.

Most Failures on Learner's Test

The record for persistence in taking and failing a test for a driver's license is held by Mrs Miriam Hargrave (b Apr 3, 1908) of Wakefield, Yorkshire, England, who failed her 39th driving test in 8 years on Apr 29, 1970, when she "crashed" through a set of red lights. She finally passed her 40th driving test on Aug 3, 1970. She spent $720 on 212 driving lessons and could no longer afford to buy a car. In 1978, she was reported to dislike right-hand turns.

Mrs Fannie Turner (b 1903) of Little Rock, Ark, passed her *written* test for a driver's license on her 104th attempt in Oct 1978.

Telephones

There were approximately 285,723,398 telephones in the world on Jan 1, 1984, it was estimated by the American Telephone and Telegraph Co. The country with the greatest number was the US with 114,349,000 (about the same number as in all of Europe), equivalent to 483 for every 1,000 people.

The greatest total of calls made in any country is in the US, with 434,569 million in 1984 (1,837 calls per person).

The city with most telephones is NYC, which had 5,808,145 (821 per 1,000 people) as of Jan 1, 1985. In 1985, Washington, DC, reached the record of 1,730 telephones per 1,000 people.

Largest Switchboard

The world's biggest switchboard is that in the Pentagon, Wash, DC, with 25,000 lines and an annual phone bill of $8.7 million.

Optical Fiber

The longest distance at which signals have been transmitted without repeaters is 156.3 miles at the British Telecom research laboratory at Martlesham Heath, Suffolk, Eng in Feb 1985. The laser wavelength was 1,525 nm and the rate was 35 megabits/ sec.

Longest Telephone Cable

The longest submarine telephone cable is the Commonwealth Pacific Cable (COMPAC), which runs for 9,340 mi from Sydney, Australia *via* Norfolk Island, Fiji, and Hawaii to Port Alberni, Canada.

Postal Services

The country with the largest mail is the US, whose people posted 153.9 billion letters and packages, including 78.9 billion first class, in the fiscal year ending Sept 1987. The US Postal Service then employed 790,577 people with the world's largest vehicle fleet—158,758 cars and trucks.

The US also takes first place in the average number of letters which each person mails during one year—635.

5. EDUCATION

Colleges and Universities

The Sumerians had scribal schools soon after 3500 BC. The oldest existing educational institution is the University of Karueein, founded in 859 AD in Fez, Morocco. The University of Bologna (Italy) was founded in 1088.

Although Harvard, originally founded in 1636 as Newtowne College (with the sole purpose of preparing men for the ministry), is thought of as the first American college, this is actually not the case. Although Harvard is the oldest *surviving* college, the first school founded in the United States never saw a graduating class. It was established at Henricopolis, Virginia, in 1619, and was forced to cease operation because of the Indian massacres of 1622.

The university with the greatest enrollment in the world is the State University of New York, which had 156,175 students enrolled in 1984–85. Its oldest college, at Potsdam, NY, was founded in 1816.

Smith College has always been exclusively for women, right up through the revolution of the 60s, but it did not appoint a woman president—Jill Ker Conway—until 1975.

Brown University was chartered in 1764 as Rhode Island College. After the Revolutionary War, this school, the smallest of the later-named "Ivy Leaguers," advertised that it would assume the name of any person who could help the institution out by donating $6,000. Nicholas Brown, a Providence merchant, won the title with his bid of $5,000.

Yale tried in 1966 to convince Vassar to move from Poughkeepsie over to New Haven, thus joining the two schools. Vassar said a firm "No."

Bids for building the $3.4-billion University of Riyadh, Saudi Arabia, were accepted in June 1978. The University will house 15,000 families and have its own mass transportation system.

The largest existing university building is the M. V. Lomonosov State University on the Lenin Hills, south of Moscow. It stands 787.4 ft tall, has 32 stories and 40,000 rooms. It was constructed in 1949–53.

The most northerly university is Inupiat University of the Arctic at Barrow, Alaska on Lat 71°16′N. Eskimo subjects are featured in the curriculum.

Highest Endowment

The greatest single gift in the history of higher education has been $125 million to Louisiana State University by C. B. Pennington in 1983.

Youngest Professors

The youngest at which anybody has been elected to a chair (full professorship) in a university is 19, in the case of Colin MacLaurin (1698–1746), who was admitted to Marischal College, Aberdeen, Scotland as Professor of Mathematics on Sept 30, 1717. In 1725 he was made Professor of Mathematics at Edinburgh University on the recommendation of Sir Isaac Newton, who was a professor at Cambridge, aged 26.

In July 1967, Dr Harvey Martin Friedman, PhD (b Sept 23, 1948) was appointed Assistant Professor of Mathematics at Stanford University, Calif, on Sept 1, 1967, just 3 weeks before his 19th birthday.

Youngest College President

Ellen Futter at age 31, only a decade after her own graduation, became the youngest college president, appointed to head Barnard in May, 1981. In September, 1981, she gave birth to a 5-pound 9-ounce girl—on her 32nd birthday. The last previous time a Barnard College head became pregnant, in 1901, she informed the board of trustees and was promptly dismissed.

Most Durable Professor

Dr Joel Hildebrand (1881–1983), Professor Emeritus of Physical Chemistry at the University of California, Berkeley, first became an Assistant Professor in 1913, and 68 years later, in 1981 published his 275th research paper.

Youngest Undergraduates

The most extreme recorded case of undergraduate juvenility was that of William Thomson (1824–1907), later Lord Kelvin, who entered Glasgow University aged 10 years 4 months in Oct 1834, and matriculated on Nov 14, 1834.

Dr. Merrill Kenneth Wolf (b Aug 28, 1931) of Cleveland, O, took his B.A. in music from Yale Univ in Sept 1945 in the month of his 14th birthday.

Ruth Lawrence (b 1971) of Huddersfield, W Yorkshire, Eng, was accepted for entrance to Oxford at the age of 12, and graduated two years later (July 4, 1985) with a first class degree, top of 191 entrants.

Jay Luo of Garden City, Mich (b Apr 4, 1970) graduated from Boise State Univ, Idaho, with a B S degree in math *cum laude* on May 16, 1982, at the age of 12 years 42 days.

Fraternity Facts

The oldest Greek letter fraternity in the US is Phi Beta Kappa, founded on December 6, 1776 at the College of William and Mary. Since it was later turned into an honor society, history notes that the oldest general (or social) fraternity in continuing existence is Kappa Alpha Society, founded in 1825 at Union College, Schenectady, NY.

The largest fraternity is Sigma Alpha Epsilon, with 181,900 initiates, located at the University of Alabama and founded on March 9, 1856.

The fraternity with the most active campus chapters is Tau Kappa Epsilon, which boasts 272 individual campus locations.

Youngest Doctorate

Carl Witte of Lochau, Germany was made a doctor of philosophy when age 12 on Apr 13, 1814, at the Univ of Giessen, Germany.

The youngest to receive a Doctor of Medicine degree is Avi

Ben-Abraham (b Nov 18, 1957, Kfar-Saba, Israel) who graduated with his MD *summa cum laude* on Mar 4, 1976 from the Univ of Perugia, Italy, at the age of 18 years 3 months.

Most Graduates in Immediate Family

Mr & Mrs Albert Kunz of Bloomington, Ind, saw all their 8 sons and 5 daughters graduate from Indiana Univ between 1932 and 1956.

Largest School

South Point High School, Calcutta, India, had an enrollment of 12,350 regular students in 1983–84.

Most Schools Attended

The documented record for the greatest number of schools attended by a pupil is 265 by Wilma Williams, now Mrs R. J. Horton, from 1933 to 1943 when her parents were in show business in the US.

Lectures and Speakers

Bob Jones of Wellington, New Zealand, in 1980, addressed a seminar of 1,048 people in Auckland on property. He received US $140,000 (NZ $200,000) equal to $11,666 per hour. In March 1981, it was reported that both Johnny Carson and Bob Hope commanded fees of $40,000 an appearance.

---

6. RELIGIONS

Oldest Religious Custom

Human burial, which has religious connotations, has been known from *c.* 60,000 BC among *Homo sapiens neanderthalensis* in the Shanidar cave, N Iraq. The earliest named prophet was Zoroaster (Zarathustra) dated to *c.* 600 BC. He has 250,000 followers today.

Largest Religious Membership

Religious statistics are necessarily only approximate. The test of adherence to a religion varies widely in rigor, while many individuals, particularly in the East, belong to two or more religions.

Christianity is the leading religion, with some 1.62 billion adherents in 1986. The Vatican statistics office reported that in 1986 there were 900,545,000 Roman Catholics. The largest non-Christian religion is Islam (Muslim) with about 560 million followers.

Largest Clergy

The largest religious organization is the Roman Catholic Church, with 138 cardinals, 729 archbishops, 3,092 bishops, 403,480 priests and 917,432 nuns in 1987. There are about 420,000 churches.

World Jewry

The total of world Jewry was estimated to number 16,000,000 in 1987. The highest concentration was in the US, with 5,834,650 of whom 1,742,500 are in the NY area. The total in Israel is 3,537,000. The total in Tokyo is only 750.

Largest Temple

The largest religious building ever constructed is Angkor Wat (City Temple), enclosing 402 acres, in Cambodia (now Kampuchea). It was built to the God Vishnu by the Khmer King Suryavarman II in the period 1113–1150. Its curtain wall measures 1,400 × 1,400 yd and its population, before it was abandoned in 1432, was at times 80,000. The whole complex of 72 major monuments, begun *c.* 900 AD, extends over 15 × 5 miles.

The largest Buddhist temple is Borobudur, near Jogjakarta, Indonesia, built in the 8th century. It is 103 ft tall and 403 ft square.

The largest Mormon temple is in Salt Lake City, Utah, completed in Apr 1983, with a floor area of 253,015 sq ft. At the adjoining Tabernacle, the choir on Feb 15, 1987 broadcast its 3,000th consecutive weekly radio program.

Largest Synagogue

The largest synagogue is the Temple Emanu-El on Fifth Ave at 65th St, NYC. The temple, completed in Sept 1929, has a frontage of 150 ft on Fifth Ave and 253 ft on 65th St. The sanctuary proper can accommodate 2,500 people, and the adjoining Beth-El Chapel seats 350. When all the facilities are in use, more than 6,000 people can be accommodated.

Largest Mosque

The largest mosque ever built was the now ruined al-Malawiya mosque of al-Mutawakil in Samarra, Iraq, built in 842–852 AD and measuring 401,408 sq ft (9.21 acres) with dimensions of 784 × 512 ft.

The largest mosque is the Merdeka Mosque in Djakarta, Indonesia, which was begun in 1962. The cupola spans 147.6 ft in diameter and the capacity is in excess of 50,000 people.

Smallest Church

The smallest church is the Union Church at Wiscasset, Maine, with a floor area of 7 ft × 4½ ft.

Largest Church

The largest church is the basilica of St Peter, built between 1492 and 1612 in Vatican City, Rome. Its length, measured from the apse, is 611 ft 4 in. Its area is 162,990 sq ft. The inner diameter of the famous dome is 137 ft 9 in and its center is 390 ft 5 in high. The external height is 457 ft 9 in.

The elliptical Basilique de St Pie X at Lourdes, France, completed in 1957 at a cost of $5,600,000, has a capacity of 20,000 under its giant span arches and a length of 656 ft.

The crypt of the underground Civil War Memorial Church in the

Guadarrama Mountains, 28 miles from Madrid, Spain, is 853 ft in length. It took 21 years (1937–58) to build, at a reported cost of $392 million and is surmounted by a cross 492 ft tall.

Largest and Smallest Cathedrals

The largest is the cathedral church of the Episcopalian Diocese of NY, St John the Divine, with a floor area of 121,000 sq ft and a volume of 16,822,000 cu ft. The cornerstone was laid on Dec 27, 1892, and work on the Gothic building was stopped in 1941, then restarted in earnest in July 1979. In NY it is referred to as "Saint John the Unfinished." The nave is the longest in the world, 601 ft in length, with a vaulting 124 ft in height.

The cathedral covering the largest area is that of Santa María de la Sede in Seville, Spain. It was built in Spanish Gothic style between 1402 and 1519 and is 414 ft long, 271 ft wide and 100 ft high to the vault of the nave.

The smallest church in the world designated as a cathedral is that of the Christ Catholic Church, Highlandville, Mo. Consecrated in July 1983, it measures 14 × 17 ft and has seating for 18 people.

Tallest Spires

The tallest *cathedral* spire is on the Protestant Cathedral of Ulm in Germany. The building is early Gothic and was begun in 1377. The tower, in the center of the west façade, was not finally completed until 1890 and is 528 ft high.

The tallest *church* spire is that of the Chicago Temple of the First Methodist Church on Clark St, Chicago. The building consists of a 22-story skyscraper (erected in 1924) surmounted by a parsonage at 330 ft, a "Sky Chapel" at 400 ft and a steeple cross at 568 ft above street level.

Most Valuable Sacred Object

The sacred object of the highest intrinsic value is the 15th-century gold Buddha in the Temple of Three Friends in Bangkok, Thailand. It is 10 ft tall and weighs an estimated 6 tons. At the current value of $457 per fine ounce, its value has been calculated at $87.7 million for the gold alone. The gold under the plaster exterior was only found in 1954.

Biggest Demonstrations

A figure of 2,700,000 was published from China for the demonstration against the USSR in Shanghai Apr 3–4, 1969, following border clashes, and one of 10 million for the May Day celebrations of 1963 in Peking.

Minarets and Pagodas

The tallest minarets are the four of 450 ft 9 in being built for a new mosque in Shah Alam, Selangor, Malaysia. The tallest free-standing stone tower is the Qutb Minar, south of New Delhi, India, built in 1194 to a height of 238 ft.

The tallest pagoda is the Phra Pathom Chedi at Nakhon Pathom,

Thailand, which was built for King Mongkut in 1853–70. It rises to 377 ft.

The oldest pagoda in China is Sung-Yo Ssu in Honan, built with 15 12-sided stories in 523 AD, though the 326-ft-tall Shwedagon Pagoda, Rangoon, Burma is built on the site of a 27-ft-tall pagoda dating to 585 BC.

Largest Crowd

The greatest recorded number of human beings assembled with a common purpose was an estimated 12,700,000 at the Hindu feast of Kumbh-Mela, which was held at the confluence of the Yamuna (formerly called the Jumna), the Ganges and the invisible "Sarasvati" at Allahabad, Uttar Pradesh, India, on Jan 19, 1977. The holiest time during this holiest day since 1833 was during the planetary alignment between 9:28 and 9:40 a.m., during which only 200,000 achieved immersion to wash away the sins of a lifetime.

Popes, Cardinals and Bishops

LONGEST PAPAL REIGN: Pius IX, Giovanni Maria Mastai-Ferretti (1848–1878), 31 years 236 days

SHORTEST PAPAL REIGN: Stephan II (752), 2 days

LONGEST-LIVED POPE: St Agatho (d 681), ?106 years; Leo XIII, Gioacchino Pecci (1810–1903), 93 years 140 days

YOUNGEST ELECTED POPE: Benedict IX—Theophylact (*c.* 1020–1056) in 1032, at 11 or 12 years—3 terms as Pope

LAST MARRIED POPE (before celibacy rule): Adrian II (867–872)

LAST POPE WITH CHILDREN: Gregory XIII—Ugo Buoncompagni (1502–1585) had a son; elected 1572

SLOWEST ELECTION: Gregory X—Teobaldi Visconti, 31 months, Feb 1269—Sept 1, 1271

FASTEST ELECTION: Julius II, on first ballot, Oct 21, 1503

LAST NON-CARDINAL POPE: Urban VI—Bartolomeo Prignano (1318–89), Archbishop of Bari, Apr 8, 1378

SLOWEST CANONIZATION: St Leo III, over span of 857 years (816–1673)

OLDEST CARDINAL: Georgio da Costa (b Portugal, 1406, d Rome Sept 18, 1508), aged 102 years

OLDEST LIVING CARDINAL: Julijans Vaivods (b Latvia, Aug 18, 1895)

YOUNGEST CARDINAL: Luis Antonio de Bourbon (b July 25, 1727) elected Dec 19, 1735, aged 8 years 137 days

YOUNGEST LIVING CARDINAL: Alfonso Lopez Trujillo of Colombia (b Nov 18, 1935) appointed when aged 47 years 76 days

LONGEST-SERVING CARDINAL: Cardinal Duke of York, grandson of James VII of Scotland and II of England (1747–1807), 60 years 10 days

LONGEST-SERVING BISHOP: Bishop Louis Francois de la Baume de Suze (1603–90) 76 years 273 days from Dec 6, 1613

Non-Italian Popes

The current Pope John Paul II, elected Oct 16, 1978 (b Karol

Wojtyla, May 18, 1920, at Wadowice, near Krakow, Poland) is the first non-Italian Pope since 1522.

Saints

There are 1,848 "registered" saints (including 60 St Johns), of whom 628 are Italians, 576 French and 271 from the British Isles. The first US-born saint is Mother Elizabeth Ann Bayley Seton (1774–1821) who was canonized Sept 14, 1975. The total includes 79 Popes.

The shortest interval that has elapsed between the death of a saint and his canonization was in the case of St Anthony of Padua, Italy, who died on June 13, 1231 and was canonized 352 days later on May 30, 1232.

The other extreme is represented by Pope St Leo III who died on June 12, 816, and was made a saint in 1673—857 years later.

Largest Funeral

The funeral of C. N. Annadurai (d Feb 3, 1969) Madras (India) Chief Minister was, according to some press reports, attended by 15 million. The longest funeral was probably that of Vice Admiral Viscount Nelson on Jan 9, 1806. Ticket holders were seated in St Paul's Cathedral, London by 8:30 AM. Many were unable to leave until after 9 PM.

The queue at the grave of the *chansonier* and guitarist Vladimir Visotsky (d July 28, 1980) stretched 6.2 mi.

WORST ACCIDENTS & DISASTERS IN THE WORLD

	Deaths		
Pandemic	75,000,000	Eurasia: The Black Death (bubonic, pneumonic and septicaemic plague)	1347–51
Genocide	*c.* 5,000,000	Mongol extermination of Chinese peasantry	1311–40
Famine	*c.* 30,000,000[1]	Northern China (revealed May 1981)	1959–61
Influenza	21,640,000	Worldwide: Influenza	Apr–Nov 1918
Earthquake	1,100,000	Near East and E. Mediterranean	*c.* July 1201
Circular Storm	1,000,000[2]	Ganges Delta isles, Bangladesh	Nov 12–13, 1970
Flood	900,000	Yellow (Hwang-ho) River, China	Oct 1877
Landslide	180,000	Kansu Province, China	Dec 16, 1920
Atomic Bomb	141,000	Hiroshima, Japan	Aug 6, 1945
Conventional Bombing	*c.* 140,000[3]	Tokyo, Japan	Mar 10, 1945
Volcanic Eruption	92,000	Tambora Sumbawa, Indonesia	Apr 5–7, 1815
Avalanche (mud)	*c.* 23,000	Nevado Del Ruiz, Colombia	Nov 13, 1985
Avalanche (ice and debris)	*c.* 18,000[4]	Yungay, Huascaran Mt, Peru	May 31, 1970
Marine (single ship)	*c.* 7,700	*Wilhelm Gustloff* (25,484 tons) torpedoed off Danzig by USSR submarine S-13	Jan 30, 1945
Dam Burst	*c.* 5,000[14]	Manchu River Dam, Morvi, Gujarat, India	Aug 11, 1979
Panic	*c.* 4,000[5]	Chungking, China (air raid shelter)	*c.* June 8, 1941
Smog	2,850	London (Eng) fog	Dec 5–13, 1952
Tunneling (Silicosis)	*c.* 2,500	Hawk's Nest hydroelectric tunnel, W Va	1931–35
Industrial (Chemical)	2,352[11]	Bhopal, India at Union Carbide plant (plus *c.* 200,000 injured)	Dec 2–3, 1984
Explosion	1,963[6]	Halifax, Nova Scotia, Canada	Dec 6, 1917
Fire (single building)	1,670[7]	The Theatre, Canton, China	May 1845
Mining	1,572[8]	Honkeiko Colliery, China (coal dust explosion)	Apr 26, 1942

	Deaths		
Riot	*c.* 1,200	NYC (anticonscription riots)	July 13–16, 1863
Road	*c.* 1,100[9]	Gasoline tanker explosion inside Salang Tunnel, Afghanistan	Nov 2 or 3, 1982
Mass Suicide	913	People's Temple Cult by cyanide, Jonestown, Guyana	Nov 18, 1978
Crocodiles (disputed)	*c.* 900	Japanese soldiers, Ramree Island, Burma	Feb 19–20, 1945
Fireworks Show[13]	>800	Dauphin's wedding, Seine, Paris	May 16, 1770
Railroad	>800	Bagmati River, Bihar State, India	June 6, 1981
Tornado	689	South Central States, US (3 hours)	March 18, 1925
Aircraft (Civil)	583	KLM-Pan Am Boeing 747 ground crash, Tenerife, Canary Islands (Single plane: Japan Airlines 747 in central Japan, 520 killed Aug 12, 1985.)	March 27, 1977
Man-Eating Animal	436	Champawat district, India, tigress shot by Col Jim Corbett	1907
Terrorism	329	Bomb aboard Air India Boeing 747, crashed into Atlantic south of Ireland. Sikh extremists suspected.	June 23, 1985 *deaths*
Bacteriological and Chemical	*c.* 300	Novosibirsk B&CW plant, USSR	Apr–May 1979

Notes.

1.—It has been estimated that more than 5 million died in the post-World War I famine of 1920–1 in the USSR. The USSR government in July 1923 informed Mr (later President) Herbert Hoover that the ARA (American Relief Administration) had since August 1921 saved 20 million lives from famine and famine-related diseases.

2.—The figure published in 1972 for the Bangladeshi disaster was from Dr Afzal, Principal Scientific Officer of the Atomic Energy Authority Centre, Dacca. One report asserted that less than half of the population of the 4 islands of Bhola, Charjabbar, Hatia and Ramagati (1961 Census 1.4 million) survived. The most damaging hurricane reported was Hurricane Frederic in 1979 with an estimated loss of $2,300 billion.

3.—The number of civilians killed by the bombing of Germany has been put variously at 593,000 and "over 635,000." Total Japanese fatalities in World War II were 600,000 (conventional) and 220,000 (nuclear).

4.—This avalanche occurred when an earthquake broke off the north peak of Huascaran, Peru's highest mountain, 22,205 ft high. It scooped up more ice and snow from the glacier below, then dirt and boulders, in all about 100 million tons, which fell upon Yungay. The earthquake killed about 60,000 people in all. A total of 10,000 Austrian and Italian troops is reported to have been lost in the Dolomite valley of Northern Italy on Dec 13, 1916 in more than 100 avalanches. Some of the avalanches were triggered by gunfire.

	Deaths		
Hail	246	Moradabad, Uttar Pradesh, India	Apr 20, 1888
Truck Bomb	243	US Marine Barracks, Beirut, Lebanon	Oct 23, 1983
Submarine	130	*Le Surcouf* rammed in Caribbean	Feb 18, 1942
Offshore Oil Plant	123	Alexander L. Kielland "Hotel," North Sea	March 27, 1980
Helicopter	54	Israeli military "Sea Stallion," West Bank	May 10, 1977
Ski Lift (Cablecar)	42	Cavalese resort, Northern Italy	March 9, 1976
Mountaineering	40[10]	USSR expedition on Mt Everest	Dec 1952
Nuclear Reactor	31[12]	Chernobyl No 4, Ukraine, USSR	Apr 26, 1986
Elevator	23	Vaal Reefs Gold Mine lift fell 1.2 miles	May 27, 1980
Lightning	21	Hut in Chinamasa Kraal near Umtali, Rhodesia (single bolt)	Dec 23, 1975
Yacht Racing	19	28th Fastnet Race, 23 boats sank or abandoned in Force 11 gale	Aug 13–15, 1979
Space	7	US Space Shuttle *Challenger*	Jan 28, 1986
Nuclear Waste Accident[15]	high but undisclosed	Venting of plutonium wastes, Kyshtym, USSR	*c.* Dec 1957

5.—It was estimated that some 5,000 people were trampled to death in the stampede for free beer at the coronation celebration of Czar Nicholas II in Moscow in May 1896.
6.—Some sources maintain that the final death toll was over 3,000 on Dec 6–7.
7.—>200,000 killed in the sack of Moscow, freed by Tartars, May 1571. The worst-ever hotel fire killed 162 at the Hotel Daeyungak, Seoul, South Korea, Dec 25, 1971. The worst circus fire killed 323 at the Gran Circus Norte-Americano, Niteroi, Brazil, on Dec 17, 1961.
8.—The worst gold mining disaster in South Africa was 152 killed due to flooding in the Witwatersrand Gold Mining Co gold mine in 1909.
9.—Some estimates ran as high as 2,700 victims from monoxide asphyxiation when Soviet military sealed off both ends of a 1.7-mi long tunnel.
10.—According to Polish sources, not confirmed by the USSR. On Mt Fuji, Japan 23 died in a blizzard and avalanche on March 20, 1972.
11.—Final certified death toll obscured by litigation.
12.—Total death estimates vary from 200 to 600 by 2006 AD (per Ukrainian Health Minister) to 75,000 (per US transplant specialist).
13.—Panic following the fireworks show caused a crush of people at the narrow exit doors. The deaths were not directly due to fireworks.
14.—The dynamiting of a Yangtze Kiang dam at Huayuan Kow by the KMT during the Sino-Japanese war in 1938 is reputed to have resulted in 900,000 deaths.
15.—More than 30 small communities in a 460 sq mi area eliminated from USSR maps since 1958. Possibly an ammonium nitrate-hexone explosion.

Chapter 11

Human Achievements

1. ENDURANCE AND ENDEAVOR

TRAVEL AND EXPLORATION

Lunar Conquest

Neil Alden Armstrong (b Wapakoneta, Ohio, of Scottish-Irish-German ancestry, Aug 5, 1930), command pilot of the *Apollo XI* mission, became the first man to set foot on the moon on the Sea of Tranquillity at 02:56 and 15 sec AM GMT on July 21, 1969. He was followed out of the Lunar Module *Eagle* by Col Edwin Eugene Aldrin, Jr (b Glen Ridge, NJ, of Swedish, Dutch and British ancestry, Jan 20, 1930), while the Command Module named *Columbia* piloted by Lt-Col Michael Collins (b Rome, Italy, of Irish and pre-Revolutionary American ancestry, Oct 31, 1930) orbited above.

Eagle landed at 20:17 and 42 sec GMT July 20 and blasted off at 17:54 GMT on July 21, after a stay of 21 hours 36 min. The *Apollo XI* had blasted off from Cape Kennedy, Fla at 13:32 GMT July 16 and was a culmination of the US space program, which, at its peak, employed 376,600 people and attained in the year 1966–67 a peak budget of $5.9 billion.

There is evidence that Pavel Belgayev was the cosmonaut selected by the USSR for a manned lunar flight in *Zond 7* on Dec 9, 1968 (212 days before the *Apollo VIII* flight), but no launch took place.

Speed in Space

The fastest speed at which humans have traveled is 24,791 mph when the Command Module of *Apollo X* carrying Col (now Brig-Gen) Thomas Patten Stafford, USAF (b Weatherford, Okla, Sept 17, 1930), Cdr (now Capt) Eugene Andrew Cernan and Cdr (now Capt) John Watts Young, USN (b San Francisco, Sept 24, 1930) reached their maximum speed on their trans-earth return flight at an altitude of 400,000 ft on May 26, 1969.

The highest speed ever attained by a woman is 17,470 mph by Jr Lt (now Lt Col) Valentina Vladimirovna Tereshkova-Nikolayev (b Mar 6, 1937) during her 48-orbit flight in *Vostok VI* June 16–19, 1963. The highest speed ever achieved by a woman aircraft pilot is 1,669.89 mph by Svetlana Savitskaya (USSR), reported on June 2, 1975.

MOST TRAVELED MAN: Parke Thompson of Akron, Ohio, on reaching the South Pole, accomplished his goal of visiting all 308 geographic areas of the world. Here he is at the Pole, where 4 nations meet.

Speed on Land

The highest speed ever claimed on land is an unofficial 739.666 mph or Mach 1.0106 in a one-way run by Stan Barrett (US) in the *Budweiser Rocket,* a rocket-engined 3-wheeled car at Edwards Air Force Base, Calif on Dec 17, 1979.

The *official* one-mile land speed record is 633.468 mph set by Richard Noble (b 1946) on Oct 4, 1983 over the Black Rock Desert, Nev, in his 17,000 thrust Rolls Royce Avon 302 jet-powered *Thrust 2,* designed by John Ackroyd.

The highest land speed recorded by a woman is 524.016 mph by Mrs Kitty O'Neil Hambleton (US), in the 48,000-hp rocket-powered 3-wheeled S.M.1 *Motivator* over the Alvard Desert, Ore, on Dec 6, 1976. Her official 2-way record was 512.710 mph and she probably touched 600 mph momentarily.

Speed on Water

The highest speed ever achieved on water is an estimated 300 knots (345 mph) by Kenneth Peter Warby (b May 9, 1939) on the Blowering Dam Lake, NSW, Australia Nov 20, 1977, in his unlimited hydroplane *Spirit of Australia.* The official world water speed record is 319.627 mph, set Oct 8, 1978, by Warby on the Blowering Dam Lake.

The record for propeller-driven craft is 229.00 mph by Eddie Hill in the *Texan,* a Kurtis top-fuel hydro drag boat, on Sept 5, 1982 at Chowchilla, Calif.

The fastest woman on water is Mary Rife (US), who has driven a drag boat, *Proud Mary,* at more than 190 mph.

Most Traveled Man

The most traveled person is Parke G. Thompson of Akron, Ohio, who has visited the complete list of 308 countries, territories and geographical areas listed by the Travelers Century Club, including the 229 recognized by the United Nations. His Jan 1988 trip to the South Pole, where 4 countries' territories meet, completed his log. He has visited every state of the US including 78 of the 87 metropolitan areas and 86 of the 100 biggest major cities; all but 2 of the Canadian provinces and their capitals; all of the states of Australia and their capitals; 14 of the Russian Soviet republics and their capitals and Siberia; 5 major cities in India; the major cities of China; 5 states of Malaysia; 7 of the United Arab Emirates, and even the most remote island in the world, Tristan da Cunha. Thompson, 70, whose first visit outside the US was to Germany at age 6, made 36 trips over 31 years (1956–87) to fulfill his goal.

The most traveled child is George Chauncey Clouse (b Dec 6, 1979) of Indiana who had been to 114 countries before his sixth birthday.

The man who had most mileage in visiting 215 countries in his time was Jesse Hart Rosdail (1914–77) of Elmhurst, Ill, a 5th grade teacher.

The most traveled man in the horseback era was probably the Methodist preacher Francis Asbury (b Birmingham, Eng), who traveled 264,000 mi in N America from 1771 to 1815, preaching 16,000 sermons.

Fastest Round-the-World Trip

The fastest time for a round-the-world journey on scheduled flights for a circumnavigation is 44 hours 6 min by David J. Springbett, 41, of Taplow, England from Los Angeles eastward via London, Bahrain, Singapore, Bangkok, Manila, Tokyo and Honolulu Jan 8–10, 1980 over a 23,068-mile route.

The F.A.I. accepts any flight, taking off and landing at the same point, which is as long as the Tropic of Cancer (22,858.754 *miles*) *as a circumnavigational flight.*

North Pole Conquests

The claims of both of the two US Arctic explorers, Dr Frederick Albert Cook (1865–1940) and Rear Adm Robert Edwin Peary, USN (1856–1920), in reaching the North Pole are subject to positive proof.

The earliest indisputable attainment of the North Pole over the sea ice was at 3 p.m. (CST) on Apr 19, 1968, by Ralph Plaisted (US) and three companions after a 42-day trek in four snowmobiles. Their arrival was independently verified 18 hours later by a US Air Force weather aircraft. The sea bed is 13,410 ft below the North Pole.

Naomi Uemara (b 1941), the Japanese explorer and mountaineer, became the first person to reach the North Pole in a solo trek across the Arctic ice cap at 04:45 GMT May 1, 1978. He had traveled 450 miles, setting out on March 7 from Cape Edward, Ellesmere Island, in northern Canada. He averaged nearly 8 miles per day with his sled "Aurora" drawn by 17 huskies.

The first woman to set foot on the North Pole was Mrs Fran Phipps, wife of the Canadian bush pilot Weldy Phipps, Apr 5, 1971. Galina Aleksandrovna Lastovskaya (b 1941) and Lilia Vladislavovna Minina (b 1959) were crew members of the USSR atomic icebreaker *Arktika* which reached the Pole on Aug 17, 1977.

The Soviet scientist Dr Pavel A. Gordienko and 3 companions were arguably the first ever to stand on the exact point Lat 90° 00′N (±300 meters) on Apr 23, 1948.

Dr Jean-Louis Etienne, 39, was the first to reach the Pole solo and without dogs, on May 11, 1986 after 63 days. On Apr 20, 1987 Fukashi Kazami, 36 of Tokyo reached the North Pole from Ward Hunt Island, northern Canada in 44 days having started on his 250 cc motorcycle on March 8.

Arctic Crossing

The first crossing of the Arctic Sea ice was achieved by the British Trans-Arctic Expedition which left Point Barrow, Alaska, Feb 21, 1968, and arrived at the Seven Island Archipelago northeast of Spitzbergen 464 days later on May 29, 1969, after a haul of 2,920 statute miles and a drift of 700 miles, compared with a straight-line distance of 1,662 miles. The team was Wally Herbert (leader), 34, Maj Ken Hedges, 34, Allan Gill, 38, Dr Roy Koerner, 36 (glaciologist), and 40 huskies. This was the longest sustained (sled) journey ever made on polar pack ice and the first undisputed conquest of the North Pole by sled. Temperatures sank to −47° F during the trek.

South Pole Conquests

The first men to cross the Antarctic circle (Lat 66° 30′ S) were the 193-crew of the *Resolution* (462 tons) under Capt James Cook (1728–79), the English navigator, and *Adventure* (336 tons) under Lt T. Furneaux, at 39° E, Jan 17, 1773.

The first person known to have sighted the Antarctic ice shelf was Capt. F. F. Bellinghausen (Russian) (1778–1852) on Jan 27, 1820 from the vessels *Vostock* and *Mirnyi*. The first person known to have sighted the mainland of the continent was Capt William Smith (1790–1847) and Master Edward Bransfield, of the British Royal Navy, in the brig *Williams*. They saw the peaks of Trinity Land 3 days later on Jan 30, 1820.

The South Pole (altitude 9,186 ft on ice and 336 ft bed rock) was first reached at 11 a.m. Dec 16, 1911, by a Norwegian party, led by Capt Roald Engebreth Gravning Amundsen (1872–1928), after a 53-day march with dog sleds from the Bay of Whales, to which he had penetrated in the *Fram*. Subsequent calculations showed that Olav Olavson Bjaaland (the last survivor, dying in June 1961, aged 88) and Helmer Hanssen probably passed within 400–600 meters of the exact pole. The other two party members were Sverre H. Hassell and Oskar Wisting.

The first woman to set foot on Antarctica was Mrs Karoline Mikkelsen on Feb 20, 1935. No woman stood on the South Pole until Nov 11, 1969, when Lois Jones, Eileen McSavenay, Jean Pearson, Terry Lee Tickhill (all US), Kay Lindsay (Australia) and Pam Young (New Zealand), arrived by air.

Antarctic Crossing

The first surface crossing of the Antarctic continent was completed at 1:47 p.m. March 2, 1958, after a 2,158-mile trek lasting 99 days from Nov 24, 1957, from Shackleton Base to Scott Base via the Pole. The crossing party of 12 was led by Dr (now Sir) Vivian Ernest Fuchs (b Feb 11, 1908).

The 2,600-mile trans-Antarctic leg of the 1980-82 Trans-Globe Expedition was achieved in 66 days on Jan 11, 1981 having passed through the South Pole on Dec 23, 1980. The 3-man party on snowmobiles comprised Sir Ranulph Fiennes (b 1944), Oliver Shepard and Charles Burton.

Polar Circumnavigation

Sir Ranulph Fiennes and Charles Burton of the British Trans-Globe Expedition traveled south from Greenwich, Eng (Sept 2, 1979), via the South Pole (Dec 17, 1980) and the North Pole (Apr 11, 1982), and back to Greenwich arriving after a 35,000 mile trek on Aug 29, 1982.

The only Arctic crossing achieved in a single season was that by Fiennes and Burton from Alert via the North Pole to the Greenland Sea in open snowmobiles.

Longest Sled Journeys

The longest totally self-supporting polar sled journey was one of 1,080 mi across Kalaallet (Greenland) (W–E) June 18–Sept 5, 1934 by a British team led by Capt Martin Lindsay, with 49 dogs. A Ross Sea party of 10 in the Antarctic sledged over 2,000 mi in 300 days from May 6, 1975 during which time 3 died.

First on Both North and South Poles

Dr. Albert P. Crary, a member of the party that made the first airplane landing at the North Pole on May 3, 1952, subsequently became Chief Scientist of the US Antarctic Research Program and led a scientific oversnow tractor traverse from McMurdo Sound on the coast to the South Pole, arriving at the South Pole on Feb 12, 1961. Crary thereby became the first person ever to have set foot at both North and South Poles, pre-empting David Porter by 18 years.

Greatest Ocean Descent

The record ocean descent was achieved in the Challenger Deep of the Marianas Trench, 250 miles southwest of Guam, when the Swiss-built US Navy bathyscaphe *Trieste,* manned by Dr Jacques Piccard (b 1914) and Lt Donald Walsh, USN, reached the ocean bed 35,820 ft (6.78 miles) down, at 1:10 p.m. Jan 23, 1960. The pressure of the water was 16,883 lb per sq in (1,215.6 tons per sq ft), and the temperature 37.4°F. The descent required 4 hours 48 min and the ascent 3 hours 17 min.

Deepest Salvage

The greatest depth at which salvage has been achieved is 16,500 ft by the bathyscaphe *Trieste II* (Lt Cdr Mel Bartels, USN) to attach cables to an "electronics package" on the sea bed 400 miles north of Hawaii, May 20, 1972.

The deepest salvage by robot was the recovery in July 1985 from the ocean floor off Ireland at 6,700 ft of 2 "black boxes" containing the flight recorders from the crashed Air-India 747 plane. The robot submarine "Scarab I" worked with a hydrophone and a side-scan radar "fish" towed by a surface ship.

Salvage by Divers

The deepest salvage operation ever achieved with divers was on the wreck of HM Cruiser *Edinburgh* sunk on May 2, 1942, in the Barents Sea off northern Norway inside the Arctic Circle in 803 ft of water. Twelve divers dived on the wreck in pairs using a bell from the *Stephaniturm* (1,423 tons) over 32 days under the direction of former RN officer and project director Michael Stewart from Sept 17 to Oct 7, 1981. A total of 460 gold ingots was recovered and divided; $26.3 million to the USSR, $13.15 million to GB and some $32.4 million to the salvage contractors, Jessop Marine Recoveries Ltd (10%) and Wharton Williams Ltd (90%). John Rossier, 28, was the first to touch the gold. The longest decompression time was 7 days 10 hours 27 min. The $71.85 million is an all-time record.

Deep Diving Records

The record depth for the extremely dangerous activity of breath-held diving is 344 ft by Jacques Mayol (France) off Elba, Italy in Dec 1983 for men. Mayol descended on a sled in 104 sec and ascended in 90 sec.

The record for women is 246 ft ¾ in by Rossana Majorca (Italy) off Syracuse, Sicily, on July 31, 1987.

The record dive with SCUBA (self-contained underwater breathing apparatus) is 437 ft by John J. Gruener and R. Neal Watson (US) off Freeport, Grand Bahama, on Oct 14, 1968.

The record dive utilizing gas mixtures (nitrogen, oxygen and helium) is a simulated dive of 2,250 ft in a dry chamber by Stephen Porter, Len Whitlock and Erik Kramer at the Duke University Medical Center, Durham, NC, Feb 3, 1981 in a 43-day trial in an 8-ft sphere.

Patrick Raude and 5 Comex divers left and returned to the bell *Petrel* at 1,643 ft off Cavalaire, France, in 1982.

Deepest Underwater Escapes

The deepest underwater rescue achieved was of the *Pisces III* in which Roger R. Chapman, 28, and Roger Mallinson, 35, were trapped for 76 hours when it sank to 1,575 ft, 150 miles southeast of Cork, Ireland, Aug 29, 1973. It was hauled to the surface by the cable ship *John Cabot* after preliminary work by *Pisces V*, *Pisces II* and the remote control recovery vessel US CURV, on Sept 1, 1973.

The greatest depth of an actual escape without any equipment has been from 225 ft by Richard A. Slater from the rammed submersible *Nekton Beta* off Catalina Island, Calif on Sept 28, 1970.

MARRIAGE AND DIVORCE

Longest Marriages

The longest recorded marriage is one of 86 years between Sir Temulji Bhicaji Nariman and Lady Nariman from 1853 to 1940 resulting from a cousin marriage when both were five. Sir Temulji (b Sept 3, 1848) died, aged 91 years 11 months, in Aug 1940 in Bombay.

An 86th wedding anniversary was also achieved by Lazarus Rowe of Greenland, NH, and Molly Webber, both born in 1725, married at 18, and died in 1829.

Longest Engagement

The longest engagement on record is one of 67 years between Octavio Guillen, 82, and Adriana Martinez, 82. They finally took the plunge in June 1969, in Mexico City.

Most Marriages

The greatest number of marriages claimed in the monogamous world is 80, by Pak Awang, a Malaysian witch doctor specializing in love charms. He says most of his marriages ended in divorce, although some of his wives died.

The greatest number of marriages verified in the monogamous world is 27 by the former Baptist minister Mr Glynn de Moss "Scotty" Wolfe (US) (b 1908), who first married in 1927. He says he has had 41 children but had only 25 mothers-in-law as he re-married two of his former wives.

Mrs Beverly Nina Avery, then aged 48, a barmaid from Los Angeles, set a monogamous world record in Oct 1957 by obtaining her 16th divorce, this one from Gabriel Avery, her 14th husband. She alleged outside the court that 5 of the 14 had broken her nose.

Giovanni Vigliotto (b Fred Jipp, NYC, Apr 3, 1936 or b Nikolai

CHILLY WEDDING: With penguins as witnesses, Bruno (photographer) married Heather (actress) in an ice cave in Antarctica on international territory at midnight. They stood 15 ft underground, with the thermometer at −15°F.

Peruskov, Siracusa, Sicily, Apr 3, 1929) was arrested in Panama City, Fla, on Dec 30, 1981, for a record 104 bigamous marriages in more than 27 US states and 14 other countries between 1949 and 1981. Four victims were aboard one ship in 1968. He said he specialized in "larceny by deception." Convicted on Mar 28, 1983, in Phoenix, Ariz, he was sentenced to a maximum of 34 years in prison (28 for fraud, 6 for bigamy) and fined $336,000.

Mass Wedding Ceremony

The largest mass wedding ceremony was one of 5,837 couples from 83 countries officiated over by the controversial Sun Myung Moon (b 1920) of the Holy Spirit Association for the Unification of World Christianity in Seoul, S Korea, on Oct 14, 1982.

Most Expensive Wedding

The wedding of Mohammed, son of Shaik Zayid ibn Sa'id al-Makhtum, to Princess Salama in Abu Dhabi in May 1981 lasted 7 days and cost an estimated $33 million including a purpose-built stadium for 20,000.

The most expensive private wedding is reputed to be that of Maria Niarchos, 20, to Alix Chevassus, 36, at her father's estate in Normandy, France on June 16, 1979. Guests consumed an estimated 12,000 bottles of champagne and red wine; the supply of caviar outweighed the demand in four football-field-sized tents. The cost is conservatively estimated at $500,000.

Mountain-Top Wedding

Pat Cardiff of Arlington, Va, first met his wife, Dorothy, in Wash, DC, and when he volunteered to go to Tanzania, Africa, as a teacher, she followed him. They decided to have a non-traditional, informal, intimate wedding and chose the peak of Mt Kilimanjaro as the site. Symbolic of what they called the "uphill struggle to attain peace and harmony" in marriage, the climb to the "altar" on the "roof of Africa" inspired the inscription inside their wedding rings: "18,640 feet and climbing."

Oldest Bridegroom and Bride

The oldest recorded bridegroom has been Harry Stevens, 103, who married Thelma Lucas, 84, at the Caravilla (Wis) Retirement Home on Dec 3, 1984.

The oldest recorded bride was Mrs Winifred Clark (b Nov 13, 1871) who was married the day before her 100th birthday to Albert Smith, 80, in South Yorkshire, Eng.

Youngest Married Couple

It was reported in 1986 that an 11-month-old boy was married to a 3-month-old girl in Bangladesh to end a 20-year feud between two families.

Unusual Weddings

Lou Szarka and Gloria E. Kearns of Clearwater, Fl, got married while in the air 2,000 ft above the ground in a glider. In three other gliders were the best man, the maid of honor and a notary public. By radio between the gliders while flying over the airport "the magic words to officially complete the marriage" were spoken by Tom Schlemmer, the notary. The stunt was sponsored by the Soaring Society of America which is affiliated with the F.A.I.

Bruno J. Zehnder, photographer, was married to actress Heather May in an ice-cave − 15 degrees F, 15 ft underground in Antarctica on Jan 27, 1985.

Golden Anniversaries

Despite the advent of the computer, records on golden (or 50th) wedding anniversaries remain largely uncollated. Unusual cases reported include that of Mrs Agnes Mary Amy Mynott (b May 25, 1887) who attended the golden anniversary of her daughter Mrs Violet Bangs of St Albans, Eng, on Dec 20, 1980, some 23 years after her own.

Triplets Lucille (Mrs Vogel), Marie (Mrs McNamara) and Alma (Mrs Prom) Pufpaff all celebrated their golden anniversaries on Apr 12, 1982, having all married in Cleveland, Minn, in 1932.

The 3 sons and 4 daughters of Mr and Mrs J. Stredwick of East Sussex, Eng, all celebrated golden weddings between May 1971 and April 1981.

Most Married Couple

Jack V. and Edna Moran of Seattle, Wash, have married each other 40 times since the original and only really necessary occasion on July 27, 1937 in Seaside, Ore. Subsequent ceremonies have included those at Banff, Canada (1952), Cairo, Egypt (1966) and Westminster Abbey, London (1975).

Oldest Divorce

Ida Stern, 91, and her husband Simon Stern, 97, of Milwaukee, Wis, were divorced on Feb 2, 1984, in the circuit court of Milwaukee.

MARINE RECORDS

New records set in the years 1984–88 are listed here. Older records can be found in editions of this book prior to 1984.

A non-stop circumnavigation is entirely self-maintained; no water supplies, equipment or replacements of any sort may be taken aboard en route.

Rowing Across Pacific

The husband-wife team, Curtis and Kathleen Saville (US) set a speed record of 193 days rowing (approx 43 mi/day) in *Excalibur Pacific*, 25 ft 5 in long, from Callao, Peru, to Australia, 1984–86.

Fastest Atlantic Crossings

The fastest crossing ever by sail was 7 days 21 hours 5 min by 2 Frenchmen, Loic Caradec and Philippe Facques, aboard an 85-ft

BOARDSAILING ACROSS THE ATLANTIC: These 2 Frenchmen, Stephane Peyron and Alain Pichavant, traveled from W Africa to Guadeloupe in the West Indies, and then to NYC, on this 31-ft sailboard, covering 3,000 mi of the journey in 24½ days. They arrived in time for the July 4, 1986 celebration.

catamaran sloop, Royale, in 1986. They traveled from Sandy Hook, NJ, to Cornwall, Eng at a rate of 39 mi per day.

The fastest rower, west to east, was Tom McClean of Britain who made the trip from St. John's, Newfoundland, Canada to Falmouth, Eng in 54 days 18 hours, arriving Aug 10, 1987.

Circumnavigation by Smallest Boat, Solo

Sergio Testa of Australia sailed an 11-ft 10-in Bermudan sloop *Acrohc Australis* from Brisbane back to Brisbane in 500 days, 1984–87, to become the smallest boat to travel around the globe.

Most Husband-Wife Circumnavigations

Al and Helen Gehrman (US) made 4 trips around the world in their 36-ft gaff ketch *Myonie*, Florida to Florida, 1961–64, 66–70, 72–76, and 79–83.

Earliest Circumnavigation by Motorboat

David Scott Cowper (GB) drove his 42-ft motorboat, the *Mabel E. Holland*, around the world alone from Plymouth, Eng, through the Panama Canal and back to Plymouth in 170 days 2 hours 15 min (average 165.7 mi/day) in 1984.

Earliest Non-Stop Circumnavigation by a Woman

Kay Cottee of Australia sailing 37-ft *First Lady* became the first non-stop woman soloist when she completed her trip from Sydney to Sydney, via Cape Horn, in 1988.

Sailing Blind

Hank Dekker, 42, in his 25-ft sloop, *Dark Star*, became the first blind man to sail alone from San Francisco to Honolulu in Aug 1983. He used Braille charts, a Braille compass, a talking clock, and a navigational system that reads the position aloud. A former race car driver, Dekker lost his sight in 1972.

Fastest Solo Circumnavigation

Philippe Monet (France) set a speed record of 127 days 12 hours 11 min, sailing alone, around the world from Brest, France, via Cape Town, back to Brest, in his 75-ft trimaran *Kriter Brut de Brut*, 1986–87.

Dodge Morgan (US) in the 60-ft-long Bermudan sloop, *American Promise*, sailed non-stop W–E via Cape Horn from Bermuda on Nov 12, 1985 and traversed 25,671 mi in 150 days 1 hour 6 min at the rate of 171.1 mi/day, returning to Bermuda Apr 11, 1986.

Most Non-Stop Solo Circumnavigations

Jon Sanders of Australia made 3 circumnavigations May 25, 1986–Mar 13, 1988 from Fremantle, Australia, back to Fremantle in his 44-ft Bermuda sloop *Parry Endeavor*. The 3 trips took 657 days.

Fastest Circumnavigation by Yacht

In the 80-ft Bermudan sloop *Switzerland* Pierre Fehlmann and his crew (Swiss) sailed from Portsmouth (Eng) around the world 1985–86 in 117 days 14 hours 13 min at a speed of 238 mi/day.

Youngest Transatlantic Rowers

Mike Nestor (GB) 23 years 299 days and Sean Crowley (GB) 24 years 146 days in the 22-ft *In Finnegan's Wake* rowed for 74 days from the Canary Islands to Guyana, South America, in 1986.

STUNTS AND MISCELLANEOUS ENDEAVORS

Accordion Playing. Pieter van Loggerenberg of Hoedspruit, Transvaal, S Africa played an accordion 85 hours in July 1987 as part of a wildlife festival.

Apple Peeling. The longest single unbroken apple peel on record is 172 ft 4 in peeled by Kathy Wafler, 17, of Wolcott, NY, in 11 hours 30 min at the Long Ridge Mall, Rochester, NY, Oct 16, 1976. The apple weighed 20 oz.

Apple Picking. The greatest recorded performance is 365½ US

HOT-AIR BALLOON WORLD CHAMPIONSHIPS: In 1984 all these balloons gathered in Albuquerque, NM, in a modern revival of the craft that began in the US in 1961. *(Split Second)*

bushels picked in 8 hours by George Adrian, 32, of Indianapolis, on Sept 23, 1980.

Baby Carriage Pushing. The greatest distance covered in 24 hours in pushing a perambulator is 345.25 miles by Runner's Factory of Los Gatos, Calif with an all-star team of 57 California runners June 23–24, 1979. A 10-man team of British Royal Marines from Lympstone, Devon, Eng, with an adult "baby" covered 252.65 mi in 24 hours, Mar 31–Apr 1, 1984.

Balancing on One Foot. The longest recorded duration for balancing on one foot is 34 hours by Shri N. Ravi in Sathy Amangalam City, Tamil Nadu, India, Apr 17–18, 1982. The disengaged foot may not be rested on the standing foot nor may any sticks be used for support or balance, but 5-minute rest breaks are allowed after each hour.

Balloon Release. The largest ever mass balloon release was one of 1,429,643 sponsored by United Way at Public Square in Cleveland, O, on Sept 27, 1986. The release was directed by BalloonArt by Treb Inc. of LA.

Band, One-Man. The greatest number of instruments played in a single rendition is 314 in 1 min 23.07 sec by Rory Blackwell in Devon, Eng, on May 27, 1985.

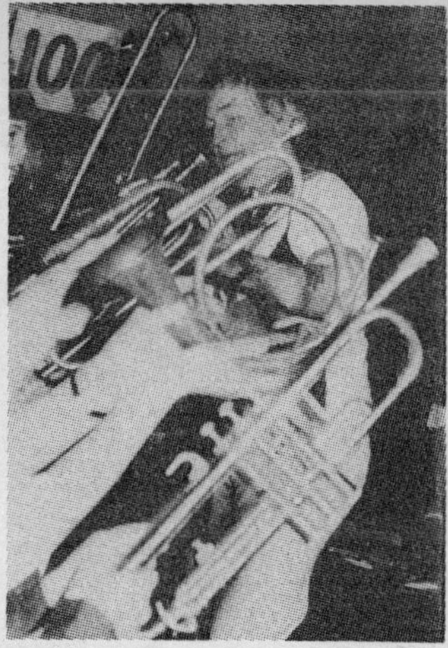

ONE-MAN BAND: Rory ▲ Blackwell (Eng) can play 314 different instruments in 1 min 23.07 sec, and 24 instruments simultaneously in a single tune.

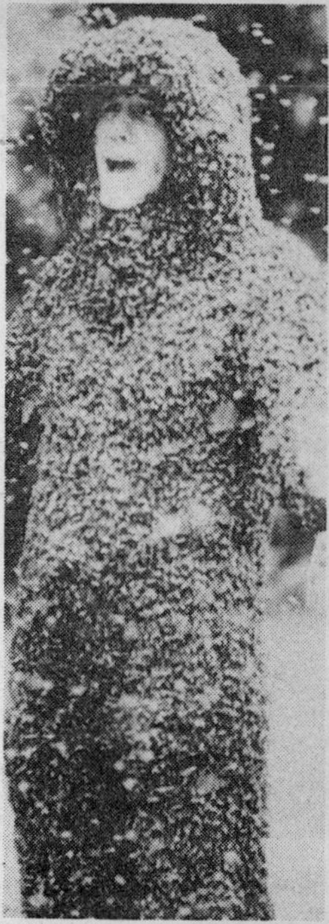

BEARD (MANTLE) OF BEES: ► Unstung, Maxwell J. Beck, 23, of Arcola, Pa, had his entire body (except around his mouth) covered by approximately 100,000 (27½ lb) buzzing bees for a Guinness TV show in Sept 1987.

► NON-STOP FOR 107 HOURS: This heavy metal group, called Vengeance K.S.A. (Eng), set a record for rock groups.

Aided by his left-footed perpendicular percussion-pounder and his right-footed horizontal 4-pronged differential beater, Blackwell played 24 (4 melody, 20 percussion) instruments in TV South West Studios, Plymouth, Eng, on May 2, 1985.

Sadhak Hurst of Brisbane, Australia played his one-man band (at least 3 instruments simultaneously) for 131 hours, Nov 16–21, 1987 in Melbourne.

Band Marathons. The longest recorded band marathon ("blow-in") for 10 or more players is 102 hours by the band of the West Midlands Fire Service in Birmingham, Eng, Oct 22–26, 1986.

The duration record for a rock group is 107 hours by 4-piece heavy metal band Vengeance K.S.A. at Take Two, Sheffield, Eng, Sept 7–11, 1987.

The duration record for a 4-man pop group is 147 hours by the "Dekorators" at Becketts Bar, Bexhill-on-Sea, Eng, Jan 8–14, 1984. *From next year in this category only one marathon will be listed.*

Barrel Jumping (on ice skates). The official distance record is 29 ft 5 in over 18 barrels by Yvon Jolin at Terrebonne, Quebec, Canada, in 1981. The female record is 20 ft 4½ in over 11 barrels by Janet Hainstock in Mich on Mar 15, 1980.

Bathtub Racing. The record for a 36-mile bathtub race is 1 hour 27 min 48.2 sec by Greg Mutton at Grafton Jacaranda Festival, NSW, Australia Nov 2, 1986. Tubs are limited to 75-in and 6-hp motors. The greatest distance for paddling a hand-propelled bathtub in 24 hours is 90.5 mi by 13 members of the Aldington (Kent, Eng) Social Club May 28–29, 1983.

Baton Twirling. Victor Cerda, Sol Lozano, Harry Little III (leader) and Manuel Rodriguez, twirled batons for 122½ hours, June 24–29, 1984, in El Sereno, Calif.

The greatest number of complete spins done between tossing a baton into the air and catching it is 10, by Donald Garcia, on the BBC *Record Breakers* program on Dec 9, 1986. The record for women is 7, by Lisa Fedick on the same program, and also by Joanne Holloway, at the UK National Baton Twirling Association Championships in Paignton, Devon, Eng. on Oct 29, 1987.

Bed of Nails. The duration record for non-stop lying on a bed of nails (sharp 6-in nails 2 in apart) is 300 hours May 3–14, 1986 by Rev Ken Owen, 48, of Glamorganshire, Wales. This included 132½ hours without a break. Much longer durations are claimed by uninvigilated *fakirs*—the most extreme case being *Silki* who claimed 111 days in São Paulo, Brazil, ending on Aug 24, 1969.

Note that the category of "Iron Maiden" (lying between 2 beds of nails with added weight on top) has been retired with the ultimate record being set at 1,642½ lb endured by Komar (Vernon E. Craig) of Wooster, Ohio at Old Chicago Towne March 6, 1977. *No further claims for publication will be entertained or published.*

Bed Pushing. The longest recorded push of a normally stationary object is 3,233 miles 1,150 yd in the case of a wheeled hospital bed by a team of 9, all employees of Bruntsfield Bedding Centre, Edinburgh, Scotland, June 21–July 26, 1979.

Bicycle Stunts. On Apr 2, 1984, at Mito Ibaragi, Japan, 16 members of the Mito-Itomi Unicycle Club rode on a single bicycle a distance of 164 ft.

The longest duration standing upright on the back wheel only of a bicycle is 1 hour 16 min 54 sec by Craig Strong (GB) at Edmonton, North London, on Jan 7, 1983.

Boomerang Throwing. The Boomerang Association of Australia's championship record for distance reached before the boomerang returns is 364.1 ft (diameter) by Bob Burwell in Nov 1981 at Albury. The longest under US rules for out-and-return is 375 ft by Peter Ruhf at Randwick, Sydney, Australia, June 28, 1982. The longest flight duration (with self-catch) is 28.9 sec by Bob Burwell at Albury, NSW, Aust, on Apr 7, 1984. The greatest number of consecutive two-handed catches on record is 653 by Bob Croll (Victoria, Aust) also on Apr 7, 1984.

Brick Carrying. The record for carrying a 9-lb brick in a nominated ungloved hand with the arm extended in an uncradled downward pincer grip is 61¾ mi by Reg Morris of Walsall in the West Midlands, Eng, on July 16, 1985.

The women's record of 22½ miles was set by Wendy Morris of Walsall, Eng, on Apr 28, 1986, with a 9-lb-12-oz brick.

Bricklaying. Robert Boll of Burbank, Ill, laid 914 bricks in 60 min to win the first US Speed Bricklaying competition at Lansing, Mich on Feb 21, 1987.

Brick Throwing. The greatest reported distance for throwing a standard 5-lb building brick is 146 ft 1 in by Geoffrey Capes at Braybrook School, Cambridgeshire, England, on July 19, 1978.

Bubble Gum Blowing. The largest bubble blown measured 22 in in diameter, created by Mrs Susan Montgomery Williams of Fresno, Calif, in her home Apr 19, 1985, while a *National Enquirer* photographer watched. He also measured with a "gumputer" calipers on a horizontal rather than a vertical basis, to eliminate any elongation due to gravity.

Camping Out. The silent Indian *fakir* Mastram Bapu "contented father" remained on the same spot by the roadside in the village of Chitra for 22 years, 1960–82.

Card Throwing. Kevin St Onge threw a standard playing card 185 ft 1 in on the Henry Ford Community College campus, Dearborn, Mich, June 12, 1979.

Carriage Driving. The only man to drive 48 horses in a single hitch is Dick Sparrow of Zearing, Iowa, 1972–77. The lead horses were 135 ft away.

BRICKLIFTING: Geoff ▲ Capes lifted 26 bricks in Brockley, S London on June 16, 1988. Before a standardized set of rules had been drawn up, Geoff had lifted 28 bricks.

MOST ON A BICYCLE: ▲ Sixteen members of the Mito-Itomi Unicycle Club of Mito Ibaragi, Japan, piled onto this bike in a record-setting stunt.

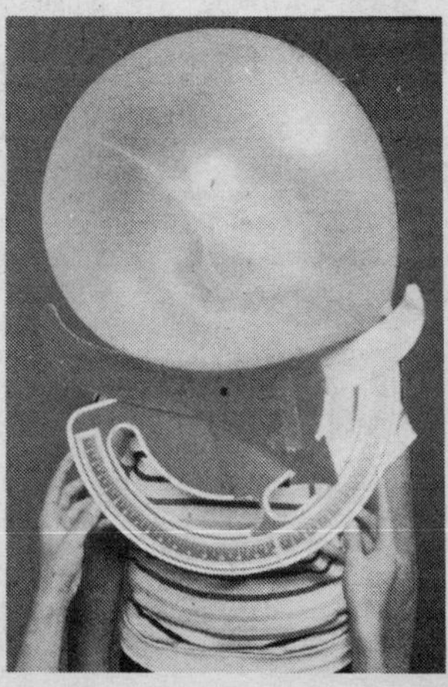

► BIGGEST BUBBLE BLOWN: Susan Montgomery Williams of Fresno, Calif, looks like a creature from outer space as she blows a record 22-in-diameter bubble, while it is being measured by a "gumputer."

Champagne Fountain. The tallest successfully filled column of champagne glasses is one 44 stories (24.7 ft) high, filled from the top and using 10,404 long-stemmed glasses, achieved by Pascal Leclerc at the Biltmore Hotel, LA, on June 18, 1984.

Clapping. The duration record for continuous clapping (sustaining an average 160 claps per min audible at 120 yd) is 67 hours 5 min by V. Jeyaraman of Tamil Nadu, India, Feb 12–15, 1988.

Coin Balancing. The tallest column of coins ever stacked on the edge of a coin is 205 Canadian 25-cent pieces on top of a Canadian Olympic Commemorative which was freestanding vertically on the base of a coin flat on the surface by Bruce McConachy (b 1963) of W Vancouver, British Columbia, for Fuji TV, Tokyo, Feb 24, 1985.

Alex Chervinsky (b Feb 22, 1908) of Lock Haven, Pa, achieved a pyramid of 390 coins on his 77th birthday.

Coin Snatching. The greatest number of British 10-pence coins (slightly larger than the US 25-cent piece) caught clean from being flipped from the back of a forearm into the same palm is 140 by Dean Gould in Hamburg, W Germany on March 19, 1988.

LARGEST CROCHETED FLAG: Terry Terrific Vona of Keansburg, NJ, sits with her son on the 14 × 19 ft American flag she made in 1983 from 300 balls of yarn. It hung once from the Perth Amboy City Hall. *(Costello)*

CIRCUS RECORDS

A table of historic circus records from 1859 to date was published in the 1985 Edition on p. 305. New records set since 1975 are below:

Flying Trapeze. Downward circles or "Muscle grinding"—1,350 by Sarah Denu (age 14) (US) Madison, Wis, May 21, 1983. Single heel hang on swinging bar, Angela Revelle (Angelique), Australia, 1977.

Highest Aerial Act. Ian Ashpole (b Jan 15, 1956) of Ross-on-Wye, Eng, performed a trapeze act suspended from a hot-air balloon 16,420 ft up over Cambridgeshire and Suffolk counties, Eng, on May 16, 1986.

Triple Twisting Double Somersault. Tom Robin Edelston to catcher John Zimmerman, Circus World, Fla, Jan 20, 1981.

Full Twisting Triple and the Quadruple Somersault. Vasquez Troupe, Miguel Vasquez to catcher Juan Vasquez at Ringling Bros, Amphitheatre, Chicago, in Nov 1981. On Sept 20, 1984, Miguel performed a triple somersault in a layout position (no turn) to catcher Juan at the Sports Arena, LA.

Triple Back Somersault with 1½ Twists. Terry Cavaretta Lemus (now Mrs St Jules) at Circus Circus, Las Vegas, Nev, in 1969.

HIGHEST AERIAL ACT: Ian Ashpole (b Jan 15, 1956) (UK) performed a trapeze act while suspended from this hot-air balloon 16,420 ft up over England May 16, 1986.

HANGING BY THEIR HAIR from a helicopter, these German circus "artists" carry off a "super-act." ◄

7-PERSON-HIGH TEETER POLE: The Bulgarian Kahaiovi Troupe performing at a Blackpool (Eng) circus in July 1986 featured 13-year-old Magdalena who ended the stunt with a somersault leap from the top. ▲

◄

BIGGEST FLYING RING AUDIENCE: Wini McKay swung high over a crowd of 85,000 people at the Los Angeles Coliseum in 1980.

MOST EXPENSIVE CIRCUS CARDS: This complete set of 20 cigarette cards of Taddy's Clowns and Circus Artists sold at auction at Phillips, London, for $30,690 in 1987.

Teeter Board. A 7-person-high pyramid perch was performed by the Bulgarian Kahaiovi Troupe at the Tower Circus, Blackpool, Eng, on July 16, 1986. It was topped by 13-year-old Magdalena, who made a somersault leap.

Trampoline. Septuple twisting back somersault to bed and quintuple twisting back somersault to shoulders by Marco Canestrelli to Belmonte Canestrelli at Madison Square Garden, NYC, on Jan 5 and Mar 28, 1979. Richard Tison (France) performed a triple twisting triple back somersault for television near Berchtesgaden, W Germany on June 30, 1981.

Flexible Pole. Double full twisting somersault to a 2-in-diameter pole by Roberto Tabak (aged 11) of the Robertos troupe in Sarasota, Fla, in 1977. Triple full twisting somersault by Corina Colonelu Mosoiann (age 13) at Madison Sq Garden, NYC, on Apr 17, 1984.

Human Pyramid (or Tuckle). Twelve (3 high) supported by a single understander. Weight 1,700 lb by Tahar Douis of the Hassani Troupe at BBC TV Studio, on Dec 17, 1979. Nine high by top-mounter Josep-Joan Martinez Lozano, 10, of the Colla Vella dels Xiquets 39 ft tall on Oct 25, 1981 in Valls, Spain.

Crawling. The longest continuous voluntary crawl (progression with one or the other knee in unbroken contact with the ground) is 28 mi by Bob DiSalle and Bobby Kunkle of Miami Univ, Ohio, Aug 4–6, 1987. The crawl, 55 laps around a measured course 2,679 ft long, took 32 hours 27 min.

The Baptist lay preacher Hans Mullikin, 39, arrived at the White House in Washington, DC on Nov 23, 1978, having crawled all but 8 of the 1,600 miles from Marshall, Tex.

Over a space of 15 months ending Mar 9, 1985, Jagdish Chander, 32, crawled 870 mi in India, to propitiate his favorite Hindu goddess Mata.

Crochet. Mrs Barbara Jean Sonntag (b 1938) of Craig, Colo, crocheted 330 shells plus 5 stitches (equivalent to 4,412 stitches) in 30 min, at a rate of 147 stitches per min, on Jan 13, 1981.

Miss Ria van der Honing of Wormerveer, The Netherlands, completed a crochet chain 38.83 mi in length on July 14, 1986.

Mrs Sybille Anthony bettered all marathons of this kind in a 120-hour crochet marathon at Toombul Shoppingtown, Queensland, Australia, Oct 3–7, 1977.

Cucumber Slicing. Norman Johnson of the Blackpool College of Art and Technology, England sliced 12 in of a 1½-in-diameter cucumber at 22 slices to the inch (total 244 slices) in 13.4 sec on Apr 3, 1983 in Cologne, W Germany.

Dancing. Marathon dancing must be distinguished from dancing mania, which is a pathological condition. The worst outbreak of dancing mania was at Aachen, Germany in July 1374, when hordes of men and women broke into a frenzied dance in the streets which lasted for hours till injury or complete exhaustion ensued.

The most severe marathon dance (staged as a public spectacle in the US) was one by Mike Ritof and Edith Boudreaux, who logged 5,148 hours 28½ min to win $2,000 at Chicago's Merry Garden Ballroom, Belmont and Sheffield, Ill, from Aug 29, 1930, to Apr 1, 1931. Rest periods were progressively cut from 20 to 10 to 5 to nil minutes per hour with 10-in steps and a maximum of 15 sec for closure of eyes.

Largest Dance. A crowd estimated at 25,000 by the local newspapers attended a "Moonlight Serenade" outdoor evening of dancing to the music of the Glenn Miller orchestra in Buffalo, NY, on July 20, 1984 on a 450-ft-long dance floor around the M&T Bank Building. An estimated total of 20,000 dancers took part in the National Square Dance Convention at Louisville, KY, on June 26, 1983.

Dancing, Ballet. The greatest number of spins called for in classical ballet choreography is the 32 in Swan Lake by Tchaikovsky. Miss Rowena Jackson (later Chatfield) (b 1925, Invercargill, New Zealand) achieved 121 such turns at her class in Melbourne, Australia, in 1940.

Dancing, Ballroom. The individual continuous record is 126 hours by Scott Michael, 31, a dancing instructor of Huntington Beach, Calif, June 20–25, 1986 at the Dance Masters Ballroom Studio, Stanton, Calif, when 27 girls worked shifts as his partner.

The most successful professional ballroom dancing champions have been Bill Irvine and Bobbie Irvine of London who won 13 world titles, 1960–72.

Dancing, Charleston. The Charleston duration record is 110 hours 58 min by Sabra Starr of Lansdowne, Pa, Jan 15–20, 1979.

Dancing, Conga. 119,986 people formed the longest conga line in the Miami Super Conga, held Mar 13, 1988 during a Cuban-American party to which all Miamians were invited for a celebration of life together.

Dancing, Disco (including Jive, Twist and Go-Go). The duration record for non-stop jiving is 97 hours 42 min by Richard Rimmer (with a relay of partners) of Surrey, England, Nov 11–16, 1979. Under the strict rules of the European Rock n' Roll Association the duration pair record is 22 hours by Mirco and Manuela Catalano at the Olympia Shopping Centre, Munich, W Germany Feb 6–7, 1981.

The longest recorded disco marathon was 462 hours 30 min by Alfie Turner of Romford, Eng, Apr 28–May 17, 1985.

Dancing Dragon. The longest dancing dragon was 448 ft 10 in long, made in Jan 1988 by members of the Singapore Dragon and Lion Athletic Association who brought it to life in dance as part of the Lunar New Year celebrations. The head was made from cloth, bamboo, cane, aluminum strips, papier mache, gauze and paints, and the body from cloth. Some 3,000 tinkling bells were sewn on its body, as were over 20,000 pieces of scale-shaped silver sequins to give it a shimmering effect.

Dancing, Flamenco. The fastest flamenco dancer ever measured is Solero de Jerez, aged 17, who, in Brisbane, Australia in Sept 1967, in an electrifying routine attained 16 heel taps per sec or 960 per min.

Dancing, High Kicking. The record for high kicks (heel to ear level) is 10,508 in 5 hours 30 min by Keith Nesbitt, in Rochester, NY, on April 16, 1988.

Tony Higo set records of 90 in 25 sec and 51 in 10 sec on Yorkshire TV on Dec 17, 1987, and 147 in 1 min on the same program on Dec 23, 1987.

Dancing, Limbo. The lowest height for a flaming bar under which a limbo dancer has passed is 6⅛ in off the floor at Port of Spain Pavilion, Toronto, on June 24, 1973, by Marlene Raymond, 15. Strictly no part of the body other than the sole or side of the foot should touch the ground, though brushing the shoulder blade does not in practice usually result in disqualification.

The record on roller skates is 5¼ in by Sandra Siviour on Mar 30, 1985, and by Tracey O'Callaghan on June 2, 1984, both at Bexley, Aust, to equal the mark set by Denise Culp of Rock Hill, SC, on Jan 22, 1984.

Dancing, Tap. The fastest *rate* ever measured for a tap dancer is 1,440 taps per min (24 per sec) by Roy Castle on the BBC-TV *Record*

Breakers program on Jan 14, 1973. Roy achieved 1 million taps in 23 hours, 44 min at the "Guinness World of Records," London, Oct 31–Nov 1, 1985.

The greatest assemblage of tap dancers ever in a single routine is 4,000 at Glasgow Airport, Scotland, on May 29, 1988.

Rosie Radiator (Rose Marie Ostler) on July 18, 1987, danced 7¾ mi in leading a column of 14 tap dancers across San Francisco.

Debating. The longest Parliamentary-style debate in the US took place at Vassar College, Poughkeepsie, NY, between 2 teams of 2, who debated continuously (except for authorized rest breaks of 5 min after each hour) for 100 hours 6 min, Jan 24–28, 1986.

With 175 formal speakers the Oxford Union Society, Eng, debated for 290 hours ending May 25, 1988.

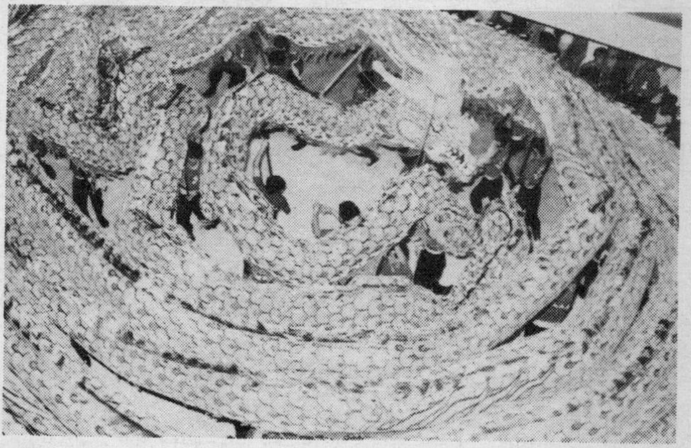

LONGEST DANCING DRAGON: For the Chinese (lunar) 1988 New Year, 30 members of the Singapore Dragon and Lion Athletic Assoc made this 448-ft-10-in long dragon with body and head of cloth. With 3,000 tinkling bells and 20,000 sequins sewn on, it was brought to life by 49 people dancing underneath.

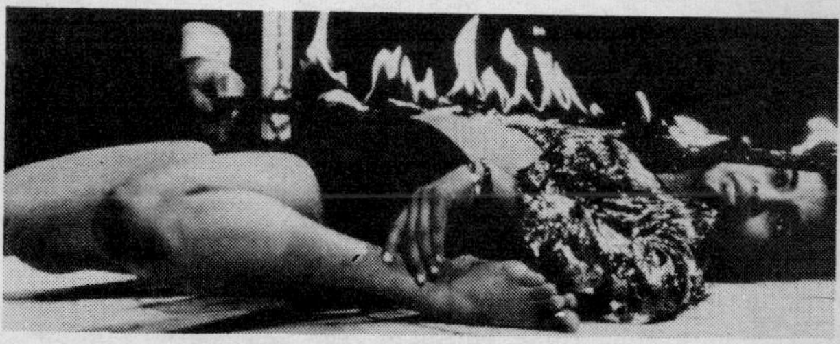

LOWEST LIMBO: Marlene Raymond, 15, slithered under a flaming bar 6⅛ in off the floor without letting any part of her anatomy except her feet touch the floor.

DOMINO TOPPLING: Single-handed, W German Klaus Friedrich set up 320,236 dominoes in formations like this, taking 31 days of 10 hours each, and on Jan 27, 1984, gave the lead domino one push, causing 281,581 to fall in progression before the line stopped. The fall took 12 min 57.3 sec.

Diving, Highest Shallow. Henri La Mothe (b 1904) set a record by diving 28 ft into 12⅜ inches of water in a child's wading pool on Apr 7, 1979 in Northridge, Calif for a Guinness TV program. He struck the water chest first at a speed of 28.4 mph.

Diving, High. The highest regularly performed head-first dives are those of professional divers from La Quebrada ("the break in the rocks") at Acapulco, Mexico, a height of 87½ ft. The leader of the 27 divers in the Club de Clavadistas is Raul Garcia (b 1928) with more than 35,000 dives. The first female accomplishment was by Mrs Barbara Winters (b Nov 12, 1953), *née* Mayer, on Dec 7, 1976. The base rocks are 21 ft out from the takeoff, necessitating a leap 27 ft out. The water is only 12 ft deep.

The world record high dive is 174 ft 8 in by Randal Dickison (US) at Ocean Park, Hong Kong, on Apr 6, 1985. The women's record is 120 ft by Lucy Wardle (US) at the same exhibition.

The greatest height reported for a dive into an air bag is 326 ft by the stuntman Dan Koko from the top of Vegas World Hotel and Casino into a 20 × 40 × 14 ft target on Aug 13, 1984. His impact speed was 88 mph. The women's record is held by Kitty O'Neil who dove 180 ft from a helicopter over Northridge, Calif onto an air cushion 30 × 60 ft on Sept 9, 1979.

Domino Stacking. Leard Wayne Woedruff, 76, of McFarland, Calif successfully stacked 242 dominoes on a single supporting domino on Sept 15, 1986.

Domino Toppling. The greatest number of dominoes set up single-handed and toppled in a row is 281,581 out of 320,236 set up by Klaus Friedrich, 22, of Weilheim, in Fuerth, W Germany on Jan 27, 1984. They fell in 12 min 57.3 sec, having taken 31 days (10 hours daily) to set up.

Students from 3 Dutch universities, working as many as 35 at a time, 12 hours a day for a month, set up 1,380,000 dominoes and toppled them on Jan 3, 1988 in Rosmalen, The Netherlands. The dominoes were arranged to illustrate European themes, such as the Ariane space project and Rembrandt's "Night Watch."

A 31-min domino-topple demonstration was staged by the National Hemophilia Foundation domino team on May 9–10, 1986, electronically linked to 6 continents by satellite spanning 35,901 curved earth miles, and using over 300,000 dominoes and 52 domino-powered stunts.

Drumming. The duration drumming record is 1,057 hours (44 days 1 hour) by Trevor Mitchell at the Brown Cow Hotel, Scunthorpe, Eng, July 5–Aug 18, 1986.

Four hundred separate drums were played in 31.78 seconds by Rory Blackwell at Finlake Country Park, Chudleigh, Devon, Eng, on May 30, 1988.

Ducks and Drakes (Stone-Skipping). The best is 29 skips (14 plinkers and 15 pitty-pats) by Arthur Ring, 69, at Midway Beach, Calif, on Aug 4, 1984, a record tied by Jerdone (Jerry) McGhee, 42, at Wimberley, Tex, Nov 18, 1986.

Egg Hunt. The greatest egg hunt on record involved about 72,000 hard boiled hen eggs, about 40,000 candy eggs, and more than 10,000 participants, spread out over the property of the Garrison family in Homer, Ga, on Easter Sunday, 1985. This was the 26th egg hunt under the same auspices.

Egg Shelling. Two kitchen hands, Harold Witcomb and Gerald Harding, shelled 1,050 dozen eggs in a 7¼-hour shift at Bowyers, Trowbridge, Wiltshire, England Apr 23, 1971. Both are blind.

Egg and Spoon Racing. Chris Riggio of San Francisco completed a 28½-mile fresh egg and dessert spoon marathon in 4 hours 34 min Oct 7, 1979.

Egg Throwing. The longest authenticated distance for throwing a fresh hen's egg without breaking is 317 ft 10 in by Risto Antikainen to Jyrki Korhonen at Siilinjarvi, Finland, on Sept 6, 1981.

Feminine Beauty. The annual Miss World contest begun in London in July 1951 and the annual Miss Universe contest, inaugurated in Long Beach, Calif, in 1952 are the world's largest. In the latter, the greatest number of countries represented has been 80 in 1983 at St Louis. The most successful country has been the US, with winners in 6 contests. All of the contestants have to spend 3 weeks training for the presentation on TV for the night the winner is decided. The city where the contest is held is reported to have to pay $800,000 for the privilege.

In the Miss World contest, the UK is the only nation to produce 5 winners. The maximum number of contestants was 72 in 1983.

Ferris Wheel Riding. The endurance record for big wheel riding is 37 days by Rena Clark and Jeff Block at Frontier Village Amusement Park, San Jose, Calif July 1–Aug 7, 1978.

Flute Marathon. The longest recorded time is 61 hours by Joseph Shury of the Sri Chinmoy Marathon Team, Toronto, Canada, Mar 21–23, 1986.

Flying Disc and Frisbee. See *Games, Throwing* in Chapter 12.

Gold Panning. The fastest time recorded for "panning" 8 planted gold nuggets with a 10-in-diameter pan is 9.23 sec by Bob Box of Ahwahnee, Calif in the 23rd World Gold Panning Championship at Knott's Berry Farm, Buena Park, Calif Mar 5–6, 1983. Box beat 86 contestants. The record for women was set at the same time by Susan Bryeans of Fullerton, Calif at 10.03 sec.

Golf Ball Balancing. Lang Martin of Charlotte, NC succeeded on Feb 9, 1980 in balancing 7 new golf balls vertically without using any adhesive, beating his own 1977 record of 6.

Grape Catching. The longest distance for catching a grape in the mouth that has been thrown from a site on the same ground level is 319 ft 8 in by Arden Chapman of Pioneer, La, July 18, 1980. The Northeast Louisiana Univ football field was used for the event. Jerry "Pete" Mercer, the thrower, stood in one end zone and on the 20th attempt, Chapman caught the grape on the track at the opposite end of the field. A slight cross wind was blowing.

The greatest height from which a grape was dropped and caught in the mouth was 660 ft 2.79 in from a Tokyo (Japan) building on Mar 1, 1986. The catcher, Paul Tavilla of Arlington, Mass, a produce merchant, surpassed his own record. "At 80 mph it hurts," he is quoted as saying.

Guitar Playing. The longest recorded solo guitar-playing marathon is one of 300 hours by Vincent Paxton at the Lord Nelson public house, Winterslow, Eng, Nov 23–Dec 6, 1986.

Hairdressing. Colin Watson and André Douglas each cut, set and styled hair continuously for 408 hours Aug 4–21, 1986 in Northcliff, Transvaal, South Africa.

The tallest hairstyle was set at the Bangz Park Ave Salon in Winter

TALLEST HAIRDO: This "beehive" from Bangz Park Ave Salon, Winter Park, Fla, is 6½ ft tall. The 120-lb model is weighted down with only 12 lb on her head. ◄

GOLF BALL BALANCING: Lang Martin's record of 7 has stood since Feb 1980. Here he is concentrating so that the dot-on-dot structure will remain standing. ►

Park, Fla with a 6½-ft-tall "beehive" designed by Christopher Morrison and Terry Carden. The 12-lb hairpiece is worn by 120-lb Laura Kelley.

Hair Splitting. The greatest reported achievement in hair splitting has been that of the former champion cyclist and craftsman Alfred West (1901–85) who succeeded in splitting a human hair 17 times into 18 parts on 8 occasions.

Handshaking. A world record for handshaking was set by President Theodore Roosevelt (1858–1919), when he shook hands with 8,513 people at a New Year's Day White House Presentation in Wash, DC, on Jan 1, 1907.

Rainer Vikström of Turku, Finland, shook 19,592 different hands in 8 hours on May 15, 1988 during Turku's Fourth Annual Spring Market.

Generally outside public life this record has become meaningless because aspirants either shake hands with anyone passing by or else shake the same hands repetitively.

Hitchhiking. The title of world champion hitchhiker is claimed by Bill Heid of Allen Park, Mich, who from 1964 to the end of 1986 obtained free rides of 324,280 mi (1,083 trips). He doesn't believe in using a thumbing technique; just approaches cars at stoplights.

Stephen Burns of Melbourne, Australia, hitchhiked around all 48

HOUSE OF CARDS WITH A FULL DECK: Actually, John Sain played with some 300 full decks when he constructed this 68-story house of cards in South Bend, Ind. Sain executed the whole project by himself, using no adhesives and never creasing the cards. (*South Bend Tribune*)

HULA HOOPLA: 1,527 people celebrated together at Disneyland, Anaheim, Calif, for the 30th anniversary of the hula hoop on Mar 25, 1988

HUMAN FLY: Daniel ("Spider Man") Goodwin, is on his way up the Bonaventure Building in LA. He also climbed the higher 1,454-ft Sears Tower in Chicago, utilizing clamps and suction cups. His tallest climb was the 1,822-ft CN Tower in Toronto, without benefit of clamps and cups.

co-terminous US states in 26 days 6 hours in an 11,438-mi trip in 56 vehicles, Sept 8–Oct 4, 1984.

Hopscotch. The longest recorded hopscotch marathon is one of 101 hours 15 min by Mark Harrison and Tony Lunn at the Studio Night Club, Leicester, Eng, Sept 30–Oct 4, 1985.

House of Cards. The greatest number of stories achieved in building free-standing houses of standard playing cards without creasing the cards or using any adhesives is 68 by John Sain, 15, a high school sophomore. His 12-ft-10-in tower, completed Aug 3, 1983, using 15,714 cards, was built in modern skyscraper form at the Univ of Notre Dame engineering school where his father is a teacher.

Hula-Hooping. The highest claim for sustaining gyrating hoops between shoulders and hips is 81 hoops by William K. Chico Johnson (b July 8, 1939) on BBC in London, Sept 19, 1983. Three complete gyrations are mandatory. The women's record is 70 hoops by Luisa Valencia in Las Vegas, Nev, in May 1987.

A claim for the longest marathon with a single hoop was 90 hours by Roxann Rose of Pullman, Wash, Apr 2–6, 1987, but she used her arm to keep the hoop whirling when tired.

Tonya Lynn Mistal, 15, of Cottonwood, Calif, went 88 hours without a drop of the hoop, July 9–14, 1986, beating her 1983 world record of 60 and topping the later record of 72 hours set by Kym Coberly.

Human Cannonball. The record distance for firing a human from a cannon is 175 ft in the case of Emanuel Zacchini, son of the pioneer Hugo Zacchini, in the Ringling Bros and Barnum & Bailey Circus, in 1940. His muzzle velocity was estimated at 54 mph. On his retirement the management was fortunate in finding that his daughter, Florinda, was of the same caliber.

An experiment on Yorkshire TV in England on Aug 17, 1978, showed that when Sue Evans, 17, was fired from a cannon, she was ⅜ in shorter in height on landing.

Human Circle (Unsupported). The highest number recorded of people who have demonstrated the physical paradox of all being seated without a chair is an unsupported circle of 10,323 employees of the Nissan Motor Co at Komazawa Stadium, Tokyo, Japan, Oct 23, 1982.

Human Fly. The longest climb achieved on the vertical face of a structure occurred in Aug 1986, when Daniel Goodwin ("Spider Man"), 30, of Calif scaled the outside of the 1,822-ft CN Tower in Toronto using neither climbing aids nor safety equipment.

Joke Telling. John Parker, alias Jay McKay, a former disc jockey, told jokes unremittingly for 52 hours (while sitting in a hot tub by his own choice) June 28–30, 1988, at the Pierre Bossier Mall, La.

The duo duration record is 52 hours by Wayne Malton and Mike Hamilton at the Howard Johnson Motor Hotel, Toronto Airport, Canada, Nov 13–16, 1975.

JUGGLING AND JOGGLING

Joggling is juggling 3 or more objects while running or jogging. The contestant must juggle every step of the way. If the object is dropped, it must be picked up at the spot of the drop before the runner resumes. Joggling records must be set in official competitions.

In an unequaled exhibition, 476 jugglers kept 1,867 objects up in the air simultaneously on July 23, 1983 in Purchase, NY, at the SUNY campus on the last day of the International Jugglers Assn's 36th Annual Convention. Each person juggled at least 3 objects.

Most Records

Albert Lucas of Las Vegas, Nev (b May 11, 1960, London, of US parents) tied the world juggling records long held by Enrico Rastelli (b Dec 19, 1896, Samara, Russia, d Dec 13, 1931, Bergamo, Italy) when he "flashed"—as opposed to "juggled"—10 balls and then 8 plates,

UPSIDE-DOWN JUGGLER: Bobby May shows how he can bounce-juggle 5 balls by rebounding them off a drum on the floor while he does a headstand on a table *(Gene S. Jones)*

on July 2, 1984 at the Hacienda Resort Hotel, Las Vegas. On the following two days, Lucas gave further evidence that he is the top juggler today by setting these world records: juggling 5 clubs for 37 min 10 sec (beating the former record of 16 min 20 sec); making 7,291 consecutive throws; juggling 7 balls for 2 min 3.48 sec; and juggling 7 rings for 3 min 23.05 sec.

He also set a new world record by juggling 12 rings in 1985 and in the same year tied the record for juggling 7 clubs.

Juggling 7 Clubs

Those tied with Lucas are Albert Petrovski (USSR), 1963, Sorin Munteanu (Romania), 1975, and Jack Bremlov (Czech) 1985.

Balancing Cigar Boxes on Chin

Bruce Block balanced 211 boxes on his chin for 9.47 sec on July 28, 1988 in St Joseph, Mich.

Non-Contested Juggling

Tony Ferko (Czech) on July 15, 1987 juggled 7 table tennis balls by blowing them into the air with his mouth and keeping them aloft simultaneously.

Ala Naite (female, Japan) in 1937 juggled 16 hoops simultaneously, using her hands and feet.

Kris Kremo pirouetted a quadruple turn with 3 cigar boxes in mid-air in 1977.

Eric Berg from Westminster, Calif surf-juggled with 3 clubs in 1988 off the California coast. He is the only one known to have juggled this way.

While jumping on a pogo stick, Ashrita Furman of Jamaica, NYC juggled 3 balls for 1 hour 13.6 sec without dropping or stopping on Aug 1, 1988 at the Empire State Building Guinness exhibit hall.

Inverted Juggling

Bobby May (US) while standing on his head juggled 5 balls by bouncing them off a drum.

Bounce Juggling

Tim Nolan of Elizabeth City, NC bounce-juggled 10 balls on July 7, 1988 at the Marriott Marquis Hotel, NYC. Nolan also bounce-juggled 7 balls in 2 min 9 sec at the same session.

Juggling 3 Balls Without Drop

Ashrita Furman of Jamaica, NYC juggled for 6 hours 7 min 4 sec in 1987. A claim for 6 hours 24 min 50 sec in England is being investigated.

Joggling 5 Objects

Bill Gillen (US) covered one mile in 8 min 28 sec on June 25, 1985. Owen Morse (US) covered 100m in 15.25 sec on July 15, 1987.

211 UNGIMMICKED CIGAR BOXES were balanced on his chin for 9.47 sec by Bruce Block, who set this new record on July 28, 1988, beating his own record of 134, set in July 1987. The cigar boxes had to be regular size and weight and not glued in any way.

◄

JOGGLING with 3 heavily weighted sports balls in competition with unburdened runners in the 1988 LA Marathon, Albert Lucas (above in 1986), holder of 11 juggling titles, gets attention from some runners as he joggles the whole 26.2 mi in 3 hours 29 min 17 sec, beating the majority of the field. In 1988, he bettered this by finishing in 3 hours 29 min 4 sec without dropping a ball. *(Bill Giduz)* ▼

◄

JOGGLING: This new sport is being demonstrated by Owen Morse who set the records for 100m joggling of 5 objects in 15.25 sec and 3 objects in 12.12 sec. *(Kevin Galloway, Tustin, Calif)*

Joggling 3 Objects

Owen Morse covered 100m in 12.25 sec on July 15, 1987.

Kirk Swenson (US) ran 1 mi in 4 min 43 sec on July 24, 1986 and ran 5 km in 16 min 55 sec on the same day.

A relay team of 4 US men (Bill Fowle, Bill Giduz, Owen Morse, Bill Gillen) ran 1 mile in 4 min 31.2 sec on July 15, 1987.

Joggling 50 Miles

Prof Helaman Pratt-Ferguson (US) ran for 16 hours 12 min on May 8, 1987.

Spinning Basketballs

By spinning 10 basketballs simultaneously on June 7, 1988 (on one finger of each hand, knees, toes, head and 3 other spots of his body) for 7 sec, 15-year-old Michael Kettman of St Augustine, Fla, set a world record.

SPINNING: Michael Kettman, 15, of St. Augustine, Fla, spun 10 basketballs on his body for 7 sec on June 9, 1988 and recorded it on videotape. *(Jim Lane/St Augustine Record)*

JUGGLING WHILE ▲
SURFBOARDING: Eric Berg shows how he does it.

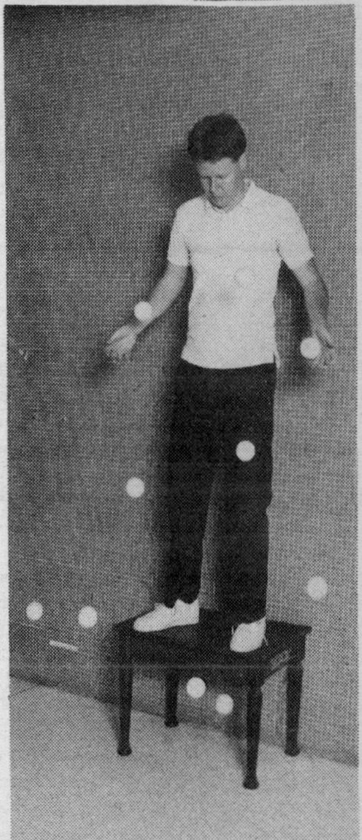

BOUNCE-JUGGLING 10 ►
BALLS: Count them! Tim Nolan has them all in hand or in air at the same moment. (*Sean Moorman*)

Karate Chop. *Note: Claims for breaking bricks and wooden blocks are unsatisfactory because of the lack of any agreed standards upon which comparisons can be made of friability and the spacing of fulcrums.*

Kissing. The most prolonged osculatory marathon in cinematic history is one of 185 sec by Regis Toomey and Jane Wyman (b Sarah Jane Faulks, Jan 4, 1914, later Mrs. Ronald Reagan) in *You're In the Army Now,* released in 1940.

The most protracted kiss underwater was one of 2 min 18 sec by Toshiaki Shirai and Yukiko Nagata on Fuji TV in Tokyo, Japan on Apr 2, 1980.

John McPherson kissed 4,444 women in 8 hours in Newcastle, Eng, on Mar 8, 1985, at a rate of 1 each 6.48 sec.

Kite Flying. The longest recorded flight is one of 180 hours 17 min by the Edmonds Community College team at Long Beach, Wash Aug 21–29, 1982. Managing the flight of the J-25 parafoil was Harry N. Osborne.

The classic record is 31,955 ft up by a chain of 8 kites over Lindenberg, (now East) Germany, on Aug 1, 1919. The record altitude for a single kite is 22,500 ft (min)–28,000 ft (max) by Prof Philip R. and Jay P. Kunz of Laramie, Wyo, on Nov 21, 1967, according to *Kite Lines* magazine.

The most kites flown on a single line is 7,150 by Sadao Harada, 69, at Kagoshima, Japan, Apr 27, 1987.

The largest kite ever flown (2,133 ft long and 8,288 sq ft in area) was the "Thai Snake" flown by Herman van den Broek and Jan Pieter Kuil for 22 min 50 sec at Uithuizen, The Netherlands, on Aug 11, 1984.

Knitting. The most prolific hand-knitter has been Mrs Gwen Matthewman (b 1927) of Featherstone, W Yorkshire, England, who in 1979 knitted 915 garments involving 11,012 oz of wool (equivalent to the fleece of 89 sheep). She has been timed to average 111 stitches per min in a 30-min test. Her technique has been filmed by the world's only Professor of Knitting—a Japanese.

The Exeter Spinners—Audrey Felton, Christine Heap, Eileen Lancaster, Marjorie Mellis, Ann Sandercock and Maria Scott produced a jumper by hand from raw fleece in 1 hour 55 min 50.2 sec on Sept 25, 1983 at BBC Television Centre, London.

Knot Tying. The fastest recorded time for tying the six Boy Scout Handbook knots (square knot, sheet bend, sheep shank, clove hitch, round turn, and two half hitches, and bowline) on individual ropes is 8.1 sec by Clinton R. Bailey Sr, 52, of Pacific City, Ore on Apr 13, 1977.

Leap Frogging. Fourteen students at Hanover High School, NH, covered 888.1 mi in 189 hours 49 min June 10-18, 1988.

Life Saving. In Nov 1974, the City of Galveston, Tex and the Noon Optimist Club unveiled a plaque to the deaf-mute lifeguard Leroy

Colombo (1905–74), who saved 907 people from drowning in the waters around Galveston Island, 1917–1974.

Lightning-Struck. The only man in the world to be struck by lightning 7 times is former Shenandoah Park Ranger Roy C. Sullivan (US), the human lightning-conductor of Virginia. His attraction for lightning began in 1942 (lost big toenail) and was resumed in July 1969 (lost eyebrows), in July 1970 (left shoulder seared), on Apr 16, 1972 (hair set on fire) and, *finally,* he hoped, on Aug 7, 1973: as he was driving along a bolt came out of a small, low-lying cloud, hit him

LARGEST KITE: The "Thai Snake," flown by two Dutchmen on Aug 11, 1984, is 2,133 ft long, and 8,288 sq ft in area.

LOG ROLLING: Julie Hughes and Jenny Owens show how they stay on the rolling logs at the annual Timber Festival in Albany, Ore.

on the head through his hat, set his hair on fire again, knocked him 10 ft out of his car, went through both legs, and knocked his left shoe off. He had to pour a pail of water over his head to cool off. Then, on June 5, 1976, he was struck again for the sixth time, his ankle injured. When he was struck for the *seventh* time on June 25, 1977, while fishing, he was sent to Waynesboro Hospital with chest and stomach burns. He could offer no explanation for his magnetism, but he donated his lightning-burnt Ranger hats to some of the Guinness World Records Exhibit Halls. In Sept 1983, reportedly rejected in love, he died of a self-inflicted gunshot wound.

Lion Taming. The greatest number of lions mastered and fed in a cage simultaneously by an unaided lion-tamer was 40, by "Captain" Alfred Schneider in 1925.

Clyde (Raymond) Beatty (b Bainbridge, Ohio, June 10, 1903, d Ventura, Calif, July 19, 1965) likewise handled more than 40 "cats" (mixed lions and tigers) simultaneously. Beatty, top of the bill for 40 years, insisted on being called a lion-trainer. More than 20 lion-tamers have died of injuries since 1900.

Log Rolling. The record number of International Championships is 10 by Jubiel Wickheim (of Shawnigan Lake, BC, Canada) between 1956 and 1969. At Albany, Ore, on July 4, 1956, Wickheim rolled on a 14-in log against Chuck Harris of Kelso, Wash for 2 hours 40 min before losing.

The youngest international log-rolling champion is Cari Ann Hayer (b June 23, 1977) who won her first championship July 15, 1984 at Hayward, Wis.

Magician, Fastest. Paul Ricksecker performed 91 separate tricks in 2 min 12½ sec at the 57th Annual Magi-Fest, Columbus, O, on Feb 6, 1988.

Merry-Go-Round. The longest marathon ride on record is one of 312 hours 43 min by Gary Mandau, Chris Lyons and Dana Dover in Portland, Ore, Aug 20–Sept 2, 1976.

Message in a Bottle. The longest recorded interval between drop and pick-up is 72 years in the case of a message thrown from the *SS Arawatta* out of Cairns, Aust, on June 9, 1910, in a lotion bottle and reported to be found on Moreton Is, Aust, June 6, 1983.

Milk Bottle Balancing. The greatest distance walked by a person while continuously balancing a full pint milk bottle on his head is now a full marathon distance of 26.2 mi by Ashrita Furman of Jamaica, NYC, on Oct 3, 1987, in Zurich, Switzerland.

Morse Code. The highest recorded speed at which anyone has received Morse code is 75.2 wpm—over 17 symbols per sec. This was achieved by Ted R. McElroy (US) in a tournament at Asheville, NC, July 2, 1939. The highest speed recorded for hand key transmitting is 175 symbols per min by Harry A. Turner of the US Army Signal Corps at Camp Crowder, Mo, Nov 9, 1942.

"WHEELIE KING" Doug Domokos alone on his record-breaking 145-mi ride at Talladega, Ala, in 1984. ▲

MOTORCYCLE ASCENT: Riding up stairs is not what bikes were intended for, but Terry McGauren, a professional stuntman, 23, got the idea that he could mount the 1,760 steps of Toronto's CN Tower on his 250-cc Yamaha. So, on the tower's 8th birthday, he did it. *(Toronto Star)* ▲

FLYING ON A MOTORCYCLE: After a short run up a takeoff ramp, Todd Seeley in his red Honda soared 246 ft to land on the tail of another ramp in Tampa, Fla. Seeley was in the air all of 3 seconds. *(Joie Chitwood's Thrill Show)* ◄

Motorcycle and Car Stunting. The longest distance ever achieved for motorcycle ramp-to-ramp long jumping is 246 ft by Todd Seeley, 24, in Tampa, Fla, Feb 28, 1988. Seeley, a stuntman for Joie Chitwood's Thrill Show has been in movies and on *Miami Vice*.

The pioneer of this form of exhibition—Evel Knievel (b Oct 17, 1938, Butte, Mont)—suffered 433 bone fractures in his career. His abortive attempt to cross the 1,600-ft wide and 600-ft deep Snake River Canyon, Idaho on Sept 8, 1974 in a rocket reputedly increased his lifetime earnings by $6 million.

Terry McGauren motorcycled up the outdoor 1,760 steps of the CN Tower, Toronto, on June 26, 1984.

Doug Domokos went 145 mi on the back wheel of his motorcycle without stop or touching down on the 2.66-mi tri-oval paved track at Alabama International Motor Speedway in Talladega, Ala, on June 27, 1984. His average speed was in excess of 50 mph, and he stopped only because he ran out of gas on the 146th mi.

Riding on the back wheel only, Janim (Jimmy) Gentile of Torrance, Calif, traveled 440 yd (¼ mi) at a speed of 120.8 mph, beating the record held previously by Ottis Lance at Penwell Raceway Park, Tex when he sped 112 mph over 440 yd on a Suzuki GS-1000.

The longest ramp jump in a car by a professional stunt driver is 232 ft by Jacqueline De Creed (*née* Creedy) in a 1967 Ford Mustang at Santa Pod Raceway, Bedfordshire, Eng, on Apr 3, 1983.

Most Miles on Motorcycle in 24 Hours. Michael Kneebone of Chicago traveled 1,502 mi from NYC to N Platte, Neb, May 12-13, 1988.

Musical Chairs. The largest game on record was one starting with 6,003 participants and ending with Tamara van der Schans on the last chair, which was held in the market place at Etten-Leur, The Netherlands on Feb 15, 1988.

Needle Threading. The record number of strands of cotton threaded through a Number 13 needle (eye ½ × 1/16 in) in 2 hours is 5,370, set by Diane Sharp on Aug 1, 1987 at the Charitable Union's centenary event, Battle Creek, Mich.

Omelet Making. The greatest number of 2-egg omelets made in 30 min is 315 by John Elkhay at the City Lights Restaurant in Providence, RI on June 29, 1985. He went on to set an endurance record of 36 hours during which he made 5,247 omelets, all of which were eaten by hungry observers or sent to worthy institutions.

Onion Peeling. The record for onion peeling is 50 lb (52 onions) in 5 min 23 sec by Alfonso Salvo of York, Pa, on Oct 28, 1980. Before the current requirement of having at least 50 onions in the 50 lb, a record of 3 min 18 sec was set by Alain St John of Plainfield, Conn on July 6, 1980.

Organ Marathons. The longest church organ recital ever sustained was one of 440 hours by Tony Peters at Sheppey Beach Social Club, Isle of Sheppey, Kent, Eng.

Paddle Boating. The longest recorded voyage in a paddle boat is 2,226 mi in 103 days by the foot power of Mick Sigrist and Brad Rud down the Mississippi River from the headwaters in Minn to the Gulf of Mexico, Aug 4–Nov 11, 1979.

Pancake Tossing. Philip Artingstall tossed a pancake 232 times in 2 min on Feb 16, 1988 at the Hawthorne Restaurant, Fordyce, Banff and Buchan, Scotland.

A crew representing Birkett Mills baked and flipped a buckwheat pancake 28 ft 1 in in diameter and 2 in deep at Penn Yan, NY on Sept 27, 1987. The pancake weighed 4,238 lb.

Parachute, Longest Fall Without Parachute. Vesna Vulovic, 23, a Jugoslavenski Aerotransport hostess, survived when her DC-9 blew up at 33,330 ft over the Czechoslovak village of Serbska Kamenice on Jan 26, 1972. She was hospitalized for 16 months after emerging from a 27-day coma, having broken many bones. She is now Mrs Breka.

ON THE JUMP: Rocky Kenoyer ▲ making one of his 403 record parachute leaps and safe landings in 24 hours from heights of 1,200 ft or more at Snohomish Parachute Center, Wash, July 3–4, 1988, to establish a record that beat the one, set only a month previously, of 301 by Dale Nelson in Pennsylvania. *(Ron Hesse/Wind Dancer)*

LONGEST DELAYED DROP IN ► A PARACHUTE was 84,700 ft (16.04 mi) from a balloon by Capt Joseph W. Kittinger of the USAF in 1960. He also was the first to cross the Atlantic solo by helium balloon in 1984, from Maine to Italy.

PARACHUTING RECORDS

First from Tower	Louis-Sébastien Lenormand (1757–1839)	Quasi-parachute	Montpellier, France	1783
Earliest Mid-Air Rescue	Miss Dolly Shepherd brought down Miss Loule May on her single chute	from balloon at 11,000 ft	Longton, Eng	June 9, 1908
First from Aircraft				
(man)	"Capt" Albert Berry	aerial exhibitionist	St Louis	Mar 1, 1912
(woman)	Mrs Georgina "Tiny" Broadwick		Griffith Park, Los Angeles	June 21, 1913
Lowest Escape	Squad Leader T. Spencer, RAF	30–40 ft	Wismar Bay, Baltic Sea	Apr 19, 1945
Longest Duration Fall	Lt Col Wm. H. Rankin, USMC	40 min, due to thermals	North Carolina	July 26, 1956
Longest Delayed Drop (man)	Capt Joseph W. Kittinger[1]	84,700 ft (16.04 miles) from balloon at 102,800 ft	Tularosa, NM	Aug 16, 1960
(woman)	E. Fomitcheva (USSR)	48,556 ft	over Odessa, USSR	Oct 26, 1977
Most Southerly	T/Sgt Richard J. Patton (d 1973)	Operation Deep Freeze	South Pole	Nov 25, 1956
Most Northerly	Dr Jack Wheeler (US)	Pilot, Capt Rocky Parsons (−25°F)	in Lat 90° 00′ N	Apr 15, 1981
Career Total (man)	Roch Charmet (France)	14,000		to Feb 1988
(woman)	Valentina Zakoretskaya (USSR)	8,000	over USSR	1964–Sept 1980

Highest Landing	Ten USSR parachutists[2]	23,405 ft	Lenina Peak	May 1969
Highest Tower Jump	Herbert Leo Schmidtz (US)	KTUL-TV Mast 1,984 ft	Tulsa, Okla	Oct 4, 1970
Connected Free Fall (Biggest Star)	Team of 126	Formation held 4.68 sec from 19,029 ft	Koksijide, Belgium	July 11, 1987
Highest Column	28-man US team	United Parachute Club	Gilbertsville, Pa	Sept 22, 1985
Lowest Indoor Jump	Andy Smith and Phil Smith	192 ft	Houston Astrodome, Tex	Jan 16–17, 1982
Most Traveled	Kevin Seaman from a Cessna Skylane (pilot, Charles Merritt)	12,186 miles	Jumps in all 50 US states	July 26–Oct 15, 1972
Oldest Man	Edwin C. Townsend	89 years	Vermillion Bay, La	Feb 6, 1986
Oldest Woman	Mrs Sylvia Brett (GB)	80 years 166 days	Cranfield, Eng	Aug 23, 1986
Lowest Mid-Air Rescue	Gregory Robertson saved Debbie Williams (unconscious)	Collision at 9,000 ft, pulled her ripcord at 3,500 ft 10 sec from impact	Coolidge, Ariz	Apr 18, 1987

[1]Maximum speed in rarefied air was 825.2 mph at 90,000 ft, breaking the sound barrier. [2]Four were killed.

Parachute, Most Jumps With 301 jumps in 24 hours over New Hanover Airport, Gilbertsville, Pa, using 5 aircraft rising to altitudes of 2,000 ft or more, as required by the US Parachuting Assn, Dale E. Nelson of Bryn Mawr, Pa (b Oct 24, 1949) set a new record on May 26–27, 1988, beating the previous record of 250 jumps. Then, on July 3–4, 1988, Rocky Kenoyer of Redmond, Wash, made 403 jumps in 24 hours at the Snohomish Parachute Center, Wash, using 7 aircraft, 10 pilots, and 50 parachute packers and handlers on the ground. He followed different rules, jumping from lower altitudes than Nelson did—1,200 to 1,500 ft—heights which are accepted by the FAA.

It is said that the king of Ayuttkaya, Siam, in 1617, was "diverted" by an ingenious athlete parachuting with two large umbrellas. Also in 1617, Faustus Verancis is reputed to have descended in Hungary with a "framed canopy."

Party Giving. The most expensive private party ever thrown was that of Mr and Mrs Bradley Martin of Troy, NY. It was staged at the Waldorf-Astoria Hotel, NYC in Feb 1897. The cost to the host and hostess was estimated to be $369,200 in the days when dollars were made of gold.

At the largest party ever, in Hyde Park, London, given by the Royal Family, 160,000 children attended in celebration of the International Year of the Child, May 30–31, 1979.

The largest Christmas Party ever staged was that thrown by the Boeing Co in the 65,000-seat Kingdome, Seattle in two shows before an audience of 103,152 people on Dec 15, 1979. It was managed by general chairman John Mathiasen and produced by Greg Thompson with a cast of 2,506. The floor was decorated with 1,000 Christmas trees, each with 100 lights; 150,000 snow-white balloons; and 3 ice ponds.

Piano Playing. The longest piano-playing marathon has been one of 1,218 hours (50 days 18 hours) by David Scott May 7–June 27, 1982, at Wagga Wagga League's Football Club, Australia. (*The non-stop category is now discontinued.*)

Piano Tuning. The record time for pitch raising (one semi-tone or 100 cents) and then returning a piano to a musically acceptable quality is 4 min 20 sec by Steve Fairchild at the Piano Technicians Guild contest at the Dante Piano Co factory, Ronkonkoma, NY, Feb 5, 1980.

Pipe Smoking. The duration record for keeping a pipe (with 3.3 grams of tobacco) continuously alight with only an initial match under IAPSC (International Association of Pipe Smokers Clubs) rules is 126 min 39 sec by the 5-time champion William Vargo of Swartz Creek, Mich at the 27th World Championships in 1975. Joe Oetli achieved 130 min 11 sec at the Iowa State Fair contest on Aug 18, 1984, using *two* matches. Longer durations have been recorded in less rigorously

POGO STICK JUMPER: Ashrita Furman (b 1954) of Jamaica, NYC, who holds other Guinness records, set 2 with his pogo stick. He made 3,647 jumps in 3 hours 40 min in 8-ft-deep water in Peru, and also went 11½ mi on Mt Fuji, Japan, for a distance record.

invigilated contests in which the foul practices of "tamping" and "gardening" are not unknown.

Plate Spinning. The greatest number of plates spun simultaneously is 84 by Dave Spathaky on BBC TV *Record Breakers* on Oct 21, 1986.

Pogo Stick Jumping. The greatest number of jumps achieved on a pogo stick is 130,077 by Guy Stewart in Reading, Ohio on Mar 8–9, 1985.

In 8-ft-deep water in the Amazon River, Peru, Ashrita Furman (b 1954) of NYC made 3,647 jumps on a pogo stick in 3 hours 40 min on Jan 11, 1987. With each jump his head came up above the surface and he breathed through mask and snorkel.

Furman also set a distance record of 11.53 mi on a pogo stick, going up and down the foothills of Mt Fuji, Japan, on Jan 8, 1986 in 8 hours 21 min. (Also see *Versatility*.)

Pole Sitting. There being no international rules, the "standards of living" atop poles vary widely. The record squat is 516 days by Mellissa Sanders in Indianapolis, Ind, in a 6 × 7-ft pole house 43 ft above ground from Oct 26, 1986 to Mar 24, 1988. She had her "pole cat" with her.

Modern records do not, however, compare with that of St Simeon the Elder (*c.* 390?–459 AD), called Stylites (Greek, *stylos* = pillar), a monk who spent his last 37 years on a stone pillar on the Hill of Wonders, Syria. This is probably the earliest example of record setting.

Potato Peeling. The greatest amount of potatoes peeled in 45 min by 5 people to an institutional cookery standard with regular kitchen knives was 685 lb 4 oz by a team in a competition held in Den Haag, The Netherlands, Sept 17, 1987.

Quizzing. The highest number of participants was 80,977 in the All Japan High School Quiz Championship televised on Dec 31, 1983. The most protracted contest was that lasting 110 hours in Long Hanborough, Eng, Mar 27–Apr 1, 1986 when two teams correctly answered 22,483 out of 37,310 questions.

Quoit Throwing. The world's record for rope quoit throwing is an unbroken sequence of 4,002 pegs by Bill Irby, Sr of Australia in 1968.

Rappeling (or Abseiling). The west face of Thor Peak, Baffin Island, Canada, allowed an abseiling or rappeling record of 3,250 ft in July 1982, by a group of 16 Mt Thor Expedition members. The longest descent down the side of a skyscraper is one of 580 ft (52 stories) in Hong Kong by Capt Martin Fuller (GB) on Sept 1, 1984.

Rocking Chair. For 453 hours 40 min (just a few hours short of 19 days), "Ramblin' Rob" McDonald sat and rocked in the window of the Pizza Factory in Mariposa, Calif, Mar 14–Apr 2, 1986.

Roller Coasting. The endurance record for rides on a roller coaster is 503 hours by M. M. Daniel Glada and Normand St-Pierre at Parc Belmont, Montreal, Canada July 18–Aug 10, 1983. The minimum qualifying average speed required is 25 mph.

Roller Skating. The longest recorded continuous roller skating marathon was one of 344 hours 18 min by Isamu Furugen at Naka Roller Skate Land, Okinawa, Japan, Dec 11–27, 1983.

Rolling Pin. The record distance for a woman to throw a 2-lb rolling pin is 175 ft 5 in by Lori La Deane Adams, 21, at the Iowa State Fair, Aug 21, 1979.

Rummage Sale. The largest known rummage sale or "white elephant sale" was held at the Cleveland, O, Convention Center on Oct 18 and 19, 1983. On the first day $294,972.53 was collected, and for the two days, a total of $427,935.21 was raised for the non-profit Garden Center of Greater Cleveland.

Safecracking. Lockmasters vie each year in a contest held at the Associated Locksmiths of America convention. For 22 years (1966–88) Sal Schillizzi (b Dec 3, 1923) of NYC held the title of fastest safecracker, winning with a "best" time of 16 min. In 1986, Franklin "Skip" Eckert (b 1953) of Medina, O, opened a safe lock in

12 min, and the next day Schillizzi surpassed this with a 9 min 40 sec safecracking. However, in the July 1988 contest, Eckert beat all records with a 3 min 59 sec safecracking.

Sand Sculpting. The longest sand sculpture on record was a 10,760-ft long "Millerpede" made with a water-saturated mound of sand mechanically piled up and meticulously carved out, which meandered along South Padre Beach, Tex on Mar 17, 1987, organized by Walter McDonald and Lucinda Wierenga and made by college students and local members of the Sons of the Beach organization.

The world's tallest sand castle, 5 stories or 52 ft 9 in tall, representing the "Lost City of Atlantis," may also be the largest, weighing an estimated 48,384 tons. Built on Treasure Island, Fla, Apr 19–26, 1986 (and torn down on May 5, 1986), it was constructed by 2,000 enthusiastic volunteers trained by the Sand Sculptures International Group. It was 257.5 ft long and 200 ft wide.

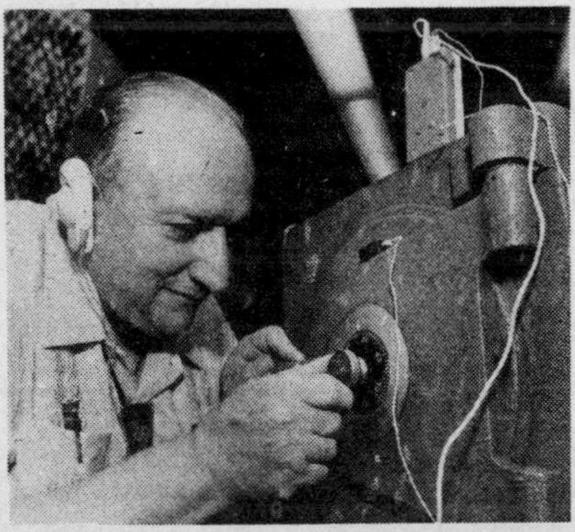

LEGAL SAFECRACKER: For 22 years, Sal Schillizzi of NYC was the winner of the safe-opening contests held at the locksmiths' convention. His record is 9 min 40 sec. (*Louis C. Liotta*) ◄

LARGEST ILLUMINATED SAND CASTLE: Made in Hollywood, this sculpture of the City of Jerusalem was built in 1986. It had 1,000 "windows" and used 160 tons of sand. (*Rex Features*) ▼

Scuba. See *Submergence*

Search, Longest. Walter Edwin Percy Zillwood (b London, Dec 1900) traced his missing sister Lena (Mrs Elizabeth Eleanor Allen, b Nov 1897, d Jan 1982) after 79 years through the agency of the Salvation Army on May 3, 1980.

See-Saw. The most protracted session for see-sawing indoors is one of 1,101 hours 40 min by George Partridge and Tamara Marquez of Auburn High School, Wash, on a suspension see-saw (indoors) on Mar 28–May 13, 1977.

Georgia Chaffin and Tammy Adams of Goodhope Junior High School, Cullman, Ala, completed 730½ hours outdoors, June 25–July 25, 1975.

Sermon. The longest sermon on record was delivered by the Rev Ronald Gallagher at the Baptist Temple, Appomattox, Va, June 26–July 1, 1983 for 120 hours.

Shaving. The fastest barber on record is Gerry Harley, who shaved 987 men in 60 min with a safety razor in Gillingham, England, on Apr 28, 1983, taking 3.64 sec per volunteer. He shaved 235 even braver volunteers with a cutthroat razor in a less perfunctory 15.3 sec per face on Aug 13, 1984. He drew blood only once.

Shoe Shining. In this category (limited to teams of 4 teenagers, an 8-hour time limit, and all shoes "on the hoof") the record is 6,780 pairs by the Sheffield (England) Citadel Band of the Salvation Army on Feb 27, 1982.

Shorthand, Fastest. The highest recorded speeds ever attained under championship conditions are: 300 words per minute (99.64% accuracy) for 5 minutes and 350 wpm (99.72% accuracy, that is, two insignificant errors) for 2 minutes by Nathan Behrin (US), in NYC in Dec 1922. Behrin (b 1887) used the Pitman system invented in 1837. Morris I. Kligman, official court reporter at the US Court House, NYC has taken 50,000 words in 5 hours (a sustained rate of 166.6 wpm). Rates are dependent upon the nature, complexity, and syllabic density of the material.

G. W. Bunbury of Dublin, Ireland, held the unique distinction of writing at 250 wpm for 10 minutes on Jan 23, 1894.

Arnold Bradley achieved a speed of 309 words per min without error using the Sloan-Duployan system with 1,545 words in 5 minutes in a test in Walsall, England on Nov 9, 1920.

Showering. The most prolonged continuous shower bath on record is one of 340 hours 40 min set by Kevin "Catfish" McCarthy at Buffalo State College (NY) Mar 29–Apr 12, 1985.

The female record is 121 hours 1 min by Lisa D'Amato, Nov 5–10, 1981, at Harpur College, Binghamton, NY.

Desquamation can be a positive danger.

Singing. The longest recorded solo singing marathon is one of 200 hours 20 min by Jorge Antonio Hidalgo Chamomo at the Piano Bar, Barcelona, Spain, Nov 7–15, 1985.

The marathon record for a choir is 78 hours 28 min by the Barnsley Junior Operatic and Dramatic Society at the Globe Theatre, Barnsley, Eng, Aug 29–Sept 1, 1987.

Acharya Prem Bhikuji (d Apr 18, 1970) started chanting the Akhand Rama-Dhoon on July 31, 1964 and devotees took this up in rotation continuing their devotions, which were still in progress in Apr 1987 at Jamnagar, India.

SKATEBOARD RECORD ▲ LONG JUMP: Paul Pearman jumping over 21 barrels.

◄ SKATEBOARD RECORD HIGH JUMP: Tony Magnuson reaching 9½ ft above the top of the ramp.

Skateboarding. David Frank, 25, covered 270.483 mi in 36 hours 43 min 40 sec in Toronto, Canada Aug 11–12, 1985.

The highest speed recorded on a skateboard is 71.79 mph on a course at Mt Baldy, Calif, in a prone position by Richard K. Brown, 33, on June 17, 1979.

The stand-up record is 53.45 mph by John Hutson, 23, at Signal Hill, Long Beach, Calif, June 11, 1978.

The record for high jump is 9½ ft above the ramp, set by Tony Magnuson on Sept 14, 1987, at Calif State U—Dominguez Hills, Carson, Calif. What is called a "high air" jump means the "greatest height in the air above the top of the ramp."

The high jump record of 9½ ft is actually held by two persons, Tony Magnuson (see above) and Christian Hosoi on May 30, 1988 at Raging Waters Amusement Park, San Jose, Calif.

At the same event, Steve Caballero in a "railslide" set an inaugural record with a 24-ft belly slide on the "Boomeramp" which is 132 ft long, 13 ft high at its highest wall and 47 ft wide. On the "long extended grind" on the lip of the ramp, Christian Hosoi set an inaugural record of 19 ft 8 in.

The longest jump from a skateboard over low barrels to land on a skateboard was the jump of 21 barrels by Paul Pearman (b Nov 10, 1960) in Augusta, Ga, at Regency Mall on May 28, 1987. In another attempt, Paul almost made it over 25 barrels 12 in wide but clipped the last barrel. The event was staged for United Cerebral Palsy who collected $500.

Christopher Von Guenthner, age 43, of Evergreen, Colo, claims an inaugural record of performing a handstand on a skateboard, traveling a distance of 803 ft on Nov 8, 1987.

Smoker, Most Voracious. Jim (The Mouth) Purol of Livonia, Mich, broke his own records by simultaneously smoking 140 cigarettes for 5 min on Jan 28, 1983 in Detroit; then on Apr 21, 1983 in Farmington, Mich he simultaneously smoked 40 cigars for 5 min; not content with that, Purol kept 38 pipes in his mouth for 5 min in Hollywood on June 9, 1983. Purol is a non-smoker.

Simon Argevitch of Oakland, Calif, whistled, hummed, gave bird imitations, sang and talked while lighting 17 cigars and smoking them at the same time July 3, 1982 in front of the Guinness Museum of World Records on Fisherman's Wharf, San Francisco, Calif.

George Anastassopoulos (b Patras, Greece Aug 20, 1911) kept account of smoking 40,730 cigars from Jan 1950 to June 1984.

Smoke-Ring Blowing. The highest recorded number of smoke rings formed with the lips from a single pull of a cigarette with cheek tapping disallowed, is 355 by Jan van Deurs Formann of Copenhagen, Denmark, achieved in Switzerland in Aug 1979.

Soap Bubble. A bubble measuring 50 ft in length was created by David Stein of NYC, the inventor of the wand, on June 6, 1988. The liquid was simple soap and water, and the special wand, called "The Bubble Thing" was used to extend the bubble horizontally.

Spitting. The record for projecting a melon seed under WCWSSA (World Championship Watermelon Seed Spitting Association) rules is

65 ft 4 in by John Wilkinson in Luling, Tex, on June 28, 1980. The greatest reported distance for a cherrystone is 65 ft 2 in by Rick Krause, at Eau Claire, Mich on July 5, 1980. Spitters who care about their image wear 12-in block-ended boots so practice spits can be measured without a tape.

Square Dance Calling. Alan Covacic called continuously for 24 hours 2 min for the Wheelers and Dealers SDC at St John's Hospital, Stone, Buck, Eng, Nov 23–24, 1984.

Stair Climbing. The 100-story record for stair climbing was set by Dennis W. Martz in the Detroit Plaza Hotel, Detroit, Mich on June 26, 1978, at 11 min 23.8 sec. Dale Neil, 22, ran a vertical mile up and down the stairs of the Peachtree Plaza Hotel, Atlanta, Ga in continuous action of 2 hours 1 min 24 sec on Mar 9, 1984. *These records can only be attempted in buildings with a minimum of 70 stories.*

Pete Squires raced up the 1,575 steps of the Empire State Building, NYC, in 10 min 59 sec on Feb 12, 1981. Janine Aiello of San Francisco, set the women's record for the event when she scaled the 1,050 vertical ft in 13 min 14 sec on Feb 14, 1985.

The record for climbing the 1,760 steps in the world's tallest free-standing structure, Toronto's CN Tower, is 8 min 28 sec by George Kapenyes, 22, of Hamilton, Ont, Canada, on Oct 27, 1985, beating 1,300 people in a charity climb. Robert C. Jezequel ran 17 round trips in 11 hours 20 min on Oct 18, 1985 without use of the elevator for a vertical height of 15,708 ft.

In the line of duty, Bill Stevenson has mounted 334 of the 364 steps of the tower in the Houses of Parliament, Eng, 4,000 times in 15 years (1968–83)—equivalent to 24.9 ascents of Mt Everest.

Standing Up. The longest period on record that anyone has stood up continuously is more than 17 years, from 1955 to Nov 1973, in the case of Swami Maujgiri Maharij while performing the *Tapasya* or penance in Shahjahanpur, Uttar Pradesh, India. When sleeping he would lean against a plank. He died aged 85 in Sept 1980.

Stilt Walking. Even with a safety wire, very high stilts are extremely dangerous—25 steps are deemed to constitute "mastery." Eddy Wolf (also known as Steady Eddy) of Loyal, Wis, mastered stilts measuring 40 ft 6½ in from ground to ankle over a distance of 27 steps without touching his safety handrail wires, at Yokohama Dreamland Park, Japan, on Mar 9, 1986. His aluminum stilts weighed 55 lb each.

Joe Long (b Kenneth Caesar), who has suffered 5 fractures, mastered 56-lb 24-ft stilts at the BBC TV Centre, London on Dec 8, 1978.

Hop pickers use stilts up to 15 ft. In 1892 M. Garisoain of Bayonne, France stilt-walked 4.97 miles into Biarritz in 42 min to average 7.10 mph.

In 1891 Sylvain Dornon stilt-walked from Paris to Moscow *via* Vilno in 50 stages for the 1,830 miles. Another source gives his time as 58 days.

The endurance record is 3,008 miles by Joe Bowen from Los Angeles to Bowen, Ky, Feb 20–July 26, 1980.

Masahami Tatsushiko (Japan), 28, ran 100 meters on 1-ft-high stilts in 14.5 sec in Tokyo on March 30, 1980.

Stone-Skipping. See *Ducks and Drakes*.

Stowaway. The most rugged stowaway was Socarras Ramirez, who escaped from Cuba June 4, 1969, by stowing away in an unpressurized wheel well in the starboard wing of a Douglas DC-8 in a 5,600-mile Iberia Airlines flight from Havana to Madrid. He survived 8 hours at 30,000 ft where temperatures were −8°F.

Stretcher Bearing. The longest recorded carry of a stretcher case with a 140-lb "body" is 127 miles in 45 hours 45 min by two 4-man teams from the Sri Chinmoy marathon team of NYC, Apr 17–19, 1981.

String Ball. The largest ball of string on record is one of 12 ft 9 in in diameter, 40 ft in circumference and weighing 10 tons, amassed by Francis A. Johnson of Darwin, Minn, between 1950 and 1978.

Submergence. The *continuous* duration record (i.e., no rest breaks) for SCUBA (self-contained underwater breathing apparatus) without surface air hoses, is 212 hours 30 min by Michael Stevens of Birmingham, Eng, in a Royal Navy tank, Feb 14–23, 1986.

Measures have to be taken to reduce the risk of severe desquamation in such endurance trials.

Swinging. The record duration for continuous swinging in a hammock is 240 hours by John David Joyce, 19, of Bryan, Tex, July 29–Aug 8, 1986.

Talking. The record for non-stop talking is 240 hours by N. S. Viswanathan at Jalakandeswarar Temple, Tamal Nadu, India, Dec 24, 1987–Jan 3, 1988.

The women's non-stop talking record was set by Mrs Mary E. Davis, who, Sept 2–7, 1958, started talking at a radio station in Buffalo, NY, and did not draw breath until 110 hours 30 min 5 sec later in Tulsa, Okla.

Dr Donald Thomas completed an after-dinner speech at City College (NYC) that lasted 32 hours 25 min. It began on Good Friday, Apr 1, 1988, and ended on Easter Sunday.

Pulling with Teeth. The "strongest teeth in the world" belong to John "Hercules" Massis (b Wilfried Oscar Morbée, June 4, 1940) of Oostakker, Belgium, who at Evrey, France on March 19, 1977, raised a weight of 513⅝ lb to a height of 6 in from the ground with a bit in his teeth. Massis prevented a helicopter from taking off using only a mouth harness in Los Angeles Apr 7, 1979, for the "Guinness Spectacular" ABC-TV show.

"Hercules" Walter Arfeuille of VlamertingeIeper, Belgium raised a weight of 545.64 lb 6.3 in from the ground with a tooth bit at Diksmuide, Belgium on Sept 11, 1983.

Joe Ponder of Love Valley, NC, claims he has stronger teeth, has

ALL TIED UP: To make the ▲ world's largest string ball, Francis Johnson of Darwin, Minn, has been adding to this ball until now, 40 ft around, it needs its own house. *(Minneapolis Star Tribune)*

LONGEST AFTER-DINNER ▲ SPEECH: Donald Thomas, speaking at City College of NY, talked for 30 hours Apr 1–3, 1988. His subject was vegetarian athletic nutrition. *(Peterson S. Grosvenor © 1988)*

◄ LIFTING WITH TEETH: Joe Ponder of Love Valley, NC, prides himself on his strong teeth, claiming he should be recognized as the world recordholder. Here he is proving he can lift a 606-lb pumpkin with teeth alone. *(Mark S. Wexler)*

lifted a 606-lb pumpkin, held back a 55,000 lb truck, a 92,000-lb train, and dangled from a helicopter using only his teeth.

Throwing. (*See Games, Chapter 12.*)

Tightrope and Wire Walkers. In this field, two names stand out—Charles Blondin (1824–97) and Steven McPeak (b Apr 21, 1945). Blondin, born in France (real name Jean-Francois Gravelet) became famous for his feats of crossing Niagara Falls between the US and Canada on a rope, and McPeak traveled (and still travels) all over the world setting up high cables to cross.

No one had crossed the 165-ft-high Niagara Falls before Blondin in 1859. On June 30, Blondin started out. A short way out, Blondin stopped, lay down on his back full length on the rope, then raised himself on one leg. The crossing took 20 minutes in all.

But his supreme act was to carry his 145-lb friend and manager, Harry Colcord, on his back while crossing. (The photo on the next page testifies to the truth of this.)

McPeak, who makes his home in Alaska now, and earns his living as a steel rigger and stage set designer, has now tied Blondin's record for carrying a person on his back. He practiced 300 times across Hoover Dam in Nevada on a 1,620-ft-long cable before carrying his 114-lb fiancée, Carly, on his back in Feb 1983. In the middle of the walk, they sat down on the wire and by intercom radio the pair got married by a minister on the ground. Then they traversed the rest of the cable.

STADIUM HIGH-WIRE WALK: Steve McPeak takes a walk across Anaheim Stadium on an 800-ft-long wire as 55,000 people watch.

TIGHTROPE WALKER ▲ SUPREME: Steve McPeak of Las Vegas has conquered mountains by walking up cable ropeways—barefoot! Here he is almost to the top of the 9,718-ft-high Zugspitze on the W German-Austrian border in 1981. For height, this beat his Rio de Janeiro climb up Sugar Loaf Mt, and every other tightrope record.

◄ ROPE-WALKING MARVEL: Charles Blondin was such an intrepid tightrope artist that he crossed Niagara Falls nine times in 1859–60. After a few crossings he carried his 145-lb friend and agent, Harry Colcord, on his back (shown here) three times. *(Francis Petrie)*

McPeak performed the highest high-wire act by crossing on a thin wire he had rigged between two peaks of the Zugspitze on the W German-Austrian border on June 25, 1981, at a height of 3,150 ft above the ground below, and 9,718 ft above sea level. He needed 181 steps to cross the snow-covered gorge.

On the same day he finished the longest wire walk, (beating his previous record set in Rio de Janeiro, Brazil), by walking on a 46.5-cm diameter cable up the Zugspitze cable car lift in 3 stints aggregating 5 hours 4 min for a total of 7,485 ft, with a one-day walk of 3,117 ft. The gradient was above 30°. At his highest, McPeak was 2,313 ft higher than at the cable car base.

The greatest height above street level in a high-wire performance was when Philippe Petit, 24, of Nemours, France crossed on a wire 1,350 ft above the street in NYC between the newly constructed twin towers of the World Trade Center on Aug 7, 1974. He shot the 140-ft-long wire across by bow and arrow. He was charged with criminal trespass after a 75-min display of at least 7 crossings. The police psychiatrist's verdict was, "Anyone who does this 110 stories up can't be entirely right."

The tightrope endurance record is 185 days by Henri Rochetain (b 1926) of France on a wire 394 ft long, 82 ft above a supermarket in St

TIRE SUPPORTER: Standing up under 96 tires piled on top of him like a clothes tree, Gary Windebank of Romsey, Eng, survived under a total of 1,440 lb.

132 TOBOGGANERS managed to get on one 102-ft-7⅜-in-long sled at Lakeland College, Vermilion, Alberta, Canada.

Etienne, France, March 28–Sept 29, 1973. His ability to sleep on the wire has left doctors puzzled.

Ashley Brophy, of Neilborough, Vic, Australia, walked 7.18 mi on a wire 147.64 ft long, 32.81 ft high at the Adelaide Grand Prix, Australia on Nov 1, 1985 in 3 hours 30 min.

Tire Supporting. The greatest number of car tires supported in a free-standing "lift" at one time is 96 by Gary Windebank of Romsey, England in Feb 1984. The total weight was 1,440 lb. The tires were Michelin XZX 155 × 13.

Tobogganing. The most people on a sled is 132, a record claimed by Lakeland College of Vermilion, Alberta, Canada, when that many students rode downhill on a 102-ft 7 ⅜-inch-long toboggan on Mar 16, 1987.

Tree Climbing. The fastest climb up a 100-ft fir spar pole and return to the ground is one of 27.16 sec by Ed Johnson of Victoria, BC, Canada in July 1982 at the Lumberjack World Championships in Hayward, Wis. The fastest time up a 29.5-ft coconut tree barefoot is 4.88 sec by Fuatai Solo, 17, in Sukuna Park, Fiji, Aug 22, 1980.

Tree Sitting. Timothy Roy entered a tree house in Norwalk, Calif on July 4, 1982, and did not come down for 431 days, on Sept 8, 1983.

Typing, Fastest. The highest recorded speeds attained with a ten-word penalty per error on a manual machine are:

One Minute: 170 words, Margaret Owen (US) (Underwood Standard), NYC, Oct 21, 1918. Five Minutes: 176 wpm net by Mrs Carole Forristall Waldschlager Bechen in Dixon, Ill, 1959.

One Hour: 147 words (net rate per min), Albert Tangora (US) (Underwood Standard), Oct 22, 1923.

Records on electric and computer-driven typewriters cannot be compared with any accuracy.

Typing, Longest. The longest duration typing marathon on a manual machine is 123 hours by Shambhoo Govind Anbhawane of Bombay, India Aug 18–23, 1986 on a Godrej Prima manual machine in Bombay, aggregating 806,000 strokes.

Les Stewart of Mudjimba Beach, Queensland, Australia has typed the numbers 1 to 544,000 *in words* on 10,770 long sheets as of May 23, 1988. His target is to become a "millionaire."

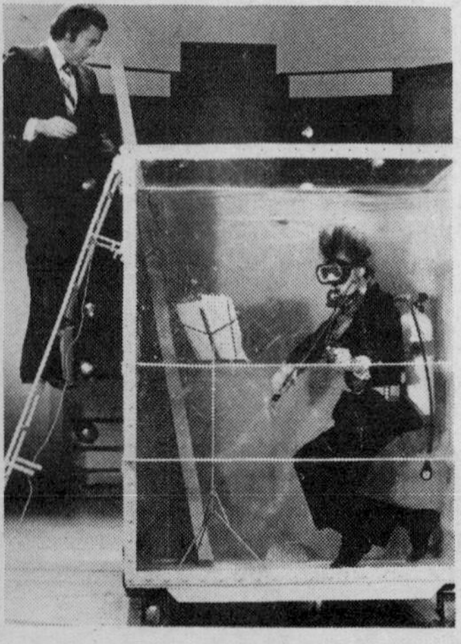

UNDERWATER ROCK-AND-ROLL BAND: With diving gear, aqua instruments and microphones, Jim ("The Mouth") Purol and 4 other wet rockers, calling themselves "Atlantis," performed at LA Swim Stadium on Nov 12, 1987.

UNDERWATER VIOLINIST: Mark Gottlieb of Olympia, Wash, repeats his record rendition of Handel's "Water Music" for David Frost's "Guinness" TV show.

Underwater Cycling. Thirty-two certified SCUBA divers in 60 hours, Nov 27–29, 1981, rode a submarine tricycle 64.96 miles on the bottom of Amphi High School pool, Tucson, Ariz, to raise money for a charity. A relay team of 32 bicycled underwater for 87.81 miles in 72 hours in Norvik, Norway, Mar 28–31, 1984. Another relay team of 32 SCUBA divers in Santa Barbara, Calif, went 75 hours 20 min on a tricycle circling around the bottom of the Diver's Den pool for 116.659 mi, June 16–19, 1988.

Underwater Violinists. The pioneer violinist to surmount the problems of playing the violin underwater was Mark Gottlieb. Submerged in Evergreen State College swimming pool in Olympia, Wash, in Mar 1975 he gave a submarine rendition of Handel's *Water Music*. His most intractable problem was his underwater *détaché*. On Oct 7, 1979 the first underwater quartet performed in the *Challenge the Guinness* TV show on Channel 7 in Tokyo, Japan.

Waiters' Marathon. Beverly Hills restaurateur Roger Bourban (b May 10, 1948) ran a full marathon of 26 mi 385 yards in full uniform in London, England, May 9, 1982, carrying a free-standing open bottle on a tray (gross weight 3 lb 2 oz) in 2 hours 47 min, using the same hand the whole way.

Walking on Hands. The duration record for walking on hands is 871 miles by Johann Hurlinger of Austria, who, in 55 daily 10-hour stints, averaged 1.58 mph from Vienna to Paris in 1900.

Shin Don-mok of S Korea completed a 50-meter inverted sprint in 17.44 sec at the Toda Sports Center, Saitama, Japan, Nov 14, 1986.

A 4-man team of David Lutterman, Brendan Price, Philip Savage and David Scannel covered 1 mi in 24 min 48 sec on Mar 15, 1987 at Knoxville, Tenn.

Walking on Water. Using outsize shoes-cum-floats Fritz Weber walked on the Main River, W Germany from Bayreuth over 185 mi to Mainz Sept 1 to Oct 15, 1983, an average of 4 mi per day.

David Kiner, 41, of Slingerlands, NY, walked from Albany to Battery Park, NYC, on the Hudson River, 155 mi in 5½ days, June 22–27, 1987, an average of 1.17 mph. He used 11-ft-long water ski shoes, called Skijaks, made of polyethylene, and a twin-bladed paddle.

Daniel Hodes, lawyer from Newport Beach, Calif, "walked" 15 mi across the rough waters of the Strait of Gibraltar in 7 hours on July 21, 1987. He also walked 18 mi across the rough waters of the English Channel in 5 hours 59 min on Sept 16, 1987. He began walking on water on Mar 6, 1987, when he traversed Cook Strait from the South to North Islands of New Zealand.

Wall Press. Sitting unsupported, back 90° flat against a wall, looks simple, but the longest anyone can stay in that position (see photo on page 493) is 1 hour, 16 min, 12 sec, a record set by Kevin DeWitt of Kennewick, Wash in Dec 1986.

VERSATILITY

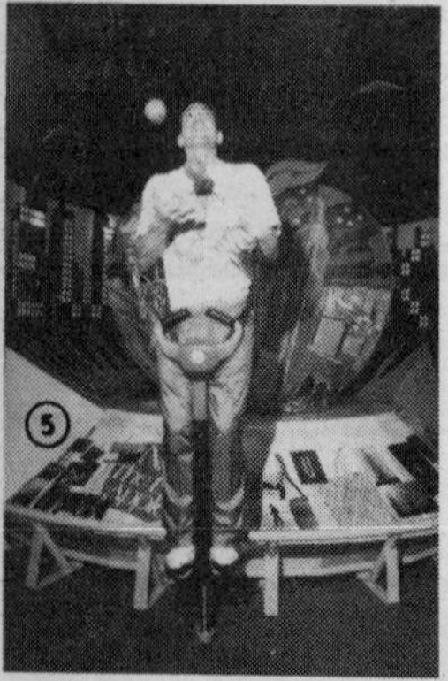

Weather Balloon Blowing. The inflation by lung power of a standard 1,000 gram meteorological balloon to a diameter of 8 ft against time was achieved by Nicholas Berkeley Mason in 57 min 7 sec for a Fuji TV program in Tokyo on Mar 9, 1986.

Wheelbarrow Pushing. The heaviest loaded one-wheeled barrow pushed for a minimum 200 level feet is one loaded with bricks weighing a gross 8,275 lb through 243 ft by John Sarich at London, Ont, Canada on Feb 19, 1987.

Wheelbarrow Racing. The fastest time reached for a 1-mile wheelbarrow race is 4 min 48.51 sec by Piet Pitzer and Jaco Erasmus of Vanderbijlpark, S Africa on Oct 3, 1987.

Wheelies. See *Motorcycle and Car Stunting*, p. 470.

Whip Cracking. The longest stock whip ever "cracked" (*i.e.*, the end made to travel above the speed of sound—760 mph) is one of 140 ft (excluding the handle), wielded by Garry Brophy at Adelaide, Australia on Oct 31, 1985.

Whistling Loudest and Longest. Roy Lomas (GB) achieved 122.5 decibels at 2½ meters in the Deadroom at the BBC Manchester (Eng), Studios on Dec 19, 1983. The whistling marathon record is by David Frank of Toronto, Canada, who completed 35 hours nonstop at the Washington Monument, DC July 17–18, 1987.

Wood Cutting and Pole Climbing. World championships for lumberjacks have been held since 1874, first in Tasmania, Australia, since 1960 in Hayward, Wis, and more recently in Albany, Ore. Records at the several sites are not precisely comparable as, for example, the poles may have or have no bark when climbed, and the logs to be sawed or chopped may be of different hardnesses. The standard for chopping is white pine of 14-in diameter, and 20-in for sawing.

The record for speed climbing of a new pole with bark is 30.17 sec by Guy German of Sitka, Alaska, set at Albany, Ore, in July 1987, beating the previous record of 30.92 sec set in 1986 at the same site.

In tree topping, Guy German was again the recordholder, winning for the second year in a row on July 5, 1987 by climbing and cutting the top off a tree of 40-in diameter and returning to the ground in 1 min 10.87 sec.

The world record of 7.85 sec for the hot power saw is held by Mel

---

◄

ASHRITA FURMAN (b 1954) of Jamaica, NYC, holds 11 competitive stamina records: (1) pogo stick jumping (up Mt Fuji); (2) pogo stick jumping underwater (in Peru); (3) milk bottle balancing on head; (4) skip-running (10 mi); (5) juggling while jumping on pogo stick; (6) and land rowing. Other records he holds (not shown) are joggling marathons, somersaulting continuously, juggling 3 balls continuously, stretcher bearing (with partner) and, now, versatility.

WALKING ACROSS THE STRAIT OF GIBRALTAR: Daniel Hodes, Calif lawyer, shows how he "walked" on water from Ceuta, N Africa to the Rock in 7 hours on July 21, 1987. *(Slim Simpson)*

WALKING DOWN THE HUDSON RIVER through NY City: Wearing 11-ft "Skijaks", David Kiner walked 155 mi from Albany, taking 57 hours over 5½ days in June 1987. *(Forbes Museum)*

Lentz of Creswell, Ore, who has won 3 times at Hayward and 7 times at Albany, but not in 1987. His father won 8 times.

Mel Lentz also holds the record of 25.38 sec for the standing block chop, 18.66 sec for the underhand block chop, and has been voted all-around champion. He has been among the winners in contests also for horizontal block chop, springboard chop, single bucking, and more.

HEAVIEST LOAD PUSHED BY MAN: John Sarich of London (Ont) Canada, has lifted on a wheelbarrow 8,275 lb of concrete blocks and is pushing it 243 ft.

WALL PRESS: Backing a human body with an arched spine against a wall and keeping it there for more than 1¼ hours is the record set by Kevin DeWitt of Kennewick, Wash, in Dec 1986. (*Bob Brawdy/Trinity Herald*)

WALK ACROSS THE AMERICAS: Starting from southern Argentina, George Meegan (GB) (b Oct 2, 1952) walked 19,019 mi before planting this British flag at Prudhoe Bay, northern Alaska. He took from Jan 26, 1977 to Sept 18, 1983 for the first complete on-foot transverse south to north of the Western Hemisphere.

WRAPPING AS AN ART FORM: Christo, the Bulgarian-born sculptor, when he isn't curtaining valleys or draping islands, is wrapping bridges. Here he is adorning Paris' famous Pont Neuf with woven fabric and rope. The French gave him permission. (*Photo © Wolfgang Volz*)

Wrapping. Christo, the sculptor who has made gigantic curtains and draped islands (see page 355), in 1985 wrapped the famous bridge, Pont Neuf, in Paris with 440,000 sq ft of polyamide fabric and 42,900 ft of rope.

Writing Small. In 1926 an account was published of Alfred McEwen's pantograph record in which the 56-word version of the Lord's Prayer was written by diamond point on glass in the space of 0.0016 × 0.0008 in.

Frank C. Watts of Felmingham, Norfolk, England, demonstrated for photographers, on Jan 24, 1968, the ability, without mechanical or optical aids, to write the Lord's Prayer 34 times (9,452 letters) within the size of a definitive postage stamp (0.84 × 0.71 in).

Tsutomu Ishii of Tokyo demonstrated his ability to write the names of 44 countries (184 letters) on a single grain of rice, and the words TOKYO JAPAN in Japanese on a human hair in Apr 1983.

Writing Under Handicap. The ultimate feat in "funny writing" would appear to be the ability to write extemporaneously and decipherably backwards, upside down, laterally inverted (mirror-style) while blindfolded, with both hands simultaneously. Three claims to this ability with both hands and feet simultaneously, by Mrs Carolyn Webb of Thirlmere, NSW, Aust, Mrs Judy Hall of Chesterfield, Va, and Robert Gray of Toronto, Canada are outstanding.

Yodeling. The most protracted yodel on record was that of Errol Bird for 26 hours in Lisburn, N Ireland, Sept 27–28, 1984. Yodeling has been defined as "repeated rapid changes from the chest-voice to falsetto and back again." The most rapid recorded is 5 tones (3 falsetto) in 1.9 sec by Donn Reynolds of Canada on July 25, 1984.

Yo-Yo. Yo-yo was a toy in Grecian times and is depicted on a bowl dated 450 BC. It was also a Filipino jungle fighting weapon recorded in the 16th century weighing 4 lb with a 20-ft thong. The word means "come-come." Though illustrated in a book in 1891 as a bandalore, the yo-yo did not become a craze until it was marketed by Donald F. Duncan of Chicago in 1926. The most difficult modern yo-yo trick is the "Whirlwind," incorporating both inside and outside horizontal loop-the-loops.

The individual continuous endurance record is 121 hours 10 min by Bob Brown of Boston, Mass June 24–29, 1985.

Dr Allen Bussey in Waco, Tex on Apr 23, 1977 completed 20,302 loops in 3 hours (including 6,886 in a single 60-min period). He used a Duncan Imperial with a 34½-in nylon string. Spins of 8,000 rpm have been recorded.

The largest yo-yo ever constructed was one by Dr Tom Kuhn weighing 256 lb, test-launched from a 150-ft crane in San Francisco on Oct 13, 1979.

EATING RECORDS

While no healthy person has been reported to have succumbed in any contest for eating non-toxic food or drinking non-alcoholic drinks, such attempts, from a medical point of view, must be regarded as *extremely* inadvisable, particularly among young people. Gastronomic record attempts should aim at improving the *rate* of consumption, rather than the volume. This book will not list any records involving the consumption of more than 2 liters (approximately 2 quarts) of beer or any at all involving liquor. Nor will this book list records for potentially dangerous categories such as consuming live ants, goldfish, quantities of chewing gum or marshmallows, or raw eggs in shells. The ultimate in stupidity—the eating of a bicycle—has, however, been recorded since it is unlikely to attract competition.

Liquidizing, processing or puréeing foodstuffs is not permitted. However, drinking during attempts is permissible.

Specific records have been claimed as follows:

Baked Beans. 2,780 cold beans one by one, with a cocktail stick, in 30 min by Karen Stevenson of Merseyside, Eng, Apr 4, 1981.

Bananas. 17 (edible weight min 4½ oz each) in 2 min by Dr Ronald L. Alkana at the University of California, Irvine on Dec 7, 1973.

Beer. Steven Petrosino drank one liter of beer in 1.3 sec on June 22, 1977, at "The Gingerbreadman," in Carlisle, Pa.

Peter G. Dowdeswell (b London, July 29, 1940) of Earls Barton, Northants, Eng, drank 2 liters in 6 sec on Feb 7, 1975. He also holds the speed record for consuming 2 Imp pints, in 2.3 sec, June 11, 1975, and for 3 Imp pints in 5.0 sec on July 6, 1985.

Champagne. 1,000 bottles per year by Bobby Acland of the "Black Raven," Bishopsgate, London.

Cheese. 16 oz of hard English cheddar in 1 min 13 sec by Peter Dowdeswell (see photo) in Earls Barton, England, on July 14, 1978.

Chicken. 27 (2-lb pullets) by "Bozo" Miller at a sitting at Trader Vic's, San Francisco in 1963. Also, 4 lb 10 oz in 10 min 37 sec by Valentin Florentino Muñoz Muñoz, Vizcaya, Spain, Apr 27, 1986.

Sean Barry ate 3 lb 12 oz of chicken in 8 min 5 sec in Cheltenham, Eng on July 5, 1986.

Clams. 424 Little Necks in 8 min by Dave Barnes at Port Townsend Bay, Wash, on May 3, 1975.

The greatest omnivore is Michel Lotito (b 1950) of Grenoble, France, known as Monsieur Mangetout, who has been eating metal and glass since 1959. Gastroenterologists have X-rayed his stomach and have described his ability to consume 2 lb of metal per day as unique. His diet since 1966 has included 10 bicycles, a supermarket cart (in 4½ days), 7 TV sets, 6 chandeliers and a low-calorie Cessna light aircraft, which he ate in Caracas, Venezuela. He is said to have provided the only example in history of where a coffin (handle and all) ended up inside a man.

NO ONE EATS as much as fast as Peter Dowdeswell of London. Here he is showing off his gluttony. A few of the records he holds are: 38 soft-boiled eggs in 75 sec, 21 hamburgers in 9 min 42 sec, and 62 pancakes in less than 7 min! ►

TREE EATER: Jay Gwaltney eating an 11-ft-tall birch sapling. He ate branches, leaves and the 4.7-in-diameter trunk over a period of 89 hours to win $10,000 as first prize in a WKQX-Chicago radio station contest called "What's the Most Outrageous Thing You Would Do?" ▼

◄ OYSTER-EATING CHAMP: Displaced as the snail-eating record holder, Thomas (Muskrat) Greene in Annapolis, Md, turning to oysters, swallowed a 6-lb mass of 288 oysters in 1 min 33 sec in July 1985.

Doughnuts. 12¾ (weighing 51 oz) in 5 min 46 sec by James Wirth, and 13 (52 oz) in 6 min 1.5 sec by John Haight, both at the Sheraton Inn, Canandaigua, NY, Mar 3, 1981.

Eels. 1 lb of elvers (1,300) in 13.7 sec by Peter Dowdeswell (see photo) at Reeves Club, Bristol, England, on Oct 20, 1978.

Eggs. (Hard-boiled) 18 in 20 sec by John Kenmuir on BBC radio, on Sept 7, 1987. (Soft-boiled) 38 in 75 sec by Peter Dowdeswell in Kilmarnock, Scotland, on May 28, 1984. (Raw, without shells) 13 in 1.0 sec by Peter Dowdeswell in Kilmarnock on May 16, 1984.

Frankfurters. 30 (2 oz) in 64 sec by Reg Morris at Miner's Restaurant, Burntwood, Eng, Dec 10, 1986.

Gherkins. 1 lb in 41.6 sec by Peter Dowdeswell at Ronelles Discotheque, Eng, on Feb 8, 1986.

Grapes. 3 lb 1 oz in 34.6 sec by Jim Ellis of Montrose, Mich, on May 30, 1976.

Hamburgers. 21 hamburgers (weighing 3½ oz each or 4½ lb of meat) and buns in 9 min 42 sec by Peter Dowdeswell at Birmingham, Eng, on June 30, 1984.

Ice Cream. 3 lb 6 oz of unmelted ice cream in 31.37 sec by Tony Dowdeswell on July 16, 1986 at the Guinness Museum, NYC.

Jelly. 20 fl but gelatinous oz in 8.25 sec by Peter Dowdeswell in Gloucestershire, Eng, on July 5, 1986.

Lemons. 12 quarters (3 lemons) whole (including skin and seeds) in 15.3 sec by Bobby Kempf of Roanoke, Va on May 2, 1979.

Meat. One whole roast ox in 42 days by Johann Ketzler of Munich, Germany, in 1880.

Milk. One Imperial quart (1.2 US quarts) in 3.2 sec by Peter Dowdeswell at Dudley Top Rank Club, England on May 31, 1975.

Oysters. Edible mass of 288 (6 lb) in 1 min 33 sec by Tommy "Muskrat" Greene in Annapolis, Md, on July 6, 1985.
The record for opening oysters is 101 in 2 min 30.41 sec by Ray Hibbs in Invercargill, New Zealand July 28, 1987.

Pancakes. 62 (each 6 in in diameter, buttered and with syrup) in 6 min 58.5 sec by Peter Dowdeswell in Northampton, England on Feb 9, 1977.

Peanuts. 100 (whole, out of the shell) singly in 46 sec by Jim Kornitzer, 21, at Brighton, England on Aug 1, 1979.

Peas. 7,175 petit pois one by one in 60 min using chopsticks by Mrs Janet Harris, Seal Hotel, Selsey, Eng, on Aug 16, 1984.

Pickled Onions. 91 (total weight 30 oz) in 1 min 8 sec by Pat Donahue in Victoria, BC, Canada, on March 9, 1978.

Pizza. 2 lb in 32 sec by John Kenmuir at Confettis Nightclub, Derby, Eng on Mar 18, 1988.

Potato Chips. 30 2-oz bags in 24 min 33.6 sec, without a drink, by Paul G. Tully of Brisbane University, Australia, in May 1969.

Potatoes. 3 lb in 1 min 22 sec by Peter Dowdeswell in Earls Barton, England on Aug 25, 1978.

Prunes. 144 in 31.27 sec by Peter Dowdeswell at Silver Stadium, Rochester, NY, on June 20, 1986.

Ravioli. 5 lb (170 squares) in 5 min 34 sec by Peter Dowdeswell in Suffolk, Eng on Sept 25, 1983.

Sandwiches. 40 (jam and butter, 6 × 3¾ × ½ in) in 20 sec by Reg Morris at Miner's Restaurant, Burntwood, Eng, Nov 25, 1986.

Sausage Meat. 6 lb in 3 min 10 sec by Reg Morris at Spring Cottage, Sheffield, W Midlands, Eng, Dec 28, 1986.

Shellfish. 100 (unshelled) whelks in 5 min 17 sec by John Fletcher in Liverpool St Station, London on Aug 18, 1983.

Shrimps. 3 lb in 3 min 10 sec by Peter Dowdeswell at Weymouth, Dorset, Eng, on Aug 7, 1985.

Snails. 38.8 oz in 1 min 5.6 sec by Andoni Basterrechea Dominguez in Vizcaya, Spain on Apr 27, 1986.

Spaghetti. 100 yd in 12.02 sec by Peter Dowdeswell in Halesowen, Eng, on July 3, 1986.

Strawberries. 2 lb in 12.95 sec by Peter Dowdeswell at Corby, Eng on July 5, 1985.

Sushi. 1½ lb in 1 min 13.5 sec by Peter Dowdeswell in Tokyo on Feb 22, 1985.

Tortillas. 74 (total weight 4 lb 1½ oz) in 30 min by Tom Nall in the 2nd World Championship at Mariano's Mexican Restaurant, Dallas, Tex on Oct 16, 1973.

Tree. 11-ft birch (4.7-in-diameter trunk) in 89 hours by Jay Gwaltney, 19, on WKQX's Outrageous Contest, Chicago, Sept 11–15, 1980. As he finished, he said, about the taste, "as far as trees go, it's not bad."

WEALTH

The comparison and estimation of extreme personal wealth are beset with intractable difficulties. Quite apart from reticence and the element of approximation in estimating the valuation of assets, as Jean Paul Getty (1892–1976) once said: "If you can count your millions, you are not a billionaire." The term "millionaire" was invented *c.* 1740 and "billionaire" in 1861.

Cornelius Vanderbilt (1794–1877) left $100 million in 1877. The earliest dollar billionaires were John Davison Rockefeller (1839–1937); Henry Ford (1863–1947); and Andrew William Mellon (1855–1937). In 1937, the last year in which all 3 were alive, a billion dollars was worth almost 20 times as much in purchasing power as it is today.

The riches of most of the world's remaining 29 monarchs are national rather than personal assets. The least fettered monarch is H M Sir Muda Hassanal Bolkiah Mu'izzaddin Waddaulah, the Sultan of Brunei (b July 15, 1946). He appointed himself Prime Minister, Finance Minister and Home Affairs Minister on Jan 1, 1984. The annual oil revenue of Brunei is $3,780 million and its foreign reserves are $14 billion, all of which are effectively at his personal disposal.

Richest People

The US was said by *Forbes* magazine to have 47 individuals and 20 families worth over $1 billion in 1987. Japan was in second place with 32 individuals and 2 families, and W Germany was in third place with 16. In all of Europe there were 44 individual and family billionaires.

Highest Income and Wealth

The world's wealthiest man is Yoshiaki Tsutsumi, 54, Japanese railway owner, with a personal net worth, according to *Forbes* magazine, of $18.4 billion. He is followed on the list of billionaires by another Japanese, former economics professor Taikichiro Mori, who owns 68 office buildings in Tokyo, and is reportedly worth $18 billion. Of the 192 individuals or families worth $1 billion or more, 27 percent are Japanese, and 8 of the top 20 individual billionaires are Japanese.

Sam Moore Walton, the Wal-Mart Stores magnate, heads the US list with $6.5 billion, but is only #7 on the world list. The 3 Reichmann brothers of Canada, as a group, rank third on the world list, with $9 billion of assets. John Kluge and H. Ross Perot are credited with $3 billion each and are second on the US list, 20th on the world list.

Some of the greatest incomes derive from the collection of royalties per barrel by rulers of oil-rich sheikhdoms, who have not abrogated personal entitlement. Shaikh Zayid ibn Sultan an-Nuhayan (b 1918), head of state of the United Arab Emirates, arguably has title to some $9 billion of the country's annual gross national product.

The highest gross income ever achieved in a single year by a private citizen is an estimated $105 million in 1927 by the Neapolitan-born gangster Alphonse ("Scarface Al") Capone (1899–1947). This was derived from illegal liquor trading and alky-cookers (illicit stills), gambling establishments, dog tracks, dance halls, "protection" rackets and vice. On his business card, Capone described himself as a "Second Hand Furniture Dealer."

Millionairesses

The world's wealthiest woman was probably Princess Wilhelmina Helena Pauline Maria of Orange-Nassau (1880–1962), formerly Queen of The Netherlands (from 1890 to her abdication, Sept 4, 1948), with a fortune which was estimated at over $300 million.

The cosmetician Sarah Breedlove (Mrs Charles Joseph) Walker (US, 1867–1919), a black woman, is reputed to have become the first self-made millionairess. She was an uneducated orphan whose fortune was founded on a hair straightener. She had been a scrubwoman and a laundress.

Biggest Dowry

The largest recorded dowry was that of Elena Patiño, daughter of Don Simón Iturbi Patiño (1861–1947), the Bolivian tin millionaire, who in 1929 bestowed $22,400,000 from a fortune at one time estimated to be worth $350 million.

RICHEST MAN: John D. Rockefeller, who made his millions with Standard Oil in the early 1900's, was an often photographed figure. He started many philanthropies, but was better known for giving away dimes to young people.

MOST MISERLY MISER: Hettie Green in the early 1900's lived on cold oatmeal, and left $95 million when she died in 1916.

Greatest Miser

If meanness is measurable as a ratio between expendable assets and expenditure, then Henrietta (Hetty) Howland Green (*née* Robinson) (US, 1835–1916), who kept a balance of over $31,400,000 in one bank alone, was the all-time world champion. She was so stingy that her son had to have his leg amputated because of the delays in finding a *free* medical clinic. She herself lived off cold oatmeal because she was too thrifty to heat it. Her estate proved to be worth $95 million.

Return of Money

Jim Priceman, 44, assistant cashier at Doft & Co Inc, returned an envelope containing $37.1 million in *negotiable* bearer certificates found outside 110 Wall Street to A. G. Becker, Inc, NYC on Apr 6, 1982. In announcing a reward of $250, the Becker Company was acclaimed as being "all heart."

The largest amount of *cash* ever found and returned to its owners was $500,000 found by Lowell Elliott, 61, on his farm in Peru, Ind. It had been dropped in June 1972 by a parachuting hijacker.

Greatest Bequests

The greatest bequests in a lifetime of a millionaire were those of the late John Davison Rockefeller (1839–1937), who gave away sums totaling $750 million.

The Scottish-born US citizen Andrew Carnegie (1835–1919) is estimated to have made benefactions totaling $350 million in the last 18 years of his life. These included 7,689 church organs and 2,811 libraries. He had started in a bobbin factory at $1.20 a week.

The largest bequest made in the history of philanthropy was made by Ryoichi Sasakawa, chairman of the Japanese Shipbuilding Industry Foundation, who made total donations of 405,732,907,012 yen (approx $1,741,000,000) during the years 1962–84. This exceeded the $500 million gift, announced on Dec 12, 1955, to 4,157 educational and other institutions by the Ford Foundation (established 1936) of NYC.

---

2. HONORS, DECORATIONS AND AWARDS

Highest US Decoration

The highest US military decoration is the Congressional Medal of Honor. Five marines received both the Army and Navy Medals of Honor for the same acts in 1918, and 14 officers and men from 1863 to 1915 received the medal on two occasions.

Top Jet Ace

The greatest number of kills in jet-to-jet battles is 16 by Capt Joseph Christopher McConnell, Jr (USAF) (b Dover, NH, Jan 30, 1922) in the Korean War (1950–53). He was killed on Aug 25, 1954. It is possible that an Israeli ace may have surpassed this total in the period 1967–70, but the identity of pilots is subject to strict security.

MOST HONORARY DEGREES: The Rev Father Theodore M. Hesburgh of Notre Dame University garnered 111 degrees, 1954–87, to set a new record.

Top Woman Ace

The record score for any woman fighter pilot is 12 by Jr Lt Lydia Litvak (USSR) in the Eastern Front campaign of 1941–43. She was killed in action on Aug 1, 1943.

Submarine Warfare

The largest target ever sunk by a submarine was the Japanese aircraft carrier *Shinano* (59,000 tons) by the *USS Archerfish* (Commander Joseph F. Enright, USN) Nov 29, 1944.

Statues

Louis Agassiz, famed Swiss naturalist who helped turn Harvard into a university and whose widow helped found Radcliffe College, had a statue erected in his honor at Stanford University, Calif. When, during the San Francisco earthquake of 1906, it fell, head-first, his contemporaries mused: "Agassiz was great in the abstract but not in the concrete."

The record for raising statues to oneself was set by Generalissimo Dr Rafael Leónidas Trujillo y Molina (1891–1961), a former President of the Dominican Republic. In March 1960 a count showed that there were "over 2,000." The country's highest mountain was named Pico Trujillo (now Pico Duarte). One province was called Trujillo and another Trujillo Valdez. The capital was named Ciudad Trujillo (Trujillo City) in 1936, but reverted to its old name of Santo Domingo on Nov 23, 1961. Trujillo was assassinated in a car ambush on May 30, 1961, and May 30 is now celebrated annually as a public holiday.

The man to whom most statues have been raised is undoubtedly Buddha. The 20th century champion is Vladimir Ilyich Ulyanov, *alias* Lenin (1870–1924), busts of whom have been mass-produced. Busts of Mao Tse-tung (1893–1976) and Ho Chi Minh (1890–1969) have also been mass-produced.

Most Decorated Soldier

Lt Col Matt Urban (US Army Ret) of Buffalo, NY is the most decorated soldier in American history. After 35 years wait he received the Congressional Medal of Honor for conspicuous gallantry in action June 14–Sept 3, 1944. He was also awarded the Silver Star with 1 oak leaf cluster, the Bronze Star with 2 oak leaf clusters, the Purple Heart with 6 oak leaf clusters, the American Campaign Medal, the European-African-Middle Eastern Campaign Medal with 1 Silver and 1 Bronze service star, World War II Victory Medal, Combat Infantry Badge, the French Croix de Guerre with Silver Gilt Star, the Fourragère from Belgium. He also received a civilian award of the New York State Conspicuous Cross with 4 Silver and 1 Gold Clusters.

Most Honorary Degrees

The greatest number of honorary degrees awarded to any individual is 111, given to Rev Father Theodore M. Hesburgh (b 1918), president

TOP SCORING AIR ACES

The "scores" of air aces in both wars are still hotly disputed. The highest figures officially attributed have been:

Country	*World War I* 1914–1918	*World War II* 1939–1945
World	75 Col René Paul Fonck (France) Gr Cordon, L. d'H., C. de G. (26 palms) Med. Mil (Belge) (d. 1953)*	352 Major Erich Hartmann (Germany)
US	26 Capt Edward Vernon Rickenbacker M.H., D.S.C. (7 o.l.c.), L. d'H., C. de G.	40 Major Richard I. Bong, M.H., D.S.C., S.S., D.F.C. (6 o.l.c.), A.M. (11 o.l.c.).
Canada	72 Lt-Col William Avery Bishop, V.C., C.B., D.S.O. and bar, M.C., D.F.C., L. d'H., C. de G.	31½ Sq-Ldr George F. Beurling, D.S.O., D.F.C., D.F.M. and bar.

*A total of 80 was attributed to Rittmeister Manfred Freiherr (Baron) von Richthofen (Germany) but fewer than 60 of these could be verified from German records. Col Fonck unofficially has been credited with as high a score as 125. The German high score is 62 by Col-Gen Ernst Udet.

of the University of Notre Dame, South Bend, Ind. These were accumulated from 1954 through June 1987.

Nobel Prize Winners

The Nobel Foundation of $8,960,000 was set up under the will of Alfred Bernhard Nobel (1833–96), the unmarried Swedish chemist and chemical engineer who invented dynamite in 1866. The Nobel Prizes are presented annually on Dec 10, the anniversary of Nobel's death and the festival day of the Foundation. Since the first Prizes were awarded in 1901, the highest cash value of the award, in each of the six fields of Physics, Chemistry, Medicine and Physiology, Literature, Peace and Economics was $220,000 (approx) in 1985.

The most awards (3) were won by the International Committee for Red Cross.

Individually, the only person to have won two Prizes outright is Dr Linus Carl Pauling (b Feb 28, 1901), Prof of Chemistry since 1931 at the Calif Institute of Technology, Pasadena, Calif. He was awarded the Chemistry Prize for 1954 and the Peace Prize for 1962. Only three others have won two Prizes. One was Madame Marie Curie (1867–1934), born in Poland as Marja Sklodowska, who shared the 1903 Physics Prize with her husband, Pierre Curie (1859–1906) and

MOST CLUSTERS AND GOLD STARS

Navy Cross	5 gold stars	Lt Gen Lewis B. Puller, USMC
Distinguished Service Cross	7 clusters	Capt Edward Rickenbacker (d 1973)
Silver Star	8 clusters	Col David H. Hackworth, USA
Distinguished Flying Cross	11 clusters	Col Francis S. Gabreski, USAF
	11 gold stars	Maj Charles Carr
Distinguished Service Medal (Army)	4 clusters	Gen of the Army Douglas MacArthur (also one Naval award)
		Gen of the Army Dwight D. Eisenhower
	3 clusters	Gen Lyman L. Lemnitzer (also one USN and one USAF award)
Distinguished Service Medal (Navy)	3 gold stars	Fleet Adm William F. Halsey
		Marine Gen Holland M. Smith
Legion of Merit	5 clusters	Maj Gen Richard Steinbach
Purple Heart	9 clusters	Sgt Raymond E. Tirva

Antoine Henri Becquerel (1852–1908), and won the 1911 Chemistry Prize outright. Another was Prof Frederick Sanger (UK) (b Aug 13, 1918) who twice shared the Chemistry Prize (1958 and 1980). The third was Prof John Bardeen (US) (b May 23, 1908) who shared the Physics Prize in 1956 and 1972.

The oldest prizeman was Prof Francis Peyton Rous (b Baltimore, 1879–1970), who worked at the Rockefeller Institute, NYC. He shared the Medicine Prize in 1966, at the age of 87.

The youngest laureate was Prof Sir William Lawrence Bragg (b Adelaide, South Australia, 1890, d 1971), of the UK, who, at the age of 25, shared the 1915 Physics Prize with his father, Sir William Henry Bragg (1862–1942), for work on X-rays and crystal structures. Bragg and also Theodore William Richards (1868–1928) (US) who won the 1914 Chemistry Prize, carried out their prize work when aged 23. The youngest Literature prizeman was (Joseph) Rudyard Kipling (UK) (1865–1936) at the age of 41, in 1907.

Who's Who

The longest entry of the 66,000 entries in *Who's Who in America* is that of Dr Glenn T. Seaborg (b Apr 19, 1912), whose record listing of 100 lines compares with the 9-line entry for Ronald Reagan.

In the British *Who's Who,* the longest entry was that of Winston Churchill, who appeared in 67 editions from 1899 (18 lines) and had 211 lines by the 1965 edition. When he died he was replaced by the romantic novelist, Barbara Cartland, who has 130 lines. The youngest entry of those who qualify without hereditary title is Yehudi Menuhin (b NYC, Apr 22, 1916), the concert violinist now living in England, who first appeared in the 1932 edition, aged 15.

Youngest Gallantry Award

The youngest age at which an official gallantry award has ever been won is 8 years in the case of Anthony Farrer who was given the Albert Medal on Sept 23, 1916 for fighting off a cougar at Cowichan Lake, Vancouver Island, Canada to save Doreen Ashburnham.

Chapter 12

Sports, Games & Pastimes

AUTO RACING

Earliest Races

There are various conflicting claims, but the first automobile race was the 201-mile Green Bay-to-Madison, Wis, run in 1878, won by an Oshkosh steamer.

In 1887, Count Jules Felix Philippe Albert de Dion de Malfiance (1856–1946) won the *La Velocipede* 19.3-mile race in Paris in a De Dion steam quadricycle in which he is reputed to have exceeded 37 mph.

The first "real" race was from Paris to Bordeaux and back (732 miles) June 11–13, 1895. The winner was Emile Levassor (1844–97) (France) driving a Panhard-Levassor two-seater with a 1.2-liter Daimler engine developing 3½ hp. His time was 48 hours 47 min (average speed 15.01 mph). The first closed-circuit race was held over 5 laps of a mile dirt track at Narragansett Park, Cranston, RI on Sept 7, 1896. It was won by A. H. Whiting, who drove a Riker electric.

The oldest auto race in the world still being regularly run is the R.A.C. Tourist Trophy, first staged on the Isle of Man on Sept 14, 1905. The oldest continental race is the French Grand Prix, first held June 26–27, 1906. The Coppa Florio, in Sicily, has been irregularly held since 1900.

Fastest Races

The fastest race in the world is the NASCAR Busch Clash, a 50-mi all-out sprint on the 2½-mile 31-degree-banked tri-oval at Daytona International Speedway, Daytona Beach, Fla. On Feb 8, 1987, Bill Elliott (b Oct 8, 1955) of Dawsonville, Ga, averaged 197.802 mph in a Ford Thunderbird to set the record. Elliott set the world record for a 500-mi race in 1985 when he won at Talladega, Ala, at an average speed of 186.288 mph. He also set the NASCAR qualifying record of 212.809 at Talladega's Alabama International Motor Speedway on Apr 30, 1987.

Fastest Drivers

The highest average lap speed attained on any closed circuit is 250.958 mph in a trial by Dr Hans Liebold (b Oct 12, 1926) (Germany) who lapped the 7.85-mile high-speed track at Nardo, Italy, in 1 min 52.67 sec in a Mercedes-Benz C111-IV experimental coupé on May 5, 1979. It was powered by a V8 engine with two KKK turbochargers with an output of 500 hp at 6,200 rpm.

The highest average lap speed in an actual race on a closed circuit is 223.401 mph by Rick Mears of Bakersfield, Calif, driving a Chevrolet-powered March on the 2-mi Michigan International Speedway, Brooklyn, Mich, July 31, 1986, during the qualifying for the Michigan 500. Mears, in the same car on the same track Nov 17, 1986, was clocked at 233.934 under simulated race conditions and has applied for certification of that time to break his 223.401 record.

The fastest average lap speed on a closed-circuit track by a woman racer is 204.223 by Lyn St. James, (US), in a Mustang Probe on the 2.66-mi Alabama International Motor Speedway in Talladega, Ala, on Nov 26, 1985.

The most Grand Prix victories is 31 in 125 races by Alain Prost (France) (b Feb 24, 1955) from July 5, 1981 through May 29, 1988. Jim Clark (1936–1968) of Scotland shares the record of Grand Prix victories in one year with 7 in 1963; Prost had 7 in 1984. The most Grand Prix starts is 176 (out of a possible 184) between May 18, 1958, and Jan 26, 1975, by (Norman) Graham Hill (1929–1975); Jacques Laffite (France) (b Nov 21, 1943), likewise had 176 starts 1974–86.

The most Grand Prix points won is 439½ by Alain Prost 1981–88.

Youngest and Oldest Grand Prix Winners and Drivers

The youngest Grand Prix driver was Michael Christopher Thackwell (b New Zealand, March 30, 1961) who took part in the Canadian Grand Prix on Sept 28, 1980, aged 19 years 182 days. The youngest Grand Prix winner was Bruce Leslie McLaren (1937–70) of New Zealand, who won the US Grand Prix at Sebring, Fla, on Dec 12, 1959, aged 22 years 104 days. The youngest world champion was Emerson Fittipaldi of Brazil (b Dec 12, 1946), who won the World Championship in 1972 at age 25 years 273 days.

The oldest Grand Prix winner was Tazio Giorgio Nuvolari (1892–1953) of Italy, who won the Albi Grand Prix at Albi, France, on July 14, 1946, aged 53 years 240 days. The oldest Grand Prix driver was Louis Alexandre Chiron (Monaco, 1899–1979), who finished 6th in the Monaco Grand Prix on May 22, 1955, aged 55 years 292 days. The oldest world champion was Juan-Manuel Fangio, who won in 1957 at age 46 years 55 days.

Indianapolis 500

The Indianapolis 500-mile race (200 laps) was inaugurated on May 30, 1911. The most successful drivers have been Anthony Joseph "A. J." Foyt, Jr (b Houston, Tex, Jan 16, 1935), who won in 1961, 64, 67 and 77, and Al Unser, Sr (b May 29, 1939) of Albuquerque, N Mex, who won in 1970, 71, 78 and 87.

The record time is 2 hours 55 min 42.48 sec (average speed 170.722

MOST GRAND PRIX ▲ VICTORIES: Alain Prost (France), shown in his Formula One car, shares the record of 7 wins in one year (1984) with Jim Clark (Scotland, 1963), and set a career record of 31 wins.

◄ **MOST NASCAR VICTORIES:** Richard Petty has won a total of 200 Winston Cup races 1958–87 in 1,044 starts, his best season being 1967 with 27 victories. He was the first driver to pass $1 million in career earnings.

mph) by Bobby Rahal (US) on May 31, 1986, driving a March Cosworth.

The one lap record is 221.565 mph by Mario Gabriele Andretti (US) (b Feb 28, 1940) in a Lola-Chevrolet on May 11, 1988.

The qualifying 4-lap record average speed is 219.198 mph by Rick Mears (US) in a Penske-Chevrolet V8 on May 22, 1988.

The record prize fund is $5,016,959 for the 1988 race. The individual prize record is the $804,853 won by Bobby Rahal in 1988.

The first and only woman to qualify for and compete in the Indianapolis 500 is Janet Guthrie (b Mar 7, 1938). She passed her rookie test in May 1976, and earned the right to compete in the qualifying rounds, but was unable to win a place on the starting line when the Vollstedt-Offenhauser she drove was withdrawn from the race after repeated mechanical failures. In the 61st running of the Indianapolis 500, in 1977, Guthrie became the first woman to compete, although her car developed mechanical problems which forced her to retire after 27 laps. In 1978, she completed the race, finishing in ninth place after 190 laps.

CART Leaders

The Indy cars, the fastest open-wheeled class of racing cars in the United States, are the American equivalent of the international Formula One series. They race under the auspices of CART (Championship Auto Racing Teams). A. J. Foyt holds the all-time record for victories with 67. Mario Andretti is the leader in earnings ($5,750,068), pole positions (64) and laps led (7,088) as of July 3, 1988.

LE MANS: Record-breaking crowd of 400,000 watches the start of the 24-hour race for touring cars called the Grand Prix d'Endurance.

MAN OF LE MANS: Jackie Ickx (Belgium) roared to 6 wins in this race, turned in the fastest race lap at almost 149 mph and has been a contender since 1969.

Most Successful Drivers

Based on the World Drivers' Championships, inaugurated in 1950, the most successful driver is Juan-Manuel Fangio (b Balcarce, Argentina, June 24, 1911), who won five times in 1951, 54–57. He retired in 1958, after having won 24 Grand Prix races (2 shared) in 51 starts.

The most successful driver in terms of earnings is Darrell Waltrip (b Feb 5, 1949) of Franklin, Tenn, whose career earnings reached $8,136,963 through May 8, 1988. Richard Lee Petty (b Randleman, NC, July 2, 1937) has 200 NASCAR Winston Cup wins, 1958–87. Petty's best season was 1967 with 27 wins. Geoff Bodine won 55 races in 1978. Bill Elliott holds the single year's record of $2,383,187 in NASCAR events in 1985.

Le Mans

The greatest distance ever covered in the 24-hour *Grand Prix d'Endurance* (first held May 26–27, 1923) on the old Sarthe circuit (8 miles 650 yd) at Le Mans, France, is 3,314.222 miles by Dr Helmut Marko (b Graz, Austria, Apr 27, 1943) and Jonkheer Gijs van Lennep (b Bloemendaal, Netherlands, March 16, 1942) driving a 4,907-cc flat-12 Porsche 917K Group 5 sports car June 12–13, 1971. The record for the current circuit is 3,161.938 miles (average speed 131.747 mph) in a Porsche 956 June 15–16, 1985 by Klaus Ludwig (W Ger), Paulo Barillo (Italy), and John Winter (W Ger). The race lap record (8.410-mile lap) is 3 min 25.1 sec (average speed 148.61 mph) by Jackie Ickx (Belgium) in a Porsche 962C in 1985. The practice lap record is 3 min 14.8 sec (av. speed 156.62 mph) by Hans Stuck (W Ger) in a Porsche 962C on June 14, 1985.

The most wins by one man is 6 by Jackie Ickx (b Belgium, Jan 1, 1940), who won in 1969, 75-77 and 81-82.

Fastest Pit Stop

Bobby Unser (US) took 4 sec to take on fuel on lap 10 of the Indianapolis 500 on May 30, 1976.

Closest Finishes

The closest finish to a World Championship race occurred when Ayrton Senna (Brazil) beat Nigel Mansell (GB) by 0.014 sec in the Spanish Grand Prix at Jerez de la Frontera Apr 13, 1986.

The closest finish in the Indianapolis 500 was in the 1982 race when the winner, Gordon Johncock, crossed the finish line just 0.16 sec before runner-up Rick Mears.

Duration Record

The greatest distance ever covered in one year is 400,000 km (248,548.5 miles) by François Lecot (1879–1949), an innkeeper from Rochetaillée, France, in a 1,900-cc 66-bhp Citroën 11 sedan mainly between Paris and Monte Carlo, from July 22, 1935 to July 26, 1936. He drove on 363 of the 370 days allowed.

Land Speed Records

The highest speed attained by any wheeled land vehicle is 739.666

FASTEST STOCK CAR: At 212 mph, Bill Elliott drove this Ford Thunderbird to a speed record at Talladega, Ala, Apr 30, 1987. Elliott has record earnings of over $2 million in one year. (*NASCAR*)

HIGHEST AVERAGE SPEED: This Mercedes-Benz C111-IV experimental coupe was recorded on May 5, 1979 at 250.958 mph.

DRAG RECORD: Eddie Hill became the new king of dragsters with 2 major record performances in 1988.

mph or Mach 1.0106 (making it the only land vehicle to break the sound barrier) *in a one-way stretch* by the rocket-engined *Budweiser Rocket*, designed by William Frederick, and driven by Stan Barrett at Edwards Air Force Base, California, on Dec 17, 1979. The vehicle, owned by Hal Needham, has a 48,000-hp rocket engine with 6,000 lb of extra thrust from a sidewinder missile. The rear wheels (100-lb solid discs) lifted 10 in off the ground above Mach 0.95, acting as 7,500-rpm gyroscopes.

The official 1-mi land speed record, which is for the average of a two-way run, was set on Oct 4, 1983 when Richard Noble (GB) drove a jet-powered car, *Thrust 2*, at 633.468 mph at Black Rock Desert, Gerlach, Nev. The previous record, 622.287, was set by Gary Gabelich and had stood for 13 years.

The most successful land speed record breaker was Major Malcolm Campbell (1885–1948) (UK). He broke the official record nine times between Sept 25, 1924, with 146.157 mph in a Sunbeam, and Sept 3, 1935, when he achieved 301.129 mph in the Rolls-Royce-engined *Bluebird*.

Drag Racing

The lowest elapsed time recorded by a piston-engined dragster is 4.99 sec from a standing start for 440 yd by Eddie Hill at Ennis, Tex, on Apr 9, 1988. The highest terminal velocity recorded at the end of a 440-yd run is 288.73 mph by Hill at Gainesville, Fla, on Mar 18, 1988.

BASEBALL

Earliest Games

The Reverend Thomas Wilson, of Maidstone, Kent, England, wrote disapprovingly, in 1700, of baseball being played on Sundays. The earliest game on record under the Cartwright (Alexander Joy Cartwright, Jr, 1820–92) rules was on June 19, 1846, in Hoboken, NJ, where the "New York Nine" defeated the Knickerbockers 23 to 1 in 4 innings. The earliest all-professional team was the Cincinnati Red Stockings in 1869, who had 56 wins and 1 tie that season.

Night Baseball

The first night game was played on June 2, 1883 (M.E. College vs professionals from Quincy, Ill). The major leagues were slow to adopt this change of program, then considered radical. The Cincinnati Reds were the first big-league team to play under lights when they hosted the Philadelphia Phillies on May 24, 1935. President Franklin D. Roosevelt pressed a button at the White House to flick the switch at Crosley Field. Wrigley Field, home of the Chicago Cubs, no longer remains unlit.

Home Runs

Henry L. (Hank) Aaron (b Feb 5, 1934, Mobile, Ala) broke the major league record set by George H. (Babe) Ruth of 714 home runs in a lifetime when he hit No. 715 on Apr 8, 1974. Between 1954 and 1974 he hit 733 home runs for the Milwaukee and Atlanta Braves in the National League. In 1975, he switched to the Milwaukee Brewers in the American League and in that year and 1976, when he finally retired, he hit 22 more, bringing his lifetime total to 755, the major league record.

A North American record of almost 800 in a lifetime has been claimed for Josh Gibson (1911–47), mostly for the Homestead Grays of the Negro National League, who was elected in 1972 to the Baseball Hall of Fame in Cooperstown, NY. Gibson is said to have hit 75 round-trippers in one season, in 1931, but no official records were kept.

The most officially recorded home runs hit by a professional player in the US in one season is 72, by Joe Bauman, of the Roswell, NM team, a minor league club, in 1954. The major league record is 61 in 161 games of a 162-game season by Roger Maris (1934–1985) of the NY Yankees, in 1961. George Herman "Babe" Ruth (1895–1948) hit 60 in a 154-game season in 1927.

The longest home run "officially" measured was 618 ft by Roy Edward "Dizzy" Carlyle (1900–56) in a minor league game at Emeryville Ball Park, Calif, July 4, 1929. Babe Ruth hit a 587-ft

HOME RUN HEROES: Josh Gibson (left) hit 800 homers in the Negro leagues, but died in 1947 just 3 months before the first black, Jackie Robinson, got into the major leagues. Mickey Mantle (right) can claim 2 "longest" major league home runs—one an officially measured 565 ft and the other a trigonometrically measured 643 ft. (*NY Yankees*)

homer for the Boston Red Sox vs NY Giants in an exhibition game at Tampa, Fla, in 1919. The longest measured home run in a regular-season major league game is 565 ft by Mickey Mantle (b Oct 20, 1931) for the NY Yankees vs Washington Senators on Apr 17, 1953, at Griffith Stadium, Wash DC.

> Mantle's homer in Detroit on Sept 10, 1960, which ascended over the right field roof and is said to have landed in a lumberyard, was measured trigonometrically in 1985 to have traveled 643 ft.

Shortest and Tallest Players

The shortest major league player was surely Eddie Gaedel, a 3-ft-7-in, 65-lb midget, who pinch hit for the St Louis Browns vs the Detroit Tigers on Aug 19, 1951. Wearing number ⅛, the batter with the smallest ever major league strike zone walked on four pitches. Following the game, major league rules were hastily rewritten to prevent the recurrence of such an affair.

The tallest major leaguer was John Alexander Gee (1915–88), a 6-ft-9-in pitcher who spent 6 seasons in the National League: 1939, 41, 43–46.

Youngest and Oldest Players

The youngest major league player of all time was the Cincinnati pitcher Joe Nuxhall, who started his career in June 1944, aged 15 years 10 months 11 days.

Leroy "Satchel" Paige (1906?–82) pitched three scoreless innings for the Kansas City Athletics at approximately age 59 in 1965. Baseball's color barrier had kept him out of the major leagues until 1948, when he was a 42-year-old "rookie," and his record of 6 wins and 1 loss helped the Cleveland Indians win the pennant. His birthday is listed as July 7, 1906, but many believe he was born earlier. The Atlanta Braves carried Paige on their roster in 1968 to allow him to qualify for a pension.

One Day Wonder

John Paciorek of the Houston Colt '45s had a perfect day at bat in his only game in the majors in 1963 with 3 singles, 2 walks, 4 runs scored, and 3 rbi's, for a 1.000 average.

Fastest Base Runner

Ernest Evar Swanson (1902–73) took only 13.3 sec to circle the bases at Columbus, Ohio, in 1932, averaging 18.45 mph.

Most Stolen Bases

While Lou Brock holds the career record for most bases stolen with 938, this was topped in the Japanese league by Yubaka Kikomoto with 1,059.

MAJOR LEAGUE ALL-TIME RECORDS
(Including 1987 season)

Individual Batting

Most years
25 Roderick (Bobby) Wallace, Cleve NL 1894–98; St L NL 1899–1901, 1917–18; St L AL 1902–16
Edward Collins, Phil AL 1906–14, 1927–30; Chi AL 1915–26

Highest percentage, lifetime (5,000 at-bats)
.367 Tyrus R. Cobb, Det AL, 1905–26; Phil AL, 1927–28

Highest percentage, season (500 at-bats)
.438 Hugh Duffy, Bos NL, 1894
Modern Record
.424 Rogers Hornsby, St L NL, 1924

Most games played
3,562 Peter Rose, Cin NL, 1963–78; Phil NL, 1979–83; Mont NL, 1984; Cin NL, 1984–86

Most consecutive games played
2,130 Henry Louis (Lou) Gehrig, NY AL, June 1, 1925 through Apr 30, 1939

Most runs batted in, season
190 Lewis R. (Hack) Wilson, Chi NL, 155 games, 1930

Most runs batted in, game
12 James L. Bottomley, St L NL, Sept 16, 1924

Most runs batted in, lifetime
2,297 Henry L. (Hank) Aaron, Mil NL, 1954–65, Atl NL, 1966–74; Mil AL, 1975–76

Most runs, lifetime
2,244 Tyrus R. Cobb, Det AL, 1905–26; Phil AL, 1927–28

Most runs, season
196 William R. Hamilton Phil NL 1894
Modern Record
177 George H. (Babe) Ruth NY AL 1921

Most runs, game
6 Held by 12 players. Most recent: Spike D. Owen, Bos AL Aug 21, 1986

Most base hits, lifetime
4,256 Peter Rose, Cin NL, 1963–78; Phil NL, 1979–83; Mont NL, 1984; Cin NL, 1984–86

Most base hits, season
257 George H. Sisler, St L AL, 154 games, 1920

Most hits in succession
12 M. Frank (Pinky) Higgins, Bos AL, June 19–21 (4 games), 1938
Walter Dropo, Det AL, July 14, July 15, 2 games, 1952

Most base hits, game
9 John H. Burnett, Cleve AL, July 10, 1932 (18 innings)

Most base hits, consecutive, game
7 Wilbert Robinson, Balt NL, June 10, 1892, 1st game (7-ab), 6-1b, 1-2b
Renaldo Stennett, Pitt NL, Sept 16, 1975 (7-ab), 4-1b, 2-2b, 1-3b
Cesar Gutierrez, Det AL, June 21, 1970, 2nd game (7-ab) 6-1b, 1-2b (12-inning game)

Most times at bat, lifetime
14,053 Peter Rose, Cin NL, 1963–78; Phil NL, 1979–83; Mont NL, 1984; Cin NL, 1984–86

Most consecutive games batted safely, season
56 Joseph P. DiMaggio, NY AL (91 hits—16-2b, 4-3b, 15 hr), May 15 to July 16, 1941

Most total bases, lifetime
6,856 Henry L. (Hank) Aaron, Mil NL, 1954–65; Atl NL, 1966–74; Mil AL, 1975–76

Most total bases, season
457 George H. (Babe) Ruth, NY AL, 152 gs (85 on

1b, 88 on 2b, 48 on 3b, 236 on hr), 1921

Most total bases, game
18 Joseph W. Adcock, Mil NL (1-2b, 4-hr), July 31, 1954

Most one-base hits (singles), season
202 William H. (Wee Willie) Keeler, Balt NL, 128 games, 1898

Modern Record

198 Lloyd Waner, Pitt NL, 1927

Most two-base hits, season
67 Earl W. Webb, Bos AL, 151 games, 1931

Most three-base hits, season
36 J. Owen Wilson, Pitt NL, 152 games, 1912

Most home runs, season
61 Roger E. Maris, NY AL (162-game schedule) (30 home, 31 away), 161 gs, 1961
60 George H. (Babe) Ruth, NY AL (154-game schedule) (28 home, 32 away), 151 gs, 1927

Most home runs, lifetime
755 Henry L. Aaron, Mil NL, 1954 (13), 1955 (27), 1956 (26), 1957 (44), 1958 (30), 1959 (39), 1960 (40), 1961 (34), 1962 (45), 1963 (44), 1964 (24), 1965 (32); Atl NL, 1966 (44), 1967 (39), 1968 (29), 1969 (44), 1970 (38), 1971 (47), 1972 (34), 1973 (40), 1974 (20); Mil AL, 1975 (12), 1976 (10)

Most home runs, bases filled, lifetime
23 Henry Louis (Lou) Gehrig, NY AL, 1923–1939

Most consecutive games hitting home runs
8 R. Dale Long, Pitt NL, Don Mattingly, NY AL, 1987

4,577 STRIKEOUTS is the record total achieved by Nolan Ryan in his career, begun in 1968 with the Mets, then the Angels, and in 1987 the Astros.

Most home runs with bases filled, season
6 Don Mattingly, NY AL, 1987

Most home runs, with bases filled, game
2 Anthony M. Lazzeri, NY AL, May 24, 1936
James R. Tabor, Bos AL (2nd game), July 4, 1939
Rudolph York, Bos AL, July 27, 1946
James E. Gentile, Balt AL, May 9, 1961 (consecutive at-bats)
Tony L. Cloninger, Atl NL, July 3, 1966
James T. Northrup, Det AL, June 24, 1968 (consecutive at-bats)
Frank Robinson, Balt AL, June 26, 1970 (consecutive at-bats)
Don Mattingly, NY AL, 1987

Most home runs, one doubleheader
5 Stanley F. Musial, St L NL, 1st game (3), 2nd game (2), May 2, 1954; Nathan Colbert, SD NL, 1st game (2), 2nd game (3), Aug 1, 1972

Most bases on balls, game
6 James E. Foxx, Bos AL, June 16, 1938
Andre Thornton, Clev AL, May 2, 1984 (16 inns)

Most bases on balls, season
170 George H. (Babe) Ruth, NY AL, 152 games, 1923

Most hits, pinch-hitter, lifetime
150 Manuel R. Mota, SF NL, 1962; Pitt NL, 1963–1968; Mont NL, 1969; LA NL, 1969–1980

Most consecutive home runs, pinch-hitter
3 Delbert Unser, Phil NL, June 30, July 5, 10, 1979
Leondaus (Lee) Lacy, LA NL, May 2, 6, 17, 1978 (one walk in between)

Most consecutive pinch hits
9 David E. Philley, Phil NL, Sept 9, 11, 12, 13, 19, 20, 27, 28, 1958; Apr 16, 1959

BASE STEALER SUPREME: Rickey Henderson, while with the Oakland A's in 1982, stole 130 bases in 149 games. *(Steve Babineau photo)*

Base Running

Most stolen bases, lifetime
938 Louis C. Brock, Chi NL, 1961–64; St L NL, 1964–79

Most stolen bases, season since 1900
130 Rickey Henderson, Oak AL, 149 games, 1982

Most stolen bases, game
7 George F. (Piano Legs) Gore, Chi NL, June 25, 1881

Most stolen bases, game (continued)
William R. (Sliding Billy) Hamilton, Phil NL, 2nd game, 8 inn, Aug 31, 1894

Modern Record

6 Edward T Collins, Phil AL, Sept 11 and again Sept 22, 1912

Most times stealing home, lifetime
46 Tyrus R. Cobb, Det AL, 1905–26; Phil AL 1927–28

Fewest times caught stealing, season (50+ attempts)
2 Max Carey, Pitt NL, 1922 (53 atts)

Pitching

Most years
25 James Kaat, Wash AL 1959–60; Minn AL 1961–73; Chi AL 1973–75; Phil NL 1976–79; NY AL 1979–80; St L NL 1980–83

Most games, lifetime
1,070 J. Hoyt Wilhelm, NY-St L-Atl-Chi-LA (448) NL, 1952–57, 69–72; Clev-Balt-Chi-Cal (622) AL, 1957–69

Most complete games, lifetime
751 Denton T. (Cy) Young, Clev-St L-Bos NL (428); Bos-Clev AL (323), 1890–1911

Perfect game—9 innings
1880 John Lee Richmond, Worcester vs Clev NL, June 12 1–0
John M. Ward, Prov vs Buff NL, June 17 AM 5–0

1904 Denton T. (Cy) Young, Bos vs Phil AL, May 5 3–0
1908 Adrian C. Joss, Clev vs Chi AL, Oct 2 1–0
†1917 Ernest G. Shore, Bos vs Wash AL, June 23 (1st g) 4–0
1922 C. C. Robertson, Chi vs Det AL, Apr 30 2–0
*1956 Donald J. Larsen, NY AL vs Bklyn NL, Oct 8 2–0
1964 James P. Bunning, Phil NL vs NY, June 21 (1st g) 6–0
1965 Sanford (Sandy) Koufax, LA NL vs Chi, Sept 9 1–0
1968 James A. (Catfish) Hunter, Oak AL vs Minn, May 8 4–0
1981 Leonard H. Barker II, Cleve AL vs Tor, May 15 3–0
1984 Michael Witt. Cal Al vs Texas, Sept 9, 1984 1–0

Special mention
1959 Harvey Haddix, Jr, Pitt vs Mil NL, May 26, pitched 12 perfect innings, allowed hit in 13th and lost.

Most games, season
106 Michael G. Marshall, LA NL, 1974

Most games won, season
60 Charles Radbourn, Providence NL, 1884

Most complete games, season
74 William H. White, Cin NL, 1879

Modern Record

48 John D. Chesbro, NY AL, 1904

Lowest earned run average, season
0.90 Ferdinand M. Schupp, NY NL, 1916 (140 inn)
1.00 Hubert B. (Dutch) Leonard, Bos AL, 1914 (222 inn)
1.12 Robert Gibson, St L NL, 1968 (305 inn)

Most innings pitched, game
26 Leon J. Cadore, Bklyn NL, May 1, 1920
Joseph Oeschger, Bos NL, May 1, 1920

Most games won, lifetime
511 Denton T. (Cy) Young, Clev NL (239) 1890–98; St L NL (46) 1899–1900; Bos AL (193) 1901–08; Clev AL (29) 1909–11; Bos NL (4) 1911

Most consecutive games won, lifetime
24 Carl O. Hubbell, NY NL, 1936 (16); 1937 (8)

Most strikeouts, season
505 Matthew Kilroy, Balt AA, 1886 (Distance 50 ft)
383 L. Nolan Ryan, Cal AL, 1973 (Distance 60 ft 6 in)

Most strikeouts, career
4,577 L. Nolan Ryan, NY NL, Cal AL, Houston NL, 1968–87

Most strikeouts, game (9 inn) since 1900
20 Roger Clemens, Bos AL vs Seat, Apr 29, 1986

Most strikeouts, extra-inning game
21 Thomas E. Cheney, Wash AL vs Balt (16 inn), Sept 12, 1962 (night)

Most no-hit games, lifetime
5 L. Nolan Ryan, Cal AL, 1973 (2)–74–75; Hou NL, 1981

Most consecutive no-hit games
2 John S. Vander Meer, Cin NL, June 11–15, 1938

Most consecutive games won, season
19 Timothy J. Keefe, NY NL, 1888 Richard W. (Rube) Marquard, NY NL, 1912

Most shutout games, season
16 George W. Bradley, St L NL, 1876
Grover C. Alexander, Phil NL, 1916

---

† Starting pitcher, "Babe" Ruth, was banished from game by Umpire Brick Owens after an argument. He gave the first batter, Ray Morgan, a base on balls. Shore relieved and while he pitched to second batter, Morgan was caught stealing. Shore then retired next 26 batters to complete the "perfect" game.

* World Series game.

ACE PITCHERS OF THE 1980's: Dwight Gooden (above) of the NY Mets and Roger Clemens (right) of the Boston Red Sox both had a rare season in which they won 20 more games than they lost. Gooden did it in 1985 and Clemens in 1986.

◄ MOST CONSECUTIVE INNINGS PLAYED: Cal Ripken, Jr, the Baltimore Oriole shortstop, has played all of every inning for 910 games in a unique record of 8,243 innings, 1982–87. *(Jerry Wachter)*

Most shutout games, lifetime
113 Walter P. Johnson, Wash AL, 21 years, 1907–27

Most consecutive shutout games, season
6 Donald S. Drysdale, LA NL, May 14, 18, 22, 26, 31, June 4, 1968

Most consecutive shutout innings
58 Donald S. Drysdale, LA NL, May 14-June 8, 1968

Most saves, season
46 Dave Righetti, NY AL, 1986

Most saves, lifetime
341 Roland (Rollie) Fingers, Oak AL, 1968–76; SD NL 1977–80; Mil AL 1981–85

Fielding

Best percentage, season, by position

First Base: 1.000
Steven Garvey, SD NL, 1984

Second Base: .9966
Robert Grich, Cal AL, 1985

Third Base: .9894
Donald Money, Mil AL, 1974

Shortstop: .9912
Lawrence Bowa, Phil NL, 1979

Outfield: 1.000
Curtis Flood, St L NL, 1966 (based on most chances handled without an error—396)

Catcher: 1.000
Warren (Buddy) Rosar, Phil AL, 1946

Pitcher: 1.000
Randall Jones, SD NL, 1976 (based on most chances handled without an error—112)

Consecutive games, no errors, by position

First Base: 193
Steven Garvey, SD NL, 1983–85

Second Base: 91
Joe Morgan, Cin NL, 1977–78

Third Base: 97
James Davenport, SF NL, 1966–68

Shortstop: 72
Edwin Brinkman, Det AL, 1972

Outfield: 266
Donald Demeter, Phil NL–Det AL, 1962–65

Catcher: 148
Lawrence P. (Yogi) Berra, NY AL, 1957–59

Pitcher: 385
Paul Lindblad, KC-Oak AL, 1966–74

World Series Records

Most series played
14 Lawrence P. (Yogi) Berra, NY, AL, 1947, 49–53, 55–58, 60–63

Highest batting percentage (75 at bats, min), total series
.391 Louis C. Brock, St L NL, 1964, 67–68 (g-21, ab-87, h-34)

Highest batting percentage, 4 or more games, one series
.625 4-game series, George H. (Babe) Ruth, NY AL, 1928

Most runs, total series
42 Mickey C. Mantle, NY AL, 1951–53, 55–58, 60–64

Most runs, one series
10 Reginald M. Jackson, NY AL, 1977

Most runs batted in, total series
40 Mickey C. Mantle, NY, AL, 1951–53, 55–58, 60–64

Most strikeouts, one series
23 in 4 game series
Sanford (Sandy) Koufax, LA NL, 1963
18 in 5 game series
Christy Mathewson, NY NL, 1905
20 in 6 game series
C. A. (Chief) Bender, Phil AL, 1911
35 in 7 game series
Robert Gibson, St L NL, 1968
28 in 8 game series
W. H. Dinneen, Bos AL, 1903

Most strikeouts, one pitcher game
17 Robert Gibson, St L NL, 1968

Most base hits, total series
71 Lawrence P. (Yogi) Berra, NY AL, 1947, 49–53, 55–58, 60–63

Most home runs, total series
18 Mickey C. Mantle, NY AL, 1952 (2), 53 (2), 55, 56 (3), 57, 58 (2), 60 (3), 63, 64 (3)

Most home runs, one series
5 Reginald (Reggie) M. Jackson, NY AL, 1977

Most home runs, game
3 George H. (Babe) Ruth, NY AL, Oct 6, 1926; Oct 9, 1928
Reginald (Reggie) M. Jackson, NY AL, Oct 18, 1977

Most runs batted in, game
6 Robert C. Richardson, NY AL, (4) 1st inn, (2) 4th inn, 1960

Most hits, 7-game Series
13 Martin Barrett, Bos AL, 1986
Louis Brock, St L NL, 1968
Robt Richardson, NY AL, 1960

Most Series Won
22 New York AL, 1923, 1927, 1928, 1932, 1936–39, 1941, 1943, 1947, 1949–53, 1956, 1958, 1961, 1962, 1977, 1978

Pitching in most series
11 Edward C. (Whitey) Ford, NY AL, 1950, 53, 55–58, 60–64

Most victories, total series
10 Edward C. (Whitey) Ford, NY AL, 1950 (1), 55 (2), 56 (1), 57 (1), 60 (2), 61 (2), 62 (1)

Most games won, one series
3 games in 5-game series
Christy Mathewson, NY NL, 1905
J. W. Coombs, Phil AL, 1910

Ten others won 3 games in series of more games.

Most victories, no defeats
6 Vernon L. (Lefty) Gomez, NY AL, 1932 (1), 36 (2), 37 (2), 38 (1)

Most shutout games, total series
4 Christy Mathewson, NY NL, 1905 (3), 1913

MOST HITS, MOST AT-BATS, MOST GAMES: Pete Rose, spark plug of the Cincinnati Reds (with the Phillies for 5 years), now manager of the Reds, ended the 1986 season with 4,256 hits (65 more than Cobb) in 3,562 games and 14,053 times at the plate.

Most shutout games, one series
3 Christy Mathewson, NY NL, 1905

Most strikeouts, one pitcher, total series
94 Edward C. (Whitey) Ford, NY AL, 1950, 53, 55–58, 60–64

HOME RUN KING: Hank Aaron rewrote the record book in the 1970's. The great outfielder broke Babe Ruth's record (714) and finished with 755 homers in the major leagues.

Most Strikeouts

Bobby Bonds in 1970, right fielder for the San Francisco Giants, fanned 189 times in 157 games.

Fewest Strikeouts

Joe Sewell in 1929, while playing third base for the Cleveland Indians, played in 115 consecutive games, going to bat 437 times without once striking out. In his career stretching 14 years he only struck out 114 times.

Most Strikeouts in an Inning

Nineteen different pitchers hold the record of 4 in an inning. How? The catcher misses on a third strike and the batter gets on base, so the hurler has to fan another batter. The latest pitcher to have 4 K's (strikeouts) in one inning was Bobby Witt of the Texas Rangers, Aug 2, 1987.

Most Foul-Offs

Luke Appling, shortstop for the White Sox in the 1930's, fouled off 14 consecutive pitches from Dizzy Trout of the Tigers. On the 15th pitch, Trout threw his glove instead of the ball.

Hit by Pitch

Don Baylor, outfielder-first baseman and designated hitter, who played with 6 American League teams from 1970 through 1987 (most recently with the Minnesota Twins), holds the major league record for getting hit by pitch the most times: 255. The previous record of 243 was held by Ron Hunt, National League infielder from 1963 to 1974, who still holds the record of 50 in one season (1970).

Baylor, a powerful righthanded batter, stands close to the plate and gets hit most frequently on the left shoulder and arm. No matter how hard he gets hit, he never rubs the injured area.

Catcher's Interference

Steve Lombardozzi, Minnesota second baseman, probably set a major league record in 1986 in getting on base the most times in a single season because of catcher's interference, 11. (Records were not kept until fairly recently.)

When Connie Mack was a catcher in the National League with Washington and Pittsburgh from 1886 to 1896, he became so adept at tipping a bat that he would rarely be called for catcher's interference.

Consecutive Innings

Calvin Ripken, Jr, (b Aug 24, 1960) of the Baltimore Orioles set what is believed to be a record for playing every inning of consecutive games, when he played 8,243 innings over 910 games, 1982–87. Ripken played the first six games at third base, beginning June 5, 1982, then moved to shortstop for the duration of the streak, which came to an end Sept 14, 1987, when the manager pulled him from a game because he felt the streak was distracting the slumping Orioles. The manager was his father, Cal Ripken, Sr. Young Ripken still had a streak of 927 consecutive games at the close of the 1987 season. The known previous best for consecutive innings had been no longer than 534 games by Buck Freeman, Boston Red Sox, 1901–05.

Fastest Pitcher

The fastest recorded pitcher is (Lynn) Nolan Ryan (b Jan 31, 1947) who, on Aug 20, 1974 (then of the California Angels, now of the Houston Astros) at Anaheim Stadium, Calif, was measured to pitch at 100.9 mph.

Unanimous Choice for Rookies of the Year

For only the second time in 40 years the Baseball Writers Association of America was unanimous in choosing Mark McGwire, the Oakland Athletics first baseman, as the 1987 American League Rookie of the Year. McGwire set records with 49 homers breaking all rookie records in the majors, and also hit 5 homers and scored 9 runs in 2 games.

For the National League Rookie of the Year, the writers were again unanimous in selecting Benito Santiago, catcher for the San Diego Padres.

Do-Everything Record

Two major league ballplayers, Bert Campaneris (b Mar 12, 1942) and Cesar Tovar (b July 3, 1940), have the distinction of playing each of the nine field positions in a single major league game. Campaneris did it first, on Sept 8, 1965, when his team, the Kansas City Athletics, announced he would. He played one inning at each position, including the full eighth inning as a pitcher and gave up just one run. Tovar duplicated the feat on Sept 22, 1968, when he played for the Minnesota Twins. He pitched a scoreless first inning and retired the first batter, none other than Campaneris. On June 4, 1983, Mike Ashman, a minor league player for the Albany-Colonie A's of the Eastern League, improved upon the Campaneris-Tovar feat by playing 10 positions, including designated hitter, in a game against Nashua.

Do-Nothing Record

Toby Harrah of the Texas Rangers (AL) played an entire doubleheader at shortstop on June 26, 1976, without having a chance to make any fielding plays, assists or putouts.

9 Games Won by 9 Different Pitchers

The pennant-winning St. Louis Cardinals of 1985 established an unusual streak record, according to Paul Ferrell. In one stretch of 10 games, the Red Birds won 9, with those victories being recorded by 9 different pitchers.

Date	*Winning Pitcher*	*Opposing Team*
Sept 14	Bill Campbell	Chicago
Sept 15	Danny Cox	Chicago
Sept 16	John Tudor	Pittsburgh
Sept 16	Bill Perry	Pittsburgh
Sept 17	Joaquin Andujar	Pittsburgh
Sept 18	Bob Forsch	Philadelphia
Sept 19	Matt Keough (Lost)	Philadelphia
Sept 20	Todd Worrell	Montreal
Sept 21	Jeff Lahti	Montreal
Sept 22	Ken Dayley	Montreal

On Sept 23, Lahti defeated Pittsburgh, and on the 24th Rick Horton became the 10th Cards pitcher in 11 days to win a game when he throttled the Pirates. For September the Cardinals posted a 21–9 record and went 101–61 for the season.

Longest Major League Career

James "Deacon" McGuire (1865–1936), a catcher-infielder, played in 26 seasons for 12 different teams in three major leagues (American Association, National and American) 1884–1912. He also managed Washington in the National League (1898) and Boston (1907–08) and Cleveland (1909–11) in the American League.

Longest Throw

The longest throw of a 5–54-oz (regulation) baseball is 445 ft 10 in by Glen Gorbous (b Canada) Aug 1, 1957. Mildred "Babe" Didrickson (later Mrs George Zaharias) (1914–56) threw a ball 296 ft at Jersey City, NJ, July 25, 1931.

Longest Shutouts

Four pitchers have hurled 18-inning shutout games in the majors: Carl Hubbell, NY Giants, 1933; Walter Johnson, Wash Senators, 1918; Ed Summers, Det Tigers, 1908; John Montgomery Ward, Providence NL, 1882.

Most Strikeouts, Career

Nolan Ryan of the Houston Astros pitched his 4,000th strikeout on July 11, 1985 against the NY Mets, his former team. By the 1987

SLUGGERS: Although his home run records have been surpassed, Babe Ruth (left) is unlikely to be forgotten. His .625 batting average in the 1928 World Series is the best ever, as is his career slugging percentage of .690. Roger Maris (right) watches his 60th home run fly into the seats at Yankee Stadium. Maris then hit his record-breaking 61st in the last game of the 1961 season.

season's end his total had risen to 4,577. Ryan was the first to eclipse Walter Johnson's (Wash AL) record of 3,508 which he set between 1907 and 1927 and which stood for 55 years until April 27, 1983.

Dwight Gooden (b Nov 16, 1964) of the Mets in the 1984 All-Star Game in San Francisco struck out 6 consecutive AL batters.

Gooden, in 1985, became the youngest pitcher to win the coveted Cy Young Award. He won it by unanimous vote of the 24 sportswriters who make the selection.

Managers

Connie Mack (1862–1956) managed in the major leagues for 53 seasons—3 with Pittsburgh (NL), 1894–96, and 50 with the Philadelphia Athletics (AL), the team he owned, 1901–50. He amassed a record 3,776 regular-season victories (952 victories ahead of John McGraw). Eddie Stanky managed the Texas Rangers (AL) for one day (June 23, 1977) before deciding he did not want the job—even though his team beat Minnesota, 10–8. It is believed to be the shortest term for anyone who signed a managerial contract (that is, excluding interim managers).

Charles D. "Casey" Stengel (1890–1975) set records by managing the NY Yankees (AL) in 10 World Series and winning 7 of them, including 5 in a row (1949–53).

Longest and Shortest Major League Games

The Brooklyn Dodgers and Boston Braves played to a 1–1 tie after 26 innings on May 1, 1920.

WORLD SERIES HERO: Reggie Jackson got the name "Mr October" by hitting 5 home runs for the NY Yankees in the 1977 Series and attaining a record slugging average of .755. ▲

8 BASEBALLS IN HAND: ► Robert Link of St Petersburg, Fla, shows how he held 8 baseballs in one hand without any adhesives in June 1987.

LITTLEST MAJOR LEAGUER: Eddie Gaedel, a 26-year-old 3-ft-7-in pinch hitter for the St Louis Browns, walked on 4 pitches in an Aug 19, 1951 official game against the Detroit Tigers.

The NY Giants needed only 51 min to beat the Philadelphia Phillies, 6–1, in 9 innings on Sept 28, 1919. (A minor league game, Atlanta vs Mobile in the Southern Association on Sept 19, 1910, took only 32 min, it is claimed.)

The Chicago White Sox played the longest ballgame in elapsed time—8 hours 6 min—before beating the Milwaukee Brewers, 7–6, in the 25th inning on May 9, 1984 in Chicago. The game took 2 days, actually. It started on Tuesday night and was still tied at 3–3 when the 1 A.M. curfew caused suspension until Wednesday night.

Attendances

The World Series record attendance is 420,784 (6 games with total gate receipts of $2,626,973.44) when the Los Angeles Dodgers beat the Chicago White Sox 4 games to 2, Oct 1–8, 1959.

The single game record is 92,706 for the fifth game (gate receipts $552,774.77) at the Memorial Coliseum (no longer used for baseball), LA, Oct 6, 1959.

The all-time season record for attendance for both leagues has been 52,029,664 in 1987 (27,278,822 AL; 24,750,842 NL).

An estimated 114,000 spectators watched a game between Australia and an American servicemen's team in a "demonstration" during the Dec 1, 1956 Olympics in Melbourne, Australia.

An estimated 115,000 fans watched the Tellings Strollers play the Hanna Cleaners for the "Class A" amateur baseball championship at Cleveland's Brookside Stadium in Sept 1914. Brookside Stadium, shaped like a huge amphitheatre, had only a few thousand seats behind home plate, and so most of the fans sat along the bluffs directly above the playing field.

Longest Game in Baseball History

The longest game was a minor league game in 1981 that lasted 33 innings. At the end of 9, the score was tied, 1–1, with the Rochester (NY) Red Wings battling the home team Pawtucket (RI) Red Sox. At the end of 21 it was tied, 2–2, and at the end of 32, the score was still 2–2, when the game was suspended. Two months later, play was resumed and 18 minutes later, Pawtucket scored one run and won. The winning pitcher was the Red Sox' Bob Ojeda, whose teammates included Marty Barrett at 2B, Wade Boggs at 3B, and Rich Gedman catching. The Rochester cleanup batter was Cal Ripken, Jr. The 33rd inning was witnessed by 54 newspaper reporters, got a top-of-page headline in *The New York Times*, and was carried by the national TV networks!

Ball Drop from a Dirigible

Joe Sprinz, later catcher for the Cleveland Indians, in 1939 was playing for the Seals of the Pacific Coast League, when Lefty O'Doul was his manager. The San Francisco World's Fair was drawing crowds to Treasure Island in the Bay when someone dreamed up the stunt of dropping baseballs from a dirigible from 1,200 ft up for the Seals' players to try to catch. Sprinz was the only one who had dared to try.

"I had to shade my eyes, I saw the ball all the way, but it looked the size of an aspirin tablet," he said later. "The ball hit me in the mouth, my lips were lacerated very badly, 12 cracks in my upper jaw, lost 5 teeth, was knocked out." And he dropped the ball.

Rained-Out Game in Covered Stadium

The only time in baseball history a game in a covered stadium was called because of rain was on June 16, 1976, in Houston. Flooding around the Astrodome prevented anyone getting into the stadium and the game between Houston and Pittsburgh was called.

Running Bases in Reverse

Herman (Germany) Schaefer of the Washington Senators in 1910 stole first base. This was after he had stolen second with a runner on third. Dissatisfied because the catcher had not thrown to second to allow a double steal to begin, he stole first on the next pitch to try again. A new baseball rule (7.08 i) was instituted at once to prevent this happening again.

Baseball Memorabilia

The National Baseball Hall of Fame and Museum in Cooperstown, NY, contains a whole room devoted to Babe Ruth including a life-sized wood carving of him and his voice on records. Also it contains a wood sculpture of Ted Williams, and even razor blades used by Cy Young. In the ballparks room, there are turnstiles, lockers, dugout benches and grandstand seats from Ebbets Field, Polo Grounds and other defunct stadiums. In the library are 15,000 books and 150,000 photographs, as well as millions of press clippings, and audio and visual aids.

The greatest private collection is probably that of Barry Halper of Elizabeth, NJ, whose memorabilia is insured for $10 million. It includes over 1 million different baseball cards, 900 complete uniforms, nearly 5,000 autographed baseballs, over 1,000 bats, and at least 1,000 different examples of baseball sheet music. His newest acquisition is the fire hat that belonged to Alexander Joy Cartwright (see p. 513), the father of modern baseball, who served as fire chief in Honolulu in the 1850's.

The most valuable baseball cigarette card is still the Honus Wagner issued in 1910 which sold for $45,000 in 1987.

All Runs Unearned

The Mets scored 16 runs against the Houston Astros on July 27, 1985, winning 16–4, with all the Met runs unearned. Houston made 5 errors in the game.

BASKETBALL

Origins

Ollamalitzli was a 16th century Aztec precursor of basketball played in Mexico. If the solid rubber ball was put through a fixed stone ring placed high on one side of the stadium, the player was entitled to the clothing of all the spectators. The captain of the losing team often lost his head (by execution). Another game played much earlier, in the 10th century BC by the Olmecs in Mexico, called *Pok-ta-Pok*, also resembled basketball in its concept of a ring through which a round object was passed.

Modern basketball was devised by the Canadian-born Dr James Naismith (1861–1939) at the Training School of the International YMCA College at Springfield, Mass, in Dec 1891. The first game played under modified rules was on Jan 20, 1892. The first public contest was on March 11, 1892.

The International Amateur Basketball Federation (FIBA) was founded in 1932.

The Court

The professional 3-point shot is measured from the center of the hoop to the top of the key, namely 23 ft 9 in. This is 4 ft longer than the college 3-point distance. In the corners, the pro distance is 22 ft, or 2 ft 2 in longer than the college distance.

From the backboard to the top of the key, the pro distance is 25 ft and the college distance 21 ft. The free-throw line has always been measured from the backboard and is 15 ft, both college and pro.

Rule Change

In the 1940's coaches devised a new tactic, "freezing the ball," in order to maintain a leading score. It consisted of dribbling the ball and avoiding shooting it at the basket in order to maintain possession. In a short time this strategy became part of the entire game resulting in slow play and low scores. The lowest ever was when the Fort Wayne Pistons beat the Minneapolis Lakers 19–18, Nov 22, 1950. As attendance dropped as a result of boring play, Danny Biasone, a team owner, conceived of the "24-second rule" which requires a team to make a try at a basket within 24 seconds of gaining possession of the ball or turn possession over to the opposing team. In 1954, the NBA adopted the rule and scores increased dramatically—as did attendance. In international amateur play the 30-second rule is enforced. In college play the rule is 45 seconds.

Individual Scoring

Marie Boyd (Eichler) scored 156 points in a girls' high school basketball game for Central HS, Lonaconing, Md, in a 163–3 victory over Ursuline Academy, on Feb 25, 1924. The boys' high school record is 135 points by Danny Heater of Burnsville, W Va, on Jan 26, 1960.

In college play, Clarence (Bevo) Francis of Rio Grande College,

TOP SCORERS: Kareem Abdul-Jabbar, Mil-LA, (below) compiled 37,639 points with 15,524 field goals 1970–88, beating the 31,419 point record of Wilt Chamberlain (right, #13 in Phila uniform) who scored 100 points in one game and never fouled out of his 1,045 games played. Here he is seen jumping for a rebound.

BUCKET BRIGADE: Bevo Francis (left) scored 113 points in one game for tiny Rio Grande College in 1954. That season, he averaged 46.5 points per game. Starring for Francis Marion College, Pearl Moore (above) topped all collegiate players with 4,061 career points, 16 more than the men's college record held by Travis Grant of Kentucky State.

Ohio, scored 113 points against Hillsdale on Feb 2, 1954. One year earlier, Francis scored 116 points in a game, but the record was disallowed because the competition was with a two-year school. In women's college basketball, Annette Kennedy of State Univ at Purchase, NY, scored 70 points vs Pratt Institute on Jan 22, 1984, with 34 field goals in 43 attempts.

Wilton Norman (Wilt) Chamberlain (b Aug 21, 1936) holds the professional record with 100 points for the Philadelphia Warriors vs NY Knicks, scored in one game on Mar 2, 1962. During the same season, Wilt set the record for points in a season (4,029).

Kareem Abdul-Jabbar (formerly Lewis Ferdinand Alcindor) (b Apr 16, 1947) has scored a professional career record of 37,639 points from 1970 through the 1988 season for the Milwaukee Bucks and Los Angeles Lakers. His streak of 787 consecutive games in which he scored in double figures was broken on Dec 4, 1987, after 10 seasons. Wilt Chamberlain holds the record average of 30.1 points per game for his total of 31,419.

Pearl Moore of Francis Marion College, Florence, SC, scored a record 4,061 points during her college career, 1975–79. The men's college career scoring record is 4,045 points by Travis Grant for Kentucky State, 1969–72.

Mats Wermelin (Sweden), 13, scored all 272 points in a 272–0 win in a regional boys' tournament in Stockholm, Sweden, on Feb 5, 1974.

Longest Field Goal

The longest *measured* field goal in a college game was made from a distance of 89 ft 10 in by Bruce Morris for Marshall Univ vs Appalachian St, Feb 7, 1985. In an AAU game at Pacific Lutheran University on Jan 16, 1970, Steve Myers sank a shot while standing out of bounds at the other end of the court. Though the basket was illegal, the officials gave in to crowd sentiment and allowed the points to count. The distance is claimed to be 92 ft 3½ in from measurements made 10 years later. The longest for a woman is one of 77 ft by Cheryl Myers of Lakeland (Ind) Christian Academy in a 48–29 victory over Elkhart Baptist on Jan 20, 1987.

Most Accurate Shooting

The greatest goal-shooting demonstration was made by a professional, Ted St. Martin, now of Jacksonville, Fla, who, on June 25, 1977, scored 2,036 consecutive free throws.

In 24 hours, Robert Browning scored 16,093 free throws from a total of 23,194 taken (69.38%) at St. Mark's School, Dallas, Tex on Nov 21–22, 1987.

Fred L. Newman of San Jose, Calif, made 88 consecutive free throws while blindfolded at the Central YMCA, San Jose, Calif, Feb 5, 1978. On Dec 17, 1986 he made 338 free throws out of 356 attempts in 10 min, for an average accuracy of 94.9%.

The longest reported string of consecutive free throws made at any level of organized game competition is 126 by Daryl Moreau over 2 seasons (Jan 17, 1978–Jan 9, 1979) of high school play for De La Salle in New Orleans, La. The best reported one-game free throw performance was by Chris McMullin who made all 29 of his foul shots for Dixie College (St. George, Utah) in the NJCAA National Finals on Mar 16, 1982.

MAJOR-COLLEGE INDIVIDUAL RECORDS

(Through 1988 Season)

Points			
Most in a Game	100	Frank Selvy (Furman)	1954
Most in a Season	1,381	Pete Maravich (Louisiana St)	1970
Best Average, Season	44.5	Pete Maravich (Louisiana St)	1970
Most in a Career	3,667	Pete Maravich (Louisiana St)	1968–70
Best Average, Career	44.2	Pete Maravich (Louisiana St)	1968–70
Field Goals			
Most in a Game	41	Frank Selvy (Furman)	1954
Best Percentage, Season	74.6	Steve Johnson (Oregon St)	1981
Best Percentage, Career	67.8	Steve Johnson (Oregon St)	1976–81
Free Throws			
Most in a Game	30	Pete Maravich (Louisiana St)	1969
Best Percentage, Season	95.9	Craig Collins (Penn St)	1985
Best Percentage, Career	90.9	Greg Starrick (Ky, So Ill)	1969–72
Consecutive	64	Joe Dykstra (W Ill)	1982
Rebounds			
Most in a Game	51	Bill Chambers (Wm & Mary)	1953
3-Point Goals			
Most in a Game	12	Gary Bossert (Niagara)	1987
		Darrin Fitzgerald (Butler)	1987
Assists			
Most in a Game	22	Tony Fairly (Baptist)	1987
Blocked Shots			
Most in a Game	14	David Robinson (Navy)	1986
Division I Tournament			
Most Points in a Game	61	Austin Carr (Notre Dame)	1970
Most Points in a Tournament	177	Bill Bradley (Princeton)	1965
Most Points in a Career	358	Elvin Hayes (Houston)	1966–68
Most Rebounds in a Game	31	Nate Thurmond (Bowling Green)	1963
Most Field Goals in a Game	25	Austin Carr (Notre Dame)	1970
Most Free Throws in a Game	23	Bob Carney (Bradley)	1953
Most Blocked Shots in a Game	9	David Robinson (Navy)	1986
Most Assists in a Game	23	Mark Wade (Nev-Las Vegas)	1987
Most 3-Pt Goals in a Game	10	Freddie Banks (Nev-Las Vegas)	1987

NBA REGULAR SEASON RECORDS

(Including 1987–88)

The National Basketball Association's Championship series was established in 1947. Prior to 1949, when it joined with the National Basketball League, the professional circuit was known as the Basketball Association of America.

SERVICE

Most Games, Lifetime
1,486 Kareem Abdul-Jabbar, Mil 1970–75, LA Lakers 1976–88

Most Games, Consecutive, Lifetime
906 Randy Smith, Buf-SD-Cleve-NY 1972–1983

Most Complete Games, Season
79 Wilt Chamberlain, Phil 1962

Most Minutes, Lifetime
55,751 Kareem Abdul-Jabbar, Mil 1970–75, LA Lakers 1976–88

Most Minutes, Season
3,882 Wilt Chamberlain, Phil 1962

Most Games, No Disqualifications
1,045 Wilt Chamberlain, Phil-SF-LA 1960–73 (Entire Career)

SCORING

Most Seasons Leading League
7 Wilt Chamberlain, Phil 1960–62; SF 1963–64; SF-Phil 1965; Phil 1966

Most Points, Lifetime
37,639 Kareem Abdul-Jabbar, Mil 1970–75, LA Lakers 1976–88

Most Points, Season
4,029 Wilt Chamberlain, Phil 1962

Most Points, Game
100 Wilt Chamberlain, Phil vs NY, Mar 2, 1962

Most Points, Half
59 Wilt Chamberlain, Phil vs NY, Mar 2, 1962

> NBA Championships
>
> The most National Basketball Association titles have been won by the Boston Celtics with 16 championships between 1957 and 1988. They also hold the record for 8 consecutive championships (1959–66).

Most Points, Quarter
33 George Gervin, SA vs NO, Apr 9, 1978

Most Points, Overtime Period
14 Butch Carter, Ind vs Bos, March 20, 1984

Highest Scoring Average, Lifetime (400+ games)
30.1 Wilt Chamberlain, Phil-SF-LA 1960–73

Highest Scoring Average, Season
50.4 Wilt Chamberlain, Phil 1962

Field Goals Made

Most Field Goals, Lifetime
15,524 Kareem Abdul-Jabbar, Mil 1970–75; LA Lakers 1976–88

Most Field Goals, Season
1,597 Wilt Chamberlain, Phil 1962

Most Field Goals, Game
36 Wilt Chamberlain, Phil vs NY, Mar 2, 1962

Most Field Goals, Half
22 Wilt Chamberlain, Phil vs NY, Mar 2, 1962

Most Field Goals, Quarter
13 David Thompson, Den vs Det, Apr 9, 1978

Most 3-Point Field Goals, Game
8 Rick Barry, Hou vs Utah, Feb 9, 1980
John Roche, Den vs Sea, Jan 9, 1982

Most 3-Point Field Goals, Season
148 Danny Ainge, Bos 1988

Field Goal Percentage

Most Seasons Leading League
9 Wilt Chamberlain, Phil 1961; SF 1963; SF-Phil 1965; Phil 1966–68; LA 1969, 72–73

Highest Percentage, Lifetime
.599 Artis Gilmore, Chi 1977–82; SA 1983–87; Chi, Bos 1988

Highest Percentage, Season
.727 Wilt Chamberlain, LA 1973

Free Throws Made

Most Free Throws Made, Lifetime
7,694 Oscar Robertson, Cin-Mil 1961–74

Most Free Throws Made, Season
840 Jerry West, LA 1966

Most Free Throws Made, Consecutive, Season
78 Calvin Murphy, Hou Dec 27, 1980–Feb 28, 1981

Most Free Throws Made, Game
28 Wilt Chamberlain, Phil vs NY, Mar 2, 1962
Adrian Dentley, Utah vs Hou, Jan 5, 1984

Most Free Throws Made (No Misses), Game
19 Bob Pettit, St L vs Bos, Nov 22, 1961
Bill Cartwright, NY vs KC, Nov 17, 1981

Most Free Throws Made, Half
19 Oscar Robertson, Cin vs Balt, Dec 27, 1964

Most Free Throws Made, Quarter
14 Rick Barry, SF vs NY, Dec 6, 1966
Pete Maravich, At vs Buff, Nov 28, 193
Adrian Dantley, Det vs Sac, Dec 10, 1986

Team Free Throws

Wash Bullets made 60 free throws in 69 attempts vs NJ Nets on Nov 13, 1987, to break a 38-year-old NBA record for one game.

Free Throw Percentage

Most Seasons Leading League
7 Bill Sharman, Bos 1953–57, 59, 61

Highest Percentage, Lifetime
.900 Rick Barry, SF-GS-Hou 1966–67, 73–80

Highest Percentage, Season
.958 Calvin Murphy, Hou 1981

REBOUNDS

Most Seasons Leading League
11 Wilt Chamberlain, Phil 1960–62; SF 1963; Phil 1966–68; LA 1969, 71–73

Most Rebounds, Lifetime
23,924 Wilt Chamberlain, Phil-SF-LA 1960–73

Most Rebounds, Season
2,149 Wilt Chamberlain, Phil 1961

Most Rebounds, Game
55 Wilt Chamberlain, Phil vs Bos, Nov 24, 1960

Most Rebounds, Half
32 Bill Russell, Bos vs Phil, Nov 16, 1957

Most Rebounds, Quarter
18 Nate Thurmond, SF vs Balt, Feb 28, 1965

Highest Average (per game), Lifetime
22.9 Wilt Chamberlain, Phil-SF-LA 1960–73

Highest Average (per game), Season
27.2 Wilt Chamberlain, Phil 1961

ASSISTS

Most Seasons Leading League
8 Bob Cousy, Bos 1953–60

Most Assists, Lifetime
9,887 Oscar Robertson, Cin-Mil 1961–74

Most Assists, Season
1,128 John Stockton, Utah, 1988

Most Assists, Game
29 Kevin Porter, NJ vs Hou, Feb 24, 1978

Highest Average (per game), Lifetime
10.9 Earvin (Magic) Johnson, LA Lakers 1979–87

Highest Average (per game), Season
13.9 Isiah Thomas, Detroit 1985

PERSONAL FOULS

Most Personal Fouls, Lifetime
4,461 Kareem Abdul-Jabbar, Mil 1970–75, LA Lakers 1976–88

Most Personal Fouls, Season
386 Darryl Dawkins, NJ 1984

Most Personal Fouls, Game
8 Don Otten, TC vs Sheb, Nov 24, 1949

STEALS

Most Steals, Season
301 Alvin Robertson, SA, 1986

Highest Steals Average, Season, per game
3.67 Alvin Robertson, SA, 1986

Most Steals, Game
11 Larry Kenon, SA vs KC, Dec 26, 1976

NBA PLAYOFF RECORDS (Through 1988)

Most games played, lifetime
222 Kareem Abdul-Jabbar, Mil-LA Lakers, 17 years

Most points scored, lifetime
5,595 Kareem Abdul-Jabbar, Mil-LA Lakers, 17 years

Most points, game
63 Michael Jordan, Chi vs Bos, Apr 20, 1986 (2 overtimes)
61 Elgin Baylor, LA Lakers vs Bos, Apr 14, 1962

Most field goals, game
24 Wilt Chamberlain, Phil vs Syr, March 14, 1960
John Havlicek, Bos vs Atl, Apr 1, 1973
Michael Jordan, Chi vs Cleve, May 1, 1988

Best scoring average, lifetime
29.1 Jerry West, LA Lakers, 13 years

Most free throws, lifetime
1,213 Jerry West, LA Lakers, 13 years

Most free throws, game
30 Bob Cousy, Bos vs Syr, March 21, 1953 (4 overtimes)
21 Oscar Robertson, Cin vs Bos, Apr 10, 1963

Most assists, game
24 Earvin (Magic) Johnson, LA Lakers vs Phoenix, May 15, 1984
John Stockton, Utah vs LA Lakers, May 17, 1988

Most rebounds, lifetime
4,104 Bill Russell, Bos, 13 years

Most rebounds, game
41 Wilt Chamberlain, Phil vs Bos, Apr 5, 1967

Most assists, lifetime
1,800 Earvin (Magic) Johnson, LA Lakers, 9 years

Team Scoring

The highest game total in the NBA is 370 points in the Detroit Pistons' victory over the Denver Nuggets 186–184 in 1983. The highest in college play is 282, Univ of Nevada—Las Vegas vs Utah State, 1985. Nevada won, 142–140.

The highest score recorded in a senior international match is 251 by Iraq against Yemen (33) at New Delhi in November 1982 at the Asian Games.

Olympic Champions

The US won all 7 Olympic titles from the time the sport was introduced to the Games in 1936 until 1972, without losing a single contest. In 1972, in Munich, the US run of 63 consecutive victories was broken when its team lost, 51–50, to the USSR in a much-disputed final game. The US regained the Olympic title in Montreal in

BULL'S EYE: Artis Gilmore leads the NBA with a .599 field goal percentage. ◄

MAGIC! Earvin Johnson ("magic" tactician of the LA Lakers) added to his record for assists in a career in 1987–88. Here "Magic" drives to a basket over the Boston Celtics' Greg Kite (#50) in the NBA finals. The Lakers broke the Celtics' streak of championships. *(Nathaniel Butler/NBA).* ►

1976, again without losing a game. In 1980 Yugoslavia took the Olympic gold, when the US did not play, but the US came back once more in 1984 for a record 9th title.

In women's Olympics, the USSR won in 1976 and 1980, but the US took the gold in 1984.

World Champions

The USSR has won most titles at both the Men's World Championships (inst. 1950) with three (1967, 1974 and 1982) and Women's (inst. 1953) with six (1959, 1964, 1967, 1971, 1975 and 1983).

Greatest Attendances

The Harlem Globetrotters played an exhibition to 75,000 in the Olympic Stadium, West Berlin, Germany, in 1951. The largest indoor basketball attendance was 67,596, including 64,682 tickets sold at the box office, for the Indiana Olympic Basketball Tribute at the Hoosier Dome, Indianapolis on July 9, 1984. They saw victories by the US men's and women's Olympic teams over all-star opposition. The record for a women's college game is 24,563 in Knoxville, Tenn, for a game between Univ of Tenn and Univ of Tex on Dec 9, 1987. The NBA record is 61,983 on Jan 29, 1988 in Pontiac, Mich, with the Boston Celtics vs Detroit Pistons. The Pistons also set records for largest attendance in a season (1,066,505 in 41 games, 1988) and largest attendance in a playoff game (41,732 on June 16, 1988).

Marathon

The longest game is 102 hours by two teams of five from the Singma Nu fraternity at Indiana Univ of Pennsylvania, Indiana, Penn, Apr 13–17, 1983.

Tallest and Shortest Players

The tallest player of all time is reputed to be Suleiman Ali Nashnush (b 1943) who played for the Libyan team in 1962 when he measured 8 ft tall. Aleksandr Sizonenko of the USSR national team is 7 ft 10 in tall. The tallest woman player is Iuliana Semenova (USSR) who played in the 1976 Olympics and is reputed to stand 7 ft 2 in tall and weigh 281 lb.

In the 1987 NBA season, the shortest player was Tyrone Bogues, drafted by the Wash Bullets, at 5 ft 3 in in bare feet. His teammate, Manute Bol, at 7 ft 6¾ in is the tallest in the League's history.

Youngest and Oldest NBA Players

Bill Willoughby (b May 20, 1957) made his NBA debut for the Atlanta Hawks on Oct 23, 1975, when he was 18 years 5 months 3 days old. The oldest NBA player was Bob Cousy (b Aug 9, 1928), who was 41 years 6 months 2 days old when he appeared in the last of seven games he played for the team he was coaching (Cincinnati Royals) during 1969–70.

College Coach

Richard E. Baldwin, coach at Broome Community College, Binghamton, NY, celebrated his 40th year of coaching in 1987, without ever having missed a game out of a total of 1,169 games played by his team. His record is 879 wins, 290 losses to Feb 28, 1987, his last game. He retired in June 1987.

BOWLING

Origins

Bowling can be traced to articles found in the tomb of an Egyptian child of 5200 BC where there were nine pieces of stone to be set up as pins at which a stone "ball" was rolled. The ball first had to roll through an archway made of three pieces of marble. In the Italian Alps about 2,000 years ago, the underhand tossing of stones at an object is believed the beginnings of *bocci*, a game still widely played in Italy and similar to bowling. Martin Luther is credited with the statement that nine was the ideal number of pins. In the British Isles, lawn bowls was preferred to bowling at pins. In the 16th century, bowling at pins was the national sport of Scotland. Early British settlers probably brought lawn bowls to the US and set up what is known as Bowling Green at the tip of Manhattan Island in NY but perhaps the Dutch under Henry Hudson were the ones to be credited.

In 1841, the Connecticut state legislature prohibited the game and other states followed. Eventually, a tenth pin was added to what had all along been a 9-pin game, to evade the ban.

Organizations

The American Bowling Congress (ABC), established in NY on Sept 9, 1895, was the first body to standardize rules, and the organization now comprises 3,424,204 men who bowl in leagues and tournaments. The Women's International Bowling Congress (WIBC), founded 1916, has a membership of 3,351,411. The Young American Bowling Alliance (YABA) (inst 1982), the successor to the American Junior Bowling Congress and Youth Bowling Assn, has 646,203 youth and collegiate members. The Professional Bowlers Association (PBA), formed in 1958, comprises more than 2,800 of the world's best male bowlers. The Ladies Professional Bowlers Tour has 170 members.

Lanes

In the US there were 8,031 bowling establishments with 151,312 lanes in 1986–87 and about 68 million bowlers.

The world's largest bowling center (now closed) was the Tokyo World Lanes Center, Japan, with 252 lanes. Currently the largest center is Fukuyana Bowl, Osaka, Japan, which has 144 lanes.

Highest Score in 24 Hours

The 6-man Dragons team scored 75,223 in 24 hours at Nowra Tenpin Bowl and Leisure Center, Nowra, NSW, Australia on Apr 2–3, 1988.

Marathons

Donnie Moore (b 1960), a US Navy petty officer stationed at the Jacksonville, Fla Naval Air Station, bowled 2,028 games in 217 hours, 55 min, July 15–24, 1985, for an average of 9.3 games per hour. However, he stopped for 24½ hours for medical reasons. The next best record is 195 hours 1 min by Jim Webb at Gosford City Bowl, NSW., Australia in 1984.

Chrissy Wolking of Riva, Md, aged 14 (YABA) broke the female record on Nov 29, 1987 by bowling 173 games in 18 hours averaging 9.6 games per hour.

World Championships

The Fédération Internationale des Quilleurs world championships were instituted in 1954. The highest pinfall in the individual men's event is 5,963 for 28 games by Ed Luther (US) at Milwaukee, Wis on Aug 28, 1971. In the current schedule of 24 games, the men's record is 5,261 by Rick Steelsmith (US) and 4,894 by Sandra Jo Shiery (US) is the women's record, both set in 1987 at Helsinki, Finland.

ABC LEAGUE RECORDS

Highest Scores

The highest individual score for three games is 886 by Albert "Allie" Brandt of Lockport, NY, on Oct 25, 1939. Glenn Allison (b 1930) rolled a perfect 900 in a 3-game series in league play on July 1, 1982, at La Habra Bowl, LA, Calif, but the ABC could not recognize the record when an ABC inspector determined the lanes were improperly dressed. Highest 3-game team score is 3,858 by Budweisers of St Louis on Mar 12, 1958.

The highest season average attained in sanctioned competition is 242 by John Ragard of Susquehanna, Pa, for 66 games in 1981–82.

The all-time ABC sanctioned 2-man single-game record is 600, held jointly by the team of John Crimmins (300) and Walter Schackett (300) of Detroit, Mich, on Oct 27, 1933; a team of John Cotta (300) and Steve Lanson (300) on May 1, 1981, at the Manteca, Calif, Bowling Assn Tournament; and Jeff Marz and Dave Roney of Canton, O, Nov 8, 1987 in the Ann Doubles Classic in Canton. The 2-man team series record is 1,642 by Joe Golden (865) and Frank Henberger (717) in Oakland, NJ, on Aug 10, 1987.

Consecutive Strikes

The record for consecutive strikes in sanctioned match play is 33 by John Pezzin (b 1930) at Toledo, Ohio, on March 4, 1976.

Most Perfect Scores

The highest number of sanctioned 300 games is 31 by Jim Johnson Jr of Wilmington, Del through July 18, 1988.

The maximum 900 for a three-game series has been recorded 6 times in unsanctioned competition—by Leo Bentley at Lorain, Ohio, on March 26, 1931; by Joe Sargent at Rochester, NY, in 1934; by Jim Murgie in Philadelphia, on Feb 4, 1937; by Bob Brown at Roseville Bowl, Calif, on Apr 12, 1980; by Glenn Allison at Whittier, Calif, on July 1, 1982, and by John Strausbaugh at Columbia, Pa, on July 11, 1987.

PBA RECORDS

Most Titles

Earl Anthony of Dublin, Calif, has won a lifetime total of 41 PBA titles through Oct 1986. The record number of titles won in one PBA season is 8, by Mark Roth of North Arlington, NJ, in 1978.

Consecutive Titles

Only three bowlers have ever won three consecutive professional tournaments—Dick Weber in 1959, 60, and 61, Johnny Petraglia in 1971, and Mark Roth in 1977.

Perfect Games

A total of 119 perfect (300-pin) games were bowled in PBA tournaments in 1979, the most ever for one year. Dick Weber rolled 3 perfect games in one tournament (Houston) in 1965, as did Billy

MOST TITLES IN A SEASON: Mark Roth of N Arlington, NJ, was victorious in 8 PBA tournaments in 1978. He has also beaten Earl Anthony's record for total earnings.

Hardwick of Louisville, Ky (in the Japan Gold Cup competition) in 1968, Roy Buckley of Columbus, Ohio (at Chagrin Falls, Ohio) in 1971, John Wilcox (at Detroit), Norm Meyers of St Louis (at Peoria, Ill) in 1979, and Shawn Christensen of Denver (at Denver) in 1984.

Don Johnson of Las Vegas, Nev, bowled at least one perfect game in 12 consecutive seasons (1966–77). Guppy Troup, of Savannah, Ga, rolled 6 perfect games on the 1979 tour.

Highest Earnings

The greatest lifetime earnings on the Professional Bowlers Association circuit have been won by Mark Roth who has taken home $1,278,681 through 1987. Mike Aulby holds the season earnings record with $201,200 in 1985.

Television Bowling

Nelson Burton Jr, St Louis, rolled the best series, 1,050, for four games (278–279–257–236) at Dick Weber Lanes in Florissant, Mo, Feb 11, 1984.

ABC TOURNAMENT RECORDS

Highest Individual

Highest three-game series in singles is 801 by Mickey Higham of Kansas City, Mo, in 1977. Best three-game total in any ABC event is 833 by Fran Bax of Niagara Falls, NY, in team in 1983. Jim Godman of Lorain, Ohio, holds the record for a nine-game All-Events total with 2,184 (731–749–704) set in Indianapolis, Ind, in 1974. ABC Hall of Famers Fred Bujack of Detroit, Bill Lillard of Houston, and Nelson Burton Jr of St Louis, have won the most championships with 8 each. Bujack shared in 3 team and 4 team All-Events titles between 1949 and 1955, and also won the individual All-Events title in 1955. Lillard bowled on regular and team All-Events champions in 1955 and 1956, the Classic team champions in 1962 and 1971, and won regular doubles and All-Events titles in 1956. Burton shared in 3 Classic team titles, 2 Classic doubles titles and has won Classic singles twice and Classic All-Events.

Highest Doubles

The ABC national tournament record of 558 was set in 1976 by Les Zikes of Chicago and Tommy Hudson of Akron, Ohio. The record score in a doubles series is 1,453, set in 1952 by John Klares (755) and Steve Nagy (698) of Cleveland.

Perfect Scores

Les Schissler of Denver scored 300 in the Classic team event in 1967, and Ray Williams of Detroit scored 300 in Regular team play in 1974, the first two perfect games bowled in team competition. In all, there have been only 50 300 games in the ABC tournament through 1988.

Best Finishes in One Tournament

Les Schissler of Denver won the singles, All-Events, and was on the winning team in 1966 to tie Ed Lubanski of Detroit and Bill Lillard of Houston as the only men to win three ABC crowns in one year. The best four finishes in one ABC tournament were third in singles, second in doubles, third in team and first in All-Events by Bob Strampe, Detroit, in 1967, and first in singles, third in team and doubles and second in All-Events by Paul Kulbaga, Cleveland, in 1960.

Strikes and Spares in a Row

In the greatest finish to win an ABC title, Ed Shay set a record of 12 strikes in a row in 1958, when he scored a perfect game for a total of 733 in singles. Most strikes in a row is 20 by Lou Viet of Milwaukee in 1977. The most spares in a row is 23 by Lt Hazen Sweet of Battle Creek, Mich, in 1950.

Most Tournament Appearances

Bill Doehrman of Fort Wayne, Ind, competed in 71 consecutive ABC tournaments, beginning in 1908. (No tournaments were held 1943–45.)

Youngest and Oldest Winners

The youngest champion was Ronnie Knapp of New London, Ohio, who was a member of the 1963 booster team champions when he was 16 years old. The oldest champion was Joe Detloff of Chicago, Ill, who, at the age of 72, was a winner in the 1965 Booster team event. The oldest doubles team in ABC competition totaled 165 years in

1955: Jerry Ameling (83) and Joseph Lehnbeutter (82), both from St Louis. The youngest bowler to score 300 is said to be John Jaszkowski of S Milwaukee, Wis, who performed this feat at age 11, on Mar 13, 1982. The oldest bowler to score 300 is Leo Sites of Wichita, Kans, who performed the feat on Apr 10, 1985 at age 80.

TOP WOMEN BOWLERS: Patty Ann (above) had a record 5-year average of 227.20 and has scored 27 strikes in a row. Rose Walsh (above right) became the second woman in history to roll 300 in the 67-year-old WIBC Championship Tournament. Jeanne Maiden (right) has a record 13 perfect games in WIBC play.

WIBC RECORDS

Highest Scores

Patty Ann of Bloomington, Ill, had a record 5-year composite average of 227.20 through the 1985–86 season. She also has the best one-season average, 232, in the 1983–84 season. Her record for the highest total in a three-game series was exceeded in 1986 by Jeanne Maiden (see photo on page 543) who rolled 864.

The highest 5-woman team score for a 3-game series is 3,379 by Freeway Washer of Cleveland in 1960. The highest game score by a 5-woman team is 1,210 by Sheraton Inn, Scranton, Pa in 1982 as well as Veltri & Sons Clothier, also of Scranton, in the 1984–85 season.

Championship Tournaments

The highest score for a 3-game series in the annual WIBC Championship Tournament is 737 by D. D. Jacobson in the 1972 singles competition. The record for one game is 300 by Lori Gensch of Milwaukee in the 1979 doubles event, by Rose Walsh of Pomona, Calif in the 1986 singles event, and by Linda Kelly of Union, Ohio, in the 1987 doubles event.

Mary Covell of Chicago participated in her 55th WIBC tournament in 1986. The oldest participant was Ethel Brunnick (b Aug 30, 1887) of Santa Monica, Calif, at age 99 in 1987. Mary Ann Keiper of St Louis was only 5 years old when she participated in the 1952 tournament. The youngest champion was Leila Wagner (b July 12, 1960) of Seattle, Wash, who was 18 when she was a member of the championship 5-woman team in 1979.

Dorothy Miller of Chicago has won 10 WIBC Championship Tournament events, the most by an individual. Millie Martorella is the only one to have won 3 WIBC Queen Tournaments, 1967, 1970, and 1971.

The highest lifetime average is 199.14 by Dorothy Fothergill of Lincoln, RI, who has bowled for 10 years but is now inactive.

Perfect Games

The most 300 games rolled in a career is 13 by Jeanne Maiden of Solon, Ohio. The oldest woman to bowl a perfect game (12 strikes in a row) was Helen Duval of Berkeley, Calif, at age 65 in 1982. Of all the women who rolled a perfect game, the one with the lowest average was Diane Ponza of Santa Cruz, Calif, who had a 112 average in the 1977–78 season.

Consecutive Strikes, Spares and Splits

The record for most consecutive strikes is 40 by Jeanne Maiden (see above). Joan Taylor of Syracuse, NY, made 27 consecutive spares. Shirley Tophigh of Las Vegas, Nev, holds the unenviable record of rolling 14 consecutive splits.

BOXING*

Boxing with gloves was depicted on a fresco from the Isle of Thera, Greece, which has been dated to 1520 BC. The earliest prize-ring code of rules was formulated in England, Aug 16, 1743, by the champion pugilist Jack Broughton (1704–89), who reigned from 1729 to 1750. Boxing, which had in 1867 come under the Queensberry Rules, formulated for John Sholto Douglas, 9th Marquess of Queensberry, was not established as a legal sport in Britain until after a ruling of Mr Justice Grantham following the death of Billy Smith (Murray Livingstone) due to a fight on Apr 24, 1901, at Covent Garden, London.

Longest Fights

The longest recorded fight with gloves was between Andy Bowen of New Orleans and Jack Burke in New Orleans, Apr 6–7, 1893. The fight lasted 110 rounds (7 hours 19 min from 9:15 p.m. to 4:34 a.m.) but was declared no contest (later changed to a draw) when both men were unable to continue. The longest recorded bare knuckle fight was one of 6 hours 15 min between James Kelly and Jack Smith at Fiery Creek, Dalesford, Australia, Dec 3, 1855. The greatest recorded number of rounds is 276 in 4 hours 30 min, when Jack Jones beat Patsy Tunney in Cheshire, England, in 1825. The longest world title fight was in 1906 when Joe Gans (US) beat Battling Nelson (Den) when Nelson was disqualified in the 42nd round of a scheduled 45-round contest.

Shortest Fights

There is a distinction between the quickest knockout and the shortest fight. A knockout in 10½ sec (including a 10-sec count) occurred on Sept 23, 1946, when Al Couture struck Ralph Walton while the latter was adjusting his mouthpiece in his corner at Lewiston, Me. If the time was accurately taken it is clear that Couture must have been more than half-way across the ring from his own corner at the opening bell.

The shortest *professional* bout occurred Apr 3, 1936 when Al Carr (Alfred Tramantano) stopped Lew Massey in 7 sec with one punch in New Haven, Conn.

The shortest world title fight was 45 sec, when Lloyd Honeyghan (b Apr 22, 1960) beat Gene Hatcher in an IBF welterweight bout on Aug 30, 1987. The shortest ever heavyweight world title fight was the James J. Jeffries (1875–1953)–Jack Finnegan bout on Apr 6, 1900, won by Jeffries in 55 sec.

Largest Receipts

The Mike Tyson–Michael Spinks fight which Tyson won in 91 sec brought in $12,150,000 at the gate in Atlantic City, NJ on June 27, 1988. Held at the Convention Center, it resulted in gross receipts that exceeded $74 million, a record for *any* sports event. The gross

* More boxing records may be found in "Guinness Boxing: The Records" by Ian Morrison (Sterling).

includes attendance live-at-site, closed circuit TV at theaters, home viewing, foreign and domestic delayed telecast.

Longest Career

The heavyweight Jem Mace (GB) (1831–1910), known as "the Gypsy," had a career lasting 50 years from 1855 to 1905, when he put on an exhibition bout with Tug Wilson, but his career is not fully documented. Kid Azteca (b Louis Villanueva Parano, 1915, Mexico City) started boxing professionally in 1929 and has a published record that includes at least one bout per year, 1932–61.

Tallest Boxer

The tallest boxer to fight professionally was Gogea Mitu (b 1914) of Rumania in 1935. He was 7 ft 4 in and weighed 327 lb. John Rankin, who won a fight in New Orleans in Nov 1967, also claimed 7 ft 4 in as did Jim Culley, the "Tipperary Giant" who boxed and wrestled in the 1940's.

WORLD HEAVYWEIGHT CHAMPIONS

Earliest Title Fight

The first world heavyweight title fight, with 3-oz gloves and 3-minute rounds, was between John L. Sullivan (1858–1918) and Dominick McCaffrey on Aug 29, 1885 in Cincinnati, O. It went 6 rounds and Sullivan won.

Longest and Shortest Reigns

The longest reign of any world heavyweight champion is 11 years 252 days by Joe Louis (b Joseph Louis Barrow, 1914–81), from June 22, 1937, when he knocked out James J. Braddock in the 8th round at Chicago until announcing his retirement on March 1, 1949. During his reign Louis made a record 25 defenses of his title.

The shortest reigns were 83 days for WBA champion James "Bonecrusher" Smith (US) (b Apr 3, 1955), who ruled Dec 13, 1986 to Mar 7, 1987; Ken Norton (US) (b Aug 9, 1945) recognized by the WBC as champion for 83 days from Mar 18 to June 9, 1978; and 64 days for Tony Tucker (US) (b Dec 28, 1958), IBF champion May 30–Aug 2, 1987.

The longest-lived heavyweight champion was Jack Dempsey, who died May 31, 1983 aged 87 years 341 days.

Oldest and Youngest

The oldest man to win the heavyweight crown was Jersey Joe Walcott (b Arnold Raymond Cream, Jan 31, 1914, at Merchantville, NJ), who knocked out Ezzard Charles on July 18, 1951, in Pittsburgh, when aged 37 years 5 months 18 days. Walcott was the oldest title holder at 38 years 7 months 23 days when he lost to Rocky Marciano on Sept 23, 1952. The youngest age at which the world heavyweight title has been won is 20 years 145 days by Mike Tyson (b June 30, 1966), who won the WBC title by beating Trevor Berbick in the 2nd round on Nov 22, 1986, in Las Vegas, Nev.

YOUNGEST HEAVYWEIGHT CHAMPION: Mike Tyson, 220 lb, who won the title when only 20 years 145 days old, holds off Tyrell Biggs with his left while readying his right for a knockout blow. He has knocked out 31 opponents and is unbeaten in 35 bouts. (*Photo courtesy of Jim Jacobs and Bill Cayton*)

Most Recaptures

Muhammad Ali Haj (b Cassius Marcellus Clay, in Louisville, Ky, Jan 17, 1942) is the only man to regain the heavyweight title twice. Ali first won the title on Feb 25, 1964, defeating Sonny Liston. He defeated George Foreman on Oct 30, 1974, having been stripped of his title by the world boxing authorities on Apr 28, 1967. He lost his title to Leon Spinks on Feb 15, 1978, but regained it on Sept 15, 1978 by defeating Spinks in New Orleans.

Heaviest and Lightest

The heaviest world champion was Primo Carnera (Italy) (1906–67), the "Ambling Alp," who won the title from Jack Sharkey in 6 rounds in NYC, on June 29, 1933. He scaled 260½ lb for this fight, but his peak weight was 270. He had the longest reach at 85½ in (finger tip to finger tip) and an expanded chest measurement of 53 in.

The lightest was Robert James Fitzsimmons (1863–1917), (b Helston, Cornwall, England) who, at a weight of 167 lb, won the title by knocking out James J. Corbett in 14 rounds at Carson City, Nev, March 17, 1897.

The greatest differential in a world title fight was 86 lb between Carnera (270 lb) and Tommy Loughran (184 lb) of the US, when the former won on points at Miami, Fla, March 1, 1934.

Tallest and Shortest

The tallest world champion was Primo Carnera, who was measured at 6 ft 5.4 in by the Physical Education Director at the Hemingway

Gymnasium of Harvard, although he was widely reported and believed in 1933 to be 6 ft 8½ in tall. Jess Willard (1881–1968), who won the title in 1915, was often described as being 6 ft 6¼ in tall, but was in fact 6 ft 5¼ in. The shortest was Tommy Burns (1881–1955) of Canada, world champion from Feb 23, 1906, to Dec 26, 1908, who stood 5 ft 7 in and weighed between 168 and 180 lb.

Heavyweight Champions through the Years

1882 John L. Sullivan (US)
1892 James J. Corbett (US)
1897 Bob Fitzsimmons (GB)
1899 James J. Jeffries (US)
1905 Marvin Hart (US)
1906 Tommy Burns (Can)
1908 Jack Johnson (US)
1915 Jess Willard (US)
1919 Jack Dempsey (US)
1926 Gene Tunney (US)
1930 Max Schmeling (Ger)
1932 Jack Sharkey (US)
1933 Primo Carnera (Ita)
1934 Max Baer (US)
1935 James J. Braddock (US)
1937 Joe Louis (US)
1949 Ezzard Charles (US)
1951 Jersey Joe Walcott (US)
1952 Rocky Marciano (US)
1956 Floyd Patterson (US)
1959 Ingemar Johansson (Swe)
1960 Floyd Patterson (US)
1962 Sonny Liston (US)
1964 Cassius Clay/Muhammad Ali (US)
1965 Ernie Terrell (US)—WBA only till 1967
1968 Joe Frazier (US)—NY State
1968 Jimmy Ellis (US)—WBA
1970 Joe Frazier (US)—undisputed
1973 George Foreman (US)
1974 Muhammad Ali (US)
1978 Leon Spinks (US)
1978 Muhammad Ali (US)—WBA
1978 Ken Norton (US)—WBC
1978 Larry Holmes (US)—WBC, IBF from 1983
1979 John Tate (US)—WBA
1980 Mike Weaver (US)—WBA
1982 Mike Dokes (US)—WBA
1983 Gerry Coetzee (So Afr)—WBA
1984 Tim Witherspoon (US)—WBC
1984 Pinklon Thomas (US)—WBC
1984 Greg Page (US)—WBA
1985 Tony Tubbs (US)—WBA
1985 Michael Spinks (US)—WBC, IBF
1986 Trevor Berbick (Canada)—WBC
1986 Tim Witherspoon (US)—WBA
1986 Mike Tyson (US)—WBC, WBA, IBF

WBC—World Boxing Council, headquartered in Mexico City. President: Jose Sulaiman, who has devoted himself to boxing for 20 years. A substantial portion of WBC's income has been spent furthering the sport, protecting the athletes and improving medical facilities. This is the most highly regarded organization.

WBA—World Boxing Association, headquartered in Panama City, Panama. President: Gilberto Mendoza.

IBF—International Boxing Federation, headquartered in NJ. President: Bob Lee.

These 3 bodies represent national federations of boxing commissions throughout the world, and have a variety of financial and political connections.

Undefeated

Rocky Marciano (b Rocco Francis Marchegiano) (1923–69) is the only heavyweight champion to retire undefeated after his entire professional career (1947–1956). His record was 49 wins (43 by KO) and no losses or draws.

TITLE DEEDS: Joe Louis (left) kept the heavyweight title for over 11 years, the longest reign at any weight class. Known as "The Brown Bomber," Louis successfully defended his title a record 25 times. Louis' largest purse, earned in his 8th round KO of Billy Conn in 1946, was $625,916—a far cry from today's high-priced bouts. Ringside seats cost a then-record $100.

Youngest and Oldest

The youngest at which any world championship has been won is 17 years 176 days by Wilfredo Benitez (b Sept 12, 1958) of Puerto Rico, who won the WBA junior-welterweight title, Mar 6, 1976.

The oldest world champion was Archie Moore (b Archibald Lee Wright, Collinsville, Ill, Dec 13, 1913 or 1916), who was recognized as a light-heavyweight champion up to Feb 10, 1962, when his title was removed. He was then between 45 and 48. Bob Fitzsimmons (1863–1917) had the longest career of any official world titleholder with over 31 years from 1883 to 1914. He had his last world title bout on Dec 20, 1905 at the age of 42 years 208 days.

Most Fights Without Loss

Edward Henry (Harry) Greb (US) (1894–1926), who was blind in one eye, was unbeaten in 178 bouts, but these included 117 "no decisions" 1916–23 and 5 were unofficial losses. Of boxers with complete records Packey McFarland (US) (1888–1936) had 97 fights (five draws) in 1905–15 without a defeat. Pedro Carrasco (b Spain, Nov 7, 1943) won 83 consecutive fights from Apr 22, 1964 to Sept 3, 1970, and then drew once and had a further nine wins before his loss to Armando Ramos in a WBC lightweight contest on Feb 18, 1972.

Olympic Gold Medals

In the 1984 Olympics, US boxers won a record total of 9 of the 12 gold medals.

Only two boxers have won three Olympic gold medals: southpaw László Papp (b 1926, Hungary), who took the middleweight (1948) and the light-middleweight titles (1952 and 56), and Cuban heavy-

YOUNGEST BOXER to win a world title was Wilfred Benitez (right), who captured the light-welterweight title when he was only 17½ years old. Benitez is one of only a handful of fighters who have won world titles in 3 different weight classes. (*Raymon Kopff*)

weight Teofilo Stevenson (b Mar 23, 1952), who won the gold medal in his division for three successive Games (1972, 76 and 80). The only man to win two titles in one meeting was Oliver L. Kirk (US), who took both the bantam and featherweight titles at St Louis, Mo, in 1904, but he only needed one bout in each class.

The oldest man to win an Olympic gold medal in boxing was Richard K. Gunn (1871–1961) (GB), who won the featherweight title on Oct 27, 1908, in London, aged 38.

Longest and Shortest Reigns

Joe Louis's heavyweight duration record of 11 years 252 days stands for all divisions.

The shortest reign was that of Tony Canzoneri who held the light-welterweight title for 33 days, May 21–June 23, 1933. By ruling Joe Burman was awarded the bantamweight title on Oct 19, 1923, when Joe Lynch pulled out of the championship contest at the last minute at 3 PM, and at 11 PM the same night Burman was knocked out and lost the title to Abe Goldstein in Madison Sq Garden, NYC.

Most Recaptures

The only boxer to win a world title five times at one weight is Sugar Ray Robinson (b Walker Smith, Jr, in Detroit, May 3, 1921) who beat Carmen Basilio (US) in the Chicago Stadium on March 25, 1958, to regain the world middleweight title for the fourth time. The other title wins were over Jake LaMotta (US) in Chicago on Feb 14, 1951; Randy Turpin (UK) in NYC on Sept 12, 1951; Carl "Bobo" Olson (US) in Chicago on Dec 9, 1955; and Gene Fullmer (US) in Chicago on May 1, 1957.

Most Titles Simultaneously

The only man to hold world titles at three weights simultaneously was Henry "Hammering Hank" Armstrong (b Dec 12, 1912) of the US, at featherweight, lightweight and welterweight from Aug to Dec 1938.

Thomas Hearns (b Oct 18, 1958) became the first man ever to hold world titles at 4 different weights but could not hold them simultaneously. On Oct 29, 1987 he won the WBC Middleweight title after holding WBA Welterweight since 1980, WBC Super-Welterweight since 1982 and WBC Light Heavyweight in 1987.

Amateur World Championships

Two boxers have won three world championships (instituted 1974): Teofilo Stevenson (Cuba), heavyweight 1974, 1978 and 1986, and Adolfo Horta (b Oct 3, 1957) (Cuba), bantam 1978, feather 1982 and lightweight 1986.

Longest and Shortest Title Fights

The longest world title fight (under Queensberry Rules) was between the lightweights Joe Gans (1874–1910), of the US, and Oscar "Battling" Nelson (1882–1954), the "Durable Dane," at Goldfield, Nev, Sept 3, 1906. It was terminated in the 42nd round when Gans was declared the winner on a foul.

The shortest title bout was 40 sec from the starting bell when welterweight champion Lloyd Honeyghan knocked out Gene Hatcher on Aug 30, 1987, at Marbella, Spain, to retain his WBA and IBF titles. This beat the previous mark of 52 sec when Sugar Ray Robinson on Aug 25, 1950, defended his middleweight title against Jose Basora.

Most Title Bouts

The record number of title bouts in a career is 37, of which 18 ended in "no decision," by 3-time world welterweight champion Jack Britton (US) (1885–1962), from 1915 to 1922.

Most Frequent Championship Fights

Henry Armstrong (US) between Oct 9 and Oct 30, 1939, fought 5 times for the welterweight title and won each time.

> George Foreman is the only US champion in any weight class to have won, defended, and lost his crown all outside the US. To win his title he defeated Joe Frazier in Kingston, Jamaica, Jan 22, 1973. He defended it against Jose Roman in Tokyo, Japan, Sept 1, 1973, and against Ken Norton in Caracas, Venezuela, Mar 26, 1974. He lost it to Muhammad Ali in Kinshasa, Zaire, Oct 30, 1974. As world champion, this native of Marshall, Tex never fought in his own country.

Most Knockdowns in Title Fights

Vic Toweel (South Africa) knocked down Danny O'Sullivan of London 14 times in 10 rounds in their world bantamweight fight at Johannesburg, Dec 2, 1950, before the latter retired.

ALL FIGHTS

Highest Earnings in Career

The largest known fortune ever made in a fighting career is an estimated $69 million (including exhibitions) amassed by Muhammad Ali from Oct 1960 to Dec 1981, in 61 fights comprising 551 rounds.

Most Knockouts

The greatest number of knockouts in a career is 145 (129 in professional bouts) by Archie Moore (1936 to 1963). The record for consecutive KO's is 44, set by Lamar Clark of Utah at Las Vegas, Nev, Jan 11, 1960. He knocked out 6 in one night (5 in the first round) in Bingham Canyon, Utah, on Dec 1, 1958.

Referee Counted Out

While Ruby Goldstein was refereeing a light-heavyweight title bout on June 25, 1952, he was overcome by the intense heat at the end of the 12th round and had to be replaced.

GREATEST EARNER: Muhammad Ali (right) seems to be knocking the stuffing out of Joe Frazier in the "Thriller in Manila" when he won $6½ million. Ali's earnings in his 61 fights totaled about $69 million, making him the highest paid in any sport. (*AP*)

Double Knockouts

In 1887, an earlier Jack Dempsey (Ireland) retained his world middleweight title by knocking out Johnny Reagan (US) in two rings! The fight began in Huntington, Long Island, NY, but in the 8th round, the tide flooded the ring, so the fighters and spectators boarded a tug and continued the bout some 25 miles away.

Danny Lopez (US) had to knock out Mike Ayala twice on June 17, 1979, in San Antonio to make his victory stick. In the 11th round Ayala was counted out but his followers complained to the referee that their man was up at the count of 9, so Lopez did it a second time in the 15th round.

Closest Call

With just one second to go in the 15th and final round of their light-heavyweight title bout, Victor Galindez (Arg) knocked out Richie Kates (US).

Fighter Endures Plane Crash

Featherweight Willie Pep (1942–50) was severely injured in a plane crash in 1947. Told he would never fight again, maybe not even walk without crutches, Pep defied everyone, came back in 5 months to win the first of 26 consecutive bouts, and retain his world title.

Greatest "Tonnage"

The greatest "tonnage" in a world title fight was 488¾ lb when Primo Carnera (259½ lb) fought Paolino Uzcudun (229¼ lb) of Spain, in Rome, Italy, Oct 22, 1933.

The greatest "tonnage" recorded in any fight is 700 lb, when Claude "Humphrey" McBride of Okla at 340 lb knocked out Jimmy Black of Houston at 360 lb in the 3rd round at Oklahoma City, June 1, 1971.

Smallest Champions

The smallest man to win any world title has been Netranoi Vorsingh (b Apr 22, 1959) (Thailand), WBC light-flyweight champion from May to Sept 1978, at 4 ft 11 in tall. Jimmy Wilde (b Merthyr Tydfil, 1892, d 1969, UK), who held the flyweight title from 1916 to 1923, was reputed never to have fought above 108 lb.

Most Fights

The greatest recorded number of fights in a career is 1,024 by Bobby Dobbs (US) (1858–1930), who is reported to have fought from 1875 to 1914, a period of 39 years. Abraham Hollandersky, *alias* Abe the Newsboy (US), is reputed to have had 1,309 fights in the 14 years from 1905 to 1918, but many of them were one-round exhibition bouts. Len Wickwar, an English lightweight who fought between 1928–47, had 463 documented fights.

The Real McCoy

A boxer named Charles "Kid" McCoy in the 1890's is responsible for an expression that got into the language. With 10 marriages to his credit, incidentally, McCoy had a trick of making believe he was ill or in difficulty, so his opponent would be fooled into letting up on him, then suddenly regaining his strength, which led his opponents into asking: "Which is the real McCoy?"

CYCLING

Earliest Race

The earliest recorded bicycle race was a velocipede race over 2 km (1.24 miles) at the Parc de St Cloud, Paris, on May 31, 1868, won by Dr James Moore (GB) (1847–1935).

The first American bicycle race was held May 24, 1878 in Boston's Beacon Park. Winner C. A. Parker of Harvard University covered the 3-mi course in 12 min, 27 sec.

The time-trial was devised in 1889–90 by F. T. Bidlake to avoid the congestion caused by ordinary mass road racing.

Most World Titles

World championships, contested annually, were first staged for amateurs in 1893 and for professionals in 1895. The most wins at a particular event is 10 consecutively by Koichi Nakano (Japan) (b Nov 14, 1955), professional sprint champion 1977–86. The most wins at a men's amateur event is 7 by Daniel Morelon (France) (b July 28, 1944), sprint 1966–7, 69–71, 73, 75; and Leon Meredith (UK) (1882–1930), 100-km motor-paced 1904–5, 1907–9, 11, 13.

The most women's titles is 7 by Beryl Burton (UK) (b May 12, 1937), pursuit 1959–60, 62–63, 66 and road 1960, 67; and by Yvonne Reynders (Belgium) pursuit 1961, 64–65 and road 1959, 61, 63, 66.

Greg LeMond is the only American ever to win the World Professional Road Championship, taking the title Sept 4, 1983, at Altenrhein, Switzerland.

SPEEDIEST BIKER: John Howard, riding in the vacuum created behind a large-tail racing car on a specially designed 46-lb bicycle, sped more than 152 mph on Bonneville Salt Flats in July 1985. *(Al Gross)*

Highest Speed

John Howard (b Aug 16, 1947) of Encinitas, Calif, achieved 152.284 mph on July 20, 1985, riding a specially designed 46-lb bike with hydraulic forks and motorcycle wheels, at Bonneville Salt Flats, Utah. A former Olympic cyclist, he rode behind a car that gave him considerable help with a large tail section designed to cut down on air resistance and give a slipstreaming effect.

The greatest distance ever covered in one hour is 76 miles 604 yd by Leon Vanderstuyft (Belgium) on the Montlhéry Motor Circuit, France, Sept 30, 1928. This was achieved from a standing start paced by a motorcycle ahead. (Cycling rules permit a motorcycle to precede a bicycle in an event of over 10 km.) The 24-hour record behind pace is 860 miles 367 yd by Sir Hubert Ferdinand Opperman (b May 29, 1904) in Melbourne, Australia on May 23, 1932.

COAST-TO-COAST CYCLING*

US Transcontinental

Date	*Name*	*Mileage*	*Start-Finish*	*Days:Hours:Min*
Men				
6/29/61	Jerry Hornig		San Francisco to NYC	17:05:15
4/22/72	Peter Duker		Santa Monica to NYC	18:02:38
3/17/73	Paul Cornish		Santa Monica to NYC	13:05:20
8/26/78	John Marino		Santa Monica to NYC	13:01:20
6/28/80	John Marino		Santa Monica to NYC	12:03:41
7/14/81	Lon Haldeman		Santa Monica to NYC	10:23:27
8/14/82	Lon Haldeman	2,986	Santa Monica to NYC	9:20:02 Great American Bike Race '82
8/29/84	Pete Penseyres	3,047.4	Huntington Beach to Atlantic City, NJ	9:13:13 Race Across America '84
7/31/85	Jonathan Boyer	3,120.2	Huntington Beach to Atlantic City, NJ	9:02:06 Race Across America '85
7/14/86	Pete Penseyres	3,107.3	Huntington Beach to Atlantic City, NJ	8:09:47 McDonald's Race Across America '86
Women				
6/15/82	Ann Kovich		Santa Monica to NYC	14:14:54
7/13/82	Susan Notorangelo		Santa Monica to NYC	11:16:15
8/1/85	Susan Notorangelo-Haldeman	3,120.2	Huntington Beach to Atlantic City, NJ	10:14:25 Race Across America '85
7/16/86	Elaine Mariolle	3,107.3	Huntington Beach to Atlantic City, NJ	10:02:04 McDonald's Race Across America '86
Trans-Canada				
6/28/82	Wayne Phillips	3,800	Vancouver, B.C. to Halifax, Nova Scotia	14:22:47

U.S. Transcontinental Tandem West-East				
5/17/87	Pete Penseyres-Lon Haldeman	2,920	Huntington Beach, Calif to Atlantic City, NJ	7:14:55
US Transcontinental East-West				
7/2/81	Lon Haldeman (solo/unpaced)		NY to Santa Monica	12:18:49
7/7/81	Len Vreeland (solo/recumbent)		NY to Santa Monica	14:21:13
US Double Transcontinental				
10/84	Victor Vincente		Santa Monica to NY to Santa Monica	36:08:00
7/14/81	Lon Haldeman		NY to Santa Monica to NY	24:02:34
US 24-Hour Outdoor Track (San Diego Velodrome)				
4/2/84	Jim Elliott	502.3 mi		
US 24-Hour Indoor Track (Olympic Velodrome, Montreal, Canada)				
3/14/85	Michael Secrest	516 mi, 427 yd		
US 24-Hour Roller Record				
1/21/77	Bruce Hall	792.209 mi		
5/14/83	Richard Gunther	838.7 mi		
US Transcontinental West-East				
9/10/84	Sean O'Keefe 11 years (born 6/6/73), youngest to cross US on a bicycle		Santa Monica to NY	24 days
US West Coast				
6/27/84	Michael Shermer		Seattle to San Diego	3:23:49

*US records from the Ultra Marathon Cycling Association, as of September 1986, courtesy of John Marino.

Human-Powered Speed Record

Fred Markham (b May 9, 1957) of Aptos, Calif, became the first person to pedal a bicycle 65 mph on a level course, unpaced and unaided by wind. Riding on Big Sand Flat, Calif, on May 12, 1986, Markham pedaled a 31-lb covered recumbent to a record 65.484 mph. (His speed was calculated over a distance of 200 m.) He took approximately 2 mi to build up to top speed. The bike was covered with DuPont Kevlar to reduce wind resistance. Nearly all steel parts were replaced with lighter titanium or aluminum substitutes. Markham and bike designer Gardner Martin shared an $18,000 prize that was awarded by DuPont to the first cyclist to break 65 miles per hour under the above-specified conditions.

24-Hour Distance Record

The 24-hour record on the road is 515.8 miles by Teuvo Louhivouri of Finland on Sept 10, 1974.

Indoors, unpaced, the 24-hour record is 516 mi 427 yd by Michael Secrest (b Jan 20, 1953) of Flint, Mich, who cycled this distance at the Montreal (Canada) Olympic Velodrome Mar 13–14, 1985.

One-Hour Distance Records

The greatest distance covered in 60 min unpaced is 31 mi 1,381 yd by Francesco Moser (Italy) at Mexico City on Jan 23, 1984. The International Cycling Union (UCI), which recognizes both sea-level and high-altitude hour records, classifies Moser's Mexico City distance in the high altitude category because it was achieved on a track located at an elevation greater than 600 m (above mean sea level). Moser also holds the sea-level 60 min distance record of 30 mi 1,665.6 yd in Milan, Italy on Oct 3, 1986.

The indoor 60 min distance record is 30 mi 1,742 yd by Viatcheslav Ekimov (USSR), ridden on the Olympic Velodrome in Moscow in Nov 1986.

Jeannie Longo of France holds the sea-level, indoor and high-altitude 60 min unpaced women's records. She cycled 27 mi 147 yds in Oct 1986 in Milan, Italy, for the sea-level mark and 27 miles 1,441 yds, Sept 20, 1986, in Colorado Springs, Colo for the altitude mark and then 27 mi 1,338 yds on Nov 7, 1986 in Paris for the indoor record.

Tour de France

For the first time in 83 years the Tour de France was won by a non-European, Greg LeMond (b June 26, 1961) of Reno, Nevada. He beat the field in 1986, including his teammate Bernard Hinault (b Nov 14, 1954) (France) who won in 1978, 79, 81, 82 and 85. This race takes about 23 days to stage annually. The longest ever was in 1926 when it lasted for 29 days. It is estimated that as many as 10 million people watch some part of it.

The greatest number of wins in the Tour de France (inaugurated 1903) is 5 by Jacques Anquetil (b Jan 8, 1934) (France), who won in 1957, 1961–64; Eddy Merckx (b June 17, 1945) (Belgium) who won five titles (1969–72, 1974); and Bernard Hinault (see above) who also won 5 times.

The closest race ever was in 1968 when after 2,898.7 mi over 25 days (June 27–July 21) Jan Jannssen (Netherlands) (b May 19, 1940) beat Herman van Springel (Belgium) in Paris by 38 sec. The longest course was 3,569 miles on June 20 to July 18, 1926. The length of the course is usually about 3,000 miles, but varies from year to year.

The fastest average speed was 24.18 mph by Pedro Delgado in 1988. The greatest number of participants were 209 starters in 1987.

Cycling's Triple Crown

In 1987, Stephen Roche (b Nov 28, 1959) of Dublin, Ireland became only the second cyclist in history to win the Tour of Italy, the Tour de France and the World Road Championship all in the same year. Eddy Merckx of Belgium did it in 1974.

FIRST AMERICAN WINNER of Tour de France: Greg LeMond of Reno, Nev, became the only non-European in 83 years to win the 23-day race in 1986. He was also the only American to win the World Professional Road Championship in Switzerland in 1983. *(All-Sport)*

FASTEST WOMAN CYCLIST: Jeanne Longo (France) (b Oct 31, 1958) dominates the field, having set women's records for unpaced, 60-min runs at sea level, altitude and indoor. *(Mike Powell/All Sport)*

Coast-to-Coast Cycling

The US transcontinental men's unpaced record (West Coast to East Coast) has been cut in half since 1972. Pete Penseyres, 43, of Fallbrook, Calif, set the current mark of 8 days 9 hours 47 min in July 1986 during the Race Across America (3,107.3 mi, Huntington Beach, Calif to Atlantic City, NJ). The US transcontinental women's record of 10 days 2 hours 4 min, held by Elaine Mariolle of Berkeley, Calif, was also set during the '86 RAAM.

Pete Penseyres and Lon Haldeman of Harvard, Ill, set a transcontinental tandem bicycle record of 7 days, 14 hours, 55 min (Huntington Beach, Calif to Atlantic City, NJ) in May 1987. It was the fastest-ever US crossing on a bicycle.

Wayne Phillips of Richmond, BC, rode across Canada from Vancouver, BC, to Halifax, Nova Scotia, covering the 3,800 miles in 14 days 22 hours 47 min June 13–28, 1982.

Longest One-Day Race

The longest single-day "massed start" road race is the Bordeaux-to-Paris, France, event of 342 to 385 miles. Usually paced over all or part of the route, the highest average speed in 1981 was 29.32 mph by Herman van Springel (Belgium) (b Aug 14, 1943) for 363.1 mi in 13 hours 35 min 18 sec.

Touring

The most participants in a bicycle tour were 27,220 in the 56-mile London-to-Brighton Bike Ride on June 15, 1986.

The longest cycle tour on record is the more than 402,000 miles amassed by Walter Stolle (b Sudetenland, 1926), an itinerant lecturer. From Jan 24, 1959 to Dec 12, 1976, he covered 159 countries, had 5 bicycles stolen and suffered 231 other robberies, along with over 1,000 flat tires. From 1922 to Dec 25, 1973, Tommy Chambers (1903–84) of Glasgow, Scotland, rode a verified total of 799,405 miles.

John Hathaway of Vancouver, Canada, covered 50,600 miles, visiting every continent, from Nov 10, 1974 to Oct 6, 1976.

Veronica and Colin Scargill, of Bedford, England, traveled 18,020 miles around the world, on a tandem, Feb 25, 1974–Aug 27, 1975.

Six-Day Races

The greatest number of wins in six-day races is 88 out of 233 events by Patrick Sercu (b June 27, 1944), of Belgium, 1964–83.

Endurance

Tommy Godwin (1912–75) (GB) in the 365 days of 1939 covered 75,065 miles or an average of 205.65 miles per day. He then completed 100,000 miles in 500 days to May 14, 1940. Jay Aldous and Matt DeWaal cycled 14,290 miles on a round trip from Place Monument, Salt Lake City, Utah, in 106 days, Apr 2–July 16, 1984.

Nicholas Mark Sanders (b Nov 26, 1957) of Glossop, Eng, circumnavigated the world (13,035 road miles) in 78 days, 3 hours 30 min between July 5 and Sept 21, 1985.

Carlos Vieira cycled for 191 hours "non-stop" at Leiria, Portugal

June 8–16, 1983. The distance covered was 1,496.04 mi, and he was moving 98.7% of the time.

Daniel Buettner, Bret Anderson, Martin Engel and Anne Knabe cycled the length of the Americas, from Prudhoe Bay, Alaska to the Beagle Channel, Ushuaia, Argentina from Aug 8, 1986–June 13, 1987. They cycled a total distance of 15,266 mi.

Highest Altitude

Adrian Crane (UK) cycled from the lower summit of Mount Chimborazo, an altitude of 20,561 ft, to the town of Riobamba, Ecuador, at 9,022 ft on May 11, 1986. His brother Richard and cousin Nicholas Crane held the previous record, from Mount Kilimanjaro, Tanzania, at 19,340 ft.

Bicycle Balancing

David Steed (b 1959) of Tucson, Ariz, balanced on his bicycle for 24 hours 6 min non-stop Mar 10–11, 1986 at the NYC Coliseum. Sitting astride his bike in a carpeted area of about 15 ft by 15 ft, Steed remained upright without a break, without touching a foot to the floor and without either of his bike wheels ever making a complete revolution forward or backwards.

Roller Cycling

The greatest distance achieved in 24 hours is 1,560.73 mi by Piet Vitten (Neth) at Midden, Beemster, The Netherlands on Mar 8–9, 1980. James Baker (US) achieved a record 129.1 mph on rollers at the Univ of Arizona in Tucson on Dec 6, 1986.

In a marathon try, Gilbert Bil rode 85 hours 24 min at De Weesper, Amsterdam, The Netherlands, Oct 10–14, 1986.

FISHING

Origins

From time immemorial men have fished the seas and rivers of the world for food, but fishing for pleasure and leisure seems to have been practiced in Egypt, according to wall paintings, from the 5th Dynasty, 2470–2320 BC. On tomb inscriptions, Amenemhat, a prince of Beni Hasan, is described as "overseer of the swamps of enjoyment," a reference interpreted as fishing grounds.

Freshwater Casting

The longest freshwater cast ratified under ICF (International Casting Federation) rules is 574 ft 2 in by Walter Kummerow (W Germany), for the Bait Distance Double-Handed 30-g event held at Lenzerheide, Switzerland, in the 1968 Championships.

The longest Fly Distance Double-Handed cast is 257 ft 2 in by Sverne Scheen (Norway) also set at Lenzerheide in Sept 1968.

Longest Fight

The longest recorded fight between a fisherman and a fish is 32 hours 5 min by Donal Heatley (NZ) (b 1938) with a black marlin (estimated length 20 ft and weight 1,500 lb) off Mayor Island off Tauranga, New Zealand, Jan 21–22, 1968. It towed the 12-ton launch 50 miles before breaking the line.

World Championships

The *Confédération Internationale de la Pêche Sportive* championships were inaugurated as European championships in 1953. They were recognized as World Championships in 1957. France won 12 times between 1956 and 1981 and Robert Tesse (France) took the individual title uniquely three times, 1959–60, 65. The record weight (team) is 76 lb 8 oz in 3 hours by W Germany in the Neckar at Mannheim, W Germany on Sept 21, 1980. The individual record is 37 lb 7 oz by Wolf-Rüdiger Kremkus (W Germany) at Mannheim on Sept 20, 1980. The most fish caught is 652 by Jacques Isenbaert (Belgium) at Dunajvaros, Yugoslavia on Aug 27, 1967.

Most Fish Caught in a Season

In 77 days of fishing from Apr 1 to Oct 31, 1984, David Romeo of East Meadow, NY, caught on rod and reel 3,001 largemouth bass in the fresh waters of NY State and Florida, the most ever caught in a season. Mr. Romeo, who doesn't like eating fish but enjoys catching them, threw back all but 24 of them for this and legal reasons. His log books helped the environment conservation people to make "informed bass management decisions."

Largemouth Bass

A record of 22 lb 4 oz for a fish caught in Montgomery Lake, Georgia, by George W. Perry was set on June 2, 1932, and although millions of fishermen have tried to break this record since then, it still stands.

Largest Catches

Yet to be ratified is the largest fish ever caught by rod and line: A great white shark, 18 ft 9 in long, weighing 3,450 lb was landed off Montauk Marine Basin, LI, NY in August 1986 by Donnie Braddick and Frank Mundus. The shark fought for two hours, but this could not be accepted as a record because the men used a 150-lb test nylon line, heavier than the 130-lb IGFA limit.

The largest fish ever caught on a rod is an officially ratified man-eating great white shark (*Carcharodon carcharias*) weighing 2,664 lb, and measuring 16 ft 10 in long, caught by Alf Dean at Denial Bay, near Ceduna, South Australia, on Apr 21, 1959. In June 1978 a great white shark measuring 29 ft 6 in in length and weighing over 10,000 lb was harpooned and landed by fishermen in the harbor of San Miguel, Azores.

A white pointer shark weighing 3,388 lb was caught on a rod by Clive Green off Albany, W Australia, on Apr 26, 1976, but this will remain unratified as whale meat was used as bait.

The largest marine animal ever killed by *hand* harpoon was a blue

CAUGHT 3,001 BASS in one season: The champ David Romeo of East Meadow, NY holds up a 5 lb-5 oz, $21\frac{5}{8}$-in-long catch he made in 1986. *(Photo by Bruce Cooper)*

DUEL WITH SWORDFISH: Don Mann caught each of the 9 IGFA®-recognized species of billfish within one year.

RECORD CATCH: E. Lane Nichols III holds a prize 46 lb-8 oz red snapper that he caught Oct 1, 1985 in Destin, Fla.

whale 97 ft in length by Archer Davidson in Twofold Bay, NSW, Australia, in 1910. Its tail flukes measured 20 ft across and its jaw bone 23 ft 4 in.

The biggest single freshwater catch ever ratified was on the Snake River, Idaho, in 1956 when Willard Cravens caught a white sturgeon weighing 360 lb. However, that may not be the last word as two years previously, in the same river, Glenn Howard claims to have caught one which weighed 394 lb.

The heaviest game fish caught on rod and line is a 468-lb sturgeon by Joey Pallotta on July 9, 1983 off Benicia, Calif. An 834-lb freshwater sturgeon was *landed* by Garry Oling from the Fraser River, Albion, Brit Columbia, on Aug 11, 1981.

Most Valuable Fish

It was a modern version of an old fairy tale. When Al McReynolds went fishing one stormy night, the fish he caught brought fame and fortune. In this case, the magic was supplied by ABU-Garcia, a leading manufacturer of fishing tackle, through a contest that offered a $250,000 reward for landing an all-tackle world record fish in one of four categories.

McReynolds, 36, and his friend Pat Erdman were fishing from a jetty in their hometown, Atlantic City, NJ, on the night of Sept 21, 1982, when McReynolds hooked and, after a 2-hour fight, landed a 78-lb-8-oz striped bass—a world record for rod and reel. As one ordeal had ended, another began. McReynolds had to wait for the IGFA and ABU-Garcia to determine that the record was legitimate—a process that took nearly 5 months. Testing even included having the fish x-rayed to determine no stones or weights had been added to make the fish heavier.

It all ended happily on Feb 11, 1983, at the Explorers Club in NYC when McReynolds received a check for $250,000—the most money ever paid for a fish.

A claim has been made that two fishermen won $500,000 each in a fishing contest in Puget Sound, Wash in 1983. The objective was to catch one of 8 tagged fish. The two reportedly succeeded and split the $1 million prize.

Spear-Fishing

The largest fish ever taken underwater was an 804-lb giant black grouper by Don Pinder of the Miami Triton Club, Fla, in 1955.

Smallest Catch

The smallest fish ever to win a competition was a smelt weighing 1/16 of an oz, caught by Peter Christian at Buckenham Ferry, Norfolk, England, on Jan 9, 1977. This beat 107 other competitors who failed to catch anything.

FOOTBALL

Origins

The origin of modern football stems from the "Boston Game" as played at Harvard. Harvard declined to participate in the inaugural meeting of the Intercollegiate Football Association in NYC in Oct 1873, on the grounds that the proposed rules were based on the non-handling "Association" code of English football. Instead, Harvard accepted a proposal from McGill University of Montreal, which played the more closely akin English Rugby Football. The first football match under the Harvard Rules was thus played against McGill at Cambridge, Mass, in May 1874. Most sports historians point to a contest between Rutgers and Princeton at New Brunswick, NJ, on Nov 6, 1869, as the first football game, but many American soccer historians regard this contest as the first intercollegiate *soccer* game. (Rutgers won the game, 6 goals to 4, and there were 25 players to a side.) In Nov 1876, a new Intercollegiate Football Association, with a pioneer membership of 5 colleges, was inaugurated at Springfield, Mass, to reconcile the conflicting versions of the sport. It was not until 1880 that the game, because of the organizational genius of Walter Camp of Yale, began to take its modern form. Among other things, he reduced the number of players on a side to 11, which it is today (and defined their positions), and also replaced the scrum with the line of scrimmage.

Professional football dates from the Latrobe, Pa vs Jeannette, Pa match at Latrobe, in Aug 1895. The National Football League was founded in Canton, Ohio, in 1920, although it did not adopt its present name until 1922. The year 1969 was the final year in which professional football was divided into separate National and American Leagues, for record purposes.

Most Prolific Recordbreaker

After he finished his 4-year career at Portland State U in 1980, Neil Lomax held 90 NCAA football records and was tied for two other records, mostly on the basis of his passing feats. No other football player, past or present, has been remotely close to holding that many records—in any college sport.

All-America Brothers

Twice have three brothers made All-America at the same school. The first trio were the Wistert brothers at Mich, all of whom were tackles. Francis was honored in 1933, Albert in 1942, Alvin in 1948–49. At Oklahoma, defensive lineman Lucious Selmon was an All-America in 1973 and he was followed by his brothers Leroy, a defensive tackle, and Dewey, an offensive guard, in 1975.

First Televised Football Game

Fordham U, NYC, was the host to Waynesburg, a Pa school, in the first football game ever televised—in 1939. Fordham won, 34–7.

College Series Records

The oldest collegiate series still contested is that between Yale and Princeton dating from 1873, or 3 years before the passing of the Springfield rules, with 110 games played through the 1987 season. The most regularly contested series is between Lafayette and Lehigh, who have met 123 times, 1884 to 1987.

Yale University became the only college to win more than 700 games when it finished the 1979 season with a total of 701 victories in 107 seasons. Yale has 743 wins in 115 seasons to the end of 1987.

MODERN MAJOR-COLLEGE INDIVIDUAL RECORDS (Through 1987 Season)

Points			
Most in a Game	43	Jim Brown (Syracuse)	1956
Most in a Season	174	Lydell Mitchell (Penn State)	1971
	174	Mike Rozier (Nebraska)	1983
Most in a Career	393	Derek Schmidt (Fla State)	1984–87
Touchdowns			
Most in a Game	7	Arnold Boykin (Mississippi)	1951
Most in a Season	29	Lydell Mitchell (Penn State)	1971
	29	Mike Rozier (Nebraska)	1983
Most in a Career	59	Glenn Davis (Army)	1943–46
	59	Tony Dorsett (Pittsburgh)	1973–76
Field Goals			
Most in a Game	7	Mike Prindle (W Mich)	1984
		Dale Klein (Nebraska)	1985
Most in a Season	29	John Lee (UCLA)	1984
Most in a Career	80	Jeff Jaeger (Washington)	1983–86
Most Consecutively (Career)	30	Chuck Nelson (Washington)	1981–82
Other Season Records			
Yards Gained Rushing	2,342 yd	Marcus Allen (So Cal)	1981
Highest Average Gain per Rush (min. 150 attempts)	9.35 yd	Greg Pruitt (Oklahoma)	1971
Most Passes Attempted	511	Robbie Bosco (Brigham Young)	1985
Most Passes Completed	338	Robbie Bosco (Brigham Young)	1985
Most Touchdown Passes	47	Jim McMahon (Brigham Young)	1980
Most Yards Gained Passing	4,571 yd	Jim McMahon (Brigham Young)	1980
Most Passes Caught	134	Howard Twilley (Tulsa)	1965
Most Yards Gained on Catches	1,779 yd	Howard Twilley (Tulsa)	1965
Most Touchdown Passes Caught	18	Tom Reynolds (San Diego St)	1969
Most Passes Intercepted by	14	Al Worley (Washington)	1968
Highest Punting Average (min. 30 punts)	49.8 yd	Reggie Roby (Iowa)	1981

RUSHING RECORD of 2,105 yds in one season was set by Eric Dickerson (LA Rams) in his peak year 1984, eclipsing O.J. Simpson's record of 2,003 which had held for 11 years.
(UPI—Bettmann Archive)

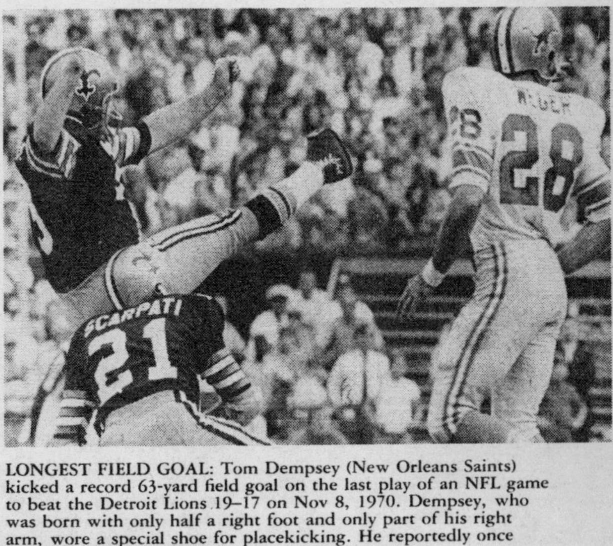

LONGEST FIELD GOAL: Tom Dempsey (New Orleans Saints) kicked a record 63-yard field goal on the last play of an NFL game to beat the Detroit Lions 19–17 on Nov 8, 1970. Dempsey, who was born with only half a right foot and only part of his right arm, wore a special shoe for placekicking. He reportedly once kicked a 57-yarder without a shoe in a semipro game.

ALL-TIME NATIONAL FOOTBALL LEAGUE RECORDS
(Through 1987 Season)

SERVICE

Most Seasons, Active Player
26 George Blanda, Chi Bears, 1949–58; Balt, 1950; AFL: Hou, 1960–66; Oak, 1967–75

Most Games Played, Lifetime
340 George Blanda, Chi Bears, 1949–58; Balt, 1950; AFL: Hou, 1960–66; Oak, 1967–75

Most Consecutive Games Played, Lifetime
282 Jim Marshall, Cleve, 1960; Minn, 1961–79

Most Seasons, Head Coach
40 George Halas, Chi Bears, 1920–29, 33–42, 46–55, 58–67

SCORING

Most Seasons Leading League
5 Don Hutson, GB, 1940–44
Gino Cappelletti, Bos, 1961, 63–66 (AFL)

Most Points, Lifetime
2,002 George Blanda, Chi Bears, 1949–58; Balt, 1950; AFL: Hou, 1960–66; Oak, 1967–75 (9-td, 943-pat, 335-fg)

Most Points, Season
176 Paul Hornung, GB, 1960 (15-td, 41-pat, 15-fg)

Most Points, Rookie Season
144 Kevin Butler, Chi Bears, 1985 (51-pat, 31-fg)

Most Points, Game
40 Ernie Nevers, Chi Cards vs Chi Bears, Nov 28, 1929 (6-td, 4-pat)

Most Consecutive Games, Scoring
151 Fred Cox, Minn 1963-73

Touchdowns

Most Seasons Leading League
8 Don Hutson, GB, 1935–38, 41–44

Most Touchdowns, Lifetime
126 Jim Brown, Cleve, 1957–65 (106-r, 20-p)

Most Touchdowns, Season
24 John Riggins, Wash (24-r), 1983

Most Touchdowns, Rookie Season
22 Gale Sayers, Chi Bears, 1965 (14-r,6-p, 1-prb, 1-krb)

Most Touchdowns, Game
6 Ernie Nevers, Chi Cards vs Chi Bears, Nov 28, 1929 (6-r)
William (Dub) Jones, Cleve vs Chi Bears, Nov 25, 1951 (4-r, 2-p)
Gale Sayers, Chi Bears vs SF, Dec 12, 1965 (4-r, 1-p, 1-prb)

Most Consecutive Games Scoring Touchdowns
18 Lenny Moore, Balt, 1963–65

Points After Touchdown

Most Seasons Leading League
8 George Blanda, Chi Bears, 1956; AFL: Hou, 1961–62; Oak, 1967–69, 72, 74

Most Points After Touchdown, Lifetime
943 (out of 959 attempts) George Blanda, Chi Bears, 1949–58; Balt, 1950; AFL: Hou, 1960–66; Oak, 1967–69, 72, 74

Most Points After Touchdown, Season
66 Uwe von Schamann, Miami 1984

Most Points After Touchdown, Game
9 Marlin (Pat) Harder, Chi Cards vs NY, Oct 17, 1948
Bob Waterfield, LA vs Balt, Oct 22, 1950
Charlie Gogolak, Wash vs NY Giants, Nov 27, 1966

Most Consecutive Points After Touchdown
234 Tommy Davis, SF, 1959–65

Field Goals

Most Seasons Leading League
5 Lou Groza, Cleve, 1950, 52–54, 57

Most Field Goals, Lifetime
373 Jan Stenerud, KC 1967–69; GB 1980–83, Minn 1984–85

Most Field Goals, Season
35 Ali Haji-Sheikh, NY Giants, 1983

Most Field Goals, Game
7 Jim Bakken, St L vs Pitt, Sept 24, 1967

Most Consecutive Games, Field Goals
31 Fred Cox, Minn, 1968–70

Highest Percentage, Lifetime
79.62 Morten Andersen, NO, 1982–87 (125–157)

Highest Field Goal Percentage, Season
95.24 Mark Mosely, Wash, 1982 (20–21)

Most Consecutive Field Goals
23 Mark Mosely, Wash, 1981–82

Longest Field Goal
63 yd Tom Dempsey, NO vs Det, Nov 8, 1970

RUSHING

Most Seasons Leading League
8 Jim Brown, Cleve, 1957–61, 63–65

Most Yards Gained, Lifetime
16,726 Walter Payton, Chi Bears, 1975–87

Most Yards Gained, Season
2,105 Eric Dickerson, LA Rams, 1984

Most Yards Gained, Game
275 Walter Payton, Chi Bears vs Minn, Nov 20, 1977

Longest Run from Scrimmage
99 Tony Dorsett, Dall vs Minn, Jan 3, 1983 (td)

Highest Average Gain, Lifetime (799 att)
5.2 Jim Brown, Cleve, 1957–65 (2,359–12,312)

Highest Average Gain, Game (10 att)
17.1 Marion Motley, Cleve vs Pitt, Oct 29, 1950 (11–188)

Most Touchdowns Rushing, Lifetime
110 Walter Payton, Chi Bears 1975–86

Most Touchdowns Rushing, Season
24 John Riggins, Wash, 1983

Most Touchdowns Rushing, Game
6 Ernie Nevers, Chi Cards vs Chi Bears, Nov 28, 1929

PASSING

Most Seasons Leading League
6 Sammy Baugh, Wash, 1937, 40, 43, 45, 47, 49

Most Passes Attempted, Lifetime
6,467 Fran Tarkenton, Minn, 1961–66, 72–78; NY Giants, 1967–71

Most Passes Attempted, Season
623 Dan Marino, Miami, 1986

Most Passes Attempted, Game
68 George Blanda, Hou vs Buff, Nov 1, 1964 (AFL) (37 completions)

Most Passes Completed, Lifetime
3,686 Fran Tarkenton, Minn, 1961–66, 72–78; NY Giants, 1967–71

Most Passes Completed, Season
378 Dan Marino, Miami, 1986

Most Passes Completed, Game
42 Richard Todd, NY Jets vs SF, Sept 21, 1980 (59 attempts)

Most Consecutive Passes Completed
20 Ken Anderson, Cin vs Hou, Jan 2, 1983

Longest Pass Completion (all tds)
99 Frank Filchock (to Farkas), Wash vs Pitt, Oct 15, 1939
George Izo (to Mitchell), Wash vs Cleve, Sept 15, 1963
Karl Sweetan (to Studstill), Det vs Balt, Oct 16, 1966
C. A. Jurgensen (to Allen), Wash vs Chi Bears, Sept 15, 1968

HEADED FOR THE SUPER BOWL: Owner George Halas (standing center, in raincoat and baseball hat) coached the Chicago Bears for 40 seasons, piling up a record 325 victories. Here he watches Gale Sayers in 1965 take off around end. The Bears did not win their first Super Bowl until Jan 1986, long after Halas had passed away.

RUSHING RECORDHOLDER: Walter Payton of the 1986 Super-Bowl Champion Chicago Bears set a record of 77 games with 100 yds or more gained. In 1977 he broke the record for yds gained in one game (275). He rushed 16,726 yds in his career. *(UPI—Bettmann Archive)*

Jim Plunkett (to Branch) LA Raiders vs Wash Oct 2, 1983
Ron Jaworski (to Quick) Phil vs Atl, Nov 10, 1985

Most Yards Gained Passing, Lifetime
47,003 Fran Tarkenton, Minn, 1961–66, 72–78; NY Giants, 1967–71

Most Yards Gained Passing, Game
554 Norm Van Brocklin, LA vs NY Yanks, Sept 28, 1951 (41–27)

Most Yards Gained Passing, Season
5,084 Dan Marino, Miami, 1984

Most Touchdown Passes, Lifetime
342 Fran Tarkenton, Minn, 1961–66, 72–78; NY Giants, 1967–71

Most Touchdown Passes, Season
48 Dan Marino, Miami, 1984

Most Touchdown Passes, Game
7 Sid Luckman, Chi Bears vs NY Giants, Nov 14, 1943
Adrian Burk, Phil vs Wash, Oct 17, 1954
George Blanda, Hou vs NY Titans, Nov 19, 1961 (AFL)
Y. A. Tittle, NY vs Wash, Oct 28, 1962
Joe Kapp, Minn vs Balt, Sept 28, 1969

Most Touchdown Passes, Consecutive Games
47 John Unitas, Balt, 1956–60

Passing Efficiency, Lifetime (1,500 att)
63.61 Joe Montana, SF 1979–87; (2,084–3,276)

Passing Efficiency, Season (100 att)
70.55 Ken Anderson, Cin, 1982 (309–218)

Passing Efficiency, Game (20 att)
90.91 Ken Anderson, Cin vs Pitt, Nov 10, 1974 (22–20)

Passes Had Intercepted

Most Passes Intercepted, Game
8 Jim Hardy, Chi Cards vs Phil, Sept 24, 1950 (39 attempts)

Most Consecutive Passes Attempted, None Intercepted
294 Bryan (Bart) Starr, GB, 1964–65

Fewest Passes Intercepted, Season (Qualifiers)
1 Joe Ferguson, Buff, 1976 (151 attempts)

Lowest Percentage Passes Intercepted, Lifetime (1,500 att)
2.72 Joe Montana, SF 1979–87 (3,276–89)

Lowest Percentage Passes Intercepted, Season (Qualifiers)
0.66 Joe Ferguson, Buff, 1976 (151–1)

PASS RECEPTIONS

Most Seasons Leading League
8 Don Hutson, GB, 1936–37, 39, 41–45

Most Pass Receptions, Lifetime
752 Steve Largent, Sea, 1976–87

Most Pass Receptions, Season
106 Art Monk, Wash, 1984

Most Pass Receptions, Game
18 Tom Fears, LA Rams vs GB, Dec 3, 1950 (189 yd)

Most Consecutive Games, Pass Receptions
152 Steve Largent, Seattle, 1976–87

Most Pass Receptions by a Running Back, Game
17 Clark Gaines, NY Jets vs SF, Sept 21, 1980

Most Yards Gained Pass Receptions, Game
309 Stephone Paige, KC vs SD, Dec 22, 1985

Longest Pass Reception (all tds)
99 Andy Farkas (Filchock), Wash vs Pitt, Oct 15, 1939
Bobby Mitchell (Izo), Wash vs Cleve, Sept 15, 1963
Pat Studstill (Sweetan), Det vs Balt, Oct 16, 1966
Gerry Allen (Jurgensen), Wash vs Chi Bears, Sept 15, 1968

Cliff Branch (Plunkett), LA Raiders vs Wash, Oct 2, 1983
Mike Quick (Jaworski), Phil vs Atl, Nov 10, 1985

Touchdowns Receiving

Most Touchdown Passes, Lifetime
99 Don Hutson, GB, 1935–45

Most Touchdown Passes, Season
22 Jerry Rice, SF, 1987

Most Touchdown Passes, Game
5 Bob Shaw, Chi Cards vs Balt, Oct 2, 1950
Kellen Winslow, SD vs Oak, Nov 22, 1981

Most Consecutive Games, Touchdown Passes
13 Jerry Rice, SF, 1987

PASS INTERCEPTIONS

Most Interceptions by, Lifetime
81 Paul Krause, Wash (28), 1964–67; Minn (53), 1968–79

Most Interceptions by, Season
14 Richard (Night Train) Lane, LA Rams, 1952

Most Interceptions by, Game
4 By 17 players, twice by Jerry Norton St L vs Wash, Nov 20, 1960; St L vs Pitt, Nov 26, 1961

Most Touchdowns Interception Returns, Lifetime
9 Ken Houston, Hou 1967–79; Wash 1973–80

Longest Return
103 Vencie Glenn, SD vs Den, Nov 29, 1987

PUNTING

Most Seasons Leading League
4 Sammy Baugh, Wash, 1940–43
Jerrel Wilson, AFL: KC, 1965, 68; NFL: KC, 1972–73

Most Punts, Season
114 Bob Parsons, Chi, 1981

Most Punts, Lifetime
1,154 Dave Jennings, NY Giants 1974–84, NY Jets 1985—87

Longest Punt
98 yd Steve O'Neal, NY Jets vs Den, Sept 21, 1969 (AFL)

Most Punts, Game
15 John Telchik, Phila vs NY Giants, Dec 6, 1987

Average Yardage Punting

Highest Punting Average, Lifetime (300 punts)
45.1 yd Sammy Baugh, Wash, 1937–52 (338)

Highest Punting Average, Season (20 punts)
51.4 yd Sammy Baugh, Wash, 1940
(35)

Highest Punting Average, Game (4 punts)
61.8 yd Bob Cifers, Det vs Chi Bears, Nov 24, 1946

KICKOFF RETURNS

Yardage Returning Kickoffs

Most Yards Gained, Lifetime
6,922 Ron Smith, Chi Bears, 1965, 70–72; Atl, 1966–67; LA, 1968–69; SD, 1973; Oak, 1974

Most Yards Gained, Season
1,345 George (Buster) Rhymes, Minn 1985

Most Yards Gained, Game
294 Wally Triplett, Det vs LA, Oct 29, 1950 (4)

Longest Kickoff Return for Touchdown
106 Al Carmichael, GB vs Chi Bears, Oct 7, 1956
Noland Smith, KC vs Den, Dec 17, 1967 (AFL)
Roy Green, St L vs Dall, Oct 21, 1979

Average Yards Kickoff Returns

Highest Average, Lifetime (75 returns)
30.6 Gale Sayers, Chi Bears, 1965–71

PUTTING THE FOOT IN ▲ FOOTBALL: Steve O'Neal (#20) of the NY Jets follows through on his punt from the end zone in Denver's Mile High Stadium. The line of scrimmage (from which punts are measured) had been the 1-yd line. The ball, which sailed well over the receiver's head, bounced and rolled to the Denver 1-yd line—a 98-yd punt! *(Pro-Football Hall of Fame)*

◄

STRONG ARM: Fran Tarkenton set lifetime NFL records by attempting 6,467 passes and completing 3,686 of them during his 18-year career with the NY Giants and Minn Vikings. Tarkenton, who holds career passing records for touchdowns (342) and yards gained (47,003), was elected to the Hall of Fame in 1986.

Highest Average, Season (15 returns)
41.1 Travis Williams, GB, 1967 (18)

Highest Average, Game (3 returns)
73.5 Wally Triplett, Det vs LA Rams, Oct 29, 1950 (4–294)

Touchdowns Returning Kickoffs

Most Touchdowns, Lifetime
6 Ollie Matson, Chi Cards, 1952 (2), 54, 56, 58 (2)
Gale Sayers, Chi Bears, 1965, 66 (2), 67 (3)
Travis Williams, GB, 1967 (4), 69, 71

Most Touchdowns, Season
4 Travis Williams, GB, 1967
Cecil Turner, Chi Bears, 1970

Most Touchdowns, Game
2 Thomas (Tim) Brown, Phil vs Dall, Nov 6, 1966
Travis Williams, GB vs Cleve, Nov 12, 1967
Ron Brown, LA Rams vs GB, Nov 24, 1985

PUNT RETURNS
Yardage Returning Punts

Most Yards Gained, Lifetime
3,291 Billy Johnson, Hou 1974–80, Atl 1982–87

Most Yards Gained, Season
692 Fulton Walker, LA Raiders 1985

Most Yards Gained, Game
207 LeRoy Irvin, LA Rams vs Atl, Oct 11, 1981

Longest Punt Return (all tds)
98 Gil LeFebvre, Cin vs Brk, Dec 3, 1933
Charlie West, Minn vs Wash, Nov 3, 1968
Dennis Morgan, Dall vs St L, Oct 13, 1974

Highest Average, Lifetime (75 or more returns)
12.78 George McAfee, Chi Bears, 1940–41, 1945–50

Highest Average, Season (Qualifiers)
23.0 Herb Rich, Balt, 1950

Highest Average, Game (3 returns)
47.7 Chuck Latourette, St L vs NO, Sept 29, 1968

Most Touchdowns, Game
2 Jack Christiansen, Det vs LA Rams, Oct 14, 1951; vs GB, Nov 22, 1951
Dick Christy, NY Titans vs Den, Sept 24, 1961
Rick Upchurch, Den vs Cleve, Sept 26, 1976
LeRoy Irvin, LA Rams vs Atl, Oct 11, 1981
Vai Sikahema, St L vs Tampa, Dec 21, 1986

Most Touchdowns, Lifetime
8 Jack Christiansen, Det, 1951–58
Rick Upchurch, Den, 1975–83

Most Touchdowns, Season
4 Jack Christiansen, Det, 1951
Rick Upchurch, Den, 1976

FUMBLES

Most Fumbles, Lifetime
105 Roman Gabriel, LA Rams, 1962–72; Phil, 1973–77

Most Fumbles, Season
17 Dan Pastorini, Hou, 1973
Warren Moon, Hou 1984

Most Fumbles, Game
7 Len Dawson, KC vs SD, Nov 15, 1964 (AFL)

Longest Fumble Return
104 Jack Tatum, Oak vs GB, Sept 24, 1972

Most Opponents' Fumbles Recovered, Lifetime
29 Jim Marshall, Cleve, 1960; Minn, 1961–79

Most Opponents' Fumbles Recovered, Season
9 Don Hultz, Minn, 1963

Most Opponents' Fumbles Recovered, Game
3 by 9 players 1949–85

SUPER BOWL RECORDS
(Through 1988 Game)

Most points, lifetime
24 Franco Harris, Pitt, 4 games (4 td)

Most points, game
18 Roger Craig, SF vs Miami, Jan 20, 1985 (3 td)

Most field goals, lifetime
5 Ray Wersching, SF, 2 games

Most field goals, game
4 Don Chandler, GB vs. Oak, Jan 14, 1968
Ray Wersching, SF vs Cin, Jan 24, 1982

Longest field goal
48 Jan Stenerud, KC vs Minn, Jan 11, 1970
Rick Karlis, Den vs NY Giants Jan 25, 1987

Most extra points, game
6 Ali Haj-Sheikh, Wash vs Den Jan 31, 1988

Most yards rushing, lifetime
354 Franco Harris, Pitt, 4 games

Most yards rushing, game
204 Tim Smith, Wash vs Den, Jan 31, 1988

Most yards passing, lifetime
932 Terry Bradshaw, Pitt, 4 games

Most yards, passing, game
340 Doug Williams, Wash vs Den Jan 31, 1988

Most passes completed, lifetime
61 Roger Staubach, Dallas, 4 games

Most passes completed, game
29 Dan Marino, Miami vs SF, Jan 20, 1985

Most touchdown passes, lifetime
9 Terry Bradshaw, Pitt, 4 games

Most touchdown passes, game
4 Terry Bradshaw, Pitt vs Dallas, Jan 21, 1979
Doug Williams, Wash vs Den, Jan 31, 1988

Longest completed pass
80 Jim Plunkett to Kenny King, Oak Raiders vs Phil, Jan 25, 1981
Doug Williams to Ricky Sanders, Wash vs Den, Jan 31, 1988

Best passing pct, game
.880 Phil Simms, NY Giants vs Den (22 of 25), Jan 25, 1987

Most yards receiving, lifetime
364 Lynn Swann, Pitt, 4 games

Most yards receiving, game
193 Ricky Sanders, Wash vs Den, Jan 31, 1988

Most receptions, lifetime
16 Lynn Swann, Pitt, 4 games

Most receptions, game
11 Dan Rose, Cin vs SF, Jan 24, 1982

Most interceptions, game
3 Rod Martin, Oak Raiders vs Phil, Jan 25, 1981

Longest punt
62 Rich Camarillo, NE Patriots vs Chi Bears, Jan 26, 1986

Longest punt return
34 Darrell Green, Wash vs LA Raiders, Jan 22, 1984

Longest kickoff return
98 Fulton Walker, Miami vs Wash, Jan 30, 1983

Longest Streaks

The longest collegiate winning streak is 47 straight by Oklahoma. The longest unbeaten streak is 63 games (59 won, 4 tied) by Washington from 1907 to 1917. Macalaster University of St Paul, Minn, ended a record 50-game losing streak when, with 11 sec remaining in the game, a 23-yd field goal beat Mount Senario, 17–14, on Sept 6, 1980. It was Macalaster's first victory since Oct 11, 1974.

Statistical Leader

Oklahoma became the first team in major college football history to win 6 team championships in 1986 and then do it again in 1987 giving them 12 titles in 2 seasons. In the latest year, they led in rushing offense (428.2 yd per game), scoring offense (43.5), scoring defense

(7.5), total defense (208.1 rushing-passing yd allowed per game), pass defense (102.4) and total offense (499.7).

Worst Attendance

The worst attendance for a college football game was recorded on Nov 12, 1955 at Pullman, Washington. The game was between Wash State and San Jose State. It was played in spite of high winds and a temperature of 0°F. Total paid attendance: 1.

Highest Score

The most points ever scored (by one team and both teams) in a college football game was 222 by Georgia Tech, Atlanta, Ga, against Cumberland University of Lebanon, Tenn on Oct 7, 1916. Tech also set records for the most points scored in one quarter (63), most touchdowns (32) and points after touchdown (30) in a game, and the largest victory margin (Cumberland did not score).

Coaching Records

The longest-serving head coach was Amos Alonzo Stagg (1862–1965), who served Springfield in 1890–91, Chicago from 1892 to 1932 and College of the Pacific from 1933 to 1946, making a total of 57 years. He later served as an assistant coach to his son.

The record for most victories by a coach of a professional team is 325, by George Halas (1895–1983), who coached the Chicago Bears, 1920–29, 33–42, 46–55, 58–67.

Through 1987, the 68-year-old Eddie Robinson compiled a 341–117–15 record at Grambling State University (Louisiana), the winningest coach in college football history. The previous record of

SUPER PASSING: Phil Simms (NY Giants), most valuable player in the 1987 Super Bowl, set 2 major records, completing 10 passes in a row and finishing with 22 out of 25 attempts for a record .880 percentage.

323 had been set by Paul "Bear" Bryant in 1982. Bryant had coached at Maryland (1945), Kentucky (1946–53), Texas A&M (1954–57) and Alabama (1958–82).

NFL Champions

The Green Bay Packers have won a record 11 NFL titles from 1929 through 1967. The Packers also won the first two Super Bowls (instituted Jan 1967), when the games were a competition between NFL and AFL champions. The Pittsburgh Steelers have the most Super Bowl victories with 4 (1975–76, 79–80). The 1972 Miami Dolphins had the best record for one season, including playoffs and Super Bowl (played Jan 1973), with 17 wins and no losses or ties.

Shortest Touchdown Pass

When the Dallas Cowboys had only 2 inches to go for a touchdown against the Washington Redskins on Oct 9, 1960, quarterback Eddie LeBaron did the unexpected. Knowing that everyone was looking to a powerful thrust at the line by the heaviest plunging back on his team, LeBaron took the ball from center and instead of handing it off to his fullback, slipped into the pocket and unleashed a short pass over the left side to his left end Bielski to set a world record for the shortest distance gained by a pass for a touchdown—2 inches.

Pro Playoff Heroes

On Jan 9, 1988, Anthony Carter, one of the smallest players in the National Football League at 166 lb, had one of the biggest days ever in playoff history. The Minnesota Vikings' wide receiver gained 227 yds, a record for postseason games, on 10 catches against the San Francisco 49ers.

Other outstanding playoff records include Bernie Kosar, the Cleveland Brown quarterback who passed for 489 yds against the NY Jets in 1986; Eric Dickerson, then of the Los Angeles Rams, who rushed for 248 yards against the Dallas Cowboys in 1985, and Daryle Lamonica, playing for the Oakland Raiders when he threw 6 touchdowns passes against the Houston Oilers in 1969.

GAMES AND PASTIMES

BRIDGE (CONTRACT)

Bridge (corruption of Biritch) is thought to be either of Levantine origin, similar games having been played there in the early 1870's, or to have come from the East—probably India.

Auction bridge (highest bidder names trump) was invented *c.* 1902. The contract principle, present in several games (notably the French game *Plafond, c.* 1917), was introduced to bridge by Harold S. Vanderbilt (US) on Nov 1, 1925, during a Caribbean voyage aboard the SS *Finland*. The new version became a worldwide craze after the US vs GB challenge match between Rumanian-born Ely Culbertson

(1891–1955) and Lt-Col Walter Thomas More Buller (1887–1938) at Almack's Club, London, Sept 1930. The US won the 200-hand match by 4,845 points.

Most Players

The biggest tournament, called the Epson World Bridge Championship, held on June 3, 1988, was contested by 84,352 players playing the same hands at 2,500 centers.

In N Amer alone, there are 4,120 bridge clubs, according to the Amer Contract Bridge League (ACBL).

Most World Titles

The World Championship (Bermuda Bowl) has been won most often (13 times) by Italy's Blue Team between 1957 and 1975, and by the US team between 1950 and 1987. Italy also won the Olympiad in 1964, 68 and 72. Giorgio Belladonna (b 1923) was on all these Italian winning teams. The US won a record 4 times in the women's world championship for the Venice Trophy.

Possible Auctions

The number of possible auctions with North as dealer is 128,745,650,347,030,638,120,231,926,111,609,371,363,122,697,557.

Perfect Deals

The mathematical odds against dealing 13 cards of one suit are 158,753,389,899 to 1, while the odds against a named player receiving a "perfect hand" consisting of all 13 spades, for example, are 635,013,559,599 to 1. The odds against each of the four players receiving a complete suit ("perfect deal") are 2,235,197,406,895,366,368,301,559,999 to 1.

Most Durable Player

Oswald Jacoby (b Dec 8, 1902), Dallas, Tex, d 1984) was a world-rank competitor for 52 years after winning his first world title in 1931. In Oct 1967, he became the first player to amass 10,000 master points. He retired in July 1983 but came back in Nov 1983 to be part of a team that won the North America team championship. (He also won the World Backgammon title.)

Most Master Points

In the latest ranking list based on Master Points awarded by the World Bridge Federation, the leading male player in the world was Giorgio Belladonna, a member of Italy's Blue Team, with 1,821¼ points, followed by four more Italians. The world's leading woman player is Jacqui Mitchell (US) with 347 points.

As for master points awarded by the American Contract Bridge League, the leader was Barry Crane of Los Angeles (b 1927 Detroit, murdered July 5, 1985) who won a total of 35,137.6 points. Only 4 other players have even reached 25,000. The leader currently is Paul Soloway with 29,153 points to June 15, 1988. The most master points scored in a year is 3,270 by Grant Baze (US) in 1984.

Youngest Life Masters

Sam Hirschman of Southfield, Mich, became a Life Master in the ACBL on July 21, 1988, at the age of 11 years 9 months 5 days, beating the previous youngest master by 29 days.

Adair Gellman of Bethesda, Md, became the youngest-ever female Life Master at age 14 years 6 months 4 days on Oct 24, 1983, breaking a record that had stood for 6 years. Then on Nov 5, 1983, just 12 days later, she was toppled from her peak by a still younger lady, Patricia Thomas of Las Cruces, NM, who was 14 years and 28 days.

Oldest Active Players

Jay Feigus of Middletown, NJ at age 95 in Mar 1988 won a pairs title with Edwin Utan in a field of 90 pairs at the Univ of Scranton. His earliest was a 1929 Goldman Pair Championship.

Mrs Julia Chadwick of Torquay, Eng, now 102, at the age of 98 won two events in 1985.

CHECKERS

Checkers, also known as draughts, has origins earlier than chess. It was played in Egypt in the second millennium BC. The earliest book on the game was by Antonio Torquemada of Valencia, Spain in 1547. There have been four US vs GB international matches (crossboard) in 1905, 27, 73, and 83, three won by the US and one by GB.

Asa Long (b 1904) of Toledo, Ohio, was the youngest player ever to win a US National checkers tournament (aged 18 years 2 months) in 1922, and also the oldest player to duplicate this (aged 79 years 11 months) in 1984 at Tupelo, Miss, a span of 62 years. He was also world champion 1934–48, and won 4 other US Nationals—1929, 37, 39, and 82.

Walter Hellman (US) (1916–75) won a record 8 world titles during his tenure as world champion 1948–75.

Dr Marion Tinsley (Tallahassee, Fla) has been undefeated in match play internationally from 1947 to 1988. Melvin Pomeroy (US) was internationally undefeated from 1914 until his death in 1933.

Most Opponents

Nathan Cohen of Portland, Maine, played 172 opponents, 5 to 10 at a time, in 4 hours on July 26, 1981, and won every game, in an exhibition at a picnic.

Con McCarrick (Ireland) was reported as having played a record 154 games simultaneously, winning 136, drawing 17, and losing one, in 4½ hours at Dundalk, County Louth, Ireland, Mar 14, 1982.

Gary Davis played 177 games of checkers simultaneously at Marketown, Mt District, NSW, Australia on July 4, 1987.

Longest and Shortest Games

In competition the prescribed rate of play is not less than 30 moves per hour with the average game lasting about 90 min. In 1958 a match between Dr Marion Tinsley (US) and Derek Oldbury (GB) lasted 7 hours 30 min. The shortest possible game is one of 20 moves, composed by Alan Malcolm Beckerson (GB).

The longest session is 138 hours 28 min by Greg Davis and Mark Schumacher at Denny's Restaurant, Nunawading, Australia, Aug 26–Sept 1, 1985.

WOMEN'S CHESS CHAMPION: Nona Gaprindashvili (USSR) held the world title for 16 years, during which she defended it successfully 4 times. (*AP*)

CHESS

The game originated in ancient India under the name Chaturanga (literally "four-corps")—an army game. The name chess is derived from the Persian word *shah.* The earliest reference is from the Middle Persian Karnamak (*c.* 590–628), though there are grounds for believing its origins are from the 2nd century, owing to the discovery, announced in Dec 1972, of two ivory chessmen in the Uzbek Soviet Republic, datable to that century. The *Fédération Internationale des Echecs* was established in 1924. There were an estimated 7 million registered players in the USSR in 1973.

The game of chess has led to the publication of at least 20,000 books, more than for any other game.

Most Opponents

Vlastimil Hort (b Jan 12, 1944) (Czechoslovakia), in Seltjarnes, Iceland, Apr 23–24, 1977, played 550 opponents, including a record 201 simultaneously. He only lost ten games.

Eric G. J. Knoppert (Neth) (b Sept 20, 1959) played 500 games of 10-min chess against opponents averaging 2,002 on the Elo scale in 67 hours 58 min, Sept 13–16, 1985. He scored 413 points (1 for win, ½ for draw), a success rate of 82.6%.

The record for most consecutive games played is 663 by Vlastimil Hort over 32½ hours at Porz, W Germany on Oct 5–6, 1984. He played 60–100 opponents at a time, scoring over 80% and averaging 30 moves per game.

George Koltanowski (Belgium, later of US) tackled 56 opponents "blindfold" and won 50, drew 6, lost 0 in 9¾ hours at the Fairmont Hotel, San Francisco, on Dec 13, 1960.

WORLD CHESS CHAMPIONS: Anatoliy Karpov (left) (USSR) played 45.2 games a year 1975–85 to become the most active champion. When Gary Kasparov (right) (USSR) first defeated Karpov he became the youngest world champion at 22 years 210 days. Most recently Kasparov retained his title in a match that earned him $2 million.

Longest Games

The master game with the most moves on record was when Yedael Stepak (b Aug 21, 1940) (Israel) beat Yaakov Mashian (b Dec 17, 1943) (Iran, later Israel) in 193 moves in Tel Aviv, Israel, March 23–Apr 16, 1980. The total playing time was 24½ hours.

The slowest reported move (before modern rules) in an official event is reputed to have been played by Louis Paulsen (1833–91) (Germany) against Paul Charles Morphy (1837–84) (US) on Oct 29, 1857. The game ended in a draw on move 56 after 15 hours of play, of which Paulsen used most of the allotted time. Grandmaster Friedrich Sämisch (1896–1975) (Germany) ran out of the allotted time (2½ hours for 45 moves) after only 12 moves, in Prague, Czechoslovakia, in 1938.

The slowest move played, since time clocks were introduced, was at Vigo, Spain in 1980 when Francisco Trois (b Sept 3, 1946) took 2 hours 20 min for his seventh move *v.* Luis M. C. P. Santos (b June 30, 1955).

World Champions

World champions have been generally recognized since 1886. The longest undisputed tenure was 26 years 337 days by Dr Emanuel Lasker (1868–1941) of Germany, from 1894 to 1921. Robert J. (Bobby) Fischer (b Chicago, March 9, 1943) is reckoned on the officially adopted Elo system to be the greatest Grandmaster of all time at 2,785.

Gary Kimovich Kasparov (USSR) (b Apr 13, 1963) at 2,740 is currently the highest ranked player. He successfully defended his world championship title in Spain against Karpov late in 1987, but almost lost it through making a blunder. Needing only two draws to win, Kasparov got careless and sacrificed a rook, only to find that he had lost a game. Now he had to win to salvage a tie. He did just that. In astonishing play he carefully backed Karpov into a hopeless position and won the game, retained his title and a pot of more than $2 million!

The most active world champion has been Anatoliy Yevgenyevitch Karpov (USSR) (b May 23, 1951) who in his tenure as champion, 1975–85, averaged 45.2 competitive games per year, played in 32 tournaments and finished first in 26.

The women's world championship was held by Vera Menchik-Stevenson (1906–44) (USSR, later GB) from 1927 till her death, and was successfully defended a record 7 times. Nona Gaprindashvili (USSR) (b May 3, 1941) held the title from 1962 to 1978, and defended successfully 4 times. The highest-rated woman player is also the youngest champion, Maya Chiburdanidze (b Jan 17, 1961) of Tbilisi (USSR) at 2,530. She won the women's title in 1978 in a women-only match at the age of 17.

The youngest male world champion is Gary Kasparov who, at 22 years 210 days on Nov 9, 1985, beat Anatoliy Karpov. The oldest was Wilhelm Steinitz (1836–1900) (Czech) who was 58 years 10 days old when he lost his title to Lasker on May 26, 1894.

Ariel Avigad-Vernon, at 7 years 237 days, defeated Nick Dumyk, an adult with an Expert rating by the US Chess Federation, on Dec 5, 1987 at the Manhattan Chess Club in NYC.

José Raúl Capablanca (1888–1942) (Cuba) lost only 34 games in his adult career, 1909–39, for the fewest games lost by a world champion. He was unbeaten from Feb 10, 1916, to Mar 21, 1924, and was world champion from 1921 to 1927.

THROWING

In boomerang throwing, the longest distance for throw-and-return was 396.98 ft achieved by Christian Jabet (France) on Apr 5, 1986 near Lyon, France. Dr. Larry Ruhf (US) set a record of 2 min 31 sec for keeping a boomerang aloft in a throw-and-catch contest in Catskill, NY, sponsored by the US Boomerang Assoc and Palenville Interarts, Inc.

The longest independently authenticated throw of any inert object heavier than air is 1,257 ft, for an Aerobie flying ring, by Scott Zimmerman on July 8, 1986 at Fort Funston, Calif.

In Frisbee (flying disc) throwing, Don Cain of East Brunswick, NJ set the record for maximum time aloft by keeping a flying disc in the air for 16.72 sec in Phila, Pa, on May 26, 1984. For women, the time-aloft record is 11.47 sec, set in Sonoma, Calif, by Denise Garfield on Oct 5, 1980.

The greatest distance achieved for throwing a flying disc, running, and catching it is 291 ft by Pekka Ranta (Finland) on June 6, 1986 at Tali, Finland. The women's record is 196.9 ft by Judy Horowitz of NYC on June 29, 1985 at LaMirada, Calif.

The world record for outdoor distance is 612 ft 11½ in by Michael Canci (Australia) on Apr 11, 1987, at Bunbury, W Australia. The indoor distance record is held by Van Miller of Tempe, Ariz, with a 399-ft toss at Flagstaff, Ariz, on Sept 18, 1982.

Bethany Porter (US) holds the women's outdoor distance record at 409 ft 2½ in, set on Aug 21, 1987 at Fort Collins, Colo, while the women's indoor distance record belongs to Suzanne Fields, of Boston, who threw 229.6 ft in Cedar Falls, Iowa, Apr 26, 1981.

The 24-hour group distance record is 428.02 miles set in Vernon, Conn, by the South Windsor Ultimate Frisbee Disc Team, July 8–9, 1977. The outdoor pair distance record for 24 hours has been set at 303.38 mi by Leonard Muise and Gabe Ontiveros at Torrance, Calif,

THROWING ACROSS NIAGARA FALLS: Scott Zimmerman, record holder with an Aerobie throw of 1,257 ft, shows how he threw a flying disc from the Canadian side to the American. *(Denis Cahill/St. Catherine's Standard)*

FASTEST DISC THROW: Alan Bonopane holds the record for tossing a frisbee—74 mph. *(Donnell A. Tate Photography)*

Aug 3–4, 1986. Jamie Knerr and Keith Biery set the indoor 24-hour pair distance mark with 298.37 miles, Aug 14–15, 1982, at Allentown, Pa.

The Prince George's Community College Flying High Club set the group marathon mark with 1,198 hours, June 1–July 22, 1983. The two-person marathon record is held by Jamie Knerr and Keith Biery, who played 110 hours 40 min in Allentown, Pa, Aug 23–27, 1981.

Alan Bonopane threw a professional model Frisbee disc at a speed of 74 mph and his teammate Tim Selinske made a clean catch of the throw on Aug 25, 1980 in San Marino, Calif.

GOLF

Origins

It has been suggested that golf originated with Scottish shepherds using their crooks to knock pebbles into rabbit holes. This may be apocryphal, but somewhat firmer evidence exists. A stained glass window in Gloucester Cathedral, dating from 1350, portrays a golfer-like figure, but the earliest mention of golf occurs in a prohibiting law passed by the Scottish Parliament in March 1457, under which "golff be utterly cryit doune and not usit."

The Romans had a cognate game called *paganica*, which may have been carried to Britain before 400 AD. The Chinese National Golf Association claims the game is of Chinese origin ("*Ch'ui Wan*—the ball-hitting game") from the 3rd or 2nd century BC. There were official ordinances prohibiting a ball game with clubs in Belgium and Holland from 1360. Gutta-percha balls succeeded feather balls in 1848, and were in turn succeeded in 1902 by rubber-cored balls, invented in 1899 by Coburn Haskell (US). Steel shafts were authorized in the US in 1925.

Golf was first played on the moon in Feb 1971 by Capt Alan Shepard (US), commander of the Apollo XIV spacecraft.

Oldest Clubs

The oldest club of which there is written evidence is the Gentleman Golfers (now the Honourable Company of Edinburgh Golfers) formed in March 1744—10 years prior to the institution of the Royal and Ancient Club of St Andrews, Fife, Scotland. However, the Royal Burgess Golfing Society of Edinburgh claims to have been founded in 1735. The oldest existing club in North America is the Royal Montreal Club (Nov 1873) and the oldest in the US is St Andrews, Westchester County, NY (1888). An older claim is by the Foxbury Country Club, Clarion County, Pa (1887).

Longest Courses and Holes

The world's longest course is the par-77, 8,325-yd International GC, Bolton, Mass, from the "Tiger" tees, remodeled in 1969 by Robert Trent Jones. Its 16th hole of 270 yd is the longest par 3 in the world.

The longest par 4 is the 6th hole of the Dwight D. Eisenhower Golf Club at City of Industry, Calif, at 500 yd. The longest par 5 is the 17th hole of the Palmira Golf Club in St Johns, Ind, at 710 yd. The longest par 6 is the 17th hole of Black Mt GC, NC, at 747 yd, and the longest hole (par 7) is the 948-yd 7th at Koolan Is, W Australia.

Floyd Satterlee Rood used the entire United States as a course, when he played from the Pacific surf to the Atlantic surf from Sept 1963 to Oct 1964 in 114,737 strokes. He lost 3,511 balls on the 3,397.7 mi trail.

Highest and Lowest Courses

The highest golf course in the world is the Tuctu Golf Club in Morococha, Peru, which is 14,335 ft above sea level at its lowest point. Golf has, however, been played in Tibet at an altitude of over 16,000 ft.

The lowest golf course in the world is the par-70 Furnace Creek Golf Course, Death Valley, Calif, at a disputed average of 178–272 ft below sea level.

Biggest Bunkers

The world's biggest trap is Hell's Half Acre which stretches 200 yd across the fairway at the 585-yd 7th hole of the Pine Valley course, Clementon, NJ. Highest bunker is the 19-ft deep 115-yd-long trap along the 16th hole at the new PGA West course in Palm Springs, Calif.

Largest Green

Probably the largest green in the world is that of the par-6, 695-yd 5th hole at International GC, Bolton, Mass, with an area greater than 28,000 sq ft.

Lowest Scores for 9 and 18 Holes

Three professional players are recorded to have played a long course (over 6,000 yd) for a score of 57: Bill Burke at the Normandie Golf Club, St Louis (6,389 yds, par 71) on May 20, 1970; Tom Ward at the Searcy (Ark) Country Club (6,098 yds, par 70) in 1981; Augie Navarro at the Sim Park Golf Course (Wichita, Kans) in 1982.

Alfred Edward Smith (1903–85), the English professional at Woolacombe, achieved an 18-hole score of 55 (15 under bogey 70) on his home course on Jan 1, 1936.

Nine holes in 25 (4, 3, 3, 2, 3, 3, 1, 4, 2) was recorded by A. J. "Bill" Burke in his round of 57 (32 + 25) (see above), and by teenager Douglas Beecher at the Pitman (NJ) Country Club (3,150 yd, par 35) in 1976. The tournament record is 27 by Mike Souchak (US) (b May 1927) for the second nine (par 35) first round of the 1955 Texas Open; Andy North (US) (b Mar 9, 1950) second nine (par 34), first round, 1975 BC Open at En-Joie GC, Endicott, NY; and Jose Maria Canizares (Spain) (b Feb 18, 1947), first nine, third round, in the 1978 Swiss Open on the 6,811-yd Crans-Sur course, and by Robert Lee (GB) (b Oct 12, 1961) first nine, first round, in the Monte Carlo Open on the 6,249 yd Mont Agel course on June 28, 1985.

The US PGA tournament record for 18 holes is 59 (30 + 29) by Al

Geiberger (b Sept 1, 1937) in the second round of the Danny Thomas Classic, on the 72-par, 7,249-yd Colonial CC course, Memphis, Tenn, June 10, 1977.

In non-PGA tournaments, Samuel Jackson Snead (b May 27, 1912) had 59 in the Greenbrier Open (now called the Sam Snead Festival), at White Sulphur Springs, W Va, on May 16, 1959; Gary Player (South Africa) (b Nov 1, 1935) carded 59 in the second round of the Brazilian Open in Rio de Janeiro on Nov 29, 1974; and David Jagger (GB) also had 59 in a Pro-Am tournament prior to the 1973 Nigerian Open at Ikoyi Golf Club, Lagos, and Miguel Martin (Spain) in the Argentine Southern Championship at Mar de Plata on Feb 27, 1987.

Women's Lowest Scores

The lowest recorded score on an 18-hole course (over 6,000 yd) for a woman is 62 (30 + 32) (9 under par) by Mary (Mickey) Kathryn Wright (b Feb 14, 1935), of Dallas, on the Hogan Park Course (6,286 yd) at Midland, Tex, in Nov 1964, and 62 (11 under par) by Vicki Fergon in the 2nd round of the 1984 San Jose Classic.

Wanda Morgan (b March 22, 1910) recorded a score of 60 (31 + 29) on the Westgate and Birchington Golf Club course, Kent, England, over 18 holes (5,002 yd) on July 11, 1929.

The LPGA record for 9 holes is held by Pat Bradley who scored 28 (7 under par) in Denver, Colo, Aug 24, 1984, and 28 (8 under par) by Mary Beth Zimmerman in the 1984 Rail Charity tournament.

Lowest Scores for 36 Holes

The record for 36 holes is 122 (59 + 63) by Sam Snead in the 1959 Greenbrier Open (now called the Sam Snead Festival) (non-PGA), May 16–17, 1959. Horton Smith (1908–63), twice Masters champion, scored 121 (63 + 58) on a short course (4,700 yd) on Dec 21, 1928.

Lowest for a woman is 129 (64–65) by Judy Dickinson in 1985 in the S&H Golf Classic.

Lowest Scores for 72 Holes

The lowest recorded score on a first-class course is 255 (29 under par) by Leonard Peter Tupling (b Apr 6, 1950) (GB) in the Nigerian Open at Ikoyi Golf Club, Lagos, in Feb 1981, made up of 63, 66, 62 and 64 (average 63.75 per round).

The lowest 72 holes in a US professional event is 257 (60, 68, 64 and 65) by Mike Souchak in the 1955 Texas Open at San Antonio.

The lowest for a woman is 242 (21 under par) by Trish Johnson in the Eastleigh Classic in Eng July 25–27, 1987. Nancy Lopez shot 268 (66–67–69–66) in the 1985 Henredon Classic for the lowest finish in a US tournament.

Lowest Score with One Club

Playing only with a 6-iron, Thad Daber of Durham, NC, won the 1987 World One Club Championship with a record score of 70 (2 under par) on the 6,037-yd Lochmere Golf Club course in Cary, NC.

Longest Drive

In long-driving contests 330 yd is rarely surpassed at sea level.

In an official PGA long-driving contest at 5,200-ft altitude in Denver, Colo, at the John F. Kennedy Golf Course, on a clear day with a slight wind against him, Jack L. Hamm of Denver drove a ball 406 yd on July 12, 1986. The contest required the drive to land on a 40-yd wide fairway.

Liam Higgins (Ireland) drove a Spalding Top Flite ball 634.1 yd on an airport runway at Baldonnel Military Airport, Dublin, Ireland, Sept 25, 1984.

The longest on a sea-level course is 515 yd by Michael Hoke Austin (b Feb 17, 1910) of Los Angeles, in the US National Seniors Open Championship at Las Vegas, Nev, Sept 25, 1974. Aided by an estimated 35-mph tailwind, the 6-ft-2-in 210-lb golfer drove the ball on the fly to within a yard of the green on the par-4, 450-yd 5th hole of the Winterwood Course. The ball rolled 65 yd past the flagstick.

Arthur Lynskey claimed a drive of 200 yd out and 2 miles down off Pikes Peak, Colo, (14,110 ft) June 28, 1968.

HIGH DRIVE: Saul Ballesteros, 22, of Chicago, on a climb of Mt McKinley, Alaska, took time out to tee up and with a 1-iron drove a ball from 20,320 ft up off the south face.

LONGEST DRIVE: With a 406-yd drive in an official PGA driving contest, Jack L. Hamm of Denver, Colo, set a new world record on July 12, 1986. He had a slight wind against him on a clear day at 5,200-ft altitude; the contest was on a 40-ft wide fairway.

The longest drive by a woman was 531 yd by Helen Dobson at RAF Honington, Eng, Oct 31, 1987.

A drive of 2,640 yd (1½ miles) across ice was achieved by an Australian meteorologist named Nils Lied at Mawson Base, Antarctica, in 1962. On the moon, the energy expended on a mundane 300-yd drive would achieve, craters permitting, a distance of a mile.

Biggest Winning Margin

The greatest margin of victory in a major tournament is 21 strokes by Jerry Pate (b Sept 15, 1953) (US) in the Colombian Open with 262 on Dec 10–13, 1981.

Cecilia Leitch won the Canadian Ladies Open Championship in 1921 by the highest margin for a major title, 17 up and 15 to play.

Most Tournament Wins

The record for winning tournaments in a single season is 18 (plus one unofficial), including a record 11 consecutively, by Byron Nelson (b Feb 4, 1912) (US), March 8–Aug 4, 1945.

Sam Snead has won 84 official US PGA tour events to Dec 1979, and has been credited with a total 134 tournament victories since 1934.

Kathy Whitworth (b Sept 27, 1939) (US) topped this with her 88th LPGA victory through 1985, her 23rd year on the tour. Mickey Wright (US) won a record 13 tournaments in one year, 1963.

Jack Nicklaus (US) is the only golfer who has won all five major titles (British Open, US Open, Masters, PGA and US Amateur) twice, while setting a record total of 20 major tournament victories (1959–86). His remarkable record in the US Open is 4 firsts, 8 seconds and 2 thirds. Nicklaus has accumulated 71 PGA tournament wins in all.

In 1930 Bobby Jones achieved a unique "Grand Slam" of the US and British Open and British and US Amateur titles.

Longest Putt

The longest recorded holed putt in a major tournament was one of 86 ft on the vast 13th green at the Augusta National, Ga, by Cary Middlecoff (b Jan 1921) in the 1955 Masters Tournament.

Bobby Jones was reputed to have holed a putt in excess of 100 ft on the 5th green in the first round of the 1927 British Open at St Andrews, Scotland.

Bob Cook (US) sank a putt measured at 140 ft 2¾ in on the 18th at St Andrews, Scotland, in the International Fourball Pro-Am Tournament on Oct. 1, 1976.

Highest Earnings

The greatest amount ever won in official US PGA golf prizes is $4,976,980 by Jack Nicklaus through 1987.

The record for a year in US PGA events is $925,941 by Curtis Strange (b Jan 20, 1955) in 1987. Worldwide earnings of over $1 million in 1 year were reported by Greg Norman (Aust) in 1986.

The highest LPGA career earnings by a woman is $2,426,320 by Pat Bradley (b Mar 24, 1951) through 1987. In 1986 she set a season record of $492,021, beating Nancy Lopez' 1985 winnings of $416,472.

HIGHEST EARNINGS: Besides winning 20 major tournaments (71 in all) for a record, Jack Nicklaus (right) has earned $4,976,980 through 1987 in prize money. Nicklaus is the only golfer who has won all 5 major titles twice. *(E. D. Lacey)* Arnold Palmer (above) prepares to putt as his many followers, known as Arnie's Army, look on. Palmer won the Masters 4 times and played on 6 winning teams in World Cup play. He was the first golfer to reach $1 million in career earnings.

Marathon Golf

The most holes played on foot in a week (168 hours) is 1,128 by Steve Hylton at the Mason Rudolph Golf Club (6,060 yd), Clarksville, Tenn, Aug 25–31, 1980. The most holes in 24 hours is 401 by Ian Colston, 35, at Bendigo Golf Club, Victoria, Aust, par 73 (6,061 yd) on Nov 27–28, 1971.

Using golf carts for transport, Charles Stock played 783 holes in 24 hours at Arcadia Country Club in Lyndhurst, Ohio, July 20, 1987. Terry Zachary played 391 holes in 12 hours on the 6,706-yd course at Connaught Golf Club, Alberta, Canada on June 16, 1986. Dr. R. C. "Dick" Hardison, aged 61, played 236 holes under USGA rules in 12

MOST WINS IN MAJOR TOURNAMENTS			
US Open	Willie Anderson (1880–1910)	4	1901–03–04–05
	Robert Tyre Jones, Jr (1902–71)	4	1923–26–29–30
	W. Ben Hogan (b Aug 13, 1912)	4	1948–50–51–53
	Jack William Nicklaus (b Jan 21, 1940)	4	1962–67–72–80
US Amateur	Robert Tyre Jones, Jr	5	1924–25–27–28–30
British Open	Harry Vardon (1870–1937)	6	1896–98–99, 1903–11–14
British Amateur	John Ball (1861–1940)	8	1888–90–92–94–99, 1907–10–12
PGA Championship (US)	Walter C. Hagen (1892–1969)	5	1921–24–25–26–27
	Jack W. Nicklaus	5	1963–71–73–75–80
Masters Championship (US)	Jack W. Nicklaus	6	1963–65–66–72–75–86
US Women's Open	Elizabeth (Betsy) Earle-Rawls (b May 4, 1928)	4	1951–53–57–60
	"Mickey" Wright (b Feb 14, 1935)	4	1958–59–61–64
US Women's Amateur	Mrs Glenna Vare (*née* Collett) (b June 20, 1903)	6	1922–25–28–29–30–35

hours at Sea Mountain GC, Punaluu, Hawaii, July 31, 1984, maintaining an average score of 76 per round, with an average time per hole of 3.05 min. His best round was a 68, achieved in 49 min 58 sec, including a second nine of 30 in 24 min 28 sec. He used seven fore caddies and 26 electric golf carts, which he drove himself.

Largest Tournament

The Volkswagen Grand Prix Open Amateur Championship (UK) attracted a record 321,778 (206,820 men and 114,958 women) competitors in 1984.

US Open

This championship was inaugurated in 1895. The lowest 72-hole aggregate is 272 (63, 71, 70, 68) by Jack Nicklaus (b Jan 21, 1940) on the Lower Course (7,015 yd) at Baltusrol Golf Club, Springfield, NJ, June 12–15, 1980. The lowest score for 18 holes is 63 by Johnny Miller (b Apr 29, 1947) of Calif on the 6,921-yd, par-71 Oakmont, Pa, course on June 17, 1973, and Jack Nicklaus and Tom Weiskopf (b Nov 9, 1942), both on June 12, 1980.

The longest delayed result in any national open championship occurred in the 1931 US Open at Toledo, Ohio. George von Elm (1901–61) and Bill Burke (1902–72) tied at 292, then tied the first replay at 149. Burke won the second replay by a single stroke after 72 extra holes.

US Masters

The lowest score in the US Masters (instituted at the 6,980-yd Augusta National Golf Course, Ga, in 1934) was 271 by Jack Nicklaus in 1965 and Raymond Floyd (b Sept 4, 1942) in 1976. Jack Nicklaus has won most often—6 times. The lowest round is 63 by Nick Price (b Jan 28, 1957) (Zimbabwe) in 1986. The oldest champion was Jack Nicklaus at 46 years 114 days in 1986, and the youngest was Severiano Ballesteros (Spain) aged 23 years 4 days in 1980.

Fastest Rounds

With such variations in lengths of courses, speed records, even for rounds under par, are of little comparative value. Rick Baker completed 18 holes (6,142 yd) in 25 min 48.47 sec at Surfer's Paradise, Queensland, Australia, Sept 4, 1982, but this test permitted striking the ball while it was still moving. The record for a still ball is: James Carvill (Ireland) (b Oct 13, 1965) played a round at Warrenpoint Golf Club, Co Down, Ire, in 27 min 9 sec on Jun 18, 1987.

Seventy-seven players completed the 18-hole 6,502 yd Kern City course, Calif, in 10 min 30 sec on Aug 24, 1984 using only one ball. They scored 80!

Most Balls Hit in One Hour

The most balls driven in one hour, over 100 yds and into a target area, is 1,064 (from 1,290 attempts) by David Morris at Abergele Golf Club, Clwyd, Wales, May 21, 1988.

Biggest Prize Putt

Jack Nicklaus' total earnings went up by $240,000 when he sank an 8-foot putt on the 18th green of the Desert Highlands course in Scottsdale, Ariz, on Nov 25, 1984 in a "Skins" match against Arnold Palmer, Gary Player and Tom Watson. All three of his opponents missed their birdie putts from farther distances and Nicklaus won the accumulated prize money.

Richest Prize

The greatest first-place money was $1,000,000 won by Ian Woosman (Wales) on Dec 6, 1987 at Sun City, Bophuthatswana, S Africa.

Highest Altitude

Saul Ballesteros of Chicago drove 3 golf balls off a tee on the south face near the summit of Mt McKinley, Alaska, 20,320 ft above sea level on May 31, 1987, using a 1-iron. It matched a feat by Timothy J. Ayers (US) on May 23, 1984.

Longest Span

Jacqueline Ann Mercer (*née* Smith) (b Apr 5, 1929) won her first

LEADING PROS: Severiano Ballesteros (Spain) (above left) began winning major tournaments in 1979 when he was victorious in the British Open. Then he won the Masters in 1980 and 1983, and the British Open again in 1984. Here he is preparing to enter the water to retrieve an errant shot. *(Phil Sheldon)* Nancy Lopez (above) in 1985 set a season record by winning $416,472, only to be beaten in 1986 by Pat Bradley (left) who earned $489,749 in tournament play. Bradley shot a record 28 for 9 holes in 1984. *(Lopez photo by All-Sport; Bradley photo LPGA by SPORTSELL)*

South African title at Humewood GC, Port Elizabeth, in 1948, and her fourth title at Port Elizabeth GC on May 4, 1979, 31 years later.

British Open

The Open Championship was inaugurated in 1860 at Prestwick, Strathclyde, Scotland. The lowest score for 9 holes is 28 by Denis Durnian (b June 30, 1950) at Royal Birdale, Southport, Eng, in the second round on July 15, 1983.

The lowest scoring round in the Open itself is 63 by Mark Hayes (US, b July 12, 1949) at Turnberry, Strathclyde, Scotland, in the second round on July 7, 1977, and by Isao Aoki (Japan) (b Aug 31, 1942) in the third round at Muirfield, July 19, 1980. Greg Norman (b Feb 10, 1955) (Aust) equaled the record of 63 at Turnberry, July 18, 1986. Henry Cotton (b Jan 26, 1907) (GB) at Royal St George's, Sandwich, Kent, England, completed the first 36 holes in 132 (67 + 65) on June 27, 1934.

The lowest 72-hole aggregate is 268 (68, 70, 65, 65) by Tom Watson (US) (b Sept 4, 1949) at Turnberry, Scotland, ending on July 9, 1977.

Youngest and Oldest Champions

The youngest winner of the British Open was Tom Morris, Jr (1851–75) at Prestwick, Ayrshire, Scotland, in 1868, aged 17 years 249 days. The oldest British Open champion was "Old Tom" Morris (1821–1908) who was aged 46 years 99 days when he won in 1867. In modern times, the oldest was 1967 champion Roberto de Vicenzo (Argentina), when aged 44 years 93 days.

The oldest US Amateur Champion was Jack Westland (b Dec 14, 1904) at Seattle, Wash, on Aug 23, 1952, aged 47 years 253 days. The oldest US Open champion was Raymond Floyd at 43 years 284 days on June 15, 1986. Isabella "Belle" Robertson (b Apr 11, 1936) won the 1986 Scottish Women's Championship aged 50 years 43 days.

US PGA Championship

The Professional Golfers' Association championship was first held in 1916 as a match play tournament but since 1958 it has been contested over 72 holes of stroke play. It has been won a record five times by Walter Hagen between 1921 and 1927, and Jack Nicklaus between 1963 and 1980. The oldest champion was Julius Boros at 48 years 18 days in 1968 and the youngest was Gene Sarazen aged 20 years 5 months 20 days in 1922. Since 1958 the greatest margin of victory has been the seven-stroke lead by Nicklaus in 1980. The lowest aggregate was 271 by Bobby Nichols at Columbus, Ohio in 1964, and the lowest round was 63 by Bruce Crampton in 1975, Ray Floyd in 1982, and Gary Player in 1984. The lowest score for 36 holes has been 131 by Hal Sutton (65, 66) in 1983. The 54-hole mark is 202 (69, 66, 67) by Raymond Floyd in 1969.

US Women's Open

This tournament was first held in 1946, and currently is played over 72 holes of stroke play. Betsy Rawls won a record four times between 1951 and 1960, and this was equalled by Mickey Wright between 1958 and 1964. The oldest champion was Fay Crocker (Uru) at 40

OUTSIDE CHOICE: Laura Davies was the first Briton to win the US Women's Open since the tournament began, when she took the 1987 title. *(All-Sport)*

years 11 months in 1955, while the youngest was Catherine Lacoste (France) at 22 years 5 days in 1967, when she became the only amateur player to win the title. The greatest margin of victory was by Babe Didrikson Zaharias who beat Betty Hicks by 12 strokes in 1954. The lowest aggregate score has been 280 (70, 70, 68, 72) by Amy Alcott in 1980, and the lowest round was 65 by Sally Little in 1978. The record for 36 holes is 139 by Carol Mann and Donna Caponi in 1970, the latter going on to a 54-hole score of 210.

US Amateur

Initially held in the same week and at the same venue as the first US Open in 1895. Bobby Jones won a record five times between 1924 and 1930, having first qualified for the tournament in 1916, aged 14 yr 5½ months, the youngest ever to do so. The oldest player to win the title was Jack Westland, aged 47 years 8 months 9 days in 1952, while the youngest was Robert Gardner at 19 years 5 months in 1909. (Three years later, in 1912, Gardner broke the world pole vault record becoming the first to clear 13 ft.)

US Women's Amateur Championship

Instituted in Nov 1895, and currently 36 final holes of match play after 36 qualifying holes of stroke play. Glenna Collett Vare won a record 6 titles between 1922 and 1935. The oldest champion was Dorothy Campbell-Hurd (GB) aged 41 years 4 months when winning her third title in 1924, and the youngest was Laura Baugh at 16 years 2 months 21 days in 1971. Margaret Curtis beat her sister, Harriot, in the 1907 final—they later presented the Curtis Cup for competition between the US and GB.

Most Shots One Hole

The highest number of strokes taken at a single hole in a major tournament was achieved in the inaugural (British) Open Championship at Prestwick, Scotland, in 1860, when an unnamed player took

21. In the 1938 US Open, Ray Ainsley achieved instant fame when he took 19 strokes at the par-4 16th hole. Most of them were in an attempt to hit the ball out of a fast-moving brook. Hans Merrell of Mogadore, Ohio, took 19 strokes on the par-3, 222-yd 16th during the Bing Crosby tournament at Cypress Point Club, Del Monte, Calif, on Jan 17, 1959. At Biarritz, France in 1888 it was reported that Chevalier von Cittern took 316 for 18 holes, thus averaging 17.55 strokes per hole.

The story to top them all concerns a lady player in the qualifying round of a tournament in Shawnee-on-Delaware, Pa in the early part of the century. Her card showed she took 166 strokes for the short 130-yd 16th hole. Her tee shot landed and floated in a nearby river, and, with her meticulous husband, she set out in a boat and eventually beached the ball 1½ mi downstream. From there she had to play through a forest until finally she holed the ball. A. J. Lewis, playing at Peacehaven, Sussex, Eng, in 1890 had 156 putts on one green without holing the ball.

Ryder Cup

The biennial Ryder Cup (instituted 1927) professional match between the US and GB (Europe since 1979) has been won by the US 21½–5½. William Earl "Billy" Casper (b San Diego, Calif, June 24, 1931) has the record of winning most matches, with 20 won out of 37 (1961–75). Neil Cales (GB) played in a record 40 matches (1961–77).

In 1987, Ian Woosnam (Wales) (b 1958) 5 ft 4½ in, played a starring role against the US at Muirfield Village, Ohio, as GB won.

HOLES-IN-ONE

Golf Digest was notified in 1987 of 41,406 holes-in-one.

Longest

The longest straight hole shot in one is the 10th hole (447 yd) at Miracle Hills GC, Omaha, Neb. Robert Mitera achieved a hole-in-one there on Oct 7, 1965. Mitera, aged 21 and 5 ft 6 in tall, weighed 165 lb. A two-handicap player, he normally drove 245 yd. A 50-mph gust carried his shot over a 290-yd drop-off. The group in front testified to the remaining distance.

The women's record is 393 yd by Marie Robie of Wollaston, Mass, on the first hole of the Furnace Brook GC, Sept 4, 1949.

The longest dogleg achieved in one is the 480-yd 5th hole at Hope CC, Ark, by Larry Bruce on Nov 15, 1962.

Most Eagles in One Round

Keith Kollmeyer had four 3's on par-5 holes in one round at the Waialae Country Club, Honolulu, Hawaii, on June 11, 1988, tying the 1981 record set by Ken Harrington at the Silver Lake C.C. in Cuyahoga Falls, O.

Consecutive

There is no recorded instance of a golfer performing three consecutive holes-in-one, but there are at least 16 cases of "aces" being achieved in two consecutive holes, of which the greatest was Norman L. Manley's unique "double albatross" on two par-4 holes (330-yd 7th and 290-yd 8th) on the Del Valle CC course, Saugus, Calif, on Sept 2, 1964.

The first woman ever to card consecutive aces is Sue Prell, on the 13th and 14th holes at Chatswood GC, Sydney, Australia, on May 29, 1977.

The closest recorded instances of a golfer getting 3 consecutive holes-in-one were by the Rev Harold Snider (b July 4, 1900) who aced the 8th, 13th and 14th holes of the par-3 Ironwood course in Phoenix, Ariz, on June 9, 1976, and the late Dr Joseph Boydstone on the 3rd, 4th and 9th at Bakersfield GC, Calif on Oct 10, 1962.

Most Aces

The most aces in one year is 33 by Scott Palmer (b Nov 22, 1958) June 5, 1983–May 31, 1984, all on holes between 130 and 350 yd in length in San Diego County, Calif. He also made 4 aces in 4 consecutive rounds, Oct 9–12, 1983.

The greatest number of holes-in-one reported in a career is 97, also by Scott Palmer (see above) through June 1988. Of these aces, 26 were shot on short courses, but none were on holes of less than 100 yd.

Douglas Porteous, 28, aced 4 holes over 39 consecutive holes—the 3rd and 6th on Sept 26, and the 5th on Sept 28 at Ruchill GC, Glasgow, Scotland, and the 6th at the Clydebank and District GC Course on Sept 30, 1974. Robert Taylor holed the 188-yd 16th hole at Hunstanton, Norfolk, England, on three successive days—May 31, June 1 and 2, 1974. On May 12, 1984, Joe Lucius of Tiffin, Ohio, aced for the 13th time the par-3, 141-yd 15th hole at the Mohawk Golf Club. Lucius has 10 aces for the 10th hole on the same course, and 31 aces in all.

Youngest and Oldest

The youngest golfer recorded to have shot a hole-in-one was Scott Statler of Greensburg, Pa, now of Los Alamitos, Calif. At the age of 4 years 172 days on July 30, 1962, he shot an ace on hole 7 of Statler's Par 3 Golf Course, Greensburg, Pa. *Golf Digest* credits Tommy Moore (6 yrs 1 month 7 days) of Hagerstown, Md with being the youngest for an ace he shot on a 145-yd hole in 1969.

The oldest golfer to have performed the feat is Otto Bucher (Switz) (b May 12, 1885) aged 99 years 244 days on Jan 13, 1985 when he aced the 130-yd 12th hole at La Manga GC, Spain.

The oldest woman to score an ace is Erna Ross, aged 95 years 257 days, who holed-in-one on the 112-yd 17th hole of the Everglades Club, Palm Beach, Fla, on May 25, 1986.

The oldest player to score his age is C. Arthur Thompson (1869–1975) of Victoria, BC, Canada, who scored 103 on the Uplands course of 6,215 yd when age 103 in 1973.

GYMNASTICS

Earliest References

Tumbling and similar exercises were performed *c.* 2600 BC as religious rituals in China, but it was the Greeks who coined the word gymnastics. A primitive form was practiced in the ancient Olympic Games, but it was not until Johann Friedrich Simon began to teach at Basedow's Gymnasium in Dessau, Germany, in 1776 that the foundations of the modern sport were laid. The first national federation was formed in Germany in 1860 and the International Gymnastics Federation was founded in Liège, Belgium in 1881. The sport was included at the first modern Olympic Games at Athens in 1896.

Current events for men are: floor exercises, horse vault, rings, pommel horse, parallel bars and horizontal bar, while for women they are: floor exercises, horse vault, asymmetrical bars, and balance beam.

World Championships

In Olympic years, the Olympic title is the World Championship title.

The greatest number of individual titles won by a man in the World Championships (including 6 Olympics) is 10 by Boris Shakhlin (USSR) between 1954 and 1964. He was also on three winning teams. The women's record is 12 individual wins and 5 team titles by Larissa Semyonovna Latynina (b Dec 27, 1934, retired 1966) of the USSR, between 1956 and 1964, including Olympics. She has the most medals, 33, of which 18 are Olympic medals. Japan has won the men's team title a record 10 times (including 5 Olympics) between 1960 and 1978 and the USSR the women's team title on 17 occasions (including 8 Olympics) out of 20 since 1952.

American Cup Titles

Olympic gold medalist Mary Lou Retton (b 1968) of Fairmont, W Va won her first American Cup in 1983 in NYC and has not relinquished the title since that competition. She is the only female gymnast to hold the title for three straight years. US gymnast Kurt Thomas won the title three years in a row from 1978 to 1980.

World Cup Titles

Gymnasts to have won two World Cup (inst 1975) overall titles are three men, Nikolai Andrianov (USSR), Aleksandr Ditiatin (USSR) and Li Ning (China) (b Sept 8, 1963) and one woman Maria Filatova (USSR) (b July 19, 1961).

Modern Rhythmic Gymnastics

This recent addition to the female side of the sport incorporates exercises with different hand-held apparatus, including ribbons, balls, ropes, hoops and Indian clubs. The most overall titles won in world championships is 3 by Maria Gigova (Bulgaria) in 1969, 71, and 73 (shared), while the most individual apparatus titles is 9 by Gigova and

A PERFECT "10": Nadia Comaneci (Romania) (left and right above) was 14 years old when she made Olympic history as the first gymnast ever to be awarded a perfect score. Her unprecedented feat came during the 1976 Olympics in Montreal. She went on to earn 6 more 10's for a remarkable total of 7 flawless routines (4 on uneven parallel bars and 3 on the balance beam).

BEST ALL-AROUND OLYMPIC GYMNAST: Mary Lou Retton (US) won the gold medal in this category, silver medal in the vault and bronze medal in the uneven parallel bars in the 1984 Games.

Galina Shugurova (USSR). The latter has also won a record total of 14 medals. This category of the sport was included in the Olympic Games for the first time in 1984.

Wall Press (Samson's Chair)

Sitting unsupported, back 90° flat against a wall, looks simple, but the longest anyone can stay in that position (see p. 489) is 1 hour, 16 min, 12 sec, a record set by Kevin DeWitt of Kennewick, Wash July 31, 1986.

Youngest International Competitors

Pasakevi "Voula" Kouna (b Dec 6, 1971) was aged 9 years 299 days at the start of the Balkan Games at Serres, Greece on Oct 1, 1981, when she represented Greece. Olga Bicherova (b Oct 26, 1966) won the women's world title at 15 years 33 days in Nov 1981. The youngest men's champion was Dmitri Belozerchev (USSR) at 16 years 315 days at Budapest, Hungary in 1983.

Chinning the Bar

The greatest number of continuous chin-ups (from a dead hang position) is 170 by Lee Chin Yong (b Aug 15, 1925) at Backyon Gymnasium, Seoul, S Korea on May 10, 1983. Robert Chisnall (b Dec 9, 1952) performed 22 one-arm (his right) chin-ups, from a ring, 18 two-finger chins and 12 one-finger chins, from a nylon strap on Dec 3, 1982 at Queen's Univ, Kingston, Ont, Canada.

PUSH-UP CHAMPION: Paul Lynch of London holds the record for one-arm push-ups with 3,857 in 5 hours, set on June 6, 1987. He also set a new record for 2-arm push-ups (correct position shown here) at 32,573 in 24 hours in Sept 1987. *(Jon Arns)*

Push-Ups

Paul Lynch (GB) did 32,573 push-ups in 24 hours at Bedford Hall, London, Sept 12–13, 1987, and also holds the record for 3,857 one-arm push-ups in 5 hours in London's Guinness World of Records, June 6, 1987.

John Decker did 5,010 finger-tip push-ups in 5 hours at a department store in Manchester, Eng, June 19, 1987.

Harry Lee Welch, Jr did 100 one-finger consecutive push-ups in Durham, NC on Mar 31, 1985.

ROPE JUMPING

The longest recorded rope-jumping marathon (with 5-min rest break after each hour) was one of 13 hours 30 min 49 sec by Edwin Langerwij (b Jan 19, 1967) at Reismalen, The Netherlands on May 16, 1987.

Other rope-jumping records made without a break and with no faults:

Most turns in 1 minute	418	Tyrone Krohn	Middletown (NY) HS	July 10, 1984
Most turns in 10 seconds	128	Albert Rayner	Birmingham, Eng	Nov 19, 1982
Most turns in 1 hour	13,160	Robert R. Commers	Connellsville, Pa	Mar 19, 1988
Most doubles (with cross)	2,110	Sean Birch	Kerry, Ireland	Oct 19, 1986
Double turns	10,133	Katsumi Suzuki (Japan)	Saitama	Sept 29, 1979
Treble turns	381	Katsumi Suzuki (Japan)	Saitama	May 29, 1975
Quadruple turns	51	Katsumi Suzuki (Japan)	Saitama	May 29, 1975
Quintuple turns	6	Hideyuki Tateda (Japan)	Aomori	June 19, 1982
Duration	1,264 miles	Tom Morris (Aust)	Brisbane-Cairns	1963
Most on a single rope (minimum 12 turns obligatory)	181	(165-ft rope)	Greeley, Colo.	June 28, 1988
Most turns on single rope (team of 90)	163	Students at Nishigoshi Higashi Elementary School	Kumamoto, Japan	Feb 27, 1987
On a tightrope (consecutive)	58	Bryan Andrew (*née* Dewhurst)	TROS TV, The Netherlands	Aug 6, 1981
Skip-running	10 mi in 76 min 33 sec	Ashrita Furman (US)	Zurich, Switz	May 26, 1987

ROPE-SKIPPERS GALORE: A record-breaking 181 rope-jumpers set a mark for most on a single rope. The 181 did the obligatory 12 turns on a 165-ft rope on June 28, 1988 at the International Rope Skipping Organization Championships at Greeley, Colo.

SKIP-RUNNING: Ashrita Furman set another world record when he ran 10 miles like this in 76 min 33 sec in May 1987, to add to his somersaults, pogo stick, and jumping jacks records. He now has 10 in all. (*See p. 490*)

HUMAN SUSPENSION BRIDGE: 300 gymnasts of NSA constructed this bridge in Worcester, Mass on July 10, 1988, and held the position for over 45 sec. The human ladder towers were 25 ft high and the bridge "cables" were 7 ft off the floor at the lowest point. (*Nichiren Shoshu Soka Gakkai of America*)

LARGEST AEROBIC DISPLAY: At the annual Czechoslovakian Spartakiad at the Strahov Stadium in Prague, the field is marked off for 13,284 gymnasts to perform simultaneously. Before as many as 200,000 spectators per day, the display goes on for 4 days with a total of about 180,000 participants.

Chung Kwun Ying (Hong Kong) did 2,750 handstand push-ups at Government City Hall, Hong Kong, on May 18, 1986. In one hour he did 1,985.

In one year (1985) Adam Parsons, a retired Lt Col in the USAF, did 1,293,850 documented push-ups in Akron, Ohio.

Jumping Jacks

The greatest number of side-straddle hops is 104,538 by Louis Scripa, Jr, in Sacramento, Calif, Dec 2, 1986. In 12 hours 23 min the record is 45,027 by Ashrita Furman on Dec 4, 1986, in San Francisco.

Parallel Bar Dips

Chris Peverell performed 1,861 parallel bar dips in 1 hour on Feb 8, 1988 at Clacton, Essex, Eng.

Somersaults

Ashrita Furman (US) performed 8,341 forward rolls over 12 miles 390 yards in 10½ hours on Apr 30, 1986, performing from Lexington to Charlestown (Boston), Mass. Shigeru Iwasaki (b 1960) backwards somersaulted over 50 m (54.68 yd) in 10.8 sec in Tokyo, March 30, 1980.

Sit-Ups and Leg Raises

Lou Scripa, Jr of Sacramento, Calif did 100,003 sit-ups in 50 hours, Aug 5–7, 1985. During the first 24 hours he did 60,405. These were done with his legs straight, with no weights or anyone holding his legs.

Tim Kides of W New York, NJ, set a record for leg raises—25,000 in 11 hours 57 min 15 sec on Oct 14, 1986.

Pommel Horse

Lee Thomas (GB) did 75 consecutive double circles on BBC television on Dec 12, 1985.

Rope Jumps in One Hour

Robert R. Commers (b May 15, 1950) of Connellsville, Pa, set a new record by rope jumping 13,160 revolutions with zero faults in one hour on Mar 19, 1988, beating the old record by 664 jumps.

HARNESS RACING

Origins

Trotting races were held in Valkenburg, Netherlands, in 1554. In England the trotting gait (the simultaneous use of the diagonally opposite legs) was known in the 16th century. The sulky first appeared in harness racing in 1829. Pacers thrust out their fore and hind legs simultaneously on one side.

Greatest Winnings

The greatest award won by any harness horse is the $3,225,653 won by the pacer "Nihilator," who was victorious in 35 of 38 races, 1984–85. He also holds the single season winnings record with $1,864,286 in 1985.

The greatest amount won by a trotting horse is $2,753,666 by "Ideal du Gazeau" (France) to July 23, 1983.

The largest purse ever was $2,161,000 for the Woodrow Wilson 2-year-olds race over 1 mi at Meadowlands, NJ, on Aug 16, 1984, of which a record $1,080,500 went to the winner "Nihilator" driven by Billy O'Donnell (b May 4, 1948).

Highest Prices

The highest price ever paid for a pacer is for "Nihilator," who was syndicated for $19.2 million in 1984, topping the record of $10 million set by his father, "Niatross," in 1979.

The highest price paid for a trotter is $5.25 million for "Mystic Park" by Lana Lobell Farms from Allen, Gerald and Irving Wechter of NY and Robert Lester of Florida, announced on July 13, 1982.

Most Successful Driver

The most successful sulky driver in North America has been Herve Filion (Canada) (b Quebec, Feb 1, 1940) who achieved 10,395 wins and earnings of more than $56 million from the start of his career, 1953, through the 1987 season. A fellow Canadian, Michel Lachance, broke Filion's 1974 season record of 637 victories by winning 770 races in 1986. Filion won the North American championship for the 13th time in 1982. The greatest earnings in a year is $10,207,372 by Billy O'Donnell, who won 419 races in 1985.

TROTTING CHAMP: "Mack Lobell," trained by Chuck Sylvester, driven by John D. Campbell, set the mile record at 1 min 52 sec at Springfield, Ill, on Aug 21, 1987. *(U.S. Trotting Assoc.)*

HARNESS RACING RECORDS AGAINST TIME

TROTTING			
Time Trial (mile track)	1:53.4	"Prakas" (driver William O'Donnell) (Can) at Du Quoin, Ill	Aug 31, 1985
Race Record (mile)	1:52	"Mack Lobell" (driver John D. Campbell) (US) at Springfield, Ill	Aug 21, 1987
PACING			
Time Trial (mile track)	1:49.2	"Niatross" (driver, Clint Galbraith) (US) at Lexington, Ky	Oct 1, 1980
Race Record (mile)	1:49.6	"Nihilator" (driver, William O'Donnell) (Can) at East Rutherford, NJ	Aug 3, 1985

HOCKEY

Origins

There is pictorial evidence of a hockey-like game (Kalv) being played on ice in The Netherlands in the early 16th century. The game probably was first played in North America on Dec 25, 1855, at Kingston, Ontario, Canada, but Halifax also lays claim to priority.

The International Ice Hockey Federation was founded in 1908. The National Hockey League was inaugurated in 1917. The World Hockey Association was formed in 1971 and disbanded in 1979 when 4 of its teams joined the NHL.

World Championships and Olympic Games

World Championships were first held for amateurs in 1920 in conjunction with the Olympic Games, which were also considered as World Championships up to 1968. From 1977 the World Championships have been open to professionals. The USSR has won 20 world titles since 1954, including the Olympic titles of 1956, 64, 68, 72, 76, 84 and 88. Canada won 19 titles between 1920 and 1961, including 6 Olympic titles (1920, 24, 28, 32, 48 and 52). The longest Olympic career is that of Richard Torriani (b Oct 1, 1911) (Switzerland) from 1928 to 1948. The most gold medals won by any player is 3; this was achieved by 4 USSR players in the 1964, 68 and 72 Games—Vitaliy Davidov, Aleksandr Ragulin, Anatoliy Firssov and Viktor Kuzkin. Goalie Vladimir Tretiak (USSR) won 3 golds (1972, 1976 and 1984) as well as a silver in 1980.

Longest Season

The only man ever to play 82 games in a 78-game season is Ross Lonsberry. He began the 1971–72 season with the Los Angeles Kings where he played 50 games. Then, in January, he was traded to the Philadelphia Flyers (who had played only 46 games at the time) where he finished out the season (32 more games).

Brad Marsh (b Mar 31, 1958) played 83 games (17 with Calgary and 66 with Philadelphia) during an 80-game season in 1981–82.

Longest Career

Gordie Howe (b March 31, 1928, Floral, Saskatchewan, Canada) skated 25 years for the Detroit Red Wings from 1946–47 through the 1970–71 season, playing in a total of 1,687 NHL regular-season games.

After leaving the Red Wings, he ended a 2-year retirement to skate with his two sons as teammates and played for 6 more seasons with the Houston Aeros and the New England Whalers of the World Hockey Association, participating in 497 games.

With the incorporation of the (now Hartford) Whalers into the NHL for the 1979–80 season, Gordie Howe skated in all 80 regular season games (for a record total of 1,767) in his record 26th year in that league. The remarkable 52-year-old grandfather was again selected as an NHL all-star, more times than any other player. Including Howe's 157 NHL playoff appearances, he skated in 2,421 "major league" games in all.

Fastest Scoring

Toronto scored 8 goals against the NY Americans in 4 min 52 sec on March 19, 1938.

The St. Louis Blues were protecting a 6–4 lead in an NHL game against the Bruins in Boston on Dec 19, 1987 when Ken Linseman scored for the Bruins with 10 sec left. As the Blues' Doug Gilmour took to the ensuing center-ice face-off circle, the Bruins kept their goalie on the bench, hoping for an added advantage. But Gilmour slapped the face-off toward the Bruin goal. It went in, giving the two teams goals just 2 sec apart, faster than any pair of goals in NHL history.

The fastest goal ever scored from the opening whistle came at 5 sec of the first period. This occurred twice, most recently by Bryan Trottier of the NY Islanders vs Boston Bruins on Mar 22, 1984. The previous time was by Doug Smail of the Winnipeg Jets against St Louis on Dec 20, 1981. Claude Provost of the Canadiens scored a goal against Boston after 4 sec of the opening of the second period on Nov 9, 1957.

The Boston Bruins set an NHL record with three goals in a span of 20 sec against the Vancouver Canucks on Feb 25, 1971. Left winger John Bucyk began the record-breaking feat with a goal at the 4 min 50 sec mark of the third period. Center Ed Westfall scored 12 sec later at 5 min 2 sec, while defenseman Ted Green rounded out the surge with a goal at the 5 min 10 sec mark.

The fastest scoring record is held by Bill Mosienko (Chicago) who scored 3 goals in 21 sec against the NY Rangers on March 23, 1952. In a playoff game Pat LaFontaine of the NY Islanders scored 2 goals in 22 sec vs Edmonton Oilers, May 19, 1984.

Gus Bodnar (Toronto Maple Leafs) scored a goal against the NY Rangers at 15 sec of the first period of *his first NHL game* on Oct 30, 1943. Later in his career, while with Chicago, Bodnar again entered the record book when he assisted on all 3 of Bill Mosienko's quick goals.

MOST STANLEY CUP GOALS: Mike Bossy, right wing of the NY Islanders, has the most goals (85) in Stanley Cup play. ►

GOAL ORIENTED: Wayne Gretzky showed he was no flash-in-the-pan when, in 1982, he began breaking assist and most-points records and also set a goal-scoring record by netting 92 goals, including a record 10 hat tricks. In 1984, he scored 10 hat tricks again (total of 41 to the end of the 1987 season) and in 1986, a point record of 215 and an assist record of 163 in a season. *(Edmonton Oilers)* ▼

LONGEST CAREER: Gordie Howe played in the NHL for 26 seasons and collected career records for most games (1,767), goals (801), and points (1,850), was selected as an all-star a record 21 times, and also collected 500 stitches in his face. ▼

Several fast scoring feats have been reported from non-NHL competition: Kim D. Miles scored in 3 sec for Univ of Guelph vs Univ of W Ontario on Feb 11, 1975; Steve D'Innocenzo scored 3 goals in 12 sec for Holliston vs Westwood in a high school game in Mass on Jan 9, 1982; Clifford "Fido" Purpur, 38, scored 4 goals in 25 sec for the Grand Forks Amerks vs Winnipeg All Stars in Grand Forks, ND, on Jan 29, 1950. In team play, the Skara Ishockeyclubb, Sweden, scored 3 goals in 11 sec against Orebro IK at Skara on Oct 18, 1981; the Vernon Cougars scored 5 goals in 56 sec against Salmon Arm Aces at Vernon, BC, Canada, on Aug 6, 1982; the Kamloops Knights of Columbus scored 7 goals in 2 min 22 sec vs Prince George Vikings on Jan 25, 1980.

MVP Most Times

Wayne Gretzky (b Jan 26, 1961) of the Edmonton Oilers won the Hart Trophy, the most valuable player of the NHL, for the 8th consecutive year in 1987, at age 26. No player in any North American major league sport had been honored so often.

His latest feat is surpassing Gordie Howe's lifetime assist record of 1,049. Gretzky needed only 9 years to achieve what Howe did in 26.

Then in August 1988 Gretzky made his biggest news of all: He was traded to the Los Angeles Kings.

Team Scoring

The greatest number of goals recorded in a World Championship match has been 58–0 when Australia beat New Zealand on Mar 15, 1987.

The Edmonton Oilers set an NHL record of 446 goals in the 1983–84 season.

The NHL record for both teams is 21 goals, scored when the Montreal Canadiens beat the Toronto St Patricks at Montreal 14-7 on Jan 10, 1920. The most goals ever scored by one team in a single game was set by the Canadiens, when they defeated the Quebec Bulldogs on March 3, 1920 by a score of 16-3.

The most goals in a period is 9 by the Buffalo Sabres in the second period of their 14–4 victory over Toronto on March 19, 1981.

The Detroit Red Wings scored 15 consecutive goals without an answering tally when they defeated the NY Rangers 15-0 on Jan 23, 1944.

Longest Game

The longest game was 2 hours 56 min 30 sec (playing time) when the Detroit Red Wings eventually beat the Montreal Maroons 1-0 in the 17th minute of the sixth period of overtime at the Forum, Montreal, at 2:25 A.M. on March 25, 1936, 5 hours 51 min after the opening faceoff. Norm Smith, goaltender for the Red Wings, turned aside 92 shots in registering the NHL's longest single shutout.

NATIONAL HOCKEY LEAGUE ALL-TIME RECORDS

(Through 1987–88 season; the number of a year refers to the season that commenced in the year before.)

REGULAR SEASON

Service

Most Seasons
26 Gordie Howe, Det, 1947–71; Hart, 1980

Most Games, Lifetime
1,767 Gordie Howe, Det, 1947–71; Hart, 1980

Consecutive Games Played
964 Doug Jarvis, Mon-Wash-Hart, Oct 8, 1975–Oct 10, 1987

Scoring

Most Points, Lifetime
1,850 Gordie Howe, Det, 1947–71; Hart, 1980

Most Points, Season
215 Wayne Gretzky, Edm, 1986

Most Points, Game
10 Darryl Sittler, Tor vs Bos, Feb 7, 1976

Most Points, Period
6 Bryan Trottier, NY Isl vs NY Ran, Dec 23, 1978

Consecutive Games Scoring Points
51 Wayne Gretzky, Edm, Oct 5, 1983–Jan 27, 1984

Most Goals, Lifetime
801 Gordie Howe, Det, 1947–71; Hart, 1980

Most Goals, Season
92 Wayne Gretzky, Edm, 1982

Most Goals, One Period
4 Harvey Jackson, Tor vs St L, Nov 20, 1934
Max Bentley, Chi vs NY Ran, Jan 28, 1943
Clint Smith, Chi vs Mont, Mar 4, 1945
Red Berenson, St L vs Phil, Nov 7, 1968
Wayne Gretzky, Edm vs St L, Feb 18, 1981
Grant Mulvey, Chi vs St L, Feb 3, 1982
Bryan Trottier, NY Isl vs Phil, Feb 13, 1982
Al Secord, Chi vs Tor, Jan 7, 1987

Most Goals, Game
7 Joe Malone, Que Bulldogs vs Tor St Pat, Jan 31, 1920

Most Hat Tricks (3 or more goals in a game), Lifetime
43 Wayne Gretzky, Edm, 1980–88

Most Hat Tricks, Season
10 Wayne Gretzky, Edm, 1982, 1984

Consecutive Games Scoring Goals
16 Harry Broadbent, Ottawa, 1921–22

Most Assists, Lifetime
1,086 Wayne Gretzky, Edm 1980–88

Most Assists, Season
163 Wayne Gretzky, Edm, 1986

Most Assists, Game
7 Billy Taylor, Det vs Chi, Mar 16, 1947
Wayne Gretzky, Edm vs Wash, Feb 15, 1980; vs Chi Dec 11, 1985; vs Que Feb 14, 1986

Most Assists, Period
5 Dale Hawerchuk, Win vs LA, Mar 6, 1984

Goaltending

Games Played, Lifetime
971 Terry Sawchuk, Det-Bos-Tor-LA-NY Ran, 1950–70

Shutouts, Lifetime
103 Terry Sawchuk, Det-Bos-Tor-LA-NY Ran, 1950–70

Shutouts, Season
22 George Hainsworth, Mont, 1929

Consecutive Scoreless Streak
461 min 29 sec Alex Connell, Ottawa, 1927–28

Consecutive Games Without Defeat
32 Gerry Cheevers, Bos, Nov 14, 1971–Mar 27, 1972

Most Saves, One Game
70 Roy Worters, Pitt Pirates

vs NY Americans, Dec 24, 1925

Most Victories, Season
47 Bernie Parent, Phil, 1974

Penalties

Most Minutes Penalized, Lifetime
3,976 David (Tiger) Williams, Tor-Van-Det-LA-Hart, 1975–87

Most Minutes Penalized, Season
472 Dave Schultz, Phil, 1975

Most Minutes Penalized, Game
67 Randy Holt, LA vs Phil, Mar 11, 1979

STANLEY CUP

Most Games, Lifetime
185 Denis Potvin, NY Isl, 1974–88

Most Points, Lifetime
252 Wayne Gretzky, Edm, 1980–88

Most Points, Season
47 Wayne Gretzky, Edm, 1985

Most Points, Game
7 Wayne Gretzky, Edm, vs Calg, Apr 17, 1983; Edm vs Win, Apr 25, 1985; Edm vs LA, Apr 9, 1987

Most Goals, Lifetime
85 Mike Bossy, NY Isl, 1978–87

Most Goals, Season
19 Reggie Leach, Phil, 1976
Jarri Kurri, Edm, 1985

Most Goals, Game
5 Maurice Richard, Mont vs Tor, Mar 23, 1944
Darryl Sittler, Tor vs Phil, Apr 22, 1976
Reggie Leach, Phil vs Bos, May 6, 1976

Most Assists, Lifetime
171 Wayne Gretzky, Edm, 1980–88

Most Assists, Season
31 Wayne Gretzky, Edm, 1988

Most Assists, Game
6 Mikko Leinonen, NY Ran vs Phil, Apr 8, 1982
Wayne Gretzky, Edm vs LA, Apr 9, 1987

Most Shutouts by Goalie, Lifetime
14 Jacques Plante, Mont, 1953–63; St L, 1969–70

Most Victories by Goalie, Lifetime
88 Billy Smith, NY Isl, 1975–88

Longest Streaks

In the 1981–82 season, the NY Islanders won 15 consecutive regular season games, Jan 21–Feb 20, 1982. The Detroit Red Wings also won 15 from Feb 27–Apr 5, 1955, but that streak included 6 playoff games. The longest a team has ever gone without a defeat is 35 games, set by the Philadelphia Flyers with 25 wins and 10 ties from Oct 14, 1979, to Jan 6, 1980.

Penalties

The most any team has been penalized in one season is the 2,621 min assessed against the Philadelphia Flyers in 1980–81. The most penalty-filled game was a contest between Boston and Minnesota in Boston on Feb 26, 1981, with a total of 84 penalties (42 by each team) for 406 min (211 min by Minnesota).

Stanley Cup

This cup, presented by the Governor-General Lord Stanley (original cost $48.67), became emblematic of world professional team supremacy 33 years after the first contest at Montreal in 1893. It has been won most often by the Montreal Canadiens, with 23 wins in 1916, 24, 30–31, 44, 46, 53, 56–60 (a record 5 straight), 65–66, 68–69, 71, 73, 76–79, 86. Henri Richard of Montreal played in his eleventh finals in 1973.

Winners from 1970 are:

1970 Boston Bruins
1971 Montreal Canadiens
1972 Boston Bruins
1973 Montreal Canadiens
1974 Philadelphia Flyers
1975 Philadelphia Flyers
1976 Montreal Canadiens
1977 Montreal Canadiens
1978 Montreal Canadiens
1979 Montreal Canadiens
1980 New York Islanders
1981 New York Islanders
1982 New York Islanders
1983 New York Islanders
1984 Edmonton Oilers
1985 Edmonton Oilers
1986 Montreal Canadiens
1987 Edmonton Oilers
1988 Edmonton Oilers

HORSE RACING

Origins

There is evidence that men were riding horses, as distinct from riding in chariots pulled by horses, in Assyria and Egypt *c* 1400 BC. However, early organized racing appears to have been confined to chariots, for which the Roman method used riders with a foot on each of two horses. The first racing on horseback was by the Greeks in the 33rd Olympic Games in 648 BC. The earliest recorded race in Britain was at Netherby, Cumbria in 210 AD between Arabian horses brought to Britain by the Roman Emperor, Lucius Septimius Severus. The first recognizable regular race meeting was that held at Smithfield, London at the weekly horse fairs on Fridays in 1174. The first known prize money was a purse of gold presented by Richard I (the Lion-heart) in 1195 for a race between knights over a distance of 3 mi.

Organized horse racing began in New York State at least as early as March 1668. The original Charleston (Va) Jockey Club, organized in 1734, was the world's first.

Racing colors (silks) became compulsory in 1889.

All thoroughbred horses in the world today are descended from at least one of three great stallions, which were imported into Britain in the 17th and 18th centuries. The "Darley Arabian" was brought from Aleppo, Syria by the British Consul Richard Darley of Yorkshire *c* 1704; the "Byerley Turk" was brought to England from Turkey *c* 1685 and used by Captain Byerley as a charger in Ireland; and the Godolphin Barb—the latter word derived from the Barbary Coast of North Africa—was originally brought from France by Edward Coke in about 1735 and then acquired by the Earl of Godolphin.

Largest Prizes

The richest races ever held are the Breeders' Cup 7-race meetings, run most recently at Santa Anita Park, Calif, on Nov 1, 1986, which paid $10 million total in prize money. This included a total purse of $3 million to the top winners of the 1¼-mi Breeders' Cup Classic.

Speed (see table)

"Big Racket" reached 43.26 mph in setting his ¼-mi record in 1945. "Fiddle Isle" sped 37.76 mph over 1½ mi on Mar 21, 1970, and "John Henry" duplicated this speed in his record run on Mar 16, 1980. Both times were recorded at Santa Anita Park, Arcadia, Calif.

Victories

The horse with the best win-loss record was "Kincsem," a Hungarian mare foaled in 1874, who was unbeaten in 54 races (1876–79), including the English Goodwood Cup of 1878.

The longest winning sequence is 56 races, in Puerto Rico 1953–5, by "Camarero," foaled in 1951. He had 73 wins in 77 starts altogether. The most wins in a career is 137 from 159 starts by "Galgo Jr" (foaled 1928) in Puerto Rico between 1930 and 1936; in 1931 he won a record 30 races in one year. The only horse to win the same race in 7 successive years was "Doctor Syntax" (foaled 1811) in the Preston Gold Cup, 1815–21.

Greatest Winnings

The most won in a single race is $2.6 million by "Spend a Buck" on May 27, 1985 at Garden State Park in Cherry Hill, NJ. This included a $2 million bonus for also winning the Kentucky Derby and 2 preparatory races at Garden State Park. His total for 1985 was $3,552,704, also a record.

The greatest amount ever won by a horse is $6,597,947 by the gelding "John Henry" (foaled 1975) from 1977 to July 1985, when he was retired.

"All Along," who raced 1981–1984, is the leading money winner among fillies with a career total of $3,015,764. "All Along" also set the one-year record with $2,138,963 in 1983.

Owners

The most lifetime wins by an owner is 4,775 by Marion Van Berg in N America in the 35 years up to his death in 1971.

The most winners by an owner in one year is 494 by Dan R. Lasater (US) in 1974. The greatest amount won in a year is $5,743,134 by Eugene Klein (US) in 1987. His total winnings 1983–87 were $18,309,316.

Largest Grandstand

The largest at a racecourse is at Belmont Park, Long Island, NY, which seats 30,000 and is 440 yd long.

Longest Race

The longest recorded horse race was one of 1,200 miles in Portugal.

GREATEST MONEY-WINNING HORSE: The gelding "John Henry," who won $6,597,947 in purses before retiring in 1985, is shown here with jockey Bill (Willie) Shoemaker up. *(Gerry Cranham)*

WINNINGEST JOCKEY: Bill (Willie) Shoemaker, winner of the 1986 Kentucky Derby, is only 94 lb and 4 ft 11 in tall, and has made over $117 million for the owners of the 8,759 winners he has ridden.

won by "Emir," a horse bred from Egyptian-bred Blunt Arab stock. The holder of the world record for long distance racing and speed is "Champion Crabbet," who covered 300 miles in 52 hours 33 min, carrying 245 lb, in 1920.

Topmost Tipster

The only recorded instance of a racing correspondent forecasting ten out of ten winners on a race card was at Delaware Park, Wilmington,

HORSES' SPEED RECORDS

Distance	*Time mph*	*Name*	*Course*	*Date*
¼ mile	20.8s.43.26	•*Big Racket* (Mex)	Mexico City, Mex	Feb 5, 1945
½ mile	44.4s.40.54	*Sonido* (Ven)	‡Caracas, Ven	June 28, 1970
	44.4s.40.54	*Western Romance* (Can)	Calgary, Can	Apr 19, 1980
	44.4s.40.54	*Northern Spike* (Can)	Winnipeg, Can	Apr 23, 1982
⅝ mile	53.6s.41.98 †	*Indigenous* (GB)	‡*Epsom, Eng	June 2, 1960
	53.89s.41.75 ††	*Raffingora* (GB)	‡*Epsom, Eng	June 5, 1970
	55.2s.40.76	*Chinook Pass* (US)	Seattle, Wash	Sept 17, 1982
¾ mile	1m.06.2s.40.78	*Broken Tendril* (GB)	*Brighton, Eng	Aug 6, 1929
	1m.07.2s.40.18	*Grey Papa* (US)	Longacres, Wash	Sept 4, 1972
	1m.07.2s.40.18	*Petro D. Jay* (US)	Phoenix, Ariz	May 9, 1982
Mile	1m.31.8s.39.21	*Soueida* (GB)	*Brighton, Eng	Sept 19, 1963
	1m.31.8s.39.21	*Loose Cover* (GB)	*Brighton, Eng	June 9, 1966
		Traditional Miss (GB)	Chepstow, Wales	June 27, 1981
		Traditional Miss (GB)	Chepstow, Wales	Aug 31, 1981
1¼ miles	1m.57.4s.38.33	*Double Discount* (US)	Arcadia, Calif	Oct 9, 1977
1½ miles	2m.23.0s.37.76	•*Fiddle Isle* (US)	Arcadia, Calif	Mar 21, 1970
		•*John Henry* (US)	Arcadia, Calif	Mar 16, 1980
2 miles	3m.16.75s.	*Il Tempo* (NZ)	Trentham, Wellington, NZ	Jan 17, 1970
2½ miles	4m.14.6s.35.35	*Miss Grillo* (US)	Pimlico, Md	Nov 12, 1948
3 miles	5m.15.0s.34.29	*Farragut* (Mex)	Aguascalientes, Mex	Mar 9, 1941

*Course downhill for ¼ of a mile. †Hand-timed. ††Electrically timed. ‡Straight courses. •World record speeds.

Del, on July 28, 1974, by Charles Lamb of the *Baltimore News American*.

Triple Crown

Eleven horses have won all three races in one season which constitute the American Triple Crown (Kentucky Derby, Preakness Stakes and the Belmont Stakes). This feat was first achieved by "Sir Barton" in 1919, and most recently by "Seattle Slew" in 1977 and "Affirmed" in 1978.

The only Triple Crown winner to sire another winner was "Gallant Fox," the 1930 winner, who sired "Omaha," who won in 1935. The only jockey to ride two Triple Crown winners is Eddie Arcaro (b Feb 19, 1916), on "Whirlaway" (1941) and "Citation" (1948).

Most Valuable Horses

The most expensive horse ever is the 1983 Irish Derby winner "Shareef Dancer." Reportedly 40 shares in the horse were sold at $1 million each in 1983 by his owner, Sheikh Mohammed bin Rashid al Maktoum.

The highest price for a yearling is $13.1 million for "Seattle Dancer" on July 23, 1985, in Keeneland, Ky, by Robert Sangster and partners.

Dead Heats

There is no recorded case in turf history of a quintuple dead heat. The nearest approach was in the Astley Stakes at Lewes, England, on Aug 6, 1880, when "Mazurka," "Wandering Nun" and "Scobell" triple dead-heated for first place, just ahead of "Cumberland" and "Thora" who dead-heated for fourth place. Each of the five jockeys thought he had won. The only three known examples of a quadruple dead heat were between "Honest Harry," "Miss Decoy," "Young Daffodil" and "Peteria" at Bogside, England, on June 7, 1808; between "Defaulter," "The Squire of Malton," "Reindeer" and "Pulcherrima" in the Omnibus Stakes at The Hoo, England, on Apr 26, 1851; and between "Overreach," "Lady Go-Lightly," "Gamester" and "The Unexpected" at Newmarket, England, on Oct 22, 1855.

Since the introduction of the photo-finish, the highest number of horses in a dead heat has been three, on several occasions.

Most Horses in a Race

In the Grand National (England) on Mar 22, 1929, there were 66 horses.

Trainers

The greatest number of wins by a trainer is 496 in one year by Jack Van Berg in 1976, and 4,400 in his career to 1986. The greatest amount won in a year is $17,502,110 by D. Wayne Lucas (US) in 1987. The only trainer to saddle the first 5 finishers in a championship race is Michael Dickinson in the 1983 Cheltenham Gold Cup. On Dec 27, 1982, he won a record 12 races in one day.

Jockeys

The most successful jockey of all time is William Lee (Bill or Willie) Shoemaker (b at 2½ lb on Aug 19, 1931) now weighing 94 lb and standing 4 ft 11 in. (His wife is nearly 1 ft taller than he is.) From Mar 1949 through May 1988, he rode 8,759 winners in nearly 40,000 mounts, earning more than $117,500,000.

The jockey with most earnings is Laffitt Pincay, Jr (b Dec 29, 1946, Panama City, Panama) who has earned a record $127,115,976, 1966 to Dec 6, 1987, including $13,415,049 won in 1985, the most ever won by a jockey in a single year.

Chris McCarron (US), (b 1955), won a total of 546 races in 1974 out of 2,199 mounts.

Shoemaker has won the most stakes races lifetime (986). Jorge Velasquez won the most in a year (57 in 1985).

The most winners ridden on one card is 8 by Hubert S. Jones, 17, out of 13 mounts at Caliente, Calif, on June 11, 1944 (of which 5 were photo-finishes); by Oscar Barattuci at Rosario, Argentina, on Dec 15, 1957; by Dave Gall from 10 mounts at Cahokia Downs, East St Louis, Ill, on Oct 18, 1978; by Chris Loseth, 29, out of 10 mounts at Exhibition Park in Vancouver, BC, Canada on Apr 9, 1984, and by Robert Williams from 10 rides at Lincoln, Neb, Sept 29, 1984.

The youngest jockey was Australian-born Frank Wootton (1893–1940) (Eng champion 1909–12), who rode his first winner in Africa, aged 9 years 10 months. The oldest jockey is Bill Shoemaker (see above) who won the Kentucky Derby in 1986 at the age of 55.

The lightest jockey recorded was Kitchener (Eng) (d 1872), who won the Chester Cup on "Red Deer" in 1844 at 49 lb. He is said to have weighed only 35 lb in 1840.

ICE SKATING

Origins

The earliest skates were made of animal bones, such as those found in France and thought to be 20,000 years old. The first reference to skating is in early Norse literature *c.* 200 AD but the earliest report of skating as a sport or pastime is in a British chronicle by William Fitzstephen of 1180. The first club was founded in Edinburgh in 1744, and the earliest artificial ice rink was opened in London in 1876.

Speed skating or racing must have taken place from the earliest times, although curved rinks, especially for racing, did not appear until the 1880s. Two Americans developed figure skating into an art. E. W. Bushnell invented steel blades in 1848 and thereby provided the precision skate needed for ever more intricate figures, and the first true innovator and teacher was Jackson Haines. He was a ballet master who transferred the artistry of the dance to the ice when he went to Vienna in 1864. Louis Rubinstein was a founder of the Amateur Skating Association of Canada in 1878, the first national governing body in the world. In 1892 the International Skating Union was set up at Scheveningen, Netherlands.

Longest Race

The longest race regularly held was the "Elfstedentocht" ("Tour of the Eleven Towns") in The Netherlands, covering 200 km (124 miles 483 yd). The fastest time was 6 hours 5 min 12 sec by Jan-Roelof Kruithof (Neth) on Feb 25, 1979 at Oulu, Finland. Kruithof won the race 8 times, 1974, 76–77, 79–83. The race was transferred to Finland in 1964 and subsequently to Canada, but it was returned to The Netherlands in 1985. An estimated 16,000 skaters took part in 1986.

Largest Rink

The world's largest indoor artificial ice rink is in the Moscow Olympic arena which has an ice area of 86,800 sq ft. The largest outdoors is the Fujikyu Highland Promenade Rink complex in Japan with 285,243 sq ft.

FIGURE SKATING

Most Difficult Jumps

Many of the most difficult jumps in skating are named after their originators, such as the Axel (after Axel Paulsen of Norway) and the Salchow (after Ulrich Salchow of Sweden).

The first woman to attempt a jump in major competition is said to have been Theresa Weld (US) who was reprimanded for her "unfeminine behavior" in the 1920 Olympic events. Cecilia Colledge (GB) was the first woman to achieve two turns in the air a few years later. In the 1962 World Championships Donald Jackson (Can) performed the first triple Lutz in a major competition and in the 1978 championships Vern Taylor, another Canadian, achieved the first triple Axel. Among women, the first triple Salchow was done by Sonja Morgenstern (E Ger) in 1972, and the first triple Lutz by Denise Beilmann (Switz) in the 1978 European championships. Incidentally, the latter has a spin named after her.

The first quadruple twist was performed by Marina Tcherkasova and Sergei Shakrai (USSR) in a pairs competition in Helsinki in 1977. They were able to achieve this because of the unusual difference in size between the tiny 12-year-old girl and her tall male partner.

A backward somersault jump was successfully negotiated by Terry Kubicka (US) in the 1976 world championships but it was immediately banned as being too dangerous.

Kurt Browning (Canada) was the first to achieve a quadruple jump in competition—a toe loop in the World Championships at Budapest, Hungary on Mar 25, 1988.

Highest Marks

The highest tally of maximum "six" marks awarded in an international championship was 29 to Jayne Torvill and Christopher Dean (GB) in the World Ice Dance Championships at Ottawa, Canada, Mar 22–24, 1984. This comprised 7 in the compulsory dances, a perfect set of 9 for presentation in the set pattern dance and 13 in the free dance, including another perfect set from all 9 judges for artistic presentation. They previously gained a perfect set of 9 "sixes" for artistic presentation in the free dance at the 1983 World Championships in

MOVIE STAR Sonja Henie (Norway) earned an estimated $47 million in ice shows and films after winning 3 Olympic golds in 1928-32-36 and 10 world titles. ◄

HIGHEST FIGURE SKATING MARKS: Jayne Torvill and Christopher Dean (GB) have been leading all competition with maximum sixes for all 9 judges since 1983. ▼

Helsinki, Finland, and at the 1984 Olympic Games in Sarajevo, Yugoslavia. In their career Torvill and Dean received a record total of 136 "sixes."

Donald Jackson (Canada) was awarded 7 "sixes" (the most by a soloist) in the world men's championship at Prague, Czechoslovakia, in 1962.

World Titles

The greatest number of individual world men's figure skating titles (instituted 1896) is 10 by Ulrich Salchow (1877–1949), of Sweden, in 1901–05, 07–11. The women's record (instituted 1906) is also 10 individual titles, by Sonja Henie (Apr 8, 1912–Oct 12, 1969), of

MOST DIFFICULT JUMP-LIFT: Marina Tcherkasova was only 12 years old when she and Sergei Shakrai first performed their unique quadruple twist lift in 1977. Shakrai was 18 years old at the time. *(Popperfoto)*

Norway, between 1927 and 1936. Irina Rodnina (b Sept 12, 1949), of the USSR, has won 10 pairs titles (instituted 1908)—four with Aleksiy Ulanov (1969–72) and six with her husband Aleksandr Zaitsev (1973–78). The most ice dance titles (instituted 1952) won is 6 by Aleksandr Gorshkov (b Oct 8, 1946) and his wife, Ludmilla Pakhomova (1946–86), both of the USSR, in 1970–74 and 76. They also won the first ever Olympic ice dance title in 1976.

Olympic Titles in Figure Skating

The most Olympic gold medals won by a figure skater is 3 by Gillis Grafström (1893–1938), of Sweden, in 1920, 24 and 28 (also silver medal in 1932); by Sonja Henie in 1928, 32 and 36; and by Irina Rodnina in the pairs event in 1972, 76 and 80.

Distance

Robin Cousins (GB) (b Mar 17, 1957) achieved 19 ft 1 in in an Axel jump and 18 ft with a back flip at Richmond Ice Rink, Surrey, Eng on Nov 16, 1983.

SPEED SKATING

World Titles

The greatest number of world overall titles (instituted 1893) won by any skater is 5 by Oscar Mathisen (Norway) (1888–1954) in 1908–09, 12–14, and Clas Thunberg (1893–1973) of Finland, in 1923, 25, 28–29 and 31. The most titles won by a woman is 5 by Karin Kania *née* Enke (b June 20, 1961) (E Ger) 1982, 84 and 86–88. Enke also won a record 6 overall titles at the World Sprint Championships 1980–81, 1983–84, and 1986–87.

SPEED SKATING DOUBLE GOLD MEDALIST: At the 1984 Winter Olympics, Karin Enke Kania (E Ger) won 2 golds and in 1986 regained 4 of her world records. ◄

AMERICAN SPEEDSTER: ▲ His unprecedented 5-event sweep of the 1980 Olympic speed skating competition made Eric Heiden the first Olympic athlete to earn 5 individual (that is, not relay or team) gold medals at one Games.

◄ FASTEST WOMAN ON SKATES: Bonnie Blair (US) won the 500-meter race in the 1988 Olympics in record time. *(Bob Martin / All-Sport)*

Olympic Titles

The most Olympic gold medals won in speed skating is 6 by Lidia Skoblikova (b March 8, 1939), of Chelyabinsk, USSR, in 1960 (2) and 1964 (4). The male record is held by Clas Thunberg (see above) with 5 gold (including 1 tied gold) and also 1 silver in 1924 and 1 tied bronze in 1928; and by Eric Heiden (US) (b June 14, 1958) who won 5 gold medals, all uniquely at one Games at Lake Placid, NY, in 1980.

Barrel Jumping (on ice skates)

The official distance record is 29 ft 5 in over 18 barrels by Yvon Jolin at Terrebonne, Quebec, Canada, in 1981. The women's record is 20 ft 4½ in over 11 barrels by Janet Hainstock in Mich on Mar 15, 1980.

WORLD SPEED SKATING RECORDS

(Ratified by the I.S.U.)

Distance	*min:sec*	*Name and Nationality*	*Place*	*Date*
MEN				
500 m	36.23*	Nick Thometz (USA)	Medeo, USSR	Mar 26, 1987
	36.45	Jens-Uwe May (E Ger)	Calgary, Canada	Feb 14, 1988
1000 m	1.12.05	Nick Thometz (USA)	Medeo, USSR	Mar 27, 1987
1500 m	1.52.06	Andre Hoffman (E Ger)	Calgary, Canada	Feb 20, 1988
3000 m	3.59.27	Leo Visser (Neth)	Heerenveen, Netherlands	Mar 19, 1987
5000 m	6.47.01	Leo Visser (Neth)	Heerenveen, Netherlands	Feb 14, 1987
10,000 m	13.48.20	Tomas Gustafson (Swe)	Calgary, Canada	Feb 21, 1988
WOMEN				
500 m	39.10	Bonnie Blair (USA)	Calgary, Canada	Feb 22, 1988
1000 m	1.18.11	Karin Kania (*née* Enke) (GDR)	Calgary, Canada	Dec 5, 1987
1500 m	1.59.30	Karin Kania (GDR)	Medeo, USSR	Mar 22, 1986
3000 m	4.11.94	Yvonne van Gennip (Neth)	Calgary, Canada	Feb 23, 1988
5000 m	6.43.59	Yvonne van Gennip (Neth)	Calgary, Canada	Feb 28, 1988
10,000 m	15.25.25	Yvonne van Gennip (Neth)	Heerenveen, Neth	Mar 19, 1988

*Unofficial (represents an average speed of 30.87 mph.)

Marathon

The longest recorded skating marathon is 109 hours 5 min by Austin McKinley of Christchurch, NZ, June 21–25, 1977.

24 Hours

Martinus Kuiper (Neth) skated 339.68 mi in 24 hours in Alkmaar, Neth on Dec 12–13, 1987.

MARATHONS (Running)

The inaugural marathon races were staged in Greece in 1896. There were two trial races before the first Olympic marathon at Athens. The race commemorated the legendary run of an unknown Greek courier, possibly Pheidippides, who in 490 BC ran some 24 miles from the Plain of Marathon to Athens with the news of a Greek victory over the numerically superior Persian army. Delivering his message—"Rejoice! We have won"—he collapsed and died. The Olympic races were run over varying distances until 1924 when the distance was standardized at 26 miles 385 yd, the distance first instituted in the 1908 Games in London.

There are no official records for the distance but the fastest times ever run are 2 hours 6 min 50 sec by Belaine Desimo of Ethiopia among men (1988) and 2 hours 21 min 6 sec by Ingrid Kristiansen of Norway among women (1985).

In the NYC marathon in 1987, there were 21,141 finishers out of 22,523 starters.

The oldest man to complete a marathon was Dimitrion Yordanidis (Greece), aged 98, in Athens, Greece on Oct 10, 1976. He finished in 7 hours 33 min. Thelma Pitt-Turner (New Zealand) set the women's record in August 1985, completing the Hastings, New Zealand marathon in 7 hours 58 min at the age of 82.

Backwards Marathon

Yves Pol (France) ran a marathon backwards in 3 hours 57 min 57 sec in France on Aug 30, 1987 in front of 30 spectators.

Most Marathons Run

Jay F. Helgerson (b Feb 3, 1955) of Foster City, Calif, ran a certified marathon (26 miles 385 yd) or longer, each week for 52 weeks from Jan 28, 1979 to Jan 19, 1980, totalling 1,418 racing miles.

Sy Mah (b 1926), an instructor at Toledo University (Ohio), has run 468 "marathons" of 26.2 mi or longer 1966–Aug 16, 1987 for a total of 11,660 mi. He paces himself to take 3½ hours for each run.

THE BOSTON MARATHON, the oldest US race of its kind, was won 7 times by Clarence Demar.

BALANCING A BOTTLE on a tray is the way Roger Bourban runs in every marathon.

THE NYC MARATHON, with 22,000 or more runners, gets its start on the Verrazano Bridge.

MOTORCYCLING

Earliest Motorcycle

On Nov 10, 1885, a single-track vehicle, powered by an internal-combustion engine designed by Gottlieb Daimler, was ridden a little over 7 mi from Canstatt to Unterkheim, Germany. Daimler's vehicle, due to its engine location and basic design features which remain current today, is universally acknowledged as the world's first motorcycle, predating the first automobile—also by Daimler—by several months.

In the early days many races were for both motorcycles and cars, and often took the form of long-distance inter-city or inter-country events. These were heavily criticized following the aborted Paris to Madrid race of 1903 which resulted in a number of deaths of competitors and spectators. In 1904 the International Cup Race was held in France for motorcycles only, and on a closed road circuit. However, in 1905 the race was held again, and this is recognized as the first international motorcycling event. The venue was Dourdon near Paris, and it was organized by the newly formed Fédération Internationale des Clubs Motocyclistes (FIM). The race was a success and was won by an Austrian named Wondrick.

Earliest Races and Circuits

The first motorcycle race was held on an oval track of 1 mi at Sheen House, Richmond, Surrey, England, on Nov 29, 1897, won by Charles Jarrott (1877–1944) on a Fournier.

The Auto-Cycle Union Tourist Trophy (TT) series was first held on the 15.81-mile "Peel" ("St John's") course on the Isle of Man on May 28, 1907, and is still run on the island, on the "Mountain" circuit.

Longest Circuit

The 37.73-mile "Mountain" circuit on the Isle of Man, over which the two main TT races have been run since 1911, has 264 curves and corners and is the longest used for any motorcycle race.

Fastest Circuits

The highest average lap speed attained on any closed circuit is 160.288 mph by Yvon du Hamel (Canada) (b 1941) on a modified 903-cc four-cylinder Kawasaki Z1 on the 31-degree banked 2.5-mile Daytona International Speedway, Fla, in March 1973. His lap time was 56.149 sec.

The fastest road circuit is the Portstewart-Coleraine-Portrush circuit in Londonderry, N Ireland. The lap record (10.1 mile lap) is 4 min 53.2 sec (average speed 124.060 mph) by John Glyn Williams (1946–78) on a 747-cc four-cylinder Yamaha on lap five of the 750-cc event of the North-West 200, on May 21, 1977. Minor circuit changes prior to 1986 have resulted in slower times.

The TT circuit (Isle of Man) speed record is 118.54 mph for one lap by Joey Dunlop on a Honda on June 6, 1988.

Fastest Race

The fastest track race in the world was held at Grenzlandring, W Germany, in 1939. It was won by Georg "Schorsh" Meier (b Germany Nov 9, 1910) at an average speed of 134 mph on a supercharged 495-cc flat-twin BMW.

The fastest road race is the 500-cc Belgian Grand Prix on the

QUICK AS A VINK: Henk Vink of The Netherlands set world records in 1977 for 1 kilometer and for 440 yds on his Kawasaki in 2-way runs from standing starts.

FASTEST VELOCITY: Elmer Trett sped 201.34 mph at the end of a 440-yd run from a standing start to set the record for highest terminal velocity.

CROSS-US TREK: In this 260-lb 125-cc revised Suzuki, without refueling, Matt Guzzetta rode 2,443 mi from San Diego to Daytona Beach on 11.83 gallons in Mar 1984, for a record 214.37 mpg.

Francorchamps circuit. The record time for this 10-lap 87.74-mile race is 38 min 58.5 sec (average speed of 135.068 mph) by Barry Sheene (UK) on a 495-cc four-cylinder Suzuki on July 3, 1977.

Longest Race

The longest race is the Liège 24 Hours, run on the Francorchamps circuit. The greatest distance ever covered is 2,761.9 miles (average speed 115.08 mph) by Jean-Claude Chemarin and Christian Leon of France on a 941-cc four-cylinder Honda on the Francorchamps circuit on Aug 14–15, 1976.

Speed Records

Official world speed records must be set with two runs over a measured distance within a time limit (one hour for FIM records, two hours for AMA records).

Donald Vesco (b Loma Linda, Calif, Apr 8, 1939) riding his 21-ft-long *Lightning Bolt* streamliner, powered by two 1,016-cc Kawasaki engines on Bonneville Salt Flats, Utah, on Aug 28, 1978, set AMA and FIM absolute records with an overall average of 318.598 mph and had a fastest run at an average of 318.66 mph.

The world record average speed for two runs over 1 km (1,093.6 yd) from a standing start is 16.68 sec by Henk Vink (b July 24, 1939) (Netherlands) on his supercharged 984-cc 4-cylinder Kawasaki, at Elvington Airfield, N Yorkshire, England on July 24, 1977. The faster run was made in 16.09 sec.

The world record for two runs over 440 yd from a standing start is 8.805 sec by Henk Vink on his supercharged 1,132-cc 4-cylinder Kawasaki, at Elvington Airfield, N Yorkshire, England, on July 23, 1977. The faster run was made in 8.55 sec.

The fastest time for a single run over 440 yd from a standing start is 7.08 sec by Bo O'Brechta (US) riding a supercharged 1,200-cc Kawasaki-based machine at Ontario, Calif, in 1980. The highest terminal velocity recorded at the end of a 440-yd run from a standing start is 201.34 mph by Elmer Trett at Indianapolis, on Sept 5, 1983.

World Championships

Races are currently held for the following classes of motorcycles: 50 cc, 125 cc, 250 cc, 350 cc, 500 cc, and sidecars.

Most world championship titles (instituted by the *Fédération Internationale Motocycliste* in 1949) won are 15 by Giacomo Agostini (b Lovere, Italy, June 16, 1942) in the 350-cc class 1968–74 and in the 500-cc class 1966–72 and 75. Agostini is the only man to win two world championships in five consecutive years (350 and 500 cc titles 1968–72). Freddie Spencer (US) in 1985 became the first ever to win world titles at both 250 and 500 cc in the same year. Agostini won 122 races in the world championship series between Apr 24, 1965, and Sept 25, 1977, including a record 19 in 1970, also achieved by Stanley Michael "Mike" Hailwood, (b Oxford, England, 1940, d 1981) in 1966.

A record 3 world trials championships have been won by Yrjö Vesterinen (Finland) (1976–8) and by Eddie Lejeune (Belgium).

Klaus Enders (Germany) (b 1937) won 6 world sidecar titles, 1967, 69–70, 72–74.

QUICK TRIP: Fran ▲ Crane; accepting certificate, crossed the US by motorcycle in 44 hours 20 min in 1988.

► MOTO-CROSS RACE in progress. André Malherbe (Belgium) almost takes flight on his way to victory in the 500-cc contest in 1980.

Angel Roldan Nieto (Spain) (b Jan 25, 1947) won a record seven 125-cc titles, 1971–72, 1979, and 1981–84.

Cross-US Trek

Fran Crane (b Nov 5, 1946) of Santa Cruz, Calif, traveled from NYC to San Francisco (2,974 mi) in a time of 44 hours 20 min June 9–11, 1988 for the best time by either a man or woman. She drove a BMW K100.

Matthew P. Guzzetta, 31, of Don Vesco Products, Spring Valley, Calif, claims to have ridden a 260-lb, 125-cc revised Suzuki motorcycle whose shell he designed and built, from San Diego, Calif, to Daytona Beach, Fla, without refueling, Mar 3–17, 1984. With a writer friend, Gerald Foster, he covered the 2,443 mi on 11.83 gallons, for a record consumption of 214.37 mph. In a snowstorm, they had to put the motorcycle in a van for 36 mi.

Youngest and Oldest Champions

Alberto "Johnny" Cecotto (b Caracas, Venezuela, Jan 25, 1956) was the youngest person to win a world championship. He was aged 19 years 211 days when he won the 350-cc title on Aug 24, 1975. The oldest was Hermann-Peter Müller (1909–76) of W Germany, who won the 250-cc title in 1955, aged 46.

Moto-Cross (Scrambling)

This is a very specialized sport in which the competitors race over rough country including steep climbs and drops, sharp turns, sand, mud and water. The sport originated in England in 1924 when some riders competed in "a rare old scramble." Until the Second World War it remained a British interest but the Moto-Cross des Nations was inaugurated in 1947, and became an annual event, with the current rules formulated in 1963. In 1961 the Trophée des Nations, for 250 cc machines, was introduced by the FIM. World championships had been instituted in 1957.

Joël Robert (b Chatelet, Belgium, Nov 11, 1943) has won six 250-cc moto-cross (also known as "scrambles") world championships (1964, 68–72). Between Apr 25, 1964, and June 18, 1972, he won a record fifty 250-cc Grands Prix. He became the youngest moto-cross world champion on July 12, 1964, when he won the 250-cc championship aged 20 years 244 days.

OLYMPIC GAMES

An entire book, the *Guinness Book of Olympic Records* (Bantam), is available.

RODEO: STAMPEDE! This chuckwagon race is the feature of the annual Calgary (Canada) rodeo, and also was held in connection with the Winter Olympics in 1988. It has drawn crowds as big as 150,000.

ITALIAN WINS POWERBOAT RACE: Renato della Valle drove this Ego Rothman to a record 4 consecutive victories (1982-85) in the 199-mile race off the English shore from Cowes to Torquay. *(Steve Powell/All Sport)*

SKIING

Origins

The most ancient ski in existence was found well preserved in a peat bog at Höting, Sweden, dating from *c.* 2500 BC. However, in 1934 a Russian archaeologist discovered a rock carving of a skier at Bessovysledki, USSR, which dates from *c.* 6000 BC. These early skiers used the bones of animals whereas wooden skis appear to have been introduced to Europe from Asia. The first reference in literature is in a work by Procopius *c.* 550 AD who referred to "Gliding Finns." Additionally in the Scandinavian sagas there occur gods of skiing. By 1199, the Danish historian Saxo was reporting the military use of troops on skis by Sigurdsson Sverrir, the Norwegian King.

The modern sport did not develop until 1843 when the first known competition for civilians took place at Tromso, Norway. The first ski club, named the Trysil Shooting and Skiing Club, was founded in Norway in 1861. Twenty years later ski bindings were invented by Sondre Nordheim, from Morgedal in the Telemark area, and the people of this region were the pioneers of the sport. The legendary "Snowshoe" Thompson, whose parents were Norwegian, was the earliest well-known skier in the US (1856) although skiing took place here in the 1840s. It was not until Olaf Kjeldsberg went to Switzerland in 1881 that the sport began to take hold in that country, and in 1889 one of the earliest of British exponents, Arthur Conan Doyle, began skiing at Davos, Switz. The first downhill race—as opposed to the Scandinavian races across country—was held at Kitzbuhel, Austria in 1908. The International Ski Federation (FIS) was founded on Feb 2, 1924. The Winter Olympics were inaugurated on Jan 25, 1924, and Alpine events have been included since 1936. The FIS recognizes both the Winter Olympics and the separate World Ski Championships as world championships.

Most Olympic Victories

Marja-Liisa Haemaelainen (Fin), after having twice won the women's World Cup title in Nordic, 1983–84, won all 3 individual gold medals in the 1984 Olympics.

The most Olympic gold medals won by a man for skiing is 4 by Sixten Jernberg (b Feb 6, 1929), of Sweden, in 1956–64 (including one for a relay). In addition, Jernberg has won 3 silver and 2 bronze medals for a record 9 Olympic medals. Four were also won by Nikolai Zimjatov (b June 28, 1955) (USSR) in 1980 (30 km, 50 km and on the team for 4 × 10-km relay) and in 1984 (30 km).

The only woman to win 4 Olympic gold medals is Galina Koulakova (b Apr 29, 1942) of USSR who won the 5 km and 10 km (1972) and was a member of the winning 3 × 5-km relay team in 1972 and the 4 × 5-km team in 1976. Koulakova also has won 2 silver and 2 bronze medals, 1968, 76, 80.

The most Olympic gold medals won in men's Alpine skiing is 3, by Anton "Toni" Sailer in 1956 and Jean-Claude Killy in 1968.

Most Alpine World Titles

The World Alpine Championships were inaugurated at Mürren, Switzerland, in 1931. The greatest number of titles won has been 13 by Christel Cranz (b July 1, 1914), of Germany, with 7 individual—4 Slalom (1934, 37–39) and 3 Downhill (1935, 37, 39); and 5 Combined (1934–35, 37–39). She also won the gold medal for the Combined in

FOUR-EVENT WINNER, Pirmin Zurbriggen of Switzerland, in 1987 won World Cups in downhill, slalom, super-giant slalom and overall skiing. (*Steve Powell / All Sport*) ►

SLALOM STAR: Ingemar Stenmark (Sweden) has won 85 World Cup events and 2 Olympic gold medals, far surpassing anyone else, but unusually, he has never raced downhill. (*All Sport*) ▼

WINTER WONDER: Jean-Claude Killy (France) thrilled his countrymen when he swept all 3 Olympic gold medals in the 1968 Winter Olympics in Grenoble, France. Killy also won the Alpine Combination world title that year and 2 other world titles in 1966. ►

the 1936 Olympics. The most titles won by a man is 7 by Anton "Toni" Sailer (b Nov 17, 1935), of Austria, who won all 4 in 1956 (Giant Slalom, Slalom, Downhill and the non-Olympic Alpine Combination) and the Downhill, Giant Slalom and Combined in 1958.

Most Nordic World Titles

The first world Nordic championships were those of the 1924 Winter Olympics at Chamonix, France. The greatest number of World titles won is 9 by Galina Koulakova (b Apr 29, 1942) (USSR), 1970–78. She also won 4 silver and 4 bronze medals for a record total of 17. The most won by a man is 8, including relays, by Sixten Jernberg (b Feb 6, 1929) (Sweden), 1956–64. Johan Grottumsbraaten (1899–1942), of Norway, won 6 individual titles (2 at 18 km cross-country and 4 Nordic Combined) in 1926–32. The record for a jumper is 5 by Birger Ruud (b Aug 23, 1911), of Norway, in 1931–32 and 1935–37. Ruud is the only person to win Olympic titles in each of the dissimilar Alpine and Nordic disciplines. In 1936 he won the ski-jumping and the Alpine downhill (which was not then a separate event, but only a segment of the Combined event).

World Cup

The Alpine World Cup was instituted in 1967, and extended to include Nordic in 1981.

The most by a man is 85 by Ingemar Stenmark (b Mar 18, 1956) (Sweden), 1974–87, including a record 10 in one season in 1979. Franz Klammer (Austria) (b Dec 3, 1953) won a record 35 downhill races, 1974–85.

The women's cup has been won 6 times by the 5-ft-6-in 150-lb Annemarie Moser (*née* Proll) (Austria) in 1971–75 and 79. From Dec 1972 to Jan 1974 she completed a record sequence of 11 consecutive downhill victories. She holds the women's record of 62 individual event wins (1970–79).

Alexander Zavialov (USSR) (b June 2, 1955) has two wins, 1981 and 1983, in the cross-country or Nordic World Cup (inst 1979). Also with two wins are Marja-Liisa Haemaelainen (Finland) in 1983 and 1984, and Gunde Svan (Sweden) in 1984 and 1985. The jumping World Cup (inst 1980) has been twice won by Armin Kogler (Austria) (b Sept 4, 1959) 1981–2, and by Matti Nykanen (Finland) 1983 and 1985.

Duration

The record distance covered in 48 hours of Nordic skiing is 319 mi 205 yd by Bjorn Lokken (Norway) (b Nov 27, 1937) Mar 11–13, 1982.

In 24 hours Teuvo Rantanen covered 249.35 miles at Jyväskylä, Finland Feb 1–2, 1986. The women's record is 205.05 miles by Sisko Kainulaisen of Finland at Jyväskylä on Mar 23–24, 1985.

The longest time spent in downhill skiing under regulated conditions is 83 hours by Dave Phillips and Gerry O'Neill at Grouse Mt, N Vancouver, Canada, Feb 20–23, 1986. No time was wasted waiting for the lift.

Luc Labrie at Daie Comeau, Quebec, Canada, skied alone for 138 hours, Feb 20–25, 1984.

TRIPLE WINNER IN 1984 OLYMPICS: Marja-Liisa Haemaelainen (Fin) dominated the women's cross-country skiing events, taking all three individual gold medals.

Highest Speed—Cross Country

Bill Koch (US) (b Apr 13, 1943) on Mar 26, 1981 skied ten times around a 5-km (3.11-mi) loop on Marlborough Pond, near Putney, Vt. He completed the 50 km in 1 hour 59 min 47 sec, an average speed of 15.57 mph. A race includes uphill and downhill sections; the record time for a 50-km race is 2 hours 10 min 49.9 sec by Gunde Svan in the 1985 World Championships, an average speed of 14.25 mph. The record for a 15-km Olympic or World Championship race is 38 min 52.5 sec by Oddvar Braa (Nor) (b Mar 16, 1951) at the 1982 World Championships, an average speed of 14.38 mph.

Closest Verdict

The narrowest winning margin in a championship ski race was one hundredth of a second by Thomas Wassberg (Sweden) (b March 23, 1956) over Juha Mieto (Finland) in the Olympic 15 km cross-country race at Lake Placid, NY on Feb 17, 1980. His winning time was 41 min 57.63 sec.

The narrowest margin of victory in an Olympic Alpine event was 2/100ths of a sec by Barbara Cochran (US) over Daniele De Bernard (France) in the 1972 slalom at Sapporo, Japan.

Longest Run

The longest all-downhill ski run in the world is the Weissfluhjoch–Küblis Parsenn course (7.6 miles long), near Davos, Switzerland. The run from the Aiguille du Midi top of the Chamonix lift (vertical lift 9,052 ft) across the Vallée Blanche is 13 miles.

Longest Jump

The longest ski jump ever recorded is one of 636 ft by Piotr Fijas (Poland) at Planica, Yugoslavia, on Mar 14, 1987.

The women's record is 110 m (361 ft) by Tina Lehtola (Fin) (b Aug 3, 1962) at Ruka, Finland, on Mar 29, 1981.

Steepest Descent

Sylvain Saudan (b Lausanne, Switzerland, Sept 23, 1936) achieved a descent of Mt Blanc on the northeast side down the Couloir Gervasutti from 13,937 ft on Oct 17, 1967, skiing gradients of about 60 degrees.

Highest Altitude

Jean Atanassieff and Nicolas Jaeger (both France) skied down from 26,900 ft to 20,340 ft on Mt Everest in 1978.

Highest Speed—Downhill

The highest speed claimed for a skier is 139.030 mph by Michael Pruffer (France) and the fastest by a woman is 133.234 mph by Tara Mulari (Fin). Both times were achieved on Apr 16, 1988 at Les Arcs, France.

At the Les Arcs venue on Apr 18, 1987 Patrick Knauff (France) set a one-legged record of 115.012 mph.

The highest average race speed in the Olympic downhill was 64.95 mph by Bill Johnson (US) (b Mar 30, 1960) at Sarajevo, Yugoslavia, on Feb 16, 1984. The fastest in a World Cup downhill is 67.00 mph by Harti Weirather (Austria) (b Jan 25, 1958) at Kitzbuhel, Austria on Jan 15, 1982.

Most Competitors—Alpine

1,700 downhill skiers competed at Are, Jamtland, Sweden, on Apr 30, 1984.

Longest Races

The world's longest ski races are the Grenader, run just north of Oslo, Norway, and the König Ludwig Lauf in Oberammergau, W Germany. Both are 90 km (55.9 miles). The Canadian Ski Marathon at 160 km (99 miles) is longer, but is run in two parts on consecutive days.

The world's greatest Nordic ski race is the Vasaloppet, which commemorates an event in 1521 when Gustavus Vasa (1496–1560), later King of Sweden, fled 85.8 km (53.3 miles) from Mora to Sälen, Sweden. He was overtaken by loyal, speedy scouts on skis, who persuaded him to return eastwards to Mora to lead a rebellion and become the king of Sweden. The re-enactment of this return journey is now an annual event at 89 km (55.3 mi), contested by nearly 11,000 skiers. The fastest time is 3 hours 48 min 55 sec by Bengt Hassis (Swe) on Mar 2, 1986.

The Vasaloppet is now the longest of 10 long distance races, constituting the world loppet, staged in 10 countries.

The longest downhill race is the *Inferno* in Switzerland, 9.8 miles from the top of the Schilthorn to Lauterbrunnen. In 1981 there was a record entry of 1,401, with Heinz Fringen (Switz) winning in 15 min 44.57 sec. The record time of 15 min 26.44 sec was set in 1987 by Veli Grossniklaus (Switz).

Backflip on Skis

The greatest number of skiers to perform a back layout flip while holding hands is 28 at Bromont, Quebec, Canada, on Feb 10, 1982.

Longest Lift

The longest gondola ski lift is 3.88 mi long at Grindelwald–Männlichen, Switzerland (in two sections, but one gondola). The longest chair lift was the Alpine Way to Kosciusko Châlet lift above Thredbo, near the Snowy Mountains, NSW, Australia. It took from 45 to 75 min to ascend the 3.5 mi, according to the weather. It has now collapsed. The highest is at Chacaltaya, Bolivia, rising to 16,500 ft.

BACKFLIP: The record for this popular stunt (sometimes called "hotdogging") has increased from 19 (as shown here) to 28 in just a few years. *(Gary McMillin)*

SOCCER

Origins

Ball-kicking games were played very early in human history.

A game with some similarities termed *Tsu-chu* was played in China in the 3rd and 4th centuries BC. One of the earliest references to the game in England is a Royal Proclamation by Edward II in 1314 banning the game in the City of London. A soccer-type game called Calcio was played in Italy in 1410. The earliest clear representation of the game is in a print from Edinburgh, Scotland, dated 1672–73. The game became standardized with the formation of the Football Association in England on Oct 26, 1863. Eleven players on a side was standardized in 1870.

Highest Team Scores

The highest score recorded in any first-class match is 36. This

NET WEIGHT: At 6 ft 3 in and 311 lb, Fatty Foulke was the most massive goalkeeper ever. One of his greatest exploits came off the field, however, when, appearing at the dinner table early one evening, Foulke ate the team's entire meal before any of his teammates arrived.

ATHLETE OF THE CENTURY: Pelé celebrates one of his 1,285 goals, this one with the NY Cosmos of the NASL. In a seemingly premature poll of 20 international newspapers, the tremendously popular Brazilian soccer star was named "Athlete of the Century" by the French sports magazine "L'Equipe." Jesse Owens was runner-up. ◄

occurred in the Scottish Cup match between Arbroath and Bon Accord on Sept 12, 1885, when Arbroath won 36–0 on their home ground. But for the lack of nets and the consequent waste of retrieval time, the score might have been even higher. Seven goals were disallowed for offside.

The highest margin recorded in an international match is 17, when England beat Australia 17–0 at Sydney June 30, 1951. This match is not listed as a *full* international.

World Cup

The World Cup Competition, which has been held 13 times through 1986, takes on new meaning for US citizens because the 15th tournament was awarded to the US to be played at several sites across the country in 1994.The *Fédération Internationale de Football Association* (FIFA), which was founded on May 21, 1904, instituted the first World Cup on July 13, 1930, in Montevideo, Uruguay. Thirteen nations took part then, playing for a trophy named after Jules Rimet, the late Honorary President of FIFA from 1921–1954. The first team to win the competition three times was to keep the trophy, a feat achieved by Brazil in 1970.

The only countries to win three times have been Brazil (1958, 62, 70) and Italy (1934, 38, 82). Brazil was also second in 1950, and third in 1938 and 1978, and uniquely has taken part in all 13 Finals.

Antonio Carbajal (b 1923) played for Mexico in goal in a record 5 competitions, in 1950, 54, 58, 62 and 66, playing in 11 games in all. Uwe Seeler (W Ger) (b Nov 5, 1936) shares with Wladyslaw Zmuda (Poland) (b June 6, 1954) the record for the most appearances in final tournaments, playing in 21 games. Pelé is the only player to have been with 3 World Cup winning teams, all for Brazil. The youngest World Cup player ever was Norman Whiteside, who played for N Ireland vs Yugoslavia, aged 17 years 42 days on June 17, 1982.

The record goal scorer has been Just Fontaine (France) with 13 goals in 6 games in the final stages of the 1958 competition. Gerd Müller (W Ger) (b Nov 3, 1945) scored 10 goals in 1970 and 4 in 1974 for the highest aggregate of 14 goals. Fontaine and Jairzinho (Brazil) are the only two players to have scored in every game in a final series, as Jairzinho scored 7 in 6 games in 1970. The most goals scored in the final game is 3 by Geoffrey Hurst (b Dec 8, 1941) for England vs W Germany in 1966. Three players have scored in 2 finals: Vava (real name, Edwaldo Izito Neto) (Brazil) in 1958 and 62, Pelé in 1958 and 70, and Paul Breitner (W Ger) in 1974 and 82.

The highest score in a World Cup match is New Zealand's 13–0 defeat of Fiji in a qualifying match at Auckland on Aug 16, 1981. The highest score in the Finals Tournament is Hungary's 10–1 win over El Salvador at Elche, Spain, on June 15, 1982. The highest match aggregate in the Finals Tournament is 12 when Austria beat Switzerland in 1954.

The highest-scoring team in a Finals Tournament has been W Germany, which scored 25 in 6 games in 1954 for the highest average of 4.17 goals per game. England has the best defensive record, conceding only 3 goals in 6 games in 1966. Curiously, no team has ever failed to score in a World Cup Final.

The fastest goal scored in World Cup competition was one in 27 sec by Bryan Robson for England vs France in Bilbao, Spain, on June 16, 1982.

World Cup Winners

	Winner	*Locale*
1930	Uruguay	Uruguay
1934	Italy	Italy
1938	Italy	France
1950	Uruguay	Brazil
1954	W Germany	Switzerland
1958	Brazil	Sweden
1962	Brazil	Chile
1966	England	England
1970	Brazil	Mexico
1974	W Germany	W Germany
1978	Argentina	Argentina
1982	Italy	Spain
1986	Argentina	Mexico

Marathons

The longest outdoor game played was 74½ hours by two teams trying to establish a record at Liswerry Leisure Centre, Gwent, Wales, June 23–26, 1983. The indoor soccer record is 104 hours 10 min set by two teams from Rockhampton, Queensland, Australia, Nov 17–22, 1985.

Individual Scoring

The most goals scored by one player in a first-class match is 16 by Stephan Stanis (*né* Stanikowski, b Poland, July 15, 1913) for Racing Club de Lens vs Aubry-Asturies, in Lens, France, on Dec 13, 1942.

The record number of goals scored by one player in an international match is 10 by Sofus Nielsen (1888–1963) for Denmark vs France (17–1) in the 1908 Olympics and by Gottfried Fuchs for Germany, which beat Russia 16–0 in the 1912 Olympic tournament (consolation event) in Sweden.

An undocumented 1,329 goals were scored in a 43-year first-class career by Artur Friedenreich (1892–1969) of Brazil.

The most goals scored in a specified period is 1,216 by Edson Arantes do Nascimento (b Baurú, Brazil, Oct 23, 1940), known as Pelé, the Brazilian inside left, in the period Sept 7, 1956 to Oct 2, 1974 (1,254 games). His best year was 1959 with 126 goals. His *milesimo* (1,000th) came in a penalty for his club, Santos, in the Maracaña Stadium, Rio de Janeiro, on Nov 19, 1969, when he was playing in his 909th first-class match. He came out of retirement in 1975 to add to his total with the New York Cosmos of the North American Soccer League. By his retirement on Oct 1, 1977 his total had reached 1,281 in 1,363 games. He added 4 more goals later in special appearances.

Franz ("Bimbo") Binder (b Dec 1, 1911) scored 1,006 goals in 756 games in Austria and Germany between 1930 and 1950.

Longest Matches

The world duration record for a first-class match is 3 hours 30 min (with interruptions), in the Copa Libertadores championship in Santos, Brazil, Aug 2–3, 1962, when Santos drew 3–3 with Penarol FC of Montevideo, Uruguay.

A match between St Ignatius College Preparatory of San Francisco and Bellarmine College Preparatory of San Jose lasted 4 hours 56 min (230 min playing time) at San Francisco on Feb 6, 1982.

Goalkeeping

The longest that any goalkeeper has succeeded in preventing any goals being scored past him in international matches is 1,142 min for Dino Zoff (Italy) from Sept 1972 to June 1974.

The biggest goalie on record was Willie J. ("Fatty") Foulke of England (1874–1916) who stood 6 ft 3 in and weighed 311 lb. By the time he died, he tipped the scales at 364 lb. He once stopped a game by snapping the cross bar.

Ball Control

Allan Abuto Nyanjong (Kenya) headed a ball non-stop for 5 hours at Coronado High School Gym, El Paso, Tex, on Apr 25, 1987.

Nyanjong also juggled a regulation soccer ball for 16 hours 27 min 52 sec non-stop with feet, legs and head without the ball ever touching the ground at the Hyatt Regency Crystal City, Arlington, Va, Jan 16, 1988.

Janusz Chomontek of Gdanieck, Poland kept a ball up while he traveled a distance of 18.641 miles in 8 hours 25 min 20 sec on Sept 19, 1987.

Crowds

The greatest recorded crowd at any soccer match was 205,000 (199,854 paid) for the Brazil vs Uruguay World Cup final in Rio de Janeiro, Brazil, on July 16, 1950.

SOFTBALL

Origins

Softball, as an indoor derivative of baseball, now 100 years old, was invented by George Hancock at the Farragut Boat Club of Chicago, in 1887. Rules were first codified in Minneapolis in 1895 as Kitten Ball. The name Softball was introduced by Walter Hakanson at a meeting of the National Recreation Congress in 1926. The name was adopted throughout the US in 1930. Rules were formalized in 1933 by the International Joint Rules Committee for Softball and adopted by the Amateur Softball Association of America. The International Softball Federation was formed in 1950 as governing body for both fast pitch and slow pitch, and reorganized in 1965.

Pitchers

While softball pitchers, who stand 50 ft from the plate and hurl a 12-in spheroid, can't seriously be compared with major league hardball pitchers who stand 60½ ft from the plate, one pitcher, Eddie "The King" Feigner, set records that make major league stars look pale by comparison. In his 33-year span from 1946 through 1978, Feigner pitched in 6,177 games, won 5,144 (more than 10 times as many as Cy Young's 511 victories in the major leagues), lost 815, and struck out a total of 100,468 batters (more than 20 times Nolan Ryan's big league total of 4,577).

Along the way, Feigner once won 187 games in a row (more than 7 times as many as Carl Hubbell's 24 in a row), threw 1,581 shutouts (15 times as many as Walter Johnson's 110), and notched 216 perfect games (more than 40 times as many as Nolan Ryan's major league record of 5).

Big league hitters have on frequent occasion tried to hit fast pitch softball and they've generally failed. Babe Ruth, Hank Greenberg and Ted Williams have all been struck out. In the mid-1930s while facing a softball pitcher in an exhibition at Madison Square Garden (NYC)

Babe Ruth missed a dozen straight pitches and finally, in sheer frustration, grabbed the ball and hit it with his hang fungo style. After the ball hit the roof with enormous impact, Ruth growled, "I just wanted to see if it would go."

Slow Pitch vs Fast Pitch

Slow pitch softball, unlike hardball and fast pitch softball, gives the batter something to hit and statistics become astronomical. For example, Mike Macenko, the 6-ft-3-inch 260-lb second baseman for the "Men of Steele" (Grafton, Ohio's entry in the U. S. Amateur Softball Association) slammed 844 homers and drove in almost 2,000 runs in the 1987 season. (Seasons generally run for 300 games.) Macenko has hit as many as 9 homers in a single game, and once he clubbed a shot that was tape-measured at 508 ft.

Marathons

The longest fast pitch marathon is 61 hours 36 min 33 sec by two teams of 9 (no substitutes) belonging to the Marines of the 2nd Radio Battalion at Camp Lejeune, NC, May 3–5, 1984. The game went 266 innings and the score was 343–296.

The longest slow pitch softball game was 111 hours 2 min by Brigade Service Support Group 1 vs Marine Aircraft Group 24 at Kareoke Marine Corps Air Station, Hawaii, Sept 3–8, 1986.

World Championships

The US has won the men's world championship (instituted in 1966) four times, 1966, 68, 76 (shared) and 80. The US has also won the women's title (instituted in 1965) 4 times, in 1974, 78, 86 and 87.

In 1981, junior world championships for boys and girls were started, with Japan winning both divisions that year. In 1985, New Zealand won the boys' world championship and China the girls' division.

SWIMMING

Earliest References

Egyptian hieroglyphics, *c.* 3000 BC, indicate swimming figures, and a bronze of a diver dating from *c.* 510 BC was found near Perugia, Italy. Both Julius Caesar and Charlemagne were known to be good swimmers. Competitions took place in Japan in 36 BC, and that country was the first to take to the sport in a major way with an Imperial edict by the Emperor Go-Yozei decreeing its introduction in schools. In Britain, sea bathing was practiced as early as 1660 at Scarborough, but competitive swimming was not introduced until 1837, when competitions were held in London's artificial pools organized by the National Swimming Society, founded in that year. Australia was in the forefront of modern developments and an unofficial world 100-yd championship was held in Melbourne in 1858. With the foundation of the Amateur Swimming Association (though not known by this name till later) in Britain in 1869 came the distinction between amateurs and professionals.

The first recognizable stroke style seems to have been the breaststroke, although the "dog-paddle" technique may well have preceded it. From this developed the sidestroke, which is the breaststroke performed sideways, a style which was last used by an Olympic champion in 1904, when Emil Rausch (Ger) won the 1-mi event. About the middle of the 19th century, some American Indians had swum in London exhibiting a style resembling the crawl. An Englishman, John Trudgen, noted a variation of this style while on a trip to South America in the 1870s. His forerunner to the modern crawl used the legs in basically a breaststroke way. However, from ancient carvings and wall paintings it would seem that the trudgen stroke was in use in early times.

Another "throwback" was the front or Australian crawl which is credited to a British emigrant to Australia, Frederick Cavill, and his sons, who noticed the unusual style of South Sea Island natives, and modified it to their own use. American swimmers developed this even further by variations of the kicking action of the legs. At the beginning of the 20th century some had shown their prowess by attempting the breaststroke on their backs, and later the crawl action was tried in the same position. Thus the backstroke was born. In the 1930s the idea of recovering the arms over the water in the breaststroke was developed, and led to a drastic revision of the record book, until the new style was recognized as a separate stroke, the butterfly, in 1952. Also in the 1930s came the introduction, mainly in the US, of medley events in which swimmers use all four major strokes during one event, a real test of all-around ability.

World Titles

In the world swimming championships (instituted in 1973), the greatest number of medals won is 10 by Kornelia Ender of E Germany (8 gold, 2 silver) in 1973 and 75. The most by a man is 8 (5 gold, 3 silver) by Ambrose "Rowdy" Gaines (US, b Feb 17, 1959) in 1978 and 1982. The most gold medals is 6 by James Montgomery (b Jan 24, 1955) in 1973 and 1975.

The most medals in a single championship is 7 by Matt Biondi (US) in 1986 with 3 gold, 1 silver and 3 bronze. The women's record is 6, shared by Tracy Caulkins (US) (b Jan 11, 1963) in 1978 with 5 gold and a silver; by Kristin Otto (E Ger) with 4 gold and 2 silver in 1986; and by Mary Meagher (US) with 1 gold, 3 silver, and 2 bronze in 1986. She won a record 48 US titles before she retired in 1984.

The most successful country in the championships has been the US with a total of 57 swimming, 11 diving and 8 synchronized swimming titles. However, in women's swimming events alone E Germany has a record total of 44 victories.

Other than relays, the only gold medalist in the same event at three championships is Phil Boggs (US) in springboard diving.

The most medals won by a woman is 8 by Dawn Fraser, who in addition to her 4 golds won 4 silvers (400 m freestyle 1956, 4 × 100 m freestyle relay 1960 and 1964, 4 × 100 m medley relay 1960); by Shirley Babashoff (US) who won 2 golds (4 × 100 m freestyle relay 1972 and 1976) and 6 silvers (100 m freestyle 1972, 200 m freestyle

1972 and 1976, 400 m and 800 m freestyle 1976, and 400 m medley 1976); and by Kornelia Ender (E Germany) who, in addition to her 4 golds, won 4 silvers (200 m individual medley 1972, 4 × 100 m medley 1972, 4 × 100 m freestyle 1972 and 1976).

Most Individual Gold Medals

The record number of individual gold medals won is 4 shared by four swimmers: Charles M. Daniels (US) (1884–1973) (100 m freestyle 1906 and 1908, 220 yd freestyle 1904, 440 yd freestyle 1904); Roland Matthes (E Germany) (b Nov 17, 1950) with 100 m and 200 m backstroke 1968 and 1972; and Mark Spitz and Mrs Patricia McCormick.

MOST RECORDS: A young Mark Spitz (17 years old in this photo) is congratulated after setting a world record early in his career. Spitz might be considered the most successful swimmer ever. Of his 9 Olympic gold medals (including the unequaled haul of 7 in 1972), 8 were won in world record time. In his 6-year career, Spitz set a total of 26 world records. *(UPI)*

SPRINT CHAMPION: Matt Biondi (US) broke the 100 m world record 3 times in 1985-86, shortening the time from 49.36 sec to 48.74 sec. He also held the record for 50 m, and was the anchor man on the record-breaking US 4 x 100 m relay team. *(All-Sport)*

SWIMMING WORLD RECORDS (MEN)

At distances recognized by the Fédération Internationale de Natation Amateur as of July 16, 1983. FINA no longer recognizes any records made for non-metric distances. Only performances in 50-m pools are recognized as World Records.

Distance	*min:sec*	*Name and Nationality*	*Place*	*Date*
		FREESTYLE		
50 m	22.18	Peter Williams (S Africa)	Indianapolis, Ind	Apr 10, 1988
100 m	48.74	Matthew Biondi (US)	Orlando, Fla	June 24, 1986
200 m	1:47.44	Michael Gross (W Ger)	Los Angeles	July 29, 1984
400 m	3:47.38	Arthur Wojdat (Poland)	Orlando, Fla	Mar 27, 1988
800 m	7:50.64	Vladimir Salnikov (USSR)	Moscow, USSR	July 4, 1986
1,500 m	14:54.76	Vladimir Salnikov (USSR)	Moscow	Feb 22, 1983
4 × 100 m Relay	3:17.08	US National Team	Tokyo	Aug 17, 1985
		(Scott McCadam, Michael Heath, Paul Wallace, Matthew Biondi)		
4 × 200 m Relay	7:13.10	W Germany	Strasbourg, France	Aug 19, 1987
		(Peter Sitt, Rainer Henkel, Thomas Fahrner, Michael Gross)		
		BREASTSTROKE		
100 m	1:01.65	Steve Lundquist (US)	Los Angeles	July 29, 1984
200 m	2:13.34	Victor Davis (Canada)	Los Angeles	Aug 2, 1984
		BUTTERFLY STROKE		
100 m	52.84	Pedro Pablo Morales (US)	Orlando, Fla	June 23, 1986
200 m	1:56.24	Michael Gross (W Ger)	Hanover, W Ger	June 27, 1986
		BACKSTROKE		
100 m	54.91	David Berkoff (US)	Austin, Tex	Aug 12, 1988
200 m	1:58.14	Igor Polyansky (USSR)	Erfurt, E Ger	Mar 3, 1985

continued

INDIVIDUAL MEDLEY

200 m	2:00.56	Tamas Darnyi (Hungary)	Strasbourg, France	Aug 23, 1987
400 m	4:15.42	Tamas Darnyi (Hungary)	Strasbourg, France	Aug 9, 1987

MEDLEY RELAY

(Backstroke, Breaststroke, Butterfly Stroke, Freestyle)

4 × 100 m	3:38.28	US National Team (Richard "Rick" Carey, John Moffett, Pablo Morales, Matthew Biondi)	Tokyo	Aug 18, 1985

SWIMMING WORLD RECORDS (WOMEN)

FREESTYLE

Distance	*min:sec*	*Name and Nationality*	*Place*	*Date*
50 m	24.98	Yang Wenyi (China)	Guangzhou, China	April 10, 1988
100 m	54.73	Kristin Otto (E Ger)	Madrid, Spain	Aug 19, 1986
200 m	1:57.55	Heike Friedrich (E Ger)	E Berlin	June 18, 1986
400 m	4:05.45	Janet Evans (US)	Orlando, Fla	Dec 20, 1987
800 m	8:17.20	Janet Evans (US)	Orlando, Fla	Mar 23, 1988
1,500 m	15:52.10	Janet Evans (US)	Orlando, Fla	Mar 26, 1988
4 × 100 m Relay	3:40.57	East Germany (Kristin Otto, Manuella Stellmach, Sabina Schulze, Heike Friedrich)	Madrid, Spain	Aug 19, 1986
4 × 200 m Relay	7:55.47	E Germany (Manuella Stellmach, Astrid Strauss, Anke Moehring, Heike Friedrich)	Strasbourg, France	Aug 18, 1987

		BREASTSTROKE		
100 m	1:07.91	Silke Hoerner (E Ger)	Strasbourg, France	Aug 21, 1987
200 m	2:27.27	Allison Higson (Canada)	Montreal	May 29, 1988
		BUTTERFLY STROKE		
100 m	57.93	Mary Meagher (US)	Milwaukee	Aug 16, 1981
200 m	2:05.96	Mary Meagher (US)	Milwaukee	Aug 13, 1981
		BACKSTROKE		
100 m	1:00.59	Ina Kleber (E Ger)	Moscow	Aug 24, 1984
200 m	2:08.60	Betsy Mitchell (US)	Orlando, Fla	June 27, 1986
		INDIVIDUAL MEDLEY		
200 m	2:11.73	Ute Geweniger (E Ger)	E Berlin	July 4, 1981
400 m	4:36.10	Petra Schneider (E Ger)	Guayaquil, Ecuador	Aug 1, 1982
		MEDLEY RELAY (Backstroke, Breaststroke, Butterfly Stroke, Freestyle)		
4 × 100 m Relay	4:03.69	E German National Team (Ina Kleber, Sylvia Gerasch, Ines Geissler, Birgit Meineke)	Moscow	Aug 24, 1984

Most World Records

Men: 32, Arne Borg (Sweden) (b 1901), 1921–29. Women: 42, Ragnhild Hveger (Denmark) (b Dec 10, 1920), 1936–42. Under modern conditions (only metric distances in 50-meter pools) the most is 26 by Mark Spitz (US, b Feb 10, 1950), 1967–72, and 23 by Kornelia Ender (now Matthes) (E Germany, b Oct 25, 1958), 1973–76.

Hveger's record of 42 gained for her the name "Golden Torpedo." Her records came in 18 different events. She was a virtual certainty to win at the 1940 Olympic Games, but, of course, war intervened. Retiring in 1945, she made a comeback for the 1952 Games and placed fifth in the 400 m freestyle.

Long Distance Swimming

A unique achievement in long distance swimming was established in 1966 by Mihir Sen of Calcutta, India. He swam the Palk Strait from Sri Lanka to India (in 25 hours 36 min, Apr 5–6); the Straits of Gibraltar (Europe to Africa in 8 hours 1 min on Aug 24); the Dardanelles (Gallipoli, Europe, to Sedulbahir, Asia Minor, in 13 hours 55 min on Sept 12); the Bosphorus (in 4 hours on Sept 21) and the entire length of the Panama Canal (in 34 hours 15 min, Oct 29–31). He had earlier swum the English Channel in 14 hours 45 min on Sept 27, 1958.

The longest ocean swim was one of 128.8 miles by Walter Poenisch (US) (b 1914), who started from Havana, Cuba, and arrived at Little Duck Key, Fla (in a shark cage and wearing flippers) 34 hours 15 min later, July 11–13, 1978.

The greatest recorded distance ever swum is 1,826 miles down the Mississippi from Ford Dam, near Minneapolis, to Carrollton Avenue, New Orleans, July 6 to Dec 29, 1930, by Fred P. Newton, then 27, of Clinton, Okla. He was in the water a total of 742 hours, and the water temperature fell as low as 47° F. He protected himself with petroleum jelly.

The longest swim using the highly exhausting butterfly stroke exclusively was 40.6 miles from Gun Cay, the Bahamas to near Florida by twins James and Jonathan di Donato (b Oct 24, 1953) (US) June 23, 1985. They were stopped by foul weather after 20 hours 6 min.

The longest duration swim ever achieved was one of 168 continuous hours, ending on Feb 24, 1941, by the legless Charles Zibbelman, *alias* Zimmy (b 1894), of the US, in a pool in Honolulu, Hawaii.

The longest duration swim by a woman was 129 hours 45 min by Vicki Keith of Kingston, Ont, Canada, June 5–10, 1986. She covered about 78 mi in a pool.

The greatest distance covered in a continuous swim is 299 miles by Ricardo Hoffmann (b Oct 5, 1941) from Corrientes to Santa Elena, Argentina, in the River Paraná in 84 hours 37 min, Mar 3–6, 1981.

Bering Straits Swim

The first person to swim across from Alaska to the Soviet Union (2.7 mi), Lynne Cox (b Calif 1957) made the swim in 2 hours 5 min Aug 7–8, 1987. Because of heavy tides and strong currents she had to swim as much as 6 mi from Little Diomede, Alaska to Big Diomede,

GREATEST MILEAGE IN 24 HOURS: Alyson Gibbons (UK) set the women's record of 42.05 mi in a 25m pool in Birmingham, Eng, in Sept 1985. The men's record is 60.08 mi by Evan Barry (Aust) in a 50-yd pool on Dec 19-20, 1987, in Brisbane, Australia.

CONQUEROR OF BERING STRAIT: Lynne Cox (b 1957) became the first to swim from the US to Russia across the 2.7-mi channel between Alaska and Siberia. It took her 2 hours 5 min, Aug 7-8, 1987. ▼

HOLDER OF 3 RECORDS: ▲ Janet Evans of the US is the new queen of women freestylers, with records in distances of 400,800 and 1,500 meters. *(All-Sport)*

a military outpost in the Soviet Union. The water was 44°F and her body temperature dropped to 94° during the swim. Cox had previously swum the English Channel in 1972 in 9 hours 57 min, a record at that time.

Fastest Swimmers

The fastest speed measured in a 50 m pool is by Peter Williams (South Africa) who achieved a speed of 5.04 mph at Indianapolis, on April 10, 1988. The women's record is by Yang Wenyi (China), 4.48 mph.

Greatest Lifetime Distance

Gustave Brickner (b Feb 10, 1912) of Charleroi, Pa, recorded 38,512 mi of swimming in the 59 years from 1926 to his retirement in Nov 1986.

Treading Water

The duration record for treading water (vertical posture in an 8-ft square without touching the pool sides or bottom or lane markers) is 98½ hours set by Reginald (Moon) Huffstetler of Belmont, NC, at The Reef in Myrtle Beach, SC, May 20–24, 1986.

Albert Rizzo trod water in the sea at Gzira, Malta, for 108 hours 9 min Sept 7–12, 1983.

Fastest Channel Crossings

The official Channel Swimming Association record is 7 hours 40 min by Penny Dean (b March 21, 1955) of California, who swam from Shakespeare Beach, Dover, England to Cap Gris Nez, France on July 29, 1978.

The fastest crossing by a relay team is 7 hours 17 min by 6 Dover (Eng) lifeguards from England to France on Aug 9, 1981.

Closest Race

In the women's 100 m freestyle final in the 1984 Olympics, Carrie Steinseifer (US) and Nancy Hogshead (US) won in a tie at 55.92 sec, and were both awarded gold medals. It was not in record time, but it was the only dead heat in Olympic swimming history.

Diving Titles

Greg Louganis (US) (b Jan 29, 1960), won 5 world diving titles, highboard in 1978, and both highboard and springboard in both 1982 and 1986, as well as 2 Olympic golds in 1984. At Guayaquil, Ecuador, he became the first to score over 700 points for the 11-dive springboard event with 752.67 on Aug 1, 1982. He went on to be awarded a score of 10.0 by all 7 judges for his highboard inward 1½ somersault in the pike position. In the 1984 Olympics, Louganis won two gold medals and set record totals of 754.41 for springboard and 710.91 for highboard.

Klaus Dibiasi (Italy, b Austria, Oct 6, 1947) won a total of 5 Olympic diving medals (3 gold, 2 silver) in 4 Games from 1964 to 1976. He is also the only diver to win the same event (highboard) at

DIVING CHAMPION: Greg Louganis (US), considered by many to be the best diver in the world in the 1980's, is one of two divers to earn perfect 10's from all 7 judges for one dive. He achieved the feat while winning his 2nd and 3rd world championships. In the 1984 Olympics he won 2 gold medals and set new world records for springboard and highboard.

3 successive Games (1968, 72 and 76). He also won 4 medals (2 gold, 2 silver) in world events in 1973 and 1975.

Irina Kalinina (USSR) (b Feb 8, 1959) has won 5 medals (3 gold, one silver, one bronze) in 1973, 1975 and 1978.

Perfect Dive

In the 1972 US Olympic Trials, held in Chicago, Michael Finneran (b Sept 21, 1948) was awarded a score of 10 by all seven judges for a backward 1½ somersault 2½ twist (free) from the 10-m platform, an achievement then without precedent. Greg Louganis matched this feat in 1982.

Underwater Swimming

Paul Cryne (UK) and Samir Sawan al Aw swam 49.04 mi underwater in a 24-hour period at Doha, Qatar Feb 21–22, 1985 using sub-aqua equipment. They were swimming underwater for 95.5% of the time.

The first underwater cross-Channel swim was achieved by Fred Baldasare (US), aged 38, who completed a 42-mile swim from France to England with SCUBA in 18 hours 1 min, July 10–11, 1962.

Tony Boyle, Eddie McGettigan, Laurence Thermes and Gearoid Murphy swam a relay of 332.88 mi underwater in 168 hours using sub-aqua equipment at the Mosney Holiday Centre, Co. Meath, Ireland, June 22–29, 1985.

Relay Records

The New Zealand national relay team of 20 swimmers swam a record 113.59 mi in Lower Hutt, NZ in 24 hours, passing 100 mi in 20 hours 47 min 13 sec on Dec 9–10, 1983.

The most participants in a one-day swim relay is 2,135, each swimming a length, organized by the Syracuse (NY) YMCA, Apr 11, 1986.

The longest duration swim relay was 216 hours 50 min 16 sec for 373.57 mi by a team of 20 at Katowice, Poland, Feb 17–26, 1987.

The fastest time recorded for 100 miles in a pool by a team of 20 swimmers is 21 hours 41 min 4 sec by the Dropped Sports Swim Club of Indiana State University at Terre Haute, Ind, Mar 12–13, 1982. Four swimmers from the Darien YMCA, Conn, covered 300 miles in relay in 122 hours 59 min 40 sec, Nov 25–30, 1980.

TENNIS

Origins

The modern game of lawn tennis is generally agreed to have evolved as an outdoor form of the French Royal Tennis or *Jeu de Paume* from the 11th century. "Field Tennis" was mentioned in an English magazine (*Sporting Magazine*) on Sept 29, 1793. In 1858 Major Harry Gem laid out a "court" on the lawn of a friend in Birmingham, Eng, and in 1872 he founded the Leamington Club. In Feb 1874, Major Walter Clopton Wingfield of England (1833–1912) patented a form called "sphairistike," which was nicknamed "sticky," but the game soon became known as lawn tennis. The US Lawn Tennis Association (USLTA) was founded in 1881.

Amateurs were permitted to play with and against professionals in Open tournaments starting in 1968.

"Grand Slams"

The "grand slam" is to hold at the same time all four of the world's major championship titles: Wimbledon, the US Open, Australian and French championships. The first time this occurred was in 1935 when Frederick John Perry (GB) (b 1909) won the French title, having won Wimbledon (1934), the US title (1933–34) and the Australian title (1934).

The first player to hold all four titles in the same calendar year was J. Donald Budge (US) (b June 13, 1915), who won the championships of Wimbledon (1937), the US (1937), Australia (1938), and France (1938). He subsequently retained Wimbledon (1938) and the US (1938). Rodney George Laver (Australia) (b Aug 9, 1938) achieved this grand slam in 1962 as an amateur and repeated as a professional in 1969 to become the first two-time grand slammer.

Three women have achieved the grand slam: Maureen Catherine Connolly (US) (1934–69), in 1953; Margaret Jean Court (*née* Smith) (Australia) (b July 16, 1942) in 1970 and Martina Navratilova (US) (b Prague, Czech, Oct 18, 1956) in 1983–4. Navratilova won 6 successive grand slam singles titles in 1983–4 and with Pamela Howard Shriver (US) (b July 4, 1962) won 8 successive grand slam tournament women's doubles titles and 109 successive matches in all events from April 1983 to July 1985. The most singles championships in "grand slam" tournaments is 24 by Margaret Court (11 Australian, 5 French, 5 US, 3 Wimbledon), 1960–73. The men's record is 12 by Roy Emerson (Australia) (b Nov 3, 1936) (6 Australian, 2 each French, US, Wimbledon), 1961–67.

AT THE TOP: Steffi Graf (W Germany, b June 14, 1969) rose to #1 in the world in 1988, a year in which she ended Martina Navratilova's Wimbledon streak. (*Carol Newsom / Virginia Slims*)

SUPERSTAR: Martina Navratilova, easily the top money-winning woman athlete in the world, is one of 3 women who have won the "grand slam" (1983-84). She had a streak of 74 singles victories in 1984 and 109 doubles victories 1983-85. (*USTA*)

In doubles, the only men to win a "grand slam" are Frank Sedgman (Aust) and Ken McGregor (Aust) in 1951. Margaret Smith Court (Aust) and Ken Fletcher (Aust) won it in mixed doubles in 1961. Martina Navratilova (US) and Pam Shriver (US) managed a "grand slam" in doubles in 1983–84, the same year Martina got her "grand slam" in singles.

WIMBLEDON RECORDS

The first Championship was in 1877. Professionals first played in 1968. From 1971 the tie-break system was introduced, which effectually prevents sets proceeding beyond a 17th game, i.e., 9–8.

The record crowd for one day was 39,813 on June 26, 1986. The record for the whole championship was 400,032 in 1986.

In 1988, Steffi Graf (b June 14, 1969) of W Ger beat Martina Navratilova, 5–7, 6–2, 6–1 to end Navratilova's streak of 6 straight Wimbledon women's singles titles. Stefan Edberg, 22, of Sweden defeated Boris Becker, 4–6, 7–6, 6–4, 6–2, for the men's singles title.

Most Wins

Six-time singles champion Billie Jean King (*née* Moffitt) has also won 10 women's doubles and 4 mixed doubles during the period 1961 to 1979, to total a record 20 titles.

The greatest number of singles wins was 8 by Helen N. Moody (*née* Wills) (b Oct 6, 1905) (US), who won in 1927–30, 32–33, 35 and 38. This record was tied by Martina Navratilova in 1978, 79, and 82–87.

The greatest number of singles wins by a man since the Challenge Round (wherein the defending champion was given a bye until the final round) was abolished in 1922, is 5 consecutively by Bjorn Borg (Sweden) in 1976–80. The all-time men's record was 7 by William C. Renshaw, 1881–86 and 1889.

The greatest number of doubles wins by men was 8 by the brothers Doherty (GB)—Reginald Frank (1872–1910) and Hugh Lawrence (1875–1919). They won each year from 1897 to 1905 except for 1902. Hugh Doherty also won 5 singles titles (1902–06) and holds the record for most men's titles with 13.

The most wins in women's doubles was 12 by Elizabeth "Bunny" Ryan (US) (1894–1979). The greatest number of mixed doubles wins was 7 by Elizabeth Ryan, giving her a record total of 19 doubles wins 1914–34.

The men's mixed doubles record is 4 wins: by Elias Victor Seixas (b Aug 30, 1923) (US) in 1953–56; by Kenneth N. Fletcher (b June 15, 1940) (Australia) in 1963, 65–66 and 68; and by Owen Keir Davidson (Australia) (b Oct 4, 1943) in 1967, 71 and 73–74.

Youngest Champions

The youngest champion ever at Wimbledon was Charlotte (Lottie) Dod (1871–1960), who was 15 years 285 days old when she won in 1887.

The youngest male champion was Boris Becker (W Ger) (b Nov 22, 1967) who won the men's singles title in 1985 at 17 years 227 days.

The youngest-ever player at Wimbledon is reputedly Miss Mita Klima (Austria), who was 13 years old in the 1907 singles competition.

YOUNGEST WIMBLEDON ► WINNER: Boris Becker (W Ger) was not yet 18 when he beat the favorites and was victorious in 1985. (*Photo by David L. Boehm / Tamron*)

WON WIMBLEDON MATCH ▲ AT 14: Kathy Rinaldi, who in 1981 was the youngest ever to be victorious on a Wimbledon court, turned professional a month later. (*All-Sport*)

► WIMBLEDON WINNER in 1988: Stefan Edberg (Sweden) beat the top-ranked players for his first major championship. (*Michael Baz / Advantage International*)

The youngest player to win a match at Wimbledon is Kathy Rinaldi (b March 24, 1967) (US), who was 14 years 91 days old on June 23, 1981.

Oldest Champions

The oldest champion was Margaret Evelyn du Pont (*née* Osborne) (b Mar 4, 1918) (US) who was 44 years 125 days old when she won the mixed doubles in 1962 with Neale Fraser (Aust). The oldest singles champion was Arthur Gore (GB, 1868–1928) at 41 years 182 days in 1909.

US CHAMPIONSHIPS

The USTA Championships were first held in 1881 and continued until 1969. The Tournament was superseded in 1970 by the US Open Championships which had first been held in 1968, and are now held at Flushing Meadow, New York.

Most Wins

Margaret Evelyn du Pont (*née* Osborne) won a record 25 titles between 1936 and 1962. She won a record 13 women's doubles (12 with Althea Louise Brough), 9 mixed doubles and 3 singles. The men's record is 16 by William Tatem Tilden, including 7 men's singles, 1920–25, 1929—a record for singles shared with Richard Dudley Sears (1861–1943), 1881–87; William A Larned (1872–1926), 1901–02, 1907–11; and at women's singles by Molla Mallory (*née* Bjurstedt) (1892–1959), 1915–16, 1918, 1920–22, 1926 and Helen Moody (*née* Wills), 1923–25, 1927–29, 1931.

Youngest and Oldest

The youngest champion was Vincent Richards (1903–59) who was 15 years 139 days when he won the doubles with Bill Tilden in 1918. The youngest singles champion was Tracy Ann Austin (b Dec 12, 1962) who was 16 years 271 days when she won the women's singles in 1979.

The oldest champion was Margaret du Pont who won the mixed doubles at 42 years 166 days in 1960. The oldest singles champion was William Larned at 38 years 242 days in 1911.

Fastest Service

The fastest service ever *measured* was one of 163.6 mph by William Tatem Tilden (1893–1953) (US) in 1931.

A serve by Steve Denton (US) (b Sept 5, 1956) was timed at 138 mph at Beaver Creek, Colo on July 29, 1984, and is the record for fastest service timed with modern equipment.

Longest Game

The longest known singles game was one of 37 deuces (80 points) between Anthony Fawcett (Rhodesia) and Keith Glass (GB) in the first round of the Surrey championships at Surbiton, Surrey, England, on May 26, 1975. It lasted 31 min.

A junior game lasted 52 min (9 deuces) between Noelle Van Lottum and Sandra Begijn in the semi-finals of the under-13 Dutch National Indoor Championships in Ede, Gelderland, Holland on Feb 12, 1984.

The longest rally in tournament play is one of 643 times over the net between Vicky Nelson and Jean Hepner at Richmond, Va in October 1984. The 6 hour 22 min match was won by Nelson 6–4, 7–6. It concluded with a 1 hour 47 min tiebreaker, 13–11, for which one point took 29 min.

US OPEN CHAMPION and ▲ No. 1 in the world 1985-87: Ivan Lendl, the Czech who now lives in the US, has been winning almost all the mjor tournaments except Wimbledon. *(David L. Boehm / Tamron)*

►

$500,000 FOR A SINGLE MATCH: This, the greatest reward for one challenge match, was won by Jimmy Connors over John Newcombe in Las Vegas, Nev, in Apr 1975. Connors is shown here playing at Stratton, Vt. *(David L. Boehm)*

The longest tiebreaker was the 26–24 for the fourth and decisive set of a first round men's doubles at the Wimbledon Championship on July 1, 1985. Jan Gunnarsson (Sweden) and Michael Morterven (Denmark) defeated John Frawley (Australia) and Victor Pecci (Paraguay) 6–3, 6–4, 3–6, 7–6.

Tennis Marathons

The longest recorded tennis singles match is one of 120 hours 9 min by Mark Humes and Bill Victor at The City of Reno Tennis Center, Reno, Nev, May 20–25, 1986.

The duration record for doubles is 102 hours by Bobby McWaters, Jim Knapp, Jason Thomas and Ed Vantregt of Myrtle Beach High School, SC, Oct 25–29, 1987, at Kingston Plantation, SC. The organizer and coach was Bob Detwiler.

Highest Earnings

Ivan Lendl won the largest single prize of $583,200 in the inaugural 3-day Skins Stakes in W Palm Beach, Fla in 1987, when he beat Pat Cash in the final.

The greatest reward for playing a single match is the $500,000 won by James Scott (Jimmy) Connors (US) (b Sept 2, 1952) when he beat John Newcombe (Australia) (b May 23, 1944) in a challenge match at Caesars Palace Hotel, Las Vegas, Nev, Apr 26, 1975.

The record for career earnings is held by Martina Navratilova, who won $12,724,417 thorugh 1987. The men's record is $12,298,031 by Ivan Lendl through 1987, not including special contests such as the Skins Match (above).

The single season record for men is $2,028,850 by Ivan Lendl in 1982 (and including the Volvo Masters tournament held in January 1983). The women's record is $2,173,556 in 1984 (including a $1 million "Grand Slam" bonus) by Martina Navratilova in 1984.

Grand Prix Masters

The first WCT Masters Championships were staged in Tokyo, Japan in 1971 and have been held annually in NYC since 1977. Qualification to this annual event is by relative success in the preceding year's Grand Prix tournaments. John Patrick McEnroe (US) (b Feb 16, 1959) has won a record five titles, 1979, 1981, 1983–5.

Tennis Olympics

Tennis was part of the Olympic program up until 1924 and it was also a demonstration sport at Mexico City in 1968 and LA in 1984. It was reinstated to the Games proper in 1988.

Davis Cup

The most wins in the Davis Cup (instituted 1900), the men's international team championship, have been (inclusive of 1982) by the US with 28.

Roy Emerson (b Nov 3, 1936) (Australia) played on 8 Cup-winning teams, 1959–62, 1964–67.

Nicola Pietrangeli (Italy) (b Sept 11, 1933) played a record 163 rubbers, 1954 to 1972, winning 120. He played 109 singles (winning 78) and 54 doubles (winning 42). He took part in 66 ties.

Wightman Cup

The most wins in the Wightman Cup, contested annually by women's teams from the US and GB (instituted 1923) have been 49 by the US and 10 by GB through 1987. Virginia Wade (b July 10, 1945) (GB) played in a record 21 ties and 56 rubbers between 1965 and 1985. Christine Evert (b Dec 21, 1954) (US) won all 26 of her singles matches, 1971–85. She was selected by the Women's Sports Foundation in 1985 as the "greatest American Woman Athlete of the last 25 years."

Federation Cup

The most wins in the Federation Cup (instituted 1963), the women's international team championship, is 12 (to 1986) by the US. Virginia Wade (GB) played each year from 1967 to 1983, in a record 57 ties, playing 100 rubbers, including 56 singles (winning 36) and 44 doubles (winning 30). Christine Evert won her first 29 singles matches, 1977–86. Her overall record from 1977–87 is 35 wins in 37 singles and 15 wins in 19 doubles matches.

TRACK AND FIELD

Earliest References

There is evidence that running was involved in early Egyptian rituals at Memphis *c.* 3800 BC, but usually track and field athletics date from the ancient Olympic Games. The earliest accurately known Olympiad dates from July 776 BC, at which celebration Coroibos won the foot race of 164–169 yd. The oldest surviving measurements are a long jump of 23 ft 1½ in by Chionis of Sparta *c.* 656 BC, and a discus throw of 100 cubits (*c.* 152 ft) by Protesilaus.

Earliest Landmarks

The first time 10 sec ("even time") was bettered for 100 yd under championship conditions was when John Owen, then 30 years old, recorded 9⅘ sec in the AAU Championships at Wash, DC, on Oct 11, 1890. The first recorded instance of 6 ft being cleared in the high jump was when Marshall Jones Brooks (1855–1944) jumped 6 ft 0⅛ in at Marston, near Oxford, England, on March 17, 1876. (He is reputed to have done much of his jumping while wearing a high hat.) The first man over 7 ft was Charlie Dumas (US) who jumped 7 ft 0½ in in June 1956. The breaking of the "4-minute barrier" in the one mile was first achieved by Dr Roger Gilbert Bannister (b Harrow, England, March 23, 1929), when he recorded 3 min 59.4 sec on the Iffley Road track, Oxford, at 6:10 p.m. on May 6, 1954. John Walker (NZ) became the first man to run the mile in less than 4 min 100 times by Feb 17, 1985, in Auckland, NZ. His time was 3:54.57.

LONGEST WINNING STREAK: Edwin Moses (US) was finally beaten in May 1987 in the 400 m hurdles after 9 years 281 days. He had won 122 consecutive times. Moses holds the record for the fastest time, 47.02 sec.

MOST RECORDS IN ONE DAY: Jesse Owens, rated by many as the greatest athlete of the 20th century, and top vote-getter in the inaugural election for the US Olympic Hall of Fame, not only won 4 Olympic golds in one Games (1936), but set 6 world records in one hour at Ann Arbor, Mich (3 to 4PM, May 25, 1935). Here he shows his starting style. *(Photo Atlantic Richfield Co—ARCO Jesse Owens Games and Mary Evans)* ▼

HISTORIC JUMP: Bob Beamon (US) is in midflight of his 29-foot-2½-inch long jump at the 1968 Olympics in Mexico City. The high altitude and a tail wind possibly helped Beamon shatter the record by 1 ft 9 in. The next best jump has been 28 feet 10¼ in by Carl Lewis in 1983. ▼

Most Records

The greatest number of official world records (in events on the current schedule) broken by one athlete is 14, by Paavo Nurmi (Fin) at various events between 1921 and 1931, and by Iolanda Balas (Rom) in the high jump from 1956 to 1961. Nurmi also set eight marks in events no longer recognized, giving him a grand total of 22.

The only athlete to have his name entered in the record book 6 times in one day (in fact, within one hour) was J. C. "Jesse" Owens (US) (1913–80) who at Ann Arbor, Mich, on May 25, 1935, equaled the 100-yd running record with 9.4 sec at 3:15 p.m.; long-jumped 26 ft 8¼ in at 3:25 p.m.; ran 220 yd (straight away) in 20.3 sec at 3:45 p.m.; and 220 yd over low hurdles in 22.6 sec at 4 p.m. The two 220-yd runs were ratified as 200-m world records.

World Championships

The first-ever track and field world championships were staged at Helsinki, Finland, Aug 7–14, 1983. The most gold medals won was 3 by Carl Lewis (US) in the 100 m dash, long jump, and 4 × 100 m relay; and by Marita Koch (E Ger) in the 200 m dash, 4 × 100 m relay, and 4 × 400 m relay. With a silver medal in the 100 m dash, Koch was the top medal winner with 4.

In the 2nd world championships held in Rome in 1987, Lewis won gold medals at long jump and 4 × 100 m relay, also silver at 100 m, so he has won a record 5 gold at the two meets.

Fastest Speed

The fastest speed recorded for a man was 26.32 mph and 22.5 mph for a woman. Analysis of each 10 m of Aug 30, 1987 race in Rome shows that Ben Johnson (Canada) in setting his 100-m world record of 9.83 sec (av. speed 22.76 mph) ran the stretch between 50 and 70 m at a peak speed 26.32 mph, matched by Carl Lewis (US) running alongside him between 80 and 90 m at the same 26.32 mph.

Evelyn Ashford (US) in the 1984 sprint relay ran the final 100 m leg at a speed of 22.5 mph.

Standing Long Jump

Joe Darby (1861–1937), the famous Victorian professional jumper from Dudley, Worcestershire, England, jumped a measured 12 ft 1½ in *without* weights at Dudley Castle, on May 28, 1890. Arne Tverrvaag (Norway) jumped 12 ft 2¼ in in 1968. The best long jump by a woman is 9 ft 7 in by Annelin Mannes (Norway) at Flisa, Norway Mar 7, 1981.

Most Olympic Gold Medals in Field and Track

The most Olympic gold medals won in field events is 10 individual medals by Ray C. Ewry (US) (1874–1937) with:

Standing High Jump	1900, 1904, 1906, 1908
Standing Long Jump	1900, 1904, 1906, 1908
Standing Triple Jump	1900, 1904

The most gold medals won by a woman is 4, a record shared by Francina E. Blankers-Koen (Netherlands) (b Apr 26, 1918) with 100

DECATHLON CHAMPION: In the shot put, Daley Thompson (GB) scored most points (4,550) in the first day and a world record total of 8,847 points in the 1984 Olympic Games in LA. ◄

POLE-VAULT ► RECORDHOLDER: Sergei Bubka (USSR) has broken the world record 9 times. His 19 ft 10¼ in leap was made June 9, 1988.

ONE-LEGGED HIGH JUMPER: Arnie Boldt of Canada leaped 6 ft 8¼ in (2.04 m) high in Rome Apr 3, 1981, proving that he is not greatly handicapped. ◄

TOP RIVALS: Ben Johnson (Canada) (far right) broke the record for 100 m in beating Carl Lewis (US) (center) on Aug 30, 1987, in Rome. The new mark of 9.83 beat the old mark by 0.10 sec. *(Claus Anderson)*

m, 200 m, 80 m hurdles and 4 × 100 m relay (1948); Betty Cuthbert (Australia) (b Apr 20, 1938) with 100 m, 200 m, 4 × 100 m relay (1956) and 400 m (1964); and Barbel Wöckel (*née* Eckert) (b March 21, 1955) (E Germany) with 200 m and 4 × 100 m relay in 1976 and 1980.

The most gold medals at one Olympic celebration is 5 by Nurmi in 1924 and the most individual is 4 by Alvin C. Kraenzlein (US) (1876–1928) in 1900 with 60 m, 110 m hurdles, 200 m hurdles and long jump.

Most Olympic Medals in Track and Field

The most Olympic medals won in track is 12 (9 gold and 3 silver) by Paavo Johannes Nurmi (Finland) (1897–1973) with:

1920 Gold: 10,000 m; Cross-Country, Individual and Team; silver: 5,000 m.
1924 Gold: 1,500 m; 5,000 m; 3,000 m Team; Cross-Country, Individual and Team.
1928 Gold: 10,000 m; silver: 5,000 m; 3,000 m Steeplechase.

The most medals won by a woman athlete is 7 by Shirley de la Hunty (*née* Strickland) (b July 18, 1925) (Australia) with 3 gold, 1 silver and 3 bronze in the 1948, 1952 and 1956 Games. A recently discovered photo finish indicates that she finished third, not fourth, in the 1948 200 m event, thus unofficially increasing her total to 8. Irena Szewinska (*née* Kirszenstein) of Poland has also won 7 medals (3 gold, 2 silver, 2 bronze) in 1964, 1968, 1972 and 1976. She is the only woman ever to win Olympic medals in track and field in 4 successive Games.

WORLD INDOOR TRACK AND FIELD RECORDS

MEN

Event	min : sec	Name and Nationality	Place	Date
		RUNNING		
50 m	5.55	Ben Johnson (Can)	Ottawa, Canada	Jan 31, 1987
60 m	6.41	Ben Johnson (Can)	Indianapolis, Ind	Mar 7, 1987
200 m	20.36	Bruno Marie-Rose (Fra)	Lievin, France	Feb 22, 1987
400 m	45.41	Thomas Schonlebe (E Ger)	Vienna, Austria	Feb 9, 1986
800 m	1:44.91	Sebastian Coe (GB)	Cosford, England	Mar 12, 1983
1,000 m	2:16.62	Robert Druppers (Neth)	The Hague, Neth	Feb 20, 1988
1,500 m	3:35.82	Jose-Luis Gonzalez (Spain)	Oviedo, Spain	Mar 1, 1986
Mile	3:49.78	Eamonn Coghlan (Ire)	E. Rutherford, NJ	Feb 27, 1983
3,000 m	7:39.2	Emiel Puttemans (Bel)	Berlin, W Ger	Feb 18, 1973
5,000 m	13:20.4	Suleiman Nyambui (Tanzania)	New York	Feb 6, 1986
5,000 walk	18:11.41	Roland Weigel (E Ger)	Vienna, Austria	Feb 13, 1988
	ft in	**FIELD EVENTS**		
High Jump	7 11¼	Carlo Thranhardt (W Ger)	Berlin, W Ger	Feb 26, 1988
Pole Vault	19 7	Sergei Bubka (USSR)	Turin, Italy	Mar 17, 1987
Long Jump	28 10¼	Carl Lewis (US)	New York	Feb 26, 1984
Triple Jump	58 3¼	Mike Conley (US)	New York	Feb 27, 1987
Shot Put	73 ½	Werner Gunthor (Switz)	Magglingen, Switz	Feb 8, 1987
	sec	**HURDLING**		
50 m	6.25	Mark McKoy (Can)	Kobe, Japan	Mar 5, 1986
60 m	7.46	Greg Foster (US)	Indianapolis, Ind	Mar 6, 1987
	min : sec	**RELAYS**		
4×200 m	1:22.32	Italy	Turin, Italy	Feb 11, 1984
4×400 m	3:05.9	Soviet Union	Vienna, Austria	Mar 14, 1970
4×800 m	7:17.8	Soviet Union	Sofia, Bulgaria	Mar 14, 1971

WOMEN

Event	min : sec	Name and Nationality	Place	Date
		RUNNING		
50 m	6.06	Angella Issajenko (Can)	Ottawa, Canada	Jan 31, 1987
60 m	7.00	Nellie Cooman (Hol)	Madrid, Spain	Feb 23, 1986
200 m	22.27	Heike Drechsler (E Ger)	Indianapolis, Ind	Mar 7, 1987
400 m	49.59	Jarmila Kratochvilova (Czech)	Milan, Italy	Mar 7, 1982
800 m	1:56.40	Christine Wachtel (E Ger)	Vienna, Austria	Feb 13, 1988
1,000 m	2:34.8	Brigitte Kraus (W Ger)	Dortmund, W Ger	Feb 19, 1978
1,500 m	4:00.8	Mary Slaney (US)	New York	Feb 8, 1980
Mile	4:18.86	Doina Melinte (Romania)	E Rutherford, NJ	Feb 13, 1988
3,000 m	8:39.79	Zola Budd (GB)	Cosford, England	Feb 8, 1986
5,000 m	15:25.04	Brenda Webb (US)	Gainesville, Fla	Jan 30, 1988
3,000 walk	12:05.49	Olga Krishtop (USSR)	Indianapolis, Ind	Mar 6, 1987
	ft in	**FIELD EVENTS**		
High Jump	6 8¾	Stefka Kostadinova (Bul)	Indianapolis, Ind	Mar 8, 1987
Long Jump	24 ¼	Heike Drechsler (E Ger)	New York	Feb 27, 1987
Shot Put	73 10	Helena Fibingerova (Czech)	Jablonec, Czech	Feb 19, 1977
	sec	**HURDLING**		
50 m	6.71	Cornelia Oschkenat (E Ger)	Berlin, E Ger	Feb 9, 1986
	6.71	Cornelia Oschkenat (E Ger)	Berlin, E Ger	Feb 24, 1987
60 m	7.74	Yordanka Donkova (Bul)	Sofia, Bulgaria	Feb 25, 1987
	min :sec	**RELAYS**		
4×200 m	1:32.55	S. C. Eintracht Hamm (W Ger)	Dortmund, W Ger	Feb 18, 1988
4×400 m	3:34.38	West Germany	Dortmund, W Ger	Jan 30, 1981
4×800 m	8:24.72	Villanova (US)	Oklahoma City	Mar 14, 1987

WORLD TRACK AND FIELD RECORDS (MEN)

World Records for the men's events scheduled by the International Amateur Athletic Federation. Note: On July 27, 1976, IAAF eliminated all records for races measured in yards, except for the mile (for sentimental reasons). All distances up to (and including) 400 m must be electrically timed to be records. When a time is given to one-hundredth of a second, it represents the official electrically timed record.

A—These records were set at high altitudes—Mexico City 7,349 ft.

RUNNING

Event	*min:sec*	*Name and Nationality*	*Place*	*Date*
100 m	9.83	Ben Johnson (Canada)	Rome	Aug 30, 1987
200 m	19.72A	Pietro Mennea (Italy)	Mexico City	Sept 12, 1979
400 m	43.39	Butch Reynolds (US)	Zurich	Aug 17, 1988
800 m	1:41.73	Sebastian Coe (GB)	Florence, Italy	June 10, 1981
1,000 m	2:12.18	Sebastian Coe (GB)	Oslo	July 11, 1981
1,500 m	3:29.46	Said Aouita (Morocco)	W Berlin	Aug 23, 1985
1 mile	3:46.32	Steve Cram (GB)	Oslo	July 27, 1985
2,000 m	4:50.81	Said Aouita (Morocco)	Paris	July 16, 1987
3,000 m	7:32.1	Henry Rono (Kenya)	Oslo	June 27, 1978
5,000 m	12:58.39	Said Aouita (Morocco)	Rome	July 22, 1987
10,000 m	27:13.81	Fernando Mamede (Portugal)	Stockholm	July 2, 1984
20,000 m	57:24.2	Jos Hermens (Neth)	Papendal, Neth	May 1, 1976
25,000 m	1 hr. 13:55.8	Toshihiko Seko (Japan)	Christchurch, NZ	Mar 22, 1981
30,000 m	1 hr. 29:18.8	Toshihiko Seko (Japan)	Christchurch, NZ	Mar 22, 1981
1 hour	13 miles 24 yd 2 ft	Jos Hermens (Neth)	Papendal, Neth	May 1, 1976

FIELD EVENTS

Event	*ft*	*in*	*Name and Nationality*	*Place*	*Date*
High Jump	7	11¼	J.N.P. Sjoberg (Sweden)	Stockholm	June 30, 1987

Pole Vault	19	10¼	Sergei Bubka (USSR)	Bratislava, Czech	June 9, 1988
Long Jump	29	2½A	Robert Beamon (US)	Mexico City	Oct 18, 1968
Triple Jump	58	11½	Willie Banks (US)	Indianapolis, Ind	June 16, 1985
Shot Put	75	8	Ulf Timmerman (E Ger)	Khania, Greece	May 22, 1988
Discus Throw	243	0	Jurgen Schult (E Ger)	Neubrandenburg, E Ger	June 6, 1986
Hammer Throw	284	7	Yuri Sedykh (USSR)	Stuttgart, W Ger	Aug 30, 1986
Javelin Throw*	343	10	Uwe Hohn (E Ger)	East Berlin	July 20, 1984

HURDLING

Event	*min:sec*	*Name and Nationality*	*Place*	*Date*
110 m (3′6″)	12.93	Renaldo Nehemiah (US)	Zurich	Aug 19, 1981
400 m (3′0″)	47.02	Edwin Corley Moses (US)	Coblenz, W Ger	Aug 31, 1983
3,000 m Steeplechase	8:05.4	Henry Rono (Kenya)	Seattle, Wash	May 13, 1978

RELAYS

4 × 100 m	37.83	US Team (Sam Graddy, Ron Brown, Calvin Smith, Carl Lewis)	Los Angeles	Aug 11, 1984
4 × 200 m	1:20.26†	University of Southern California (US) (Joel Andrews, James Sanford, William Mullins, Clancy Edwards)	Tempe, Ariz	May 27, 1978
4 × 400 m	2:56.16A	US Olympic Team (Vincent Matthews, Ronald Freeman, G. Lawrence James, Lee Edward Evans)	Mexico City	Oct 20, 1968
4×800 m	7:03.89	Great Britain Team (Peter Elliott, Garry Cook, Steve Cram, Sebastian Coe)	London	Aug 30, 1982
4×1,500 m	14:38.8	W German Team (Thomas Wessinghage, Harald Hudak, Michael Lederer, Karl Fleschen)	Cologne, W Ger	Aug 17, 1977

DECATHLON

8,847 points (1985 scoring)	Francis Morgan "Daley" Thompson (GB)	Los Angeles	Aug 8–9, 1984

* Old javelin—new javelin with center of gravity moved forward was introduced in 1986—record under new rules is 287 ft 7 in by Jan Zelezny (Czech) (b June 16, 1966) at Nitra, Czech, on May 31, 1987.

WORLD TRACK AND FIELD RECORDS (WOMEN)

RUNNING

Event	*min:sec*	*Name and Nationality*	*Place*	*Date*
100 m	10.49	Florence Griffith Joyner (US)	Indianapolis, Ind	July 16, 1988
200 m	21.71	Marita Koch (E Ger)	Potsdam, E Ger	July 21, 1984
	21.71	Heike Dreschler (E Ger)	Stuttgart, W Ger	Aug 29, 1986
400 m	47.60	Marita Koch (E Ger)	Canberra, Australia	Oct 6, 1985
800 m	1:53.28	Jarmila Kratochvilova (Czech)	Munich	July 26, 1983
1,000 m	2:30.6	Tanyana Providokhina (USSR)	Podolsk, USSR	Aug 20, 1978
1,500 m	3:52.47	Tatyana Kazankina (USSR)	Zurich, Switz	Aug 13, 1980
1 mile	4:16.71	Mary Decker Slaney (US)	Zurich, Switz	Aug 21, 1985
2,000 m	5:28.69	Maricica Puica (Romania)	London, Eng	July 11, 1986
3,000 m	8:22.62	Tatyana Kazankina (USSR)	Leningrad	Aug 26, 1984
5,000 m	14:37.33	Ingrid Kristiansen (Norway)	Stockholm, Sweden	Aug 5, 1986
10,000 m	30:13.74	Ingrid Kristiansen (Norway)	Oslo, Norway	July 5, 1986

FIELD EVENTS

Event	*ft*	*in*	*Name and Nationality*	*Place*	*Date*
High Jump	6	10¼	Stefka Kosadinova (Bulgaria)	Rome	Aug 30, 1987
Long Jump	24	8¼	Galina Christyakova (USSR)	Leningrad, USSR	June 11, 1988
Shot Put	74	3	Natalya Lisovskaya (USSR)	Moscow, USSR	June 7, 1987
Discus Throw	244	7	Zdena Silhava (Czech)	Nitra, Czech	Aug 26, 1984
Javelin Throw	258	10	Petra Felke (E Ger)	Leipzig, E Ger	July 29, 1987

Event	min:sec	Name and Nationality	Place	Date
HURDLES				
100 m (2′9″)	12.25	Ginka Zagorcheva (Bulgaria)	Drama, Greece	Aug 8, 1987
400 m (2′6″)	52.94	Marina Stepanova (USSR)	Tashkent, USSR	Sept 17, 1986
RELAYS				
4 × 100 m	41.37	E Germany (Silke Gladisch, Sabine Rieger, Ingrid Auerswold, Marlies Göhr)	Canberra, Australia	Oct 6, 1985
4 × 200 m	1:28.15	E Germany (Marlies Göhr, Romy Müller, Barbel Wöckel, Marita Koch)	Jena, E Ger	Aug 10, 1980
4 × 400 m	3:15.92	E Germany (Gesine Walther, Sabine Busch, Dagmar Ruebsam, Marita Koch)	Erfurt, E Ger	June 3, 1984
4 × 800 m	7:50.17	USSR (Nadezha Olizarenko, Lyubov Gunina, Lyudmila Borisova, Irina Padyalovskaya)	Moscow, USSR	Aug 7, 1984
HEPTATHLON				
7,215 points		Jackie Joyner-Kersee (US)	Indianapolis, Ind	July 15–16, 1988

Oldest and Youngest Record Breakers

The greatest age at which anyone has broken a world track and field record is 41 years 196 days in the case of John J. Flanagan (1868–1938), who set a world record in the hammer throw on July 24, 1909. The female record is 36 years 139 days for Marina Stepanova (USSR) (*née* Makeyeva, b May 1, 1950) when she ran 400 m hurdles in 52.94 sec in Tashkent, USSR, Sept 17, 1986.

The youngest individual record breaker is Wang Yang (b Apr 9, 1971) (China) who set a women's 3,000 m walk record in 21 min 33.8 sec at Jian, China on Mar 9, 1986, when aged 14 years 334 days. The male record is 17 years 198 days by Thomas Ray (1862–1904) when he pole-vaulted 11 ft 2¼ in on Sept 19, 1879.

Oldest and Youngest Olympic Champions

The oldest athlete to win an Olympic gold was Irish-born Patrick J. "Babe" McDonald (US) (1878–1954) who was aged 42 years 26 days when he won the 56-lb weight throw at Antwerp, Belgium on Aug 21, 1920. The oldest female champion was Lia Manoliu (Romania) (b Apr 25, 1932) aged 36 years 176 days when she won the discus at Mexico City on Oct 18, 1968.

THREE WORLD RECORDS IN 20 DAYS: Steve Cram (GB) set a new record in running 1500 m on July 16, 1985 (3:29.67), in the mile run on July 27 (3:46.32), and 2000 m race on Aug 4 (4:51.39). On Aug 10 he came in with the world's second best time in 1000 m, against a head wind. Shown here, he exults over his victory in the mile. He set a better mark in the 1500 m in 1985. (*IAAF Mobil Grand Prix*)

The oldest Olympic medalist was Tebbs Lloyd Johnson (1900–84), aged 48 years 115 days when he was third in the 1948 50,000 m walk. The oldest woman medalist was Dana Zatopkova aged 37 years 248 days when she was second in the javelin in 1960.

The youngest gold medalist was Barbara Pearl Jones (US) (b March 26, 1937) who was a member of the winning 4 × 100 m relay team, aged 15 years 123 days, at Helsinki, Finland, on July 27, 1952. The youngest male champion was Robert Bruce Mathias (US) (b Nov 17, 1930) aged 17 years 263 days when he won the decathlon at London, Aug 5–6, 1948.

Longest Winning Sequence

Iolanda Balas (Romania) (b Dec 12, 1936) won 140 successive high jump competitions from 1956 to 1967. The record for track races is 122 at 400-meter hurdles by Edwin Corley Moses (US) (b July 31, 1955) from 1977 to his defeat by Danny Harris (US) (b Sept 7, 1965) in Madrid on June 4, 1987.

24-Hour Record

The greatest distance run on a standard track in 24 hours is 170 miles 974 yd by Dave Dowdle (b Nov 7, 1954) (Gloucester AC) at Blackbridge, Gloucester, England, May 22–23, 1982. The best by a woman is 133 miles 939 yd by Lynn Fitzgerald (b Sept 9, 1947) (Highgate Harriers) in the same race.

Mass Relay Record

The record for 100 miles by 100 runners belonging to one club is 7 hours 53 min 52.1 sec by Baltimore Road Runners Club of Towson, Md, on May 17, 1981. The women's mark is 10 hours 47 min 9.3 sec by a team from the San Francisco Dolphins Southend Running Club, on Apr 3, 1977.

The longest relay ever run was 10,524 mi by 2,660 runners at Trondheim, Norway, Aug 26–Oct 20, 1985. Twenty members of the Melbourne Fire Brigade ran around Australia on Highway No. 1 in 43 days 23 hours 58 min, July 10–Aug 23, 1983. The most participants is 4,800 (192 teams of 25), in the Batavierenrace, 103.89 mi from Nijmegen to Enschede, The Netherlands, won in 9 hours 30 min 44 sec on Apr 23, 1983.

Running Backwards

The fastest time recorded for running 100 yd backwards is 12.8 sec by Ferdie Adoboe (Kenya, now US) in Amherst, Mass, on July 28, 1983.

Anthony ''Scott'' Weiland, 27, ran the Detroit marathon backwards in 4 hours 7 min 54 sec on Oct 3, 1982.

Donald Davis (b Feb 10, 1960) (US) ran 1 mi backwards in 6 min 7.1 sec at the University of Hawaii on Feb 21, 1983.

Arvind Pandya (India) ran LA–NY in 107 days, Aug 18–Dec 3, 1984.

Rob Cooper of Toronto, Ohio, claims his 5,000 m (3.1 mi) run backwards in Schenley Park, Pittsburgh, in 37 min 16 sec is a record without compare.

Longest Race

The longest races ever staged were the 1928 (3,422 miles) and 1929 (3,665 miles) transcontinental races from NYC to Los Angeles. The Finnish-born Johnny Salo (1893–1931) was the winner in 1929 in 79 days, from March 31 to June 18. His elapsed time of 525 hours 57 min 20 sec gave a running average of 6.97 mph. His margin of victory was only 2 min 47 sec.

Three-Legged Race

The fastest recorded time for a 100-yd three-legged race is 11.0 sec by Olympic medalists Harry L. Hillman (1881–1945) and Lawson Robertson (1883–1951) in Brooklyn, NYC, on Apr 24, 1909.

Six-Day Race

The greatest distance covered by a man in six days (*i.e.* the 144 permissible hours between Sundays in Victorian times) was 635 miles 1,385 yards by Yiannis Kouros (Greece) (b Feb 13, 1956) at Colac, Australia on Nov 26–Dec 1, 1984. On the same occasion Eleanor Adams (UK) (b Nov 20, 1947) set the women's record at 500 mi 1,452 yds.

Pancake Race Record

The annual "Housewives" Pancake Race at Olney, Buckinghamshire, England, was first mentioned in 1445. The record for the winding 415-yd course (three tosses mandatory) is 61.0 sec, set by Sally Ann Faulkner, 16, on Feb 26, 1974. The record for the counterpart race at Liberal, Kansas, is 58.5 sec by Sheila Turner (b July 9, 1953) in 1975.

Dale R. Lyons (b Feb 26, 1937) (GB) has run several marathons during which he tosses a 2-oz pancake repeatedly en route in a 1½ lb pan. His fastest time is 3 hours 6 min 48 sec in London, Apr 20, 1986.

Fastest 100 Miles

The fastest recorded time for 100 miles is 11 hours 30 min 51 sec by Donald Ritchie (b July 6, 1944) at Crystal Palace, London, on Oct 15, 1977. The best by a woman is 15 hours 24 min 46 sec by Eleanor Adams (GB) (b Nov 20, 1947) at Honefoss, Norway, July 12–13, 1986.

Blind 100 Meters

The fastest time recorded for 100 m by a blind man is 11.4 sec by Graham Henry Salmon (b Sept 5, 1952) of Loughton, Essex, England, at Grangemouth, Scotland, on Sept 2, 1978.

Fastest 100 Kilometers

Donald Ritchie ran 100 km in a record 6 hours 10 min 20 sec at Crystal Palace, London, on Oct 28, 1978. The women's best, run on a road, is 7 hours 27 min 22 sec by Chantal Langlace (b Jan 6, 1955) (France) at Amiens, France on Sept 6, 1980.

Trans-America Run

The fastest time for the cross-US run is 46 days, 8 hours 36 min by Frank Giannino Jr (b 1952) (US) for the 3,100 miles from San Francisco to NYC, Sept 1–Oct 17, 1980.

When Johnny Salo won the 1929 Trans-America race from NYC to LA, his total elapsed time of 525 hours 57 min 20 sec gave him a margin of only 2 min 47 sec over second-place Peter Gavuzzi—after 3,665 miles.

ALL IN THE FAMILY: Sisters-in-law Jackie Joyner-Kersee (above, throwing the javelin) and Florence Griffith Joyner, both of the US, set world records in the US Olympic Trials on the same day (July 16) in 1988. Joyner-Kersee broke her own mark in the heptathlon, and Joyner set hers in the 100-m dash. *(Focus on Sports)*

The women's Trans-America record is 69 days 2 hours 40 min by Mavis Hutchinson (South Africa) (b Nov 25, 1924) Mar 12–May 21, 1978.

Trans-Canada Run

The only woman to have run across Canada from Victoria, BC, to Halifax, Nova Scotia, a distance of 3,824 mi in 6½ months, touching all 10 provinces, is Kanchan Beryl Stott of Ottawa, Ont. It was probably the longest run ever made by a woman.

Greatest Mileage

Douglas Alistair Gordon Pirie (b Feb 10, 1931) (GB), who set 5 world records in the 1950s, estimated that he had run a total distance of 216,000 miles in 40 years to 1981.

The greatest distance run in one year is 15,472 miles by Tina Maria Stone (b Naples, Italy, Apr 5, 1934) of Irvine, Calif, in 1983.

Ron Grant (Aust) (b Feb 15, 1943) ran around Australia, 8,316 miles in 217 days 3 hours 45 min, running every day Mar 28–Oct 31, 1983.

Ernst Mensen (1799–1846) (Norway), a former seaman in the British Navy, is reputed to have run from Istanbul, Turkey, to Calcutta, in West Bengal, India, and back in 59 days in 1836, so averaging an improbable 92.4 miles per day.

Max Telford (b Hawick, Scotland, Feb 2, 1935) of New Zealand ran 5,110 miles from Anchorage, Alaska, to Halifax, Nova Scotia, in 106 days 18 hours 45 min from July 25 to Nov 9, 1977.

The greatest non-stop run recorded is 352.9 miles in 121 hours 54 min by Bertil Järlåker (Sweden) at Norrköping, Sweden, May 26–31, 1980. He was moving 95.04% of the time.

Downhill Mile

Mike Boit (Kenya) ran what is believed to be the fastest mile ever when he won the Molenberg Mile in 3 min 28.36 sec over a carefully measured downhill course along Queen Street, Auckland, NZ, on Apr 16, 1983. The course had an overall vertical drop of nearly 208 yd.

Standing High Jump

The best high jump from a standing (as opposed to a running) position is 6 ft 2¾ in by Rune Almen (b Oct 20, 1952) (Sweden) at Karlstad, Sweden, on May 30, 1980. The best jump by a woman is 4 ft 11 in by Grete Bjørdalsbakke (b June 23, 1960) (Norway) at Orsta, Norway on Dec 12, 1979.

> The longest-ever solo run is 10,608 miles by Robert J. Sweetgall (US) (b Dec 8, 1947) around the perimeter of the 48 states, starting and finishing in Wash, DC, Oct 9, 1982–July 15, 1983.

SPORTS AND GAMES ENDURANCE MARATHONS

Backgammon—151 hours 11 min by Dick Newcombe and Greg Peterson at Rockford, Ill, June 30–July 6, 1978.

Badminton (singles)—83 hours 25 min by Henry Marais and Jaco Visser at Quartermaster, Pretoria, S Africa, Jan 1–4, 1988. (doubles)—86 hours 22 min by Cameron McMullen, Michael Patterson, Stephen Breuer and Michael Bain at Rhyl, Clywd, Wales, July 18–21, 1987.

Basketball—102 hours by Sigma Nu Fraternity at Indiana U, Indiana, Pa, Apr 13–17, 1983.

Bowling (Ten Pin)—195 hours 1 min by Jim Webb at Gosford City Bowl, NSW, Aust, 1984.

Bridge (Contract)—186 hours 38 min by Johnathan Noad, Jeremy Cohen, Robert Pinder and Andrew Gale at Ariel Hotel, Hayes, Middlesex, Eng, Sept 20–28, 1986.

Checkers—138 hours 28 min by Greg Davis and Mark Schumacher at Denny's Restaurant, Nunawading, Victoria, Aust, Aug 26–Sept 1, 1985.

Chess—200 hours by Roger Long and Graham Croft at Dingles, Bristol, Eng, May 11–19, 1984.

Cribbage—124 hours 15 min by 4 students from St Anselm's College, Wirral, Merseyside, Eng, July 14–19, 1986.

Croquet—120 hours 25 min by Jane Langan, Miles Harbot, Jo Gill and Daryl Shorthose at Birmingham U, Eng, June 14–19, 1986.

Curling—(4 players) 67 hours 55 min at the Capital Winter Club, Fredericton, NB, Canada, Apr 9–12, 1982. (pair)—43 hours 2 min by Brian Rankin and David Senior at Bradford, W Yorkshire, Eng, July 5–7, 1988.

Darts—168 hours 4 min by David Dingley and Michael Poole at The Three Horseshoes, Malvern, Worcestershire, Eng, Nov 1986.

Ice Skating—109 hours 5 min by Austin McKinley at Christchurch, New Zealand, June 21–25, 1977.

Judo—245 hours 30 min by 5 of 6 people at Smithfield RSL Youth Club, NSW, Aust, Jan 3–13, 1984.

Joggling (3 balls)—3 hours 22 min 32.51 sec by Ashrita Furman while competing in a marathon run on July 4, 1988 at Salmon, Idaho. Albert Lucas ran in the 1988 Los Angeles Marathon, alongside more contestants, joggling 3 balls without drop for 3 hours 29 min 17 sec.

Juggling (3 balls without drop)—6 hours 7 min 4 sec by Ashrita Furman in 1987.

Pool—345 hours 52 min by Gary Drummond and John Small at Clackamannan College, Alloa Central, Eng, June 17–July 1, 1988.

Racquetball—50 hours 2 min by Robert Sauve and Vic Sabramsky in Whitby, Ont, Canada, Aug 20–22, 1987.

Roller Skating—344 hours 18 min by Isamu Furugen at Naha Roller Skate Land, Okinawa, Japan, Dec 11–27, 1983.

Scrabble—153 hours by Peter Finan and Neil Smith at St Anselm's College, Wirral, Merseyside, Eng, Aug 18–25, 1984. (Against various opponents)—155 hours 48 min by Ken Cardozo at "Perfect Pizza," Fulham, Eng, Dec 5–11, 1984.

Skiing (Alpine)—138 hours by Luc Labrie at Daie Comeau, Que, Can on Feb 20–25, 1984. (With no waiting for lifts)—87 hours 28 min by John Mordini at Kissing Bridge, NY, Jan 11–14, 1988.

Soccer—64 hours 44 min by two teams from Stewart's, Lake Park, Fla, Aug 31–Sept 3, 1984.

Softball (fast pitch)—61 hours 36 min 33 sec by two teams of 9 (no substitutes), Marines of the 2nd Radio Battalion at Camp Lejeune, NC, May 3–5, 1984. (slow pitch)—111 hours 2 min by Brigade Service Support Group-1 and Marine Aircraft Group-24 at Kareohe Marine Corps Air Station, Hawaii, Sept 3–8, 1986.

Squash—126 hours 1 min by P. Etherton and L. Davies at Tannum Sands, Queensland, Aust, July 7–12, 1987.

Table Tennis (singles)—147 hours 47 min by S. Unterslak and J. Boccia at Dewaal Hotel, Cape Town, S Africa, Nov 12–18, 1983. (doubles)—101 hours 1 min 11 sec by Lance, Phil and Mark Warren and Bill Weir at Sacramento, Calif, Apr 9–13, 1979.

Tennis (singles)—120 hours 9 min by Mark Humes and Bill Victor at The City of Reno Plumas Tennis Center, Reno, Nev, May 20–25, 1987. (doubles)—102 hours by 4 high school players from Myrtle Beach, SC, Oct 25–29, 1987 at Kingston Plantation, SC.

Trampolining—266 hours 9 min by Jeff Schwartz at Glenview, Ill, Aug 14–25, 1981.

Volleyball—118 hours 30 min by students of Krugersdorp HS, S Africa, Mar 30–Apr 4, 1988.

Water Polo—25 hours 34 min by 2 teams of 7 from Shrewsbury School, Shropshire, Eng, Nov 29–30, 1986.

NEWLY VERIFIED RECORDS

The following records were received and verified too late to be included in the main section of this book.

Oldest Authentic Centenarians (Ch. 1). Madame Calment of Arles, France, is 113 years old, according to a claim which has just been verified that she was born on Feb 21, 1875.

Largest Meeting of Twins (Ch. 1). 1,810 sets met at Twinsberg, Ohio, Aug 6–7, 1988, for their 13th annual Twins Day Festival.

Longest Separated Twins (Ch. 1). Twins Philip and Barbara McAuley of Preston, Lancashire, Eng (b May 27, 1916), became separated when over a year old on June 30, 1917. Officers of the Salvation Army reunited them for the first time after almost exactly 70 years in London, June 29, 1987.

Melons (Ch. 2). A watermelon weighing 270 lb, 91 in long and 43 in in circumference around the center, was reported to have been grown in 1987 by Foye Rogerson of Robersonville, NC.

Pop Concert Attendance (Ch. 6). When the Beach Boys appeared at the Parkway Party in Philadelphia on July 4, 1985, estimates of the crowds in the street were as high as 1 million.

Weightiest Magazine (Ch. 6). The September 1987 issue of Vogue ran to 828 hernia-inducing pages.

Most Honored Entertainer (Ch. 6). Bob Hope never received an Oscar but he has been awarded more honors by the US than any other civilian, namely, the Medal of Freedom (1969); Congressional Gold Medal (1963); Medal of Merit (1966); Distinguished Public Service Medal (1973); and the Distinguished Service Gold Medal (1971). He is also an Hon. CBE (1976) and was appointed Hon. Brigadier of the US Marine Corps. He has 44 honorary degrees.

Fastest Propeller-Driven Aircraft (Ch. 8). McDonnell Douglas expects its projected MD-91X, powered by counter-rotating multi-bladed fans, to cruise at about Mach 0.78/514 mph.

Lawn Mower Ride (Ch. 8). The longest drive was 3,031 mi when Steve Perritt of Standlake, Oxfordshire, Eng, drove a Kubota G3HST across England in 30 driving days from Feb 14 to Mar 18, 1988.

Solar-Powered Cars (Ch. 8). General Motors Sunraycer ($8 million, Australian) won a 1,988 mi race of steam-driven cars from Darwin to Adelaide, S Australia on Nov 6, 1987.

Survival after Shipwreck (Ch. 8). The longest survival at sea was 142 days when a 30-ft-long Costa Rican fishing boat, *Cairo III*, containing 5 men, ran out of gas and was stranded in the Pacific Jan 24–June 14, 1988. The men started out from Puntarenas, Costa Rica, and ran into trouble when their motor conked out. They drifted until they were sighted by the crew of a Japanese tuna boat 700 mi southeast of Hawaii, who brought them to Oahu. Being fishermen, they never went hungry, according to the captain, Gerardo Obregon Obando.

Cheese (Ch. 9). The largest cheese ever created was a cheddar of 40,060 lb made Mar 13–14, 1988 at Simon's Specialty Cheese, Little

LARGEST TELEPHONE: This phone (13 ft × 15 ft) and handset (10 ft high), weighing 6,720 lb, is operational. It was exhibited at the Glasgow Garden Festival in Scotland in May 1988. To raise the handset to this vertical position a hydraulic lift is needed.

Chute, Wis, subsequently taken on tour in a specially-designed, refrigerated "Cheesemobile."

Largest Community Garden (Ch. 9). The Wayne County (Mich) Senior Citizens have increased the area of their plots to 1,450,000 sq ft—580 gardens of 50x50 ft in 1988, with 385,000 sq ft of this being new ground, and beating the Dayton garden of 952,475 sq ft.

Coin Display (Ch. 10). A carpet of 1,945,223 one-franc Belgian coins (0.83 in diameter—approx same size as U.S. quarter) 25.384 mi long was laid in Geel, Belgium, by members of Mepp-Stegeta on June 25, 1988.

Ice Cream Sundae (Ch. 10). The largest weighed 54,914.8 lb, made by Palm Dairies, Ltd, in Edmonton, Alberta, Canada, on July 24, 1988. It consisted of 44,689.5 lb of ice cream, 9,688.1 lb of syrup and 537.2 lb of topping.

Largest Milk Shake (Ch. 10). A milk shake of 282 gallons was made in a 300-gallon stainless steel mixer on July 9, 1988, in Coral Springs, Fla, at Mullins Park.

Largest Hamburger (Ch. 10). A 5,100-lb hamburger of ground beef was cooked on July 9, 1988, in Coral Springs, Fla at Mullins Park.

LONGEST CONTINUOUS HOME CONSTRUCTION:
For complete story, see page 250

Sausage (Ch. 10). The longest continuous sausage ever made was 13.125 mi long, made at the premises of Keith Boxley, near Wolverhampton, Eng, in 15 hours 33 min, June 18–19, 1988.

Strawberry "Bowl" (Ch. 10). A strawberry "bowl" weighing 3,324-½ lb was amassed on July 7, 1988, by the Kinsmen Club of Portage la Prairie, Manitoba, Canada.

Youngest Undergraduate (Ch. 10). Adragon Eastwood De Mello (b Oct 5, 1976) obtained his B.A. in mathematics from the Univ of Calif in Santa Cruz on June 11, 1988, aged 11 years 8 months.

Bicycle Stunts (Ch. 11). 19 members of the Jago Sport Club of Semarang, Central Java, Indonesia, mounted on and rode a single bicycle for 656 ft 2 in on June 30, 1988.

CPR (Cardio-Pulmonary Resuscitation). (Ch. 11). The longest time that a team of 2 continuously performed CPR (15 chest compressions alternating with 2 ventilations, i.e., mouth-to-mouth resuscitation) is 80 hours by Christopher Currie and Kevin Pilkington, July 7-10, 1988, in Penrith, Cumbria, Eng.

Joke Telling (Ch. 11). Felipe Carbonell of Lima, Peru, told jokes for 72 hours at the Alfa Hotel, Lisbon, Portugal, Mar 18–21, 1986.

Golf, Fastest Rounds (Ch. 12). Forty-eight players completed a round of 18 holes in 9 min 51 sec on the 7,108-yd Kyalami course near Johannesburg, S Africa, on Feb 23, 1988, using only one ball. They scored 73.

INDEX

A

Abbreviations 201
Abseiling 476
Absorbency 167
Academy Awards 238–39
Acceleration, 41, car 289
Accelerator, particle 185, 187–88
Accidents 428–30
Accordion playing 441
Accountants 343
Accuracy, clock 337, basketball free throws 532–33
Aces, air 502, 504
Aces, golf 596
Acrobatics 597–603
Acromegaly 3
Actors and actresses, theatre 227, television 232, motion picture 237–39
Addax 61
Administrative building 246
Advance, author's 209
Advertiser 343
Advertising, rates 215, commercials, television rates 234, signs 264–65, agency 343
Aerial, ropeways 330, act 448, 449
Aerobic display 602
Aerospace company 343
After-dinner speech 482
Age, human 8–9, 14, 15–16, 17, 20, 21, of motherhood 17, whales, cow, elephants 53, pinnipeds 56, bats 56, primates 56, 59, birds 76, 78, plants 105, earth 130, meteorites 151, moon soil 153, universe 162, language 199, authoress 209, Oscar winners 239, ships and boats 277, of marriages 385, judge 396, auto drivers 418, bridegroom and bride 438, oldest divorcers 439, male and female marathoners 622; see also **Longevity**
Ages, marriage 385, 438
Agriculture 372–77
AIDS (Acquired Immune Deficiency Syndrome) 34
Air aces 502, 504
Airborne bird 76
Aircraft 308–26, disaster 429; see also **Airlines**
Aircraft carriers 281
Air forces 391
Airliners 313–14
Airlines 343, 414–15
Airports 319–21
Air safety 319
Airships 325
Airstrip ticket 415
Air-supported structure 247
Albatross 75, 78
Alcohol 168
Alcoholic beverages 168, 365, bottles 169–70, 365
Algae 115, 116, 122–23
Alimony 395
All-America brothers 565
Alligators 81
Alphabets 199–200
Alphorn 219
Altitude records, animal 53, 87, birds 77, crustaceans 95, flowering plants 114, bacteria 124, lakes 138, 383, aurorae 160, manned space flight 165, astronomical observatory 173, spa, restaurant 251, bridge 258, dam 261, hovercraft 287, railroad station 305–6, aircraft unassisted 317, airport, plane landing 320, helicopter, 320, autogyro 321, 322, flying boat 322, balloons 324–25, airship, model aircraft 325, 326 aerial ropeway 330, countries 379, cities and capitals 382, 383, gun projectile 392–93, South Pole 434, mountaintop wedding 438, trapeze act 448, kites 466, highwire act 485, 486, cycling 561, golf course 585, golf drive 587, 591, skiing 634, ski lift 635, running 664, 665
Aluminum producer 343
Amber 178
Ambergris 51
Ambulances 296, 297
"American Dream" 289, 291
Amphibians 48, 86–87
Amphibious vehicle 298
Amphitheatres 224, 225
Amputation 36
Amusement parks 253–55
Anacondas 85
Anagrams 201
Anatomy, human 24–43
Anechoic room 188
Anesthesia 36
Animals 44–105
Animal town 48
Anniversaries, wedding 436–38, golden 439
Antarctic crossing 435
Anteater 48, 49, 62
Antelopes 51, 60, 61
Anthems 224
Antique 353
Antique sales at auction, watch 339, art, art nouveau Babe Ruth memorabilia, bed, blanket, bottles, carousel art, carpet, ceramics, chess set, cigarette cards 366–68, fire chief's trumpet 367, 370, corkscrew 368, doll, dollhouse, duck decoy cookie jars, earrings 367, 368, needlework sampler 368, 369, firebucket 368, furniture glass, hat, jade, mechanical toy, mirrors, musical box, paperweight, photograph, pistol, playing cards, porcelain and pottery 370, jewels 369, 370, 371, shoes 369, 370, silver, stained glass, sword, table, tapestry, teddy bears, toy soldiers, typewriter, walking stick and hat 370–72, weathervane 372
Antlers 60–61
Apartments 248–49
Appendectomy 36
Apples 107, peeling, picking 441–42
Aquamarine 174
Aquarium 125
Aqueducts 259
Arachnids 92–94
Arches, natural 138–39, bridge 257, aqueduct 259, steel 268
Archipelago 132
Arctic crossing 434
Arena 253
Aria 222
Armadillos 52
Armed forces 391
Armies 391
Arm span, human 1, starfish 92
Arrangement, flower 116
Arrest, mass 398
Art, prehistoric 190, exhibitor museum, gallery 194, auctioneering 344, 353, 366, thefts 400
Artichoke 107
Articulation 39
Artificial heart 32, 33
Artificial insemination 373
Artists 190–94
Arts and entertainment 190–243
Ascendants 20
Aspidistra 112
Assets 341
Asteroids 151, 157
Astronauts 163–64, 165; see also **Space flight**
Athlete, "of the Century" 636, "greatest American

Women . . . of the last 25 years" 657
Atlantic crossings, see **Transatlantic crossings**
Atlas 207
Atmospheric temperature 142
Atolls 132
Atomic, particles 166, power 328, bombs 393–94, 428, 429, waste fatalities 430
Attendance, concert, rock festival 220, movie-going 236, amusement parks, international fairs 253, murder trial 394, barbecues 408, Hindu feast, funeral 426, 427, parties 474, baseball 528, basketball 537–38, worst 576, see also **Crowds**
Auctions, orchid 118, wine 169, camera 171–72, gems 174, 175, 176, 177, 180, 344, paintings 191–92, drawing 192, sculptures, mobile 197, 198, medieval English manuscript 129, illustrated manuscripts, musical manuscript 203, 204–05, printed documents 206, autographs, expense account 211, musical instruments 215, 217, flowers 244, clock 337, watches 339, corporate take-over, art 343, 344, land 352, manuscript 353, dollhouse 368, coin collections 403–04, postage stamps 419
Auctions, possible bridge 578
Audience, concert 218, 220, radio 230, television 231, circus act 449; see also **Attendance, Crowds**
Aurorae 160
Authors, see **Writers**
Autographs 212
Autogyros 322
Automobiles, see **Cars**
Auto racing 507–13
Avalanches 137, 147, 428, 429–30
Avocado 107
Awards, entertainment 502–6, 238–39, 240–41, 243

B

Babies 21–24
Baboon 58
Baby carriage pushing 442
Backflip on skis 635
Backgammon 673
Backward, marathon 622, running 669
Bacteria 123–24
Bacteriological and chemical deaths 429
Badminton 673
Bail 394
Balance 183
Balanced rock 130
Balancing, one-foot 442, coins 447, balls 456, 457, cigar boxes 462, 463, milk bottle 468, on bicycle 561
Ball, string 482
Ball control 639
Ballet dancing 451
Balloons 322–25, release 442
Ballroom, 256, dancing 451–52
Bamboo 118, 120
Bananas, eating 496
Banana split 412
Band 219, marching 221, one-man 442–43, marathons 443, 444
Bank, assets 351, robbery 400
Bankruptcy 342
Banks 351
Banner 195
Barbecue 408
Barges 283–84
Barometer 183
Barometric pressure 145
Barrel jumping on ice skates 444, 621
Bars 255–56
Barter deal 342
Base, running 518, stealer 518, runner 515
Baseball 513–29, night 513
Baseball game, longest 528
Base hits 516, 517, 522
Basin, river 135
Basket 353
Basketball 530–38, 673, juggling 464
Bass (fish) 562, 563, 564
Bass, double 216–17
Bathtub 353, racing 444
Bathyscaphe 127, 283, 435
Baton Twirling 444
Bats 34, 51, 54, 56, 57
Battery 329
Batting, individual 516–18, World Series 521–22
Battleships 281
Bay 127
Beach, pleasure 254
Beans, lima 109, eating baked 496
Beard 29–30, of bees 443
Bears 52–53
Beauty 456
Beds 353, 366, of nails, pushing 444–45
"Beefalo" 377
Beer 169, bars 255–56, speed drinking 496
Bees 97, beard of 443
Beet 107, sugar 374
Beetles 46, 50, 95, 96, 97, 407
Begonia 112, 113
Bench 358
Bequests 502, to dog 68, to cat 73
Bering Straits swim 646–48
Beryl 174
Best sellers, books 208–09, sheet music 223, records 241–42
Bibles 203, 206–07, 210
Biceps measurement 13, 28
Bicycle manufacturers 344
Bicycles 301–03, stunts on 445, 446, 561
Bicycling, see **Cycling**
Bigamy 438
"Big tree" 119, 121–22
Bikini 357
Bill, bird 79–80, platypus 82
Billboard 264
Billionaires 500, 502
Biography (book) 210
Biplane 315
Birds 47, 49, 74–80, extinct 103
Bird-spotter 80
Birth dates, coincidental 22, 24
Birth rate 384
Births 16–24, multiple 16, 17, 18, 19, premature 21, 23, postmortem 21, multiple (livestock) 373–74, royal 387
Bishop, longest-serving 426
Bite, human 31
Black holes, 159
Black mamba 83
Blackout 329
Blanket 353, 354, 366
Blast furnace 330
Blind, sailing 441, running 670
Blindness, color 34
Blood, groups, donor, recipient 34–35, temperatures 48
Blooms 111, 115, 116
Blowing, weather balloon 491
Boardsailing 440
Boar racing, wild 375
Boas, 84
Boat racing, see **Powerboat racing**
Boats, see **Ships**
Boilers 329
Bombers 314
Bombs 428, 430, atomic 393–94, 428, 429, truck 430
Bond signing 212
Bones 24, 215, 616, 630
Bonsai plants 119
Books 203, 204–05, 206–07, 208–10, 213, overdue 213
Bookstores 344
Boomerang throwing 445
Boots, spitters' 481
Borings, earth 274–76
Both poles, first on 435
Bottle caps 364
Bottles 169–70, 366, 367, collection 364, messages in, milk bottle balancing 468
Bouncing babies 23
Boundary 380
Bowling 538–44, 673
Box office gross 236
Boxing 545–54
Brain, human 25, animal 48
Brass instrument 219
Bravery 478
Breach of contract 395
Bread 408
Breakwater 265

Breath-held diving 436
Breeder, youngest 54
Breweries 344
Bricks 445, 446
Bridegroom and bride 438
Bridge (contract) 577–79, 673
Bridges 257–58, natural 138–39, tunnel 263, wrapping 494, 495
Brightness, stellar 150, 158, 159, fireball 152, solar 154, planet 156, super-nova 159, man-made 186
Bristlemouth (fish) 90
British royalty 387, 408
Broadcaster 229
Broadcasting, see **Radio broadcasting, Television**
Broadway and off-Broadway runs 225–26
Broccoli 107
Brown Bomber 546, 549, 551
Brush 194
Bubble chamber 183
Bubble gum blowing 445, 446
Buddhist temple 424
"Bug" 229
Buildings, opera houses 222–23, theatres 224, movie theatres 235–36, oldest 244, for working 244–47, for living 248–51, for entertainment 251–56, demolished 274, university 421
Bull 373, 377
Bunker, biggest 585
Burial, human 423
Burrower 44
Buses 296
Business 341–77
Bustard, Kori 74
Butter fat yield 375
Butterflies, preserves 97–98
Butterfly strokers 641, 643, 645 , 646, for distance 646

C

Cabbage 107, 110
Cab driver 295
Cable, telephone 420
Cable car 330, disaster 430
Cable crosser 484–87
Cactus 115, 117
Cakes 408
Calculator 339
Calories 44, fruit 107
Camel, roasted 414
Cameras 170–71
Camping out 445
Canals 259, 260
Canal tunnel 263
Canaries 80
Candle 353
Candlepower 186
Candy 407
Cannon 392
Cannonball, human 460
Canoe 277, 279
Canonizations 427
Cantaloupe 109
Canyons, see **Gorges**
Capacious aircraft 315, 316
Capital cities 382, 383, 433
Capuchin monkey 58, 59
Capybara 59, 60
Carat 174–77
Cardinals 426
Cards, Christmas 213, post 359, 364, cigarette 364, 368, credit 364, playing 370, throwing 445, circus 450, house of 458, 460
Car ferry 285
Cargo vessel 283
Carnivores 52–53
Carousel 253, 255, art 366
Carp 91
Carpets 354, 366–68
Carriage driving 445
Carrot 107
Cars 288–98, rocket-powered 290, vintage 291, 364, manufacturer, factor 344, ramp jump 470, duration record 511
CART leaders 510
Cartoonist 211
Casting, freshwater 561
Castles 248, 477
Catalytic cracker 330
Catapulting, military 391
Catcher's Interference 524
Caterpillar crawler 295
Catfish 88
Cathedrals 425, spire 425
Cathode-ray tube 230
Cats 54, 55, 70–72
Cattle 372–73, 377, horns 63, station 372–73
Cauliflower 107
Cave art, prehistoric 190, 196
Caves 139
Caviar 91
Celery 107
Celestial body, remotest visible 161–62
Cello 217
Cemetery 266
Centenarians 8, 15–16
Centillion 182
Centipedes 98
Centrifuges 183–84
Ceramics 368
Chain stores 344–46
Chair 354, 368
Chair lifts 635
Chameleons 82
Champagne, fountain 447, drinking 496
Champagne cork flight 170
Chandelier 354, salad bowl 362
Channel, walking across 489, swimming 647, 648, relay swimming 648
Chanting 479
Character, most portrayed 237–38
Charleston 452
Charming, worm 100
Checkers 579–80, 673
Cheese 375, eating 496
Cheetah 51
Chelonians 83
Chemical fumes 428
Chess 580, 581–82, 673, set 368
Chest measurement 26–28, 547, gorilla 58
Chevrotain 61
"Chicken gun" 319
Chickens 78, 80, ranch 372, plucking 376, eating 496
Children 16–23, royal 387
Chimney demolition 274
Chimpanzees 58
Chinning the bar 599
Chocolate, factory 345, Easter egg 408
Choirs 219, 479
Chorus lines 226, 228
Christmas, trees 117, 122, cards, 213, party 474
Churches 424–25, spire 425
Cicadas 97
Cigarettes 355, 364, plant 348, 350, lighter 355, 364, cards 364, 368
Cigars 355, bands 364, box balancing 462, 463
Circle, unsupported 460
Circling US 672
Circular storm 428
Circulation, newspaper, periodical 214
Circumnavigation, sailing solo 278, automobile 293, amphibious vehicle 298, flights 310–11, 433, helicopter 321, marine, motorboat 440, 441, cycle 560; see also **Round-the-World**
Circum-polar flight 311
Circus cards 450
Circuses 251, fire toll 430, records 448–50
Cities 382
Clams 48, 100, 101, eating 496
Clapping 447
Clergy 423
Cliffs, sea 140, planetary ice 156
Climbing, cat 73, aircraft 317, stairs 332, tree 487, pole 493
Clockface, floral 337
Clocks 336–37, 338
Clothes 355–57
Clouds 144
Clover 112–13
Coaching records, football 576–77
Coastline 378
Cobra 84, 85
Cockatoo 78
Cockroach 95
Coffin 1, 10, 11
Coincidental birth dates 24
Coin display 406
Coins 402–04, 405–06, balancing, snatching 447
Cold 141, 144, 189
Collard 107
Collections, teeth 31, 365,

Rolls-Royces 291, vintage cars 291, 364, miniature bottles, bottle caps, cigar bands, cigarettes, cigarette cards, cigarette lighters, credit cards 364, keys, matchbox labels, postcards, salt and pepper shakers, soaps, spirits and liqueurs, watches 364–65, art 366, coins 403–4, stamps 419
College football records 565–66, 576
College president, youngest 422
Colleges 421, 422, 423
Collision, ship 285
Colony 379, 381
Color, sensitivity, blindness 34
Columnist 211
Columns 266, cave 139, monumental 268
Coma 31
Comets 151, 155
Comic strips 211
Commerce 341–50
Commercial buildings 244, 246
Commercials, television 234
Communications 420
Community garden 373
Compact discs 243
Compensation, legal 395
Composers 220, popular 223–24
Computers 339–40, human 25, company 345, fraud 401
Concerts 219–20, 241
Conchs 101
Concrete structure 261
Condors 74, 77
Conga dancing 452
Conjunction, planetary 156
Consecutive, innings, games 524, holes-in-one 596, hockey goals 608, hockey games 610, horse race victories 612, high jump competitions, hurdles races 669
Constitutions 388
Construction, continuous home 250–51
Containerships 279, 283
Continents 129–30, 131
Contracts, television 233, breach of 395
Contrived names 203
Conveyor belt 330–31
Cookie jars 367
Coral 102
Coriander 106
Cork flight, champagne 170
Corkscrew 368
Corn 107, 110, 374
Coronation robe 357
Corporate seal 342
Correspondence 213
Corundum 174, 177
Costumes, movie 238
Countries 378–82, 388, 389, 397–98, 401–03, least taxed, richest 401–02, worst inflation 402
Couples 5, 7–8, disparate 10, 13, youngest married, most married 438, 439
Courses, golf 584–85
Court trials 394–96
Covered bridge 257
Cow 53, 373, 374, 377
Crabs 44, 94, 95
Crane (bird) 78
Cranes (mechanical) 331
Craters 146, 148, moon 153
Crawling 451
Credit cards 364
Crematorium 266
Crepe 408, 409
Cribbage 673
Crime and punishment 397–401
Criminal organization 397
Criticism, theatre 228
Crocheting 447, 451
Crocodiles 81, 429
Crop yields 374
Croquet 673
Cross-country skiing 630, 632, 633, 634
Crossword puzzles 208, 215
Crowds 425, 426, classical concert 218, sports 252, 510, 639, dance 451; see also **Attendance**
Crustaceans 94–95
Crypt of Civilization 363
Crystals 174, 178
Cuckoo clock 338
Cucumber 107, 108, slicing 451
Curling 673
Currency 402–04
Currents 128, electric 184
Curtain calls 222
Curtains 355
Customs, religious 423
Cut, finest 183–84
Cycling 301–03, 554–61, underwater 489, one hour, twenty-four hours, speed record 558, touring 560, endurance 560–61

D

Dahlia 113
Damages 395
Dams 261–62, 428, 430
Dancing 451–53
Darts 673
Day at bat, best 515
Day's run under sail 278
Dead heats, horse racing 615, Olympic swimming 648
Death, leading cause 31, highest mortality 34, snakebite 85, earthquake 145–46, volcanic explosion 148–49, space flight 164, 165, 430, rate 384, infant 385, compensation award for 395, accidents and disasters 428–30
Debating 453
Decaplets 18
Decathlon 660, 665
Deceleration 41, 50, 77
Decompression time 436
Decorations 502, 503–05
Decoy, duck 356, 368
Deer 60–61
Deer bot-fly 96
Defamation suits 396
Degrees, honorary 503, 504–05
Dehydration, insect 46
Delayed drops, parachuting 471, 472
Delivery vehicles, nuclear 394
Deltiology 359
Demolitions 274
Demonstrations 425
Density, wood 121, earth's core 126, moon 152, planets 156, gem mineral 175, population 380–82, traffic 415
Dentists 31, 386
Department store 345
Deposits, gas 275
Depressions 134
Depth, whale 50, pinniped 55–56, bird 78, turtle 83, toad 87, fish 91, starfish 92, crustacean 95, sponge 103, plant roots 106, underwater plant life 116, oceans 127, fjord 128, depressions 134, lake 138, caves, gorge 139, 140, earthquake hypocenter, volcanic crater 145, earth's craters 151–52, moon craters 153, Venusian canyon 156, night clubs 251, canal lock 261, railroad tunnel 263, spiral staircase 272, subterranean 272, drilling, seabed drilling 274–75, water well, steam well 275, submarines 283, airport 320, mine elevator 331–32, town 382, road, pass 418, ocean descent, diving, underwater escapes, salvage 435–36, golf course 585
Descendants 20, protozoan 123
Descent, whales 50, pinnipeds 55–56, diving, ocean, salvage 435–36, parachute 471, 472–73, 474, rappeling 476, skiing 634
Desert 140
Destroyer 282
Detectable sound 38–39
Diamonds 130, 174, 175, 176, 180, 181, 371, synthetic 176
Diaries 204, 205
Dictionaries 205–06, 210
Diesel-engined car 291
Differential, married couple's height 10, weight 13, monkeys' sizes 58, male and female marine worms 100, figure-skating couple 617
Dik-dik 60
Dinosaurs 103–05

Dirigible, ball drop from 528–29
Disasters 145–48, 428–30
Disco dancing 452
Discomfort, humidity and 141
Discrete object, largest 161
Discs, see **Records, Compact Discs**
Diseases 34, 428, most 37
Dish, largest 414
Dish telescopes 173
Distance to city centers, airport 321
Distant object 161–62, visible 161
Distilleries 345
Diving, animal 50–51, 55–56, bird 78, depth, salvage by 435–36, shallow, high 454; see also **Swimming**
Divorces 385, 395, 439
Doctorates 422–23
Doctors 32, 33, 36–37, 386, 422–23
Document 206
Dogs 66–70, 72, 372
Dog sled race 67
Dollhouse 368
Dolls 355, 368
Dolphins 51–52, 56
Domes 266
Domesticated animals, mammals 64–74, 372–77, birds 76, 80, 372, 374, 376
Domino, toppling, stacking 454, 455
Donor, blood 35
Doors 246, 266
Double knockouts 553
Doughnuts, eating 498
Downhill mile 672
Dowry 501
Dragline excavator 331
Dragon, shopping mall 349, dancing 452
Dragonfly 97
Drag racing 512, 513
Drawbridge 258
Drawing 192
Dream 40
Dredger 284
Dress 355–57
Drilling and mines 274–75
Drink 168–70
Drivers 418, licenses 418, racing 508–13, sulky 604
Drives, golf 586–88
Driving, two-wheel 293, round-the-world 293, in reverse 294, 295, longest trip 298, carriage 445
Drop, roller coaster 254–55
Drugs 168, prescription 168
Drum 219
Drumming 455
Drydock 266
Dryness 145
Ducks 74, decoys 356, 368, laying 374
Ducks and drakes 455
Dump truck 296
Dunes, sand 134
Durability, light bulb 186, musicians 217, actors 227, radio programs 230, 424, TV shows and performers 233–34, movie film 237, phonograph records, 240, 241, car 292, railroad station 305, airplane pilot 317, batteries 329, clocks 336, driver 418, professor 422, boxers 546, bridge player 578
Dwarfs 5–10
Dwellings, elevation 382

E

Eagles 78, 79, golf 595
Earnings, blurb writer 209–10, musicians 221, singers 222, 228, 232, 241, sports people 229, 509, 511, 541, 549, 553, 552, 564, 588, 589, 591, 592, 604, 613, 655, 656, TV stars 228, 233, movie actors 237, 618, stuntman 238, 470
Earrings 368
Ears 73
Earth 126, 154, 155, rotation 182, land area 378
Earth mover 298, 299
Earthquakes 145–46, 428
Earthworms 99, attracting 100
Easter egg 408
Eaters 47, human 496–99
Eating records 495–99, 636
Echo 184
Eclipses 154–55
Economic records 401–20
Education 421–23
Eels 91, electric 92, eating 498
Eggplant 107
Eggs, animal 49–50, bird 49, 79, heaviest 79, 374, fish 91, insect 96, laying rate, yolks, goose, duck 374, Easter 408, stunts with 455, omelet making 470, eating 498
Eider ducks 74, 79
Eland 60
Elections 389–90, papal 426
Electric current 184
Electric fish 92
Electric plane 318
Electric shock 43
Electrons 166
Elements 126, 166
Elephant bird 49
Elephants 48, 51, 53, 62
Elephant seal 55
Elevators, grain 247, canal-lock 261, passenger, involuntary entrapment 331, fatalities 430
Embassy 247
Embroidery, see **Tapestries**
Emerald 174, 176, 179
Emigration 384
Employer 342
Encore, operatic 222
Encyclopaediae 206
Endeavors, miscellaneous, and stunts 441–95
Endowment, highest 421
Engagement 437
Engineering 329–36, monument to 245
Engines, car 292; see also **Steam engines**
English Channel, walking across 489, swimming 648
Enrollment, university 421, school 423
Entertainers 228
Entertainment, arts and, 190–243, structures for 251–56
Entrapment, involuntary 331
Equator, circumference 126
Error, postage stamp 419
Eruptions 147, 148
Escalators 332
Escapes, underwater 436
Estuary 136
EVA suits 355
Everest, Mount 132, 133, 430
Excavation, canal 259
Excavators 331–32
Exhibitor, art 194
Expense account 212
Explosions 148–149, 151, 428, 430
Extinct animals 103–05
Extrasensory perception 40–41
Extra-terrestrial vehicle 164
Extra-vehicular-activity suits 355
Eye, human 34, animal 49, 100; see also **Sight**

F

Fabrics 357
Fairs 254
Falabella horse 65
Falcons 47, 77, 79
Falls, without parachute 471
Family, richest 500
Famine 428, 429
Fangs 85
Farms 372, 373
Fashion shows 228
Fasting 39
Feathers 79
Felines 54, 55; see also **Cats**
Female head of state 388
Female vote 389
Fences 266
Ferns 118
Ferris wheels 254, riding 456
Ferry 286, 287
Fiber, optical 420
Field goals, basketball 530–32, 533, 534–35, 536, football 566, 567, 569, 575
Fighter plane 315
Fights, most undefeated 550
Figure skating 616, 617–19
Fillibusters 388
Film rentals 236
Film rights 236
Films, movie 236, 237
Finance 350–51, 401–06

Fine 396
Fingers 28, nails 29, 30
Fireball 152
Fire bucket 368
Fire-eating 43
Fire engine 298
Fires, forest 122, gas 275, fatalities 428, 430
Fire-walking 43
Fireworks 357, show 429, 430
Fishes 88–92
Fishing 561–64, catch 345, 561–64, fight 562
Fjords 128
Flagpole 266–67
Flags 357
Flame 184
Flamenco dancing 452
Flare 275
Fleas 97
Flexible pole 450
Flies 46
Flight, bird 47, 74–75, chicken 80, insect 96, space 163–65, 314–15, champagne cork 170, hovercraft 282, 286, 287, aircraft 308–26, human-powered 318, duration 317, balloons 322–25, airships, model aircraft 325, 326, paper airplane 326, kite 466, 467
Float, space 165
Floating bridge 258
Floats, parade 357
Flood 428
Floor 244, 246
Floral clock 337
Flow, ocean currents 128, river 135–36, waterfalls 137
Flowers 105, 106, 112–14, 115
Flute 215, marathon 456
Fly, human 459, 460
Flying boats 315–16, 322
Flying disc 582–84
Flying fox 56
Flying hours 317–18
Flying ring 449
Flying trapeze 448
Fogs 145
Foods and drinks 407–14, abstinence from 39–40, consumption 407–14, 495–99, 636, 638
Football 565–78
Forest 118–20, fire 122
Forging 333
Fork-lift truck 333
Forts 248
Forward passing 569–71, 576, shortest touchdown pass 577
Fossils, hominid 14–15, plant 106
Foul-offs 523
Fountain 267, champagne 447
Fountain pen, jeweled 360
Frankfurters, eating 498
Fraternities 422
Frauds 400, 401
Free throws, basketball 532–33, 535, 536
Freight train 304, 308
Frequency, highest measured 184
Freshwater casting 561
Friction 184
Frisbee, see **Flying disc**
Frogs 86, 87
Frontiers 379–80
Frozen embryo birth 24
Fruits 107, 108, 109, 110, 111, 112, 114
Fuel economy, cars 292, 293
Fumes, chemical 428
Fumigation 185
Funeral 427
Fungi 123
Furnace, blast 330
Furniture 358, 368
Furs 61

G

Gaboon viper 85
Gaining weight 13–14
Galaxies 158, 159, 161
Gallantry award 506
Galleries 194
Gambling losses 404
Games 577–84
Garages 247
Garage sales, see **Rummage sale**
Garbage scow 284
Gardens 105, community 373
Garlic 107
Gas, deposits, tank 275, flare 275, turbine 329, pipeline 333–34
Gasoline, -driven car 288, consumption by car 293, by motorcycle 625, 628
Gastropods 101
Gauges, railroad 306
Geckos 83
Geese 74, 76, egg 374
Gems 174–81, 369, 370
Generators 328
Genocide 397, 428
Gerbils 72
Gestation period, animal 48, mammal 53–54; see also **Incubation**
Geysers 149
g forces 41, 50, bird 77, flea 97
Gherkins, eating 498
Giantesses 3, 5, 21–22
Giants 1–3, 4, 10, shoes for 1, 361
Gigayear 162
Gingerbread house 409
Ginseng 407
Giraffe 45, 46
Girth, tree 119, 121
Glaciers 136
Gladiolus 113
Glass 358, 370, stained 196, 370, thinnest 358
Goalkeeping, soccer 636, 638
Goat 61–62, 372, 374–75, 377
Gobies 89–90
Go-karting 293
Gold, nuggets 178, rush 276, bathtub 353, cigarette lighter 355, coffin, pens 358, 359, reserves 402, coin 402–03, 405, Buddha 425, mine disaster 430, ocean salvage 436, panning 456
Golden records 240–41, 243
Goldfish 91
Golf 584–96, shoes 361
Golf ball balancing 456, 457
Googol 182
Gorges, 140
Gorillas 57–58, 59
Gourd 107–09
Government 386–90
Grade, railroad 306
Gradient, street 415–16, cable walk 486
Graduates in family 423
Graham's number 182
Grain elevator 247
Grammy awards 243
Grand Canyon 140
Grandparents, multiple great- 20
Grand slams, baseball 517, golf 588, tennis 650–52
Grandstand 612
Grapefruit 109
Grapes, bunch, vine 111, 114, vineyard 376, catching 456, eating 498
Grass 118, 120
Grave site 352
Green, golf 585
Greyhound 68, 69, 70
Grill 358
Grocery stores 346
Ground figures 197
Groups, singing 240, 242, 243
Growth, animal 48, plant 106, seaweed 77, grass bamboo 118, tree 120, 122
Guide dog 68
Guinea pig 72
Guitars 217, 218, playing 456
Gulf 127
Guns 392–93
Gusher, oil 275
Gymnastics 597–603, circus 448–50
Gyroplanes 322

H

Hailstones 142, 145, 430
Hair 28, 29, strongest 28, hanging by 449, splitting 457
Hairdressing 456–57
Halites 134
Halley's Comet 155
Ham, radio 230
Hamburgers 409, eating 498
Hamsters 72
Hands, giants 1, span 221, shaking 457–58, walking on 489, eight baseballs in one 527
Hangars 247
Hangings 398

Harbor, artificial 414
Hardness 174
Harem 252
Hares 60, 74
Harness racing 603–05
Harp 218–19
Hat 370, 371–72
Hat tricks 607, 609, 610
Head of state, female 388
Hearing, human 38–39, 56
Heart, stoppages 31, 41, transplants 32, 33, artificial 32, 33, whale 44
Hedgehog-tenrec 62
Hedges 114
Height, human 1–10, animal 45, 46, 51–53, 54, 57–58, 60, 61–62, horse 65, dog 67–68, bird 74, 75, sponges 103, collard plant, corn, okra 107, 109, pepper plant, tomato plant 108, 109–12, garden plants 111, 112–14, inflorescence 114, cactus 115, 117, orchids 116, bamboo, ferns 118, 120, trees 120–21, 122, sea-mountain 127, waves 129, iceberg, mountain wall 129, 130, mountains 132–33, sand dunes 134, waterfall 137, natural arch, natural cavern, stalagmite, cave column 138–40, sea cliffs, waterspouts 143, clouds 144, volcanoes 146, 148, geysers 149, lunar mountains 152, planetary mountain 156, aurorae 160, Soviet rocket 163, guitar 218, building doors 246, 266, office buildings 246, apartment buildings 248–49, hotel 250, carousel 253, 255, Ferris wheels, roller coaster 254–55, man-made structure, self-supporting tower 256, bridges 257, 258, aqueduct 259, canal-lock elevator, dams 261, monuments 268, advertising signs, columns, 264–66, fences, flagpole, fountain, ice palace, lampposts 266–67, 269, lighthouse 267–68, obelisk, pyramids, scarecrow 270–71, scaffolding 269, 270–71, snowman 271, stairs, swing, statue, totem pole, trash dump 272–73, water tower, windows 273, 274, gas tank 275, oil gusher, gas flare, oil platforms 276, bicycle 302, unicycle 302, 303, windmills 326, mobile crane, excavator 331, forging press 333, power lines 335, clock 336, 337 watch 339, basket, headboard, candle, chair 353, 354, curtains, dolls 355, duck decoy 356, vase 363, soldier 391, cakes, chocolate Easter egg 408, university building 421, cross, cathedral spire, church spire, minarets, pagoda 425–26, champagne fountain, column of coins 447, aerial act 448, human pyramid 450, lowest limbo 452, 453, high diving 454–55, grape catching, tallest hairdo 456, house of cards 457, 458, 460, rappeling 476, sand castle 477, stilts 481–82, high-wire acts 484–87, baseball players 515, basketball players 538, boxers 546
Helicopters 320–22, fatalities 430, circus act from 449
Helipad 321–22
Heliport 321
Helium liquefying plant 187
Heptathlon (women's) 667, 671
Herbs 106
Herds 54
Hibernation 54
Hiccoughing 37
Highest numbers 182
High jump 657, 659, 662, 664, 666, 669, from skateboard 480, standing 658, 672, one-legged 660
High kicks 452
Highways 416–18
High wire walking 484–87
Hijack ransom 401
Hill figure 197
Himalayan ibex 63
Hit by pitcher 523
Hitchhiking 458–60
Hitting streak 516
Hockey 605–11, career 606, 607
Holes 184–86, 187, golf 584–85, 595–96
Holes-in-one 595–96
Hollyhock 113
Home runs 513–14, 515, 517, 518, 523, 524, 526
Homes 248–51
Homicides 397–98
Honey, wild 97
Honors 502–06
Hop field 377
Hopscotch 460
Horns, animal 62–64, 95
Horse racing 611–16
Horses 64–66, 196, 372, 377, race 46, 64–65, 611–13, 614–15, most valuable 46, 615, carriage driving 445
Hospitals 385–86
Hotdogging, see **Backflip on skis**
Hotels 250, 346, demolition 274, fire toll 430
House of cards 458, 460
Houses 250–51
Housing 385
Hovercraft 282, 286, 287
Hula hooping 459, 460
Human beings 1–43
Human-powered, ships 278–79, railcars 305, flight 318, paddle boat 471
Human suspension bridge 602
Humidity 141
Hummingbirds 76, 77
Hundred-kilometer run 670
Hunger strike 39–40
Hurricane damage 143, 429
Hutia 47
Hydroelectric tunnel 264
Hydrofoils 283
Hydroplane 432
Hyperventilation 43

I

Ibex, Himalayan 63
Ice 142, Palace 267, skating 269, 616–22
Icebergs 129
Icebreaker 284–85
Ice cave, wedding in 437, 439
Ice cream, sundae 413, 414, eating 498
Ice shows 228–29
Ice skating 616–22, 673
Ice sled 298
Illness, see **Diseases**
Immigration 384
Immolation 102
Imprisonment, wrongful 395
Income, per capita, national 401–02, personal 500
Incubation 78–79
Independent country 378–79, 380
Index 205
Indianapolis 500 508–10, 511
Industrial building 244
Industry 341–50
Inebriation 201
Inexpensive car 292
Infant mortality 385
Infectious diseases 34
Inflation 402
Inflorescence 114
Influenza 428
Insectivores 62, extinct 103–04
Insects 95–98
Instant replay 253
Institutionalization 386
Insurance 346
Interval between twins 19
Invertebrate, largest 100
Inverted juggling 461, 462
Investment gain 351
Investment house 350
I.Q. 26
Iron 126, lung 36, maiden 444
Iron Curtain 380
Irrigation, canal 260, tunnel 264
Islands 131–32, 378, 379, 381
Isolation 41–43, 131–32
Ivory 62

J

Jade 178, 370
Jazz records 240
Jelly 410, eating 498
Jellyfishes 102
Jet aces 502
Jet-engined car 290, 513
Jet-engined flight 311, 313–14, 315
Jet stream 142
Jetty 267
Jewel robbery 400
Jewels 369, 370, 371; see also **Gems**
Jewry 424
Jig-saw puzzles 358
Jiving (dancing) 452
Jockey 613, 616
Jogging 461–64, 673
Joke telling 460
Journeys, hovercraft 287, rail 304–05
Judges 396
Judicial matters, litigation 394–96, crime and punishment 397–401
Judo 673
Juggling 461–64, 639, 673
Jumping 63, 64, barrel 444, motorcycle 469, 470, pogo stick 475, rope 600, 601
Jumping jacks 603
Jumps, kangaroo 64, dog 68–70, frog 87, flea 97, motorcycle 469, 470, ramp by car 470, parachute 471–74, figure skating 617, 618, 619, ski 632, 634, 635, track and field 657, 658, 659, 660, 662, 663, 664, 665, 666, 669, 672
Junks 279
Jury award 342

K

Kangaroos 64, 373
Karate chop 466
Keys 364
Kicking, high 452
Kidnappings 400–41, ransoms 400–01
Kidney transplant 37
Killer whale 45, 46
Killings 397–98, 428–30
Kings 387
Kissing 466
Kitchen 267
Kite flying 466, 467
Kiwi (bird) 79
Knife 358
Knitting 466
Knockdowns 552
Knockouts 545, 546, 547, 549, 552, 553
Knots, carpet 354
Knot tying 466
Kohlrabi 109
Kojah 61
Komodo monitor 81–82
Kremlin Square landing 309
Krill 47

L

Labor 406–07, disputes 406
Lagoon 132, 138
Lakes 132, 134, 135, 137, 138, artificial 262
Lampposts 267
Land 129–40, urban sale, auction 352
Landings, on aircraft carrier 281, airport, air base 320, 321
Landowner 352
Landslide toll 428
Land speed 289, 290, 432, 511–13
Lanes, bowling 539
Language and literature 198–215
Laryngectomy 36–37
Laser beams 186, 187, 420
Last word 203
Lathe 333
Lava flow 146, 148
Lawn mowers 298, 299
Lawsuits 394–96
Leap frogging 466
Learner's tests (driving) 420
Lease 396
Leaves 115–16
Lecture speakers 423
Legacy, to dog, 68, to cat, 73
Legislators 387–88, 389–90
Leg raises 603
Legs 98, 99
Le Mans *Grand Prix d'Endurance* 508, 509, 510, 511
Lemons 109, eating 498
Lemurs 57, 58
Leopard 51
Lethal chemical 167
Letters 213, mailed 420
Letters (writing symbols) 198, 201, 265
Lettuce 109
Levees 262
Libraries 213
Lice 96
License plates 288–89
Licenses, drivers' 418
Life expectation 385
Life insurance 346
Life Masters (bridge) 579
Life Savers 407
Life saving 466–67
Life span, see **Longevity**
Lifetime distance swimming 648
Lifting operation 333, 446
Light, beam, bulb, pulse, brightest 185, 186
Lighter 364
Lightest humans 12–13
Lighthouses 267–68
Lightning 143, fatalities, 430, -struck 467–68
Light-year 150, 158, 159, 161, 162
Lily 113, 115, 116
Lima bean 109
Limbo dancing 452, 453
Limousine, Presidential 291, largest 289, 292
Liners, passenger 280–281
Lines of sight 134
Linguists 199
Lion taming 468
Liquor 168
Listener response, radio 230
Literary correspondence, shortest 213
Literature and language 198–215
Litigation 394–96
Litters, mammal 53, 373–74, dog 68, 72, cat 71–73, pets 72
Livestock births 373–74, 375–76
Livestock sales records 377
Living standards 385–86
Living things, number, concentration 47
Living world 44–125
Lizards 81–82, 84
Load hauling 296, dogs 67, train 304
Lobsters 94–95
Locks, canal 261
Locomotives 303, 304, 307
Log rolling 467, 468
London Bridge 353
Long-distance, driving 293, swimming 646
Longevity, dwarf 8, human 14, 15–16, 46, 53, twins 20, quadruplets, triplets 21, clam 46–47, tortoise 47, 83, mammal 53, animals, 53, 56, 58–60, 61, 62, 64, 70, 72, caged pets 76, 80, birds 78, domestic birds 76, reptiles 80, 81, 82, 84, amphibians 86, fish 91, spiders, crustaceans, 94, 95, insects 97, mollusks 100, oldest living things 105, bonsai plants 119, trees 118, nuclear particles 166, language 200, newspaper 214, TV show 233–34, vessels afloat 277–78, battery life 329, clock 336, sheep 373–74, cities 382, reigning monarchs 386, officeholders 389, army 391, working careers 407, drivers 418, pagodas 425–26, marriages 436–37, auto racers 507, college coach 538, boxing careers 546, 551, heavyweight champion, 547, bridge player 578, hockey career 606, 607; see also **Age; Life expectation**
Longhorn, Texas 63
Long jump skateboarding, 479, 480
Lops 73
Losses, theatrical 228, movie 238, business 342, 351, insurance company 346, investment 351, gambling 404

Loudness, see **Sound**
Love letters 213
Luminosity, stellar 150, 159, solar 154, super-nova 159, quasars 161
Lunar, see **Moon**
Lynx 61

M

Machine, slowest 333
Machinery 329; see also **Engineering**
Mach number 264, 290, 304, 308, 311, 314, 315, 432, 513
Magazines 214
Magician 468
Magnet 186
Magnetic fields 186–87
Magnitude 150, 152, 156, 159
Mail 213, 420
Major league games, longest and shortest 526–28
Mallee fowl 78
Mammals 50–74, 82
Man, origins of 14–15
Managers, baseball 526
Mandrill 58
Man-eater, deaths by 429
Manned flight, longest 164, 165
Manufactured articles 353–63
Manuscripts, medieval English 199, illustrated da Vinci, Einstein, musical 203–05, illuminated 203, 353
Maps 207
Marathons, dog training 70, motorcycle riding 301, model train 308, sheep-shearing 376, military road march 392, accordion playing 441, band 443, 444, clapping, crocheting 447, 451, dance 451–53, debating 453, drumming 455, Ferris wheel riding, flute, guitar hairdressing 456, hopscotch, hula-hooping 460, joke telling 460, kissing, kite flying 466, leap frogging 466, merry-go-round ride 468, omelet making, organ playing 470, piano playing 474, piano playing 474, quizzing, rocking chair 476, roller coasting, roller skating 476, see-saw, sermon 478, showering 478, singing, skateboarding 478–80, square dance calling, standing up 481, submergence, hammock swinging 482, talking 482, tree sitting, typing, underwater cycling, waiters' 487–88, 489, 623, whistling 493, yo-yo 495, basketball 538, 673, bowling 539, 673, cycling 561, checkers 580, 673, Frisbee 584, golf 589–90, rope jumping 600, ice skating 622, 673, foot racing 622, 623, skiing 632, 634–35, 674, soccer 638, softball, 640, 674, swimming 646, 650, tennis 656, 674, running while pancake tossing 670
Marble 178
Marches 392
Marching band 221
Marigold 113, 115
Marine circumnavigation 440–41
Marine disaster 428
Marine insurance 346
Marine records, circumnavigation, transatlantic, transpacific 439–41
Maritime fraud 400
Market 348
Marlin 562
Marmosets 57, 58
Marriage 436–39, ages 385, 438, papal 426, on high wire 484
Married couples, tallest 5, midgets 7–8, disparate sizes 10, youngest, oldest divorced, most 438–39
Marsupials 64
Maser beams 337
Mashed potatoes 412
Mass, killing 397, suicide 398, 429, hanging, arrest 398, communications 414–20, wedding ceremony 438, running relays 669
Mast, radio 256, sailing ship 279
Master points 578–79
Matchbox labels 364
Mathematical, proof, puzzle 183
Mathematics, human ability at 25
Matter 166
Maze 268
Meanings, word 200
Measured frequency 184
Measurement, time 337
Measures, time 182, balance 183
Meat, eating 498
Mechanical toy 370
Mechanical world 277-340
Medals, Olympic 350–51, 597, 598, 605, 619, 620, 621, 630, 631–32, 648–49, 658, 659–61, 668–69
Medical insurance 346
Medicine, pill taking 35
Megabits 340
Melons 109, 110
Membership, religious 423
Memorabilia, baseball 529
Memory, human 25
Merchandise, see **Stores**
Merchandise market 348
Merchant shipping 414
Merganser 47, 74
Merry-go-round 253, 255, ride 468
Message in a bottle 468
Metabolism 48
Meteorites 151, 156
Meteorological records, see **Weather**
Meteors 150
Microphones 187, 229
Microscopes 184–86, 187
Midgets 5–10
Migration, bird 74
Mileage, car, gasoline 292, balloons 322–24, year's driving 511, year's cycling 560, longest horse race 612–13, lifetime of swimming 648
Military and defense 390–94
Military awards 502, 503, 504, 505
Milk, yields 374–75, drinking 498
Milk bottle balancing 468
Milking 374–75
Milk shake 410
Millionaires 500, 501, 502
Millionairesses 501, 502
Millipedes 99
Minaret 425
Minerals 174
Mineral water 346
Mines, disaster 275, 429, 430
Miniature, portrait 192, bicycles 301–03, railways 307, 308, bottles 364, tools, mosaic, pocketknife 365
Mint 405–06
Mirages 149
Mirrors 327, 328, 370
Miser 501, 502
Moats 248, 252
Mobile 198
Model, railways 307, 308, 370, aircraft 326
Mole-rat 44
Mollusks 100-01
Monarchs 386–87, 500
Money, return of lost 502
Money and finance 401–06
Monkeys 58–60
Monoliths 130
Monuments 268, prehistoric 270
Moon 152–53, probes 152, landings 153, 164, 165, conquest 431, golf on 584, 588
Moose 60–61
Morse code 468
Mortality 34, infant 385
Mortars 393
Mortician 350
Mosaic 196
Mosques 424
Mosses 118
Most fights 554
Motherhood 16–24
Mothers-in-law 437
Moths 47, 49, 77, 97–98
Motion, proper 150
Motionlessness 41, 42
Motion pictures 235–39
Motor-cross (scrambling) 627, 628

Motorcycles 293, 300–01, 624–25, midgets 9, stunting 470
Motorcycling 624–28
Motor trip 298
Mountaineering disaster 430
Mountains 132–34, submarine 127, salt 134, moon 152
Mount Everest 133, 430
Mouse 47, 60, 72, marsupial 64
Mouser 73
Moustaches 30
Movie-going 236
Movie review 228
Movies, see **Motion pictures**
Movie theatres 235–36
Movie viewer 238
Moving, apartment house 249
Moving sidewalks 332
Multiple births (livestock) 373–74
Muntjac 61
Murals 193, 196
Murder 397–98
Muscles 26–28
Museums 194
Mushrooms 123, farm 373
Music 215–24; see also **Records**
Musical box 370
Musical chairs 470
Musical instruments 215–19
Musical manuscript 204–05
Musical notes, human voice 38, electronic 187, double bass viol 216–17
Musicals, long-run 226
Musicians 217, 221
MVP most times 608

N

Nails, bed of 444
Nails, finger 30
Names 160, 202–03
National, anthems 224, wealth per capita 401–02
Natural bridge 138–39
Natural organ 216
Natural world 126–49
Naturist resort 270
Navies 391
NBA Championships 534–36
Necks, human 27, dog 28, cat 67, 71
Needles 358
Needle threading 470
Needlework sampler 368, 369
Negative, photographic 170–71
Neon sign 264
Nerve fibers 48
Nerve gas 167
Nests 78
Newspapers 214
NFL Championships 568–71, 577
NHL records 609–10
Night clubs 251–52
Nobel Prizes 505–06
Noise 187; see also **Sound**
Non-stop, anthem playing 224, motorcycle ride 301, round-the-world flight 310–11, flights 317, solo marine circumnavigation 440–41, lying on bed of nails 444, talking 482, cycling 560–61, soccerball juggling 639, run 672
Nonuplets 18
Noodle making 410
Northern Lights 160
North Pole conquests 433–34
North-to-south drive 293
North-West Passage 285
Notes, see **Musical Notes**
Novels 208–09
Nuclear, particles 166, submarines 282–83, reactor 328, arsenal, delivery vehicles 394, reactor leak, waste accident 430
Nudist camp 270
Nuggets, gold 178
Numerals 181–83
Nuts, see **Peanuts**
Nuts (mechanical) 333
Nylon 359

O

Oarfish 89
Obelisks 266, 270
Observatories 172–73
Oceanaria 125
Oceans 127–29, descent 435
Octopus 101
Office, term of 389
Office buildings 245, 246
Offshore oil plant disaster 430
Oil, field 275, gushers, platforms 275, 276, spills 275–76, 346, tanks, pipelines 333–34, refinery 347
Oil plant disaster, offshore 430
Okra 109
Olympic Games 537, 550–51, 597, 598, 605, 619, 620, 621, 628, 630, 631, 641, 642, 648–49, 656, 659–61, 668–69
Omelets 410, making 470
Omnivore 496
One day wonder 515
One hole, most shots 594–95
One-man band 442–44
One-man concerts, attendance 220, price 222
One-man shows 227
Onions 109, peeling 470, eating pickled 499
Opal 177
Opera 222–23, houses 222–23
Operations 32, 35–37
Opossums, 52, 54, water, 54
Opponents, checkers, 579, chess 580, 581
Optical fiber 420
Orange 109
Orangutan 56
Orbiter, space shuttle 164, 165, 314, 315, 430
Orbit, moon 152, earth 154, planets 156, 157, satellites, man in 163–64, 165, woman in 165, 315, 431
Orchids 106, 118
Organized crime 397
Organs 215–16, playing 470
Organ transplants, see **Transplants**
Origins of man 14
Oryx 60
Oscars 238–39
Ostriches 74, 75, 79
Otters, sea 52, 61
Overdue book 213
Ox, eating whole 498
Oysters, eating, opening 498

P

Pacific crossings, see **Transpacific**
Paddle boating 471
Paddlewheeler 277, 286
Paella 410
Page size, newspaper 214
Pagodas 425–26
Paintbrush 194
Painters, see **Artists**
Painting 190–96
Palaces 248, 267, 269
Palindromes 200
Panama Canal transit 259
Pancakes 410, tossing 471, eating 498, race 670
Panda 45
Pandemic 428
Pangram 201
Panic toll 428, 430
Pantyhose, new use for 102
Paper, airplane 326, company 347, money 402
Paperweight 370
Parachuting 471, 472–73, 474
Parallel bar dips 603
Park 125
Parking, lot 247, tickets 418
Parrots 80
Parsnip 109
Participants, quiz 476, bridge tournament 578, sports 590, 602, 615, 617, 622, 623, 634, swimming relay 650, running relay 669
Particle accelerators 185, 187–88
Particles, sub-nuclear 166
Party giving 474
Pass, lowest 418
Passenger liners 280–81
Passenger load, airliner 314, airship 325, airline 343
Passengers, air 319, 343
Passing, football, 566, 567, 569–71, 573, 575, 577
Pastry 410
Patent, television 230, case 396
Patient, coma 31, iron lung, "sickest" 36, 37
Pay-out, life insurance 346
Peanuts 108, 109, eating 498
Pear 109
Pearls 177, 180, 181, black 177

Peas, eating 498
Peeling, apple 441, onion 470, potato 476
Penalties, hockey 610
Pendulum 337, 338
Penguins 78, 437
Peninsula 131
Penknife 358
Pens 359
Pepper 109–12
Per capita income 401–02
Perfect development 28
Perfect dive 648, 649
Perfect numbers 181
Perfect, bowling scores 540–41, deals 544, 578, dives 648, 649
Performers 220, 221–23, 226, 227, 228, 232, 233, 236, 238–42, 243
Perfume 167, shower 167
Periodicals 214
Permafrost 143
Persistent candidate 390
Personal injury damages 395
Personal names 202
Petrels 77, 78
Petunia 114
Pharmaceutical company 347
Phillumenist 364
Philodendron 114
Phoenix fowls 79
Phonograph 239
Phonographic identification 243
Photograph 370
Photographic store 347
Photography 170–72
Physical extremes (terrestrial) 183–89
Physicians 386
Physiology, human 24–43
Pi 182, memorizing 26
Pianists 221
Pianos 215, compositions 221, playing, tuning 474
Pickles, eating gherkins, eating pickled onions 498, 499
Pictographs 198
Pier 270, pleasure 254
Pies 411
Pigs 372, 373, 375, 377
Pill taking 35
Pilots 317
Pineapple 112
Pinnacle, rock 131
Pinnipeds 55–56
Pipe 359, smoking 474–75
Pipelines 333–34
Piranhas 90
Pistol 359, 370
Piston engines, car, 290, 292, aircraft 315
Pitch 39, 56
Pitchers 517, 518–19, 520, 522–23, 524, 525, softball 639–40
Pit stop 511
Pizza 411, 412, eating 499
Place names 201–02
Plague 34, deaths 428
Planes, see **Aircraft**
Planetaria 173
Planets 156–58
Planigales 64
Plants 105–18, collector 106
Plasma (gas) 166, 189
Plateau 134
Plate spinning 475
Platforms, oil 276, 346, railroad 306
Platinum, discs 240, 243, bikini 357
Platypus 82
Playing cards 370
Playoff heroes, pro football 577
Plays 225, 227, 228
Playwright 227
Pleasure, beach, pier 254
Poems 212
Poets laureate 212
Pogo stick jumping 475, while juggling 462
Poisoning, mass 398, 429
Poisons, animal 85, 87, 91, 93, 102, toadstool 123, organism 167, man-made 167
Polar conquests 432, 433, 434, 435
Polar lights 160
Polder 262
Poles, flag 266–67, totem 272, flexible, 450
Pole sitting 475–76, climbing 493
Pole vaulters 660, 662, 664
Political and social records 378–90
Political division 378
Pony 64
Pool 673
Popes 123, 426–27
Pop festival 220
Popsicle 412
Population 380–82, natural increase 381, 384
Porcelain and pottery 370
Porcupine 60
Porpoise 50
Portraits 192
Ports 414
Postage stamps 419
Postal services 420
Post cards 359, 364
Posters 194–96
Postmortem birth 21
Potato chips 412, eating 499
Potatoes 112, picking 374, mashed 412, peeling 476, eating 499
Powder, finest 168
Power, producers 326–29, lines 335
Powerboat racing 629
Power-driven vessels 277
Power plant 327, 328, solar 327, 328
Precious stones 174–81, 369, 370
Precipitation, see Rainfall
Pregnancies 21–23
Prehistoric, rocks 130, art 190, 196, structures 244, monuments 270
Premature birth 21, 23
Prescription drug 168
Presidential limousine 291
Press, forging 334
Pressure, submarine 50, 51, 56, 126, 127, 435, 436, earth's core 126, barometric 145, volcanic 147, physical 188, mechanical 334
Primates 14, 56–58
Prime numbers 181
Printed books 203–07, 208–10
Printers 210–11
Printing 203–07, 208–10, machine 334
Prisons 399, sentences 398
Prison term 398
Private houses 250
Prizes, radio 230, Nobel 505–06, auto racing 508–09, golf 591, horse racing 611, 612
Procaryota 123–24
Producers, Broadway, 227, television 234–35, motion picture 237
Production, car longest in 291–92
Production, TV 233
Production-car engine 292
Professors 421–22
Profit, 342, 351
Prohibition 407
Prolific, human mother 16, dog 68, 72, cat 71, 72, rabbits 73, painters 192–94, art teacher 193, writers 208, composers 220, fashion shows 228, TV producer, scriptwriter 235, cow 373, monarchs 387, recordbreaker 565
Proofreading 210
Proof spirits 168
Propeller-driven aircraft 317
Propellers, screw 277, largest 284, aircraft 317
Proper motion 150
Prophet 423
Protista 122–23
Protophyta 122–23
Protozoans 122–23
Prunes, eating 499
Psychiatrists 386
Psychologists 386
Publication, largest 206
Public relations 347
Publisher's advance 209
Publishing 209–10, 347; see also **Books**
Pudu 61
Puffballs 123
Pulling with teeth 482–84
Pulsars 161
Pulse, light 186
Pulse rate 33
Pummel horse 603
Pumpkins 111, 112, 483–84
Punishment, crime and 397–401

Push-ups 599–603
Putts 588, prize 591
Puzzles, crossword 208, 215, jig-saw 358
Pygmies 10
Pyramids 270, human 450
Pythons 85

Q

Quadruplets 16, 18, 21
Quahog 46–47, 100
Quasars 161
Queens 387
Queleas 78
Quiet 188
Quilts 359
Quindecaplets 17
Quintuplets 18
Quizzing 476
Quoit throwing 476
Quotations 207

R

Rabbits 73–74
Rabies 34
Race runner 84
Racing, bathtub 444, egg and spoon 455, wheelbarrow 493, auto 507–13, cycling 554–61, harness 603–05, horse 611–16, speed skating 616, 619–20, motorcycle 624–28, powerboat 629, skiing 630–32, 633–34, swimming 641–46, 657–59, running 661, 662–67, 668, 669, 670, 671, 672, walking 668, three-legged 670
Racquetball 673
Radar installations 334–35
Radio broadcasting 229–30
Radio telescopes 173, 265
Radishes 112
Raft, survival on 287
Railroad lines 306
Railroads 303–08, 415 bridges 257, 258, tunnels 263, busiest system 307, model 307, 308, 370, disaster 429
Rainbow 143
Rainfall 143, 145
Rally, tennis 655
Ramp jump 470
Range, vocal 38, temperature 141, rocket 162, light visibility 267, submarine missile 282, gun 392–93
Ranges, mountain 134
Ransoms 400–01
Rappeling 476
Rarity, animal 47–48, pinniped 56, primate 58, antelope 60, deer 61, dog 67
Rats 62, 72
Rattlesnakes 85
Ravioli, eating 499
Real estate 352
Real McCoy 554
Recaptures, boxing title 547, 548, 551
Recordbreaker, sports 565
Recorded sound 239–43
Recording, video tape 231
Recording artists, see **Singers**
Records (phonograph) 239–43
Record-setting viii, 659
Records in a day 658, 659
Red shifts 161
Reef 132
Refinery, oil 347
Reflector telescopes 172
Refracting telescopes 172
Refuelings, flight 310, 311, 313, 317
Refuse 284
"Refuseniks" 384
Registration plates, auto 288–89
Reigns 386–87, sports 546, 549, 551
Rejections, by publishers, 208, 209
Relay swims 641, 642, 643, 644, 645, 648, 650
Religions 423–27
Remoteness, tree 122, islands 131–32, visible heavenly body 161, body in space 161–62, man-made object 163, town from sea 382–83
Rents 352
Repetitious painter 192–94
Reproductivity 16–24, 123; see also **Litters**
Reptiles 81–86, extinct 103–04
Rescue, underwater 436
Reserves, gold 402
Reservoirs 262
Residences 248–51
Resort, naturist 270
Restaurant chain 347, school 349
Restaurants 252, 253, 256
Retailer 345–46
Retail merchandise, see **Stores**
Return of money 502
Reverse, driving in 294, 295, stock split 351, running bases in 529
Review, theatre 228
Revue 225
Rhododendron 114
Rhythmic gymnastics 597–99
Ribbon worms 46, 101–02
Rice farm 376
Richest, cat 73, men, people 500–01
Ring size 1
Riot toll 429
Riverboat 285, 286
Rivers 135–36
Road fatalities 429
Road load 296
Roads 415, 418
Road tunnels 263
Road vehicles 288–303
Robberies 399, 400
Rock climbing 130
Rock crystal 178
Rocket-engined cars 290, 432, 511–13
Rocketry and missiles 162–65
Rockets 162–63
Rocket sled, on ice 298, on rails 304
Rocking chair 476
Rocks 130
Rodents 59, 60, 72
Rodeo 629
Roles 228
Roll calls attended 388
Roller coasters, 254–55, riding 476
Roller cycling 561
Roller skating 476, 673
Rolling pin throwing 476
Roofed structure 319
Roofs, air-supported 247, retractable, one-piece 252
Rookies of year, unanimous 524
Roots 106
Ropes 359–61, wire 335–36, jumping 600, 601, 603
Ropeways, aerial 330
Rose tree 114
Roulette 404
Rounds, golf 591
Round-the-world, driving 293, amphibious vehicle 298, helicopter 321, via poles 435; see also **Circumnavigation**
Rowers, transocean 439, 441
Royal Lavalite 181
Royalty 386–87 British 387, wealthiest 500
Ruby 175, 177
Rugs 354
Ruler, most married 387
Ruling house 386
Rummage sale 476
Run, ski 633
Running, marathon, 622–23, track and field 657–72, backwards 669, blind 670
Runs, railroad, longest 306, straightest 306
Runs, theatrical 225–27, 228
Runway, airport 321
Rushing, football 566, 567, 569, 575

S

Sacred object 425
Safecracking 476
Safety, air 319
Sailfish 90
Sailing blind 441
Sailing ships 278, 280
Sails 278
Saints 427
Salad 412
Salad bowl chandelier 362
Salamanders 48, 86
Salami 412
Salaries, legislators' 387–88
Sale, rummage 476
Sales (volume) 341
Salt 134
Salt and pepper shakers 364
Salvadori monitor 82
Salvage 435–36
Sampler, embroidered needlework 368, 369

Sand dunes 134
Sand sculpting 477
Sandwiches, eating 499
Sapphire 177, 180
Satellites, natural 157, artificial 155, 163
Sausages 358, 412, eating sausage meat 499
Saving of life 397
Scaffolding 269, 270–71
Scarecrow 271
Scarf 361
Scheduled flights 319
Schools 423
Scientific building 246
Scientific world 166–89
Scores, football 576, golf 585–86, 590–91, 593, 594
Scoring basketball 530–32, 533, 534, 535, 536, bowling 540, 542, 544, hockey 605–08, figure skating 617–18, soccer 635–38
Scotlandite 174
Scrabble 673–74
Scrambling, see **Moto-cross**
Screams 38
Screen, movie 236
Scriptwriter, television 235
Scuba diving 436, duration 482
Sculptures 196–98
Sea, clearest 127–28
Sea cliffs 140
Sea dam 262
Sea lions 55, 56
Seals 55, 56
Sea-mountain 127
Search, longest 478
Searchlight 186
Sea snakes 85, 86
Seaway 260
Seaweed 116
Sea-worms 46, 47, 100, 101–02
Second 182
Security fences 266
Seeds 116, 122, spitting 480–81
See-saw 478
Seismic wave 129
Self-made millionairess 501
Seller, slowest 210
Sensitivity, touch 28, color 34
Sentences, prison 398
Septuplets 17
Sequoias, giant 119, 120–121
Sermon 478
Service, tennis 654
Sets, radio 229, TV 231, 234
Sewage works 271
Sewerage tunnel 264
Sex, size difference between sexes 10, 13, 58, 100, ratio 384
Sex attractant 49
Sextuplets 19
Shakespeare's plays 227
Sharks 49–51, 89, 90, 104, 562
Sharpest vision 33–34
Sharpness 188
Shaving 478
Sheep 373–74, 376, 377, station 373, shearing 376
Sheet music 223
Shellfish, eating 499
Shelling, egg 455
Shells 101
Shipbuilding 285, 347
Shipping, line 348, merchant 414
Ships 277–87
Shipwrecks 277, 287, 428, 430
Shipwreck survival 287
Shock, electric 43
Shoes 2, 360, 361, 369, 370, 399
Shoe shining 478
Shopping centers 348
Shorthand 478
Shouting 38
Shovel, mechanical 295, 335
Showering 478
Show room, theatre 225
Shows, fashion, ice, wrestling 228–29
Shrews 62, primate 57
Shrimps, eating 499
Shutouts, longest 525
Siamese twins 17–19
"Sickest" patient 37
Sidewalks, moving 332
Sight, human 33–34, bird 79, lines of 134; see also **Eye**
Signatures, see **Autographs**
Signs, advertising 264–65
Silence 188
Silicosis 428
Silver 178, 361, 370, 406
Simultaneous games, chess 579
Simultaneous monarchs 387
Simultaneous titleholder 551
Singers 38, 219, 222, 223, 228, 232, 240–42; see also **Records**
Singing, voice range 38, marathon chanting 479; see also **Songs**
Sire, dog 68
Sitting, in unsupported circle 460, pole 475–76, tree 487
Sit-ups 603
Six-day racer, bicycle 560, on foot 670
Size differences between sexes 10, 13, 58, 100
Skateboarding 479–80
Skating, roller 476, 673, ice, figure, speed 616–22, 673
Skid marks 294
Skiing 630–35, 674; see also **Water skiing**
Ski lifts 635, disaster 430
Skip-running 601
Skull 25
Slalom, snow 631–32
Sled journeys 67, 435
Sleeplessness 41
Slide, ski 254
Slimming 13
Slooow-seller (book) 210
Sloth 52
Slot machines 405
Slowest machine 333
Slow vs fast pitch 640
Slowworm 82
Smell, sense of 49, smelliest animal 44, substance 167
Smiths 203
Smog toll 428
Smoke-ring blowing 480
Smokers 355, voracious, whistling 480
Smoking, pipe 474–75, 480
Snails 52, eating 101
Snakebites 85
Snakes 83–86
Sneezing 37
Snore 37
Snow avalanche 428, 429–30
Snow construction 271
Snowfall 144
Snowman 271
Snowmobiling 299, 300
Snow Train, Arctic 295
Soap bubble 480
Soaps 365
Soccer 635–39, 674, stadium 252
Sofas 361
Softball 639–40, 674
Soft drinks 348
Solar-powered, vehicle 294, flight 313
Solar power plant 327, 328
Solar system, man-made object leaves 163
Soldiers 391, toy 371, decorations 502, 504, 505
Solo circumnavigation 440–41
Somersaults 448, 450, 603, 635
Songs 223, 240–42
Song writers 223–24; see also **Composers**
Sound 37–39, 44, pitch 39, insects 97, highest note 187, loudest whistle 493
South Pole conquests 434
South-to-north drive 293, 294
Space 152–65
Space flight 163–65, 431, fatalities 164, 165, 430
Space programs, costs of 164
Space shuttle 164, 165, 314–15, disaster 164, 430
Space telescopes 173
Space "walk" 165
Spaghetti, eating 499
Span, giant's arm 1, antler 61, water buffalo horns 62–64, starfish's arms, spider's legs 92, claw 94, natural arches 138–39, space ***Explorer*** 164, hand 221, bridge 257, helicopter rotor 320, power line 335, between winnings 591–93; see also **Wing span**
Sparrows 77
Spas 251
Speak, ability to 198
Spear-fishing 564
Speeches 239, 388, 423

Speed skating (ice) 619–21
Spices 407
Spiders 92–94
Spinning, basketballs 464, plates 475
Spiral staircase 272
Spires 425
Spirits, see **Alcoholic beverages**
Spitting 480–81
Sponges 103
Sports 507–77, 584–674
Spreading plant 114–15
Springbok 54
Sprinters, women 659–61, 663, 666, 669, 671
Square dance calling 481
Squash 111, 112
Squash (sport) 674
Squid 48, 49, 100
Squirrel 54
Stadiums 247, 252, 266, 529, rained-out game is covered 529
Stained glass 196, 370
Stairs 272, climbing 481
Stalactites 140, 216
Stalagmite 140
Stampede, human 430
Stamps, postage 419
Standard cars 291
Standards of living 385–86
Standing up 481
Stanley Cup 607, 610–11
Starfishes 92, 132
Stars 150, 158–59
"Star Wars" 392
Stations, railroad 306
Statues 269, 270, 272, 503
Stature, variable 10; see also **Height**
Steam engines, ship 277, car 288, 294, 507, train 303, airplane 308
Steam well, geothermal 275
Steel company 348
Stibiotantalite 175
Stick insect 95
Stilt walking 481–82
Stink 44, 167
Stock exchanges 351
Stockings, nylon 359
Stocks 351
Stolen bases 515, 518, 529
Stone (calculus) 35
Stonefish 91
Stone-skipping 455
Stones, precious 174–81
Stores, chain, department, grocery 344–46, photographic 347
Storm toll 428
Stowaway 482
Straits 129
Strawberries 112, 413, 414, eating 499
Streets, 415–16, 417
Strength, beetle 46, primate 58, dogs 67
Stretcher bearing 482
Strikeouts 517, 519, 521, 523, 525–26
Strikes bowling 540, 542, 544
Strikes, 406, hunger 39–40
String ball 482
Stringed instruments 216–19
Structures 244–46, tallest 256, concrete 261, strongest 262, largest roofed 319
Students 422–23
Stuffed camel 414
Stunt man 238
Stunts and miscellaneous endeavors 441–95
Sturgeon 91, 564
Subject of operation 36
Submarine cable 420
Submarine canyon 140
Submarine depression 134
Submarine drilling 275
Submarine mountains 127, 134
Submarine pipeline 334
Submarines 282–83, fatalities 430, target 503
Submarine tunnels 263–64
Submergence, unaided 43, bird 78, longest duration 436, 482
Sub-nuclear particles 166
Subterranean lake 137
Subterranean penetrations 275
Subways 306–07, tunnel 263–64
Suffrage, woman 389
Sugar beet 374
Sugar mill 348
Suicide 398, mass 398, 429
Suite, hotel 251
Sun 154–55, approach to 163
Sundae 413, 414
Sundial 337
Sunfish 89, 91
Sunflower 114
Sunken treasure 406
Sunshine 144, 145
Sunspots 154
Super Bowl records 574–75
Super-nova 159
Supersonic flight 311–14
Supersonic pneumatic tunnel 264
Surfboarding while juggling 462, 465
Surgery 32, 35–37
Survival, in coma 31, in iron lung 36, without food or water 39, on raft 287
Sushi, eating 499
Suspension bridges 257, 258, human 602
Swallowing 35, sword 35
Swamp 140
Swans 74, 77, 79
Sway, wind 256
Sweet potato 112
Swifts 74, 77
Swimming, birds 74, 75, 77, human sport 640–50, diving 641, 648–49
Swing 272
Swinging 482
Switchboard 420
Sword 371, swallowing 35
Swordfish 90, 563
Sword swallowing 35
Symphonies 220–21
Synagogue 424
Synchrotrons 187–88
Synonyms 201

T

Table 361, 371
Tablecloth 361
Table tennis 674
Tail, comet's 155
Takeoffs, airplane 316, 318
Takeoff weight 311
Take-overs 343
Talkative bird 80
Talking 39, 482, 483
Tamarin 58–60
Tandem bicycle 301, 302, 303, cross-country record 560
Tanker 283
Tanks, oceanarium, aquarium 125, gas 275, oil 333
Tanzanite 181
Tap dancing 452–53
Tape recordings 239
Tapestries 361–63, 371
Tasmanian tiger 47
Tattoos 40
Taxation 401
Taxi, fleet, fare 295
Tea 404
Teddy bear 371
Teeter board 450
Teeth 30–31, collection 31, 365, decay 34, pulling with 482–84
Tektites 152
Telephones 420
Telescopes 172–73
Television 230–35, first football game on 565
Television programs, longest 233
Temperature 141, 142, 144, human body 32, 33, endured 43, mammal 48, earth's core 126, ranges, equable, atmosphere 141–42, land 141, 142, 144, lightning 143, moon, sun 153, 154, planets 156, flame 184, man-made terrestrial 189, deep-sea 435
Temperature-Humidity Index 141
Temples 244, 424
Temple tower 274
Tennis 650–57, 674
Tenrecs 54, 62
Tent 272
Teratorn 103
Term of office 389
Terns 74, 78
Terrorist killing 429
Test-tube, baby 22, 24, 58, primate 58
Theatre 224–28
Theatregoers 227
Thefts 400
Theorem 183

Thermometer 189
Thread snake 85
Three-legged race 670
Throwing, boomerang 445, 582–84, brick 445, card 445, egg 455, rolling pin 476, baseball 525, flying ring, flying disc (Frisbee) 582–84
Thunder 145
Thylacine (Tasmanian tiger) 47
Ticket, airstrip 415
Tickets, parking 418
Tidal power station 328–29
Tidal wave 129
Tides 128
Tigers 54, 55, Tasmanian 47, man-eating 429
Tightrope walking 484–87
Time, in space, on moon 164, 165, measure 182, measurer 337, capsule 363, served 398
Timepieces 336–39
Tipster, horse-racing 613–15
Tires 296
Tire supporting 487
Title flights, boxing 546, 547, 548, 549, 550, 551, 552, 553, 554, 550
Title recaptures, boxing 547, 548, 551
Titles, bowling 540
Toads 86, 87
Toadstool 123
Tobacco company 348–50
Tobogganing 487
Toes 28
Toll, Panama Canal swimmer 260
Toll plaza, bridge 415
Tomato 108, 111, 112
Tomb 272
Tongue-twister 201
Tongue, whale 44
Tools, stone 15
Toothed mammal 53
Topaz 174, 178, 179
Tornado toll 429
Torpedoing, wartime 428
Tortilas, eating 499
Tortoises 47, 52, 83
Totem pole 272
Toucan 79
Touchdown pass 577
Touch sensitivity 28
Toughest, animal 46, insect 96, bacteria 124
Tour de France 558–59
Tournament wins, golf 588, 590–91, 592, 593, 594, 595
Tow, longest 295
Towers 244, 246, 256, water, ziggurat 273, 274, free-standing 425
Towns 382–83
Toys, store, longest soft 350, at auction 370, 371
Track and field 657–72
Tractor 296
Trade unions 406
Traffic 415, lights 416
Trailer tour 298
Trainers, dog 70, horse 615
Train robbery 400
Trampolining 450, 674
Trans-America, balloonists 324, south-north walk 494, cyclists 556–57, 560, golf game 585, motorcyclists 624, 625, 626, 627, 628, foot races 671
Transatlantic crossings, radio transmission 229, television 231–32, ships, 280, amphibious vehicle 298, flight 309–10, by balloon 322–23, marine records 439–40, 441, rowing 440, 441
Trans-Canada, cyclist 560, run 672
Transformer 335
Transistor 340
Transmission lines 335
Transocean rowers 440, 441
Transpacific crossings, ship 280, amphibious vehicle 298, flight 310, by balloon 322, rowing 440
Transplants, heart 32, triple 32, kidney 37
Transportation 414–18, 420
Trapeze, flying 448
Trash dump 272–73
Travel, motor trip 298, rail journey 304–05, and exploration 431–36
Traveled men 432–33
Treading water 648
Treasure 406
Treaty 388
Tree frogs 86
Trees 118–22, climbing 487, sitting 487, eating 499
Trencherman 497
Trials 394–96
Tribes, tallest, shortest 9, 10
Tributaries 135
Trip, see **Travel**
Triple Crown, cycling 559, horse racing 615
Triple transplant 32
Triplets 16, 18, 21
Trotters, see **Horse racing**
Truck 297, 298, dump 296
Truck bomb toll 430
Truffles 407
Tsunami 129
Tuatara 48
Tuba 219
Tubes 188
Tugs 284
Tumbling, see **Somersaults**
Tumor 35
Tuna 90
Tunneling 264, deaths 263 428
Tunnels 263–64, wind 264
Turbines 326, 329, ship 280
Turkeys 80, theatrical 228, farm 372, gutting, plucking 376
Turnip 112
Turtles 83, 84
Tusks 62
Twenty-four hours, go-karting mileage 293, countries by rail 304, plowing 374, baby carriage pushing 442, cross-country motorcycle mileage 470, auto race mileage 511, bowling score 539, cycling distance 558, 561, push-ups 599, sit-ups 603, ice skating 622, skiing 632, swimming 647, running 669
Twins 3, 8, 9, 10–11, 16, 17–19, 20
Two-wheeldriving 293
Typesetting machines 334
Typewriters 363, 371
Typhoon 145
Typing 487, 488

U

Ultralight plane 313
Unclimbed mountain 133
Undefeated boxers 549, 550
Undergraduates 422
Underground, see **Subterranean**
Undertaker 350
Underwater, duration 43, 78, 435–36, 482, pressure 50, 51, 56, 127, mountains 127, 134, depression 134, tunnel 264, drilling 275, rescue, escape 436, kiss 466, pogo stick jumping 475, violinists 488, 489, cycling 489, rock-and-roll band 488, swim, Channel swim, relay swim 649; see also **Submarine**
Unearned runs 529
Unicycles 302, 303, tallest 303
Unions 406
Universe 150, 161–62
Universities 421–23
UN speech 388
Unsupported circle 460
Used cars 291

V

Vacuum 189
Valve 335
Variable stature 10
Vases 363
Vegetables 107, 108, 109, 110, 111, 112
Vehicles 293, 294, 295, 296, 297, 298, 299, 300, extra-terrestrial 164, nuclear delivery 394
Velocity 255, space vehicle 163, highest 189
Venom, see **Poisons**
Venusian canyon 156
Versatility, magician 468, athlete 490
Vexillology 357
Video, see **Television**
Video tape, rentals 231 recording 231
Viewing, television 231
Vines 111, 114

Vineyards 376
Vintage wines 168–69
Viol, double bass 216–17
Violence, movie 238
Violinists 217, 488, 489
Violins 217, 218, 488, 489
Violoncello 217
Viroids 124
Viruses 124
Viscosity 189
Visible objects 161, 189
Vision, see **Sight**
Visual acuity 33–34
Vocabulary 199
Vocal range 38
Voices 38
Volcanoes 146–49, eruption toll 428
Volleyball 674
Voltages 189, 335
Vultures 77

W

Waists 11, 13, 26, 27
Waiters' marathon 489
Waiting rooms 305
Walker, slowest 44
Walking, on stilts 481–82, tightrope 484–86, on hands 489, on water 489, 492
Walking stick 371–72
"Walk" in space 165
Wallet 363
Wall press 489, 493, 599
Walls 247, 248, 273, mountain 130
Wars 390–91
Warship 282
Wasps 96
Watches 339, 365
Water, speed on 432, walking on 489
Waterbed 353
Water buffalo 62
Waterfalls 137
Water fleas 95
Watermelon 109, 110, seed spitting 480–81
Water pipeline 334
Water polo 674
Water-raising instrument 329
Waterspout 143
Water tower 273
Waterwheel 273
Waves 129
Wealth, national 401–02, personal 500–02; see also **Earnings**
Weasels 53
Weather 141–45
Weather balloon blowing 491
Weathervane 372
Webs 93
Weddings 438–49; see also **Marriage**
Weeds 115
Weight, humans 1, 2, 3, 6, 7, 9, 10–14, 18, 20, 21–23, differential 13, loss 13, gaining 13–14, animal 44, 47, 50, 51, 52–53, 54, 55, 56, 57–58, 60, 61, 62, 64, 65, 67, 68, 70–71, 73, tusks 62, birds 77, 80, ostrich egg 79, poultry 80, reptiles 81, 82, 83, amphibians 86, 88, fish 89, 90, starfish, spiders 92, 93, crustaceans 94, 95, insects 95, 96, mollusks 100–01, sponge, extinct birds 103, dinosaurs 105, fruits and vegetables 107–12, 114, 116, seeds 122, bacteria 124, earth, all oceans 127, Soviet rocket 162, orbited space object 164, nuclear particles 166, telescope mirror 172, space telescope 173, magnet 186, mobile 198, index 205, largest publication 206, map 207, newspaper issue 214, grand piano 215, guitar 218, radio set 229, TV sets 234, door 266, oil platform (heaviest object moved) 276, ship 281, Presidential limousine 291, truck 297, mechanical shovel 295, tractor 296, planes 311–13, helicopter, helicopter altitude lift 321, forging, lifting operation, mechanical nuts 333, wire ropes 335–36, watch 339, dress 355–56, flag 357, gold coffin 358, silver water jugs, salad bowl chandelier 361, 362, cattle, hog, lamb, goat 375–76, cannon, military tanks, guns 392, chocolate Easter egg 408, gold Buddha 425, pancake 471, sand castles 477, wheelbarrow pushing 491–93, heavyweight boxing champs 547, 554, game fish 562–64, soccer goalie 636, 638; see also specific animals
Weight changes 13–14
Wells 275
Wetness 144
Whale factory 284
Whales 44, 45, 46, 47, 50–51, 53, 562–63, whistle 44, ambergris 51
Wheat field 377
Wheelbarrow pushing 491, 493
Wheelbarrow racing 493
Wheelies 293, 469, 470
Whip cracking 493
Whisk(e)y distilleries 345
Whistles 215
Whistling loudest 493
White elephant sale, see **Rummage sale**
Who's Who entries 506
Wild boar race 375
Wills 396; see also **Bequests**
Wimbledon 650–51, 652–54
Wind 145, tunnels 264
Windows 274, stained glass 196
Windshield wipers 295
Wine 168–70, bottles 169–70, auction, tasting 169, cellars 274
Wing beat, bird 77
Wing span, bat 51, 57, bird 75, insects 97, 98, extinct birds 103, aircraft 313, 314, 315, 316, 318, 320, 321
Winnings, racing dog 69, harness racers 603–05, horserace 612, 613
Winning streak, football 575, hockey 610, race horses 612, track and field 658, 669
Wins in one day 658
Wire rope 335–36, walking 484–86
Woman suffrage 389
Wombat 64
Women, height 3, 5–7, 8, 10, weight 12–14, age 16, 17, brain weight 25, bearded 29–30, tattoos 40, fire-eating 43, in space 165, 315, 431, highest-priced painting 192, song writers 224, most Oscars 238, 239, vocalists 240, 241, 242, 243, supersonic flier 311, head of state 388, undergraduate 422, speed records 431, 432, at North Pole, at South Pole 433, 434, marine diver 436, non-stop solo round-world sail 440–41, barrel jumping 444, baton twirling brick carrying, bubble gum blower 444, 445, 446, crocheting records 447, 451, circus acts 448–50, dancers 451–53, debaters 453, high divers 454, gold panning 456, hula-hooping 460, human cannonballs 460, juggling 462, knitter 466, log rolling 467, 468, parachuting 471, pole sitting 475, rolling pin throwing 476, see-sawing 478, showering 478, stair climbing 481, non-stop talker 482, typists 487, writing under handicap 495, champion eaters 496, 498, millionairesses, miser 501, 502, ace 503, Nobel Prize winner 505, auto racers 508, 509, throwing baseball 525, basketball players 531, 532, 538, bowling 539, 543, 544, cyclists 555, 558, 559, 560, bridge players, checkers player 578, 579, chess champions 580, 582, Frisbee throwing 582, golfers 586, 588, 591–93, 594, 595, 596, sports earnings 588, 592, 656, gymnasts 597–99, ice skaters 617–21, marathoners 622, motorcyclist 627, 628, skiers 630–34, softballers 640, swimmers 641, 642,

644–45, 646, 647, 648, divers 649, in tennis 650–51, 652, 654–55, 656–57, in track events 659–61, 663, 666–67, 669, 670, 671, in field events 659, 661, 662, 663, 666, 669, 671, walkers 668, distance runners 666, 670, 672, heptathlon 667, 671,
Woodcocks 75
Wood cutting 493
Wooden, buildings 247, ships 279, flying boat 315–17, doll 368
Woodpeckers 77, 78–79
Woods 121
Wool 377
Word processor 340
Words 199–201
Working careers 407
World Cups, gymnastics 597, Nordic (skiing) 632, Alpine (skiing) 632, ski-jumping 632, soccer 636–37
World Series 521–23, attendance 528
Worm charming 100
Worms 46, 47, 48, 99, 100, 101–02
Wrapping 494, 495
Wreaths 116
Wrecker 298
Wrecks, ship 277, 287
Wrestling 13, 229
Wristwatches 339
Writers 207–10
Writing, earliest English 199
Writing, small 495, under handicap 495
Writing shorthand 478
Wrongful imprisonment 395

Y

Yachts 285, disaster 430
Yak 53
Yawning 37
Yodelling 495
Yolks, egg 374
Yo-Yo 495

Z

Zeppelin, see **Airships**
Zero birth rate 380
Ziggurat 274
Zipper 363
Zoos 125
Zorilla 44
Zucchini 122

Index compiled by Henry W. Engel